THE FIRST AFGHAN WAR
1838–1842

THE FIRST AFGHAN WAR
1838-1842

BY

J. A. NORRIS

CAMBRIDGE
AT THE UNIVERSITY PRESS
1967

CAMBRIDGE UNIVERSITY PRESS
Cambridge, New York, Melbourne, Madrid, Cape Town, Singapore,
São Paulo, Delhi, Dubai, Tokyo

Cambridge University Press
The Edinburgh Building, Cambridge CB2 8RU, UK

Published in the United States of America by Cambridge University Press, New York

www.cambridge.org
Information on this title: www.cambridge.org/9780521130967

© Cambridge University Press 1967

First published 1967
This digitally printed version 2010

A catalogue record for this publication is available from the British Library

Library of Congress Catalogue Card Number: 67–21962

ISBN 978-0-521-05838-4 Hardback
ISBN 978-0-521-13096-7 Paperback

For Josephine

CONTENTS

Contents

A NOTE ON NAMES

In the first half of the nineteenth century the English transliteration of personal and place names common in the East was far from standardized. In this work the author has in general used the modern spelling in his narrative, while retaining the old spelling in quotations from contemporary writings. He has, however, followed the old style in transliterating the name of the Maharajah of Lahore —'*Runjeet* Singh'. This spelling is a better guide to pronunciation than the more modern 'Ranjit'. He has also favoured the form *Muhammad* whenever that name occurs in his narrative. In referring to Dost Muhammad Khan he follows an old practice by calling him sometimes the Dost (Friend) and sometimes the Emir (Commander or Prince). In the narrative Shah Shuja is sometimes 'king' and sometimes 'shah' but never 'emir.'

ACKNOWLEDGEMENTS

Transcripts of Crown-copyright material in the British Museum and Public Record Office appear by permission of the Controller of Her Majesty's Stationery Office.

Unpublished Crown-copyright material in the India Office Library and the India Office Records transcribed in this book appears by permission of the Secretary of State for Commonwealth Affairs.

The author gratefully acknowledges assistance given by the Keeper of Manuscripts and staff of the Manuscript Students' Room at the British Museum; by the Secretary and Search Room staff at the Public Record Office; by the Keeper of the India Office Records; and by the Librarian and his assistants at the India Office Library.

The author is particularly grateful to the India Office Librarian for lending him books published more than a century ago.

Research work done by Mr Robert A. Huttenback for his book on *British Relations with Sind, 1799–1843, An Anatomy of Imperialism* has lightened the author's task in more than one chapter. He wishes to acknowledge his debt to Mr Huttenback and the University of California Press.

Over a long period the author has owed much to his teachers, and particularly to the late Francis Lockwood, sometime headmaster of William Ellis School, to Christopher Rieu, and to Dr T. R. Henn, Fellow of St Catharine's College, Cambridge. If this book shows any understanding of military matters the credit is due to his association with the Territorial Battalion of the Queen's Own Royal West Kent Regiment.

To his wife the author owes the inspiration and encouragement which made this book possible.

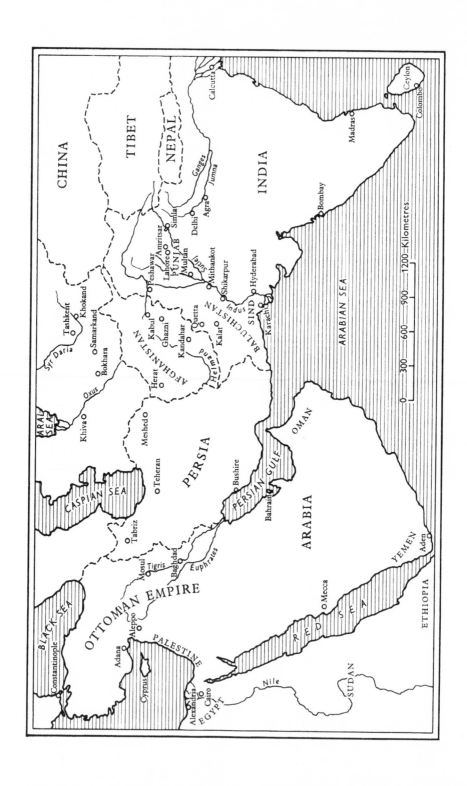

INTRODUCTION

The events known in history as the First Afghan War have had many reporters, but few of them appear to have examined the voluminous original sources in detail. Some have long remained content to reproduce the contemporary judgements and partisan comments of nineteenth-century writers without discrimination. To a very large extent this is the influence of Sir John William Kaye's long reign as an unchallenged historian of Victorian India. His books are solid monuments, not unlike the statue of Sir Charles Napier in Trafalgar Square. One does not lightly question the skill of the sculptor in catching a likeness. The passer-by does not, unless he has a particular interest in the subject, question the values of the men who placed Napier next to Nelson in a gallery of heroes. Nevertheless, it becomes necessary from time to time to look with the eye of irreverence at the work of established authorities. Sir John William Kaye was a man of strong opinions and prejudices, ever ready with a moral judgement and a fine rhetorical flourish to arguments which were often based on incomplete or circumstantial evidence. His honesty is not in question, and the author of this work has the greatest respect for Kaye's scholarship and integrity, but it is surely time at last to re-examine the evidence calmly, taking into account a mass of evidence to which Kaye can never have had access. It is also time to replace the episode in its proper context. The third edition of the *Oxford History of India* provides a signpost:

It is in the interaction of British policy towards Russia in the Near and Middle East that the explanation of much that happened in the two Afghan Wars is to be found...Events in one theatre cannot therefore be understood without reference to events in the other; the Afghan Wars were essentially a part of the general Eastern Question.[1]

Few have shown the Afghan War of 1838 in that light. Sir Llewellyn Woodward's recent volume[2] in the *Oxford History of England*, 'The Age of Reform', includes a long section on British policy in the Near East from 1827 to 1841, without once mentioning Afghanistan. He gives seven lines to the question of Cabinet responsibility for the First Afghan War. *The Cambridge History of British Foreign Policy* sees the connexion between British policy in the Ottoman Empire and British policy in Persia and Afghanistan, but gives only a dozen pages to the First Afghan War.[3] The same strange separatism is apparent in Sir Charles Webster's study of Palmerston's Foreign Policy. Having accepted that Palmerston was right about Russian ambitions in Central Asia, and that British aims in the First Afghan War were justifiable, Sir Charles Webster says:

Whether the same objectives could have been obtained with less blood-shed and intrigue is a question of Indian strategy and politics, and not of British foreign policy.[4]

W. A. J. Archbold, author of the account given in the *Cambridge History of the British Empire*, drew a sketch for the standard work that could have been written in 1929. But it was only a sketch, revealing to the disciples of Kaye and Durand that the last word had by no means been spoken in 1851. One of the few things on which the author finds it possible wholeheartedly to agree with the authors of *The Rise and Fulfilment of British Rule in India*, on the other hand, is their statement that 'the writing of Indian history is over-run with cant'.[5] Kaye started a fashion for comment on the First Afghan War, and many have copied him since he wrote:

Throughout the entire period of British connection with Afghanistan, a strange moral blindness clouded the vision of our statesmen: they saw only the natural, the inevitable results of their own measures, and forgot that those measures were the dragon's teeth from which sprung up the armed men.[6]

On the shelf of the author's local public library there is a much borrowed work on the history of the British Army. It is not the standard work by Sir John Fortescue, but a more modest 'Short History' by Captain Eric Sheppard of the Royal Tank Corps, written in 1925. He gives an account of the First Afghan War, starting with a piece of rhetoric worthy of Kaye himself:

We now come to one of the darkest chapters in our history—one of the few, indeed almost the only one, which has to tell not only of defeat but of disgrace, of shame as well as of sorrow. For once our arms were employed in a cause which has met with universal condemnation at the hands of posterity, and in the course of an unjust aggression met with condign defeat; and though our ruined prestige was later in some measure repaired, the objects for which we took up arms were in the ultimate outcome left unattained. This ill-conceived and ill-starred campaign is known to history as the First Afghan War.[7]

Sir John Fortescue called it 'the insane enterprise which is known as the First Afghan War'.[8] Archbold's calmer verdict was that the invasion of Afghanistan was 'a terrible mistake',[9] while L. J. Trotter, the author of a biography of Lord Auckland, called that Governor's policy a blunder and a crime.[10] And just as the policy has met with little but criticism, the chief actors have been pelted with abuse for the last one hundred and twenty years. Auckland has been accused of 'straightforward wickedness',[11] of being a 'conscientious mediocrity',[12] of being a 'bumbling'[13] weakling without a settled policy of his own. Poor Ellenborough, the 'wild elephant'[14] of Westminster and Calcutta, was blamed and ridiculed even by his own Tory colleagues, the duke of Wellington and a few others excepted. He has been written down as a vain and bullying pseudo-Napoleon, and as one who lost his nerve at a moment of crisis in April 1842. The talented and likable Alexander Burnes and the 'spunky'[15] and always optimistic William Hay Macnaghten have also suffered at the hands of historians. Neither lived to tell his own tale, and Burnes in particular has suffered because of the spiteful innuendoes of Charles Masson, a traveller and archaeologist who kept the Bengal government supplied with Kabul rumours until Burnes came on the scene and made him redundant in September 1837.[16] Those who have accepted Masson's version of Burnes as a licentious lightweight have all ignored the wise advice given by George Buist, a great editor of the *Bombay Times* and a model for journalists in any age. He wrote: 'In quoting Mr Masson on this subject [the activities of the Russian agent Vitkievitch in Kabul] we are bound to state, that whatever he writes in reference to Captain Burnes bears an appearance in the last degree suspicious.'[17]

It is the author's belief that historians have not yet done justice to those who were responsible for this first war of Victoria's reign. There is no shortage of source material in English, but some scholars seem only to have skimmed the surface. The author also believes that the study of the origins, events, and outcome of the First Afghan War can teach valuable lessons about the nature of imperialism, the growth of Asian nationalism, the realities of power politics, and the British national character. It is certainly not his intention to 'whitewash' what was unworthy in the record of British involvement in Afghanistan. Nevertheless, he hopes that the result of his studies will throw light into some hitherto murky corners of British imperial history, and he would be content if his work served a purpose similar to that of the restorer of an old painting, for there is a very thick layer of dirt and varnish on the generally accepted picture of the First Afghan War.

ANGLO-RUSSIAN RIVALRY
TO 1830

CHAPTER I

EARLY THREATS TO THE BRITISH EMPIRE IN INDIA

...The ships of the English swarm like flies; their printed calicoes cover the whole earth, and by the side of their swords the blades of Damascus are blades of grass. All India is but an item in the ledger-books of the merchants, whose lumber rooms are filled with ancient thrones!—whirr! whirr! all by wheels!—whiz! whiz! all by steam!...

The Pasha to the Traveller in Kinglake's *Eothen* (1844)

...Of His Majesty and the Royal Family and many other circumstances connected with England they spoke with a knowledge that surprised me, and once observed that English sailors and Beloche soldiers were the best in the world. They knew the character and fall of the Emperor Napoleon, but were ignorant of his death. Of vaccine inoculation they had heard by report, and when I explained its advantages they declared their intention of establishing it in Sinde, and requested me to assist them with the means of doing so. Among other subjects I told them of the grand discovery of steam engines; but in this, and respecting the revenues of Great Britain they evidently considered I was making use of a Traveller's privilege...

From a conversation between Dr James Burnes and the Emirs of Sind, in *Narrative of a Visit* (1829)

When Dost Muhammad Khan of Kabul returned home in April 1843, he came fresh from one of the 'lumber rooms' of 'ancient thrones' maintained by the Honourable East India Company. He had been a comfortable and well endowed guest of the Governor General for two years and a few days from the date of his surrender at Kabul.[1] He did not rush back to Kabul the moment he was released in November 1842; he knew too much about Afghan politics for that. He took his time. He visited Lahore, capital of his late enemy the Maharajah Runjeet Singh, and the Sikh Durbar received him, we are told, with the honours due to an Afghan prince.[2] He had to conciliate the wild tribesmen who dominated the mountain passes between Peshawar and Kabul. He had to make sure that the factions at Kabul were truly ready to have him back, and he had to promise favours here and there to smooth his way back to the throne from which he had been plucked in 1839.

The two years of enforced residence in British India had worked

3

a change in Dost Muhammad Khan. He now appreciated the full
extent of British power in the world; he had come to understand
that his 'hosts' were for the time being the most powerful nation
on the face of the earth, that the Russians might have more men
and a greater expanse of national territory, but that the British,
more than any other people, had engines and engineers, innumer-
able ships and guns, and an unlimited self-confidence. They
accepted no bounds and no barriers to the advance of British influence in the untamed regions of the earth. Yet, by a strange para-
dox, these conquerors were not primarily intent upon territorial
aggrandizement. They worshipped one God; they were people of
the book; but their god of every day seemed to be an idol called
Commerce. Dost Muhammad Khan could recall the words of the
Simla Manifesto of 1 October 1838. Lord Auckland stated that his
government originally entered into treaties with the Emirs of Sind
in order, 'by opening the navigation of the Indus, to facilitate the
extension of Commerce, and to gain for the British nation in
Central Asia that legitimate influence which an interchange of
benefits would naturally produce'. It was impossible to dismiss
these men as meddling infidels. Dost Muhammad could respect
them and be wary of them. He could even feel friendly towards
individuals. Lord Auckland's sister and Lord Auckland himself
had treated him kindly and with consideration. At the Queen's
Birthday Ball in Calcutta in May 1841 they had taken the trouble to
amuse him and his suite in a place apart, where they would not
have to watch those prancing, red-faced officers and their shame-
less, half-naked women.[3]

But now Dost Muhammad was re-entering his own country. He
must reign and he must rule in a land where the British and their
sepoys had killed and been killed. On the journey from Jalalabad
to Kabul he could see the rotting corpses of one battle and the
bleaching bones of another, freshly exposed by the melting of the
snow. In Kabul itself he would be shown the signs of Britain's
vengeance for the massacre of an army and the murder and
mutilation of a British envoy. The great roofed bazaar of Kabul,
'the architectural pride of Central Asia',[4] was now in ruins. The
fortress at Ghazni, barring an invader's route from Kandahar to
Kabul, had been blown up and burned by General Nott's sappers
and miners in the previous September. Many Afghans were still
mourning their dead and nursing their wounds, having paid the

heavy price for their triumph over British arms in the winter of 1841–2. It was fitting, among tribes long accustomed to the rituals of revenge, that the British forces returning to Kabul in the summer of 1842 should be known as an army of retribution. Dost Muhammad, on his return, saw how heavily his people had paid, and we need not wonder why he held his country aloof from British India for so long thereafter. It should not surprise us that he appointed his son, Muhammad Akbar Khan—the murderer of Macnaghten—as his vizier, or chief minister, as soon as he was re-established in the Bala Hissar at Kabul. Eleven years later the marquess of Dalhousie could only describe Anglo-Afghan relations as 'sullen quiescence on either side, without offence but without goodwill or intercourse'.[5] The only departure from that state of affairs had occurred in 1849, when Dost Muhammad, hoping perhaps to revive his claim to Peshawar, momentarily allied himself with his old enemies the Sikhs against the British. Subsequent events, including the annexation of the Punjab, made him more receptive to the diplomatic overtures made by Dalhousie's government in 1855. He never again quarrelled with British India, and in return the British made it a rule not to meddle in his internal affairs. The rule did not long survive him, but that is another story.

Why should the British in India have meddled in the affairs of nations beyond the Sutlej and the Indus in the first place? To find the correct answer to that question we do not need to go back as far as the early history of the Levant Company, whose charter of 1592 authorized trade with India overland through Ottoman territories. But it is useful to remember that the voyagers and venturers of the sixteenth century, the 'master o' the *Tiger*' and his like,[6] started the commerce that eventually led Britain into Central Asia. The merchants with their 'ledger-books' acquired armies and navies, generals and governors general, territory and taxes. For a few years after the conquest of Bengal some of the worst Englishmen in India did their worst, plundering, and jobbing, and profiteering their way into early graves or to wealth and purchased honours in England. The Regulating Act of 1773 included clauses designed to prevent any repetition of the 'flagrant errors' of the recent past. The Government in London now shared control of Indian affairs with the East India Company. Then in 1784 Pitt's India Act effectively subordinated the Company to the

5

Crown. A Board of Control consisting of six Privy Councillors—and including at least two ministers of the Crown—was established with the right to issue orders to the Company's servants in India. The Secret Committee of the Court of Directors of the East India Company became in time a forwarding agency for instructions from the president of the Board of Control. From 1793 onwards the president received a salary and functioned to all intents and purposes as a Secretary of State for India, often with a seat in the Cabinet. From 1812 onwards he invariably held a seat in the Cabinet.

The period of the consolidation of government control over Indian affairs coincided with the onset of new fears of invasion from the north-west. Every threat to Britain's communications by land and sea with India loomed as a menace to her Indian Empire. Now that the American Colonies had become independent, India was doubly precious to the British Crown. King William IV expressed a widespread and enduring feeling in October 1836 when he urged upon John Cam Hobhouse 'the necessity of watching the western frontier of India', and added: 'Now this is a fine country, but it is nothing without its colonial possessions, especially India.'[7]

To many Englishmen in the confident years after Waterloo, India was the badge of greatness. But there was a radical minority which rejected the general attitude. William Cobbett had written in April 1808:

There is a constant, never-ceasing war in India. There is not always actual fighting; but there are always going on preparations for fighting; what right, in God's name, what right have we to do this? How is it possible for us to justify our conduct, upon any principle of morality?...[8]

Cobbett also hated Nabobs, but he was already out of date. India in the first quarter of the nineteenth century became a jewel in the imperial crown, a living proof of Britain's world power and of her military and maritime supremacy. It demonstrated her capacity for just and efficient government. A few thousand British officers and men ran and supplemented a native army which kept eighty million people under control. Some simply relished the glory of this feat, like latter-day Romans. But others were beginning to see the inevitable result of Britain's moral and educational

6

impact upon India. The nation as a whole was inheriting grave responsibilities from the merchants, and by 1833 the Company was ready to wind up its commercial activities and devote itself to administration. In the House of Commons debate on the Bill which brought about that change, Macaulay said:

...To have found a great people sunk in the lowest depths of slavery and superstition, to have so ruled them as to have made them desirous and capable of all the privileges of citizens would indeed be a title to glory all our own. The sceptre may pass away from us. Unforeseen accidents may derange our most profound system of policy. Victory may be inconstant to our arms. But there are triumphs which are followed by no reverses. There is an empire exempt from all natural causes of decay. These triumphs are the pacific triumphs of reason over barbarism; that empire is the imperishable empire of our arts and our morals, our literature and our laws.[9]

Whether one viewed India as a colonial possession pure and simple, like King William, or as a looter's paradise, like Cobbett, or as a field for the propagation of British enlightenment, like Macaulay, the fact remained that India was now a place where the national prestige was at stake. The defence of such a prize would justify the taking of great risks, as it did in the First Afghan War. Meanwhile, the existence of the empire in India was profoundly affecting British foreign policy, and the distance and difficulty of communication between London and Calcutta were creating a distinctively Indian foreign policy which sometimes led statesmen to think of Britain as two powers, one European and one Asiatic. In certain circumstances it might become possible for Britain to have an ally in Europe who was at the same moment an enemy in Asia. Moreover, an Asiatic power could act boldly without the inhibitions of sophisticated European states. Much would depend on the personality of the Governor of Bengal at the moment of crisis. Would he take arms against a sea of troubles, or would he stay still within his existing frontiers and let trouble come to him?

In 1798, when Napoleon led his army into Egypt[10] and set his sights on India, the new Governor of Bengal was the Earl of Mornington, not a man to sit still and await aggression. Tipu Sultan of Mysore had just invited into his territory a small French force to help him against the encroaching British. In the north Zaman Shah of Kabul was trying to restore the Afghan Empire to its former greatness—a course of action which could lead him into conflict with Persia, the Punjab, Sind, or the British.

All these threats faced Mornington during the first few months of his term as Governor. Nelson saved him much anxiety by destroying the French fleet at Aboukir Bay[11] and bottling up Napoleon's army in Egypt. Mornington, who received the news of the invasion of Egypt in October, first determined to neutralize the actual French threat on Indian soil. Tipu would not relinquish his alliance with the French, and on 4 May 1799 he died in the rubble of his fortress at Seringapatam, defeated by an army which contained a contingent led by the future duke of Wellington.

But there was still a potential menace from France or Afghanistan, or both together. Mornington instructed the Governor of Bombay to cultivate good relations with the Shah of Persia and the Emirs of Sind, with a view to checking French and Afghan ambitions. The Governor of Bombay deputed merchant diplomats from Bushire for this task. In Sind there ruled a family of parvenu Baluchi princes, the Talpuras. Four brothers shared power in Hyderabad, having ousted the Kalora family in 1783. They were probably no worse than any previous rulers of their neglected country, but the British found them grasping and oppressive. Indeed the British in India, who periodically squeezed advantages out of them and their descendants from 1800 onwards, eased their conscience with the thought that anything must be better for the people of Sind than subjection to such masters.

Since 1757 Sind had been in theory subordinate to the Kingdom of Afghanistan. During the early years of the Talpura supremacy the emirs paid their annual tribute, and in 1786 Timur Shah recognized their leader as Governor of Sind, but the payments ceased when the Sindians found that they could defy Timur with impunity. In Afghan eyes, nevertheless, Sind remained under Afghan suzerainty.

In 1798 Zaman Shah, more forceful than his father Timur, was pressing his claims for tribute from Sind, and the usurped Kalora family was plotting to recover its lost dominions. The British merchant diplomatists therefore found a receptive audience when they proposed the establishment of closer relations between Sind and British India. The result was a commercial agreement, signed in the spring of 1800. Now, as later, Britain could not let any other power control, with or without Ottoman approval, her communications with the East. Now, as later, Britain could not afford to neglect the ancient invasion routes into northern India. But the French threat did not last long, and Wellesley[12] was not disposed to quarrel at the end of 1800 when the principal Sind emir, Fath Ali, curtly terminated the commercial agreement which had been concluded in the period of danger. By that time Wellesley could afford to relax. Zaman Shah's threats had caused Fath Ali to send the British merchants packing, but Zaman's downfall now gave both Fath Ali of Hyderabad and Wellesley breathing-space again. For the time being neither the British nor the Afghans thought of pressing their attentions on Sind. The Afghans, for their part, were deep in dynastic quarrels, and the British were negotiating treaties with Persia as a better long-term guarantee against both French and Afghan ambitions. The Commercial and Political Agreements between Britain and Persia were signed at the beginning of 1801.[13] A few months later the French threat receded even further. Thanks partly to British naval and military action and partly to the obstinate resistance of the Egyptians, the French expeditionary force had to evacuate Egypt. During the remainder of his term as Governor General, Wellesley had his hands full in India itself. Of the Treaty of Bassein, concluded on the last day of 1802, it has been said:

The treaty unquestionably must be accepted as giving the British the Empire of India, for it reduced the head of the Maratha Confederacy to a position of complete inferiority, and, in matters external, of absolute subordination, to the British.[14]

By the end of 1803 the British under Wellesley had pacified all but Holkar among the Maratha leaders. While they were so engaged the pattern of external relations was changing again in the north-west. In 1801 the Persians had to surrender Georgia to the Russians, and in the following year they took advantage of Afghan divisions to annex the province of Khorasan, which had previously paid tribute to Afghanistan. This was to be a recurring pattern. A Russian success against Persia would be followed by a Persian thrust against Afghans and Turcomans.

Another recurring feature of external relations in this period was a tendency on the part of the Sind emirs to make overtures to the British whenever they felt nervous about the intentions of their neighbours. In 1803 Shah Shuja, another of the grandsons of the founder of the Afghan Empire, ousted his brother Mahmud and

9

became king of Kabul. Shuja soon renewed the pressure of Afghan claims on the Sind emirs, and for a time he exacted tribute again. The British would not lift a finger to help the emirs; they refused even to receive an envoy from Sind as long as their financial claims, arising from the rupture of October 1800, remained unsettled. Sind and Persia were alike neglected now that the French were far away and Zaman Shah was blind and powerless. The Persians, looking for help against Russian pressure, signed a treaty[15] with France in 1807, receiving a general as ambassador and officers as instructors for their army. Gilbert Elliot, first earl of Minto, who became Governor General in that year, quickly understood the danger. He did not see any immediate risk of invasion, but he wrote that 'many considerations denoted conclusively the extension of the enemy's views' to India.[16]

The French, as we have seen, had long since evacuated Egypt, where the Albanian Muhammad Ali was now Pasha and intent upon destroying the power of the Mameluke Beys.[17] In British eyes Muhammad Ali was far too ambitious. Not for the last time, by any means, in their imperial history, they extended support in 1807 to more tractable men, notably to the Mameluke Elfi Bey. A British expedition landed in Egypt in support of Elfi and other Mamelukes, only to discover that Elfi Bey was already dead. The expedition met with disaster, and British heads were paraded on Egyptian pikes in Cairo. Like the French before them, the British withdrew, leaving Muhammad Ali alone to develop his Egyptian estate, nominally on behalf of the Ottoman Sultan.[18] He was not unduly disturbed by his Ottoman overlord, however. In Constantinople the reactionary Janissaries had just weakened the Porte still further by substituting their nominee, Mustafa IV, for the mildly reformist Selim III.

But in 1807 British India faced a much more dangerous threat to its security than the ambitions and hostility of Muhammad Ali. After the Peace of Tilsit between Napoleon and the Tsar the British Government had to prepare for the possibility of a French and Russian invasion of India. Already Persia, in her weakness, was gradually yielding ground to the Russians on and around the Caspian. French influence was already strong at the Persian Court.

Accordingly, on 2 March 1808, the Secret Committee of the Court of Directors of the East India Company dispatched the British Government's instructions to Lord Minto. He was to take measures to prevent a hostile army from crossing the Indus, and he was to cultivate to the utmost of his power 'the favourable opinion and co-operation not only of all states and countries to the Eastward of the Indus, but also of the Afghan government and even of the Tartar tribes to the Eastward of the Caspian'. The states eastward of the Indus clearly included Sind and the Punjab; the Tartar tribes occupied the region which we now know as Turkmenistan. These instructions excluded Minto from treating with Persia, for the Home Government was sending its own envoy. But in April 1808 Sir John Malcolm, who had negotiated the treaties of January 1801, was already on his way from Bombay to Persia. The British Resident in Muscat, Captain David Seton, with a small escort of Bombay Native Infantry, set out shortly after Malcolm's departure and headed for Hyderabad and the court of the Sind emirs, for in March it had been discovered that the emirs were looking for alliance with Persia against their Afghan suzerain, and rumours had reached Bombay that the French (now so influential in Persia) had been making overtures to Sind. Later in the year Minto sent Mountstuart Elphinstone to Afghanistan and Charles Metcalfe to the Punjab.

Captain Seton's mission was to negotiate with the Sind emirs for commercial facilities and the reception of a British political agent in their country. He was to use the British claim for an indemnity (for losses incurred in 1800) as a means of obtaining concessions if necessary, and he was to make discreet inquiries about the plots and intentions of Persia and Afghanistan. Speed was essential if Seton was to forestall Persian initiatives, but Seton took his time, and a Persian envoy reached Hyderabad first. Poor Seton, unaware that missions would soon be on their way to Kabul and Lahore, and anxious to counter the extravagant promises of the Persian envoy, came to an agreement with Ghulam Ali and his family in Hyderabad. The East India Company would drop all claim to the indemnity and open factories (what we should call trading stations) at Tatta and Hyderabad. The Company and the Emirs would give each other assistance, and neither side would protect the enemies of the other. In other circumstances Seton might have been able to justify his action in going so far beyond his brief. He could have pleaded that the Persian envoy had promised Persian and French help to make Ghulam Ali Governor of Kabul and Kandahar—two of the principal cities of Afghanistan—in return for French use of Sind ports. But Sind's potential enemies included two of the countries to which Lord Minto was enjoined to send ambassadors. Shah Shuja of Afghanistan and Runjeet Singh of the Punjab were hardly likely to listen to British overtures if they knew that Britain was in alliance with Sind. Therefore, in October 1808, Lord Minto repudiated Seton's treaty and authorized fresh negotiations. This time he stipulated that there must be no commitment to help Sind against the Afghans.

So it was that Nicholas Hankey Smith, the British agent at Bushire, became one of the ambassadors appointed to secure the frontiers of India against aggression in 1808. The doctor accompanying Smith's mission to Hyderabad was required to be capable of conducting local researches; the sepoys of his escort had to have some knowledge of surveying. A nineteen-year-old ensign in the Company's service, Henry Pottinger, was a member of Smith's mission. He had left Britain at the age of sixteen to make a career in India, and this first taste of adventure set him on the road to a baronetcy for services in Sind thirty years later.

Whatever Smith's mission brought back in the way of intelligence and local knowledge, it had but little to show for its diplomacy. The emirs and the British swore eternal friendship and promised to exchange ambassadors regularly. The emirs promised not to 'allow the establishment of the tribe of the French in Sind'. But they declined to grant new commercial facilities or to receive a British political agent, for the British made no military commitment of any kind. The emirs resumed their accustomed feudal stance; they turned their backs on Europeans and the nineteenth century, watched the Indus slide past their fortresses, and slaughtered game in their well-stocked private forests. They gained twenty years more of medieval isolation, so that talk of steam engines in 1828 was to be treated as a traveller's tale.

In the meantime French influence at Teheran was still strong enough to keep Sir John Malcolm at a distance. He kicked his heels at Bushire for a month until 11 June 1808, then returned to India without even making contact with the Persian Court. Sir Harford Jones, the plenipotentiary sent from London with promises and presents, waited until the coast was clear, made his way to the Persian Court, and, to the chagrin of Malcolm and Minto, negotiated the preliminary Anglo-Persian Treaty of 12 March 1809. He gained advantage from the fact that the Persians had begun to see the one-sidedness of their French treaty. Also, his credentials were more imposing than Malcolm's. The new Anglo-Persian agreement was a preliminary treaty of friendship and union, intended as the basis of a later and more permanent arrangement. It cancelled all other Persian treaties with European states, and contained the promise that the Shah would not permit the passage of any European force through Persia, 'either towards India or towards the ports of that country'. If Persia should be threatened by a European invader, Britain would supply an armed force or a subsidy, with warlike stores and officers, to oppose the threat. In return Persia promised to help Britain to defend India if the Afghans or any other power invaded it. The penultimate article of the treaty caused trouble many years later. It stated that Britain would not take part in any war between Persia and Afghanistan, except to mediate if asked to do so by both parties. The eighth and final article, however, offered a loophole in 1838. It stipulated that in accordance with these defensive articles the Shah of Persia would not enter into any engagements inimical to Britain or 'pregnant with injury and disadvantage' to British territories in India.

Sir Harford Jones thus succeeded where the Company's envoy had failed, and in doing so he established a precedent and brought Persia for a time within the orbit of the Foreign Office. Indian official pride was appeased by the appointment of Sir John Malcolm to lead the mission which went to Teheran in 1810 to ratify the treaty. The Foreign Office continued to exercise influence, shared with the Company, until 1826, when the East India Company regained complete control and the envoy carried credentials from the Governor General of Bengal. But the envoy was also given a letter of notification from the Foreign Office—enough to maintain the connexion with London but not enough to convince other powers that the envoy had any authority. This division of responsibility helped to weaken influence in Persia at a critical period, and so contributed to the causes which made the First Afghan War.

But what mattered in the middle of 1809 was that the Sind emirs were about to consent, and that the Shah of Persia had already consented, to keep the French at arm's length. At the end of February Mountstuart Elphinstone, one of three members of a family which plays a big part in our story, arrived at Peshawar, then the winter capital of the king of Kabul. There he found Shah Shuja,

13

grandson of the Durrani Emperor Ahmed Shah, apparently secure in possession of the throne. This was the first official contact between Britain and Afghanistan. Archbold has called Elphinstone's treaty[19] with Shuja a useless measure against 'an imaginary Franco-Persian combination'. We have to remember that Elphinstone could not yet know of Jones's success in Teheran. Under his treaty the 'servants of the heavenly throne' (Shuja's turbulent subjects) were bound, in the cause of mutual defence, to prevent the passage through Afghanistan of French and Persian troops on their way to India, and Britain promised to pay the cost of their service to the extent of her ability. Like the Sindians and the Persians, the Afghans were to exclude Frenchmen from their kingdom. Their treaty had a very short life. Indeed it was hardly worth the labour of the clerk who penned it for the Governor General's signature, for Fath Khan, Barukzai, the Warwick of Afghanistan, helped Mahmud to recover his throne from Shuja at the battle of Nimla, on the road from Jalalabad to Kabul. Nevertheless, in the early summer of 1809, among the splendours of Peshawar, Shuja and Elphinstone concluded their brief and optimistic treaty. 'The veil of separation', they said, 'shall be lifted up from between them, and they shall in no manner interfere in each other's countries.' The words enshrine the only lasting achievement of Elphinstone's mission to Peshawar. The veil of separation was well and truly lifted.

Elphinstone was only thirty when he negotiated his treaty with Shah Shuja. His host at Peshawar was about the same age. The negotiators at Amritsar in April 1809 were also young for such responsibility. Charles Metcalfe and Runjeet Singh concluded a treaty which committed the British in India and the Ruler of the Punjab to live in perpetual friendship. Britain would refrain from interference in the Rajah's territories north of the Sutlej, and the Rajah would ensure that there were never more Sikh troops on the left bank, that is south, of the Sutlej than he needed for internal security in his territories there. The treaty was short and simple. Its only ambiguity, to an oriental mind, lay in the expression: north of the Sutlej. It became necessary, at some cost, to convince Runjeet Singh in 1836–7 that the expression did not apply to any territories to which he laid claim west of the Indus. A glance at the map will show how tempting it could be for an interested party to treat the Indus below Mithankot as a prolongation of the Sutlej.

Within a year of these treaties the British Government felt secure enough in its Indian possessions to order a reduction in military expenses 'within the narrowest bound that may be consistent with the publick security and interests'.[20] Napoleon and Alexander were still allies, but they were fully occupied in Europe. For the time being all was peace in the north-west. But the British in India had not been content to leave the Sind emirs entirely in isolation. On 2 January 1810 Lieutenant Henry Pottinger and Captain Charles Christie left Bombay to explore Sind and Baluchistan, then hardly known and rarely visited by Europeans, and to find out what was going on in western Afghanistan and southern Persia. We should call it a reconnaissance. To Pottinger and Christie it was a high and dangerous adventure, requiring the use of disguise for some of the way. They parted company beyond Baluchistan. Christie went to Herat and Pottinger headed west into southern Persia. They met again in Isfahan. Pottinger was the lucky one of the two. He returned to Bombay at the beginning of 1811 with his report. Christie stayed behind during the frontier fighting which broke out in that year between Persia and Russia, and died during a Russian attack in 1812.[21] Henry Pottinger eventually published an account of his adventures, having made his mark as a promising young officer.

The Treaty of Gulistan, concluded after British mediation in 1813, excluded Persian warships from the Caspian and gave Russia vast tracts of Persian territory on the shores of that sea.[22] Britain, during the two years of sporadic fighting in northern Persia, had first given Persia some help in accordance with the Anglo-Persian Treaty of 1809. Napoleon's invasion of Russia, however, complicated matters for the British Government, which now found itself in alliance with both combatants in the war on the Caspian. Hence the mediation in 1813. In the following year an attempt was made to reduce the risk of future wars between Persia and Russia. One article of the definitive Anglo-Persian Treaty of 25 November 1814 provided for a frontier settlement, to be negotiated with British help.

The treaty just mentioned, in the charming Persian style which distinguishes many contemporary documents, was introduced as 'these happy leaves, a nosegay plucked from the thornless Garden of Concord'. It broadened and completed the treaty of 1809. The Shah of Persia would prevent any European army from invading India through his territory, and would do his best to induce Central Asian neighbours to do the same. Britain would not interfere in internal Persian disputes, even if one of the parties to a dispute offered her a province for her help. Another article—the one which proposed a Persian–Russian frontier settlement—insisted that the treaty was defensive, and even included a simple definition of aggression: an attack upon the territories of another state. The definition was necessary because the next article provided for an annual subsidy of 200,000 tomauns (about £150,000), to be used exclusively for the raising and disciplining of an army and to be payable in time of war only if the British were satisfied that Persia was the victim and not the aggressor. As in 1809, the Shah promised to help Britain in the event of an Afghan invasion of India, and Britain promised not to intervene in any quarrel between the Shah and Afghanistan unless asked by both to mediate.

At that stage the possibility of Afghan invasions was very remote. A Barukzai nobleman, the Fath Khan already mentioned, was the true ruler of most of Afghanistan, the Sadozai Mahmud a mere cipher. Under Fath Khan's influence the Barukzai family prospered everywhere but in Herat. Fath Khan's brother, Dost Muhammad Khan, began to assert his leadership in the years between 1809 and 1818. Those years of dynastic quarrels inside Afghanistan culminated in the atrocious murder of Fath Khan in revenge for an offence committed by Dost Muhammad against the ruling family of Herat. Those who have tended to idolize Dost Muhammad in previous accounts of the First Afghan War have neglected the early part of his life, in which he shared to the full in the general Afghan taste for the sweets of vengeance and the excitement of war. The *Asiatic Journal* (in an article published in 1838 and quoted by George Buist) said that the Afghans 'are neither irritable nor implacable, but retain a long remembrance of injuries not retaliated: revenge is esteemed a duty'. We should remember this in all that we read about the First Afghan War.

In 1818, then, the quarrel between Barukzais and Sadozais in Afghanistan turned into a blood feud. Fath Khan was first blinded, then hacked to pieces. Mahmud Shah fled to Herat, where he died in 1829. The Barukzais blinded the man who surrendered Kabul to them. It took Dost Muhammad eight more years to fight his way to the top, and he stayed there until the British and the Sikhs had him deposed in favour of Shah Shuja.

Shuja himself travelled far and with fluctuating fortunes after Fath Khan gave his throne to Mahmud. Runjeet Singh's hospitality cost him the Koh-i-Noor diamond in 1813, and he suffered many humiliations, but he never lost the conviction that he was the rightful sovereign of Kabul and the empire based on Kabul. At the end of 1815 he came to rest at Ludhiana. The British in India, never reluctant to give sanctuary to what Emily Eden once called 'black Chevaliers[23] de Saint Georges', awarded him a pension in 1818. By this time, it must be remembered, Afghanistan had become a byword for anarchy. The country's internal divisions might reduce the risk of invasion from the north-west, but the constant strife was always unsettling. Runjeet Singh, in his prime, profited by Afghan disunity, detaching Multan, Kashmir, and Peshawar from their none too solid connexion with Kabul by the end of 1819. Britain, as we have seen, had taken out an insurance policy, the premium being Shah Shuja's annual pension. Further south she now moved much closer to Sind. The treaty with Cutch, signed in 1816, was extended in 1819, so that Cutch became a protected state. (In 1825 Henry Pottinger, by then a major, became Political Resident in Cutch.)

The days of Sind's isolation now begin to be numbered, and already the stage is set for the triumphs and tragedies of 1838–42. In Afghanistan Shuja's family and Dost Muhammad and his brothers are irreconcilable enemies; Runjeet Singh, by becoming suzerain of Peshawar and diverting the tribute into Sikh coffers, has started a quarrel which only his death will end; the British in India, by taking Cutch under their protection, have laid the foundations of a forward policy along the Indus; the conduct of British relations with Persia in times of stress is now liable to be taken out of the Indian Government's hands by the Foreign Office; the treaty with Persia forbids British interference in Persian quarrels with Afghanistan, except as a mediator, and does not foresee the possibility of Persian subjection to Russian control; and it is now the British Cabinet at Westminster that frames and directs from a distance the foreign and defence policies of British India.

The next nineteen years—the years between Queen Victoria's birth and coronation—unfold the gradual preparations for Britain's fateful leap into Central Asia.

CHAPTER 2

BRITAIN RECOGNIZES THE RUSSIAN THREAT

The Directors are much afraid of the Russians. So am I, and the Russians begin to threaten us. They hint that they have open to them the route to Baghdad, and they announce the presence in Petersburg of an Afghan chief, and of ambassadors from Runjeet Singh. I feel confident we shall have to fight the Russians on the Indus, and I have long had a presentiment that I should meet them there, and gain a great battle. All dreams, but I have had them a long time.

LORD ELLENBOROUGH, *Political Diary*, 3 September 1829

The Concert of Europe, which Castlereagh saw as an instrument for bringing back the world to peaceful habits, was shaken almost from the start by the military antics of the Russian Emperor. The British Government at that time was inclined to show less alarm than some others in the face of Russian ambitions in the Balkans. Both Castlereagh and Canning seem to have thought that it was possible to manage Alexander, and Canning[1] attempted to manage Nicholas I, with considerable early success. But British diplomacy alone could hardly suffice to check the Russian advance southwards and eastwards from their European heartland. Awareness of this fact dawned slowly, as we shall see, and there came a time when scepticism about Russian designs in Asia became the luxury of a minority. Codrington's guns at Navarino Bay wrecked the Holy Alliance as well as Ibrahim's fleet.[2] Wellington gave up trying to manage the Russians, feeling cheated by Nicholas, and allowed Britain to become the increasingly angry spectator of Russian successes against Turkey and Persia.

In 1820, however, Russia had no immediate cause for quarrel with either Turkey or Persia, and there could be but little talk of Anglo-Russian rivalry in Central Asia while the frontier of British India rested on the Sutlej and the Russians were still feeling their way round the northern shore of the Caspian. We have already noticed that Cutch came under British protection in 1819. As was to be expected, the proximity of British troops to Sind resulted in friction. A war was avoided, and the fruit of the Governor General's peaceful policy was the treaty of 9 November 1820. Its object was to prevent frontier disputes and to promote and strengthen friendship between Sind and British India. The previous treaty had excluded the 'tribe of the French' from Sind. The new treaty excluded *all* Europeans, and Americans for good measure.

This was the era of long and dangerous journeys among the Khanates of Central Asia, by both Russian and British travellers. One Russian envoy who visited Khiva in 1819–20 later wrote that the possession of Khiva could give Russia command of all the riches of Asia. 'It would become the point of reunion for all the commerce of Asia, and would shake to the centre of India the enormous commercial superiority of the dominators of the sea'.[3] This was very probably wishful thinking, but we shall see that Russians were not alone in expecting great advantage from the development of trade with the states of Central Asia. Who would get there first? The Russians stood at one end of ancient caravan routes, long and punishing to armies; the British were so near and yet so far from controlling the unexplored and long neglected Indus.

This is not the place for an essay on the birth of the modern Greek nation, but the War for Greek Independence does play a part in the development of Anglo-Russian rivalry in Asia. From 1821 onwards the Russians, making use of the vague rights accorded to them in the Treaty of Kutchuk Kainardji in 1774, kept up a constant pressure on the Ottoman Porte, ostensibly on behalf of the Sultan's Christian subjects. The British Government hoped, by diplomatic means, to keep the peace between Russia and Turkey. Therefore, both Castlereagh and Canning aimed at a compromise settlement of the quarrel between the Sultan and his Greek subjects as a means to that larger end. It is one of the more amusing ironies of history that the conservative Canning, who would probably have voted against the Reform Bill in 1832, received most of the credit among liberals for defending the cause of freedom and constitutional government against the forces of reaction. Peace between Russia and Turkey was what he wanted most of all. It was essential, for the preservation of the balance of power in Europe, to maintain the Ottoman Empire. At the same time it was essential to Britain's position in Asia that the power seated astride her communications with India should be both friendly to her and at peace with its neighbours.

2-2

In those days there were two routes between the Mediterranean and the Indian Ocean. The older of the two, for British merchants, led through Syria and the Pashalik of Baghdad to the Persian Gulf; the other went overland from Alexandria to Suez and was as yet little developed. It is immediately apparent that the existence of an ambitious Egyptian Pasha with a strong and efficient army could be a source of annoyance to Britain as well as to Egypt's Ottoman suzerain. In 1820 the British had to warn Muhammad Ali not to try conclusions with Abyssinia, and he turned his aggressive attentions elsewhere.[4] By 1826 he had an army of 90,000 men,[5] and his artillery was equal to the best in Europe. In February 1825 part of this formidable army landed in Europe at the request of the Sultan. Ibrahim and his troops arrived in the Morea with a mission much to their taste—to extinguish the Greek rebellion and to prepare the province for Egyptian colonization.[6] Ibrahim's intention was not immediately obvious, but quite early in 1826 Canning both understood the plan and knew what he must do. On 10 February 1826 he wrote his instructions to his cousin Stratford Canning, ambassador to the Porte. Britain, he said, would interpose her maritime power between the Morea and Egypt unless the Porte disavowed its intention to allow Egyptian colonization and ordered Ibrahim to halt.[7]

From that time until his death Canning worked to prevent Russia from intervening alone and to construct a Greek settlement which the Sultan might be brought to accept after the minimum of coercion. The Egyptian venture in the Morea was to be condemned on all counts—as an invitation to Russian intervention, as an affront to Christian feelings throughout Europe, as yet another means of strengthening Muhammad Ali at the expense of the Ottoman Sultan,[8] and as a corporate atrocity against the Greeks, whose struggle, though by no means as clean and heroic as many believed, had captured the imaginations of English men and women. In Wellington's view Canning's policy was altogether too hard on the Sultan. The duke was no romantic. He saw complicated situations with the clarity of a great general, and he had a flair for identifying distant threats to the national interest. But the events of 1827 and 1828 also called for skill at the arts of diplomacy and compromise, in which Wellington did not excel. The advantage gained at Navarino Bay was wasted under his administration.[9]

In the Public Record Office there is a letter from Ellenborough to

Bengal through the Secret Committee of the Company, showing just how great a change there was in British policy in the East when Wellington took office a few months after the Battle of Navarino Bay. We know that the Speech from the Throne on 29 January 1828 referred to the battle as an 'untoward event', and as a 'deeply lamented' conflict with the naval force of an ancient ally.[10] On 6 June a letter left Bengal addressed to the Secret Committee. Its writer rather rashly assumed that Britain would be at war with Turkey after what had happened at Navarino Bay. But the president of the Board of Control when that letter arrived at the end of November was Edward Law, Lord Ellenborough, who was as close to the duke of Wellington (and as much in sympathy with him) as any man in the Cabinet. On 2 December 1828 Ellenborough haughtily dismissed the rash assumption:

We believe you may now trust that it will be the constant object of His Majesty's Government to maintain the friendship which has almost uninterruptedly subsisted between this country and Turkey. It is our interest, both as an European and as an Asiatic state, that the Ottoman Porte should preserve all its present power; and in all future intercourse with the dependencies of that Empire you will make the maintenance of the integrity of the Turkish Dominions the unvaried object of your policy...[11]

When Ellenborough wrote his letter, Russia and Turkey had been at war for eight months. Britain was still bound by the Treaty of London to prevent hostilities between Turkey and Greece, and with some reluctance Wellington allowed the French to flush the remaining Turkish/Egyptian troops out of the Morea in the summer and autumn of 1828.[12] But Britain remained neutral in the dispute between Russia and Turkey. Wellington viewed the Russian proceedings with extreme distaste, never deluding himself that the Turks might win, and powerless to act on their behalf.

At this point it is necessary to leave the Russian-Turkish conflict for a while and return to the year before Canning's death. In passing we should also note that 1826 was the year in which Dost Muhammad achieved supremacy at Kabul. But what most concerns us about that year is the outbreak of war between Russia and Persia. The Treaty of Gulistan had left part of the frontier still in dispute where it ran between Erivan and Lake Gokcha. It is notoriously difficult to fix the responsibility for an act of aggression, or even to obtain an internationally acceptable definition of the word. What is certain in this instance, however, is that after fruit-less negotiations, in which a British envoy acted as mediator, Russian troops occupied Gokcha, and that the Persians, their national spirit fully roused, attacked Russian positions in the area in 1826 with considerable early success.[13] The British envoy judged that Persia was the aggressor within the meaning of the Anglo-Persian Treaty of 1814.

The Russians in the frontier area had been caught off their balance. They rallied with the arrival of reinforcements, and the Persian troops had no further success in 1826. They fared little better in 1827, registering only one success and failing to follow it up. The Russians utterly routed them at Tabriz. Negotiations opened in November. The subsequent treaty[14] humiliated Persia all the more because the Russians could afford to be relatively lenient. They did not keep Tabriz but withdrew behind the line of the River Aras for most of the distance between Erivan and the Caspian. Russian attention was distracted by the imminent prospect of hostilities with Turkey.[15] Though the short-term effects of the settlement on Persia were comparatively light, the long-term effects were momentous, and amply confirmed Ellenborough's fears expressed soon after he took over the Board of Control for the first time:

...What we apprehend is not the conquest of the Persian...monarchy, but the establishment at the Court of Teheran of a Russian influence which would practically place the resources of Persia at the disposal of the Court of St Petersburgh.[16]

Such was the effect of the Treaty of Turkmanchai between Russia and Persia. We have already noted that Britain considered Persia to have been the aggressor in 1826. The duke of Wellington remarked:

...I think that Mr. Canning did not behave handsomely or wisely in leaving the Persians to the moderation and mercy of the Emperor Nicholas. We were bound to mediate in their favour; and we ought to have started, not by taking their part, for the Persians were really in the wrong, but by moderating both parties; and by showing the Russians what we stated in respect to the Turks, that we must look to the conclusion of the contest...[17]

If he had been Prime Minister at the beginning of the Russian-Persian War he would have warned Russia, as he warned her over

Turkey, not to go too far. Britain would be watching the contest, for the result might injure her own interests in Asia.

After the Treaty of Turkmanchai the Shah of Persia needed money urgently to pay his indemnity to the Tsar, and the British envoy made use of the opportunity to free Britain from the embarrassing third and fourth articles of the 1814 treaty. Under those articles Britain was bound, in the event of foreign aggression against Persia, to support the Shah with money for the raising and training of an army. The annual sum mentioned in the treaty was equivalent to £150,000. In this instance Britain did not consider herself under any obligation to pay the subsidy, for in her eyes Persia was the aggressor. But the British envoy, Lieutenant Colonel John Macdonald Kinneir of the East India Company, arranged to make a single payment of £150,000 to the Shah in return for the cancellation of the subsidy articles in the Anglo-Persian Treaty.[18] Wellington's Cabinet applauded the envoy's action, for Persia's enemy was still ostensibly Britain's ally. They saw no prospect of making Persia strong enough to overcome the Russians, and they considered that there was a cheaper way of keeping Persia in one piece. Ellenborough wrote to Bentinck with instructions for transmission to the envoy in Teheran. The Shah should be told that the abrogation of particular articles of a treaty would not change Anglo-Persian relations, for their 'amity has always rested not upon the words of treaties but upon a deliberate consideration of the material interests of the two states'. At the same time he asked Bentinck to deliver a warning to the Shah through the envoy. The Shah was not to engage in the quarrels of European states, for 'we will not stretch forth our hand to save the Crown of Persia should its government break faith and be disposed to seek advantage for itself in the distress of powers with which it is at peace'.[19] In other words, Persia must keep its hands off Turkey. At the end of 1828 there were already signs that the defeated Shah was seeking solace on his western frontier, and he might also look for gain in the direction of Afghanistan one day, with Russian encouragement.

Ellenborough's fears were shared in India. In June 1828 Sir Charles Metcalfe, as a member of the Governor General's Supreme Council, wrote a minute in which he said:

...Were we ever to expect any essential aid from Persia, in the time of our own need, we should most assuredly find ourselves miserably deceived and disappointed. If ever Russia be in a condition to set forth an army again India, Persia most probably will be under her banners.[20]

Ellenborough had been appalled when he took over at the India Board in September 1828. On the 15th we find him settling in at his new office, with its view of the Thames:

...I spoke to Lord Melville[21] of the affairs of Persia, to which I must direct my immediate attention. We must bring our Persian diplomacy into a line with what we adopt elsewhere with regard to Russia. I dare say I shall find our Resident there is acting in the Russian interests under instructions given as far back as 1813, or earlier.

Ten days later he wrote:

I am sure we have too much sacrificed our interests on the side of India to a weakness in favour of Russia. All our exertions at Teheran have been for Russian interests. The possession of Erivan gives them now the command of an entrance into both Persia and Armenia...Sir J. Malcolm fears they will be compelled, as we were in India, to make new conquests to secure those they have already made. They have already been within 300 miles of Mosul, where the Tigris becomes navigable to the Persian Gulf, and there seems to be nothing to oppose them.[22]

And again at the beginning of October:

...Our influence in Persia has been much weakened by our vacillating conduct. I must endeavour to retrieve our affairs there.[23]

Part of the trouble was the result of the inability of the British and Indian Governments to pursue a consistent course of representation in Persia. We have seen how the Foreign Office assumed the responsibility in 1809, soothing the injured pride of men in Calcutta by allowing the Indian Government to convey the ratification of the 1809 treaty to Teheran. For several years Westminster and Calcutta shared the responsibility; the ambassador or chargé d'affaires would be an official of the Company in India, holding credentials from the Crown. But from 1826 to 1835 the envoy was usually a Company official with no credentials and with only a letter of notification from the Foreign Office. Colonel Macdonald Kinneir had to negotiate with the Russians without proper diplomatic status. In September 1828 Ellenborough discussed the question of British representation in Persia with the duke of Wellington. The duke thought it better to leave the Resident in Persia dependent on the East India Company, thus giving him 'a freer scope as the representative of a great Asiatic power'. This would relieve Britain's 'Indian policy from the embarrassment to which our European connections with Russia may give rise'.[24] This is a point to be remembered when we come to the end of 1838. Wellington thought it expedient to separate relations with Russia in Europe from relations with Russia in Asia. It was very convenient on occasion to treat British India as a separate and autonomous Asiatic power. Ellenborough at this time thought that 'our policy in Europe and Asia ought to be the same—to pull down the Russian power'. Palmerston eventually placed in Teheran an envoy sent from London, and in doing so he took Ellenborough's line, so that the British Government could control all that happened from Teheran to Calcutta from 1836 onwards. But the effort involved him in subterfuges which have in great measure concealed the truth of the First Afghan War ever since.

In 1828 all this was a decade away. With hardly a pause for breath, the Russians in 1828 crippled the independence of Persia and set out to discipline the Ottoman Porte. Wellington and his colleagues—including some who had serious misgivings about the conservatism of British policy at home and abroad[25]—reaffirmed their devotion to the Turkish alliance. In February Prince Lieven presented Wellington with a memorandum: Russia would co-operate with Britain in the Balkans; but, if Britain demurred, Russia would act alone. Wellington stood aside, and vetoed French proposals which would have continued the pressure of the three 'Navarino powers' on Turkey.[26] We have already noted that he only reluctantly allowed the French to clear the Sultan's forces from the Morea that summer. Ellenborough, ever inclined to dramatize his political experience, wrote in his diary: 'I look forward with horror to the war, not only as affecting the general interests of Europe, but as a war shocking to humanity.'[27]

In June we find Ellenborough enumerating the terrible privations of the advancing Russian army and concluding that such punishment will be 'the judgement of Providence on unprincipled ambition'.[28] Wellington did not share his emotional reaction to the news, but in September he somewhat cynically acknowledged that things must be very bad for the Russians when generals die.[29] One remembers with a jolt that they were remarking upon the misfortunes of a power with which Britain and France were still bound by treaty to work for a settlement of the Greek problem. The

Wellington government was in a very unhappy position. Public opinion might be wakening to the Russian menace, but what concerned many *voters* was the plight of the Greeks. Wellington's preference for the Turks, or, more fairly, his refusal to take sides in the local quarrel while taking the course which he considered most helpful to British interests, was far from popular. The argument between those who feared and those who trusted Russia was only just starting.[30]

The Treaty of London, what Wellington called 'the Greek Treaty', irritated the British Government at every turn. Wellington admitted that Britain could do nothing for the Turks until the Greek question was settled. 'We can do nothing, because we cannot pretend to enter into a contest to save the Turks, in breach of an engagement and at the risk of a contest with France...'[31] Ellenborough conveyed the Cabinet's feelings when he wrote in his diary:

I have always been for getting out of the treaty. We have been dragged along very unwillingly—we have been subjected to much humiliation. We seem to have gained nothing by all our compliances. We have been led on from the violation of one principle to that of another. Our position has discouraged Turkey. We have been made the tools of Russia, and have been duped with our eyes open.[32]

That was at the end of April 1829. Wellington's comment may be found in a letter written to his Foreign Secretary, Lord Aberdeen, on the 22nd of that month. He saw France still in possession of the Morea, and Russia 'on the high road to efface the name of Turkey from the list of Powers of Europe, while we are looking on and holding the candle...'.[33] In July the Turkish resistance began to collapse. Ellenborough read Lord Heytesbury's letters from St Petersburg, where he was ambassador, and found them and him 'very Russian'.[34] At the end of August both Wellington and Ellenborough were lamenting the Russian success. Wellington complained that the British Government had 'made the greatest sacrifice of opinions, principles, and national pride and prejudice to its allies'. In return those allies had 'not performed their promises'.[35] Ellenborough wrote that the Russians had quite dispersed the Turkish army in Asia. 'Every success of theirs in that quarter', he wrote, 'makes my heart bleed. I consider it a victory gained over me, as Asia is *mine*.'[36]

Britain recognizes the Russian threat

The British Government's depression was at its lowest in September and October 1829, when the full implications of the Russian-Turkish peace treaty[37] were analysed in London. The Turks had finally yielded on the Greek question, and they had yielded much else besides. The correspondence between the Foreign Secretary and the British ambassador at St Petersburg shows ample and sometimes amusing evidence of the mood in London. At the end of September Lord Heytesbury wrote that the world must be prepared

ere long to see the Emperor of Russia assume the novel character of Friend, Ally, and Protector of the Ottoman Empire...The Turkish Sultan will probably be as submissive hereafter to the orders of the Czar as any of the Princes of India to those of the Company...A dismemberment of the Empire could offer no advantages to Russia equal to this.[38]

Lord Heytesbury appeared to view the prospect with great complacency. But Wellington, Aberdeen, and Ellenborough, those most intimately concerned with the framing of the policy to be followed after Adrianople, saw no reason to be complacent. Wellington speaks first:

...all parties in Europe must view this Treaty of Peace in the same light as we do. They may not have such reasons as we may have to look with jealousy and anxiety at its consequences; but they must all consider it in the same light as the death blow to the independence of the Ottoman Porte, and the forerunner of the dissolution and extinction of its power...[39]

Ellenborough speaks next:

...That Russia will attempt, by conquest or by influence, to secure Persia as a road to the Indus, I have the most intimate conviction. It is evident that the latter and surer mode, that of influence, is the one she now selects...[40]

By the end of October Aberdeen had examined the Treaty of Adrianople from every angle and concluded that he and his colleagues had been right from the start. In spite of all protestations to the contrary, the Emperor Nicholas had used the quarrel over Greece and the façade of his alliance with France and Britain to secure for Russia a great increase of military power. Aberdeen wrote:

Under the present treaty the territorial acquisitions of Russia are small, it must be admitted, in extent, although most important in their character...The cession of the Asiatick fortresses with their neighbouring districts not only secures to Russia the uninterrupted occupation of the coast of the Black Sea; but places her in a situation so commanding as to control at pleasure the destiny of Asia Minor. Permanently advanced into the centre of Armenia, in the midst of a Christian population, Russia holds the keys, both of the Persian and the Turkish provinces; and whether she may be disposed to extend her conquests to the East or to the West, to Teheran or to Constantinople, no serious obstacle can arrest her progress...[41]

There are moments in the study of history when three or four words may sum up a whole era. Aberdeen wrote the phrase that most clearly expressed the situation after the Treaty of Adrianople —'Russia holds the keys'. In this long dispatch to Heytesbury he dissected every article of the treaty in such a way that his every comment became an accusation. In broad effect the dispatch accused the Emperor Nicholas of cheating his British allies. Nevertheless, Aberdeen instructed Heytesbury to read the dispatch to Count Nesselrode and to use every 'caution and explanation' to 'prevent its producing an unpleasant effect'.[42] How could Heytesbury be expected to convey what amounted to a lecture on Russian duplicity to the Russian Foreign Minister without giving offence? The task was clearly impossible. Heytesbury replied at the end of November:

Notwithstanding all the caution which I used, and the explanations which I gave, in obedience to your Lordship's instructions, the communication of your Lordship's despatch No. 22 has produced anything but a favourable impression. Indeed I have never seen Count Nesselrode so much moved by anything since I have had the honour of being in relation with him...[43]

To make matters worse, the French had sent a note full of compliments about the Emperor's magnanimity and moderation, and the Austrians had been politely non-committal, giving no great pleasure but causing no discernible offence.[44]

Aberdeen's reply to Heytesbury's account of the uncomfortable interview with Count Nesselrode was a little masterpiece of controlled anger. Nesselrode had hinted that Russia could find plenty of material for a polemical reply if the British wanted a paper war. Aberdeen said:

Nothing can be further from our desire than to engage in a 'paper war' or any other sort of war with Count Nesselrode; but we had pledged ourselves to deliver our true opinion, when we should be informed of the conditions of the peace, respecting the character of the war which has been carried on by Russia against the Porte. We believe that we have spoken the truth.

Notwithstanding our opinion of the falsehood and ambition of the Emperor Nicholas, and of his government, our desire to avoid any misunderstanding is as sincere as if we believed them to be possessed of honesty and principle...My despatch was certainly not calculated to produce an agreeable impression...When you give an account in your publick despatch of the manner in which Count Nesselrode received your communication it is no doubt very proper to detail all his expostulation and remonstrances; but I think you might at the same time have given us a little of your own share in the dialogue. You will recollect that your duty was not only to read my despatch to him, but to support and enforce its reasoning by every means in your power. In short, to be animated by the same spirit; and, if possible, to make it more efficacious. I cannot help thinking, however, that you are a little like Candide, in the 'best possible of all worlds,' and I have only to hope that you will open your eyes to the realities of things...[45]

The British Government now believed that one of the 'realities of things' in Europe and Asia was the 'unprincipled ambition' of the Emperor Nicholas and his ministers. A great change had come over the world since the death of Alexander I in 1825. The living proof of that change, in the British view, was the Treaty of Adrianople. Russia had set herself up as a determined rival of the British in Asia, and Russia, as Aberdeen said, held the keys in Asia Minor.

In October 1829 there had appeared a book by the visionary Colonel de Lacy Evans—his second in just over a year. The first, appearing in 1828, had discussed the *Designs of Russia*. Now his theme was the *Practicability of an Invasion of British India*. There is evidence that he wrote it in a hurry, and with knowledge of the Treaty of Adrianople. Ministers in London were deeply impressed. Within forty-eight hours of reading the book Ellenborough sent copies to Macdonald Kinneir in Persia and Malcolm in Bombay.[46] In effect Evans visualized a Russian march from the Caspian to Khiva, followed by an advance as far up the Oxus in boats as possible and a march across the Hindu Kush to the Indus. Ellenborough wrote:

...I think it clear that the invasion of India could not be attempted till the third year; but when should we begin to take precautions? A government wholly Asiatic would not be still if the Russians took possession of Khiva; but ours, chained by European politics, would hardly move if they entered Cabul. We ought to have full information as to Cabul, Bokhara, and Khiva. My letter of last year directed the attaining of information; but I dare say nothing has been done.[47]

On the following day Ellenborough again contemplated the possibilities suggested by Evans:

Upon the subject of the invasion of India my idea is that the thing is not only practicable but easy, unless we determine to act as an Asiatic Power. On the acquisition of Khiva by the Russians we should occupy Lahore and Cabul. It is not on the Indus that an enemy is to be met. If we do not meet him in Cabul, at the foot of the Hindu Koosh, or in its passes, we had better remain on the Sutlege. If the Russians once occupy Cabul they may remain there with the Indus in their front, till they have organised insurrection in our rear, and completely equipped their army...[48]

What Ellenborough, the British Government, and the British in India most lacked was reliable information about the geography, politics, and economy of the Central Asian states. Ellenborough became obsessed with the idea of opening up Central Asia to British influence before the Russians got there. Within a few weeks of reading the book by Evans he was considering the navigability of the uncharted Indus. He read all available accounts by travellers and surveyors and began to envisage fleets of naval and merchant craft of up to 200 tons plying between Lahore and the sea: '...And no British flag has ever floated upon the waters of this river. Please God it shall, and in triumph, to the source of all its tributary streams.'[49]

A week later Ellenborough had an opportunity to discuss all these thoughts with the Prime Minister, who had also read and been disturbed by Evans's book. Wellington found that he and Ellenborough had been thinking along very similar lines, especially on the question of gathering information about the countries between the Caspian and the Indus. But he was ever a sensible and practical foil for Ellenborough's more extravagant notions. He quietly observed that the British in India could easily beat a Russian army of up to 30,000 men moving down from Kabul. Their very presence in Afghanistan, however, would put Britain to enormous military expense. Ellenborough proposed that the Indian Government should be authorized to act as an Asiatic power, ignoring the effect of its actions on Britain in Europe, if the Russians moved towards Kabul. Wellington, more cautious, said the Governor General could be allowed to spend money freely to counter a Russian advance, without waiting for further orders, but should not have discretion to advance to meet the Russians with an army without instructions from home.[50] Ellenborough's account of the conversation with Wellington does not, in the author's view, by any means rule out the possibility that a Governor General in such circumstances might receive instructions from home to advance to meet the Russians.

However that may be, the conversation between the duke of Wellington and Lord Ellenborough on Wednesday 16 December 1829 had momentous results. It led Ellenborough, with Wellington's full approval, to set in motion the policies and machinery that made the First Afghan War. The first two chapters of this study have, the author hopes, placed the quarrel squarely in its proper context of European rivalries on the road to Asia. The next part of the story charts the collision course on which Britain embarked at the end of 1829.

BRITISH AIMS IN CENTRAL ASIA
1830–1838

CHAPTER 3

WELLINGTON'S ADMINISTRATION
AND THE MASTER PLAN

...The Home Government have got frightened at the designs of
Russia, and desired that some intelligent officer should be sent to
acquire information in the countries bordering on the Oxus and the
Caspian; and I, knowing nothing of all this, come forward and
volunteer precisely for what they want. Lord Bentinck jumps at
it...

LIEUTENANT ALEXANDER BURNES,
aged 26, to his sister, September 1831

National legend has it that Arthur Wellesley, the first duke of
Wellington, was the archetypal conservative, lamenting any and
every change in the social and economic structure of his country.
If this were a true and complete account of the duke one would find
all the evidence needed, surely, in the history of his only term of
office as Prime Minister in his own right. But the account does not
stand up for long when one considers the circumstances in which
he exercised power from January 1828 until November 1830.
Party did not mean much to him. He saw himself as a defender of
the national interests at home and overseas in a period of revolution.
Reforms and improvements continued during his term of office.
The railway age opened while he was Prime Minister; his Home
Secretary created a metropolitan police force; the Test and Cor-
poration Acts were repealed; Catholics won their emancipation.
But none of these was the product of revolutionary zeal on the
duke's part. The Preface to the Book of Common Prayer precisely
conveys the spirit of Wellington's policy at the time. We have only
to apply what it says to the constitution instead of to the Church of
England:

...Accordingly we find, that in the reign of several Princes of blessed
memory since the Reformation, the Church, upon just and weighty considerations her thereunto moving, hath yielded to make such alterations
in some particulars, as in their respective times were thought convenient:
Yet so, as that the main Body and Essentials of it (as well in the chiefest
materials, as in the frame and order thereof) have still continued the same
unto this day, and do yet stand firm and unshaken, notwithstanding all

35

the vain attempts and impetuous assaults made against it, by such men as are given to change, and have always discovered a greater regard to their own private fancies and interests, than to that duty they owe to the publick...

We have already observed that Wellington was no faction fighter. He grew up as a soldier, after all, and not as a party politician. Melbourne was much better than he at keeping quarrelling colleagues united; indeed it was a Tory faction that brought Wellington down in November 1830.[1] He would soon have gone, in any case, but some of his own men hastened his departure by turning on him. It was Wellington's care to keep the 'main body and essentials' of the constitution 'firm and unshaken', but without 'too much stiffness in refusing' reforms. The author sees the duke of Wellington as a general planning and conducting his greatest defensive battle at this period. But the fortress which he was defending was not merely the moated castle of a selfish aristocracy; it was the British constitution and empire.

The frame and order of things were threatened both at home and abroad in the years of Wellington's ministry. To the Balance of Power in Europe he applied the principle practised at home. The integrity of the Ottoman Empire was an essential part of the European structure. Nicholas I of Russia was subverting the peace and stability of Europe when he made war on Turkey, and the peace and stability of Europe were more important in Wellington's scale of values than the welfare of the Greek rebels. Yet there was no objection in principle to the autonomy of the Greeks. What was objectionable was the method of those working for that end. It may be useful to shake an apple tree if you have no ladder, but it is absurd to cut it down to get at the crop. Aberdeen wrote in November 1829:

...we have fallen upon what seems to be the best and most expeditious way of settling the Greek question...The prospect of terminating the whole affair by giving an independent existence to Greece with restricted limits has been felt as a great advantage by all of us...[2]

When Aberdeen wrote those words he and his colleagues were undeniably making the best of a bad job. They were relieved to have the Greek affair settled, and collectively furious with Nicholas I because of his ill treatment of the Ottoman Porte. They now had to work out a plan of counter-action, for the next Russian thrust would pass between the Caspian and Aral Seas and would be aimed at India.

As we saw earlier, Wellington and Ellenborough came to a most important agreement in conversation on Wednesday 16 December 1829. Two days later Ellenborough conferred with the chairman and deputy chairman of the East India Company's Court of Directors known to him as the 'chairs'. He wrote in his diary:

>...I told them of my conversation with the Duke and went over the same ground. They acquiesced in all I said. We shall have the mission to Scinde and to Lahore, and the commercial venture up the Indus, and the instruction to Macdonald. In short, all I want.[3]

We shall see soon what Lord Ellenborough meant by these last two sentences. One can image the scene at this meeting of the president of the Board of Control and the chairman and deputy chairman of the Court of Directors. The president eloquently explains the policy of opening up Central Asia to British commerce and political influence as a counter to the Russian advance. He clinches his argument by telling them that the duke of Wellington approved of the policy and the proposals now before them only on Wednesday. What stronger backing could such a policy have in 1829? 'They acquiesced in all I said...In short, all I want.' We must remember that the 'chairs' could have refused and forced Ellenborough either to amend his proposals or to send them in defiance of their wishes. He had the power to defy them. If he insisted, the Secret Committee would have to sign the dispatch whether its three members liked it or not, and whether the 'chairs' liked it or not. But the chairman and deputy chairman of the Court of Directors, expressing the corporate will of the Court, acquiesced. So far the evidence for this comes only from Ellenborough's private journal, which necessarily remained secret until long after his death. But there is further evidence in Wellington's papers. Ellenborough had met the 'chairs' on Friday. On Saturday he wrote to the duke:

>...The Chairs lend themselves most willingly to the project of repelling the Russian commerce from Cabul and Bokhara, by carrying our goods directly up the Indus...The Chairs enter thoroughly into your view of the nature of the danger to be apprehended from the advance of the Russians towards the frontier of India. I have made them see it as a question of expense...[4]

British Aims in Central Asia 1830–1838

Ellenborough told the duke that he had already asked Aberdeen to obtain information through Heytesbury about Russian activity in Asia, and that a copy of the request was also going to the Resident in Persia, through the Government of Bengal. He wanted to know the tonnage of the shipping regularly using Caspian ports, the number of commercial and naval vessels on the Caspian, the value of the annual trade on that sea, the frequency and size of caravans to Bokhara, and the value of the trade carried by that route. He wanted the information annually, and he wanted it collected without 'exciting any observation'. He told the Governor General to see that watch was kept on Russian military movements on or near the Caspian, and on any 'establishments which may be formed by them on the Eastern shore of the Caspian, having professedly a Commercial object'. He was particularly anxious to know as soon as possible if the Russians made any move towards the northern shore of the Aral Sea.

It will at all times be a matter of interest with the Board to obtain full and correct information as to the Military and Political situation of the states of Khiva and Bokhara, and Khokand—and as to the nature and extent of any commerce carried on by the subjects of Russia with the people of those countries—and it will be a source of satisfaction to them should means be found for keeping them constantly informed upon these points.[5]

British Commerce in the days of Cobden had a special mystique. There was nothing sordid about the flood of machine-made goods from British factories to the markets of the world. 'Commerce', said Cobden, 'is the grand panacea...Not a bale of merchandise leaves our shores but it bears the seeds of intelligence and fruitful thought to the members of some less enlightened community...' This British Commerce, this transmitter of progress and propagator of enlightenment, was now to be used as part of Britain's counter-action against the advance of Russian influence into Central Asia. Ellenborough wrote:

...Read Meyendorff's 'Tour in Bokhara.' It contains all the information I want as to the commerce between Bokhara and Russia. We can easily supply Bokhara with many things the Russians now furnish, and with all Indian goods cheaper by the Indus than the Ganges; but what the Bokharians are to send us in return I do not well see, except turquoises, lapis lazuli, and the ducats they receive from Russia. We may get shawls cheaper by navigating the Indus.[6]

The dispatch from the Foreign Office to Heytesbury took about a week to reach St Petersburg, and in acknowledging it on 18 January he showed that he was less apprehensive than his colleagues in London about the activities of the Russians in Asia. He considered that the Russians, no less than any other nation, had an undeniable right to look to their commercial interests, 'even though they should be found in competition with those of any other, even friendly state'. Certainly the attention of the Russians was openly directed towards India, and it was certainly their primary object to establish commercial relations *at least* with the states between the Caspian and the Indus. But, he added:

...whatever wild thoughts may be germinating in the heads of the Russians generally, the Emperor and his Government have, I am convinced, too thorough a consciousness of the real weakness of the country to entertain for an instant serious thought of ever embarking in so gigantick an enterprise as the marching of an Army to India...[7]

In Heytesbury's view, what Britain had cause to fear was the disruptive influence of Russian agents, who 'invariably outstrip the orders of their Government'. To counter them it would be expedient to place British agents in Kabul and Bokhara. Clearly he was unrepentantly sanguine about Russian policy in the East. He may possibly have had some influence on his colleagues afterwards, but in January 1830 he was not believed by Aberdeen, Wellington, and Ellenborough. Though his views were communicated to the Government of Bengal there was no amendment to the dispatch which Ellenborough drafted on 12 January. Ellenborough wrote:

...we can neither feel justified in reposing upon the good faith and moderation of Russia, nor in permitting the apprehensions her policy and her power are calculated to excite to be altogether done away by reflection upon the difficulties she would have to encounter in the attempt to approach the Indus...We dread therefore, not so much actual invasion by Russia, as the moral effect which would be produced amongst our own subjects and amongst the Princes with whom we are allied, by the continued apprehension of that event. We look with dismay on the financial embarrassment in which we should be involved by the necessity of constant military preparations, not only to meet an European army in the field but to preserve tranquility in our own provinces and in our tributary states. If such should be the consequence of any approximation of the Russians to the north of India, it is our interest to take measures for the prevention of any movement on their part beyond their present limits. But the efficacy of such measures must depend upon their being taken promptly, and you cannot take them promptly unless you are kept constantly informed of everything which passes on the Russian frontier in Asia, in Khiva, and in Bokhara...

Even if Russia did not plan an invasion as such, she might well take up a controlling position in Central Asia and thus come within a single campaign of Kabul, occasioning such 'vast expenditure as would be ruinous to our finances'. This would check the course of British policy in Europe, and would affect Britain as both an Asiatic and a European power. Here Ellenborough anticipated and rejected Heytesbury's argument that Russia might have a legitimate commercial interest in advancing towards Khiva and Bokhara. 'No commercial benefit could suffice to recover for her the cost of conquest and occupation.' Britain's counter-action should be pecuniary and commercial. Pecuniary means should be employed with caution but without parsimony, but no military move or treaty involving military aid could be made without previous authority from England.

While you take such measures for your own future safety as a commanding necessity may require, you will be careful not to adopt a line of conduct which might needlessly lead to collision in Europe.

The object of British policy should be to substitute British influence for Russian influence in Bokhara, using commercial means. But this was impossible while we depended upon the Ganges and a long overland route to Bokhara. The Indus would provide a better route, and if we used it we could 'not but hope that we might succeed in underselling the Russians and in obtaining for ourselves a large portion at least of the internal trade of Central Asia'. But we must not allow the chiefs of Sind and the Punjab to believe that we think of conquest, 'our first object being to introduce English goods and not Englishmen into Cabul and Central Asia'.

Lord Amherst, the previous Governor General, now once more established on his Kentish estate at Sevenoaks, had suggested making a gift of dray horses to Runjeet Singh in return for his gift of horses to King George IV some years before. The horses would go from England to Bombay and thence up the Indus, preferably in a well-armed and well-manned vessel. The escort to the horses should be an able and discreet officer who might take advantage of his visit to Lahore to acquire a knowledge of local conditions. He would be officially no more than an escort, but in his informal conversation with Runjeet Singh he might impress upon him the commercial value of the Indus and canals, for canals might one day link the Persian Gulf with the Bay of Bengal. Ellenborough foresaw that the whole scheme would fall to the ground without the co-operation of the Sind emirs. Bentinck should take care to make the passage of the horses acceptable to them:

We are far from desirous of having any collision with the people of Sind, but we cannot permit any jealous feeling on their part to close the navigation of the Indus should it appear to offer results not only commercially but politically important.

In concluding his instructions to Bentinck, Lord Ellenborough warned him to do nothing rashly, but authorized him to 'risk something for the attainment of a great object'.[8]

The selection of the 'able and discreet officer' would be the first and least difficult of the tasks given to the Government of India. It is clear that Ellenborough, with the approval of the Cabinet, was mapping out a policy for the next decade or more. It is also clear that he and his colleagues in London were well aware of the risks and dangers. For the first time in the history of the British in India they were to venture beyond the Indus and the Hindu Kush.

It is true that the British Government ordered Bentinck not to make any military move or treaty without previous authority from home, and that the declared first object of the new policy was to introduce English goods, not Englishmen, into Central Asia. The cautious, pragmatic influence of the duke of Wellington was strong in the section of the dispatch which made those conditions. But the policy was one that would only succeed in the long term if Englishmen, acting beyond the Sutlej, the Indus, and the Hindu Kush, spread their influence and their money far and wide. Cotton piece goods and mercantile enlightenment alone could never effectively bar the Russian advance towards Kabul. Englishmen would have to accompany the English goods and guard those 'pecuniary means' which Bentinck was enjoined to employ without parsimony. In a sense, the escort to the dray horses was a symbol of all that was to follow. We have already observed that Ellenborough looked forward to seeing the British flag floating upon the waters of the Indus to the source of its tributary streams. His words

could be interpreted as a dream of conquest or as a vision of pro-
cessions of British merchant vessels flying the Red Ensign. Whatever he meant, these were private thoughts. In a public dispatch
he must be more circumspect. It was enough to warn Bentinck that
the Sind emirs must not be permitted to stand in the way of navigation on the Indus. Herein lies the source of much future trouble on
the western frontiers of India. The new policy of the British
Government for Central Asia would stand or fall by the success of
its servants in opening up the Indus to commerce. The intro-
spective Sind emirs were unlikely to smile upon the project; their
coldness and suspicion towards the British were notorious. If
necessary, they would have to be 'persuaded'. But Afghans and
Sikhs also had an interest in the welfare of Sind as a potential
source of tribute. One collision would infallibly lead to another
once the British were established in Sind, and yet they must
establish themselves there or fail in their attempt to block the
Russian advance into Central Asia.

This, then, was the meaning of the historic dispatch of 12 January 1830. Let us discount all subsequent recriminations of party
politicians and the pulpit rhetoric of Kaye and his followers. Here
was a policy approved and therefore decreed by the great national
hero, Wellington, as a means of defending the Indian Empire.
British national interests and international order were menaced by
Russian ambition. Whose influence should be paramount in Asia
for the next hundred years—that of a half-civilized Russia under
its autocrat or that of the enlightened 'missionary of freedom, peace
and good government'? The duke of Wellington and his Cabinet
had no doubts about the answer, and their Whig successors carried
on where they left off.

By the time the master plan reached India the life of Wellington's
government was nearly over. In February Greece had gained her
independence under international guarantee. In June 'poor Prinny'
died at last, and with him died an age. Alexandrina Victoria,
daughter of the widowed duchess of Kent, had just passed her
eleventh birthday. Her sailor uncle, the duke of Clarence, came to
the throne as William IV at the age of 65, causing Charles Greville
to remark that if he did not go mad he might make a 'very decent
king'.[9] In July we find Palmerston exulting over the victory of the
constitutionalists in France. 'The reign of Metternich is over, and
the days of the Duke's policy might be measured by algebra, if not

by arithmetic.'[10] We may also note in passing that 1830 was the year of the ruthless suppression by the Russians of the national revolt in Poland. The duke, meanwhile, was pursuing his chosen course, one which did not yet include any provision for parliamentary reform. On 2 November he told the House of Lords that the existing system of representation possessed 'the full and entire confidence of the country'.[11] The defender of the constitutional 'frame and order' of things sadly misjudged the mood of the country. He may have thought that he was dealing only with 'the vain attempts and impetuous assaults' of 'such men as are given to change', but in fact a whole nation was knocking at his door, and the windows of Apsley House would soon be smashed by a mob. He might protest that he was not opposed to all reforms and progressive change. He had attended the opening of the Manchester and Liverpool Railway[12] and given the signal for the hectic expansion of the national railway network in the next two decades. That was not enough. The modern political leader must also give his blessing to constitutional reforms, ungrudgingly. Under this pressure he might have remained Prime Minister for a few months longer, but by now the Tories were a sick and divided party. Had not Wellington knocked a prop from under the constitution by emancipating the Catholics? Some High Tories thought so, and they voted against their own leader on the Civil List. The duke took his leave of King William, and Earl Grey was commissioned to form a government on 16 November.

In the Grey administration Viscount Melbourne took over Peel's place as Home Secretary. Palmerston moved into Aberdeen's seat at the Foreign Office. Charles Grant followed Ellenborough at the India Board. All three were men who had resigned from Wellington's Government in May 1828. They and their colleagues, old Whigs or new, more accurately reflected the national desire for reform. A brisk and businesslike skirmish with the borough-mongers should be enough to win the battle; no one with any substantial following wanted to revive the duke's high-minded but agonizingly Fabian tactics.

While people at home were arguing about reform and, as usual, yawning over the contents of the Indian mails, the new Central Asian policy was moving from talk to action. The January dispatch reached Bentinck in the summer of 1830. He did not have to look far for a suitable escorting officer for the Maharajah's dray horses.

In Cutch, working as assistant to the Resident (Lieutenant Colonel Henry Pottinger) was a young officer with a high reputation as a linguist and with a passion for travel and exploration. His name was Alexander Burnes, and he was only 25. With Bentinck's approval the Governor of Bombay appointed Lieutenant Burnes as the escort to the dray horses towards the end of the year. Alexander's older brother, Dr James Burnes, had been on a mission to Sind in 1827-8, officially to give medical attention to Murad Ali, whom he described as an 'Asiatic Tiberius or Philip the Second'. James Burnes's optimistic account of his journey, with those of more prosaic surveyors, fired Ellenborough's imagination during his first term of office at the Board of Control.

For instance, James Burnes had written:

...it is scarcely possible to conceive a more easy, or as far as the people generally are concerned, a more willing conquest, were our victorious arms turned in that direction...Were such an event to happen, as happen in all probability it will, from causes as uncontrollable as those which have led to the already mighty extension of our Empire, there is no district which would better repay the fostering care of a mild and enlightened management than Sinde...Then the River Indus might once more become the channel of communication and wealth, between the interior of Asia and the Peninsula of India, and Sind herself, equally interesting to us from classic association and from sympathy in her present sufferings, would rise renewed to claim a due importance in the scale of nations, and to profit by the benefits which nature has bestowed upon her.[13]

This youthful enthusiasm and the assumption of noble motives for the eventual conquest of Sind are not necessarily invalidated by what follows. The author quotes from a letter written by Sir John Malcolm, who, as Governor of Bombay, sent James Burnes to Sind in 1827 and Alexander Burnes up the Indus three years later. Malcolm wrote it in a letter to a colleague at Calcutta, and enclosed a copy of that letter in one to Wellington a few months later. The date of the original letter to John Bax in Calcutta is 23 July 1830:

...I shall hope some demonstration on the part of Russia will make men alive to the value of this presidency, (Bombay) and that circumstances may admit of our settling on the Indus. The revenues of Scind would go far to meet our deficit and add to our strength, but this is a distant speculation, and dependent upon many contingencies...[14]

In August Sir John Malcolm circulated a minute on the navigability of the Indus,[15] a fact which, together with the letter just quoted, shows that the Home Government's policy did not come as a surprise to those in authority in India. Indeed, the Bombay Government had had officers watching and surveying as much as they dared of the Indus for many years. Most of the work had taken place on the eastern perimeter of the Indus system. There was a long gap between Henry Pottinger's reconnaissance with Christie in 1810 and Dr James Burnes's mission to Sind in 1827. The invitation from Murad Ali had come as a complete surprise[16] after a long period of sullen silence, but the British were then very receptive to any and every friendly word from that quarter.

Lord William Bentinck and his colleagues at once complied with the orders from London, but not without comment. Some parts of Ellenborough's dispatch stuck in the throats of a group which he once lightly dismissed as 'Mr Elphinstone and all the Indians.'[17] At the end of October 1830 Charles Metcalfe, a man who favoured consolidation within existing frontiers and who strongly argued against becoming involved and ensnared beyond the Indus, objected strongly to the methods proposed by Ellenborough. He had said in November 1828 that he could not imagine the utility of precipitating a hostile collision with Russia.[18] Now he said:

...The scheme for surveying the Indus under the pretence of sending a present to Rajah Runjeet Singh seems to be highly objectionable. It is a trick, in my opinion, unworthy of our government, which cannot fail, when detected, as most probably it will be, to excite the jealousy and indignation of the powers on whom we play it...It is not impossible that it will lead to war.[19]

Bentinck included this and other comments from Metcalfe in a dispatch dated 7 November 1830. The dispatch reached England some months later. Charles Grant had by then been in office quite long enough to send amendments to the previous Government's Indus policy if he wished, but none was sent. At the end of July, however, he stirred himself to answer Bentinck's dispatch through the Secret Committee. He presumed that the Bombay Government had lost no time in carrying the proposals of his predecessor into effect, and declared that he and his colleagues were anxiously awaiting news of the result. Then Grant said that he was disposed to agree with Metcalfe's minute:

...Desiring to hold ourselves uncommitted as to particular expressions and shades of opinion in that minute, we have no hesitation in recording our cordial concurrence in the general principles which it lays down for the management of our Indian Empire...

Grant stated that it would be best to avoid this 'species of policy' in future:

...It must not, however, be overlooked that there are objects, connected with the matter before us, which may unobjectionably engage attention...To acquire information respecting the course and navigation of the Indus, and the tribes that inhabit its banks, is highly important, as well with a view to more remote consequences of various kinds, as to the extension of British Commerce...

One can see that Grant was anxious to appease Metcalfe and those who agreed with him, without abandoning Ellenborough's objectives. The specific dangers of his dispatch had become 'remote consequences of various kinds' in Grant's. But they are clearly the same consequences. Meanwhile Grant told Bentinck that it was his Government's duty to use every lawful and honourable effort to the end stated—but not 'measures of the class which we have already censured'. It was then that Grant made his only serious amendment to Ellenborough's dispatch. He recommended open, undisguised, and honourable negotiations with the principal states on the Indus and its tributary streams, starting with the Sind emirs, and using only persuasion:

...Let it be at once explained that our motive is to extend our commerce and *only* our commerce, along the waters of the Indus, and that it would become the government of Schinde to act in the same spirit and to concur in the promotion of what must necessarily prove a common advantage...[20]

But if persuasion failed, then Bentinck must abstain from resorting to any other means and must immediately report back to the Secret Committee. Thus Grant attempted to soften the original instruction in which Ellenborough appeared to permit a hectoring tone towards the Sind emirs. The substance of the policy remained the same. Metcalfe's basic complaint had been against the methods proposed by Ellenborough.

Six dapple-grey horses (one of which, a mare, died before the ship reached Bombay) and a friendly letter from Ellenborough to the ruler of Lahore were on their way to India in the summer of

1830. Alexander Burnes received his orders in Bombay, where he fitted out his expedition and took delivery of the dray horses. In January he and his companions sailed for Cutch, hoping to gain quick passage through Sind. They met with storms at sea and hostility on land. It was perhaps just as well that they did not appear off Sind in the well-armed vessel recommended by Ellenborough. The princes who had been so friendly in their dealings with James Burnes wanted nothing to do with his brother, even in the guise of an ambassador bearing gifts. In the recent past their snub would have been accepted with a shrug of resignation; the emirs were incorrigible. But now the Bombay Government had instructions—not yet amended—to be rough if necessary. 'We cannot permit any jealous feeling on their part to close the navigation of the Indus should it appear to offer results not only commercially but politically important.' In March the emirs yielded to the persuasions of Colonel Pottinger, who was a hard negotiator and righteously ruthless when the occasion demanded.[21] He reminded them how fragile was their security against the ambitions of Afghan, Sikh and Khosa neighbours, and how much they relied in reality upon the willingness of the British to restrain the covetous. The mission consequently began to make progress. Alexander Burnes and Ensign John Leckie, young and enthusiastic subalterns with a taste for adventurous exploration, led their little team to Lahore, taking soundings and bearings and making detailed notes as they went.[22] Burnes duly presented the dray horses to the Maharajah, and the Maharajah gratefully placed them in the hands of the palace grooms.[23] It is said that they died in luxury, far from their Kentish meadows, from overfeeding.

At this time Lord William Bentinck was on tour in the northern and north-western provinces with William Macnaghten. Burnes found them at Simla, where they listened with growing interest to his report.[24] Burnes seems to have been a good talker and a courtier of some charm. When he volunteered to go to Bokhara Bentinck was delighted, for Ellenborough was most insistent on the need for complete information about the states beyond the Indus, and Burnes was the man to collect it. In the two years since he had become Pottinger's assistant in Cutch, Alexander Burnes had convinced some severe judges of his personal merit—Pottinger, Malcolm, Macnaghten, and Bentinck himself.

In October Bentinck and his suite, including Burnes, had a brief ceremonial encounter with Runjeet Singh at Rupar.[25] It is as well to remember that successive Indian Governments had placed a very high value on the friendship and alliance of Runjeet Singh; one cannot properly understand the First Afghan War without being constantly aware of the fact. It has been well said that 'the Lahore kingdom was one of the few really successful buffer states in history'.[26] Much of the credit for the success and longevity of the alliance, starting with the Treaty of Amritsar in 1809, belonged to Runjeet Singh. British and Sikh soldiers had a healthy respect for each other, and the policy laid down by the Home Government in January 1830 depended not only on the opening of the Indus to British commerce but also on the maintenance of the alliance with the Sikhs. At Rupar in October 1831 the Governor General and the Maharajah reaffirmed their alliance and came to an understanding about their relations with Sind and Afghanistan.

Confident of the Maharajah's approval and inspired by Burnes's report on the Indus, Lord William Bentinck now issued instructions to Colonel Pottinger. He was to open negotiations with the rulers of Hyderabad and Khairpur at the earliest opportunity with a view to obtaining facilities for British commerce on the Indus. The relationship between what follows and the dispatch which Ellenborough drafted in January 1830 is very clear:

The Secret Committee of the Honourable Court of Directors have expressed great anxiety to obtain the free navigation of the Indus with a view to the advantages that might result from substituting our own influence for that derived by Russia, through her commercial intercourse with Bokhara, in the countries lying between Hindustan and the Caspian Sea, as well as because of the great facilities afforded by the River for the disposal of produce and manufactures of the British dominions, both in Europe and India.[27]

At a place called Ludhiana, suitably enough half-way between Simla and Lahore, resided two Afghan pensioners of the British. One was the old and blind Zaman Shah, and the other was Shah Shuja. Both were grandsons of the Afghan Emperor Ahmed, and Shuja, as we have observed before, nursed the hope that he might one day return to Kabul in triumph. In August 1831 Alexander Burnes called on them on his way from Lahore to Simla. Shuja welcomed Burnes to his exiguous court, and sighed: 'Had I but my kingdom, how glad I should be to see an Englishman at Cabool,

48

and to open the road between Europe and India.'[28] When Burnes left Simla again in December, to start his Central Asian travels, he spent ten more days in Ludhiana. Burnes shows us that Shuja at the end of 1831 was again dreaming of returning to Kabul as King, and we can understand that Shuja expected that the revived British interest in Central Asia might one day be of use to him.

CHAPTER 4

RECONNAISSANCE ALONG THE INDUS

...Dost Mahommed Khan...enquired into the state of the Mahommedan principalities in India, and as to the exact power of Runjeet Singh, for sparing whose country he gave us no credit. He wished to know if we had any designs upon Cabool...

ALEXANDER BURNES, *Travels into Bokhara*[1]

...Imperialism is a monkey riding a donkey...

From a modern Arabic saying

I

Lord William Cavendish Bentinck occupies a secure niche in the history of Britain in India as the Governor who put into practice what Macaulay preached in the great debate on the renewal of the Company's Charter. He brought about some 'pacific triumphs of reason over barbarism'. He set out to rule India in the interests of the people, not only by putting order in the place of anarchy and policing the frontiers, but also by introducing reforms in the social life of the masses. He suppressed thugs and banned the burning of widows. He ended flogging in the Company's armed forces, and he assumed some responsibility for the education of Indians. He found a huge deficit when he arrived in July 1828, and in March 1835 he left behind him a handsome surplus. 'His victories', G. M. Trevelyan has said, 'were those of peace.'[2]

This is a true judgement, and Bentinck's was a noble achievement, but it should not blind us to the fact that he zealously applied the policy framed by Wellington and his colleagues to counter the Russians in Central Asia. The line of responsibility for the First Afghan War passes through him. It was he who conferred with Runjeet Singh at Rupar in October 1831 about the opening of the Indus to commerce and all that that entailed in changed relations with Sind; it was he who sent Alexander Burnes to collect information and intelligence about the states of Central Asia in conformity with the Home Government's new policy; it was he who sent Henry Pottinger to Hyderabad to negotiate commercial treaties with the Talpura princes; above all, it was he who professed neutrality and disinterest but allowed Shah Shuja four months' advance of pension when that king without a kingdom set off with Runjeet Singh's blessing in a bid to recapture Kabul. It was his good fortune to serve in India during the period of reconnaissance and planning. Bentinck's groundwork was essential for the attempt to project British power into Central Asia. His 'Minute Upon the Dangers Confronting the British Empire in India', composed shortly before he sailed for home, is one of the most convincing documents in the defence of the British Government and Lord Auckland. It is discussed later in this chapter.

At home, in 1831 and 1832, Indian affairs caused even less excitement than usual. Ellenborough's unpublished journals, so recently full of forebodings about the Russian threat to India, show his preoccupation with the battle for and against parliamentary reform. But in 1832 a number of elderly gentlemen who had seen long service in India emerged from their houses in the Marylebone and Mayfair squares to give evidence before the Select Committee of the House of Commons on the affairs of the East India Company. They made it quite clear that the Russian threat was not simply a figment of Ellenborough's fevered imagination.[3]

In 1831 the Reform Bill appeared briefly, in its first version, and vanished in the wreckage of the first Parliament of William IV's reign. The Whigs increased their majority in May 1831, but still the Lords rejected reform. The Bill reached the statute-book at the third attempt, becoming law in June 1832, but not before the nation had caught a whiff of civil war and Wellington had had his windows broken by a mob. The drama of parliamentary reform had hardly reached its last act when the British Government found itself in the middle of a crisis in the eastern Mediterranean. Sultan Mahmud II had promised Muhammad Ali, Pasha of Egypt, the management of his Syrian provinces as part of the reward for services rendered against the rebellious Greeks. But Muhammad Ali was expected to content himself with Crete when the time came to redeem promises made in desperation. In July 1831 his son Ibrahim publicly voiced the hope that the Egyptian fleet would soon carry Muhammad Ali to Constantinople. In October the Pasha declared war on his master, and during the next fifteen months the Egyptian army under Ibrahim advanced, by way of Homs and Hama, Beilan, Konya, and Kutayha, to within striking

distance of Constantinople itself. Palmerston viewed these proceedings with increasing alarm, especially when he found that this
'active Arabian sovereign' had caused the Sultan to look to the
Russians for help. It was mortifying to see that what really deterred
Muhammad Ali was the threatening attitude of the Russians. Lord
Aberdeen had been proved right. Within three and a half years of
the Treaty of Adrianople the Emperor Nicholas had found an
opportunity to act as the sole protector of the Ottoman Porte. The
staff of the British and French embassies in Constantinople saw a
Russian naval squadron and 15,000 men arrive to rescue the Sultan
from his Egyptian enemies. The French interest in the affair was
not one of pure devotion to the preservation of the European
balance of power, for Muhammad Ali had many admirers in Paris.
Had it not been for Britain's objections, the French and the
Egyptians might have joined forces to strip the Sultan of all his
North African domains in 1830. Britain's interest in the Turkish-
Egyptian quarrel combined concern for the stability of Europe with
alarm about the safety of her communications with India. In the
end it was British and Austrian diplomacy that persuaded the
Sultan to concede the Convention of Kutayha in April 1833, and
Russian power that stayed the Pasha's hand. Muhammad Ali
agreed to withdraw, but he held the Sultan to his previous offer of
Syria, and he gained Adana into the bargain. The Sultan remained
his overlord, exacting annual tribute. Sultan Mahmud's protec-
tors, the Russians, who had never had to fire a shot, stayed in
Turkey until the middle of July 1833. Palmerston soon discovered,
that summer, that the Russians had not left empty-handed. They
took with them a Treaty of Alliance, the Treaty of Unkiar
Skelessi, and a secret article which gave Russia the right to exclude
foreign warships from the Dardanelles and the Black Sea.[4] In
effect, as the British Government had feared at the time of the
Treaty of Adrianople, Turkey had come under formal Russian protection. The British Government protested to the Emperor and the
Sultan, men seriously began to think that Britain would one day
have to go to war with Russia, and the Whigs were not alone in
opposing Russian policy. The continuity of Britain's Eastern policy
at a time of acute party conflict at home was remarkable.

II

We now return to the early stages of the Central Asian adventure. In January 1832 Henry Pottinger arrived in Hyderabad with instructions to negotiate a commercial treaty with Murad Ali, the head of the Talpura family. He was also to negotiate one with the Talpura cousin who then ruled at Khairpur, and this was difficult at the outset because Murad Ali claimed that the Khan of Khairpur was his subordinate. But Henry Pottinger's will prevailed. Rustum Khan of Khairpur signed first, on 4 April. Murad signed on the 20th. Pottinger obtained facilities for British commerce, including the promise of uninterrupted traffic on the Indus, but the ever distrustful Sind emirs still wanted as little as possible to do with Europeans.

Both Murad Ali and Rustum refused to receive British Residents at their capitals, but they agreed that there should be a system of just and reasonable tolls to make it worth the merchant's while to send his goods by that route. Murad Ali stipulated that armed vessels and military transport and stores must be barred from using the river, that no Englishman should be allowed to settle in Sind, and that all merchants using the river should carry British passports. One clause of his treaty deserves special notice because the whole of Sind was annexed to the British Empire in India only eleven years later. The clause said: 'The two contracting parties bind themselves never to look with the eye of covetousness upon the possessions of each other.'

All that Sind emirs had ever wanted was to be left alone. Their Baluchi soldiers were brave and warlike, expert with sword and shield, but the emirs knew better than to tangle with the modern British army across the border. They were hardly likely to risk annihilation by coveting British possessions in India, and since they liked nothing better at any time than to be left alone to enjoy the comfortable revenues of their estate, the clause could only affect Britain. The British in India had made a promise which would never be less than embarrassing to them in the years ahead. The Sind emirs, on the other hand, had behaved in a manner which modern nationalists could applaud today; they had kept their independence entire in the face of strong imperialist pressure. But it would be a mistake to view the relationship between Britain and Sind in modern nationalist terms, for Sind was not a nation but a family fief. The independence which the emirs guarded so jealously was only another name for the right to enjoy exclusive possession of the revenues of Sind. The treasure hoarded in their crumbling fortresses was their personal property. Conquest had given them rights, and they acknowledged few responsibilities. James Burnes once treated one of them with quinine and they confiscated his whole stock for the family's exclusive use. All this does not alter the fact that the British were exerting a pressure which would one day lead to annexation. If, as the Arab saying goes, imperialism is a monkey riding a donkey with a goad in his hand, the monkey crossing the Indus was a very determined creature and the donkey was excessively stubborn.

Meanwhile Henry Pottinger had done well for his Government. The route was now open—for the Khan of Bahawalpur and Runjeet Singh had also given their consent—from the sea to the foot of the mountain barrier eight hundred miles away. Thus the first object of Britain's Central Asian policy was attained within three years of the Treaty of Adrianople which prompted it. But the first experimental voyages on the Indus were not a huge success. One of the minor injustices of the history of this period is that Alexander Burnes is sometimes blamed for encouraging too much optimism among British officials in India about the commercial capacity of the Indus. In fact his report on the voyage of the dray horses gave a fair picture of the difficulties. Certainly there was an uninterrupted navigation from the sea to Lahore, but

this extensive inland navigation, open as I have stated it to be, can *only* be considered traversable to the boats of the country, which are flat-bottomed, and do not draw more than four feet of water when heavily laden. The largest of these carry about seventy five tons English: science and capital might improve the build of these vessels; but in extending our commerce, or in setting on foot a flotilla, the present model would ever be found the most convenient. Vessels of a sharp build are liable to upset when they run aground on the sand-banks. Steamboats could ply, if constructed after the manner of the country, but no vessel with a keel could be safely navigated...[5]

The early difficulties were as much political as navigational, and Burnes had given warning about both. The people and princes, he said, were ignorant and barbarous—the former plundering and the latter over-taxing the merchants who ventured on to their great waterway. He was proved right. Within a year of signing the commercial treaties, Henry Pottinger had to negotiate new terms. He insisted upon a uniform toll on all boats on the Indus, and he made provision for the settlement of disputes between merchants and toll-collectors. But Nur Muhammad, who had succeeded his father Murad Ali in October 1833, was just as adamant in refusing to receive a British Resident at Hyderabad. Once again he refused in the face of considerable pressure. In every negotiation conducted in Sind, Henry Pottinger had the great advantage of being able to frighten the emirs. Who would restrain their enemy Runjeet Singh if the British did not? Who but the British had it in their power to check the tribesmen who were such a nuisance on the border between Cutch and Sind? The thought of the instructions from London, the fear that every day brought the Russians a little closer to the Indus, made Pottinger more ruthless. He won his uniform toll, but still Nur Muhammad would not receive a Resident.[6]

III

While Pottinger was negotiating in Sind, Alexander Burnes was exploring the 'market' in Central Asia. He left Ludhiana on the first stage of his mission on 2 January 1832. With him were Surgeon James Gerard from the Bengal Presidency; Muhammad Ali, a surveyor trained in Bombay; Mohan Lal, a Kashmiri Hindu who was one of the first Indians to receive an English education and who joined the mission as Burnes's munshi; and the Surati servant Ghulam Husain who cooked for them. Their first halt was at Lahore,[7] and Burnes makes it very clear that Runjeet Singh, faithful ally though he might be, was not given the full, nor even the true, story of the mission's task:

Runjeet made the most particular enquiries regarding our journey; and, since it was no part of my object to develop the entire plans we had in view, we informed his Highness that we were proceeding towards our native country. He requested me to take a complimentary letter to the King of England, which I declined, on the excuse of its endangering my safety in the intermediate territories...[8]

Burnes and his companions stayed at Runjeet's court until 11 February. There had been much talk of commerce on the Indus and its probable beneficial effect on the revenues of the riverine states, but one would look in vain through Burnes's work for a specific statement of the British Government's long-term objective in Central Asia. 'His Lordship', said Burnes, 'was of opinion that a knowledge of the general condition of the countries through which I was to travel would be useful to the British Government, independent of other advantages which might be expected from such a journey.'[9] This coy remark was doubtless an act of deliberate discretion. Commercial rivalry could be implied; strategic considerations were not to be mentioned at all. In the winter of 1833, when Burnes reached London, he had an audience with the King, who said: 'You are intrusted with fearful information; you must take care what you publish.'[10] We can see that Burnes either took or did not need the king's advice. Kaye hints that the India Board censored the book.

From the middle of March to the middle of April 1832 Burnes and his companions were the guests of Sultan Muhammad Khan at Peshawar. Sultan (his name, not a title) was the brother of Dost Muhammad, and the brothers were enemies even then, for Sultan Muhammad paid a yearly tribute of horses and rice to Runjeet Singh, who held one of his sons as a hostage for his good behaviour at Lahore. Burnes observes that Sultan sighed over the disgrace of being so bound to Runjeet. Sultan's behaviour was doubly disgraceful in the eyes of Dost Muhammad, because he, as Emir of Kabul, considered Peshawar his. During one conversation with Sultan Muhammad and others in Peshawar, Burnes records,

...the subject of the Russians was introduced, and a Persian in the party declared that his country was quite independent of Russia. The chief, with much good humour, remarked that their independence was something like his own with the Seiks, unable to resist, and glad to compromise...[11]

Before we leave Peshawar with Burnes and his companions let us take note of a circumstance which has been ignored by Victorian moralists in their comments on the behaviour of the British garrison at Kabul in the years of the occupation. Burnes was introduced to four of the Peshawar chief's younger sons, not one of whom was more than twelve. They were precocious youngsters, and they drew attention to the immorality of the women of Kabul, 'which last is a proverb, given in a couplet'.[12] Burnes was too shy, or too conscious of his English audience, to quote the couplet. But Mohan Lal was more explicit, and the following proverb, which he quoted, may be the one mentioned by Burnes:

The flour of Peshawar is not without the mixture of barley,
And the women of Cabul are not without friends.[13]

In another place, Burnes remarked that 'Cabool seems to have
been always famed for its revels'.[14] There is no need to labour the
point, but it balances the effect of Kaye's almost prurient comment:

...There are truths which must be spoken. The temptations which are
most difficult to withstand, were not withstood by our English officers.
The attractions of the women of Caubul they did not know how to
resist. The Afghans are very jealous of the honour of their women; and
there were things done in Caubul which covered them with shame and
roused them to revenge. The inmate of the Mahomedan Zenana was not
unwilling to visit the quarters of the Christian stranger...The scandal
was open, undisguised, notorious...[15]

On the afternoon of 1 May 1832, Alexander Burnes caught his
first glimpse of Kabul. His first impressions were not very favourable, but within a fortnight he was writing to his mother that
'...truly, this is a paradise...'.[16] He liked the place, he liked the
people, and he much admired Dost Muhammad and his brother
and vizier, Nawab Jubbar Khan. He formed the opinion that Dost
Muhammad was the 'most rising man in the Cabool dominions'.[17]
He had met two of the fallen Sadozai princes, Shuja and Zaman,
and could compare their character with that of the most energetic
Barukzai leader. The comparison led him to conclude that the
'supremacy of the Barukzye family in Cabool is acceptable to the
people, and I even think favourable to the prosperity of the
country'. Burnes considered that the dynasty of the Sadozais had
passed away, 'unless it be propped up by foreign aid...'.

...It is more difficult to revive than to raise a dynasty; and in the common chain of events, if the country is to be ruled by another king, we
must look for another family to establish its power in Cabool; and this,
in all probability, will be the Barukzyes...

Continuing his argument in favour of Dost Muhammad he
declared that on the death of Runjeet Singh the Emir of Kabul
might secure a thorough supremacy over the country and even
recover part of the old Afghan Empire. Then, as Dost Muhammad
was already favourably disposed towards the British Government,
it would be possible to form a connexion with him at 'no great
expenditure of the public funds'. Indeed Burnes thought that such
an alliance would be especially valuable because Dost Muhammad's

57

'country lies on the great road by which the manufactures of Britain are imported'.[18] It is clear, however, that Burnes understood that such an alliance was difficult—even impossible—as long as Runjeet Singh lived. Here is part of his description of a farewell meeting with Dost Muhammad in May 1832:

...Dost Muhammad pleased us as much as ever; he kept us till long past midnight, and gave us a full insight into the political affairs of his country, and the unfortunate differences that exist between him and his brothers. He expressed hopes of being able to restore the monarchy, evinced a cordial hatred towards Runjeet Singh, and seemed anxious to know if the British Government would accept his services as an auxiliary to root him out; but I replied that he was our friend...[19]

The conversation just described took place at a time when Runjeet Singh still had seven years to live. The cordial hatred between him and Dost Muhammad remained throughout the years as an obstacle to British purposes in Central Asia. It was impossible to maintain alliances with Runjeet Singh and Dost Muhammad at the same time, yet Britain needed the active co-operation of both countries if her Central Asian policy was to succeed. Burnes recognized the obstacle as early as 1832.

From Kabul the four travellers, who had been disguised as Afghans since leaving Lahore, rode across the Hindu Kush to Tashkurghan, otherwise known as Kulum. There they could look across the 'plains of Tartary' at the country sloping down to the Oxus.[20] Their path then led by way of Kunduz and Balkh to Bokhara, which they reached on 27 June 1832. They exchanged their turbans for sheepskin caps with the fur inside, and made one or two other modifications to their dress so that they would be as inconspicuous as possible. Burnes obtained promises of protection from the vizier, but he was unable to gain an audience with Bahadur Khan, the ruler of Bokhara. 'What have travellers to do with courts?' the vizier reasonably inquired.[21] Burnes did not press the point. He contented himself with a glimpse of the 'Commander of the Faithful' on his way to prayers, and devoted the remaining weeks of his stay in Bokhara to a study of the commerce of the Central Asian states:

...Russia possesses such an extent of inland navigation, that she can bring the whole of her goods to the confines of Asia by water-carriage; and it is the superiority and cheapness of our manufactures that alone enable us to appear in the contest by the Indian route. We must surrender to her, I imagine, all trade in metals, and other weighty articles made from them; but we may successfully compete with her in our manufactures...A more extended exportation of British goods into these countries, in particular of white cloths, muslins, and woollens, I am assured by the first merchants, and even by the Vizier of Bokhara, would have the immediate effect of driving the Russians from that branch of commerce...The transport of merchandise by the route of Cabool costs little; and, if Russia navigates the Volga, the greatest of the European rivers, Britain can command like facilities, by two more grand and equally navigable streams, the Ganges and the Indus.[22]

Knowing the policy, and understanding the importance of cotton exports in a period of very rapid industrial expansion, we should not be surprised at the impact of Burnes's report on official and commercial opinion at home. Between 1830 and 1843 British exports of cotton piece goods to the rest of the world rose from 445 million to 919 million yards annually. In 1830 Britain's total domestic export trade was valued at £38,300,000; in 1843 it was £52,300,000. In 1843 India was absorbing British goods valued at just over 10 per cent of that total (£5,689,000). In 1830 there were 298 steamships under United Kingdom registration; the number had almost trebled by 1843.[23] This was the situation into which Burnes inserted the news that the Russians could be knocked out of the cotton and woollen markets in Central Asia, on condition that British merchants made full use of the Indus and the Ganges. The Government welcomed the news for political and strategic, as well as commercial, reasons. Burnes had just confirmed that the Oxus, running for six hundred miles between Kunduz and the Aral Sea, was navigable and remarkably straight for all but fifty miles of its length.[24] Those fifty miles represented the length of the marshy delta of the Oxus on the approach to the Aral Sea. In Burnes's own words: '...the many facilities which have been enumerated point it out as the channel of merchandize, or the route of a military expedition...'.[25]

The evidence of Burnes confirmed official fears and vindicated official policy. The Indus must be opened fully to commerce, the products of Lancashire and Yorkshire must go on sale in Bokhara and the rest of Central Asia, and British influence, following in the wake of British trade, must be used to prevent the Russians from advancing up the Oxus.

We left Alexander Burnes and his companions at the moment when they were starting their survey of Central Asian commerce. This occupied them in Bokhara until the end of the third week in July, when they took their leave of the vizier and set out for the Persian frontier. They entered Meshed on 14 September. It would be tedious to follow them through the remainder of their journey. We need only note that Gerard, whose health had not stood the strain of constant discomfort and exposure, left them at the end of September and returned to India by way of Herat and Kandahar, and that Burnes had audiences with the Crown Prince and the Shah of Persia during this last stage of his travels. By this time he had mastered the flowery style of Persian correspondence and official intercourse. When Fath Ali Shah asked him what was the greatest wonder which he had seen in his travels Alexander Burnes could not resist the temptation to show off. His choice of words came perilously close to parody, but he did not give offence: 'Centre of the Universe, what sight has equalled that which I now behold, the light of your Majesty's countenance, O attraction of the world!'

These words did not, and were not expected to, come from the heart. But when the Shah asked him which city he had most admired he gave what was clearly an honest answer: 'I told him that Cabool was the paradise of our travels...'[26]

Burnes left Teheran at the beginning of November and embarked in one of the company's warships on 10 December. He reached Bombay on 18 January 1833. From that moment his name was made. He reported to the Governor General and was sent on leave to England. We leave him now, writing up his notes for the narrative of his adventures, and little realizing how eagerly his report and views are awaited at home. More and more people are hearing the disconcerting rumour of a Russian diplomatic coup at Unkiar Skelessi.

IV

In May 1832, when Burnes left Kabul and headed for the passes over the Hindu Kush, he made a brief note in his journal about Ghazni, site of the tomb of the Emperor Mahmud who had ruled from there eight centuries earlier. By the time he came to write his book there was more to say about Ghazni:

...It is worthy of remark, that the ruler of the Punjab, in a negotiation which he lately carried on with the ex-King of Caboof, Shoojah ool

60

Moolk, stipulated, as one of the conditions of his restoration to the throne of his ancestors, that he should deliver up the sandal-wood gates at the shrine of the Emperor Mahmood—being the same which were brought from Somnat, in India, when that destroyer smote the idol, and the precious stones fell from his body. Upwards of eight hundred years have elapsed since the spoliation, but the Hindoo still remembers it, though these doors have so long adorned the tomb of Sultan Mahmood...[27]

Burnes was referring to the treaty which Runjeet Singh and Shuja concluded on 12 March 1833. Shuja was prepared to concede much in return for the support of the Sikhs, but he was a faithful Muslim and drew the line at restoring the gates of Somnath. To him the temple despoiled so long ago was heathen and the Hindus were idolaters. He also refused to hand over his eldest son, Timur, as a hostage. But Runjeet could not complain of a bad bargain. The treaty gave him all the Afghan territory between the hills and the five rivers, including Peshawar, if he could take it and keep it.

On 11 October 1832 Shuja had formally requested British help. In reply Bentinck declared that the British Government

religiously abstains from intermeddling with the affairs of its neighbours, when this can be avoided.

Your Majesty is, of course, master of his own actions, but to afford you assistance for the purpose which you have in contemplation, would not consist with that neutrality which on such occasions is the rule of guidance adopted by the British Government...[28]

Shuja was disappointed, but at least Bentinck had not forbidden the expedition. He was master of his own actions, according to the Government whose pensioner he had been for many years. He therefore asked the officiating political agent at Ludhiana, Major Faithful, to advance him part of his future pension, pleading that he had received just such an advance of pension in 1818. Major Faithful passed on the request to his Government. Shuja, he said, wanted 16,000 rupees (about £1,600 at that time), equivalent to pension payments for four months. Faithful remarked that so large an advance would give the transaction 'an appearance of countenance and support beyond what either the policy or intentions of His Lordship would admit...'. But on 13 December, when the Government replied, no mention of policy or intentions appeared in the instructions to Faithful. He was simply authorized to pay the 16,000 rupees, in accordance with the precedent set in 1818. Much later, in March 1835, Bentinck explained that, though his Government 'did not feel justified in prohibiting the movement of Shah Shooja, it had invariably refused to afford him the assistance which he had repeatedly solicited, in aid of his undertaking'.[29]

In view of what has been said earlier it is not difficult to see why Bentinck did not feel justified in prohibiting Shuja's project. He was under instructions to use 'pecuniary means' as well as commerce to check the advance of the Russians in Central Asia. Britain needed the active co-operation of both Afghanistan and the Punjab if her Central Asian policy was to work, and the Barukzai chiefs—especially Dost Muhammad—were the mortal enemies of Runjeet Singh. So it was that Shah Shuja and his newly recruited army set out from Ludhiana early in 1833, and so it was that Dost Muhammad, no doubt encouraged by his conversations with Burnes the year before, requested an alliance with the British.[30] Bentinck had been warned not to make any alliances without previous authority from London. Having rebuffed Shah Shuja, the friend of his ally Runjeet Singh, he could hardly give encouragement to Runjeet's sworn enemy. He politely rejected the Dost's advances and watched the progress of Shuja's army towards Shikarpur. When Runjeet wrote to him about Shuja's new treaty with Lahore, Bentinck once again emphasized his Government's neutrality. 'The Shah's success or otherwise depends upon the will of Providence, and the favourable disposition, or otherwise, of the inhabitants of that quarter...'[31] Bentinck's neutrality in the affair was only a form of words. How could he say that Shuja, a prince dependent for his food and drink on a monthly British stipend, was 'master of his own actions'? No one, least of all Dost Muhammad of Kabul, believed him to be neutral, and on a cool and selfish appraisal of British interests there was no reason why he should have been. Had Shuja succeeded, Britain would have had friends in two of the most important capitals in the north-west, and it would have been much easier to win the assistance of the Sind emirs because Shuja, in return for permission to march through their territory, would have abandoned his old claim to tribute. Then the triangle would have been complete. Sind, Afghanistan, and the Punjab, having settled all their old quarrels, would all serve Britain's purposes in Central Asia and their own profit. But it was all too good to be true.

For one thing, Shuja approached his former subjects as if their allegiance had never been alienated. Coriolanus at least dressed himself in a gown of humility when he asked the citizens of Rome for a consulship; Shuja could never bring himself to be anything but haughty towards his fellow Afghans. Meanwhile, the Sind emirs were growing restive. He sat too long on their doorstep, and held them too closely to their promises of money and supplies. They quarrelled with him and were worsted at the battle of Rohri on 9 January 1834. By then Shuja had gathered 30,000 men around him, including two battalions under the half-Scots, half-Indian adventurer Campbell. The emirs once again acknowledged Shuja's overlordship, though they later claimed that he had permanently abandoned his right as suzerain in 1833.

Shuja now headed for the Bolan Pass, and came in sight of the walls of Kandahar in June 1834. While his army was labouring through the Bolan and Khojak passes, the Sikhs were making sure of their part of the bargain with Shuja. On 6 May Hari Singh, Runjeet's favourite general, seized Peshawar and drove out Sultan Muhammad and his numerous family. For a while the indignity brought Dost Muhammad and Sultan Muhammad together, but not for long. Peshawar might not have fallen so easily if Dost Muhammad had not been busy in the west. Accounts of the battle of Kandahar, fought on 2 July 1834, vary according to the prejudice of the writer describing it. Some say that Shuja showed himself a coward and that a faint heart lost him the battle. The author prefers the account given by Major William Hough, the Deputy Judge Advocate General in the Army of the Indus in 1838–9, subtracting a little from Shuja's credit to make allowance for Hough's desire to please the Governor General (to whom he dedicated his book in August 1840): 'Had not Mr Campbell, the Commander of the Shah's Hindostanee troops, been wounded, the king would have won the battle; but this event threw all into confusion. The Shah lost all hope, and fled, and the army dispersed.'[32]

Dost Muhammad's success at Kandahar, where he had the help of his brother chiefs, strengthened his position in Kabul, and at the end of the year he assumed new titles—Commander of the Faithful and Commander of the Champions of Islam. He afterwards told Burnes that he had captured documents as well as guns and stores on the battlefield of Kandahar, and that these told him much about

Shuja's plans and intrigues. But he had no need of secret documents to tell him that Shuja had British and Sikh friends.

After taking refuge with his kinsmen at Herat, the defeated Shuja returned crestfallen to India. Runjeet now had to maintain a large army on the plain of Peshawar, fearing a counter-attack. In the spring of 1835 Dost Muhammad and his brother Sultan Muhammad rode down from Kabul with their army to seek revenge. The attempt ended in treachery and without bloodshed. Emissaries from the Sikhs seduced Sultan and his family into accepting estates within the territory of Peshawar. According to Buist, Dost Muhammad also wavered when he was offered similar inducements in return for renunciation of his claim to Peshawar and the sending of one of his sons as a hostage to Lahore, but this is hard to believe. We know that Dost Muhammad and his followers returned to Kabul much depressed, and vowing to recapture Peshawar one day. From now on, the quarrel between Dost Muhammad and the ruler of Lahore was irreparable. Runjeet Singh made sure that the Dost's anger stayed high by stationing a garrison of Sikhs in Peshawar and appointed as Governor the Italian Bonapartist General Paolo Avitabile. This gentleman, a native of Agerola (Amalfi),[33] was one of four senior European commanders in the Sikh army. He was also a cruel and ruthless disciplinarian, one who placed great faith in the deterrent effect of multiple hangings in public.

v

So far, in this chapter, we have considered the Near Eastern crisis of 1831–3, the negotiations and treaty with the Sind emirs, the journeys of Alexander Burnes during the same period, and Shah Shuja's attempt to recover the throne of Afghanistan with Sikh help and British acquiescence. Now let us see what happened to Alexander Burnes. He arrived in England at the end of 1833. In London he was the catch of the season. The rich and the powerful listened to him with flattering attention. They made him a member of the Athenaeum at the age of 28. The King invited him down to Brighton and listened to the thrilling account of his adventures. The book narrating his travels came out in the summer of 1834. According to Kaye, he had an important interview with Lord Ellenborough before returning to Bombay. Relying on a story which must have been current in Burnes's family, Kaye says that

Ellenborough offered to use his influence to make Burnes Secretary of Legation at Teheran and promised him the reversion of the post of Minister in charge of the Legation. The truth of the matter is less flattering to Alexander Burnes. What Ellenborough offered was a chance to serve as Second Secretary under Henry Ellis, who was sent on a special mission as ambassador to congratulate the new Shah, Muhammad Mirza, on his accession to the throne of Persia. The interview between Ellenborough and Burnes took place on 2 January 1835. This is how Ellenborough recorded it in his journal that day:

Saw at the office Lt. Burnes, who told me he thought the situation in Persia rather retrograde, and wished a day to consider it. I told him I didn't consider it is, as he was transferred to a King's mission...He expressed a hope that in the event of the Secretary of Embassy retiring he should be made Secretary. I told him I had nothing to do with it but I thought he had a fair claim...[34]

Kaye says that Burnes declined the handsome offer mentioned above on advice from friends in London. Ellenborough shows that Burnes, being ambitious, was not content to be only Second Secretary in Teheran. On 7 January he was still undecided but seemed to prefer India to Persia. On the 8th he decided for India and placed himself at the disposal of Government if they still wished to send him to Persia. Ellenborough told him that he would do what he could to obtain for him the situation he wanted, which was that of Governor General's agent in one of the states.[35] In the end Ellenborough did not exert himself for Burnes. He wrote to Lord Heytesbury, the Governor General designate, on 11 February, enclosing a printed statement of Burnes's former service (supplied by Burnes) and saying: '...What use should be made of his services in India entirely depends upon you. It is a matter in which I have no power, and if I had, I should entirely rely upon your doing what was best for the public service.'[36]

Ellenborough could never be called a warm or very sympathetic person. He was acutely conscious of his great powers and easy intimacy with great men, including Wellington. He seems to have found Burnes rather tiresome. But he *was* at first prepared to help Burnes on his way to promotion. He felt he owed him something, as well he might. Burnes, after all, had successfully carried out the first survey of the Indus, proposed by Ellenborough, and had just returned from Central Asia with all the information requested by Ellenborough in January 1830. Ellenborough, more than any other man, was responsible for the decisions which Burnes helped to carry out; he, more than any other man, owed a debt of recognition to Alexander Burnes. His journal shows that he tried to help him, but not very hard, and it is rather sad that when Burnes was dead, and a scapegoat, Lord Ellenborough repudiated him:

...I have a very indifferent opinion of him. He was intensely vain and self-sufficient and he did that which he ought not to have done. Acting as he was for a government to which I was opposed in Parliament, he wrote to me from Cabool upon the affairs of Affghanistan. I had not seen him since I was in office in 1835, and had never corresponded with him, and you may be sure that I took no notice of his letter.[37]

In this petty betrayal we see an example of the influence of 'party' upon the minds of those who shared responsibility for the Central Asian policy. Small wonder that some historians have gone astray. But we have jumped too far ahead. In March 1835 Burnes sailed again for India and his old post as assistant to Colonel Pottinger in Cutch. Pottinger quickly put him to work. He sent him to talk to Nur Muhammad in Hyderabad about arrangements for a new and more scientific survey of the Indus. This and similar missions kept Burnes busy until the end of 1836, by which time he and Pottinger were no longer on speaking terms. Their quarrel is part of the prelude to the British intervention in Afghanistan.

Now we must return to the period in which Palmerston, as Foreign Secretary, was reacting to the Treaty of Unkiar Skelessi. We left him protesting to the Turkish and Russian governments about their dangerous compact. At about the same time, in the autumn of 1833, Abbas Mirza, heir apparent to the throne of Persia, died while his son Muhammad Mirza was marching against the city of Herat and receiving Russian encouragement to press on to Khiva. As we have already noted, the embarrassing ninth article of the Anglo-Persian treaty prevented Britain from intervening in a quarrel between Persia and Afghanistan without being asked by both sides. Muhammad Mirza broke off his siege of Herat, to Palmerston's relief, and returned to Teheran to claim the title of heir apparent.[38] The Shah, meanwhile, had been pressing the British Government to give him a specific offer of protection, and Palmerston authorized Sir John Campbell to negotiate a revision of the treaty. Campbell was to persuade the Shah to delete the article about Persian quarrels with Afghanistan, offering as an inducement a form of words which the Shah might accept as a sufficient guarantee of protection without committing Britain too deeply against Russia. Palmerston had high hopes of coming to some accommodation with Fath Ali Shah. The Shah's death in November 1834 undid all Campbell's work, but Palmerston had a second line of defence. In June he had had an interview in London with Prince Lieven, the Russian ambassador. They agreed that Britain and Russia should jointly support the claims of Muhammad Mirza to the status of heir apparent and so avoid civil war among rival claimants after the Shah's death. Their agreement was timely, as we have just seen. The gist of their conversation was reported to the British representative in St Petersburg, the Hon. J. D. Bligh, who conveyed it to Count Nesselrode. But Palmerston also told Bligh to convey his anxiety at the way in which Russia had taken advantage of Persian weakness since the Treaty of Turkmanchai.[39] Nesselrode welcomed the succession agreement but irritably rejected the rest. He told Bligh of his regret that Palmerston 'should have thought it expedient to rake up topics for cavil...'[40] Nevertheless, in the summer of 1834 the two Governments agreed that the Russian and British agents in Teheran should work together for the peaceful succession of Muhammad Mirza when the time came. All this was immediately passed to Charles Grant for the information of the Governor General of India, who was advised to keep close watch for any Russian action in Persia which was inconsistent with Russian disclaimers of intrigue and ambition there.[41]

On 5 September Palmerston wrote twice to his friend Bligh in St Petersburg. First he wrote officially, asking him to tell Nesselrode that

His Majesty's Government are gratified to find that the Governments of Great Britain and Russia are acting, with regard to the affairs of Persia, in the same spirit, and are equally animated by a sincere desire to maintain, not only the internal tranquility, but also the independence and integrity of Persia.[42]

Then Palmerston wrote to Bligh privately, and in a very different tone:

...I always felt that the Insolence of Tone and menacing attitude of Russia were founded upon a belief that England was powerless and incapable of effort, and that as this Delusion gradually dispelled the language and conduct of the Russian Government would become more civil and pacific. But this makes no difference in our opinions of her systematic views, and cannot inspire any permanent confidence in the disinterredness of her policy. On the contrary everything tends to show the gigantic scale upon which her Projects of aggrandizement are formed, and how necessary it is for other nations who don't mean to be encroached upon to keep vigilant watch, and have their horses always saddled...[43]

Count Nesselrode continued to be civil and pacific when William IV surprised everyone by dismissing Melbourne and sending for Wellington (in Peel's absence abroad) in November.[44] The Tories reciprocated his outward courtesy, while remaining as vigilant as Palmerston had been. But they thought they knew better than he how to handle Count Nesselrode. During their three years of opposition they had tittered and shaken their heads over several of his diplomatic scrapes, even in the presence of the Russian ambassador and Princess Lieven. Now they made their own dispositions. One of the first things they had to do was to nominate a new Governor General. They did not consider confirming Charles Metcalfe in the post, even though his claims were strong and even though he was to act as Governor General in the interval between the departure of Bentinck and the arrival of a successor. The first person they thought of was Mountstuart Elphinstone, who had retired as Governor of Bombay in 1827, when only 48, to devote his life to travel and study. He declined the offer under some pressure from Ellenborough. At the same time the Tory Government decided to send an ambassador to the new Shah of Persia with credentials from the King. They chose Henry Ellis, and it was at this time that Ellenborough thought of placing Alexander Burnes on the mission as Second Secretary. They even toyed with the idea of sending the mission to Persia by way of St Petersburg. But we should not fall into the trap of thinking that this was a sign of softness towards Russia. Ellenborough remarks in his journal at this time that Sir Robert Peel is pleased with the plan for British representation in Persia, and with the choice of Ellis. He also remarks that the duke of Wellington has a high opinion of John McNeill, then a candidate for the post of Secretary of Legation and later Minister in succession to Ellis.[45] Ellis and McNeill had no illusions about Russian conduct in Persia. They were later to play an important part in Palmerston's and Hobhouse's concerted policy for Persia and Afghanistan.

Having dealt with the question of representation in Persia, the Cabinet thought again about candidates for the office of Governor General. It was on Saturday 10 January 1835 that Ellenborough scribbled a note to Sir Robert Peel, telling him that the chairman and deputy chairman of the Court of Directors were 'perfectly ready' to propose Lord Heytesbury, the former ambassador in St Petersburg, who had been thought so 'Russian' in 1829. Peel composed a letter to Heytesbury and sent it to Ellenborough on Monday, with this covering note:

I shall be perfectly satisfied with your decision, have not a personal wish in the matter, and only name Lord Aylmer that no name may escape consideration through inadvertence. If Lord Aylmer is out of the question the enclosed will enable you to take your course with regard to Lord Heytesbury...[46]

This last-minute mention of Lord Aylmer's name did not long detain them. Ellenborough consulted Aberdeen and the duke of Wellington. Aberdeen had no objection to Aylmer, and Ellenborough had had nothing but good reports of him, so he wrote back to Peel:

I have seen both Aberdeen and the Duke about Lord Aylmer. The Duke says he is not as able a man as Lord Heytesbury...[47]

Ellenborough said he would wait for Peel's decision. The duke's remark turned the scales in favour of Heytesbury, and Ellenborough dispatched Peel's and his own letters to the new Governor General designate. Heytesbury accepted the offer in a letter written on 16 January,[48] and within a few weeks his appointment was complete. He could begin to prepare for the journey and to dream of a glorious term of office and a place of honour in the history of British India. Meanwhile the brief Anglo-Russian honeymoon stayed sweet, and on 26 January Bligh reported to Wellington (then Foreign Secretary) that the Russians were delighted with the news that the new Shah, backed by both governments, had now entered Teheran unopposed.[49] The Russians gave all the credit to the co-operation of the British and Russian agents in Persia during the succession crisis. Again in March Bligh sent evidence of 'the perfect cordiality which, as Count Nesselrode had already informed me, had subsisted between the British and Russian representatives ever since the death of the late Shah...'.[50]

At the Board of Control Ellenborough, with Burnes's report fresh in his mind, was planning a new dispatch about the policy to be pursued among the countries bordering on the Indus. But first he sent a brief secret dispatch to Bengal announcing the grant of a free pardon to James Lewis, described as a deserter from the Bengal Horse Artillery 'who, under the name of Charles Masson, has been for several years past, engaged in scientific and historical researches in the countries bordering on the Indus, and who was recommended for a free pardon by the Governor General'.[51]

The timing of this dispatch is most interesting, for Masson himself recounts that he was appointed by the political agent at Ludhiana in February as 'agent for communicating intelligence' in Kabul to the Government of India. Masson wrote with considerable resentment of the appointment, as though he thought it an imposition, but gave no convincing reason for his anger:

> ...I might have supposed it would have been only fair and courteous to have consulted my wishes and views before conferring an appointment which compromised me with the equivocal politics of the country, and threw a suspicion over my proceedings, which did not before attach to them.[52]

Then why did he not refuse the appointment? Was it because his free pardon depended upon it? Somewhere in the India Office records there must be documents which would answer that question. However that may be, Masson learned of his appointment as 'agent for communicating intelligence' shortly after starting a journey from Kabul to Jalalabad at the beginning of March 1835. His companions on that journey were Dost Muhammad and his army. His employer at Ludhiana was Claude Wade.

On the day of Masson's departure from Kabul, Saturday 7 March, Ellenborough happened to complete his secret dispatch to Bengal on the division of power along the Indus. He had studied Burnes's report and had been impressed by what Burnes told him of Dost Muhammad Khan. '...the recent victory of Dost Mahomed at Candahar will add materially to his strength and to his disposition to use it, and we look forward to endeavours, on his part, to exercise efficient control over the whole of Affghanistan...'

If Runjeet Singh then grew jealous and came into conflict with

Dost Muhammad, the 'contest which would ensue would involve consequences of much interest to the British Government in India'. If Runjeet Singh defeated him and took possession of Afghanistan the Sikhs would be in a position to threaten every part of the frontier of British India from the Sutlej to Cutch, and the increase required in India's military forces would be 'ruinous to our embarrassed finances'. Similarly a united Afghan state with influence over Sind would acquire means of aggression against us. It would 'therefore be our obvious policy to preserve the independence of Scinde against an Affghan state, as it is now and must ever be our policy to preserve its independence against the power in possession of the Punjab'.

Ellenborough continued by saying:

It is our political interest that the Indus and its tributary streams should not belong to one state. The division of power on the Indus between the Scindians, the Affghans, and the Sikhs is probably the arrangement most calculated to secure us against hostile use of that river, while it will not probably oppose any real obstacles to the navigation of the river for commercial purposes, which should be secured by treaty...

Then Ellenborough spoke of the advantages of having a united Afghan state as neighbour to two states—Sind and the Punjab—which were in alliance with Britain. Such a state could not be a threat to the British dominions, for, '...valuing and capable of mtaintaining its independence, having more to fear than to hope from foreign aid, it would serve our purpose by making Affghanistan an impassable obstacle to any power advancing from the West...'. He briefly noted the strategic advantages of that country's position, and he ended his dispatch by saying:

It must, therefore, at all times, be a subject of much moment to us to have an accurate knowledge of all that passes in Affghanistan, with a view to our taking promptly such measures as may seem, from time to time, to be dictated by our interests; and we have full confidence that you will keep yourselves constantly informed of every movement in that country, and take whatever steps may be necessary to secure the British Dominions from distant as well as present danger.[53]

The plan was remarkably neat and tidy, but it neglected certain factors of which Ellenborough should have been aware. There is no mention of Herat. Ellenborough twice mentioned the possibility

71

of a union between Kabul and Kandahar and the territories dependent upon them, and he expected Dost Muhammad to try to exercise control over the whole of Afghanistan. Did he consider Herat to be outside Afghanistan? He certainly wrote as though he did. And yet Burnes had surely told him about the feud between the chiefs of the Barukzai family in Kabul and Kandahar and the Sadozai ruler of Herat. Nor did he mention Peshawar, which the Sikhs had owned and controlled from a distance since 1819 and which they entered in May 1834 by agreement with Shah Shuja. Yet he knew of the battle in which Shuja was defeated at Kandahar in July 1834. The twin feuds, between Barukzai and Sadozai over Herat and between Barukzai and Sikh over Peshawar, were to plague all who tried to cultivate good relations with states on and beyond the Indus. Ellenborough ignored them in this important dispatch. But he made it quite clear in March 1835 that he still wanted to open the Indus to commerce for the reasons stated in that other dispatch of five years earlier. Palmerston might well write to his brother on 10 March and say that 'on the whole Russia has not, I believe, much to choose between Whig and Tory; for I suspect that the Duke is, if possible, more hostile to Russia than I was...'.[54]

In March Sir Robert Peel suffered another defeat in Parliament. He finally gave up the struggle to stay in office on 8 April. Melbourne was not at all keen to return as leader of an all-Whig administration, and Lord David Cecil tells us that he secretly inquired whether it would be possible to arrange a coalition with some of the more moderate Tories. Certainly *The Times* was arguing at this stage in favour of a union of Whig and Tory. After an unsuccessful attempt to bring Lord Grey out of retirement Melbourne agreed to form a government. He did so on 29 April. At first he was loth to send Palmerston back to the Foreign Office, but Palmerston said he wanted the Foreign Office or nothing, and Melbourne gave in. We have already mentioned Tory disapproval of Palmerston's diplomatic methods. Let a man who worked under him at the Foreign Office explain why: 'I hope Palmerston can be made Archbishop of Canterbury or anything that would keep him out of the Foreign Office; for he nearly killed us all, and that, too, not with honest, hard work, but worry.'[55]

It is perhaps a pity that Wellington and Palmerston never worked as a team, the one in Downing Street and the other at the

Foreign Office. Wellington very successfully managed the equally impulsive Ellenborough (himself a disappointed aspirant for the post of Foreign Secretary). But the duke and Palmerston were too far apart in home politics. It was left to Melbourne to tug at Palmerston's elbow at moments of crisis. Wellington would have been a guide and counsellor; Melbourne was a less positive influence on his Foreign Secretary, but a good influence nevertheless.

And so, at the end of April, Palmerston was back at the Foreign Office, picking up the almost undisturbed threads of his Eastern policy. Sir John Hobhouse was now president of the Board of Control, and a man named George Eden, Lord Auckland, was First Lord of the Admiralty. The ministry took office on a Wednesday. On the following Monday Hobhouse wrote a short letter informing the Governor General designate that 'after the most mature deliberation and with much reluctance the King's confidential servants have come to the conclusion that it is their duty to advise His Majesty to revoke your Lordship's recent appointment to the Government of India'.[56]

There was an outburst of indignation, of course. But if the Whigs wanted a member of their own inner circle in India no one could stop them—and no one did. It has often been said since that the Whigs revoked the appointment because they considered Heytesbury too Russian. But when we look back over the six months just reviewed we see Ellis chosen as special envoy to Teheran, we see Burnes being offered a reward (which he, perhaps unwisely, spurned) for his services in carrying out the Tory policy of 1830, we see that the duke has a high opinion of John McNeill, and we see Heytesbury being selected by the triumvirate which became so hostile to the Emperor Nicholas after the Treaty of Adrianople. The selection of Heytesbury occurred during a comparatively bright period in Anglo-Russian relations, when the two countries were co-operating in Teheran. Heytesbury was an able man. He knew the Russian Government and he understood Russian feelings about Asia. He could be trusted to do as he was told and not to take undue risks. But the author can find no evidence to show that Heytesbury was in any way pro-Russian in 1835. It is arguable that the Tories, had they stayed in power for a few years longer, would have avoided the 1838 crisis in Anglo-Russian relations by skilful management of the Russians in Europe and Asia. But they believed with Palmerston that the Russians were out to weaken and subvert British power in the East. They were the authors of the plan for counter-action in Central Asia, and Ellenborough bequeathed to Hobhouse, who did not immediately amend it, a policy for the defence of India on and beyond the Indus. Holding such views, they would one day have clashed with the Russians in Asia no matter how skilful they were in diplomacy, for Russia was always advancing, always probing for weak spots in the armour of the 'dominator of the sea'.

Heytesbury lost his appointment at the beginning of May, when Lord William Bentinck was already on the way home. Bentinck was also well aware of Russian ambitions. We have seen in this chapter how he carried out the Home Government's instructions of January 1830. Now, in the last week of his administration, he looked about him and considered the state of the defences of British India. He argued that the only real danger 'with which we may be threatened must come from the north west'. He did not expect any trouble from the Sikhs as long as Runjeet Singh lived, but conditions would certainly change after that ruler's death.

...The present state of Afghanistan presents no cause of alarm to India. The success that attended the wretched army that Shah Sujah had under his feeble guidance affords the best proof of the weakness of the Afghan power. The assumption of the supremacy by Dost Mahomed Khan may possibly give greater strength and consolidation to the general confederacy. It is much to be desired that this state should acquire sufficient stability to form an intermediate barrier between India and Persia...

Bentinck then considered the

distracted state of Persia, and the possibility that Russia might assist the Shah against Herat with 20,000 men:

...the advance of the combined force would give them in the first campaign possession of Herat, the key of Cabul.

It is the interest of Russia to extend and strengthen the Persian Empire, which occupies a central position between the double lines of operation of the Autocrat to the eastward and westward, and as Persia can never be a rival of Russia the augmentation of her strength can only increase the offensive means of Russia. From the days of Peter the Great to the present time the views of Russia have been turned to the obtaining possession of that part of Central Asia which is watered by the Oxus and joins the eastern shore of the Caspian. The latest accounts from Cabul state they are building a fort between the Caspian and Khiva.

74

This is their best line of approach against India, but it can only be considered at present as a very distant speculation...

But Bentinck was immediately concerned about the possibility of a Persian invasion of Herat under Russian direction:

...What the policy of Russia might be after taking possession of Herat it is unnecessary now to consider, but it is impossible to deny that she might arrive at that point in legitimate support of her ally, the King of Persia, and it is equally difficult to deny that from that point she may proclaim a crusade against British India, in which she would be joined by all the warlike restless tribes that formed the overwhelming force of Timur...

He then gave the distances between Herat and Kandahar, Kandahar and Ghazni, Ghazni and Kabul, and Kabul and Attock, the latter being a most convenient place for the crossing of the Indus. He made the distance 1,032 miles.

The Afghan confederacy, even if cordially united, would have no means to resist the power of Russia and Persia. They probably would make a virtue of necessity and join the common cause, receiving in reward for their co-operation the promise of all the possessions that had been wrested from them by Runjeet Singh, and expecting also to reap no poor harvest from the plunder of India. But however this may be, it will be sufficient to assume the possibility that a Russian force of 20,000 men fully equipped and accompanied with a body of 100,000 horse may reach the shores of the Indus, that Runjeet Singh has no means to resist their advance, and that the invaders, having crossed the Indus into the Punjab, would find themselves in possession of the parts of India the most fertile in resources in every kind, and secure on every side from being harassed and attacked even if they had not on their side a body of irregular cavalry much more numerous and efficient than any we have to oppose them...[57]

Bentinck apologized for the extreme length of his observations, summarized here, but reflected that no one before him had had the 'opportunity of a season of peace' to consider the situation. He had already said enough to chill the blood of every Englishman who valued the Indian Empire.

Bentinck's minute was in part a plea for a big increase in the number of European troops in India, and one must make some allowance for the possibility that he was deliberately overstating his case. Nevertheless, his basic assumption, that if Herat fell it was possible for a Russian army to establish a base in Afghanistan, was much the same as that of Wellington and Ellenborough, expressed in 1829. Like Lord Ellenborough in his more recent analysis of the problem, the retiring Governor General saw the desirability of making Afghanistan sufficiently stable to form a barrier between India and Persia. Unlike Ellenborough, he gave due weight to the special problems of Herat and the lost territories of Kabul; he recognized the willingness of the Barukzai chiefs to join any alliance against Runjeet Singh which would help them to pay off old scores; he cast doubt upon the value of the Punjab as a rampart against the kind of army that Russia and her likely allies could bring down from Afghanistan; and he foresaw serious disturbances in the Punjab after the death of Runjeet Singh. Indubitably this minute is a key document in the case for a forward policy along the Indus.

Ellenborough in 1830 had looked nervously at the Russian line of advance between the Caspian and the Aral Seas and along the Oxus. At that time it seemed to him to pose a more serious threat than Persian subservience to Russia. At that time he relied on diplomacy to save the Persians from that fate. Now Bentinck showed that the threat from the western flank, through Herat, was the more immediate of the two. We shall find that without neglecting the threat from the north Palmerston and his colleagues shared Bentinck's anxiety about the western flank. The new Shah was only too willing to play Russia's game.

The new Whig administration at home quickly settled down to the task of countering Russian influence in Persia. On 1 July the Secret Committee recalled Sir John Campbell, the Company's representative in Persia, 'in order that we may learn from you more fully, when present, than we could by writing, the circumstances of the present condition' of that country.[58] At the same time the Secret Committee informed the acting Governor General (Sir Charles Metcalfe) that Henry Ellis was starting on his special embassy to Teheran. The committee instructed him to supply Ellis with credentials, so that he would speak for both the Government in London and the Government in Calcutta, and, more important, correspond with both. On 25 July Palmerston wrote officially to his ambassador to the Persian Court:

...In your confidential intercourse with the Persian Government, you must not conceal the opinion entertained by His Majesty's Government, that however cautiously Russia may be acting at present, it is from her that the great danger to Persia must arise, and against her that the defensive arrangements of Persia should be directed. You will especially warn the Persian Government against being made the tool of Russian policy, by allowing themselves to be pushed on to make war against the Affghans.

Russia has objects of her own to gain by exciting the Persian Government to quarrel with its Eastern neighbours. The attention of Persia is thus turned away from what is passing to the North and West, and the intrigues by which Russia is paving her way to encroachment upon Persia have a better chance of being carried on unobserved. Whatever may be the result of such quarrels, Russia is sure to gain. Whether Persia is successful or not, her resources will be wasted in these wars, and her future means of defence against the attacks of Russia must be diminished.

The author has reason to believe that until now the only published part of the dispatch just quoted consisted of two sentences:

...You will especially warn the Persian Government against being pushed on to make war against the Afghans.

...Whether Persia is successful or not, her resources will be wasted in these wars, and her future means of defence must be diminished...[59]

Later in this work we shall see why the British Government suppressed these and numerous other references to Russia when the time came to publish Parliamentary Papers in 1839. The fuller version of the dispatch to Ellis is taken from Palmerston's own personal copy of the papers printed for the sole use of the Cabinet in 1839. Moreover, that personal copy is marked copiously in pencil with instructions to the printer of the version presented to Parliament. The pencilled instructions told him what to omit and what to print. It seems impossible to doubt that the man who made the pencil marks was Palmerston himself.

But we must return to the end of July 1835. Palmerston has given precise instructions to Henry Ellis. Now Hobhouse, as president of the Board of Control, asks George Eden, Lord Auckland to give up the Admiralty and go to India. George Eden was a serious and efficient administrator with a creditable record of public service since the return of the Whigs to power in 1830. He was president of the Board of Trade and Master of the Mint under Grey, and Melbourne made him First Lord of the Admiralty in July 1834. Like his colleagues he had a long winter vacation from November 1834 until the end of April 1835, the time it took Peel and his friends to realize that William IV had summoned them too soon to the seats of power. Melbourne once again placed Auckland at the Admiralty, where he was a trusted and respected member of the inner circle of the party. Auckland accepted Hobhouse's offer on the 30th,[60] and on Friday 31 July he had an audience with King William, 'who was very civil to him, and said that "although they differed in politics yet he was an honest man"'.[61] It is as well to remember that Melbourne, Palmerston, Auckland and Hobhouse formed a very tight little group within the Whig party. At one stage it was thought that Melbourne might marry Auckland's sister Emily. Nothing came of it, but they remained close friends. When Emily Eden sailed for India in the *Jupiter* at the end of September, accompanying her brother and sister, Lord Melbourne wrote her a touching letter and gave her a Milton from his library. 'Very few events could be more painful to me than your going, and therefore I am not unwilling to avoid wishing you goodbye...I shall be most anxious to hear from you and promise to write. Adieu.'[62] The relationship between Palmerston and Melbourne was even closer, for Melbourne's sister, Lady Cowper, was Palmerston's dearest friend. They married at the end of 1839, as soon as they decently could after the death of Lord Cowper. Hobhouse's relationship with the Prime Minister was one which could have caused much ill feeling but did not; he had been Byron's good friend and literary executor, and Byron and Melbourne's unbalanced wife Caroline had once been lovers. One should not exaggerate the influence of these personal relationships within the Cabinet in 1835, but they do underline the easy intimacy of the little group of men who held joint responsibility for the defence of the Indian Empire. The strongest personality of the four was Palmerston's. He proposed and planned under the genial supervision of Lord Melbourne, whose restraining influence we have already noticed. Lord David Cecil says that the phrase 'For God's sake, don't!' figured frequently in messages between Downing Street and the Foreign Office, and that Palmerston respected Melbourne's advice and acted upon it more often than not.[63]

Auckland started his long journey to India at the end of September. At that moment the restless Palmerston decided to make use of David Urquhart's strongly felt antipathy to the Russian Emperor, appointing him on 29 September to the post of secretary of the embassy at Constantinople. Urquhart had travelled to Constantinople on a secret mission in 1834. He became so successful at extracting confidences from Turkish officials that he became an embarrassment, and Palmerston recalled him.[64] By the time he arrived home the Tories were in office, and Wellington was unwilling to make use of his services. But Palmerston still thought him useful, in London as well as in Constantinople. Before he set out for Turkey Urquhart published some confidential Russian correspondence in his *Portfolio*, a magazine for those interested in diplomatic affairs. Palmerston was careful not to commit any part of this transaction to writing, but his influence can be seen in it at every point. This was his first serious attempt to waken public opinion to the dangers of Russian foreign policy. Lady Cowper wrote to a friend about the *Portfolio* on 5 January 1836. She said:

The disclosure of Russian prospects is a great point gained and will I hope open the eyes of Europe to their common danger.[65]

Henry Ellis had arrived in Teheran on 3 November on his special mission of condolence and congratulation. He soon confirmed Palmerston's fears:

The Shah has very extended schemes of conquest in the direction of Afghanistan, and, in common with all his subjects conceives that the right of sovereignty over Herat and Kandahar is as complete now as in the reign of the Safavi dynasty.

This pretension is much sustained by the success of his father Abbas Meerza in the Khorassan campaign, and the suggestions of General Berowski, who naturally looks to great advantage to himself from a renewed expedition in that quarter.

Ellis found the Shah and his ministers busily planning expeditions against Herat and Kandahar, and against their Baluchi and Kurdish enemies. They were entirely satisfied with the conduct of the Russians, and all they asked from England was 60,000 muskets. As soon as he could, Ellis had an interview with the Persian ministers:

...They declared that a large portion of Affghanistan belonged to the Shah of Persia, and that he was at liberty to decide how he would deal with the Affghans as being his own subjects...I enquired how far they considered the dominion of Persia to extend; their reply was to Ghazni; on former occasions the Hajee has mentioned the occupation of Herat as a proximate enterprise, and that of Candahar as one not far distant...

79

But Ellis reminded Palmerston that the Persians and Heratis had made a treaty in 1834. Kamran, the chief of Herat, had not only flouted the treaty but had encroached on Persian territory in Seistan during his periodic slaving raids.

... Under such circumstances, even if the British Government was not restrained by the 9th Article of the existing Treaty from interfering between the Persians and the Affghans, it would be difficult to oppose an attack upon Herat, or to define the exact limit to which hostilities were to be carried against Kamran Meerza; but an attempt to annex Candahar and Ghazni to the Persian dominions, upon pretensions derived from the time of Nadir Shah, has no such justification, and could not be looked upon with indifference by the British Government.[66]

Such was the tenor of the dispatches which began to arrive on Palmerston's desk in March and April 1836. Similar messages arrived in Calcutta and awaited Auckland when his ship anchored there in March, for, from now on, the envoy in Teheran was a most important link between London and Calcutta. Holding credentials from both Crown and Company, the envoy in Teheran corresponded with both. During McNeill's time in Persia the liaison became very close and influenced decisions in both London and Calcutta. Indeed McNeill played a critical part in the events leading up to the First Afghan War, and it is worth remembering that the duke of Wellington had a high opinion of him![67]

CHAPTER 5

AUCKLAND'S FIRST YEAR IN INDIA

...the most passive policy is not always the most pacific...
AUCKLAND to Metcalfe, 28 October 1836

When Lord Auckland sailed for India in September 1835 he was subject to the same general instruction as Henry Ellis. He had by all means to keep 'his horse always saddled', but he knew of no immediate reason for placing his foot in the stirrup or his hand on his sword. Like every Governor General who ever went to India, he had high hopes of being able to do good, to preserve the peace, to protect and improve the lot of the millions under his care, and to build up a surplus in the Treasury for his successor. He spent five months at sea, cut off from the dispatches and intelligence reports reaching Palmerston and his colleagues in London, and in Calcutta he was greeted by a man with strong views about India's defences.[1] Sir Charles Metcalfe had been acting as Governor General since Bentinck's retirement in March 1835. We have already seen that he preferred to leave well alone in the north-west, recognizing a remote danger from the Russians but depending upon a strong and, if necessary, expanded Sikh buffer state to stave them off. We shall examine his views more closely later in this chapter. Meanwhile we can see that his views ran counter to those of Tory and Whig ministers and of Lord William Bentinck himself.

At the very beginning of his Governorship, therefore, Lord Auckland came under Metcalfe's influence. This was only natural in the circumstances. The burden of public business was immense, and Auckland had much to learn. He could not ignore the advice of a man who had been in India for thirty-five years. But he grew more confident in his own judgement of the interaction of European and Indian politics as the year went by, and he found that his own judgement was very close to that of the Home Government.

One of the policy-making factors that Auckland missed during his voyage to India was the publication of the Russian dispatches in the *Portfolio*. They caused a sensation for a few days, and Melbourne, not yet as wide awake to Russian ambitions as Palmerston, grew slightly nervous. He wrote a note to Palmerston on 7 January about Urquhart, who by then ought to have been at work in Constantinople: 'I think it would be well to get him off to his post. These active persons are better after all in the Levant.'[2]

One of Palmerston's active persons, Henry Ellis, was now offering grave warnings with nearly every dispatch from Teheran. On the 8th he wrote that the Russian Minister in Persia, Count Ivan Simonich, was pressing the Shah to mount his expedition against Herat without delay and telling him that the British would probably try to discourage him 'in pursuance of their known wish to see a restoration of the Affghan monarchy'. Ellis went to see the Persian ministers and told them that the British Government had no such wish, 'but would look with great dissatisfaction on the prosecution of any schemes of extended conquest in Affghanistan'. He urged the Persian ministers to tell the Shah that Britain acknowledged his right to obtain redress for wrongs done by the chief of Herat, but considered negotiation preferable to a costly war. Ellis remained sceptical when the ministers hastened to agree with him. He fully expected them to quote the ninth article of the Anglo-Persian Treaty as an excuse for ignoring Britain's advice. In fact they ignored it without even bothering to quote the treaty.[3]

On 15 January Ellis sent Palmerston a memorandum on the effect of the existing Anglo-Persian Treaty upon the interests and security of the British Empire in India. He felt 'quite assured that the British Government cannot permit the extension of the Persian monarchy in the direction of Affghanistan, with a due regard to the internal tranquillity of India'. Such an extension would

bring Russian intrigue and influence to the very threshold of our empire; and as Persia will not, or dare not, place herself in a condition of close alliance with Great Britain, but rather defers to Russia...our policy must be to consider her no longer an outwork for the defences of India, but as the first parallel, from whence the attack may be commenced or threatened.

Then, in an often quoted passage, Ellis said:

...Indeed, in the present subservient state of Persia to Russia, it cannot be denied, that the progress of the former in Affghanistan is tantamount to the advance of the latter, and ought to receive every opposition from the British Government that the obligations of public faith will permit; but, while the Russian Government is free to assist Persia in the assertion of her Sovereign pretensions in Affghanistan, Great Britain is precluded by the 9th Article of the present treaty, from interfering between the Persians and the Affghans, unless called upon to do so by both parties; and therefore, as long as this treaty remains in force, the British Government must submit to the approach of Russian influence, through the instrumentality of Persian conquests, to the very frontier of our Indian empire.[4]

In the middle of February Ellis reported that the Shah was still contemplating an attack on Herat but had lately appeared more interested in chastising the Turcomans infesting Khorasan. Ellis also remarked that the Shah would 'lose no opportunity of forming connections with the Chief of Cabool and his brothers' in order to overcome Herat.[5]

At that time Auckland was still at sea. His first reaction to Ellis's letters from Teheran was an impatient one, very different from that of Palmerston in London. At the beginning of April Auckland wrote to Stanley Clarke at India House:

Henry Ellis writes to me from Persia with greater dread of Russian aggression than we are disposed to feel here. In direct aggression I hold her to be actually powerless, and in indirect she can only become formidable under an exaggerated opinion of her power. In the meantime I look for the extension of British power and influence in the direction of the Indus much more to our merchants than our soldiers, and I am sanguine enough to hope that that river may become a peaceable thoroughfare for our commerce...[6]

In London Palmerston accepted Ellis's warnings with great seriousness. In February, after receiving the first batch of dispatches from Teheran, he sent a map to Melbourne, showing the Russian advance towards the Indian frontier. He met with a sceptical response; Melbourne observed that the remoteness of the Indian frontier from St Petersburg must always be a source of weakness to the Russian extremities.[7] At the end of the month Melbourne laid a restraining hand on Palmerston's shoulder. On a proposal that the Circassians might be encouraged to create an obstacle to the Russian advance, Melbourne said: 'I would leave the Circassians to themselves. I am against exciting people to commit themselves to a warfare in which you cannot give them effectual support.'[8]

But the return to London of John McNeill from Teheran, where he had been secretary to Henry Ellis's special embassy, helped to convince doubters. McNeill set to work to produce a slim volume entitled the *Progress and Present Position of Russia in the East,* which circulated in England in the spring of 1836. It was published without his name on the title page, but it was well known that he was the author. In effect the pamphlet was a manifesto in direct line of descent from Aberdeen's dispatch to Heytesbury on the iniquities of the Treaty of Adrianople. It contained some startling facts about Russian expansion and some striking passages on the importance of preserving Persia's independence and cultivating the friendship of the Central Asian states. The first of these to be quoted could easily have come from the pen of Lord Ellenborough:

...Great Britain, therefore, has a manifest interest in protecting the independence of Persia; an interest of such magnitude and importance that she cannot permit it to be endangered without exposing India to evils, from which every government is bound, if possible, to protect its subjects, and without subjecting herself to a diminution of her influence in Europe, as well as of her power in Asia.

The next passage certainly owes much to the influence of Ellenborough's dispatches after Adrianople:

...At the same time the state of the countries between Persia and India should not be neglected. The whole Mahomedan population of Central Asia dreads the power of Russia, and looks for countenance from England. It is while the first line of defence is entire, not under the fire of the enemy's guns, that we can prepare a second. Our Commercial relations are hourly extending in all that continent...

In a footnote on the same page McNeill pointed out that British exports to Central Asia were then running at £3½ million a year, a claim that must have gladdened the heart of Lord Ellenborough as the man who first proposed using commerce as a defensive weapon in that part of the world. But perhaps the most interesting and thought-provoking of all the statements made in McNeill's book was the one that now follows—a justification of interference in the affairs of other countries:

...The right of interference in the affairs of independent states is founded on this single principle, that as self preservation is the first duty, so it supersedes all other obligations. The just application of the principle requires that danger should be shown, not to the minor interests merely, but to the vital interests of the state which appeals to it...

If that was not sufficient warning to Russia, then the concluding paragraph of the book should have served as one:

...it is the ambition of Russia that forces upon us the necessity of endeavouring to preserve that which is obviously necessary to our own protection. If she will not give us security for the future she can have no right to complain if we should take all practicable measures to impede and obstruct the course she has so perseveringly pursued. If she attempts to justify her own aggressions, on what principle can she complain of measures of defence, however extensive? The integrity and independence of Persia is necessary to the security of India and of Europe; and any attempt to subvert the one is a blow struck at the other—an unequivocal act of hostility to England.[9]

This was in reality the voice of Palmerston. It was his way of warning Russia that he had caught her out in her intrigues in Teheran and that he would now act accordingly. We must note the stress here on the doctrine of just interference. It is crucial to a proper understanding of the First Afghan War.

Even as this manifesto was being read by cotton manufacturers and kings a new dispatch from Ellis was on the way to London and a similar message was being carried to Auckland in Calcutta. Ellis had written it at the end of February. He said he had just met and talked to an 'ambassador' from Dost Muhammad Khan of Kabul to the Shah of Persia; the 'ambassador' was empowered to make an alliance with the Shah against Herat and to seek Persian assistance against the Sikhs. Ellis reported that he had managed to persuade the supposed envoy to go back to Kabul without concluding a treaty and to urge Dost Muhammad to write to the Governor General.[10] To Lord Auckland he suggested that it would be politic to make an alliance with Dost Muhammad. Auckland was now somewhat less sceptical about Ellis's warnings. In May he composed a minute upon Ellis's Persian dispatches, indicating that, although he was less apprehensive than some others about the danger of direct Russian aggression, he

would not under-rate the value of Afghanistan as an outwork to our Indian possessions...
...I would willingly and by every means in my power cultivate alliances and friendly disposition and feelings of confidence with that and the neighbouring states...

But Auckland did not agree with Ellis, that he should enter into *military* alliances in Afghanistan, divided as that country was into separate principalities:

...I would abstain from interference. I would not be forward even in intercourse. I would endeavour to preserve peace. I would cultivate commerce and if at any time agencies half commercial and half political could find admission I should be glad to encourage them. But further than this in the present posture of affairs, and unless new emergencies should arise, I would not go—India is scarcely yet recovering into strength from the exhaustion of war and conquests; we have enough to do in the endeavour to make her strong and secure and rich within herself.[11]

This was a most significant document, for it revealed the influence of Metcalfe, especially in the concluding passage, but it could not conceal Auckland's growing awareness of the danger in the north-west. Other circumstances, clearly, could make a difference to his policy. Meanwhile, in letters home, he showed that his resistance to Ellis's advice arose partly from a lack of confidence in Ellis's judgement. For instance, he told Hobhouse at the beginning of June:

...I have had many communications from Ellis in Persia and they have made me wish for the arrival of McNeill, for I am far from coinciding with Ellis in his views and he writes, for my taste, with too much ill temper of everybody with whom he has to deal. He may be right, but I would not think so until his opinions are confirmed by others...[12]

Auckland was 'sure that nothing but the offence and jealousy of other powers'—above all the Punjab—'would be the result of an ostensible alliance with Dost Muhammad'.[13] At that time Auckland had not yet received the dispatch which Ellis sent from Teheran on 1 April. Palmerston had received it in London on 29 May. In that dispatch Ellis reported that an envoy from the Kandahar chiefs had made overtures to the Shah of Persia in the hope of negotiating an alliance. They wanted a guarantee of their internal independence, and would submit to the Shah's decision in all questions concerning foreign relations. They would join with him against Herat, and would hope for help against the Sikhs.

...The Envoy has been received with great favour, and the terms of the proposed alliance have been agreed to. He has already had his audience of leave, and returns with all expedition to Candahar...[14]

The mood in which this dispatch found Palmerston was that of the defiant concluding paragraph of McNeill's book, and by a coincidence it arrived on Palmerston's desk a few days after the gazetting of McNeill's appointment as envoy and minister plenipotentiary at the Persian Court.[15] Melbourne at this time was still privately warning his Foreign Secretary of 'the extreme danger of taking strong steps'.[16] In uttering such a warning Melbourne was acting, whether he knew it or not, in accordance with the guiding rule laid down by Lord Ellenborough in 1830—that 'while you take such measures for your own safety as a commanding necessity may require, you will be careful not to adopt a line of conduct which might needlessly lead to collision in Europe'.

Ellis's remaining dispatches from Teheran that April served only to confirm how busy Simonich had been in paying court to the Shah. All that Ellis could do before his audience of leave on 30 April was to make sure that the Shah and his ministers were in no doubt about the British attitude towards the proposed Herat expedition. But he scored one modest success. He persuaded the envoys from both Kabul and Kandahar to think again before binding themselves to the Shah. He informed Palmerston of this on 10 April, but by the time Palmerston received the news he had already made the move suggested by Ellis. Ellis declared on 10 April:

I have not hesitated to proceed thus [that is, to encourage the Kabul and Kandahar envoys to look towards the British Government for protection] from being quite convinced that the British Government can no longer, with safety to its possessions in India, refrain from intimate connection with the Afghans, whether they be subject to one chief or divided into principalities.[17]

We shall see soon how Auckland replied. But first we need to consider events in London. On 18 May Hobhouse wrote to Auckland about the new draft treaty which McNeill would be taking with him to Persia—a treaty omitting the frustrating ninth article of 1814. Hobhouse also told him that McNeill would be *his* envoy as well as the King's, and would 'correspond regularly with you and with us on the affairs of the mission and on the state of the British detachment in Persia'.[18] Palmerston and Hobhouse now made their arrangements for a really close liaison between the Foreign Office and India Board. Copies of all instructions to the British Minister in Persia, either by the Governor General of India or by the Secret Committee, should be transmitted without delay to the Foreign Office, for the information of the Secretary of State. McNeill, for his part, was to accept such instructions from the

Governor General as were consistent with the instructions sent to him by the Secretary of State. The same condition applied to instructions from the Secret Committee. Even McNeill's dispatches to the Secret Committee should go through Palmerston's office 'under flying seal for the perusal of the Secretary of State'.[19] In other words, Palmerston's views mattered more than those of Hobhouse or Auckland in the framing of British policy in Teheran. But Hobhouse regularly discussed Persian and Indian affairs with Palmerston in the Cabinet Room at 10 Downing Street, while Auckland was dependent upon infrequent dispatches, private letters and his own judgement. At the end of June Palmerston and Hobhouse came to a decision in London, and Auckland, working on much the same evidence from Teheran, came to a different decision in Calcutta. Macnaghten wrote to Ellis on his behalf, politely rejecting the suggestion that the Government of India should enter into an alliance with Kabul and Kandahar, and expressing the belief that the Shah might still be persuaded to see the error of his ways.[20] On the same day Auckland wrote privately to Hobhouse:

...Pray ask Palmerston to keep me as well informed as he may with propriety upon all the instructions which he sends to the King's ambassador in Persia. I have refused to comply with such suggestions of Ellis as might lead to a breach of our Persian alliance, and have written to McNeill a statement of very contrary views, mixed up however with strong remonstrances upon the manner in which our officers and detachments are treated and engagements with us evaded...[21]

Auckland wrote his letter to Hobhouse on Monday. At that moment in London the most popular topic of conversation was certainly not the disturbing conduct of the Russian Minister in Teheran; it was the alleged misconduct of the British Prime Minister. George Norton had accused him of adultery with his wife Caroline, and the case was due to come before the court on Thursday morning. Thursday came, and Melbourne was acquitted. The evidence offered was flimsy, the witnesses were contemptible, and the Attorney General, who conducted Melbourne's defence, was brilliant. The jury did not even leave the box. As Lord David Cecil has written:

...Even the bitterest Tory did not dare to question the justice of the verdict. 'As far as I can see,' said one acidly, 'Melbourne had more opportunities than any man ever had before and made no use of them.'[22]

On the day of the hearing Palmerston wrote to McNeill that he thought it right to communicate to Hobhouse copies of Ellis's dispatches on the overtures said to have been made to the Shah of Persia by the chiefs of Kabul and Kandahar, 'with a view to the conquest and partition of the territories of Shah Kamran of Herat. In consequence of the intelligence contained in these despatches,' Palmerston wrote, 'it has been thought advisable to address to the Governor General of India an instruction of which I enclose a copy for your confidential information.'[23]

Hitherto this direct evidence of Palmerston's initiative in the matter has not received the attention it deserves. It was certainly omitted when Palmerston authorized the publication of parts of the confidential collection of dispatches which he placed before the Cabinet in 1839. Auckland Colvin was the first to draw attention to the Secret Committee's instructions of 25 June 1836, when he sought to vindicate his father and his godfather (Lord Auckland) many years later.

The dispatch opened by referring to Ellis's dispatches of 25 February and 1 April, copies of which were enclosed in case Auckland had not already received some from Ellis in the normal way. Then it said:

...The facts above mentioned are clearly indicative of a disposition on the part of the rival chiefs of Affghanistan to engage the Shah of Persia in their views of personal aggrandizement, and from the views which the Shah himself is known to entertain in regard to Herat there is reason to apprehend that he may be disposed to countenance any scheme which may facilitate the accomplishment of a favourite object of his ambition, encouraged as he doubtless will be by the Russians to extend his influence, and through him that of their own, into countries bordering upon our Indian possessions.

Mr Ellis mentions in his letter of the 25th of February that he suggested to Hajee Hoossein Alli, the nobleman from whom he received the particulars of Dost Mahomed's overtures to the Shah of Persia, the propriety of Dost Mahomed himself opening a communication with the Governor General of India, and it is therefore possible that, before this letter reaches you, you may be in possession of an overture from this Chief, which will enable you the better to judge as to what steps it may be proper and desirable for you to take to watch, more closely than has hitherto been attempted, the progress of events in Affghanistan, and to counteract the progress of Russian influence in a quarter which, from its proximity to our Indian possessions, could not fail, if it were once established, to act injuriously on the system of our Indian alliances, and possibly to interfere with the tranquillity of our own territory. The mode of dealing with this very important question, whether by dispatching a confidential agent to Dost Mahomed of Cabul merely to watch the progress of events, or to enter into relations with this chief, either of a political or merely, in the first instance, of a commercial character, we confide to your discretion, as well as the adoption of any other measures that may appear to you to be desirable in order to counteract Russian influence in that quarter, should you be satisfied from the information received from your own agents on the frontier, or hereafter from Mr McNeill, on his arrival in Persia, that the time has arrived at which it would be right for you to interfere decidedly in the affairs of Affghanis- tan. Such an interference would doubtless be requisite, either to prevent the extension of Persian dominion in that quarter or to raise a timely barrier against the impending encroachments of Russian influence. We shall transmit to Mr McNeill a copy of this despatch for his information and guidance, and you may expect to receive from him intelligence of passing events sufficiently full and accurate to assist you in coming to a decision on the important question to which we wish to direct your immediate and most earnest attention.[24]

Palmerston and Hobhouse had left much to Auckland's discre- tion, thus showing their trust in his powers of judgement. He, on receiving Ellis's warnings and suggestions, had reacted very cautiously. He wanted a second opinion. He would be glad to encourage agencies half commercial and half political. His minute of 4 May, already quoted, tells us exactly how far he was prepared to go in recognition of Afghanistan's value as an outwork to Britain's Indian possessions. For the moment his attention was fixed upon the Indus. The early over-optimism of some officers about the navigability of the river gave way in the summer of 1836 to a more sensible attitude. It was not the fault of Alexander Burnes that some were too sanguine in their hopes of early success. Others followed his path up the Indus and came back with confirmation of his earliest impressions. Auckland was a little disappointed, but he wisely considered it premature to conclude that the project was hopeless. He thought deeply about the national plan to open the Indus to commerce, and the result of his study was a long minute suggesting 'measures for giving a new impulse to the commerce of that river by the establishment of places of entrepot, and of annual fairs...'. It is reasonable to suppose that the idea of sending Burnes through Sind and the Punjab to Kabul, to make entrepots and annual fairs acceptable to the rulers, occurred to him in July. An interesting feature of this minute of 19 August is Auckland's reference in it to Ellenborough's dispatch of 7 March 1835 as the latest general instruction from the Secret Committee about relations with states along the Indus. This, it will be remembered, counselled Bentinck and Metcalfe to maintain the division of power between Sindians, Afghans and Sikhs, and in August 1836 Runjeet Singh was making warlike gestures in the direction of Sind. Auckland ended his minute by saying:

...I may say that I am very unwilling to give the alarming colour of political speculation to a mission, the main object of which is commercial, but it is impossible to divest of political interest any observation of the countries on the Indus and to the West of that river. It is difficult to see without some anxiety the exertions made on every occasion by the Ruler of the Punjab to extend his power. All information from that quarter must be valuable, and it may not be useless ostensibly to mark that nothing which is there passing is viewed with indifference by the British Government, or escapes its notice.[25]

Three days after the signing of this minute Auckland sent a warning to Runjeet Singh.[26] On his behalf Macnaghten instructed Wade to tell Runjeet, in the friendliest possible way, that the British Government did not approve of his disposition to covet Shikarpur and other parts of Sind. 'The object of the British Government in procuring the Indus to be thrown open for navigation was to connect the different nations of Asia more firmly together by the ties of commerce and mutual convenience...' Hobhouse first heard about the old king's restlessness and Auckland's warning in a letter which Auckland wrote on 26 August: '...If we can but keep him quiet, the river may I think become the route of a very extended commerce, though the difficulties of its connection with the sea are much greater than were anticipated...'[27]

The Sikh expansionism that worried Auckland when he looked at Sind at the end of August made him less anxious about the Persian threat to Afghanistan. He told Hobhouse that Runjeet Singh was likely to be at Kabul long before the Shah of Persia, thus revealing his great respect for the strength and European efficiency of the Sikh armed forces.[28] What he did not know, apparently, was that the Sikhs had a powerful dread of the dark passes between the plains and Kabul, as well as of the accurate firearms and long knives of the Afghan tribesmen. Auckland merely shared the general opinion that the sepoys, with their European officers and a leaven of British and locally raised European regiments, were the only soldiers capable of defeating the Sikhs on their own ground. Now he was reaching across the frontier of British India and warning one of his neighbours to keep his hands off Sind. This was an important turning-point in the history of the British in India, as Auckland understood. Moreover, he was intervening to check the ambitions of a strong and respected ally. Can we blame him because he replied in discouraging terms to a letter from Dost Muhammad on the very day of the warning to Runjeet Singh ? To have given Dost Muhammad encouragement at that moment might well have destroyed the old alliance with the Sikhs.

Dost Muhammad wrote his letter on the last day of May 1836. 'The field of my hopes, which had before been chilled by the cold blast of the times, has, by the happy tidings of your Lordship's arrival, become the envy of the garden of Paradise.' In more prosaic terms he might have said that relations between him and Bentinck became very cool after Shuja's invasion of Afghanistan; perhaps a new Governor General would bring new policies. The British had given him assurances in the past, and now he needed their help:

... The late transactions in this quarter, the conduct of reckless and misguided Sikhs, and their breach of treaty, are well known to your Lordship. Communicate to me whatever may now suggest itself to your wisdom, for the settlement of the affairs of this country, that it may serve as a rule for my guidance... Whatever directions your Lordship may be pleased to issue for the administration of this country, I will act accordingly.[29]

As always, Dost Muhammad was haunted by the vision of Peshawar in the hands of the hated Sikhs and by the base treachery of his brother Sultan. When Auckland replied to this letter at the end of August, inhibited by his concern for the health of the Anglo-Sikh alliance at a time of strain, he conformed exactly to the terms of his minute of 4 May (on Ellis's dispatches). He wished the Afghans to be a flourishing and united nation, at peace with their neighbours and enjoying the benefits and comforts imparted by commerce. He indicated that he might soon send someone to discuss commercial matters with the government of Kabul. Then he said:

...I have learned with deep regret that dissensions exist between yourself and Maharajah Runjeet Singh. My friend, you are aware that it is not the practice of the British Government to interfere with the affairs of other independent states; and indeed it does not immediately occur to me how the influence of my government could be exercised for your benefit...

Auckland then asked Dost Muhammad to let him know how he could help. He hoped that in the meantime the Dost might find a way of effecting his own reconciliation with the Sikhs, '...it being not only for your own advantage, but for the advantage of all the countries in the vicinity, that two nations so situated should ever preserve unimpaired the relations of amity and concord...'.[30] This was not an unfriendly letter in the circumstances. The Anglo-Sikh alliance created at Amritsar in 1809 was an insuperable obstacle in the way of an arrangement with Dost Muhammad as long as he was the implacable enemy of Runjeet Singh. There was little else that Auckland could say, and the addition of one innocent word would have made the letter completely unobjectionable. He should really have said that 'it is not the *normal* practice of the British Government to interfere...'. Bentinck expressed the idea best when he told Shah Shuja in 1832 that Britain religiously abstains from intermeddling with the affairs of her neighbours 'when this can be avoided'.[31] The omission of 'normal' from Auckland's letter is all the more striking because it happened on the day of his historic act of interference between Sind and the Punjab.

We noticed earlier in this story that the British in India never hesitated to extract advantages from Sind by threatening to withhold protection. Once Auckland had decided to intervene beyond his own frontier between Sindians and Sikhs, by issuing a warning to Runjeet Singh, there was no turning back. The Sind emirs could not expect to get such protection for nothing. In September Auckland's Government took three important steps. Through Wade it again warned Runjeet Singh against trying to extend his 'power along the whole course of the Indus';[32] it instructed Burnes to prepare for his mission up the Indus;[33] and it commissioned Colonel Pottinger to open negotiations with the Sind emirs. Pottinger was told to seek from the emirs every additional facility and assistance which the British might require on the Indus, 'under the influence of the circumstances, which must now doubtless induce them to seek cordially the friendship of the British

Government'.[34] Those words were written by John Colvin, Auckland's private secretary. Colvin, then only 29, had a style of his own, but he was not the initiator of policy. Auckland wrote personally to officers and officials of high rank, but he normally left it to Colvin to keep up the semi-official correspondence. Auckland and his private secretary had a good understanding. The policy was the same, whoever wrote the letters; only the style changed, and Colvin was something of a romantic while Auckland, old enough to be Colvin's father, had left romantic notions far behind him, at Christ Church and Lincoln's Inn in the years before Waterloo. At this period Auckland also had the help of William Hay Macnaghten, who, as head of the Secret and Political Department, functioned as his Foreign Secretary. Emily Eden thought of him affectionately as 'our Lord Palmerston'. It was Macnaghten's responsibility to send official instructions to Pottinger at the end of September, on behalf of Auckland:

... You will in treating with the Amirs communicate with them, without reserve, in reference to the dangerous position in which they stand, and you will apprise them, that this government is sensible how essential it is, not to their interests only, but to their very existence, that the ties by which they are connected with the British Empire should be strengthened...

Once again we note the implied threat: if the Sind emirs wish to be protected from the Sikhs they must draw closer to the British and help them to make the Indus a commercial highway. The price of permanent protection against the Sikhs, without an alliance, was the acceptance of a British garrison in Sind, and not only in Sind but in the capital itself; the price of protection in this crisis only, without future commitment, was the acceptance of a British Resident.[35] A few days later, as an afterthought, Pottinger was told that he could also discuss the level of tolls on river traffic if he thought it necessary, for the prospect of a reasonable profit might help to keep the emirs interested.[36]

It is not difficult for the critic to make out a case against these proceedings, casting Auckland as the villainous monkey with his goad and the emirs as the poor overworked donkey. If the rulers of Sind wanted to maintain their medieval isolation, Britain had no right to interfere. The terms offered for protection were extortionate. It would have been more admirable to restrain the Sikhs without asking for any reward. Britain was bound by the treaty of 1832 to keep military transport and stores off the river. The same treaty bound her not to look with the 'eye of covetousness' at the possessions of the Sind emirs. And so on, until the logic of the argument leads us back to a little England with independent neighbours— Scotland, Wales, and probably Cornwall. The truth is, whether we like it or not, that Sind at that time was a crumbling and unreliable bastion in the defences of India, and the British in India could not afford not to interfere in the affairs of the emirs. The interference could even be portrayed as a moral obligation:

...We have conquered India, and as a necessary consequence of that conquest, have taken upon ourselves the government of the country, and supplanted almost all the native instruments of government that we found there; by doing so we have incurred the responsibility of protecting those who have submitted to our rule from external violence as well as from internal discord. This is a sacred duty, and we are bound by every moral obligation that connects a government with its subjects to neglect no honourable means of enabling ourselves to discharge it...[37]

So said John McNeill at the beginning of 1836. Could the terms offered to the Sind emirs be considered honourable, and thus qualify for McNeill's moral justification? Auckland had no doubt on this score:

...In interposing for the protection of Sinde from imminent danger, the British Government may justly expect to receive, in return, some corresponding advantages...[38]

But whether the means employed in performing 'the sacred duty' were honourable or not, there was one man who persisted in thinking that it was disastrous to interfere in the affairs of the North-West. Sir Charles Metcalfe wrote to Auckland from Agra, where he was now Lieutenant Governor of the North-West Provinces, urging him not to venture beyond the Indus and expressing the fear that the British would soon be involved in serious trouble if their forward policy continued. In answer to the first of these warnings Auckland cited three reasons for fearing that he would not be permitted to confine his administration to peaceful objects: Runjeet Singh's restless ambition, directed at that moment against Sind; the importance attached (but not yet properly assessed) to the free navigation of the Indus; and the advance of the Persians towards Herat once more. This letter showed how far Auckland's views had changed since the beginning of April. He had slowly come to understand that a collision might take place during his term of office, and that he would not be blessed with a 'season of peace', as Bentinck had been. Metcalfe's letter included a remark which Auckland considered worth quoting to Hobhouse: '...But, as you say, we must fulfil our destiny...'[39] That destiny, for both Metcalfe and Auckland, was that the British should become the masters of the whole of India within its natural frontiers. Where they differed was on the best means of defending those frontiers.

A few days after replying to Metcalfe Lord Auckland received the Secret Committee dispatch of 25 June, and he acknowledged it by saying that he had anticipated the Secret Committee's wishes 'to a great degree' by detailing Burnes to go on a mission by way of the Indus to Kabul.[40] Metcalfe wrote again when he fully understood the implications of the warning to Runjeet Singh. Again Auckland disagreed with him, for in a sense the pupil had overtaken the master. Auckland said he would gladly avoid all interference in the politics of the west, but the influence of European politics was already felt at Herat, and 'the elements of Discord had been long collecting in that quarter'. Auckland had made up his mind to repair the outer defences. 'I think I am right', he told Hobhouse, 'and shall be glad if I am thought so at home, but I shall be still more glad if by the course of events it shall be found that it little signifies whether I am right or wrong.' Nothing in Auckland's correspondence with Metcalfe supports the opinion of his critics that he lacked the courage of his own convictions, or that he was bumbling and inefficient. Metcalfe, for his part, registered one more protest against the policy of interference, and ended by saying that his disagreement would not affect his loyalty. He hoped that Auckland would employ him where he could be most useful if that policy involved them in a war with Runjeet Singh. He even enclosed a plan of action for use in the event of a war with the Sikhs, and Auckland passed it on to his Commander in Chief, Sir Henry Fane. Metcalfe stated his case very forcefully in his letter of 15 October:

...I lament the course which you have determined to pursue, for what is now done is but a beginning. We are, I fear, about to plunge into a labyrinth of interference from which I fear we shall never be able to extricate ourselves...

...I cannot perceive any object worth the risk of the possible consequences of this change in our policy, and this departure from that pacific system which was essential for the establishment of our political strength and financial prosperity...

It was then that Metcalfe expressed a view the exact opposite of the policy laid down in London. Ellenborough had said that the Indus territories should continue to be divided between Sindians, Afghans, and Sikhs. But Metcalfe could not see why the Sikhs should be prevented from occupying the whole of Sind. They would be equally good neighbours, and equally willing to permit the navigation of the Indus—'the mischievous and worthless cause of the coming turmoil'. Moreover, the subjugation of Sind by the Sikhs would so extend their strength as to make them weaker and more assailable if they ever became enemies of the British. In the meantime the extended Sikh power would serve to keep the invaders from the north out of India.[41]

It has been said that Metcalfe, during his year as acting Governor General, offended the Court of Directors by freeing the Indian press from official restrictions. But the study of these letters to Auckland reveals a man who could never conscientiously have carried out the forward policy prescribed by the Government in London. The freeing of the press was as nothing compared with this, and his opposition to Government policy must have weighed against him when the search for a successor to Bentinck started in the winter of 1834–5. It is facile to claim that later events proved Metcalfe right, as some have done only too willingly. What he proposed was the negative policy of inaction. When things go wrong it is always possible for those who said 'Do nothing' to claim that they were right. What they forget is that doing nothing, even for the very best reasons, invites a rival to take bolder and possibly much more dangerous action. Metcalfe backed his personal judgement against that of the duke of Wellington, joint progenitor of the Central Asian policy, Lord Ellenborough, Lord Palmerston, Lord Melbourne, and many others in Britain and India. Lord Auckland, as we have seen, had the courage of his convictions, but was not inclined to dogmatize. He had the rare gift of intellectual humility. It fell to his lot to make one of the most difficult and dangerous decisions in the history of British India, and he made it only after long and careful consideration of all the factors. Care and seriousness in the making of decisions are not indecision. This is how Auckland answered the dogmatic pronouncement of his eminent colleague:

...You almost frighten me with your black prognostics...I am far from an enthusiast upon the subject of the Indus, nor do I dream golden dreams of it, or think it the factotum of India as some in England do. But it may grow into Commercial importance. Its navigation is an avowed British project. I have been moved to secure it, and money and pains are spending and have been spent for it...It is true that this one [remonstrance with Runjeet Singh] may lead us further than we either wish or foresee, but the most passive policy is not always the most pacific; and another course might have led to evils more formidable. In all this you will differ from me and I deeply lament it, and whenever you do so I must doubt whether I am in the right. But whether I am in the right or wrong it is little good in politics to be long looking back on footsteps that are passed. Our thoughts must be given to where we may step in advance with most firmness and prudence, and a very few days will enable me to see our way more clearly...[42]

Auckland meant that he would soon hear Runjeet Singh's reply to the warning. He had judged that Runjeet would grumble, consider, and finally agree to do what the British Government wanted. He judged correctly, and by the middle of November the crisis was over. Runjeet Singh, unlike some of the senior officers round him, swallowed his pride in the interest of the alliance which had allowed him to achieve so much in twenty-seven years. But one can see that it would be difficult for Auckland to restrain him again. By yielding so gracefully, Runjeet had put the British under an obligation to him. It was now doubly difficult to make any accommodation with Runjeet's worst enemy, Dost Muhammad Khan of Kabul.

Thus it was that Auckland was able to write home to colleagues in London on 17 November that 'we are all at amity and cordiality again with Runjeet Singh',[43] and that 'my démêlé with the old Lion of Lahore is coming right'.[44] Colonel Pottinger at that time was just starting his mission to Hyderabad to negotiate with the Sind emirs, and Burnes was preparing for his own mission up the Indus. The 47-year-old colonel and the ambitious young subaltern were no longer on speaking terms. Burnes had been left in charge in Cutch while Pottinger was away at the beginning of 1836, and had evidently handled a particularly delicate local problem in a way which pleased the Bombay Government but displeased Pottinger. Alexander Burnes, who already knew how to flatter princes and play the diplomat, was no respecter of officers senior to him in his own service when he thought he was in the right. To Colonel Pottinger he must have seemed a whippersnapper, a conceited upstart. Perhaps jealousy also played a part in their quarrel. However that may be, Auckland asked Colvin to write to them. Through Colvin he appealed to Pottinger as 'an officer of long and distinguished public services', and to Burnes as 'an officer of distinguished promise'. He ordered them not to let their private feelings impede the course of their public conduct:

...To the complete success of the measures which have recently been prescribed for improving our connection with Sinde and securing and extending the navigation of the Indus, it is most essential that all the British Agents employed should be seen to be animated with one common spirit in the execution of their instructions, that there should be no suspicion of public differences...[45]

As it happened, the two men were not required to work much longer in harness at this stage of their careers, though their quarrel broke out again as soon as they found themselves in the same territory two years later. To their credit, however, they seem to have taken Auckland's advice to heart, and their work did not suffer. But their quarrel is interesting for the light which it throws on their personalities. Pottinger had worked long and hard without attracting special favour. He was stern and unbending in his public life. The Sind emirs learned to respect him. Burnes, on the other hand, made his mark without drudgery. Fame came to him early, and it turned his head. But Auckland, for one, was always ready to forgive his faults because his energy and ability were so valuable. In an age when patronage and pull counted for so much, both Pottinger and Burnes made their way on their merits. Burnes's merits were no less admirable because his zest and sparkle drew attention to them. It was not entirely a matter of vanity and self-advertisement. He was one of those favoured mortals who cannot help attracting and entertaining those about him. The only drawback was that some nursed a secret envy while they pretended to be his friends.

What concerned Auckland above all else in October and the early part of November was the 'démêlé with the old Lion of Lahore'. Towards the end of November he began to write in terms which recall the wording of the June dispatch. For instance, he told his Commander in Chief, Sir Henry Fane, that the Persians appeared to be advancing towards Herat: '...tho' the black cloud immediately upon our frontier is dispersing, a yet blacker is collecting beyond it...'[46] He used a similar phrase in his letter to

Hobhouse on the following day. He was sorry to see that the Persians were bringing their own, and consequently Russian, influence nearer to the Indian frontier, throwing

into confusion and disorder all those countries in which we were most anxious to see established tranquility and commerce.

It is not easy for us to take any step to counteract this inroad from India, and I have heard nothing from McNeill. In the first instance I can only hope that the Afghans may beat back our Persian ally—and they might do it if they too were not divided into many parties of whom some will attach themselves to the Persians, but hitherto our information is very imperfect and only comes in the shape of rumour from Caubul...[47]

Writing to Carnac on the same day, Auckland was equally uncertain. Direct interference was out of the question at this stage. '...We have nothing else at present to do than to keep ourselves strong and to wait for occasions of using our influence...'[48] Indeed, Auckland's Government was so far from interfering in Afghanistan at this stage that it had to rap Shuja over the knuckles, having found out that he, at least, had been looking beyond the horizon and into the Afghan hills. Such visions were premature. 'Peace beyond the Indus is desirable, but our interposition to preserve it in that direction has not been resolved upon...'[49]

Auckland's inclination was to wait and see what effect McNeil might have upon the Shah's policy, to watch events, and to 'wait for occasions of using our influence'. It was far too early to think of doing anything else, and in any case he wanted a period of peace and quiet so that the Burnes mission might have a chance of success. It was far too early because McNeill did not arrive in Teheran until the end of September, and the Shah at that time was in the province of Khorasan, hovering near and constantly menacing Herat. In October, however, McNeill was able to report the news that the Persian army was expected to return to Teheran for the winter, in spite of Simonich's urgent advice to the Shah to keep moving eastwards.[50] At the beginning of November, McNeill reported, the Persian army was in camp near Asterabad, low in spirits and short of food and pay. Yet Simonich was still urging the Shah to undertake a winter campaign against Herat.[51] Both Palmerston and Auckland received these messages at the turn of the year. Auckland had started his official correspondence with McNeill on 21 November, when Macnaghten wrote a letter instructing him to do all in his power to dissuade the Shah from attacking Herat and to be prepared to offer mediation between Persia and Herat. If the worst came to the worst McNeill was authorized to withdraw the whole British mission, both diplomatic and military, upon Herat.[52]

Meanwhile Burnes had sailed from Bombay with Lieutenant Robert Leech of the Bombay Engineers and Lieutenant John Wood of the Indian Navy on Saturday 26 November. They reached the mouth of the Indus on 13 December and they started their river voyage on Christmas Eve. In Burnes's own words, 'the objects of Government were to work out its policy of opening the river Indus to commerce, and establishing on its banks, and in the countries beyond it, such relations as should contribute to the desired end'.[53]

On Christmas Day Auckland put his signature to his minute on letters from Pottinger, who was still negotiating in Sind. So far Pottinger had wrung from the emirs a promise of consent at some future time to the permanent residence of a British officer in Sind. But Auckland was not very hopeful of early success in establishing what he called 'a decided political preponderance' in Sind, desirable though it was.

On us [he wrote] the Scindians ought to be led to look as their natural friends and the best Guardians of their independence. I would make it, therefore, a main object of our policy to bring the Government of the Ameers into a more avowed connection with us. The end is one which should not be abruptly pressed, and I have no doubt it will, if not now, at no very distant period, be effected...Our immediate and declared object is peace upon the Indus, and we must continue to seek it in good faith, being prepared only to make such use of events as we, with fairness, may, in order to procure for the national interests all the advantages that we have in view...[54]

So ended the first year of Auckland's term as Governor General of India. He had arrived fresh from England at the beginning of March, expecting ample leisure in which to prepare the defences of India and hoping to devote much of his time to good works in India itself. He found that the clouds in the north-west promised little leisure and much disturbance. He backed his own judgement against Metcalfe's in intervening between Runjeet Singh and the Sind emirs over Shikarpur. He foresaw the possibility of conflict in the north-west and began to prepare for it, but without precipitate action, and the June dispatch from London gave him the authority he needed just as he was beginning to understand that he might one day need it. He had a firm and efficient grip on Indian affairs.

CHAPTER 6

NEGOTIATIONS IN TEHERAN
AND KABUL

... The ear of Dost Mohamed's sagacity is closed by the cotton of
negligence. If he repent, offer obedience, and enter into a treaty
agreeably to my wish, he shall be pardoned. Should he delay, the
whole Sikh nation, being exasperated, will advance to Jalalabad,
where it will be of no avail to him to bite the hand of sorrow with
the teeth of repentance...

RUNJEET SINGH to Lord Auckland, July 1837

The Shah's discomfiture in Khorasan and his return to Teheran
allowed Auckland to breathe more easily in the winter of 1836–7.
He had enough to do to quieten his immediate neighbours,
who were ever fractious, without leap-frogging into Central Asia.
He might have to do so one day, but for the time being he was glad
of the respite which allowed him to concentrate on the Indus, Sind,
and the Sikhs. Runjeet Singh was an old man, still vigorous and in
command, but not quite the formidable leader of past years. A
paralytic stroke, from which he astonishingly recovered with facul-
ties almost unimpaired, left him more vulnerable and made him
conscious of approaching death. Perhaps this was what made him
so restless and eager for expansion. Auckland had to be ready for
all contingencies. Runjeet Singh might live for ten, perhaps twenty,
years more; but he might die next week. Auckland could see that
it was politic to plan for the possibility of violent change after
Runjeet's death. In the first week of January he wrote to Sir James
Carnac, relating how he had given a cordial welcome in Calcutta to
General Allard, the French commander of the Sikh cavalry, during
that officer's recent visit. He said that cordiality and friendship
were regarded

as due to the readiness with which Runjeet Singh has accommodated his
objects and measures to our views and wishes, and as possibly laying the
foundation for some influence upon the band of adventurers at his court,
which may be useful as well now as when the succession to his throne
may come into dispute. In truth a change in the whole form of public
affairs in that direction seems not to be far distant and we must await it
with the best preparation that we can make...[1]

102

Accordingly he asked the government of Madras to be ready to send some of its troops to the Bengal Presidency. Two days after writing to Carnac he sent the request to the Hon. John Sullivan:

> ...India has no external enemies to fear except from its north and north west, and with 17,000 men well appointed and armed in Nepal and a much larger force in the Punjab and a storm gathering beyond it I cannot but think it would be well if our force upon the Ganges and the Jumna were increased, and that your army is not relatively stronger than under present circumstances is necessary...[2]

It has so often been said, parrot fashion, that an indecisive Auckland was pushed by bolder spirits into a forward policy in 1838 that it may be well to note the date of his first prudent redeployment of troops, 7 January 1837. A few days earlier, far away in London, Palmerston had received the November dispatch in which McNeill complained that the Russian Minister was still urging the Shah to march to Herat. Palmerston very soon penned a note to the earl of Durham, the British ambassador in St Petersburg:

> I have to instruct your Excellency to ask Count Nesselrode whether Count Simonich is acting according to his instructions in thus urging the Shah to pursue a line of conduct so diametrically opposed to His Persian Majesty's real interests...

If Nesselrode admitted that Simonich was acting on his instructions, Durham was to tell him that such expeditions were unwise and injurious in the highest degree. But Palmerston was sure that Nesselrode would not accept Simonich's policy as his own, and in that case 'His Majesty's Government cannot doubt that the Russian Cabinet will put a stop to such a course of conduct, so much at variance with its own declared policy, and so averse to the best interests of an ally for whom the Russian Government professes friendship and goodwill'.[3]

Palmerston thought that he had Nesselrode in a corner. But Nesselrode said he was sure that McNeill had been misinformed; if Simonich *had* done what he was accused of doing, it was without authority from St Petersburg. 'Count Nesselrode further stated that he entirely agreed with the English Government as to the folly and impolicy of the course pursued by the Persian Monarch.'[4] At the end of February Durham was confident that Simonich would be recalled. But on this occasion Palmerston was outwitted. The embarrassment of having to recall Urquhart from Turkey in

March cannot have helped him in the contest with Nesselrode. The Russian Foreign Office produced copies of dispatches in which Simonich spoke of his efforts to dissuade the Shah from attacking Herat 'au moins avant d'en avoir mis de l'ordre dans les affaires de son pays'.[5] McNeill maintained his charges against Simonich, but Simonich was not recalled. Palmerston's consolation was that he had forced Nesselrode to declare Russian interest in turning the Shah's attention to more peaceful pursuits, and that Simonich had had to make an outward show of co-operation with McNeill.[6] Nevertheless, the Shah and his army marched towards Herat at the end of July. Russia's moral credit in this affair was running out.

The polite exchanges between London and St Petersburg took place over a period of seven months, starting in January. We left Auckland early in the New Year, redeploying troops as a precaution against any outbreak of violence in the north-west. At that moment Alexander Burnes and his companions were slowly making their way through Lower Sind. They were at Tatta on New Year's Day and at Hyderabad on the 18th.[7] 'Slow' was also the word for Henry Pottinger's progress in negotiating for the reception of a British Resident at Hyderabad and in employing Britain's good offices in the dispute over Shikarpur. On 2 January Auckland had told the Secret Committee that if Pottinger succeeded, 'of which there is every possibility, the preservation of tranquility along the whole course of the Indus will be the natural consequence'.[8] But Pottinger had only started a long and painful haggle over the price that each side should pay for proposed advantages. Of his dispatches up to the middle of January, Auckland wrote: '...I am well satisfied...They leave room enough for anxiety and much is yet to be done but as far as they go they improve the promise of an established connection with Sinde and of a growing influence in that country...'[9]

As their fear of the Sikhs receded, the emirs became more demanding and less accommodating. Runjeet Singh went on grumbling from time to time about his loss of face in the Shikarpur affair, but the alliance stood firm and he invited Auckland to attend the wedding of his grandson, Nao Nehal Singh. Auckland declined. He did not want to flaunt Britain's solidarity with the Sikhs at a time when Colonel Pottinger and Captain Burnes were trying to win friends and promote peaceful commerce among Runjeet's

neighbours. But he encouraged his Commander in Chief, Sir Henry
Fane, to attend the wedding on his behalf. John Colvin intimated
to Pottinger and Burnes that they must not allow the Sindian and
Afghan chiefs to draw false and exaggerated inferences from Fane's
visit to the Punjab. 'Ready cordiality and friendship with all parties', he wrote, 'are, I may repeat it, the Motto by which our
policy in all these matters is to be explained.'[10] But ready cordiality
with all at the same time, given the feuds dividing them, was more
difficult to achieve than Colvin implied. At about this time John
McNeill was analysing the situation in Afghanistan, and the result
of his winter thoughts in Teheran was a long memorandum which
he sent to Calcutta and London (in the form of a copy for Palmerston). Auckland received it at the end of March, and Palmerston at
the end of April. The dates are noteworthy because this was the
first mention of the possibility of restoring Shah Shuja. McNeill
very carefully weighed the merits and faults of each family—
Barukzai and Sadozai. A good case could be argued for either, and
in the end McNeill said that he was unwilling to hazard an opinion.
But he concluded:

...As soon as it may be decided to form connections with either party
I presume that there can be no doubt of the advantage of seeking by
every available means, to unite the Afghan Nation under one chief.
This, even in favourable circumstances, would be a tedious and arduous
undertaking, but I feel assured that it is an object of primary importance
to the security of India; and fortunately it is one which the British
Government, more than all the rest of the world, can contribute to
accomplish.[11]

Already we begin to see the great importance of John McNeill's
post. From Teheran he influenced the making of policy in both
London and Calcutta, though at the beginning of 1837 his more
receptive audience was in London. Auckland's natural caution and
a certain civilized opportunism can be traced in his letters to
London. For instance, he told Carnac in the middle of February
that the postponement of the Persian campaign against Herat
might now make Dost Muhammad more amenable, since he could
no longer profit by it:

...It is possible that he may consent to some concessions and secure
himself from the danger of eastern invasion by conciliating Runjeet
Singh, and that he would then combine with us in resisting aggression

from the west. But all this is extremely vague, and there would be no compensation for raising the anger and jealousy of the Sikhs by any advantages to be immediately gained beyond them. The dispersion of the Persian army has happily given us time, and we will endeavour to use it for the best. Captain Burnes will shortly be at Lahore and will proceed from thence to Cabul, and I am preparing instructions under which, without committing us to anything beyond amicable feelings, he may give us full information upon the relative strength of the parties in these countries...[12]

There lay the beginnings of an attempt to persuade Dost Muhammad and Runjeet Singh to live in harmony, but Auckland was still very unwilling to risk injury to the old Anglo-Sikh alliance for the sake of an alliance with others who might yield 'great local advantage but [are] otherwise weak and distant and little to be depended upon'. So he wrote to McNeill at the end of February under the influence of a feeling that Sikhs and Afghans might never be persuaded to act 'cordially and vigorously together'. But 'if we can but gain time I shall not despair of seeing those countries [Kabul, Kandahar, and Herat] flourishing and independent and forming in their own strength the best rampart which India can have'.[13]

Auckland wanted time, time for the civilizing effects of growing commerce to make their mark along the Indus, time for the 'conciliation of peaceful sentiments', time for the healing of old wounds. But time was never on his side. Rumours began to circulate in March that Dost Muhammad was planning to take his revenge at Peshawar. Runjeet Singh had already angered his courtiers by complying with Auckland's wishes at Shikarpur, and it would not be easy to hold him to a peaceful policy at the next crisis. McNeill was meanwhile continuing Ellis's work of trying to turn the attention of Dost Muhammad and his Kandahar brothers towards friendship with the British in India. In February he was telling envoys from Kabul and Kandahar that there was no wisdom in a connexion with Persia. To the envoy from Kabul he said that any overtures which Dost Muhammad might be inclined to make would be received in a friendly spirit by the Governor General of India, provided that the Dost showed the British distinctly that he was their friend and, as such, unwilling to form a connexion with any foreign power which might threaten British India with injury. If he *did* form such a connexion, McNeill added, 'he must be prepared to see us take such a course in regard to him as may be dictated by the necessity of our interests'.[14]

A few days after reporting his dealings with the Afghan agents to Palmerston, John McNeill received the instructions which Auckland had sent to him in November, namely, to offer mediation between Persia and Herat and to be prepared to withdraw his whole mission to Herat from Persia if all his efforts for peace failed. McNeill told Palmerston that he was in a difficult position, for Herat had given the Shah every motive for an attack by flouting treaty obligations and committing aggression on Persian territory:

...I therefore doubt whether the measures proposed by the Indian Government would have the desired effect...I am not quite satisfied, with reference to the temper and feelings of the Shah and of this Court, whether it would be advisable to produce the alienation which must result from the measures proposed by the Indian Government, unless we are prepared to go further and to insure success in the object for which we resort to threats, by convincing the Persian Government that we are prepared to act as well as threaten...[15]

Once again we see how strong and influential McNeill had become in his strategic half-way house between London and Calcutta. He had licence to question and ignore instructions from the Governor General if he judged that they were inconsistent with his brief from Palmerston. He and Palmerston agreed that Britain's object should be to preserve Herat for the sake of Indian security, even if it meant a break with Persia. But a break with Persia, leaving Herat at the mercy of the Shah and his Russian friends (or masters, according to one's point of view), was unjustifiable by itself. Therefore McNeill quietly shelved his instructions from the Government of India. By now he was in correspondence with Alexander Burnes, who eagerly looked forward to meeting Dost Muhammad again and to making Kabul and Kandahar allies against invaders from the west. It must have been in answer to a letter from Burnes that McNeill wrote in the middle of March about the advantages of making Dost Muhammad the ruler of a united Afghanistan. Sir John Kaye made much of this letter because it suited his argument that the British in India should have listened more attentively to Burnes and have promoted Dost Muhammad. In fact, if the letter is read in conjunction with McNeill's long analysis of Afghan politics, we see that he had reservations. For example:

...I sincerely wish, if the Ameer Dost Mahomed Khan and you come to a good understanding, that he were in possession of both Candahar and Herat...He ought to be precluded from receiving any other foreign representative or agent of any kind at his Court, and should agree to transact all business with foreign powers through the British agent. Unless something of this kind should be done, we shall never be secure; and until Dost Mahomed Khan or some other Afghan shall have got both Candahar and Herat into his hands, our position here must continue to be a false one.[16]

This was by no means a firm statement of preference for Dost Muhammad. The promotion of that chief depended in McNeill's view upon a good understanding between him and Burnes, and in fact it did not matter to McNeill whether Dost or 'some other Afghan' controlled all three states, as long as Afghanistan was strong and united against Persia and Russia. Auckland, meanwhile, was very grateful to McNeill for his essay on Afghan politics, sent in January. At the end of March he once again told McNeill that he thought it unwise, 'for a connection so precarious [with Kabul], to quarrel with our ancient and more powerful friends...'. In a postscript to this letter Auckland referred briefly to McNeill's comparison of the claims of Dost Muhammad and Shuja to the throne of Kabul. It is a revealing comment in more ways than one. It not only shows Auckland to be uncommitted; it draws attention to his capacity for ruthless play in the game of diplomacy: 'We have long since determined upon keeping Shah Shoojah quiet so long as he remains under our protection, and this may possibly become an useful instrument of influence in our favour with those against whom he has pretensions.'[17]

As an ardent whist player Auckland recognized a good card when he saw one. Runjeet Singh was his ace of trumps; Shuja was also a good court card. He was not prepared to throw either of them away in favour of one which could only score if other players did exactly what he wanted them to do. As well as mentioning Shuja in his private letter to McNeill, he allowed Macnaghten to say the same, more pompously, in an official dispatch dated 10 April.[18] Auckland recoiled, however, when McNeill's latest thoughts on Afghan unity reached him at the end of May 1837. McNeill deserved the trust which both Palmerston and Auckland placed in him, but his preoccupation with Herat blinded him to Auckland's problems on the other side of the Indus. Again Auckland reminded him:

...Whatever inconvenience we may occasionally find in the strength and restlessness of the Sikh ruler, it cannot be in our policy to have the Sikh power on our frontier crushed by a strong Mahomedan union, and the establishment of a powerful Kuzzilbash rule over the whole of Afghanistan, if it were at all within our reach to effect it, would be a measure of very doubtful policy in regard to our Indian possessions. Few events could however be more improbable than such a union, and it is more to be wished that the present nearly even balance of the three Afghan powers should be preserved, each, if it could possibly be inculcated, with a respect for his own independence and, as connected with it, for that of his neighbour...[19]

To sum up, Afghan unity, seen from Teheran, was a source of strength against Persians and Russians; seen from Calcutta it was a source of trouble if Dost Muhammad was to be the chosen ruler of a united Afghan nation, for Dost Muhammad and Runjeet Singh were irreconcilable enemies. In the end, as we shall see, there was a compromise. But in the first half of 1837, however, such a compromise could be only dimly seen through the confusion of Afghan politics, and Dost Muhammad had further muddied the waters by sending his son Akbar to raid the Sikhs on the plain of Peshawar at the end of April. At the battle of Jamrud neither side could honestly claim a victory, but the Sikhs suffered severely at the hands of the Afghan horsemen, and they lost one of their king's favourite generals, Hari Singh. Runjeet was furious, and we can easily see why Auckland was so unimpressed by McNeill's arguments in favour of a united Afghanistan under the Dost. The letter from McNeill reached Calcutta at the peak of the excitement and tension generated by the Afghan raid. The letter from Runjeet Singh, quoted at the head of this chapter, tells us all we need to know about the mood of the Sikhs after Jamrud. Dost Muhammad had now made it doubly difficult for Auckland to do anything for him without offending the Sikhs.

We saw in chapter 5 how Auckland debated the morality of interference beyond the Indus with Sir Charles Metcalfe, who ended the debate by sending the Governor General a plan of action for use in the event of war with the Sikhs and by promising his loyal co-operation in spite of his dissent. Lord Auckland sent the plan to Sir Henry Fane, who then started a correspondence on this topic with Metcalfe. In the course of it Fane wrote:

...a case could hardly occur which would render it wise for us to overturn the Sikh power, or to over-run the Punjab, or to extend ourselves to the Westward...Every advance you might make beyond the Sutlej to the Westward, in my opinion, adds to your military weakness...If you want your empire to expand, expand it over Oude or over Gwalior, and the remains of the Mahratta empire. Make yourselves complete sovereigns of all within your bounds. But let alone the Far West...[20]

This opinion has often been quoted as if it represented Fane's considered view of the advance into Afghanistan in 1838, whereas it was in reality part of an academic discussion between soldier and 'political' of the proper limits of the British Empire in India at the beginning of 1837. Fane wrote his letter with knowledge of the contents of McNeill's book about the *Progress and Present Position of Russia in the East.* A letter to Fane shows that it was Auckland who sent the book to him. Fane questioned the doctrine of legitimate interference, as propounded by McNeill, in what seems to have been an argumentative but good-humoured letter to Auckland. The relationship between the Commander in Chief (a Tory selected for the job by the Tory Government of 1834–5) and the Whig Governor General was friendly, and even warm, throughout their service together. The only disadvantage, as far as Auckland was concerned, was that Fane conceived it to be his duty to function as the voice of Toryism in India. He was a soldier without a deep knowledge of political and diplomatic affairs, and so his criticism tended to be unhelpful and his advice unsound. But Auckland valued his military experience and advice very highly. Auckland now replied to Fane's letter, making fun of his contention that Runjeet Singh's claim to Shikarpur was a strong one, and he defended McNeill's (and Palmerston's) statement of the right to interfere in self-defence:

...No-one will aver that it is wise and politic lightly to intermeddle in the affairs of other nations. Few will deny some right to interfere when the policy and measures of one nation are likely to become injurious to the interests or security of another. The difference always arises on the immediate case...

But Fane had also questioned the very basis of McNeill's argument against Russian expansion, as Auckland reveals in the last few lines of his reply:

...It is true enough that a cutting commentary upon the pamphlet which I sent to you might be found in the 'Progress of the English in the East.' But here we are and we must not labour the less in our vocation, or (without attempting further progress) be the less prepared for danger, whether near or far.[21]

This letter deserves close attention because we can assume that Fane's attitude was not far different from the general Tory scepticism about Russian policy at the time. Tories recognized that Russia had ambitions in Asia, and, as we have seen, their leaders were as vigilant as the Whigs in guarding against Russian intrigue. But many accepted the view put forward by Lord Heytesbury in 1830 that Russia was too backward to be a serious threat to India, that the Russians had as much right to compete for markets for their goods as the British had, and that it was precaution enough to post agents in Kabul and Bokhara. This was the public attitude of many Tories, and it gave them a stick with which to belabour the reckless Whigs, but those who were privy to the secrets of Russian ambition and intrigue could tell a different story. The Indus was chosen in 1830 as the highway for the transport of British goods to Central Asia with the express object of keeping the Russians at a distance from Afghanistan. Beyond the Indus the commercial caravan routes led across the mountains of Afghanistan and down into the plains. The Russian riposte was an attempt to exert influence in Afghanistan through the Persians who had been subservient to them since the Treaty of Turkmanchai. If they succeeded, they would exclude British goods from Central Asia and they would establish their influence in such a way that the defences of India would become too costly to be borne. At the time there were many people in Britain who did not understand what was going on. Like Fane, they underestimated the threat from Russia and, if they were also Tories, they were unwilling to express approval of Whig policies on principle.

The debate with Sir Henry Fane occupied Lord Auckland in the middle of March, several weeks before the battle of Jamrud. At the beginning of April he sent a situation report to Hobhouse, showing that he had no strong feelings against Dost Muhammad. On the contrary, he frequently showed a deep understanding of that chief's difficult position. He said:

...I have said enough in other letters, in minutes and in public dispatches, of the views of policy by which I have been guided in regard to the countries bordering on the Indus and to the westward of that river.

They are far off, and we can beyond Lahore only see a haze of confusion with which it is difficult to deal, but at this moment I am better satisfied than I have always been with the appearance of affairs. I hope that our connection with Sinde has been improved. I hope that Runjeet Singh's schemes of violence towards the south have been suspended. I would not forcibly interfere with him if he chooses to waste his means in the mountains of Cabul and Candahar. I believe Herat to be stronger than it was, and with the Turcomans to be more than a match for Persian aggression. I think too that the position of McNeill is improved, though unless Mahomed Shah learn to think a little more of home and a little less of foreign conquest, all the money and pains which we have expended upon him will be wasted. To Dost Mahomed of Cabul I can only speak words of friendliness and offer facilities of commercial intercourse and a readiness to mediate if contending parties should ask for mediation. In his pressing need he has courted Persia, and he has courted Russia, and he has courted us, but it would be madness in us, though we may wish to see his independence assured, to quarrel with the Sikhs for him...[22]

That was how Auckland felt before the battle of Jamrud. Even before the battle he had nothing to offer to Dost Muhammad but the use of good offices to restrain Runjeet Singh, and even that was dangerous for the health of the alliance with the Sikhs. Dost Muhammad, on the other hand, wanted much more than good offices. When he heard from Wade that Burnes was approaching his country he wrote to Burnes and said that he had 'a great desire to make friendship with the British Government and to drive the Sikhs from Peshawar, through the advice of that government'.[23] On 15 May Auckland drafted a polite letter to the Dost, telling him that Burnes was on his way and emphasizing the mission's commercial purposes. The 'general diffusion' of the 'blessings and comforts' of commerce among neighbouring nations was

the grand object of the British Government.

It seeks for itself no exclusive benefits; but it ardently desires to secure the establishment of peace and prosperity in all the countries of Asia. With this in view, the British Government prevailed upon the powers occupying the banks of the river to open the navigation of the Indus; and to this object indeed have all its efforts been invariably directed...[24]

Here we see some charming euphemisms. The blessings and comforts of commerce would always be more comfortable for all concerned if the commerce was British, and the establishment of peace and prosperity in the countries of Asia was strictly a British object. Britain desired no exclusive benefits, but she did desire to exclude the Russians. Also on 15 May William Hay Macnaghten sent fresh instructions to Burnes, who was by then about half-way to Kabul. The date is important because these instructions made it absolutely clear to Alexander Burnes what his future conduct must be.

...Dost Mahomed Khan has by imprudent demonstrations and threats provoked the Sikhs to extensive preparations, and is in immediate hazard of attack from that formidable state...Far from endeavouring to save himself by measures of conciliation he seems to be meditating acts of aggression so rash and violent as to place in jeopardy the very existence of his power...In any case in which specific political propositions shall be made to you, you will state that you have no authority to make replies, but that you will forward them, through Captain Wade, to the Government. If applied to, as you probably may be, for advice by Dost Mahomed Khan, in the difficulties by which he is surrounded, you will dissuade him from insisting in such a crisis on pretensions which he cannot maintain, and you will lead him, as far as may be in your power, to seek and to form arrangements of reconciliation for himself with the Sikh sovereign...

The day's work at Government House in Calcutta reminds us once again of Auckland's constant preoccupation. The countries along the whole length of the Indus had to be at peace with one another if the river's commercial promise was to be fulfilled, and if Britain was to gain the political advantage which she had desired since 1830 over the Russians in Central Asia. Therefore it is not surprising that the fresh instructions to Burnes continued as follows:

...You will observe the general feelings towards the British and the Russian Governments, the impressions prevailing of the power and resources of either, the degree in which the supposition was entertained of an intimate union between the Persian and Russian governments, and in which that supposition is likely to have influence; and you will gather all the information in your power on the commerce of Russia, and on the measures adopted by that power with the object of extending her influence in Central Asia...[25]

Burnes was being asked to repeat part of his earlier mission (the one ordered by Ellenborough), and for much the same reason.

Burnes and his companions at that moment were exploring the Chenab and Lower Sutlej and the Multan country in between. They cultivated very friendly relations with the ruler of Bahawalpur, who presented them with a history of his tribe. In return Burnes gave him a drawing of Medina, to match one of Mecca already in his possession.[26] They sailed again from Mithankot on 22 May and arrived at Dera Ghazi Khan eight days later. It was there, on 2 June, that Burnes heard the news of the battle of Jamrud. He decided to press on, writing to McNeill as he went. McNeill, it will be remembered, had proposed that 'Dost Mahomed or some other Afghan' should gain control of the whole of Afghanistan. Burnes, who was still bound by the mainly commercial instructions of the previous September, and who could not yet have received the fresh and explicit orders framed on 15 May, was already dreaming of achievements far outside his brief. Let us leave Peshawar in Runjeet's hands during his few remaining years, he wrote to McNeill. Let us encourage Dost Muhammad and promise him that after Runjeet's death he will have our influence on his side to make him master of the right bank of the Indus as far as Shikarpur. Meanwhile, turn his attention away from Peshawar towards Kandahar and Herat, for the intrigues of the Kandahar chiefs are dangerous:

...At all events I shall leave nothing undone to try and put a stop to their intercourse with the Russian Minister, and if matters go rightly we shall, I take it, be able to neutralise the power of the Candahar chiefs, or, at all events, place them in complete subjection to Dost Mahomed Khan, whose influence increases daily, and will be nought diminished by his late victory over the Sikhs...[27]

Burnes's preference for the Dost made him describe the Jamrud clash as a victory for the Afghans. He thought that the game, as he called it, was for the present all in favour of Kabul. Lest Burnes be accused of double dealing let us note here that he wrote in exactly the same sense to his masters in Calcutta. Auckland asked Colvin to answer him at the end of July. Colvin expressed Auckland's policy very clearly and once again brought (or attempted to bring) their eager young envoy down to earth:

It is satisfactory to his Lordship to perceive that you thoroughly share in the feeling which leads him to recognise, in the most explicit manner, the claims of Runjeet Singh to Peshawar and the territory dependent upon it as now held by the Sikhs. Any compromise on that point must be received by Dost Mahomed Khan as proceeding from the voluntary concession of the Sikh chieftain, and it may be reasonably anticipated that whatever pretensions he may, in the first instance, think it proper to advance, Dost Mahomed Khan will really be extremely well satisfied if he can succeed in preserving his authority from further diminution...[28]

We can see that Auckland was never prepared to twist Runjeet Singh's arm to influence Sikh policy in Peshawar. Burnes knew this at least three months before he entered Afghanistan in 1837. A minute written by Auckland in the middle of June helps us to understand still more clearly his policy towards the Sikhs, and to see how important the Anglo-Sikh alliance was to him. He could not depend upon it after Runjeet's death; but, as long as Runjeet lived and the alliance remained firm, the Punjab would be a strong rampart in the defensive system of India. Auckland wrote his minute on a memorandum which Fane had submitted on India's defences:

...It has been to the line of the Sutlej and to the British Empire in India, as at present bounded, that the Commander in Chief has confined his observations, and he has probably felt it to be matter rather for political than military speculation that the limits of the Empire may one day of necessity be changed and that a dissolution of order, and divisions and hostility beyond the Sutlej may force our interference and advance. The time indeed for so acting has not yet come and may not shortly arrive, but even in the contemplation of events so possible and so probable, we should only be confirmed in the view which his Excellency has taken of the expedience of omitting no opportunity for strengthening our military posts in this direction. But it seems to me unlikely that the first battle for India should ever be fought upon the Sutlej. In any contest with the Sikhs, except under circumstances of surprise, it would assuredly be onwards, and in the event of a formidable invasion by nations from the west under the conduct and influence of European powers, when all not for us would be against us, we should hardly leave the fertile plains of the Punjab to an enemy for the collection of his means and forces—either in alliance with the Sikhs or in defiance of them. Our main strength would probably be upon the Indus, our advanced posts beyond it...

Auckland went on to chide Fane for ignoring the potential threat to Gujerat and Bombay Presidency from any hostile force established in Sind, and for leaving out of account the advantage of having allies and a British force in Sind:

...It is upon these as well as upon commercial grounds, and for improved facilities in communicating with the Afghan states that I look to a clear connection with Sinde as of importance, and the power with the aid of steam of rapidly bringing together a British force in that country is amongst those provisions for security which should not, in my opinion, be overlooked.[29]

This minute followed naturally from Bentinck's farewell dissertation on defence, quoted in chapter 4. Leap-frogging over most of the rest of this study we may observe here that Sind was annexed in 1843 and the Punjab in 1849 at least partly because Auckland's judgement of their strategic importance was correct. He was both logical and far-sighted, and very far from being the bumbler of Victorian legend. Another of the charges levelled against him is that in 1837, at a period of crisis, he started out on a tour 'up country', leaving his council in Calcutta. He has been made to look irresponsible and cavalier in his treatment of senior colleagues. In fact he made the most elaborate preparations and gave those colleagues four months' notice of his intentions. In a minute written on 19 June 1837, he made provision against the inconvenience of his absence, taking into account the division of responsibilities and the time it would take him to return if urgently needed in Calcutta. No Governor General could have been more considerate of his council members or have given them more time and opportunity to remonstrate. It was only much later, when it became fashionable (and even politic) to disparage him, that his tour up country came in for criticism. Shortly before writing this minute he told the chairman of the Court of Directors, John Lock, that he intended going to Simla partly to escape the heat, partly to meet people along the route, and partly to be near and to get to know the Indians for whose destiny he was responsible. He also wanted to be near and to have an influence upon events in the north-west. His tour started on 21 October 1837.[30]

In June, as Auckland looked about him, there was not much progress to report. The Sind emirs were still holding out for a specific guarantee of British protection as the price for accepting a Resident at Hyderabad. The Sikh and Afghan armies were still glaring at each other from opposite sides of the entrance to the

Khyber Pass. But Runjeet Singh, it was said, against the advice of his generals, was inclined to keep the peace if Dost Muhammad would acknowledge his supremacy in the plain of Peshawar. In western Afghanistan the Kandahar chiefs were still looking for help from the Persians and Russians, and the Persians themselves were contemplating a new march against Herat with Russian encouragement. Auckland knew, from earlier letters from McNeill, that the Persians were restless, but he did not yet know that the threat was so imminent.

On the last day of June McNeill wrote to Palmerston with news that changed the whole complexion of British policy in the crisis over Herat. In February he had argued that the Shah had justice on his side in the quarrel with Herat, and that all he could do was to try to persuade the Shah to obtain redress through negotiation instead of through war. Now, at the end of June, the Shah was in a position in which he could indeed gain more by accepting Herat's terms than by going to war, for the new terms offered by the Herat government were 'so very advantageous'. McNeill therefore wrote:

...It appears to me that Persia having had it in her power to obtain by treaty all, and more than all, that she could reasonably demand, the time is come when if the Shah perseveres in his unwise determination to prosecute hostilities against the Affghans, it may be desirable and even necessary to inform him that we cannot permit our rising commerce with Central Asia to be destroyed, and the tranquillity of its kingdoms and principalities to be disturbed by his thirst for military glory; or, by hopeless attempts, ruinous to himself, and injurious to everyone [permit him] to assert antiquated pretensions [to sovereignty over Afghanistan] which his predecessors had long since abandoned...

In this same dispatch there appeared a short passage which has often been quoted, but never, to the author's knowledge, in full. Within parentheses are the previously suppressed words:

...I regarded it as of the utmost importance to our security in India that Herat should not (become dependent on Persia, in such a manner that it should follow the fate of this country, or) become available to any power which might obtain control over the councils of the Shah...[31]

A few days later McNeill wrote in the same strain to Lord Auckland, inviting *him* to deliver the remonstrance. He said he thought that the effect of such a remonstrance would be stronger if a letter were addressed to the Prime Minister of Persia by His Majesty's Secretary of State or by the Secretary to the Indian Government [but as] this is a question which people at home will hardly deal with, I must look to your Lordship for instructions respecting it. It is a question, in fact, between the Government of India and that of Persia, in which no Foreign Power has a right to interfere, and which His Majesty's Government will, therefore, in all probability hand over entirely to your Lordship . . .[32]

McNeill knew that what he proposed was dangerous. Rarely in the history of diplomacy can so many people have desired to pretend that all was perfect harmony between two European governments! Palmerston and Nesselrode were playing a very subtle game, which Palmerston won in the end, but in the summer of 1837, with everything at stake, McNeill could not afford to make a false move. The Russians must not be given grounds for quarrel in Europe. Therefore let Auckland pretend that this is entirely a matter for India and Persia to settle. Auckland did not immediately take the bait, but when we come to read the Simla Manifesto of 1 October 1838 we shall see how careful he was to paint the crisis in purely Asiatic colours.

On 23 July the Shah and his army marched from the neighbourhood of Teheran towards Herat, starting a journey which in those leisurely days took him four months. He left behind him a disgruntled McNeill, who wished to show 'disapprobation' by declining to accompany the army, and an unusually circumspect Russian Minister, Count Ivan Simonich. He, too, wished to show his disapproval, in harmony with the British envoy, and on 19 September Palmerston must have smiled when he received from St Petersburg a copy of the dispatch which Simonich wrote on the day of the Shah's departure. The Minister had had the gall to say that in spite of his representations the Shah was on his way to Herat, but that he had stayed behind.[33] Thus, for the time being, a kind of harmony was restored between the British and Russians in Persia. But what mattered was that the Shah was moving inexorably towards Herat. Either he was a brave and foolhardy man, defying the will of two powerful European states, or he had the secret blessing of one of them upon his enterprise. It is easy to guess which version Palmerston believed.

At the end of July Alexander Burnes was advancing slowly up the Indus, between Kala Bagh and Attock, when he received news of great importance from Kabul. First Dost Muhammad told him why he had attacked the Sikhs at Jamrud. He said that he had been provoked by the forts which Hari Singh had built in the area. There was a defiant tone about this letter, which Auckland duly noted. At the same time Burnes received a note from Mirza Sami Khan, the Dost's confidential secretary. A Persian envoy was on his way to Kabul: 'Before this an elchee had arrived from the King of Bokhara, but I think the Ameer will pay no attention whatever to the objects of any of them until you reach Cabool. When you come the Ameer will do as you advise...'[34]

Burnes passed the news on to Calcutta through Wade in Ludhiana. His letter was written on 1 August, and, since Burnes was the writer, it emphasized the friendliness of Dost's message. But what was friendly to Burnes, the admirer of Dost Muhammad, was not necessarily friendly in the view of those who wished the Dost to rest content with Kabul and make peace with Runjeet Singh. Wade, who had no high opinion of the Dost, could be relied upon to make the point in his own correspondence with the Government in Calcutta. Wade forwarded Burnes's dispatch, with his own comments, on 25 August, and the Governor General received them while he was in the middle of writing a letter to Hobhouse a fortnight later. At the beginning of his letter to Hobhouse he remarked that the Dost would be wise to accept

the moderate terms which I think that Runjeet Singh is disposed to offer him, and to apply himself with his brother potentates in securing from all aggression the triple power of Afghanistan. Whether he will have the sense to do this and whether Captain Burnes by his presence at Cabul or subsequently by visiting Herat and Candahar can promote these objects remains to be seen...

Auckland told Hobhouse that he thought Runjeet might agree to leave some troops in Peshawar and make over the administration of the territory to one of the Dost's brothers, in return for tribute and an acknowledgement of his supremacy. He thought that 'in the present state of things this would not be an unwise or extravagant arrangement for any party...'.

A little later Auckland added:

...Since I began this letter we have received further despatches from Cabul and Lahore. The Persian embassy was daily expected at Cabul and, as report announced, with a Russian in its train—and something less of a spirit of accommodation may be traced in the last letter of Dost Mahomed to Captain Burnes and something more of uneasiness in the communications of Runjeet Singh. We have been led by events to give more of a political character to Burnes's mission than originally belonged to it, and he will be instructed to receive and convey to us any reasonable propositions which Dost Mahomed may make for peace between Sikhs and Afghans, and if a high tone should be assumed, to point out the utter worthlessness of Persian promises and Persian alliances and the offence which such a connection must give to us. To Runjeet Singh I propose writing more explicitly than I have yet done upon Western politics so as to reassure him and to satisfy him that in acting thus beyond him we have no selfish objects and that his interests and ours are the same...[35]

On 9 September Auckland applied himself to his new problem, and the result was a minute on which Macnaghten based new instructions to Burnes. He spoke of the 'growing activity of intrigue with which Persia, from ambition or from weak servility, and Russia, from a rooted hostility to the British power, are exerting themselves'. He repeated his firmly held view that the existing division of Afghanistan was the most advantageous arrangement as far as Britain was concerned. He rejected the idea of having one extensive and consolidated monarchy in place of separate chieftainships:

...Schemes of this character, whether as tending to the aggrandizement of a member of the Barakzye or Saddozye families I have at no time adopted...But even had my views been very different I should scarcely have thought it by any means practicable. I should certainly not have thought it desirable or prudent to embark on an undertaking so important and difficult in such a country and at such a distance from our resources...

Auckland recognized that much of the excitement could be traced back to fear of Sikh encroachment on Kabul and Kandahar. This was what had first persuaded the Barukzai chiefs to make overtures to Persia, thus opening the way to the 'indirect operation of Russian intrigue and influence upon our frontiers'. He therefore considered it to be in Runjeet Singh's best interest to come to terms with the Afghans:

...They have no natural sympathy with the Persian government, and will retain no close connection with it if left secure in their remaining possessions...

He then briefly examined and rejected an alternative proposal, that Runjeet Singh should be allowed to conquer Kabul and Kandahar, for

we may be satisfied that the inhabitants of these poor and mountainous countries, inflamed, as they are, by feelings of religious bigotry and suspicious and hostile towards us as they would in this case be, would ever prove very dangerous and unprofitable subjects and neighbours.

And so he had decided to induce the Maharajah to cultivate peace, addressing him frankly and confidentially:

...Were he immoveably resolved on hostilities with the Afghans I should much regret it but in a contest between the two, if forced to side with either, I would assuredly side with him. I would however use all our management to avert this extremity for the reasons above stated. Beyond this, as regards the Eastern Division of Afghanistan, my views have never gone, though it is of course within the range of possibility that circumstances may occur which would force me to extend them...

The remainder of this minute set out precise orders for Alexander Burnes. He should understand that the Dost might now look upon him as 'an arbiter of peace' and 'a supporter of extravagant pretensions'. But Burnes would have no direct political power. He could only transmit any proposition that he considered reasonable through Wade to the Government in Calcutta. He was to point out to Dost Muhammad that the British Government wished to see established the peace and security and independence of his dominions, and that it regretted finding him 'exposed to the hazards of war on one side and excited to restlessness by interference and worthless promises on the other'. Burnes should also make it clear to the ruler of Kabul that 'our first feeling must be that of the regard for the honour and just wishes of our old and firm ally Runjeet Singh'. Then if Dost Muhammad looked for 'terms of peace adapted to a fair measure of his position, such good offices in his favour with the Maharajah as we can render would be given to him'. But if he received 'with favour every emissary and every proposition, the avowed object of which was to foment disturbances even at the hazard of his own independence, it was impossible but that the friendly feelings of the British Government must be impaired'. Burnes was authorized to put it to Dost Muhammad that Runjeet Singh might possibly allow a member of the Barukzai family to hold the Peshawar province again in return for payment of tribute, but he must first consult Wade, and he must make it clear to Dost Muhammad that the whole proposition was conditional upon his severing his connexion with Persia.

It is interesting to note here that Auckland was not optimistic about the effect of Burnes's representations to the Dost at that stage. It would be for Burnes to decide how long he stayed. Even if his negotiations failed, his political information would be useful.[36]

William Macnaghten faithfully reproduced this section of Auckland's minute in the dispatch which he sent to Burnes on 11 September.[37] Colvin followed it up with a semi-official letter two days later, so that Burnes could never claim that he had lacked precise instructions. Colvin said that Burnes was in a position in which he should regulate his conduct, marking the firm maintenance of the old alliance and friendship with Runjeet Singh as the avowed first principle of their duty and policy and 'bringing Dost Mahomed to his senses and to a just measure of his most hazardous position'.[38]

It has sometimes been hinted in previous accounts of these proceedings that Burnes's mission was a clever deception undertaken with the object of putting Dost Muhammad in the wrong. The present writer believes that the letters and minutes quoted above show how clearly Auckland's Government stated its policy to the Dost through Burnes. There could be no question of an alliance with Dost Muhammad against the Sikhs. All he could hope for was British influence upon Runjeet Singh to save him from further attacks, provided that he first ceased cultivating Persian alliances. Wade also received precise instructions. Colvin wrote to him on 13 September, explaining and enclosing Auckland's minute and saying:

...Runjeet Singh is informed without reserve that we will do nothing in Cabool without his consent, but we desire to make him feel that it is best for him and for us that Dost Mahommed should not be squeezed to death and that both of us should get rid of the inconvenience of this blustering of Persian Elchees on our Borders. The present mission may be of little consequence, but the precedent, if admitted, may be a most injurious one...

Wade was to discourage Runjeet from schemes of conquest in Afghanistan, for

...to encourage such schemes of conquest would be to rouse without being able to repress the bitter hostility of the Afghan people against ourselves. Perhaps he may be put in the position of feeling that he acts with open ungraciousness towards us in pursuing a policy which brings upon us Persian intrigues...Your negotiation is one of much delicacy, for all appearance of dictation and selfish interference is to be sedulously avoided, and your whole tone will be that of the most friendly and confidential concern...[39]

Much therefore depended on Wade, who, as we have previously observed in this study, was hostile to the Dost and an advocate for the cause of Shah Shuja. But he, too, had his carefully phrased orders, and they were by no means unsympathetic to the Dost or uncritical of Runjeet.

It was perhaps unfortunate that the latest instructions to Burnes did not reach him before he became immersed in his conversations with Dost Muhammad in Kabul, but earlier letters and dispatches should have left him in no doubt about the Government's position in the Sikh–Afghan dispute. He arrived in Kabul on Wednesday 20 September 1837 seated with the Dost's son Akbar Khan on an elephant and escorted by cavalry. On Thursday Burnes and his fellow officers had their first audience with Dost Muhammad:

...From the Ameer's audience chamber we proceeded to the Nawab Jubbar Khan, who received us in his bath, and invited us to breakfast. As we passed through the city some of the people cried out, 'Take care of Cabool!', 'Do not destroy Cabool!' and wherever we went in this fine, bustling place, we were saluted with a cordial welcome. Our visits were soon returned, both by the Ameer and by his brother the Nawab. Power frequently spoils men, but with Dost Mahomed neither the increase of it, nor his new title of Ameer, seems to have done him any harm. He seemed even more alert and intelligent than when I last saw him.[40]

Lieutenant John Wood, an officer in the Company's naval service and the eventual discoverer of the source of the Oxus, has left vivid personal impressions of Dost Muhammad. At that time, according to Wood, the Emir was about 45 and looked older. He had strong features and a stern expression; his beard was long and black, and his eyes were brilliant and intelligent. He had a good memory, listened attentively to his guests, and showed himself a practised conversationalist. Wood, who had met many 'vapouring Belochees' in his travels, could not help comparing the 'blunt and homely bearing' of the Afghan with theirs.[41]

Burnes had his first political discussion with the Emir on the Sunday after his arrival.[42] Dost Muhammad complained bitterly of Runjeet Singh's conduct, and shrewly expressed the hope that Britain would intervene in the Peshawar dispute as she had done in the dispute over Shikarpur a few months earlier. Burnes did not fall into the trap. He pointed out that we did not accept the Sikh claim to Shikarpur but had no doubt that Peshawar was Runjeet's. In this first interview Burnes also mentioned the rumour that Runjeet was contemplating some change in the management of the Peshawar territory. Burnes and Dost Muhammad met twice in the following week. Burnes reported later that they discussed Persian and Russian policy.[43] On 29 September Nawab Jubbar Khan called on Burnes at the mission's residence and put it to him that the British might now 'do something for Cabul in view of the rumours in circulation about Runjeet's intentions in Peshawar'. The rumours said that Runjeet might restore the territory to Sultan Muhammad Khan, the Dost's brother, in return for an annual tribute. The Nawab hoped that this might come about, possibly through British influence. But Dost Muhammad did not agree. As early as 4 October he told Burnes that he would be prepared to send one of his sons to Lahore to ask forgiveness if Runjeet Singh would let him hold Peshawar in return for annual tribute of horses and rice. He said that his brother Sultan could then keep his jagheers (estates) in the territory. But Peshawar might as well remain in Sikh hands as be restored to Sultan Muhammad; people would never believe that Runjeet Singh had withdrawn from the right bank of the Indus if Sultan was installed in Peshawar as Runjeet's tributary. After this long interview Burnes reported to his Government on the first phase of his negotiations. At this stage, however, he had not mentioned (being unaware of it as yet) his Government's insistence that Dost Muhammad should break with Persia before its good offices could be employed in his favour. Burnes had not stated such a condition to Dost, but he was convinced, and he told Macnaghten so in a report on Persian influence on 4 October, that the Persian envoy then at Kandahar was unlikely to come on to Kabul. '. . . It is certain, if he does so, that any offers which he may make will never be placed in the balance against those of the British Government. . .'[44]

Once these letters were on their way Burnes and his colleagues began to collect information, both political and geographical, about the country in which they were guests. Burnes could not expect to receive the Government's reply to his first reports before January.

It was at this moment that Burnes took the trouble to send an official tribute to the services of Charles Masson, properly James Lewis, 'whose high literary attainments, long residence in this country, and accurate knowledge of people and events, afford me at every step the means of coming to a judgement more correct than in an abrupt transition to Cabool I could possibly have formed ...'.[45] Masson eventually repaid Burnes's trust and kindness in a very different coin.

In this chapter we have considered the unfolding of Auckland's policy during 1837 and the opening of Burnes's mission to Kabul, referring only briefly to events in England. Queen Victoria had come to the throne on 20 June. At first she floundered among the strange names of men and places in the dispatches which she had to read. One particularly difficult dispatch came her way at the end of the first week in October. It came from John McNeill, the Minister in Teheran, and we may guess that he sent it at the end of July, when the Persian army was already on the march to Herat. The young Queen appealed to Lord Palmerston for an explanation, and he replied on Sunday 8 October with a brief lecture on the importance of Persia in British imperial policy:

...The geographical position of Persia, interposed as that kingdom is, between the southern frontiers of Russia and the northern frontiers of British India, has for many years past rendered the British government anxious to convert Persia into a barrier to prevent the Russians from attacking British India...[46]

It is very probable that the Queen and Palmerston were discussing the letter which McNeill sent from Teheran on 28 July, reporting the Shah's departure at the head of the Persian army and the return to Herat of the envoy who had brought such favourable terms in June. But Palmerston had no immediate cause for alarm.

On 21 October Auckland and his great retinue set out from Calcutta at the start of a journey of five and a half months to Simla. He had told Hobhouse that he expected to be back in Calcutta by the spring of 1839 at the latest, and had added prophetically: '...many an event is possible which may knock this fine scheme to pieces.'[47] At that moment Burnes received the instructions which Macnaghten had sent on 11 September. When Dost Muhammad came to call on him on 24 October Burnes explained that all connexion with states to the westward must be severed before the British Government could consent to use its good offices on his behalf. Dost readily concurred, and said he was beginning to regret that he ever approached the Persians. He also deprecated the behaviour of his brothers in Kandahar, who still had a Persian envoy cooling his heels at their court. The Dost and Burnes agreed to write to the Kandahar brothers, and Dost Muhammad let it be understood that he would be more than satisfied if his severance of relations with Persia resulted in a settlement of the Peshawar problem, but that he would continue to rely on British friendship whether that problem was settled or not.[48] In a private letter at the end of October Burnes dramatized his part in this episode and jumped to the conclusion that his mission had already succeeded; his vanity got the better of him:

...I have, in behalf of government, agreed to stand mediator between the parties and Dost Mahomed has cut asunder all his connection with Russia and Persia, and refused to receive the Ambassador from the Shah now at Candahar. His brothers at that city have however caressed the Persian Elchee all the more for this, and I have sent them such a Junius as I believe will astonish them. I had indeed reason to act promptly, for they have a son setting out for Teheran with presents for the Shah and the Russian Ambassador, and I hope I shall be in time to explain our hostility to such conduct. Everything here has indeed run well, and but for one deputation at the time it happened, the house we occupy would have been tenanted by a Russian agent and a Persian Elchee. I hardly know what the Government of India will think of my measures, for my line of conduct is only indicated by them, not marked out—Yet I am inspirited by their free use of laudatory adjectives regarding my proceedings hitherto...I am in a very critical position, and so they tell me—totidem verbis—but I like difficulties—they are my brandy.[49]

In this letter Burnes had also forecast that Dost Muhammad and Runjeet Singh would compromise by allowing a member of the Barukzai family, not identified in the letter, to hold Peshawar as a tributary of Lahore, 'the Chief of Cabool sending his son to ask pardon'. He was much too optimistic, and in any case it is odd that he should have spoken in the same sentence of Dost Muhammad sending a son to Lahore and a Barukzai holding Peshawar from Runjeet Singh. It is absolutely clear from Burnes's report to Macnaghten at the beginning of October that the Dost still wanted Peshawar for himself, even as a tributary of Runjeet. Moreover, Burnes's line of conduct was very clearly 'marked out'. But we should make allowance for the fact that he was exaggerating his own importance in the affair in a private letter to someone unaware of the facts. What he did not know was that Wade had not dared to submit the Dost's proposition to Runjeet, who was suspicious of British motives in sending Burnes to Kabul in the first place. Wade sent the proposal straight to Auckland, who agreed that Dost was far too ambitious for his own good. At the beginning of December Macnaghten again told Burnes that Runjeet would not let Dost Muhammad have Peshawar but might conceivably restore it to Sultan Muhammad as tributary. He also reminded Burnes that it was British policy to preserve 'the existing state of affairs in Central Asia, and to refrain from being a party to any arrangement which should give to any one chief a preponderance'. Macnaghten told Burnes that the Governor General was very pleased with his work, which included the gathering of information and the compiling of reports on Afghan and Central Asian affairs:

...It occurs, however, to his Lordship, that a few words of caution may be necessary, in regard to the pretensions of Dost Mahomed, who may perhaps be too sanguine in regard to the effect of our good offices, should they be exerted in his favour. His immediate recovery of Peshawar would seem to be hopeless, and it should, his Lordship thinks, be impressed upon that chief as his best policy at present, to seek for peace and security in his actual position, and to concentrate and strengthen his existing resources, which cannot, in his present position, but be weakened by too restless and impatient a desire to extend them.[50]

Burnes did not receive this cold blast until nearly the end of January. But he never lacked warning. He was told, from May onwards, that the Dost would not be allowed to have Peshawar, and that the most he could expect would be the restoration of the territory to Sultan Muhammad as tributary. Meanwhile a letter had arrived in Kabul in the middle of November from the Russian Minister in Teheran. Burnes immediately reported this to his Government,[51] and discussed with Dost Muhammad the growing threat to Herat. Simonich's letter was the precursor of a Russian agent, who, as McNeill had already reported to London, was on his way to Kabul.[52]

As Burnes wrote his dispatch on 15 November, the Persian army marched into Ghorian, a fortress town about forty miles from Herat. The chiefs of the place had capitulated after a siege lasting ten days. Burnes did not hear of the Persian victory until late in December, when he reported that it was the result of treachery.

Now, in November, he had equally serious news for his Government.[53] The Kandahar chiefs had just told their brother in Kabul that they had made a treaty with Persia, under which they would hold Herat after its capture. They said that all the Shah asked in return was their assistance whenever there was civil war in Persia. They also announced that the British and Russian ambassadors in Persia were going to witness and set their seals on the treaty. Burnes reported that he had immediately told Dost Muhammad that the name of Britain had been used without justification in this business. But his news meant that the Russian ambassador in Persia was prepared to give a kind of guarantee to a treaty which would change the balance of power inside Afghanistan and make Kandahar and Herat virtual dependants of the Shah.

Burnes went on waiting for the official response to his October report on the negotiations, and in the meantime he completed his report on the political state of Kabul, emphasizing once again his view of the great merits of Dost Muhammad Khan. The siege of Herat had just begun, and winter came to Kabul. By 11 December the ground was covered with snow 'and the whole of the population appeared clad in sheepskins'.[54] Had Burnes but known it, Auckland was writing flattering remarks about him to colleagues at India House:

...I receive frequent letters from Captain Burnes, who displays great activity and intelligence, and the information collected by him from the Caspian Sea to the mouths of the Indus is often of much interest. The degree of control which he may acquire for us over Afghan Politics is not yet easy to ascertain.

Dost Mahommed is sensible of his own weakness, and yet clings to the possibility of recovering Peshawar. Candahar is afraid of Herat, and would turn to Russia. Herat is the most respectable of the three powers, but exposed to the attack from Candahar and Persia. The movements of the Shah of Persia will generally be sooner known to you than they are by us here. Runjeet Singh writes letters to me warmly expressive of friendship. All the flowers in his garden drooped upon the news of the late king's death. They all revived upon learning that Victoria had succeeded to the throne. He thanks me with frankness and friendliness for my advice in favour of peace and commerce, professes his willingness to be upon terms the most amicable with the Afghans, but upon the principle of the victor, and he promises personal friendship and the settlement of every point of difficulty when we shall have the pleasure of embracing each other...[55]

In a later section of this letter, incidentally, Auckland mentioned a preoccupation which had been with him for several months. Through Wade he had persuaded Runjeet Singh to organize an experimental convoy of merchant boats from Lahore to Bombay. Now Wade had told him that the twenty-four boats would be setting out from Lahore during December, and that the shores of the Indus were for the time being untroubled.

John McNeill was passing a frustrating winter at Teheran. He had reported on the Russian agent as soon as he heard from the British officers travelling with the Shah and the army in Eastern Persia, and he assured Palmerston, who received this dispatch on 30 December, that 'the effect of the establishment of a Russian agent at Cabool must be seriously detrimental to British interests in India and in the Punjab...'.[56] At the end of November McNeill sent even more disturbing news to Palmerston. Not only had Simonich started his intrigues again after lying low for a few months; the Polish adventurer General Berowski (mentioned unfavourably by Ellis in November 1835) had instigated the arrest of one of McNeill's confidential messengers. A senior officer of the British military mission was insulted when he protested to Persian officials in the presence of the Prime Minister about the stripping and searching of the confidential messenger. The Persians afterwards claimed that the messenger was one of the Shah's subjects, and that they were entitled to arrest him because he had just come from their enemies in Herat. McNeill treated these arguments with contempt: they were not entitled to interfere with the staff of a foreign diplomatic mission in that way, even if the individual was the Shah's subject; moreover, Britain was neutral in the quarrel between Persia and Herat, and as a potential mediator had every right to communicate with Herat through its mission in Persia. McNeill told Palmerston that he had 'little doubt that the object of the whole proceeding was to exhibit to the Affghans and to the Persian army an apparent contempt for the English, with a view to diminish the moral effect which might have been produced on either party by the general belief that we were opposed to the conquest of Herat by the Persians...'.[57] Nevertheless, McNeill considered that the siege of Herat was bound to fail this time, for the army was in a very bad condition.[58]

In Kabul on the morning of Tuesday 19 December Burnes and his companions looked out from their mission residence in the hope of seeing a messenger arrive with dispatches from India. Burnes very much wanted to present Dost Muhammad with some good news, for the influence of Persian and Russian agents was growing day by day. Instead Dost Muhammad brought bad news to him. Dost Muhammad came over to the mission residence with a letter from Ghazni. A Russian agent had arrived there on his way to Kabul:

...Dost Mahomed Khan said that he had come for my counsel on the occasion; that he wished to have nothing to do with any other power than the British; that he did not wish to receive any agent from any other power whatsoever, *so long as he had a hope of sympathy from us*; and that he would order the Russian agent to be turned out, detained on the road, or act in any other way that I desired him...

What could Burnes do or say? His instructions from the very beginning had been to express friendship and sympathy without raising false hopes. Now, in effect, the Dost was asking him whether the British were prepared to do anything for him. The Russian agent was less than a hundred miles away. He might be an impostor; he might be carrying expensive presents and offers that Dost Muhammad would be unable to resist. Burnes quickly steered the conversation into another channel:

...I then stated that it was a sacred rule among civilised nations not to refuse to receive emissaries in time of peace, and that I should not take upon myself to advise him to refuse anyone who declared himself duly accredited, but that the Ameer had it in his power to show his feeling on the occasion by making a full disclosure to the British Government of the errand on which the individual had come; to which he most readily assented.

For the time being Burnes had averted the crisis. He had manœuvred himself out of the corner into which the Dost had pressed him. Instead of committing himself to a course of action which the emir might consider sympathetic, he had succeeded in placing the emir under an obligation to prove his good will towards Britain. Burnes does not say as much, but the Dost must have known of the Russian agent's approach some time before the morning of the 19th. In fact the agent entered Kabul that same afternoon. Burnes wrote:

After this the Ameer dispatched a servant on the road to Ghuznee to prevent the agent's entering Cabul without notice; but so rapid has been his journey, that he met him a few miles from the city, which he entered in the afternoon, attended by two of the Ameer's people. He has sent a letter from Count Simonich, which I have seen, and states that he is the bearer of letters from Mahomed Shah and the Emperor of Russia. I shall take any early opportunity of reporting on the proceedings of the Russian agent, if he be so in reality; for, if not an impostor, it is a most uncalled for proceeding, after the disavowal of the Russian government, conveyed through Count Nesselrode, alluded to in Mr McNeill's letter of the 19th June last...[59]

Dost Muhammad kept his word. After receiving the Russian agent for the first time, he sent Mirza Sami Khan to Burnes with an account of their conversation. As was the custom, the first interview was an exchange of compliments and formalities. The second interview revealed the Russian's hand. The Dost again sent Mirza Sami Khan to Burnes, and this time Nawab Jubbar Khan accompanied him. They told Burnes that the agent had offered Kabul an annual subsidy on the Emperor's behalf, to help Dost Muhammad against the Sikhs, in return for 'good offices'. The two interviews had taken place on Wednesday and Thursday. On Friday 22 December another gun was pointed at Burnes's head. He received a letter from the Kandahar chiefs (Dost Muhammad's brothers), saying that they were growing tired of waiting for British support and were about to send one of Kohendil Khan's sons to Persia.[60] Burnes immediately wrote back, offering money and personal assistance to protect Kandahar from the Persians. He had committed his Government. On the same day he satisfied himself that the newcomer really was a Russian agent, and that he was the bearer of a letter from the Emperor himself. Masson later spread the story that Burnes was thrown into a panic by an obvious forgery, but, eager as some people always were to believe the worst about the Burnes mission, Masson is not a reliable witness. Of course, Burnes was disturbed. He sent a copy of the Emperor's letter to his Government. It was dated 27 April and replied to the letter delivered by an emissary from Dost Muhammad. The Emperor acknowledged the Dost's message and spoke warmly of the friendship between their two countries. He would always feel 'happy to assist the people of Caubul who may come to trade into my kingdom'. He said that he would send a 'man of dignity' to return to Kabul with the Dost's emissary, and spoke of the gifts— 'the rarities of my country, which I have sent through him'.[61] On the face of it, this was a perfectly innocent letter. But it arrived in sinister circumstances, carried by an agent from Count Ivan Simonich, whose conduct at the Persian Court may be said to have made the First Afghan War inevitable.

Burnes wrote to his Government also on Saturday, explaining his action on hearing the news from Kandahar:

...In the critical position in which I was situated I saw no course left but that which I have followed. My belief is that Herat may withstand the attack of the Persians, but if not, and the Shah marches to Candahar, our own position in the East becomes endangered, and the tranquillity of all the countries that border on the Indus...[62]

In fact Burnes suspected that he had gone too far on an impulse, and that he had exceeded his instructions. He therefore noted in this letter that, if, as he thought, the Persians failed at Herat his promise would be shelved and forgotten. However that might be, he thought that it was of the first importance to detach the Kandahar Sirdars from Persia. With this in mind he issued instructions on Monday to Lieutenant Robert Leech of the Bombay Engineers, another of his companions on the mission, to go to Kandahar and to do all in his power to keep the Sirdars out of Persia's arms.[63] But first he had sat down on Saturday to write a private letter to Auckland himself. Usually he addressed his official correspondence to Macnaghten, who was very particular about the niceties of protocol. This was different. His letter was a direct appeal to Auckland in favour of Dost Muhammad. He pleaded his case with great skill. He blamed the Sikhs for aggravating Afghan differences over the years. He declared that the Afghan chiefs had long wanted a connexion with the British in India but had been rebuffed with 'cold and distant replies to their solicitations'. They all believed that Britain had encouraged Shah Shuja to attempt to recover his throne in 1834, and that he would have received British recognition very quickly if he had been successful.

...An open avowal of our anxiety for his success could not have been productive of worse consequences than the course which was actually taken, yet it did not alienate the chiefs from us...

Burnes went ont to say that the seizure of Peshawar by the Sikhs in 1834 had caused the Afghan chiefs to look for assistance in other quarters, but still they hoped for British help. Now there was a Russian messenger in Kabul:

...Though the messenger has arrived and delivered his letters, I trust that the friendly devotion of Dost Mahomed Khan in asking my advice and next handing to me all the letters brought by the emissary will remain in your Lordship's mind, as proofs of sincerity and conciliation, highly to be appreciated, and the more so as the British have as yet made no avowal of support to his power, while he has received declarations from others, the sincerity of which can no longer be questioned...

Then Burnes tried to counter Auckland's stubborn insistence on preserving the alliance with Runjeet Singh, but showed in doing so that he could not or would not understand Auckland's view, expressed earlier in this chapter. Burnes argued:

It is undoubtedly true that we have an old and faithful ally in Maharajah Runjeet Singh, but such an alliance will not keep these powers at a distance, or secure to us what is the end of all alliances, peace and prosperity, in our country and on our frontiers. I am yet ignorant of the light in which your Lordship or Maharajah Runjeet Singh have viewed the overtures of Dost Mahomed Khan regarding Peshawar...

At this point Burnes could not conceal his annoyance at the fact that Wade had sent the proposals directly to Auckland instead of submitting them to Runjeet Singh at once. He could not understand why Wade had done this:

There was nothing in them contrary to the dignity of his Highness: an independent chief offers to pay him allegiance and regular tribute, and to send a son to sue for forgiveness. His Highness need not accept the terms, and perhaps Dost Mahomed Khan will in the end be satisfied with the plain of Peshawar being given to any Barukzye, but it becomes a matter of great moment that this question should be speedily adjusted...

Burnes continued:

...In a settlement of the Peshawar affair we have, as it seems to me, an immediate remedy against further intrigue, and a means of showing to the Afghans that the British Government does sympathise with them, and at one and the same time satisfying the chiefs, and gaining both our political and commercial ends...

There was more to the same effect, and Burnes concluded by urging Auckland to write a letter of thanks to the Dost for his 'frank divulgement of all that has passed'.[64] Dost Muhammad never had a better advocate than Alexander Burnes. It is perhaps a pity that Burnes left this powerful plea so late, but the author finds it difficult to believe that Burnes's case would have altered Auckland's policy materially. The enmity of Sikhs and Afghans as long as Dost Muhammad and Runjeet Singh were in power was too deep. If confronted with an inescapable choice between the two, Auckland felt bound by twenty-eight years of alliance and by cool considerations of British self-interest in India to choose the Sikhs. Moreover, Burnes himself had little confidence at that time in the possibility that Dost Muhammad might eventually suffer his brother Sultan to re-occupy Peshawar. Had not Dost Muhammad said that that would be tantamount to having the Sikhs in the plain of Peshawar? Burnes could only say at the end of 1837 that the Dost might *perhaps* be satisfied with that solution in the end.

On Christmas Day, Alexander Burnes, having already received a courtesy call from the Russian agent, invited him to dinner. They were very much alike. Lieutenant Vitkievitch was an officer on the staff of the Governor of Orenburg, seconded for duty under Count Simonich. He was about 30 years old. According to Burnes he spoke French, Turkish, and Persian fluently, and wore the uniform of an officer of Cossacks, something rarely if ever seen in Kabul. Burnes found him gentlemanly and agreeable, intelligent, and well informed:

I never again met Mr. Vitkievitch (or, as I see it written, Vicovich), although we exchanged sundry messages of 'high consideration'; for I regret to say that I found it to be impossible to follow the dictates of my personal feeling of friendship towards him, as the public service required the strictest watch, lest the relative positions of our nations should be misunderstood in this part of Asia.[65]

So the Russian Cossack and the young man from Montrose parted company. Their meeting on a Christmas Day at the end of Ramadan in Kabul stirs the imagination still. In their persons Britain and Russia came face to face in Central Asia, and one can see from Burnes's account that they were acutely conscious of that fact. Within five years both were dead.

ADVANCE TO THE HINDU KUSH
1838–1839

CHAPTER 7

AUCKLAND BREAKS WITH DOST MUHAMMAD

...The question of Herat seems therefore to be the question of all Affghanistan, and if the place should fall without any attempt having been made to save it I feel convinced that the moral influence of that event would have a most prejudicial effect on our national reputation in all these countries; for it is no secret to anyone that the British Government has been desirous to prevent its fall; and that Russia on the contrary has been solicitous to see it in the hands of Persia. All Central Asia will regard it as a question between the greater powers...

JOHN McNEILL to Lord Auckland, 11 April 1838

In 1838 John McNeill, the doctor turned diplomat, came fully into his own. He saw what he had written in 1836 come true under his shaping influence and under the influence of critical events, and he probably did more than any other man to save the British Empire in India. His advice, his warnings, and his proposals profoundly influenced national policy and decisions taken at the highest level in London and Simla. Yet his contribution has never before been given its true weight, for reasons which will become abundantly clear in this chapter and the next. For those same reasons, shrouded in secrecy at the time, the story of the First Afghan War has hitherto been incompletely and misleadingly told. Let us now feel our way back into the world of our Early Victorian ancestors, judging nothing by hindsight and considering every movement made on land in terms of the marching speed of a foot-soldier and the fleetness of a good horse. Let us remember also that, in spite of the ever-increasing use of steam navigation, it still took from two to three months to deliver a dispatch from London to Calcutta, and vice versa.

In this and subsequent chapters we shall see how information and intelligence flowed into London and Simla from Persia, from Afghanistan and the Punjab, from Sind, from Nepal and Burma, and from Russia, Turkey and Egypt, leading Melbourne and his Cabinet and Auckland and his council to almost exactly the same conclusions and decisions. As the year opened both Governments,

Melbourne's and Auckland's, knew from McNeill that a Russian agent was on his way to Kabul, but were as yet unaware that he had arrived, and both felt confident that Herat would hold out against Persian assaults. As yet Auckland knew of no reason for going further in his measures than he had chosen to go in September, when he answered McNeill's proposal that the Indian Government should remonstrate with the Shah of Persia. At that time he had declined to be drawn into premature action:

...I can have no objection to your using towards the Government of Persia the strongest language of remonstrance upon the waste of all the resources which should be husbanded for useful purposes and their application to the fomenting of intrigues and the disturbance of tranquillity upon the Indian frontier, but you must be able to take a much better measure of the effect of such a remonstrance, and particularly in regard to your own position than I can. You found the British tenure of influence in Persia weak and most uncertain and though the tactics of Persian politics are of unlimited and almost of necessary duplicity I conceive your position to have been much improved since your arrival, and I almost hope that it may be strong enough to justify you in entering upon the frankest exposition of the measures which may strengthen or must lead to the dissolution of the British and Persian alliance. If the game of Persia is not one of the veriest fraud and if you confidently feel yourself to be gaining in strength you might be wrong in too immediately and too harshly taking this step, and it may be better for a time, to play with events, but if whilst you are felt to be the last prop of the Shah's tottering independence there is yet any disposition partly in misdirected ambition and partly in timid servility to Russian influence to try how much you will bear of direct injury to the interests of your country the higher tone of remonstrance can hardly be too soon put to the test. Upon these points and upon the general politics of the countries to the eastward of Persia I trust that in a few weeks or months I shall be able to write to you more explicitly...[1]

It has been said before, and this letter, received by McNeill just before Christmas 1837, underlines the point, that Auckland was a careful and cautious but not an indecisive man. He had at least one admirer in London. On 19 January 1838 John Hobhouse dined at the Palace, and in the drawing room afterwards the Queen asked him to express her satisfaction to Lord Auckland. 'India', she said, 'is sure to go on well under such a Governor General.'[2] The Queen had only been on the throne seven months, and she was still very much under the constitutional guidance of the Prime Minister,

Lord Melbourne. It is difficulty to imagine that she would have spoken so highly of Auckland if Melbourne had not shared that view, or if he had not planted the idea in her young head.

On his way to Simla that January Auckland daily looked out for dispatches from Kabul. He still hoped that the skilful and personable Alexander Burnes would persuade Dost Muhammad to rest content with his Kabul domains, but he well understood that the Dost was unlikely to be satisfied with 'anything that would not be offensive to Runjeet Singh'. He said as much in a letter to Hobhouse at the beginning of the month:

...and yet he ought to be satisfied that he is allowed to remain at peace, and is saved from actual invasion. But he is reckless and intriguing, and will be difficult to keep quiet, as are the other Afghans, and Sikhs, Heratees, Russians, and Persians. It is a fine embroglio of diplomacy and intrigue, with more of bluster than of real strength anywhere. Yet it is impossible not to feel that the east and the west are drawing sensibly nearer to each other...[3]

About ten days later Auckland and his assistants received Burnes's disturbing news from Kabul—of the arrival of Vitkievitch with a letter from the Emperor of Russia, of the Dost's persistence in the hope that Britain might influence Runjeet Singh in his favour at Peshawar, and of Burnes's impetuous offer of direct British assistance to Kandahar. At the same time they heard from Claude Wade at Ludhiana. In accordance with instructions from Auckland, letters from Burnes had all passed through Wade's hands. Wade and Burnes did not see eye to eye; at one stage Colvin had had to remind them to exclude all signs of disagreement from their correspondence. As in his quarrel with Pottinger, so in his quarrel with Wade, Burnes offended the older and more experienced man by refusing to defer to his opinions. The dispute with Wade was sharper, also, because Wade supported Shuja and Burnes favoured the claims of Dost Muhammad to the throne of Afghanistan. Whenever he read and passed on Burnes's dispatches from Kabul that winter Wade wrote and attached dispatches of his own. He consistently diluted the strong brew of Burnes's admiration of Dost Muhammad. The ruler of Herat had pleased McNeill by offering more than reasonable terms to the Shah of Persia; Dost Muhammad persisted in asking for terms which could only offend Runjeet Singh. With this last thought in mind, indeed, Wade had written to Macnaghten at the end of October.[4] He saw the contrast in the conduct of the two Afghan rulers (of Herat and Kabul) as 'another among the many arguments that might be adduced in proof of the impolicy on the part of the British Government of voluntarily becoming a party to any renunciation of the sovereignty of the Affghans in the present family of the Suddozyes'. At the end of November Wade learned from Macnaghten that the Governor General was inclined to agree with him. But at that stage the thought was expressed very carefully indeed. Macnaghten wrote:

...His Lordship fully concurs with you in this opinion, thinking as he does, that there can be no state of affairs in Central Asia more favourable to the interests of British India than the present division of power among the several rulers of Afghanistan, provided that each state possessed independence within itself, and were willing to maintain social relations with its neighbours; and his Lordship would therefore not be disposed to encourage a renunciation of all pretensions to sovereignty on the part of the Suddozyes, as he would also be very unwilling to encourage Shah Kamran in any design on Candahar...[5]

It was in this context that Wade wrote to Macnaghten again on 1 January. He carefully dissected the glowing report submitted by Burnes at the end of November on the merits and good government of Dost Muhammad in Kabul, and he felt bold enough (considering the encouraging response to his earlier recommendations about the Sadozai family) to say to Macnaghten:

...I submit my opinions with every deference in the wisdom of his Lordship's decision; but it occurs to me that less violence would be done to the prejudices of the people, and to the safety and well-being of our relations with other powers, by facilitating the restoration of Shah Shooja than by forcing the Affghans to submit to the sovereignty of the Ameer...

In another part of the same letter Wade quoted an opinion of his Kabul agent, Charles Masson, that the presence of one British officer with Shuja as an observer in 1834 would have swayed the uncommitted and given him enough support to regain the throne of his ancestors.[6]

Thus, in the third week of January 1838, Auckland and his staff received strong pleas on behalf of both contenders for the crown of Afghanistan—Afghanistan, that is, without Herat. They were embarrassed by the evidence that Dost Muhammad expected more

than informal protection against the Sikhs as the price of his friendship with the British, and that he was addressing his brothers in
Kandahar as though they owed him some form of allegiance. They
had never intended him to entertain such high hopes, and the
published and unpublished correspondence proves that Auckland
and Macnaghten said nothing to raise the Dost's hopes beyond the
modest level of an untroubled tenure at Kabul and, if he bowed his
knee to Runjeet and demanded pardon, some adjustment of the
administration of Peshawar in favour of the Dost's family. Auckland now wrote personally to Dost Muhammad, thanking him for
his cordial and friendly reception of the Burnes mission, and
expressing great satisfaction with his ready acceptance of British
friendship and rejection of Persian blandishments. Having disposed of his opening courtesies Auckland set out to bring Dost
Muhammad face to face with the realities of his situation. He
reminded him that it was British policy to favour the continuing
division of Afghanistan into three states—Herat, Kandahar, and
Kabul. Then Auckland said:

...In regard to Peshawur, truth compels me to urge strongly on you to
relinquish the idea of obtaining the government of that territory. From
the generosity of his nature, and his regard for his old alliance with the
British Government, Maharajah Runjeet Singh has acceded to my wish
for the cessation of strife and the promotion of tranquillity, if you should
behave in a less mistaken manner towards him. It becomes you to think
earnestly on the mode in which you may effect a reconciliation with that
powerful prince, to whom my nation is united by the direct bonds of
friendship, and to abandon hopes which cannot be realised...

Auckland also told Dost Muhammad that British good offices
had already saved him from a ruinous war; if he wanted to continue to feel the benefit of these good offices he must not form any
connexion with other powers without British sanction. Should he
be dissatisfied with the aid which Britain had given ('which is all
that I think can in justice be granted'), Burnes and his mission
would retire from Kabul and British good offices would come to
an end.

...I am persuaded that you will recognise the friendly feeling which has
led me to state the truth to you, as you can guide your actions as you
may consider most proper for yourself. I trust that the result of your
negotiations on this important subject will be such as to promote your
real advantage, to conduce to the prosperity and peace of your own

and of all neighbouring territories, which are objects very dear to me, and to preserve and increase the sentiments of regard which I have always entertained for you. . . [7]

Auckland ended as he had begun, with kind words and sincere good wishes, but his message for the ruler of Kabul was far from warm. He let Macnaghten and Colvin answer Alexander Burnes. Macnaghten wrote the formal public dispatch;[8] Colvin wrote the semi-official letter. Both included a rebuke about the unauthorized commitment of British aid to the chiefs of Kandahar, which Auckland had had to disavow. Two points emerge from all these letters, and they deserve special emphasis. Auckland feared that Burnes had unduly raised the Dost's hopes, so much so that Colvin wrote of 'his Lordship's anxiety to set the British Government quite right with Dost Mahommed Khan. It is the first and last of our duties to act with good faith.' Secondly, if Colvin accurately reflected the views of his master, Auckland still thought that it was 'in Europe and in Persia that the battle of Afghanistan will most probably be ultimately fought'. He told Burnes that Persia would hesitate before she allowed England to abandon her wholly to the mercies of Russia, and that Russia was herself 'affording us strong ground of European remonstrance. . .'.[9]

A few days later Auckland told McNeill what had happened in a letter which, as we shall soon see, shifted some of the responsibility from the shoulders of the Governor General to those of the British Minister in Persia. This was part of a long and leisurely correspondence, whose earlier stages we have already noted. Auckland had written to McNeill in September, leaving the whole question in suspense but giving McNeill guidance for his own future conduct towards the Shah. Now, on 27 January, Auckland showed that he had made up his mind. He would not deliver a formal remonstrance from the Indian Government to the Shah, partly because he, too, felt inhibited by the ninth article of the 1814 treaty and partly because the Shah was headstrong and remonstrance would probably have no practical effect:

. . .I have thought that. . .it would be best to leave you quite free to act upon your own excellent judgement and upon the instructions which you may have received from home, and the more so as the whole course of events may with you, as with us, on any day take a new turn, and may entirely change our views upon the manner of proceeding which may now appear to be the best. . .

Auckland breaks with Dost Muhammad

Auckland said that he had been surprised and disappointed by the rapid advance of the Persians and the early fall of Ghorian, but Herat appeared to be strong, well garrisoned, and well provisioned:

...In the event of the repulse of the Persians our course will be cleared of some portion of its difficulty. In the event of its complete success an opening will be given to new entanglements and to new speculations with which we must deal as best we may, though until they come nearer to us we shall have but little power of directly controlling them...[10]

By now we have seen enough of Auckland's correspondence to be able to recognize his great rule of policy—never to act precipitately or to take a step forward without first testing the ground. He would move when he was ready, and not before.

In February and March Auckland continued to watch and wait. He told the Secret Committee at the beginning of February that the home authorities ought to give serious consideration to the 'open mission of an individual charged with diplomatic powers on the part of the Russian Government to a chief almost on our frontiers'.[11] To Hobhouse he said, of the affairs of Afghanistan, Persia and the Punjab, that 'that mess is at its thickest, and we must wait for events'.[12] He did not have long to wait. The correspondence had been painfully slow, but now, as Auckland and his staff approached Simla, the gap between him and Burnes was closing fast. At the beginning of March he received the Dost's reply to the very limited offer made at the beginning of December. At the beginning Dost Muhammad had stated his full demands (transmitted by Burnes at the beginning of October); Auckland had replied by going almost to the opposite extreme. At that stage Burnes would have had to look for a compromise which both Dost Muhammad and Runjeet Singh might accept. His dispatch of 26 January, received by Auckland at the beginning of March, opened the way to just such a compromise. The Dost had been greatly disappointed to hear that he could not hope for more than the restoration of Peshawar to his brother Sultan Muhammad as tributary. He had told Burnes at the beginning of the negotiations that this would be tantamount to having the Sikhs on the plain of Peshawar. Now he argued that he would almost prefer the Sikhs to stay in Peshawar. He had no fear of a Sikh invasion, but he did fear the plots which Sultan Muhammad would be able to hatch against him if he were in the city. Burnes countered this with some very strong arguments: the advantage to be gained from having the

Sikhs once again on the left bank of the Indus; the prestige which Dost would gain among Muslims on that account; the reduction in Kabul's high military expenses; the consequent reduction in taxes; the advantage of having Kandahar, Kabul, and Peshawar in one family of brothers. But Dost Muhammad was not convinced. He felt that Runjeet Singh owed the British gratitude for keeping the peace, not he. It was then that his brother, Nawab Jubbar Khan, suggested the compromise. Let Dost Muhammad and Sultan Muhammad share Peshawar and pay equal tribute to Runjeet Singh. He, Jubbar, would be their resident representative, equally devoted to Dost Muhammad and Sultan Muhammad, in the city of Peshawar. The Emir told Burnes that without some such plan he foresaw evils 'which cannot have entered into the minds of those who are my well-wishers'.

Alexander Burnes seized upon this proposal, forgetting that his Government was not prepared to do anything until the Emir had abased himself before Runjeet Singh. He made much of the fact that the universally respected Nawab Jubbar Khan had made the proposal in the first place. He argued that even if the British Government would do no more than hold back Runjeet Singh it ought at least to protect Dost Muhammad from the plots of his brothers in Kandahar and Peshawar in the process. In other words, if Jubbar's plan was unacceptable, the British should not let Runjeet Singh re-establish Sultan Muhammad in Peshawar. Then Burnes tried to analyse Auckland's present policy of non-interference as between one chief and another. It might be preferable, he said, but its advantages were not apparent to him 'unless it is intended to put forth the ex-king at Loodiana, secure through him a footing in these countries, and sweep the present rulers from their authority, which has happily never been contemplated. Besides the very questionable nature of such a proceeding, it would not gain the objects of Government.'[13] Burnes correctly judged that the restoration of Shuja would be one of a number of possibilities to be considered in any contingency plan, but he was ahead of the planners at this stage. A letter from the Emir to Auckland, enclosed in Burnes's dispatch of 26 January, gives a clue to the origin of the remark about Shuja. The Emir must have been getting nervous:

...I have now heard of the approach of your Lordship towards Loodiana in this neighbourhood, and I have thought it therefore incumbent on me to send this friendly letter...

Nothing is hidden from your Lordship which is passing in this country. I therefore repose entire confidence in your Lordship. I am aware of the favourable disposition which your Lordship entertains towards supporting and strengthening my government. I beg your Lordship, considering me attached to the British Government, will be pleased to bestow early attention on the affairs of this quarter, as, from delaying, difficulties arise, which may not hereafter be put in order with facility.[14]

This, then, was the message conveyed to Auckland by Burnes and Dost Muhammad at the end of January, and received by him at the beginning of March. The Emir was getting impatient and suspicious, but was retreating slowly from his early statement of terms. Unhappily for Burnes, the Governor General's approach to Simla meant that important letters crossed. At the end of January Burnes had answered dispatches sent in December. At the end of February he received and answered the despatches sent by his Government on 20 and 21 January.[15] Auckland's coolness and aloofness greatly disappointed the Emir, who, although he realized that this was not the reply to his offer of compromise, sensed that he could hardly hope for more from the British than Auckland had put foward on 20 January. The Emir and his advisers discussed the matter for many hours. Even Nawab Jubbar Khan complained to Burnes when he heard the news. He told Burnes that he was puzzled by the British attitude. 'If you wish the good of this country you must either put the Ameer aside by force, or find some means of obliging him.'[16] Dost Muhammad now began to argue that if his brother Sultan was to be allowed back in Peshawar the British would have to give something more for Kabul's friendship. That something more should be a guarantee of British protection for Kabul and Kandahar against Persia, and for Kabul against plots from Peshawar once Sultan Muhammad returned there. On 5 March Nawab Jubbar Khan put these terms to Burnes as a formal proposal, which Burnes resolutely refused. He had already burned his fingers by committing his Government to helping Kandahar. It was going to be difficult enough to escape from that commitment. He could hardly consent to the new terms proposed by Dost Muhammad Khan. Therefore he refused, and asked for leave to return to India if the Emir had said his last word. But the Emir did not want to quarrel with the British; he was still sure that a single hint to the Maharajah would suffice to rescue Peshawar.

In an interview on 6 March Alexander Burnes heard this said and once again attempted to convince Dost Muhammad that British influence at Lahore was by no means as strong as he thought. Dost Muhammad then threw himself, as he put it, upon the generosity of the Governor General of India. Burnes wrote:

I congratulated the Ameer on his having seen his own interest better than to permit of friendship being interrupted between him and a nation so well disposed towards him; but that it was now my duty to tell him clearly what we expected of him, and what we could do in return...

The terms were stiff. The Emir should not correspond with Persia and Russia; he should not have contact of any kind with them without British sanction; he should dismiss Vitkievitch with courtesy; he should surrender all claim to Peshawar on his own account and agree to live on friendly terms with Runjeet Singh; he should respect the independence of Kandahar and Peshawar and co-operate in arrangements to end strife between him and his brothers:

...In return for this I promise to recommend to the Government that it use its good offices with its ancient ally, Maharajah Runjeet Singh, to remove present and future causes of difference between the Sikhs and Afghans at Peshawar; but as that chiefship belongs to the Maharajah, he may confer it on Sultan Mahomed Khan, or any other Afghan whom he chooses, on his own terms and tribute, it being understood that such arrangement is to preserve the credit and honour of all parties...

To Burnes's delight the Emir assented to all this. His only reservations were a request to have the terms as stated by Burnes in writing and a plea for the withdrawal of Sikh troops from Peshawar if and when the place was restored to an Afghan chief as tributary. Burnes advised him to 'leave these things to be settled hereafter, since the less that was now said about them the better'. And so Alexander Burnes happily wrote to the Governor General and his staff on 7 March that Dost Muhammad had agreed to comply with all the Governor General's wishes as expressed on 20 January.[17] How are we to explain the Emir's sudden change of heart? Burnes himself answered this question in a subsequent dispatch. He had shown the Emir's ministers encouraging letters from Eldred Pottinger and Charles Stoddart about the excellent state of Herat's defences and the poor performance of the Persians besieging the city. Dost Muhammad presumably understood that he could not use the Persian threat as an instrument for obtaining concessions while Herat was so strong. Nor could he expect much benefit from alliance with Persia and Russia if they were not even capable of breaching the defences of Herat. In a moment of weakness and good sense he decided to accept the British terms. But there was one condition that Burnes had not ventured to put forward. He could not bring himself to propose that Dost Muhammad should send presents to Runjeet Singh; he thought that he would be able later on to persuade him to write a letter to Runjeet expressing a desire for peace. He was always optimistic.[18]

By this time Auckland and his staff were only a dozen marches or so from Simla. On the very day that Burnes triumphantly reported Dost Muhammad's acceptance of the British terms, Macnaghten gave the Government's considered reply to the earlier compromise plan. In short, Dost Muhammad must not expect the British Government to intervene to make Sultan Muhammad (or any other Afghan) chief of Peshawar. The decision still rested entirely with Runjeet Singh. Nor must the Dost make a *sine qua non* of his claim to a share of Peshawar.[19] In fact nothing had changed. Auckland still wanted Dost Muhammad to be grateful for the British restraint on the Sikhs; he still wanted him to approach Runjeet Singh as a suppliant and to accept graciously whatever crumb fell from that chief's table. This is how Macnaghten replied on his behalf to Burnes when, at the end of March, they heard that Dost Muhammad was angling for protection against Persia and Russia:

...The Governor General does not mean to deny that Dost Mahomed is in an embarrassing position, and that he has at best but a choice of difficulties; still his Lordship cannot help thinking that should he prefer a Persian and Russian alliance to that of the British Government, he will have committed a gross error in judgement, the consequences of which he must be content to endure. Whatever may be the result, his Lordship feels confident that the disinterested good faith of the British Government cannot be doubted. Our good will towards Dost Mahomed, had he been disposed to avail himself of our offices on the only terms which could be conceded, was equally manifest. That we should engage to protect him against the powers to the westward would be, as you are aware, an infringement of our treaty with Persia, independently of other considerations.

Deeply as his Lordship will deplore the necessity of your quitting Cabul without effecting the object on which you have recently been engaged, he would not of course wish you to remain one day longer than may be consistent with the preservation of our national honour, and he feels satisfaction in reflecting that the time and mode of your departure may safely be left to your judgement and discretion...[20]

Like Alexander Burnes when confronted with the same set of circumstances, the Governor General and his staff judged that the mission to Kabul had failed. A few days later they received Burnes's announcement of the Emir's change of heart. For a moment or two Auckland allowed himself the luxury of extravagant hopes. In a letter to Hobhouse, shortly after arriving at Simla, he said that he was now more anxious about affairs in the east and south-east than about those in the west and north-west. At the beginning of April there had been disturbing reports about the siege of Herat, the diplomatic manœuvres of the Kandahar chiefs, and the attitude of the Sind emirs towards Colonel Pottinger. Russian influence was strong at Kabul and Burnes was about to retire. But suddenly all had changed. Wade had arrived at Simla with the news that Herat was still defending itself bravely:

...Then Dost Mahomed fumes against his abandonment of Peshawar, but in the end says that he can only exist by the breath of the British Government, that he will relinquish all connection to the Westward and do his best to make peace upon reasonable terms with Runjeet Singh. Runjeet Singh has given directions that the Russian agent shall not be admitted within his frontier, and the Ameers of Sinde are intimating their willingness to receive a British Resident at Hyderabad. In nearly all these accounts there is much yet of uncertainty and possibility of inaccuracy, nor can I say to what degree any one of these events may have been the consequence of another, but assuredly the prospect of affairs between our frontier and Persia is at this moment more cheering than it was—though I am looking with anxiety for further intelligence.[21]

Auckland told Hobhouse in passing that his last letter from McNeill in Teheran was dated 5 February, a fact worth bearing in mind later in this chapter. The letter also reveals that Wade was in Simla at the beginning of April—a crucial moment in the development of the crisis. But in the author's view the most significant feature of the letter is that it shows Auckland genuinely pleased to hear that Dost Muhammad has accepted the British terms. This is not the letter of a man who, in Machiavellian fashion, sent Burnes to trap the Emir of Kabul into a quarrel, as some have hinted. Auckland had no cause to disguise his feelings in a private letter to Hobhouse; he never hesitated on other occasions to discuss the details of diplomatic manœuvre. Indeed, his letters to Hobhouse during this period give no hint of any plot; they merely support the massive evidence of the official papers that he offered consistent terms to Dost Muhammad from beginning to end of the negotiation. One may argue that they were the wrong terms, but not that they were a fraud.

What had Vitkievitch been doing since Christmas, that Runjeet Singh had to give orders to keep him out of the Punjab? After initial courtesies the Emir paid little attention to him, in spite of the fact that he kept reminding him that there were valuable presents to be collected from Simonich if he would only send someone to collect them. Vitkievitch paid one courtesy call on the Emir on the occasion of the Russian New Year's Day, but that was all in January. As Burnes said at the end of the month, 'an Agent of Russia with letters highly complimentary, and promises more than substantial, has experienced no more civility than is due by the laws of hospitality and nations...'.[22] But Vitkievitch was not idle. Lieutenant Robert Leech, the officer sent by Burnes to Kandahar at the very end of 1837, reported in January that the Kandahar chiefs were quoting alluring Russian promises at him. They told him, he said, that Vitkievitch, claiming to speak for the Emperor himself, had promised money and help against the Sikhs in return for Kandahar's friendship. This was disturbing enough, but in February the Emir realised that he could not keep Vitkievitch waiting much longer; he would have to do something about the Russian letters. What one might call the Russian faction at Dost Muhammad's court was pressing him to pay less attention to Burnes and more to Vitkievitch. He drafted a letter to the Emperor, but Burnes soon intervened and suggested alterations which would make the message less objectionable to the British Government. For instance, Dost Muhammad deleted all reference to the possibility of sending an agent to accompany Vitkievitch on his return to Persia, and softened his remarks about the Sikhs. It was another of Burnes's misfortunes that he had to convey unpalatable British terms to Dost Muhammad only a few days after persuading him to amend his letter to the Emperor. That was at the end of February. As a sign of his displeasure the Emir had held up the messenger who was about to leave with the amended letters, the implication being that new and more friendly letters to the Russians might soon be substituted. As we saw earlier in this chapter,

Burnes managed to avert that crisis. But, in the days before the Emir yielded to the British terms, Burnes heard and transmitted to his Government a report that Vitkievitch was considering sending a warning to Runjeet Singh about Peshawar. Burnes expressed considerable reserve in sending the report, but he saw it as a straw in the wind. Auckland's letter to Hobhouse shows that Burnes's anxiety was shared in Government circles.

After months of uncomfortable travel across the northern plain of India Auckland and his staff relaxed in the bracing air of Simla. Their confidence in a peaceful settlement of the Peshawar problem soon ebbed. Towards the end of April they heard from Burnes that Dost Muhammad had changed his mind again. On 6 March, when Dost Muhammad yielded, Burnes had not dared to raise the question of a submissive letter from Kabul to Lahore. On the 9th he proposed that the Emir should write a friendly letter to the Maharajah, and he hinted that the Emir might also send a representative to assist at the meeting then planned between the Governor General and Maharajah Runjeet Singh. He made the proposal to two of the Emir's ministers, who gave him an equal shock by asking for a written guarantee that the British Government would 'use its most strenuous endeavours to alter the state of things at Peshawar'. Burnes refused. He refused again when the proposal was renewed on the 10th, and he began to realize that Dost Muhammad was delaying and playing for time. Vitkievitch, far from being dismissed with courtesy, was still in Kabul, and his position was growing stronger every day. Then, on 12 March, bad news for Burnes came in from Kandahar. Simonich was still in Teheran as far as anyone knew in Kabul, but his agent with the Shah's army at Herat, Mr Goutte, had promised to get Simonich's signature as a guarantee of another proposed treaty between Kandahar and Persia (Burnes's diplomatic efforts in December had scotched an earlier attempt). Burnes complained in letters to his Government: '. . . At every step it will be seen that Russian and Persian influence counteracts our proceedings in these countries.'[23] Worse news came on 16 March. Nawab Jubbar Khan came to see Burnes and shamefacedly confirmed a rumour that his brother the Emir had written to Kandahar saying he had lost all hope of gaining anything from the British:

. . . I at once requested the Nawab and the Mirza to convey my request for leave to return to India; that no more could or would be done for the

Afghans than had been stated, and that after the promise given to dismiss the Russian agent, and he was now detained, it was clear that I was bringing my own Government into disrepute by another day's stay in the city; that our Government had no desire to dictate to the Ameer of Cabool, and left it to himself to guide his own affairs as seemed most conducive to his interests, but that his late proceedings, particularly in what he had written to Candahar, and that, too, without even informing me, were conclusive proofs that my stay in Cabool was no longer advisable...[24]

On the day after this interview with Nawab Jubbar Khan he sent to India his copies of letters between Persia and Kandahar and, more important, the proposed treaty under Russian guarantee. Meanwhile, Dost Muhammad was still playing for time. He felt that his personal honour was at stake, and that he was being asked to humiliate himself before his people. He had not yet answered Auckland's last letter (of 20 January), and he had not yet dismissed Vitkievitch. One cannot help but feel sympathy with the Emir in his predicament in the middle of March 1838. He badly needs an ally. British friendship offers but little advantage and costs a great deal; perhaps British hostility would not matter so much if he had firm promises from the Persians and Russians—especially the Russians. His brothers in Kandahar are already drawing closer to those Western powers. Can he afford to remain aloof? Some such sequence of thoughts must have passed through his mind when he heard that Burnes was again threatening to pack up and go. He promised to answer Auckland's letter within eight days (i.e. by 25 March), and grumbled that the British seemed to be making the presence of Vitkievitch ('an individual of such little note') an excuse for quarrelling. He also told Burnes that he wanted to have a reply from his brothers at Kandahar before answering Auckland's letter. He added rather sourly that it was Auckland who had abandoned the Afghans, and not he who had deserted the British. Burnes saw no reason in this for postponing his departure. He wrote firmly to Dost Muhammad on the 18th:

...should the Ameer be dissatisfied with these good offices and seek connexion with other powers, then the Ameer is to consider the Governor General's letter a final answer, and not till then, since our friendship is entirely dependent on the relinquishment of alliance with any power to the West; this is well known, but I commit it to writing that there may be no misapprehension or mistake...

Advance to the Hindu Kush 1838–1839

Like a good diplomat Burnes had left a little loophole for Dost
Muhammad, who used it with alacrity. He sent Nawab Jubbar
Khan and Mirza Sami Khan back to Burnes with an apology. He
was able to do so because he had not *yet* taken the plunge into an
alliance with the Persians and Russians. He promised to send
Vitkievitch away at once. For a few hours Burnes could feel that he
had regained lost ground. The next day was Monday 19 March,
and Burnes was pleased to discover that the Emir no longer insisted
on a written statement of British pledges concerning Peshawar. It
seemed to him that he had at last persuaded the Emir that Peshawar
was not Britain's to dispose of. Later that day he received a copy
of the Emir's new letter to Auckland. All the Emir asked was 'a
little encouragement and power...'

If your Lordship is pleased to bestow a little trouble to adjust affairs
between this country and the Maharajah Runjeet Singh, who is the
great and old ally of the British, how is it possible that we should make
objection to it, or to suitable arrangements for peace?...[25]

Dost Muhammad also found an ingenious excuse for having kept
Vitkievitch so long in Kabul; the roads had been snowbound and
dangerous, and now that the winter was over Vitkievitch would be
dismissed. This was all very well, but what was a 'suitable arrangement for peace'? Burnes soon discovered that it could never include a clause compelling Dost Muhammad to cringe to Runjeet
Singh. On that Monday afternoon he politely asked the Emir to
write a letter of peaceful intent, thus renewing the proposal which
he had made in less propitious circumstances on the 9th. Back came
a determined refusal. Peace might be desirable, but the disgrace of
suing for it to Runjeet Singh would be irretrievable. In reporting
this to Auckland he said that he would much regret the absence of
this letter of peaceful intent 'if his Lordship has deemed it a necessary preliminary to adjust the existing differences...'. In fact this
was exactly what Auckland wanted from the beginning. On Friday
23 March the Emir called on Burnes. Gone was the friendly and
trusting tone of previous conversations. Instead Dost Muhammad
felt bitter and ill used. He could not understand what the British
were driving at, and he now told Burnes that he had lost 'every
description of hope from us'. Yet still he insisted that he preferred
the British to the Persians and Russians. He could only suppose
that the British had a low opinion of him:

...I am either kept in the dark or misled. Never was there such excitement in this land. The Persians are before Herat, openly aided by Russia. That power has sent an agent here, and your Government have deputed you. I wish no countenance but that of the English, and you refuse all pledges and promises, and mean, I presume, as you are people of your word, to do nothing for me; I am bound to say as I feel, or I would be deceiving myself and you...

The letter in which Burnes quoted Dost Muhammad was a long summary of the negotiations between the middle and the last week of March. Though rather long, its conclusion merits uninterrupted quotation.

...In pledging himself to have nothing to do with the powers to the West, the Ameer has so far acted in coincidence with the views of Government; but it will be seen that he is not so sensible as he was expected to be at our good offices in Peshawar, and seems to doubt of anything being done. He has been told, and now admits, that he can exercise no kind of interference in an adjustment of affairs there; but it is too evident that he will test the British by what is settled in that chiefship. If the Maharajah restores it, in whole or in part, to Sultan Muhammad Khan, he still paying tribute to Lahore, it would silence complaints in Cabul, and be to the Afghans an earnest of our sympathy of the highest value; but if something decisive is not done in this quarter, no reliance, in my opinion, is to be placed on this chief. Fear, it appears to me, of our displeasure is the lever on which he is now moved, and it has not escaped him that if Peshawar be restored, even partially, and Candahar clings to us these chiefships will become identified with the British, and thus the ruler of Cabool will find himself awkwardly situated from the conduct of his own relatives. If, on the other hand, we succeed in uniting the whole of the Barukzye family, which I believe quite practicable, we shall raise up in this country, instead of weak and divided states accessible to every intrigue alike injurious to themselves and us, a barrier which will prevent future causes of vexation, and advance commercial and political ends.

I have thus laid before his Lordship the result of all my communications with the Chief of Cabool. I have found my task here full of delicacy and difficulty, and instead of the language of persuasion, I have had occasion in my intercourse to use, as has appeared, much more explicit declarations. It now rests with his Lordship to judge if the circumstances that have occurred, and the intrigues which are passing, furnish an excuse for this chief's delays and observations, and if causes for future anxiety are removed. It has been said by one of the wisest of historians (Hume) that 'men's views of things are the result of their understanding alone, but that their conduct is regulated by their understanding, their temper, and their passions,' and such appears to have been the case with the ruler of Cabool.[26]

We have now seen how Burnes fared in March, and we can share Auckland's burden of decision at the end of April when all this information arrived in Simla. With it came a characteristic gloss on Burnes's report of events up to and including 5 March—from Claude Wade. He said that a connexion with Dost Muhammad would be 'full of peril' even if the British Government measured up to the 'extravagant expectations' which he seemed to have formed during the Burnes mission. Wade forecast that the Emir would try to temporize until the fate of Herat was decided, choosing alliance with Persia if Herat succumbed and renewing contact with the British if Herat survived.[27] We already know the course favoured by Claude Wade. But it would be foolish to assume that a spineless Auckland now let Wade and those who shared his views push him into a forward policy against his better judgement. Nothing could be further from the truth. At the end of April Auckland not only had before him the dossier of Burnes's failure in Kabul; he had news from McNeill in Teheran, and, to his relief, he had the newly ratified treaty with Sind.[28] After more than a year of tedious haggling Colonel Pottinger had persuaded Nur Muhammad and Nusseer Muhammad to accept a British Resident at Hyderabad. Auckland was now like a climber who had found a firm hand-hold after clinging for an eternity to the rock face, unable to go forward or back. Had he not said, in his Defence Minute of June 1837, that one could not ignore the advantage of having allies and a British force in Sind?

> ...It is upon these [i.e. military] as well as upon commercial grounds, and for improved facilities in communicating with the Afghan states that I look for a clear connection with Sinde as of importance, and the power with the aid of steam of rapidly bringing together a British force in that country is amongst those provisions for security which should not, in my opinion, be overlooked.[29]

In April 1838 Auckland at last had his 'clear connection' with Sind, even if military facilities were not yet available. He could now more confidently consider the possibilities of action beyond the Indus in the event of disaster at Herat. It was just as well. Up to the end of January McNeill had been moderately optimistic about the capacity of Herat to withstand a long siege. His most pressing problem was that arising from the insult to his confidential messenger. He had demanded redress, and the Shah was most unwilling to oblige him. McNeill grew more and more uneasy. At the end of February he told Palmerston that the time had come to remonstrate with the Shah about his designs on Herat and other Afghan territories to the east:

...This one act of interference would doubtless cause some immediate irritation, but it would cause less than would be produced by our interfering to protect Candahar after Herat shall have fallen, and if we must ultimately (incur the odium of) arrest(ing) the progress of Persia in Affghanistan, it appears to me that it can be most advantageously incurred for the preservation of the whole country, including so valuable a position as Herat...

The phrase in parenthesis was omitted from the collection of dispatches published in 1839. McNeill argued in his letter to Palmerston on 23 February that the embarrassing ninth article of the 1814 treaty could no longer be binding on Britain. Surely it could not be held to bind Britain to permit 'the unjust and wanton destruction by Persia of the most valuable defences of India, while the Shah appears to be acting in concert with, and promoting the influence in those countries of that very Power whose exclusion from them has become the chief object of the alliance with His Persian Majesty...'.

That part of the dispatch was published (subject to the reservation already noted) in 1839. What follows was suppressed, and one can see why. McNeill acknowledged that the Shah's campaign in Afghanistan might be decided before Her Majesty's Government or the Government of India could take any action,

but it may not be decided for many months, and there may yet be time sufficient to interfere with effect. If the Shah should be forced to raise the siege and retire, all interference would of course be uncalled for, except to prevent a repetition of the attempt at a future period; and if Herat should have fallen, it would be too late to interfere unless for the purpose of retaking it; but if the siege or blockade should endure for many months, as it not improbably may, if I were instructed to proceed to the Shah's camp, and distinctly announced to His Majesty, that we could not permit him to prosecute a war which was injurious to our interests; and that if he should determine to persevere, we should aid the Government of Herat, I am of opinion that he would feel the necessity of accepting an equitable treaty; and that if the state of his military preparations did not promise speedy success, he might even feel that such an announcement furnished him with a pretext for abandoning the enterprise without the discredit which would attend a failure; but if he had before him a prospect of immediate success, he might not be deterred even by this intimation from pursuing his own course, and it might then be necessary to go further and to inform him that even if he should take Herat, he would not be permitted to retain it.[30]

We must remember that McNeill was alone in Teheran. There was no one to advise him. Neither Palmerston nor Auckland, as far as he knew, had yet issued any specific instruction to guide him in his conduct towards the Shah. Auckland's advice, received just before Christmas, had not been particularly helpful, although it was sympathetic. Auckland had merely concluded that in a few weeks or months he would be able to write to McNeill more explicitly. We have already seen that Auckland kept his promise and wrote explicitly on 27 January, though still unsatisfactorily from McNeill's point of view. He thought it best to leave McNeill free to act upon his own 'excellent judgement' and upon the instructions which might have reached him from home. McNeill heard the gist of this message, but did not receive the letter itself, at the beginning of March. He interpreted it as sufficient authority for doing what he had proposed in his dispatch to Palmerston on 23 February, and so he packed his bags for the journey to Herat. But first he sat down to write to Palmerston and Auckland, telling them exactly what he was doing, and why. He wrote to Auckland on the 7th, and to Palmerston on the 8th.[31] On the 10th he mounted his horse and set out on the most important journey of his life. He was off to tell the Shah that if he continued the siege the Anglo-Persian alliance would not prevent the British Government from defending India effectively.

At the end of April, then, the Governor General of India went through a period of 'agonising re-appraisal'. His hopes of peace and conciliation were shattered, but at least the alliance with Runjeet Singh was firm and he had a footing in Sind at last. To the Emir Dost Muhammad Khan of Kabul he wrote of his regret at the refusal of Britain's good offices.[32] Through Macnaghten he told Burnes to leave Kabul, not knowing that the mission had already left on 26 April. Macnaghten's letter helps to clarify still further the consistent policy of the Indian Government at that time.

Auckland breaks with Dost Muhammad

Macnaghten listed three main charges against Dost Muhammad: he had promised to dismiss Vitkievitch, but broke the promise and kept the Russian in Kabul; he still refused to smooth the way to reconciliation with the Sikhs by writing to Runjeet Singh; and he still dwelt upon hopes of British assistance against Persia, 'which, although the topic may be, with him, a fair and natural subject of anxiety, was yet in no degree alluded to or contemplated in the propositions tendered for his acceptance by your government'. Burnes was to tell Dost Muhammad (though in fact he was spared the personal embarrassment of having to do so), that, if an alliance with Persia should lead him to proceedings either hostile or offensive to Britain or the Punjab, 'he will incur a new danger, probably far more serious than is to be apprehended by him, under any circumstances, from Persian enmity or estrangement'. Finally, Macnaghten gently conveyed to Alexander Burnes the Governor General's criticism of the conduct of his mission:

... He collects ... from your despatches that the hope of the restoration of Afghan power in Peshawur has been entertained by the Ameer in a far greater degree than it ever was intended by his Lordship to encourage; and great as has been the object of avoiding all open rupture, and difficult as it may occasionally have appeared to uphold the opinions and intentions of your government against the representations of the Ameer and his counsellors, his Lordship would yet have been glad to observe a more undoubted explicitness on this head, and must regret any occasion on which a charge of a departure from perfect frankness and consistency on our part can be founded ... [33]

On the same day Auckland sent a dispatch to the Secret Committee which strongly suggests a recent reading of McNeill's letter. He said, for instance, that Persia had departed from the Anglo-Persian Treaty by openly connecting herself with a European power in measures which could only be injurious to British interests in India, 'while the whole purport and effect of the stipulations to which Persia bound herself by the treaty is that she will co-operate with us in the defence of India against the aggressions of all European powers ...'.[34] He also argued that the time had come to remonstrate against the proceedings of Russian agents in Afghanistan. In a further dispatch to the Secret Committee, on 1 May, he reported that he had given orders to the Bombay Government to send a small naval and military force up the Persian Gulf, to be at McNeill's disposal if his mission to Herat failed and he decided to leave the country by way of Bushire.[35] On 1 May Macnaghten wrote to McNeill to let him know what had been done since the receipt of his letter of 7 March, in which the expedition to the Gulf was requested.[36] Then, on 3 May, Auckland wrote one of his regular private letters to Hobhouse. Already a new crisis was looming; the British representative in Ava had sent disturbing news of the warlike tendencies of the Burmese. Therefore Auckland told Hobhouse that Ava and Herat (of external politics) continued to be with him 'objects of much anxiety'. He had heard nothing from Herat of later date than 26 February, and in telling Hobhouse this he revealed an anxiety which was to trouble him throughout the crisis: '...I have so often been misled in my speculations by hasty and false representations that I can speak with but little confidence of what is likely to happen...'

In other words, he was expected to make critical decisions on often unreliable and invariably out-of-date information. Nevertheless, in this letter to Hobhouse, he predicted that Herat would be unlikely to survive a long siege:

...Candahar is waiting the event in quiet dismay, and Dost Mahomed is playing fast and loose, ready to crouch to Persia or to cringe to us, wherever strength may in the end appear to be. Runjeet Singh has remained quiet and throughout has behaved well, and I cannot trace that he has committed himself further than by saying that 'future events are in the womb of time'—and in the meantime the Russian agents seem to have thrown aside the mask and to be acting in avowed hostility to the British Government, and nothing can be more critical or more in jeopardy than our friendly relations in Persia. In weighing my proceedings you will look to the difficulties with which I have had to deal and to the little control which I could have had over passing occurrences—to the treaty of 1814 which has tied my hands...to the position of the Persian Embassy, and to the influence which Indian measures might have upon European politics—and particularly to my relations with Runjeet Singh, over whose head I have had to deal with Dost Mahomed, and who has not always smothered the mistrust with which he has viewed my endeavours to establish peace between him and the Afghans...

Auckland then disposed of an argument which some (including Wade, no doubt) had advanced: that he should have let Runjeet Singh deal with Dost Muhammad, in the belief that Runjeet could have influenced the fate of Herat from Kabul:

...I am far from being of this opinion. Runjeet Singh could ill afford to leave his turbulent provinces behind him. It was the pressure of Sikh power which induced Dost Mahomed to write to the Emperor of Russia, and first to enter into cajoleries with Persia, and its further pressure would have drawn assistance to Persian invasion from the whole of Afghanistan. I can have no doubt that the presence of Captain Burnes at Cabul has up to this time secured the neutrality of Cabul and Candahar, though unhappily this may not be sufficient to save Herat. What may follow the fall of that city it is not easy to conjecture. The Soonies of Afghanistan will hate the Sheeahs, but both will probably hate the Sikhs more than they hate each other, and all may be ready to combine with Persia and Russia for further mischief. Our alliance with Runjeet Singh will probably be drawn more closely for offence and defence, and Sinde must be made subservient, though it will be most reluctantly, to our objects. Burnes will retire, upon no very good terms, from Dost Mahomed, and for the rest, 'future events are in the womb of time'. My last letter from Mr McNeill is of the 7th of March. He was then about to set out for the Camp of the Persians and to endeavour to persuade the Shah to conclude a treaty with Herat and to return to his country. I can have little hope that he will succeed...[37]

Auckland stands revealed by that letter as a man of judgement and good sense. We leave him for the present, pondering upon various courses of action and awaiting the arrival of a Sikh delegation at Simla. Early in February Palmerston had received McNeill's report of the fall of Ghorian, previously considered a strong barrier against any advance upon Herat from the west. He had also heard of the insult to McNeill's messenger. On the 12th Palmerston wrote to McNeill expressing the Government's full approval of what he had said and done so far; he said he delayed sending further instructions until he knew the Persian Government's answer to his demand for redress and until he knew the outcome of the Shah's expedition.[38] In fact Palmerston shared at this time the complacency noted earlier in Auckland and encouraged up to the end of February by McNeill. In the middle of March Palmerston received dispatches which had left Persia at the end of December— about the Russian agent in Kabul and the rumours of Burnes's success, and about Auckland's reply to the suggestion that the Indian Government ought to remonstrate with the Shah. He now knew that Auckland was relying on McNeill's judgement and declining to throw India's weight into the scales at Herat, and he knew that McNeill might soon come to the point of severing relations with Persia. On the 16th Palmerston told McNeill that he placed such entire confidence in your judgement, discretion, and firmness, that I am satisfied that you will adopt provisionally, and until you can receive further instructions from me, that course which, under the circumstances of the case, will be most conducive to the interests of Great Britain and most consistent with her honour and dignity...

In other words McNeill had a free hand. Both Auckland and Palmerston had decided to rely on McNeill's judgement, based as it was on twenty years or more of service in Persia. But Palmerston gave his minister careful guidance, as Auckland had done, about the importance of preserving the alliance. 'You will...bear in mind that the object of Her Majesty's Government is not to seek an occasion for a rupture with Persia; but to prevent such a rupture, if it is possible to do so consistently with national honour...'[39]

The Secret Committee, alias John Cam Hobhouse, was not far behind Palmerston in taking account of McNeill's news from Teheran. On 20 March a brief and rather frightening dispatch was signed for transmission to Auckland. It informed him that Palmerston had authorized McNeill to leave Persia if he received no apology for the insult to his confidential messenger, and it said:

...In the event of Mr McNeill's retirement we leave it discretional with you to adopt such measures as may seem to you to be expedient to meet the contingency of the cessation of our relations with the Court of Persia...[40]

It is evident that neither Palmerston nor Hobhouse felt confident enough in the early spring of 1838 to issue specific instructions. Like Auckland, they wanted to know more before committing themselves. But they could see that the time might soon arrive for some more decisive action. At the beginning of April Palmerston heard from St Petersburg that the Russians were planning an expedition from Orenburg to Bokhara. This seemed to match earlier reports from Teheran of the possibility of a combined Russian and Persian expedition against Khiva. On 7 April Palmerston instructed McNeill to obtain the fullest information about the reported expedition and to send it as soon as possible to London and Simla.[41] The reports were as ominous to Palmerston and Hobhouse as they would have been to Aberdeen and Ellenborough in 1830. A week later Palmerston received at second hand an urgent plea from McNeill. It came in the form of a letter to Colonel Sheil, who had been Secretary to Legation at Teheran for a time but who was now in London and was about to return to Teheran. Sheil considered the letter so important that he contemplated seeking an interview with Palmerston, who was deep in European affairs at the time. Instead, he sent extracts from the letter, and his own comments. Here is a sample of what McNeill was writing unofficially early in February—before the official dispatch of 23 February already noted:

...My opinion is that Lord Auckland must now take a decided course, and declare that he who is not with us is against us, and shall be treated accordingly. If the Shah should take Herat we shall not have a moment to lose, and the stake will in my opinion be the highest we have yet played for. We must be secure in Affghanistan—able to check and to punish intrigues carried on there against our peace in India—able to exclude foreign agents and emissaries from all that country—as our security in India will be very greatly diminished and our expenses there very largely increased...

Sheil pointed out that it was imprudent to wait for news of the Shah's answer to McNeill's demand for redress for the insult to his messenger. For all McNeill knew at the time of writing the courier carrying the demand had been killed by brigands on his way to the Shah's camp. Palmerston sent the letter to Hobhouse—another proof of their close working partnership. He remarked that the letter deserved attention, 'but it seems to me that you can hardly come to a determination till we know the result of the siege of Herat...'. Having passed the letter on to Hobhouse he wrote to McNeill, expressing the same reservation and giving McNeill to understand that the Cabinet as a whole was not yet ready to take a strong line. Hobhouse's reply to the letter enclosing McNeill's plea for decision contained a wry comment on Cabinet attitudes:

...I should press upon you the expediency of coming to some determination respecting not only our relations with Persia, but also our diplomatic operations in the Affghan states, were it not that I know too well how much you are occupied by matters much nearer home, and were I not equally well aware of the disinclination of the Cabinet to consider any subject connected merely with our Indian Empire. I am however fully persuaded that the time will shortly arrive when you will have to speak to the Shah in very different language from that which has hitherto been held to him; if not to make some demonstration to convince him that, if he knows the way to India, we can shew him a road leading from Bushire to Ispahan...

But Hobhouse, knowing who was in command, accepted Palmerston's cautious view.[42] In a private letter to Auckland he speculated on the possibility of action in southern Persia, but went no further than Palmerston suggested. At the beginning of May he acknowledged Auckland's February dispatch. He agreed that Vitkievitch's mission to Kabul demanded special attention, that Burnes had exceeded his instructions in 'entering into premature arrangements with Afghan chiefs', and that Burnes should be withdrawn from Kabul if Dost Muhammad persisted in listening to Russian offers. But he advised caution. He reminded Auckland that the letter from the Emperor was in reply to one from Dost Muhammad, and that it was inadvisable to stir up controversy about this with the Russians, either in Teheran or in St Petersburg. Until the outcome of McNeill's representations to the Shah was known, and until more was known of the state of operations at Herat, 'it would be premature to come to any decision upon the affairs of Affghanistan'.[43]

That dispatch had hardly left London before it was overtaken by events. For the time being we must consider Burnes's remaining adventures in Kabul. The Kandahar and Kabul chiefs jointly tried to budge him from his terms. They tried in vain to get a promise of protection against the Persians. Only Jubbar Khan had the courage to say openly that the British terms were sufficient in themselves. But on 21 April Dost Muhammad made his decision. He sent for the Russian and had him escorted through the streets to the palace. After a sad exchange of notes Burnes and the Emir said goodbye on the 25th. Burnes left Kabul on the 26th, having been secretly informed by Jubbar Khan that he bitterly regretted Dost Muhammad's decision and was prepared even to help the British remove the Emir. Burnes noted but did not commit himself on this offer. On the 27th Mirza Sami Khan caught him up on the road and presented him with two horses from the Emir. Mirza Sami Khan asked whether Burnes had any more to say to the Emir:

...I said none, save that I feared he would soon find out he was trusting to those who could not befriend him, and that the gratification of enemies was a pretty clear proof in worldly affairs that all was not right; and the day of my quitting Cabool was one of rejoicing to Shah Shoojah, to Runjeet Singh, and to Mahomed Shah. We then parted...

Mirza Sami Khan turned his horse and went back to Kabul. Dost Muhammad, so Burnes was told, started trying to recover lost credit with the Shah of Persia. He told the Shah that he had kept Burnes waiting in Kabul with 'evasive discourse', but had dismissed him instantly on hearing of the Shah's arrival at Herat.[44] Burnes, meanwhile, reached Gandamak on 29 April. There he met a messenger with dispatches from his Government, including the answer to the Emir's proposals for a compromise. He later expressed his disgust about the reply in a letter to Wade; he felt that the Government had been dilatory and over-subtle:

..In the present state of parties in Afghanistan an adjustment of Peshawar affairs to preserve the honour of all parties was the base on which we could only hope to work, and I believe it will be found, on a review of all which has passed, that the delay regarding it, in whatever it may have originated, has been one of the principal causes of Dost Mahomed Khan's rejecting the good offices of the British Government; and, what is worse, of his doubts being raised, if it ever really had any serious intention of seeking to establish peace between himself and the Sikhs...[45]

From Jalalabad on 30 April Alexander Burnes sent reports showing that whatever he felt about the Peshawar affair he was most emphatic on the need for 'prompt, active, and decided counter-action' against Russian activities in Central Asia. It is always as well to distinguish between Burnes's strong sympathy for Dost Muhammad, which was a personal matter, and his equally strong conviction that the Russians must be checked in Central Asia. The one made him quarrel with Wade and sulk for a time after he left Kabul; the second made him suppress personal feelings and give his full support to the restoration of Shuja. In the past Burnes's change of heart—his transformation from partisan of Dost Muhammad into enthusiast for the restoration of Shuja—has been treated as a discreditable episode in his life. This is because other writers have neglected the considerable evidence of Burnes's concern about the ambitions of Russia in Afghanistan. Let him speak for himself:

...I have only again to repeat my most deliberate conviction, founded on much reflection, regarding the passing events in Central Asia, that consequences of the most serious nature must in the end flow from them, unless the British Government applies a prompt, active, and decided counter-action. I do not offer these as opinions founded on the periodical publications of all Europe, though the coincidence of sentiment in all parties does not want its weight, but as formed in the scene of their intrigues, and it is my duty to observe that England with her honesty has no chance in coping with a nation which makes no scruple to dazzle men's minds by promises and to overwhelm those whom she thus deceives at their own expense and at that of others...[46]

Burnes, after all, had been engaged in the business of countering the Russians in Central Asia since 1831. It is not without interest, in the author's opinion, that Burnes had already noted 'the coincidence of sentiment in all parties' on this issue.

We now leave Burnes and his companions, including Masson, for a few weeks. From Jalalabad they travelled to Peshawar, and there they stayed throughout the month of May. When we last heard of John McNeill, he was setting out for the Shah's camp at Herat. Simonich stayed behind in Teheran, but not for long. The British consul at Tabriz reported to Palmerston on 7 April that on direct orders from St Petersburg the Russian Minister had started out for Herat on 21 March.[47] The orders came too soon after McNeill's departure to be directly connected with it, and one would have to search the Russian archives to establish the real motive for sending Simonich to Herat at that stage, but one thing is certain: Count Nesselrode did not send him there to invite the Shah to desist.

McNeill arrived at the Persian camp on 6 April. On the 11th he wrote important dispatches to Palmerston in London and to Auckland in Simla. Here is part of his dispatch to Palmerston. The parentheses indicate an omission in the published version of 1839:

...(I apprehend that the Indian Government is deterred only by a scrupulous regard to good faith from taking active measures to secure the integrity, if not the independence of Herat. I trust however that there may yet be time to take a more decided course; and) I do not hesitate to repeat my conviction that if our only object were to preserve as long as possible the alliance of Persia, that object could best be effected by preventing her from taking Herat.[48]

McNeill sent with his dispatch to Palmerston a copy of the treaty under Russian guarantee between Kandahar and Persia. He also sent Palmerston a copy of his dispatch to Auckland, which was published with very few omissions in 1839. This was the dispatch quoted at the head of this chapter—a dispatch so frank that it is surprising that Palmerston allowed parts of it to go to the printers. McNeill told Auckland that the British Government would be fully justified in taking up arms to protect British interests in Central Asia. He proposed to tell the Shah that Her Majesty's Government regarded Persian actions in Afghanistan as

a flagrant violation of the spirit of the Treaty, and as destructive of the whole object of the alliance. That the British Government would therefore be fully justified in declaring the Treaty to be at an end and taking such active measures as it may find necessary to protect itself against the evils which Persia, for the furtherance of her own unjust ends, is bringing upon us...

and that he was still ready to mediate between the Shah and Kamran if the Shah relented. McNeill said that he did not know how far Russia would go to protect the Shah, but he did not think that she would risk a 'misunderstanding with England' for the sake of giving the Shah Herat.

...If circumstances should lead your Lordship to put in motion a force of British troops or of British combined with others there does not appear to be any probability that the Shah would or could abide their arrival here, and the probability is that their advance from Candahar would enable me to carry into effect the wishes of Government here; but if any other than a British force should march in this direction the Shah's contempt for Seiks and Affghans would probably induce him to try his fortune in battle...[49]

The dispatch just quoted did not reach Auckland until mid July, by which time Auckland and Fane had independently arrived at the conclusion that some British troops would have to be employed beyond the Indus. Having reported and made important recommendations to Palmerston and Auckland, John McNeill started the uphill work of persuading the Shah to withdraw. From the middle of April onwards he began to make progress, and he might well have succeeded and averted many deaths and disasters if only Simonich's orders from St Petersburg had failed to reach Teheran in March, or if Simonich's carriage had overturned on the road to Herat. For Simonich soon began to pull in the opposite direction, and the Shah was too weak and short-sighted to resist. But the crisis came in May. At the end of April, the moment at which we left the other principal characters, McNeill and Simonich were still competing.

May was a critical month for Palmerston as well as for McNeill and Auckland. On the 14th Palmerston received a sheaf of McNeill's dispatches up to and including the announcement of his departure for Herat (8 March). His first reaction was to send McNeill a copy of the Secret Committee's latest dispatch to Auckland—the one advising him not to take any premature action in Afghanistan and not to stir up a controversy with the Russians, either in Europe or in Persia. This was one way of showing McNeill how his Cabinet colleagues viewed events in Persia and Afghanistan. On the 18th he informed McNeill that the Cabinet approved of his journey to Herat to remonstrate with the Shah. On the same day he instructed McNeill to send an officer to Bokhara to find out what the Russians were doing in the territories to the north of Afghanistan. The dating of this dispatch is important because of its close proximity to his justly famous ultimatum of 21 May. It is clear that the British Government feared a joint Persian-Russian expedition into the trans-Oxus territories would quickly follow a Persian success at Herat. The officer detailed to go to Bokhara was to urge the ruler to release his Russian slaves and thus deprive the Russians of an excuse for attacking his country.[50] The alarm signal which so stimulated Palmerston's colleagues was a dispatch from the British consul general in Odessa. They had already seen a similar report from St Petersburg in April. Now they had confirmation from a man much closer to the scene of future action. Hobhouse immediately sent a copy of the dispatch to Auckland.[51]

Palmerston had great faith in McNeill. He accepted McNeill's recommendations in full and authorized him to deliver an ultimatum to the Shah. If the Shah persevered in his project of conquering Afghanistan the friendly relations between Britain and Persia would cease and Britain would 'take such steps as she may think best calculated to provide for the security of the possessions of the British Crown'.[52] Palmerston and Auckland were both acting on McNeill's advice in May, and they were both working from the same information, supplied by McNeill. We have already considered the letter which Auckland wrote privately to Hobhouse at the beginning of the month. At that moment a Sikh delegation was about to call on him in Simla, and he was already giving thought to various methods of intervening in Afghanistan. With his usual thoroughness he drew up a long and comprehensive minute 'on the crisis in Afghan affairs' on 12 May. First he reviewed the recent history of the crisis, explaining that his early policy was based upon the belief that the Shah would be dissuaded from marching on

Herat. He was critical of Dost Muhammad, whom he described as a man of 'restless and unaccommodating spirit'. This restlessness, combined with the influence of the Shah's invasion of Herat and Vitkievitch's mission to Kabul, had led Dost Muhammad to reject the British terms 'of security in his own possessions (which are all to which he has any fair claim, or that have ever been subject to his authority)'. Writing without knowledge of the latest negotiations between Persia and Kandahar, Auckland went on to take comfort in Kandahar's resolution to keep clear of alliances against Herat, thus depriving the Persian army of help which would have been 'of the utmost value'. He said that the Anglo-Persian Treaty had prevented him from giving Herat any more aid than this, 'even if difficulties of time and distance had been overcome'. As for arming Kabul and Kandahar for defence against Persia, the arms would 'more probably have been used against Sikhs than against Persians'. Moreover, the supply of armaments and subsidies to Dost Muhammad and his brothers would,

especially while such pretensions were advanced as regards Peshawur, have been attended with the absolute certainty of wholly destroying the cordiality of our alliance with the most powerful and valuable of our friends, Maharajah Runjeet Singh, while they would have involved us in responsibilities that could in no degree be compensated by any aid from chiefs so weak, and divided by so many jealousies and distractions.

The minute of 12 May is not only important as a clear statement of Auckland's dilemma. It also contains his explanation of the change in his policy, the gradual shift from extreme caution to measured counter-action. The explanation lay in the growth of Russian interference in Afghanistan:

...We could scarcely, with prudence, allow this new and more formidable element of disorder and intrigue to be established, without opposition, on our frontiers. The extraordinary excitement which has been produced in the public mind, as well in the Punjaub as in Affghanistan, in consequence of the approach of the Persian power, is also a signal to us of the mischief which might arise, were that power to acquire a settled authority or influence over all the Affghan countries.

If Herat survived the siege, Auckland continued, Britain could help her to develop her defences (as Britain had helped Persia in the past) without contravening the Anglo-Persian Treaty. But then

Britain would have to decide what to do about Kandahar and Kabul:

...Herat having escaped, both might be expected to be profuse in their declarations of devotion to us. But Dost Mahomed Khan has shown himself to be so disaffected and ambitious, that with him, at least, we could form no satisfactory connection. Although he might not, under such circumstances, furnish us with grounds for measures of direct hostility against him, he must yet be regarded as a person of more than equivocal feelings, occupying a position in which it is of the first importance to the tranquillity of our territories that we should have assured friends...

Auckland then expressed the fear that Herat would fall, thus allowing Persian influence to advance towards India. It might perhaps prove best to prevent this from happening:

...One thing is to my mind very certain, that we ought not to suffer Persian and Russian influence quietly to fix themselves along our entire western frontier, and that it is, in fairness, open to us to take the high ground with Persia of her whole demeanour having lately been estranged and unfriendly to the British nation; of her schemes in Affghanistan being in the universal belief combined with designs of aggression upon India; and of her advance, therefore, in the mere lust of conquest to a position which would enable her to take up a threatening attitude towards our Indian possessions, being a measure not merely of attack on the Affghan independence, with which we might be restricted by treaty from interfering, but one injurious, in intention and in effect, to ourselves, which we are warranted in repelling by all means in our power. Other circumstances may occur to strengthen further this language of direct and open opposition to Persia, as for instance, if satisfaction be not afforded to our government for the insults offered to Mr McNeill's gholam; insults which the Persian government has attempted to justify.

By this time Auckland had reached a decision in principle. Intervention of some kind beyond the Indus was now indispensable. To confine his defensive measures to the line of the Indus, leaving Afghanistan to its fate, would be to admit 'absolute defeat'. There were therefore two possibilities: either to give aid to the 'existing chiefships of Cabul and Candahar', or to 'permit or to encourage the advance of Runjeet Singh's armies upon Cabul, under counsel and restriction, and as a subsidiary to his advance to organise an expedition headed by Shah Shoojah'. It is to be noticed, at this stage, that Auckland was still reluctant even to consider unleashing his own army of British and Indian regiments. Of the two possibilities it is clear, from previous evidence, that he must favour the second. To give aid to Kabul and Kandahar 'would be only to give power to those who feel greater animosity against the Sikhs than they do against the Persians, and who would probably use against the former the means placed at their disposal...', whereas the other course, 'which, in the event of the successful resistance of Herat would appear to be most expedient, would, if the state were to fall into the hands of the Persians, have yet more to recommend it...'.[53] Accordingly Auckland sent Macnaghten on a mission to Runjeet Singh, who was then at Adinanagar. He was to discuss with Runjeet Singh the possibility of joint intervention along the lines already mentioned, but he was not to appear to rule out the possibility of action by the Sikhs alone. Macnaghten had a very difficult task. He had to protect British interests by preparing for operations beyond the Indus, but at the same time he had to keep the Anglo-Sikh alliance intact. For instance, Runjeet Singh's claim to Shikarpur was only in abeyance, but Shikarpur was likely to become an important military base if and when the British launched Shuja and an army led by British officers into Afghanistan. Would Runjeet Singh see that the Persian and Russian threat made it necessary to overlook minor infringements of his laws of trespass ? Macnaghten would have to find out.

On 22 May Lord Auckland formally reported to the Secret Committee that Dost Muhammad had rejected British good offices and friendship, and that Burnes had consequently left Kabul at the end of April:

... It will be evident to your Honourable Committee, on perusal of the above document [his minute of 12 May] that the emergency of affairs may compel me to act without awaiting any intimation of your views upon the events which have recently occurred in Persia and Affghanistan. But it will still be most satisfactory to me to be placed at the earliest possible period in full possession of your general opinions and instructions. In anticipation of the possibility of such an emergency, I have deemed it expedient to put matters in train by previous negotiation, in order to render whatever measures of direct interference I may be obliged to adopt as effective as possible...

Then Auckland told the Secret Committee that the preliminary negotiation would include a proposal to revive and to bring up to date the treaty of 1833 between Runjeet Singh and Shah Shuja.

169

In a postscript he drew attention to Burnes's latest information from Kabul about the progress of Russian influence—to the

unequivocal demonstrations therein noted of the extent to which Russia is carrying her system of interference on the very threshold of the British-Indian possessions:

...I need not repeat my anxiety, even though the rapid march of events may oblige me to act without your instructions, to be favoured with a communication of your views upon the present crisis at the earliest possible opportunity.[54]

In fact he had to wait a few months longer for the moral support he needed. His was a very lonely eminence, but thanks to the fore-thought of his Cabinet colleagues in 1836 he had a reliable man in Persia—one who could be depended upon to interpret Palmerston's instructions correctly and even to anticipate them. Moreover, he could always fall back on the instructions issued in June 1836 for authority to intervene in Afghanistan.

Macnaghten took a fortnight to reach Adinanagar, which was about seventy miles north-east of Lahore. He arrived on the 30th and had his first audience with Runjeet Singh on the last day of May. Before leaving Simla Macnaghten had sent orders to Alexander Burnes to meet him at Adinanagar as soon as possible. Burnes received these orders at Peshawar on the 29th, and he was on his way within twenty-four hours. But Charles Masson had *not* been invited to Adinanagar. It is clear that Masson expected to be offered employment, if not promotion. Long afterwards he wrote:

...I consented to remain at Peshawar, because I had no wish to see any persons belonging to the government, for my opinions of many of them had long been made up; I also well knew that there were difficulties which Captain Burnes, perhaps, did not foresee, but which I suspected were not to be got over; moreover I had determined on the course to adopt, simply that of advancing no pretensions, but if still neglected, and kept in a position where I could not be useful, to clear myself from embarrassment by quitting a service which had long been disagreeable to me, and which I felt to be dishonourable besides. Captain Burnes had reasonable anxiety that his conduct in the late mission might be called into question. The French officers at Peshawar also expressed solicitude for him. He was soon relieved from any apprehension on that account...[55]

That short quotation tells us a great deal about Charles Masson. We know that he was not summoned to Adinanagar, and that he had no alternative but to stay in Peshawar. Yet he claimed to have 'consented' to stay there, and he wrote scornfully of his masters. He also hinted darkly at 'difficulties' which were not to be got over. It is strange that this man's personal bitterness, not to mention his disloyalty to his friends, has for so long discoloured the true picture of Alexander Burnes. We shall see later that 'persons belonging to the government', and Burnes himself, were a good deal fairer to him than he ever was to them. But, of course, his *Narrative of Various Journeys* was published in 1842 and 1843, when the Tories were in office and it was fashionable to despise Auckland and all who could be held responsible for the disasters of 1841. The passage quoted, incidentally, presents an excellent example of Masson's technique. He was far from the centre of power. He never gained the confidence of any official more senior than Wade or Burnes, but he knew just enough to be dangerous. The Tories made full use of him when their time came. Meanwhile there is irony in the fact that, although Auckland left it to Macnaghten to decide whether to summon Masson or leave him in Peshawar, he suggested to Macnaghten that Masson's views might help to correct any bias in Burnes, and that two other members of Burnes's Kabul mission might stay in Peshawar while Masson went to Adinanagar.[56] As it happened, Macnaghten had already decided to leave Masson where he was. But on 23 May he asked Burnes and Masson separately to send him their views as to the best means of counteracting Dost Muhammad's policy of alliance with the Persians and Russians. We shall see later that Auckland was very much impressed by Masson's memorandum, and that he praised it in a letter to Hobhouse. It is difficult to avoid the impression that Charles Masson was his own worst enemy.

We must now consider the Cabinet's view of the crisis in June 1838. Hobhouse caused the Secret Committee to send Auckland a copy of Palmerston's ultimatum of 21 May and copies of two dispatches which had reached the Foreign Office at the end of May. One was the dispatch already mentioned, from the British consul at Tabriz, saying that Simonich was on his way from Teheran to Herat under orders from St Petersburg. The other was from the British ambassador in Constantinople, reporting a conversation with the Persian ambassador to the Porte. The main point of that conversation was that the Persian ambassador urged the British Government to take strong action to make the Shah give up the

siege of Herat. At the same time the Secret Committee sent copies
of its letters to Auckland on these topics to John McNeill. Sometimes, as the old saying goes, a wink is as good as a nod. Hobhouse
was gradually preparing for his own decision, and at the beginning
of June he felt justified in presenting Auckland with further evidence of the need for vigorous action. On the 16th Palmerston told
McNeill that the Russian expedition towards Khiva and Bokhara
had been postponed. But two days later he received dispatches
from McNeill up to the middle of April, including a copy of what
McNeill had written to Auckland on 11 April. Palmerston immediately sent these to Hobhouse with a covering letter, saying:
'...It seems to me that we ought now to strike; non est jam leni-
tati locus; severitatem Res ipsa postulat.'[57]

That was written on 18 June. On the 22nd he told McNeill that
the Cabinet approved of every action that he had taken up to the
date of these dispatches. We therefore have proof that the Home
and Indian Governments were thinking along similar lines in June.
Auckland, though the 11 April dispatch from McNeill had not yet
reached him, was acting in conformity with it.

At this point we should note a circumstance which alarmed
Palmerston and his colleagues in June. They heard that the Pasha
of Egypt had announced his desire to be independent of the Porte.[58]
At that time the British Government was trying to secure access to
all the markets of the Ottoman Empire for British manufactures.
Muhammad Ali, even if he had had no other motive for wishing
to be independent of the Porte, would have wanted to break away
in order to escape this threat to his highly protected economy. But
he did have other motives, and it was clear that his challenge to the
Sultan might soon lead to war. On 7 July Palmerston told his
consul general in Egypt to warn Muhammad Ali that if war came
Britain would be on the Sultan's side.[59] Palmerston feared that the
Turkish armed forces would be defeated by the Egyptians, and
that the Russians would seize the opportunity to act as sole protector of the Sultan. Once they had garrisons in Constantinople
and control of the Dardanelles they would never leave. No one
who valued India could permit Russia to establish herself in
Turkey. Palmerston therefore began to prepare the ground for one
of his greatest diplomatic successes. He told Ponsonby at the Porte
in September that their object must be 'to merge the Treaty of
Unkiar Skelessi into some more general compact of the same

nature'.[60] Ponsonby had just concluded a commercial treaty with Turkey, securing permission to trade against a tariff of no more than 3 per cent in every country owing allegiance to the Sultan.[61] Britain therefore had commercial as well as strategic reasons for buttressing Sultan Mahmud's administration.

All this was clear to Palmerston and most of his colleagues in the summer of 1838. They were involved by Russian restlessness in two simultaneous Eastern crises. They knew it to be their duty to keep the peace in Europe. They must somehow defeat the Russians without openly offending the Emperor and his Government in St Petersburg. Palmerston saw how it could be done. He would try to make the great powers jointly responsible for the protection of the Sultan, since this was in their joint interest. But Russia was one of the great powers, and it would be necessary to coax her into joining the others and relinquishing the ambition to protect Turkey alone. There was all the more reason, then, why the crisis in Persia and Afghanistan should be handled with great diplomatic delicacy. The value of the interests at stake would fully justify a certain amount of deception. In the author's view, it was the British Government's determination to avoid European war at all costs that disguised the truth and doctored the record of events in Persia and Afghanistan in 1838. The disguise has hampered historians ever since.

CHAPTER 8

BRITISH INDIA PREPARES FOR WAR

...Shah Shooja's friends write 'the faggots are all laid, it requires
but the torch of the British government to light them...'.

AUCKLAND to Hobhouse, 17 June 1838

Once Burnes was safely back in the plain of Peshawar everything
depended upon John McNeill. Only he could exert influence at
Herat. While he was in the Shah's camp Simonich could not be
confident of success for the Emperor's policy in Central Asia.
McNeill struggled mightily throughout April and May to waken the
Shah to the dangers of his situation. Simonich struggled equally
hard to keep the Shah firm in his resolve to reduce Herat. Sometimes McNeill appeared to be making progress, but Simonich had
the advantage of being able to play upon the Shah's military ambition and lust for conquest. McNeill held on, waiting day after day
for word from Palmerston that he was right to quit the Shah's
court and camp. Towards the end of May, sensing that the conventional communications with India were no longer reliable, he
decided to send Captain D'Arcy Todd,[1] a member of the British
Military Mission in Persia, to India with dispatches for Lord
Auckland, including copies of what he had written in April. On
3 June he told the Persian Foreign Secretary that he had decided
to leave for the Turkish frontier as a sign of the British Government's displeasure.[2] He added that the Queen would not feel able
to receive any Persian envoy until the Persian Government had
given reparation and satisfaction for the insults suffered by the
British Mission. On the 7th he started his long journey across
Persia, leaving Simonich with a clear field. His responsibility lay
heavily upon him. He had not read a line from Auckland since the
end of December; he only knew the gist of a letter which Auckland
had sent in January but which had not reached him before he left
Teheran for Herat in March. He was still waiting for official instructions from Palmerston. All he knew was that the Cabinet in
London and the Governor General and his council in India placed
the fullest trust in his judgement and discretion. But such generous

trust gives little comfort to the man on the spot when the time comes to make a decision. If he makes the wrong decision his trusting superiors may open their eyes wide and say that they had expected better of him. McNeill could not know whether he had decided correctly in severing relations with the Persian Court. He thought about the problem long and hard during the journey from Herat to Meshed, and the result of his thoughts was a long dispatch to Palmerston (copied to Auckland), which he wrote on 25 June. His powerful arguments reached Palmerston on 24 August and Auckland on 20 August:

...What course the Persian Government will now pursue I know not; for it has sheltered itself behind an audacious denial of notorious facts, and has thus made it more difficult for itself to grant, at a future period, the reparation which has been demanded; but if it still desires to place itself in a better position with the British Government, I presume it will endeavour to exculpate itself by blaming me...Whatever course the Persian Government may adopt, some publick act of reparation, which will prove to the people of Persia and of Central Asia, that we are not with impunity to be bearded and insulted, is, in my opinion, indispensably necessary—I will not say to restore us to our former position—but to enable us to retain one of any credit or respectability. Both the Persians and the Affghans in the Shah's camp saw with amazement the Persian Government venturing to treat a British mission as a proscribed body, and punishing persons who ventured to hold even a casual intercourse with it; while some of the members of the Russian Mission took to task, and threatened to get punished for that offence, persons who occasionally visited at my tent, taking some precautions to prevent their being discovered. I feel, that by remaining so long as I did in such a position, I lost something in the estimation of all the Asiatics who witnessed the state of things; but I was determined not to precipitate anything...

McNeill thought that his departure would certainly have made the Shah uneasy, but he did not think it probable that the departure alone would be sufficient to bring the Shah and his ministers to their senses.

...Whatever may be the sentiments of Her Majesty's Government as to the manner in which I have acquitted myself of the task circumstances had imposed upon me, I most sincerely hope that such measures may be adopted in respect to Persia, as will check the obstinate folly of the Shah and his Minister, and force them not only to respect the British Government, but to abandon their mischievous schemes in Affghanistan, where, in concert with Russia, they are doing us infinite injury, and preparing the way for a state of things which will involve the Indian Government in endless expense and anxiety, even if it should not lead to a disturbance of the peace of Europe. I cannot divest myself of the conviction that if we do not seize the present opportunity to check the advance of Persia, and to close the door against her on the side of Affghanistan, we must prepare, at no distant time, to encounter both Persia and Russia in that country. Russia is now pressing on in these countries with an eagerness which of itself might serve to convince us that she has some extensive and important plans in contemplation; and Count Simonich's announcement of an expedition to Khiva and Bokhara, coupled with the proposition that Persia should prosecute her views of conquest in Affghanistan, and that these two Powers should ultimately adjust their frontier on that side, taken in connexion with the Russian Mission to Cabool and its objects, and also with the Candahar Treaty, certainly presents a sufficiently extensive outline, which is to be filled in hereafter, and a sufficiently alarming prospect for India...

McNeill's warning of the 'endless expense and anxiety' which would be caused in India by the success of Persian and Russian schemes in Central Asia irresistibly recalls the conversation between Wellington and Ellenborough on 16 December 1829 and Ellenborough's remark that he had made the 'Chairs' see the matter as 'a question of expense'. In other words, John McNeill was advising his Whig masters, who were predisposed to agree with him in any case, to maintain the policy laid down by the duke of Wellington and the Tory Government of 1828–30. In the next important section of the Meshed dispatch McNeill even echoed the instructions issued by Ellenborough in January 1830:

...If Persia should succeed in taking Herat, while Russia subdues Khiva, and overawes Bokhara into submission, I conceive that it would be hopeless for us to attempt to preserve a footing in Affghanistan or in Persia: both these countries, in short Central Asia, would be lost to us. But if we save Herat, and secure it, as it is now completely at our disposal, all Affghanistan will be tolerably secure behind it; and in that case, even if Russia should reduce Khiva, though it would no doubt be a great evil, we should still be in a strong and very tenable position, which would enable us to oppose Russian influence by our own in Bokhara, to cause Russia much uneasiness, and even to make her position precarious in Khiva; to influence the whole of the nomade tribes of the Oxus and its tributaries, and of the Tejend and Moorghab as far as Merve; and perhaps even to force Persia to balance between us and Russia...

In the passage just quoted, the author submits, the most important phrase is: 'if we save Herat, and secure it'. Britain must not only save Herat; she must also secure it against the possibility of future attack. McNeill immediately continued his Meshed dispatch by saying:

...It may perhaps be apprehended, that our taking so decided a course might hasten the advance of Russia to the east of the Caspian; but I apprehend Russia has decided on the course she has to pursue there, and that she is not likely to be deterred by any forbearance we may practise, from following it out. But if she gets a military footing in Khiva before we shall have rescued and secured Herat, we must then, as it appears to me, retire on the line of the Indus, and send out ten or fifteen thousand more European troops to India. But even after having taken this costly precaution, our position there will be most precarious when Russia and Persia are on the opposite bank of the river, intriguing with all the discontented far and near, and tampering with the Sikhs and Scindians, with the easiest and best pass into Scinde at their command...

Here the emphasis is not simply on saving and securing Herat, but rather on doing so *before* the Russians take Khiva. This sense of urgency led McNeill to exaggerate a little the ease with which a Russian or any other army might march from Georgia to Herat, Kandahar, 'or, as I believe, to the Indus'. He continued:

...Under such circumstances, it appears to me that it would be a most hazardous policy to allow Persia to act as the pioneer of Russia, and, under protection of the Article of the Treaty, to break down the main defence of Affghanistan, and thereby make the country untenable to us, at a moment when the concert between Persia and Russia in these operations is avowed; and when numerous circumstances tend to confirm the impression, that whether Persia is an accomplice or merely a tool, the design is to injure us; and the accomplishment of that design, as it appears to me, [is] only to be prevented by vigour and decision on the part of the British Government, or rather of the Government of India. I shall therefore urge Lord Auckland, by every argument I can call to mind, to take a decided course, and to save Herat, even by attacking Persia, if that should be necessary; but I presume that the occupation of Bushire would be sufficient for the purpose...

McNeill then proposed that the Government of India should send troops into southern Persia. We have to remember that he did not yet know of the failure of the Burnes mission, and that he was anxious to see some immediate counter-action. He was correct in assuming that the quickest way of frightening the Shah would be to land troops in southern Persia. Communications between Bombay and the ports on the Persian Gulf were good. But he saw other possibilities, as the following quotation shows:

...the state of things which the obstinate perversity of the Persians has brought about, may enable the British Government to act with more freedom and less compunction on the side of Affghanistan, where the Governor General could easily put in motion such means as would force the Shah to raise the siege almost immediately. But as these means, when once put in motion, are not easily controlled, I apprehend it would in every respect be more advantageous to employ British troops in the south of Persia; and though I must confess to the personal mortification I have experienced in having been unable to effect anything while in camp, your Lordship is aware that the possibility of such a result was not unforeseen by me; and I am not sure that it may not ultimately be more advantageous to the public service that the matter should have been brought to an issue, while there may yet be time to save Herat, than that it should have been left smouldering to break out after Herat should already have fallen...

In the closing paragraphs of his letter to Palmerston he retailed a rumour to the effect that Persia and Russia had secretly agreed on an exchange of territory, Persia receiving some of her lost territory on the western shore of the Caspian and the Russians receiving Herat. McNeill did not pay much attention to the rumour at first, but when he heard other reports he was less sceptical. For instance Simonich was said to have advised the Shah to turn his attention to Sind after the fall of Herat, and the Russians were said to be advancing on Khiva:

...I had the pleasure to receive, on the 13th instant...your Lordship's private letter of the 14th of April; and I sincerely hope that Her Majesty's Government has long ago come to the decision that it is necessary to force the Shah to return from Herat. In the meantime, I fear I have gone further than your Lordship may approve, in the language I have held to the Shah, though I have not gone far enough to divert him from his purpose, which he seems determined not to abandon till he actually feels our bayonets...[3]

The author has sometimes referred to this letter as a dispatch, and it might be argued that one should draw a clearer distinction between official dispatches and private letters. But it frequently happened in those days that the less formal of the two was the more influential. On 25 June McNeill had also sent a long official dispatch, giving a blow-by-blow account of his experiences in the Persian camp before Herat.[4] Palmerston had no compunction in scoring out the word 'Private' and publishing parts of the letter just quoted as an official document. What was published, even in its emasculated form, was clearly more compelling and influential than the official dispatch. In the author's view the Meshed letter or dispatch is one of the key documents in the history of the First Afghan War. It ranks with Aberdeen's comments on the Treaty of Adrianople, with Ellenborough's Secret Committee dispatch of January 1830, and with McNeill's own pamphlet on the *Progress and Present Position of Russia in the East*, and it repays close study.

At the end of June McNeill's courier was speeding towards the Mediterranean with the Meshed correspondence; other letters, together with copies of the letter and dispatch to Palmerston, were on their way to Auckland. McNeill himself slowly made his way towards the Turkish frontier. He felt tired and dispirited. But at the beginning of July he heard the first evidence of Auckland's 'agonising re-appraisal'. He heard that a small naval force had occupied the island of Kharg in the Persian Gulf on 19 June. The landing produced a moral effect out of all proportion to the actual strength of the force sent from Bombay. He now knew that Auckland was backing him up, and his spirits revived accordingly. On he travelled, pursued by a messenger carrying the Indian Government's announcement of the failure of Burnes's mission and the official confirmation of the expedition to Kharg. Let us leave McNeill for a while and return to Herat. As soon as McNeill had left, Simonich realized that he would have to work fast. The Shah now expected his Russian friends to work the miracle for him. His inefficient army had been investing Herat for six months without making the slightest progress. His only comfort was that eventually the besieged would have to surrender or starve. But how long could he maintain the shaky fighting spirit of his ragged army? He turned to Simonich and the Polish officer, Berowski, who commanded a battalion of Russian deserters. Together they worked out a plan of attack. They would breach the walls and take the place by storm. The Shah's artillery opened the bombardment early on the morning of 24 June. As soon as the Russians saw a negotiable breach they set the infantry in motion. Wave after wave of Persian soldiers advanced to the breach, only to be thrown back by the obstinate Heratis. Berowski was killed. Simonich watched and saw his influence trickling away with every furious and unsuccessful assault. Inside the city Kamran's Minister, Yar Muhammad, had the help of Lieutenant Eldred Pottinger of the Bombay Artillery. This officer, a nephew of the Henry Pottinger who has figured prominently in previous chapters, had volunteered to make himself discreetly useful in Afghanistan during 1837, and he was already well established in Herat when the siege opened. Yar Muhammad lavishly praised him when the siege was over, as McNeill did, thus starting a legend of the kind which later made T. E. Lawrence the only hero of the Arab Revolt. Eldred Pottinger certainly made himself useful, especially during the crisis of 24 June, but he himself never claimed to have been responsible for saving the city. Auckland, with his usual clarity and good sense, later thanked Eldred Pottinger as one 'who, under circumstances of peculiar danger and difficulty, had by his fortitude, ability and judgement, honourably sustained the reputation and interests of his country'. His presence had helped to keep morale high in the beleagured city; his courage and confidence were infectious; and his technical knowledge as a gunner officer made him useful to his hosts. Like Burnes he started his career to the accompaniment of loud applause and ended it in embarrassed silence. His proper place in history is somewhere between the two extremes—roughly where Lord Auckland placed him at the time.

By nightfall on Sunday 24 June 1838 the Shah knew that he was beaten, at least for the time being, and Simonich knew that the tide was beginning to turn against him. The siege continued, or rather dragged on, throughout that summer, but the Shah's old enthusiasm was gone. It was fear of losing face that kept him there, obstinately battering at the city walls. The British had no way of knowing this at the end of June. What they saw was a concerted Persian and Russian advance in Central Asia with the express purpose of inflicting the greatest possible damage on British interests, whether commercial or political. William Macnaghten, therefore, was deep in negotiation with the Sikhs throughout the month of June. He had arrived at Adinanagar at the end of May with a draft treaty in his pocket, and with instructions to be very tactful towards Maharajah Runjeet Singh:

...Lord Auckland would prefer Roree to Shikarpore as a military post for any troops that we may send in that direction, and would of course the rather prefer it if the place be the most acceptable of the two to Runjeet Singh. But he would wish that there should not be the least appearance of our evading or mystifying our own views about Shikarpore and the right bank of the Indus. The Treaty of 1809 was a treaty for partition of Sikhs, not of Sindians, and this may be maintained with good humour, when necessary, while we are willing to avoid the appearance of occupying Shikarpore, should our not doing so be an object to Runjeet...[5]

It was always necessary to tread carefully in official dealings with the Sikhs. Those who have criticized Auckland for undue delicacy have never asked themselves, it appears, what risks he was running. If he offended Runjeet Singh he would not be able to cross the Indus and deal with the Persian and Russian advance. If, having offended Runjeet Singh, he tried to cross the Indus, he would have to fight the Sikhs. No one would have been more gratified than the Emperor Nicholas to see the British and the Sikhs fighting in 1838. Had it not been for Auckland's consistently sensible advice, the year might have ended very differently.

Auckland and Macnaghten made a good team. They complemented each other. Macnaghten was all for pressing on and taking risks; Auckland preferred to wait and prepare and then to act with vigour and decision. At the end of May Macnaghten suggested that he should immediately tell Runjeet Singh 'that we have made up our minds to support Shah Shooja and start him on his expedition'.[6] Auckland replied to Macnaghten:

...It may be well by opposing our troubles to end them, but it may be well too to consider whether we are not flying to others that we know not of...

Auckland warned Macnaghten against being over-confident in assessing Shuja's chances of success:

...Not less than three months must pass before he could collect a force sufficient for him to move with—six months will have elapsed before he can be at Candahar, eight or nine before he can reach Cabool, and in the meantime what may not have been done to counteract him?

I must say that the best reflection which in the hurry of business I can give to the contents of your letter is that our ignorance of what is passing in the Persian Camp, that the obscure responsibility of the Government here in regard to Persia and to European politics, and that the measure which I take of the hazards to be incurred, would lead me much rather

to stand still as nearly as circumstances will allow me to do so than *at
once* to take the plunge to which you would urge me...

Of course Auckland was not the only one who was nervous. Like
McNeill at Herat, Auckland and Macnaghten were under great
strain. What worried Auckland at the beginning of June was a
report that Runjeet Singh was thinking only of his own interests
and hoping to use Shuja for his own ends. Auckland was depressed
and frustrated. He told Macnaghten that it might be better to let
Runjeet have his head on the side of Kabul (without Shuja), and to
tell him that Persian advances might cause Britain to send a force
to the shores of the Indus as a first measure of defence:

...whether upon this may not also be grafted the adoption of Shah
Shoojah and of his claims to the Throne of Cabool must become matter
for future discussion and consideration as events may be further
developed and information be obtained. I must prefer this course to one
which might combine all Sikh feeling against us, and which might at
once pledge honour and strength and finance to the I think uncertain
cause of Shah Shoojah in a war, to be carried on 600 miles from our
frontier. To this consummation we may have to come at last, but I
would at least see my way more clearly than I do at present before I
venture onwards...[7]

One can well understand Auckland's reaction. He was clearly
disappointed to find his right-hand man proposing a foolhardy,
because unprepared, expedition with Shuja and without the Sikhs,
which might easily lead Britain into a war with the Punjab. But, as
it turned out, the reports about Runjeet's attitude were unnecessarily pessimistic. On Sunday 3 June Macnaghten and Runjeet
Singh settled down to business. Without any hesitation Runjeet
opted for joint action, and the following dialogue ensued:

MACNAGHTEN   Your Highness some time ago formed a treaty with
Shah Shoojah ool Moolk; do you think it would still be for your
benefit that that treaty should stand good, and would it be agreeable
to your wishes that the British Government become a party to that
treaty?

RUNJEET   This would be adding sugar to milk.

MACNAGHTEN   If such be decidedly the wish of your Highness, I do
not think that the Governor General would object to supplying Shah
Shoojah with money and officers, to enable him to recover his throne.

Then Macnaghten explained that the force under Shuja might
go by way of Kandahar while the Sikhs moved on Kabul, accom-

panied by one or two British officers to maintain liaison with Shuja's army and to co-ordinate the movements of the two armies. Runjeet assented to all this. Macnaghten tentatively raised the sensitive question of British military movements along the Indus. His Highness must not think that the British covet territory. Of course not, Runjeet Singh replied. Macnaghten though it best not to attempt too much at the first session and so he made no mention of Shikarpur.[8] He was feeling very pleased with himself when Auckland's letter of 1 June arrived and made him feel slighted. It took them nearly a fortnight to get back to normal working relations. But Auckland was pleased and relieved to see that Runjeet Singh was prepared to co-operate. He was less pleased by the sulky tone of Burnes's letters from Peshawar. Burnes *would* harp on the government's delay in dealing with Dost Muhammad's proposals for a settlement of his claim to Peshawar territories. What Burnes did not know was that Auckland had already formed a very high opinion of his abilities, and was by no means disposed to hold an inquest on his failure at Kabul. Burnes need not be 'sore and dispirited', for 'he has done his best with zeal and ability...'. Auckland made that remark in the course of a letter to Macnaghten, graciously making amends for his rather gruff letter of 1 June, and adding:

...When once the determination is made I shall be with you, for promptitude of action and perhaps even for greater promptitude of action than you may be, for if indeed the faggots are ready and only want the lighting I should doubt upon the policy of making Cabul wait upon Candahar...[9]

The faggots that awaited the lighting were a symbol for the support which awaited Shuja in Afghanistan according to Macnaghten and his informants. At the end of May Macnaghten had asked certain of his political officers to state their views as to the best method of counter-acting the policy of Dost Muhammad Khan towards Persia and Russia. By the time Burnes replied, on 2 June, he had recovered his composure. After recommending the Governor General to remonstrate with the Shah of Persia he considered the project which was at that moment the subject of negotiation with Runjeet Singh. He was the first to tell Auckland (through Macnaghten) that 'to ensure complete success to the plan, the British Government must appear directly in it; that is, it must

not be left to the Sikhs themselves'. To leave the project entirely to
Runjeet Singh would be to alienate an Afghan opinion which was
cordially disposed towards the British. Burnes agreed with Masson
that Shuja could easily recover his throne now that Dost Muhammad had gone over to the Persians, who were hated in Afghanistan.
With plenty of money, avowed British support, and the backing of
a few British and Punjabi Muslim regiments, Shuja could get his
throne back in a couple of months:

...It is, however, to be remembered always that we must appear directly,
for the Afghans are a superstitious people, and believe Soojah to have
no fortune; but our name will invest him with it.

Then Burnes argued in favour of having a united Afghanistan:

...Divide et Impera is a temporising creed at any time; and if the
Afghans are united, we and they bid defiance to Persia, and instead of
distant relations, we have everything under our eye, and a steadily
progressing influence all along the Indus...

Out of loyalty to his old friend Dost Muhammad he ended by
making one more plea for British support for the Emir. But he must
have known that there was no longer the slightest chance of winning Auckland's consent to such a change of policy. The fact that
he made the plea at all in the circumstances reflects nothing but
credit on him. It was his duty to go along with the new policy, but
he also recognized a duty to speak for an unfortunate friend:

...He is a man of undoubted ability, and has at heart high opinions of
the British nation; and if half you must do for others were done fo
him, and offers made which he could see conduced to his interests, he
would abandon Persia and Russia tomorrow. It may be said that that
opportunity has been given to him; but I would rather discuss this in
person with you, for I think there is much to be said for him. Government have admitted that at best he had but a choice of difficulties; and it
should not be forgotten that we promised nothing, and Persia and Russia
held out a great deal...[10]

What Burnes said about the restoration of Shuja was an opinion
shared by Wade, Mackeson (agent for navigation on the Indus),
and Masson. They all thought, and they all told their Government,
that Shuja could easily get his throne back. Masson assured his
Government that Shuja was very popular in Afghanistan:

...If he avowedly advanced under British auspices his success would be
prompt and certain, little or no blood would be shed—he would be

joined by all who are discontented with the Barakzai rule, and who is there that is not discontented?...Another advantage attending the case of Shah Sujah is that the British Government could support him, to any extent consistent with its own ideas or scruples, without exciting the least jealousy among the Afghans...[11]

Earlier in this story there was a reference to Masson's embittered reaction to being left at Peshawar. Auckland sent the letter just quoted to Hobhouse, and pencilled a note on its cover: 'This... gives, I think, very much the clearest view of the state of parties and politics in Afghanistan.'

Burnes, Masson, Mackeson and Wade—the men who had been closest to the crisis—all agreed that Shuja could get his throne back with ease. Masson even asserted that Shuja was very popular. It is important to remember that Auckland learned all this in the middle of June. Meanwhile Macnaghten was continuing his negotiation with Runjeet. It would be tedious to enter into the details of his talks with the Maharajah. It is enough to say that Macnaghten brought matters to a conclusion on the 26th, having successfully fended off an attempt to provide for the annexation of Shikarpur and Jalalabad by the Sikhs. From the first it had been intended that Shuja should extract one global payment of tribute from Sind in return for his renunciation of sovereignty over the territory of the emirs. Part of this large sum would go to Runjeet. In the middle of the month Colvin had to write to Henry Pottinger, asking him to find out how much the emirs had in their treasury, and to state what he considered to be a 'just composition' for Shuja's claims of sovereignty.[12] This is how Auckland expressed his dilemma to the Governor of Bombay on 15 June:

...I have nothing from McNeill later than the 7th of March—Nothing from Herat later than the 23rd and no instructions from home upon Persian affairs, or anything to guide me from thence except what can be collected from private letters—All this embarrasses me, for in the absence of information and instructions it is not easy for me to take a decided step, and yet I may be forced to take one, for in the pressure of events I cannot stand still. If Runjeet Singh will in the fear of Afghan and Persian irruption, connect himself in close alliance with us, if he will adopt the cause of Shah Shooja on the side of Cabul, allowing him to fight his own battles with British officers on the side of Candahar—If the integrity of Sinde can be permanently secured against the claims of Afghanistan and Lahore upon the payment of a reasonable sum—If the

Afghans should be disposed to accept Shah Shooja and the promise be opened to me of the establishment of a friendly power in Cabool and Candahar, it will be difficult for me to stop, and such is the tendency of my present negotiation with Runjeet Singh. He has received Macnaghten with cordiality, he has discussed all these objects with minuteness, he has advanced unreasonable pretensions and withdrawn them when told that they were unreasonable, and I am daily expecting propositions upon which I must pronounce an aye or no...[13]

Two days later Auckland wrote a similar letter to Hobhouse, equally lamenting his lack of reliable information, and also stating the advantages of the scheme proposed:

...The success of the scheme proposed would fix British influence in Afghanistan, and secure peace on the side of Sinde, and confirm friendship with Lahore, and occupy Sikh armies—but the scheme may fail. Yet Shah Shooja's friends write 'the faggots are all laid, it requires but the torch of the British Government to light them...'.[14]

Auckland was extremely careful with his torch. He continued to watch and wait, and he drew up a letter to the Commander in Chief, directing the addition of ten men to each company of the Bengal and Bombay armies.[15] But he kept the letter on his desk until he was quite sure of his ground. The negotiations at Lahore (Runjeet having moved there from Adinanagar earlier in the month) were drawing to an end when Burnes arrived from Peshawar on 17 June. Macnaghten immediately started to bombard him with questions about Afghan politics, and elicited much useful information: that Dost Muhammad had made many enemies by going over to Persia, thus contributing materially to Shuja's success; that Dost Muhammad ought to be offered the chance of working as a minister at Shuja's court, since he would be a 'dangerous antagonist' if he escaped to Persia; that the Sind emirs would be getting their 'manumission cheap at 20 lakhs of rupees' (£200,000 in 1838); that Shuja could expect, with increasing commerce, an annual income of up to 40 lakhs a year from Kabul, Kandahar and 'the hill states around'; that the presence of one or more of the Company's regiments with Shuja would be useful for prestige but not essential for success; that the whole project might fail if the Sikhs were allowed to play too big a part in the eastern sector. At first Burnes argued in favour of sending Shuja to Kabul by way of Peshawar, relying more on political agitation than on physical force, but under cross examination by Macnaghten he withdrew the suggestion and realized that Runjeet Singh would not like to see Shuja advancing through Sikh possessions unless under Sikh management. Burnes agreed with Macnaghten that operations on the side of Peshawar ought to be little more than a demonstration. But quite the most penetrating observation made by Burnes in those first few days at Lahore was this:

...it need hardly be remarked, I suppose, that the more promptly we set about compassing our ends the greater is the chance of success. Every day's delay is fraught with manifest disadvantages, for we may have to use our own army instead of that of our ally of Cabool, if we allow the plans beyond the Indus to ripen.[16]

Burnes proved to be right in this. Indeed, it would be possible to work out a mathematical formula correlating the number of days elapsed (between deciding to support Shuja and actually launching him on his way) with the number of men of the Indian army planned and eventually employed in the operations. Burnes's memorandum and his answers to questions greatly assisted the Government in the making of decision, and they proved that Burnes was by now completely absorbed in the new policy. Auckland took comfort from Burnes's attitude. He told Hobhouse:

...Burnes's letter [of 2 June] is a long one and I have not time to have it copied for you, but I have given you what is most material, and he is a good witness on this occasion, for his inclination is in favour, notwithstanding all that has pass'd, of Dost Mahommed...[17]

On 21 June Auckland's letter about the additions to the strength of the army was still on his desk, but he wrote that day to his Commander in Chief and warned him that if the negotiations at Lahore were successful 'it seems probable that they may demand a readiness of preparation and a demonstration of military strength on the banks of the Sutlej or even of the Indus'. In this letter he made the first of many references to the effect of events beyond the Indus on Indian public opinion, effects which 'are already felt, in the feverish speculations to which this Country is so alive and of which there are many ready to take advantage against us'.[18] Later in 1838 Auckland's anxiety on this score played a big part in helping him to his final decision. Another letter written on 21 June, this time by Burnes, throws light on contemporary British attitudes to Sind and on Masson's subsequent innuendoes. Burnes told Masson that the Sind 'orange is to be squeezed—how much I know not, but very much, I hope'. He also said: '...I have had the satisfaction of being told that I was sent to do impossible things at Cabool, so all my labour that did not succeed was not expected to succeed! Politics are a queer science...'[19]

Burnes was not always careful in his choice of words, and a sinister construction could be put on what he said to Masson, but he was only saying what we know already, that Auckland was never very sanguine of his chances of success. One should not be too hard on Masson, though he has done great damage to the reputation of better men. It is possible that his enemy in the Indian Government was Macnaghten, and that he had some reason for bitterness. But Auckland thought well of him: '...I hear that Mr Masson is feeling some anxiety in regard to his situation and we must take care not to forget him in our arrangements, for he deserves well...'[20]

Towards the end of June Auckland began to get worried about Runjeet Singh's delaying tactics. Runjeet seemed to be waiting for news of the fate of Herat before committing himself. Auckland went so far as to authorize Macnaghten to give up and return home if he felt that Runjeet Singh was being unreasonable. But the mood did not last long, and Auckland heard on 3 July that Macnaghten and Runjeet had signed the draft treaty at last. He wrote to one of his council members in Calcutta about the agreement:

...The settlement of all matters of discussion with Lahore, the admitted independence of Sinde, and an avowed union between the British Government and that of Lahore and Afghanistan cannot but have a good effect upon Eastern as well as Western politics. But for all this, Shah Shooja must succeed, and with British support, and to this we must next apply ourselves...[21]

Let us now look at the treaty which Runjeet Singh accepted on 26 June. The concession that finally persuaded Runjeet to sign was an additional clause providing for a disguised Afghan tribute to the Sikhs of two lakhs a year (£20,000). There were eighteen articles:

(i) Shuja would abandon all claim to territories held by Runjeet Singh on either side of the Indus, from Multan in the south to Kashmir in the north;
(ii) The people of the Khyber Pass would keep the peace;
(iii) No one would be allowed to cross the Indus in Runjeet's territories without a passport issued by his Government;

(iv) Runjeet Singh would abide by a settlement of the Sikh claim to Shikarpur;

(v) Once established in Kabul and Kandahar Shah Shuja would annually send gifts to Runjeet Singh, including 'fifty five high bred horses of approved colour and pleasant paces, eleven Persian cimeters, seven Persian poniards...' and so on;

(vi) Each party would address the other in terms of equality;

(vii) Afghan merchants in the Punjab would not be molested;

(viii) Runjeet Singh's annual gifts to Shuja would include 'fifty-five pieces of shawls...';

(ix) Officers sent to one side or the other for the purchase of horses (for instance) would be treated with due attention;

(x) No kine would be slaughtered when armies of the two states were assembled together;

(xi) Any booty would be shared;

(xii) The two states would constantly exchange missions with letters and presents;

(xiii) If one side should need military aid from the other, the force sent would have a senior officer at its head. Any Sikh auxiliary force would be composed of Muslims;

(xiv) The friends and enemies of each of the three powers would be the friends and enemies of all;

(xv) Shuja would abandon his claim to supremacy in and tribute from Sind in return for 'such sum as may be determined under the mediation of the British Government...';

(xvi) Shuja would pay two lakhs a year to Runjeet Singh for the maintenance of 5,000 troops in the Peshawar area, to be sent to his aid whenever needed;

(xvii) Shuja would neither attack nor molest his nephew the ruler of Herat;

(xviii) Shuja would not enter into any negotiations with foreign powers without the knowledge and consent of Britain and the Punjab; he would 'oppose any power having the design to invade the British and Sikh territories by force of arms, to the utmost of his ability'.[22]

In the preamble to this treaty it was stated that Runjeet Singh and Shah Shuja had entered into relations of friendship and alliance 'with the approbation of, and in concert with, the British Government'. Auckland had reason to be pleased with the neatness of the proposed settlement. He would have welcomed a little moral support from London at that stage, but, as we have already noted, the Cabinet as a whole was slow to understand the full implications of what was happening in Persia and Afghanistan before the second

half of May. Auckland said he was disgusted with the dispatches
and letters which reached him from England at a critical moment.
He was depressed by the complacency and obtuseness, as he
thought, of his colleagues in London. Colvin told Macnaghten that
a private letter from Hobhouse to Auckland (the one written in the
light of Sheil's letter to Palmerston) contained 'some very shallow
trifling...on our occupying Bushire and raising an insurrection in
the Southern Provinces of Persia. But not a word is there of public
instruction or opinion upon either Persian or Afghan politics...'²³

Hobhouse was far from popular in Simla at the beginning of
July, and not only because he was slow to issue instructions for
Auckland's guidance in a difficult crisis. He had declared his disapproval of one of Auckland's pet schemes, the new treaty with the
state of Oude. Auckland minuted:

...We are, on the one hand, positively interdicted from forming without
previous reference to England any new Treaty with any native Power
stipulating for the employment of British officers in the service of such
power. On the other we are anxiously engaged in concerting defensive
arrangements against hostile combination from without and the outbreak of restless and disorderly feeling in the heart of India...

This disappointing prohibition had come at a time, as Auckland
put it, when

...hostile influences, under the guidance of our powerful and vigilant
European rival, are predominant along the whole of the Western border
of India—while the means of injury and offence possessed by our Sikh
neighbours are daily growing, and their future prospects are full of the
presage of division and disturbance—while the formidable resources of
Nepal are ready to be thrown into the scale against us, and the leaders
of that state are almost openly seeking the occasion of arranging themselves in opposition to our supremacy—while in the centre of our Power
we have to guard against the revival of old habits of licence among a
people prone to disorder and impatient of their long and only partial
subjection—and while in the Eastern extremity of our possessions we
have before us the impending hazard of a costly war.

I would not exaggerate these dangers and we have, I trust, as it is, the
wherewithall to cope with them. But we are bound to look seriously to
our present and to the necessities which are rapidly accumulating upon
us, and I have said, I trust, sufficient to justify me in pausing before I
pronounce any opinion upon the course which, on a consideration of
these Despatches, it will be for my own honour, for the honour of the

Government, and for the good of the Empire, most becoming to adopt...[24]

The minute just quoted conveniently introduces a factor in the Indian crisis of 1838 which has received little attention in the past —that Nepal and Ava were also on the brink of war with Britain, and that the rumours of Persian and Russian advances in the north-west were already causing restless speculation throughout India. Auckland kept his head throughout this multiple crisis, and he rightly judged that the threat from the north-west had to be countered first of all. At the end of June and during the first week of July he issued his order for an increase in the strength of the Bengal and Bombay armies, and he was glad to receive from his Commander in Chief an understanding and positively co-operative letter. Fane, the man now famous for his remark about leaving alone the north-west, volunteered to lead the army which would reinstate Shuja in Kabul, even though his resignation on the ground of ill health had already been sent to the Horse Guards. Another volunteer at this stage was Macnaghten himself. Sir Auckland Colvin, the author of the first attempt to vindicate Auckland and his staff, claimed to have found proof that Macnaghten did not propose himself as envoy to Shuja's court, but he was wrong. On 1 July Auckland addressed him as follows:

...I will consider about officers, and for your last public spirited offer I can only thank you at present. I should with much unwillingness have you at a distance from me, but if it should be for good, I would, as you would, make the sacrifice...[25]

The letter to which Auckland Colvin referred as evidence that Macnaghten did not propose himself was written on 12 July. The writer was Auckland Colvin's father, Auckland's private secretary:

...It is right to let you know that a strong feeling is growing here that it will be most desirable for the public interests at whatever sacrifice to the daily care and satisfaction of Lord Auckland's administration that you should assume the diplomatic direction of Shah Shooja's expedition. The stake is so important that Lord Auckland feels that it may not become him to withhold his best card. Colonel Pottinger might in some respects do well. But...

In those flattering terms Macnaghten heard that he would have direct political control (under Auckland) of the operations carried out in execution of his Tripartite Treaty. Now the only reason for reviving this sad topic is that Masson and others made the selection of Macnaghten for the job sound like a sordid affair. The evidence of the letters is that Macnaghten indeed volunteered to go with Shuja if Auckland considered it necessary, but that he also put forward Colonel Pottinger as a candidate. Auckland considered Macnaghten the best available man for the post; he alone had the necessary influence and authority. When he volunteered, Macnaghten did not automatically assume that he would be appointed. Colvin even used a certain amount of persuasion: '... Think over this and let me be aware as fully as you like of your own opinions and inclinations. It will be a great enterprise in which a splendid reputation may be achieved...'

In the view of Auckland and his staff the success of the whole project might well depend upon the calibre of the man sent as envoy to Shuja and upon the quality of the troops sent beyond the Indus. Colvin, having tempted Macnaghten with prospects of achieving a 'splendid reputation', immediately raised the question of sending British troops to Afghanistan as well as the army to be recruited by Shah Shuja. When Colvin said 'British troops', of course he meant both Queen's and Company's regiments, sepoys and regular soldiers from England:

... The propriety of sending as many say as 5,000 of British troops with the Shah is beginning to be much admitted. They may be the cheapest as well as the most efficient, for as we must pay all and we have our own troops to pay at all events, it will apparently be the saving course to send them, instead of a huge rabble of raw levies got together at much cost and not to be depended on. Shah Shooja must of course have troops of his own, but by employing our own the amount of his force may be much and very usefully diminished...[26]

We have seen that Auckland thought of adding ten men to each infantry company in his army as early as the middle of June. At the beginning of July he received a letter from Henry Thoby Prinsep, one of his senior officials in Calcutta. Prinsep, always inclined to be rather contrary and censorious, was alarmed at the prospect of an expedition beyond the Indus. He could not see the wisdom of sending Shuja without British troops. Auckland replied on 8 July:

... With regard to Shah Shooja the reputation of failures and perhaps of personal character is in some degree against him. On the other hand the authority of Wade, Mackeson, Burnes and Masson are [sic] in his favour, and whatever weight of authority may be derived from local experience seems to admit of no other chief of a party who could be put in competition with him. Indeed no doubt is entertained of an easy and immediate success with the mere sound of his name and money. I wish that I had a perfect confidence of this being the case, but we shall see. It had already occurred as well to the Commander in Chief as to me that my escort at Ferozepore may be made army enough for any purpose. You will see by the latter part of Macnaghten's correspondence that what Runjeet Singh would most dislike is a British Army acting with him or with Shah Shooja in Peshawar. It was thrown in as a diplomatic argument that the brunt of the battle would be borne by the Sikh army and the brows raised exceedingly when it was proposed that a British Army should assist. Whatever we send of organised force must go by way of Candahar, and in the first instance I presume to Shikarpore...[27]

Those were not the words of a weak-willed figurehead. They show his characteristic style of argument: Shuja has an uncertain reputation, but the experts say that he is the only man for the task. Auckland leaves the question open, and takes the precaution of seeing that his escort on the occasion of his state visit to Runjeet Singh will be big enough 'for any purpose'. Moreover, as other letters show, Auckland at this time was on the best of terms with Sir Henry Fane. They agreed that it would be prudent to back up Shuja with some disciplined troops. In any case, and we should never forget this, they had to consider the possibility of marching to the relief of Herat. If there was any doubt about it on the 8th it was removed very soon, for on the 12th D'Arcy Todd's news of Herat reached Simla ahead of him. The news came in the form of a letter to Burnes from Todd, and it contained these words: 'A force of three or four thousand men would have obliged his Majesty to raise the siege. The *slightest* demonstration on *our* part in the Persian Gulph would have had the same effect.'[28]

It is not surprising to observe that Colvin's letter to Macnaghten about the advantage of sending British troops with Shuja was written within hours of the arrival of Todd's news from McNeill. Auckland had written to Hobhouse on the 10th:

...Macnaghten is to see Shah Shuja on his return to me and I will then discuss the treaty with him and sign or treat again. But I am not disposed to be fastidious—time is in the present posture of affairs more precious than anything else and I must go onward myself or allow intrigue and hostile influence and ultimately power to come onwards upon me...I have nothing yet directly from Herat or from McNeill or of instruction from you in regard to Persia, but I am well determined that none of the consideration towards that country which would have withheld me some months ago, shall withhold me now. All that I want is a clear field of action before me, and a fair prospect of success, and no exertion shall be wanting on my part to ensure it. You will have received my letter to the Commander in Chief and his answer to it, which was less full than I had hoped—but I have since had much cordial and confidential communication with him and he is even ready to volunteer a march to Candahar...[29]

Colvin summed up the news received from Todd on the 12th as highly interesting and important information. There was nothing in it to interrupt Auckland's measures, and there was much 'to induce only a greater promptitude and vigour in entering upon that course...'. A dispatch had just come in from the Secret Committee at last. This was the one already quoted in chapter 7, giving Auckland discretion to 'adopt such measures as may seem to you to be expedient to meet the contingency of the cessation of our relations with the Court of Persia'. Colvin said that the dispatch was admirably brief and vague.[30] Auckland again wrote to Hobhouse on the 12th, telling him that he might assume it 'for next to certain' that the plan would go forward.[31]

The remainder of July was taken up with treaty matters, as Macnaghten sought Shuja's consent and Runjeet Singh's final signature. Shuja gave little trouble but insisted firmly on his rights as monarch.[32] The British must not interfere in his country's internal affairs without his approval and concurrence. After obtaining Shuja's signature on 16 July Macnaghten took the treaty to Auckland, who had just received the Secret Committee's May dispatch. Auckland judged that that dispatch, with its warning against premature action in Afghanistan, was made out of date by the latest news from Herat and McNeill. Macnaghten laid the Tripartite Treaty before the Governor General on the 19th, and Runjeet Singh ratified it on the 23rd. By the 26th it was possible to send copies to McNeill and Pottinger, among others. The Sind emirs, if they had not already heard the news from agents, had a shock coming to them. Only a few months after accepting a British Resident at Hyderabad, they were being asked to dig into their treasure chests to buy an independence which they thought they had already won. They were also being asked to allow military stores on their river and a subsidiary British force on their territory, though the treaty of April 1838 had forbidden both. This was

Auckland at his most ruthless. But he had no choice. To save Afghanistan from Persia and Russia his army had to pass through Sind. There was no time for the protracted negotiating technique of the Sind emirs. In any case, Auckland argued, everything that was planned was in their interest, as well as Britain's.

Burnes arrived at Simla with Macnaghten and paid his respects to Lord Auckland on Friday 20 July. They had not met since 1834, when Burnes was in England. Burnes knew that Auckland had a high opinion of him, and he was an ambitious young man, as he revealed in a letter written to one of his brothers on 22 July:

...We are now planning a grand campaign to restore the Shah to the throne of Caubul—Russia having come down upon us. What exact part I am to play I know not, but if full confidence and hourly consultation be any pledge, I am to be chief. I can plainly tell them that it is aut Caesar aut nullus, and if I get not what I have a right to, you will soon see me en route to England...[33]

Poor Alexander Burnes! Great abilities and talents, widely recognized and appreciated, not least by Auckland, were marred by a lack of humility which led him, in private letters, to exaggerate his own importance. There is a parallel between the situation described above and the interview with Lord Ellenborough described in chapter 4. He was not ready in 1835 to tackle the responsibility of being Minister in Teheran, and he was not ready in 1838 to take political charge of the expedition into Afghanistan. But he thought he was ready, and he was bitterly disappointed when his superiors failed to agree with him. He was in too much of a hurry. So it was that on 29 July he applied to Auckland for long leave; he could not be Caesar, for that role was reserved for Macnaghten, and he therefore resolved to have no part in the campaign. Auckland was shocked. Within twenty-four hours he had persuaded Burnes to withdraw the application. According to Burnes the Commander in Chief, Sir Henry Fane, wanted to command the expedition and take Burnes with him as chief political officer,

...but this will not be, and I believe the chief and Macnaghten will be made a commission—Wade and myself political agents under them. I plainly told Lord Auckland that this does not please, and I am disappointed. He replied that I could scarcely be appointed with the chief in equality, and pledged himself to leave me independent quickly, and in the highest appointment! What can I do when he tells me I am a man he cannot spare? It is an honour, not a disgrace, to go under Sir Henry; and as for Macnaghten, he is secretary for all India, and goes pro tem. Besides, I am not sorry to see Dost Mahomed ousted by another hand than mine...[34]

This fragment, preserved by Kaye, tells us much about our principal characters in a few lines. Sir Henry Fane, if Burnes's account is accurate, did not want a political officer equal in rank to him. Auckland, however, wanted the military and political chiefs to be of equal rank. He had no senior officer with sufficient political sense to handle the two jobs equally well. On the other hand, Macnaghten had no military experience, and could not be expected to control both departments, but he was the best man available for the political post. It is also clear that Burnes did not much like William Hay Macnaghten. The fragment also tells us something about Lord Auckland; that he was well and truly in control of his subordinates. The Commander in Chief and Burnes favoured one course, and Auckland favoured another. Auckland's view prevailed, and the temperamental Burnes bowed to the inevitable with a good grace. Earlier, as we have seen, Auckland had not hesitated to curb Macnaghten during the negotiation with Runjeet Singh. How is it, then, that Auckland has so often been portrayed as a weakling, easily manoeuvred by subordinates into taking extreme measures against his better judgement? Masson is the culprit again. Let us consider Auckland's side of the story as well as Masson's, for Masson's version, propagated by Durand and others, has held the field for too long.

Throughout June and July Charles Masson had mouldered in Peshawar, waiting for a call that never came. Auckland wanted something to be done for him, but Macnaghten was either unwilling or too busy to reassure Masson. In desperation Masson wrote to Burnes. Burnes asked Colvin for his help, and Colvin consulted Auckland. The following letter shows that Masson did not want ordinary employment:

...You may write to Mr Masson to say that Lord Auckland is really sensible of his merits and would wish to consult his convenience and feeling as much as he with propriety can. While the present crisis lasts, his services are too valuable to his country to admit of his being detached to a distance.

He will remain probably so long as the rains last at Peshawar, but when the Shah proceeds in force towards Shikarpore he will have to move down to that quarter to join the principal political officer employed; when the object of the expedition shall have been obtained Lord Auckland will gladly consider what arrangements can be made so as best to meet his views...[35]

Masson's own comment on the message from Colvin was:

...Most assuredly this communication did not satisfy me, for it settled nothing; however, I offered no opposition...[36]

August and September passed, and Masson was still at Peshawar. In October he wrote to Macnaghten, offering his resignation from government service. At the end of November he was at Ferozepore, the assembly point for the regiments due to enter Afghanistan, and on 30 November, according to Masson, Macnaghten formally accepted his resignation. Masson reproduced Macnaghten's letter in his *Narrative of Various Journeys* in order to correct the impression that he had been dismissed from government service. It is significant that the passage which has caused most trouble over the years occurred in his narrative immediately after the description of his resignation:

...I had much conversation with Sir Alexander Burnes, and, observing that he had become fully acquainted with my views, he promised to frame a letter to Mr Colvin, which he would send for my approval. We had also much discourse on the state of affairs. I had previously learned from Dr Lord a strange account of the mode in which the *amiable* Lord Auckland had been driven into measures which his better judgement disapproved, and how he was obliged to yield to the assaults of certain females, aides de camp, and secretaries; and now I questioned Sir Alexander on the part he had taken, particularly as regarded the useless expedition. He replied that it was arranged before he reached Simla, and that when he arrived Torrens and Colvin came running to him and prayed to him to say nothing to unsettle his lordship; that they had all the trouble in the world to get him into the business, and that even now he would be glad of any pretence to retire from it...[37]

Unfortunately there are no entries in Auckland's letter-books for the vital five days starting on Sunday 15 July. But we know that Auckland's two letters to Hobhouse in the previous week showed him on the very brink of his decision. It may be as well to look a little more closely at the letter of 12 July already quoted:

...I give you a copy of a letter which has this moment arrived from Major Todd. I gather from it that all that I am doing, or preparing to do, is well justified by the avowed policy of the Persian Court, and by the hostile proceedings of the Russian agents, and you may assume it for next to certain that I shall go onwards, with many a deep feeling of regret, that I am not allowed to prosecute measures of peace and of peaceful improvement, but with a perfect conviction that the aggressions and the dangers with which we are threatened can be warded off. I can decide absolutely nothing until Macnaghten's return, and I think that I shall then be able to see my way clearly to all that is to be done, and with no fear of the results, though I shall be sorry for the money which it will cost...[38]

We also know that on Monday 16 July Auckland received the Secret Committee's dispatch of 10 May, warning him not to come to any decision upon the affairs of Afghanistan before he knew the outcome of the Herat crisis. This may have given him pause—for a few hours at most. He knew that Hobhouse was writing with no later knowledge of Herat than McNeill had given him in February and early March. Auckland, on the other hand, knew what had happened there up to the end of May, when it was clear that McNeill must soon suspend or sever relations with the Government of Persia. Moreover, he also had before him the previous Secret Committee dispatch (of 20 March), which had reached Simla only a week or so before that of 10 May. The March dispatch had left it 'discretional' with him to adopt such measures as might seem to him 'to be expedient to meet the contingency of the cessation of relations with the Court of Persia'.

The author may be wrong in assuming that Lord Auckland very quickly disposed of the reservations expressed in the Secret Committee's dispatch of 10 May. It may be that he argued the matter out with Colvin and others before coming back to his attitude of the previous week, and that they thought he was trying to get out of his responsibilities. Colvin and Torrens may even have exaggerated their part in bringing him to his decision, in order to impress Burnes and his companion Dr Lord. They may have taken Burnes on one side before he went in to pay his respects to the Governor General on Friday morning, and have urged him not to complicate matters by pleading once again for Dost Muhammad. But all these speculations come up against the firm rock of Auckland's character, however attractive they may seem. In order to believe Masson's version of remarks made to him by two men who were conveniently dead when he published, we should have to accept that Auckland was a moral weakling, and all the evidence cries out that he was not. Let his sister Emily—one of the 'certain females' so slyly mentioned by Masson—speak for him:

...Whenever there is any important public measure to be taken, I always think George must feel his responsibility—no Ministers, no Parliament, and his Council, such as it is, down at Calcutta. To be sure, as you were going to observe, *if* he ever felt himself in any doubt, he *might* feel that he has my superior sense and remarkable abilities to refer to, but as it is, he has a great deal to answer for by himself. I daresay he does it very well, for my notion is that in a multitude of counsellors there is folly—'wisdom' was a misprint. And then again, if the Directors happen to take anything amiss, they could hardly do less than recall us...[39]

Emily Eden wrote that letter to her friend Charles Greville, the diarist, on 10 July. She shows us a man with immense responsibilities who had to manage his burden almost alone. Her playful remark about her brother's ability to consult her when in doubt suggests that he was *not* accustomed to share his burden in that way; '...he has a great deal to answer for by himself'. We saw that Auckland wrote his second July letter to Hobhouse on the 12th. In August he wrote again to Hobhouse, and, although we shall return to that letter in another place, one section provides an apt comment on Masson's charges:

...I am sensible that my Trans-Indus arrangements are in many points open to objection, but I had no time to pause. There was no choice but between them and the more objectionable danger of remaining passive —and a friendly power and an intimate connection in Afghanistan, a peaceful alliance with Lahore, and an established influence in Sinde are objects for which some hazards may well be run...[40]

Auckland certainly allowed himself no time for pause once Macnaghten had handed him the treaty. We need only recall the timetable: Macnaghten arrives on the 19th; Runjeet Singh signs the treaty as accepted by Shuja on the 23rd, even though the distance between Simla and Lahore is nearly 200 miles; and copies are sent to McNeill and Pottinger on the 26th. In the author's view it is time to stop echoing Masson's rancorous comments.

Auckland and his private secretary add a postscript in letters written on Christmas Eve 1838. Auckland had just received a letter from Sir Henry Fane, who was then on his way down the

Indus, retailing Masson's grievances. This is what Auckland wrote:

I have been surprised with what you tell me of Mr Masson. I heard of his being at Ferozepore and wished to see him but was not able to accomplish my object. He deprecated all regular employment and seemed to covet irregular employment and, as it seemed to me, more particularly desired not to be subordinate to Major Wade. I wished him therefore to go to Shikarpore, where, probably, an appointment might be found for him agreeable to him and useful to us, but he has taken offence and is now on the Indus with you. I have begged Burnes and Pottinger who both know his merits and his failing to do all that is reasonable towards overcoming wilfulness. I am sorry to lose him, and thought a few weeks ago that I had done for him what he most wished when I raised his salary and marked him for the irregular employment to which he seems to be most attached. I wish he may be right in his estimate of the superfluity of our means. A very few weeks will put his opinion to the test...[41]

That last remark referred to Masson's opinion, to which he clung most obstinately, that Shuja did not need a British army to restore him to the throne. Colvin wrote to Burnes, also on Christmas Eve:

...Masson has come from Peshawar, and gone down in a huff with Lieutenant Wood. He seems not to have liked Lord's employment. You have a good influence over him, and you would do well to employ it for the purpose of retaining him at Shikarpore until Macnaghten joins and can judge more nearly of his feelings and possible usefulness. We sincerely wish to meet his views as far as can be fairly done...[42]

What matters in this distasteful episode is that Auckland and his private secretary still hoped to retain Masson's services, which they valued, at the end of 1838, and that the man whose evidence has so coloured the story of the First Afghan War was tormented by personal spite.

Now we must return to the main narrative. Whatever doubts may have troubled Auckland momentarily on 16 July had all gone by the middle of August. On the 13th he finished his long dispatch to the Secret Committee, received in London on 27 October (a date worth remembering). He said that at the time of his negotiations with Runjeet Singh his relations with other powers had been anything but satisfactory: he was threatened from the west; Ava and Nepal were contemplating war; and there were ominous signs of unrest in several native states.

In short, in almost every direction we seemed to be surrounded by undisguised foes or doubtful friends.

It occurred to me that a more intimate alliance between Runjeet Singh and the British Government would damp the spirit of disaffection all over India, and I deem it fortunate that a combination to the westward afforded me the means of engaging that powerful chief in a design which, while it will frustrate the views of our enemies on the other side of the Indus, must dishearten those who might have entertained secret views of hostility towards us in other quarters...

Auckland said that the news of the signing of the Tripartite Treaty had had exactly the effect for which he had hoped. The agitation had died down since the treaty became known. There was another, equally important consideration. Until the signing of the treaty Nepal had been hoping to interest Runjeet Singh in 'schemes hostile to the British Government'. One happy result of the treaty would be that Auckland's Government would from now on have a much greater influence over affairs in the Punjab. To sum up this section of the dispatch, Auckland considered that the treaty was conducive to the peace and stability of India and its immediate neighbours. He went on:

Of the justice of the course about to be pursued there cannot exist a reasonable doubt. We owe it to our own safety to assist the lawful sovereign of Afghanistan in the recovery of his throne. The welfare of our possessions in the East requires that we should, in the present crisis of affairs, have a decidedly friendly power on our frontier, and that we should have an ally who is interested in resisting aggression and establishing tranquility in place of a Chief seeking to identify himself with those whose schemes of aggrandizement and conquest are not to be disguised.

The Barukzais would not have been useful allies under the best of circumstances, but they were not to be attacked until they acted against the British Government. This they had done, and the British Government was 'warranted, therefore, by every consideration of prudence and justice, in espousing the cause of Shah Shooja ool Moolk'. Nevertheless, there was something to be said in excuse of Dost Muhammad's conduct, and he deserved honourable asylum after the restoration of Shuja. The expense of the military operations would be justified by the intended result—'an insurmountable and lasting barrier to all encroachments from the westward'. Auckland then wrote:

Advance to the Hindu Kush 1838–1839

I have acted in a crisis which has suddenly arisen and at a period when appearances in every quarter were the most threatening to the tranquility of the British Indian Empire, in the manner which has seemed to me essential to ensure the safety and to assert the power and dignity of our government. I have in adopting this step been deeply sensible of the responsibility which it places on me. But I have felt after the most anxious deliberation, that I could not otherwise rightly acquit myself of my trust, and a reference to the despatches of your Honourable Committee of the 25th of June 1836 and the 10th of May last have led me to look with confidence for your general approbation and support to the plans on which in the exercise of the discretion confided to me, I have resolved...

At this point Auckland recalled his earlier objection to having one consolidated monarchy in Afghanistan. He could no longer have any such objection, since that monarchy would henceforward come under direct British influence. He had determined

...to give the direct and powerful assistance of the British Government to the enterprise of Shah Shooja ool Moolk, in a degree which was not in the first instance contemplated by me, from a conviction, confirmed in the most decided manner by every opinion of authority on the subject, that the measure could not be trusted mainly to the support of the Sikh army and ruler without imminent hazard of failure, and of serious detriment to the reputation of the British name among the Afghan people...

Auckland concluded by urging the Secret Committee to send out two more iron steamboats for the Indus, but first he said:

...I need not enlarge on the additional proofs which have been furnished, since the date of my former Despatch, of the manifest design of the Russian officers to extend the interference and authority of their country to the borders of India...[43]

Let us now consider events on Auckland's side during the rest of August, and then catch up with McNeill as he approaches the Turkish frontier. We earlier noted Auckland's determination not to have his path obstructed by the Sind emirs. On 13 August Macnaghten wrote on his behalf to Colonel Pottinger. The tactics were traditional and unscrupulous. They had worked before and would no doubt work again. If the emirs were recalcitrant the Governor General would 'be precluded from offering opposition to any measures for the assertion of those claims which the Shah [meaning Shuja] may eventually determine to adopt'. Shikarpur might have to be occupied by Bombay troops, and the article prohibiting military traffic on the Indus would have to be suspended.[44] On the 15th Auckland notified the Commander in Chief of the Bombay Presidency's forces, Sir John Keane, that he had decided to enlist ten more men with non-commissioned officers to each company in Bengal and Bombay, thus raising each regiment to a complement of 800. 'I hold it to be wise under present circumstances rather to run the hazards of error on the side of superfluous preparation than on that of economy, and in the event of our moving a large force beyond the frontier I would have no point of danger unprovided for at home.' Another interesting point made in this letter to Keane (worth remembering when we come to November) was that Sir Henry Fane would command the force in support of the Shah 'if the occasion should be sufficient'.[45] As early as August, then, Fane let it be known that he would not go if the command was unworthy of a general of his seniority, or, in other words, if Herat's survival made it possible to send a smaller army.

As early as August, also, Colvin for the first time mentioned that 'no result of the siege of Herat will delay the Shah's expedition, with our direct countenance and support. Russian agents have commenced playing the game of their country with premature eagerness, and we shall have established ourselves, I doubt not, in force across the Indus before they are at all prepared to encounter us there.'[46] There we see the influence of McNeill, plainly displayed. Just three days later Auckland received McNeill's Meshed correspondence, and saw that they were at one upon the need for action. His first reference to the Meshed letters appears in a letter written on 21 August:

...It may probably be thought right to strengthen in a small degree the force at Karrack, and more formally to occupy that island, but I am little disposed to favour an expedition to Bushire. Indeed I am well convinced that if Mr McNeill had known that direct operations upon Afghanistan were projected he would not have suggested an attack upon Southern Persia. In the meantime I daily receive reports confirmatory of the check which the Persians are said to have received before Herat...[47]

In another letter written on the 21st Auckland showed that Colvin was not alone in believing that the expedition should go ahead even if Herat survived the siege:

...even though these reports should be true I shall not be the less convinced that the Govt. is acting wisely in making clear its alacrity to meet aggression wherever it may be threatened and its determination to secure the frontiers which are most exposed to such attacks. I am not therefore inclined to relax in preparation...[48]

On the 20th Colvin had written a letter which showed knowledge of Palmerston's ultimatum to the Shah of Persia. Auckland felt more confident, but 'in the measures now in progress Lord Auckland is acting on this side for himself'.[49]

On the 23rd Auckland wrote the letter to Hobhouse which was quoted as a comment on Masson's charges of irresolution. He said that he had passed a time of much anxiety and had had matters of extreme difficulty to deal with, and had taken far more of responsibility upon himself than could be agreeable:

...I am sensible that my Trans-Indus arrangements are in many points open to objection, but I had no time to pause. There was no choice but between them and the more objectionable danger of remaining passive —and a friendly power and an intimate connection in Afghanistan, a peaceful alliance with Lahore, and an established influence in Sinde are objects for which some hazards may well be run...

Auckland continued, after quoting his letter of 15 August to Keane on military arrangements:

...I may add to this that I have determined to send Mr Macnaghten with Shah Shooja. I can very ill spare him, but I have no public measure equal in importance to that which is contemplated on the side of Afghanistan, and I have none so capable as he is of promoting its success.

Here we see further evidence of Auckland's strength of purpose, and not only the evidence of remarks about Macnaghten. He also told Hobhouse in this letter that he had won an argument with Sir Henry Fane. Fane had wanted to form one division of native troops and one of Europeans (both Queen's and Company's regiments). Auckland strongly resisted this proposed segregation. Fane agreed, he said, and now they were good friends again. Finally Auckland mentioned McNeill's Meshed letters, and remarked that what McNeill said would fully justify any act of vigour against Persia.[50]

There is little more to report from Auckland's side in August. Wade, like Burnes, was disappointed that Macnaghten had the top job. Colvin had to soothe him, sending praise on the 24th and news of an increase in salary on the 27th.[51] Then, on the 28th, we find the first reference in the Auckland Papers to the ambitions of Muhammad Ali, Pasha of Egypt. Colvin acknowledged letters from an officer (Lieutenant Lynch) who had been experimenting with steam navigation on the Euphrates. Lynch had announced the 'important event of the declaration of independence by Mahomed Ali'. Colvin's advice to Lynch and to other British officers with him was to stand aloof and 'preserve a demeanour of general conciliation'. He said that the Governor General's action, if any, on that account must await instructions from home. [52] Auckland must have torn his hair, for he had hardly decided upon one great defensive measure when trouble loomed up even further west, where he had some shared responsibilities. Colvin fairly bubbled with enthusiasm at the prospect of settling accounts with Russia:

...The world, or at least the Eastern portion of it, seems on the eve of a great struggle. Mahomed Alee will certainly assert his independence from the Porte, and from Bassora to Constantinople and Cairo, there will be a convulsion in which Russia will undoubtedly appear as a prominent actor, and in which England can scarcely help being involved...[53]

Colvin was reacting exactly as Palmerston reacted in expecting a struggle, but it is interesting to note that Auckland (for whom Colvin spoke in giving advice to Lynch and his colleagues in the Pashalik of Baghdad) urged neutrality until he should have news and instructions from home. In fact, as other letters show, he had a good opinion of Egypt and a low one of Turkey at the time. He hoped that a quarrel would be avoided.

But we have moved a long way ahead of John McNeill. On receiving the news of the occupation of Kharg he ordered the British Resident in the Persian Gulf to be prepared, if the force sent from Bombay was strong enough, to occupy and defend Bushire if necessary.[54] He knew by then of the failure of the Burnes mission, and so, when he received Palmerston's dispatch of 21 May (the one containing the ultimatum), he sent Colonel Charles Stoddart back to Herat with an even stronger message to the Shah of Persia.[55] He later told Palmerston that he did so because he realized that on 21 May the British Government was unaware of the breakdown at Kabul, the treaty between Persia and Kandahar under Russian guarantee, and the landing at Kharg.[56] McNeill issued his instructions to Stoddard on 10 July. He separately ordered Stoddart, in accordance with Palmerston's wishes, to prepare to go to

Bokhara after completing his mission to Herat. While still at Herat McNeill had heard of Simonich's boast that 12,000 Russian troops were on their way towards Khiva and Bokhara. When he received Palmerston's instructions to send an officer to Bokhara he immediately complied.[57] Stoddart, had he but known it, had just received his death sentence. Palmerston's report that the Russian expedition had been postponed for the 1838 season either failed to reach him or came too late to deter Stoddart from going to Bokhara, where, after great suffering at the hands of a capricious potentate, he and another British officer were publicly beheaded in June 1842. But Stoddard had his moments of glory at Herat in August and September 1838. While he was waiting to hear from Stoddart at the end of July, McNeill reported to Palmerston on what he had done since leaving Meshed. He told him about his strengthened ultimatum, his orders to Stoddart, the failure of the Persian assault on the city of Herat on 24 June, and the occupation of Kharg island by troops from Bombay. On 1 August, from his camp near Teheran, McNeill wrote gloomily of the possible result of the Russian guarantee of the treaty between Persia and Kandahar:

...In short, if Herat should fall, and if the Treaty has really been guaranteed by Russia, and not by Count Simonich personally, Russia becomes by it indisputable mistress of the destinies, political and commercial, of all Central Asia; for Great Britain, having been forced back to the Indus, Khiva and Bokhara must submit if they are attacked; while Persia and Affghanistan will already be at her disposal...[58]

On the following day he warned Palmerston that the Russian diplomatic successes at Kabul and Kandahar might make the Shah bolder at Herat. He wrote yet again on the 3rd, this time making a stronger plea for British military action in Persia itself, on the ground that Herat needed to be saved first of all. By 5 August he was ready formally to propose to Auckland that he should send a supplementary force to the Persian Gulf, ready for a march into the interior of Persia.[59] All these letters and dispatches, written between 30 July and 5 August, reached London on 22 September, at a time when the Cabinet was fully aware of Auckland's intentions as developed up to the beginning of July. We shall soon see how McNeill's speculations and proposals were received.

CHAPTER 9

THE HOME GOVERNMENT
SUPPORTS AUCKLAND

... With respect to interference in Afghanistan, Howick will differ,
and what he says is plausible; but I am afraid his policy will not do
in the least. If all Afghanistan becomes hostile how long will
Runjeet Singh remain friendly, and how long will the various
nations within our frontier remain quiet?...

MELBOURNE to Russell, 13 October 1838

On 28 June 1838 Queen Victoria was crowned in Westminster
Abbey in accordance with the ritual used for her Uncle William's
coronation in 1831. The feudal splendours of former times were
abated, in subtle demonstration of the monarch's changed position
in society. There was no Coronation Banquet in Westminster Hall,
with Royal Stewart, Butler and Naperer in attendance. Instead
there was a Grand Review in Hyde Park, where Wellington and
Marshal Soult rode side by side down the long lines of troops. The
capital was full of visiting princes and ambassadors; and ministers
of the Crown, Palmerston prominent among them, were kept busy
with affairs of protocol and royal entertainment. But nothing could
keep Palmerston away from the Foreign Office for long. Just before
the Coronation he had sent the Cabinet's approval of all that McNeill
had done up to mid April.[1] He gave much thought to the Anglo-
Persian Treaty, and on 18 July he told Hobhouse of his opinion that

the time is come for declaring to the Schah that we consider the Treaty
of 1814 at an end.

The letter may remain, but the Spirit is fled. The Treaty was framed
upon the Basis that Persia was to be our Friend, and was to promote our
Interests. She is now avowedly assailing those Interests. By the Treaty
she was to be a Barrier to protect our Indian Possessions against Invasion; she is now demolishing all our Barriers to the East of herself, and
laying the Road open for Invasion up to our very Gate.

I think we ought to instruct McNeill to make such a formal Declaration, and that we should acquaint Auckland therewith.

At about that time both Palmerston and Hobhouse heard the
news that Auckland had sent troops and ships to Kharg and that

Burnes had instructions to withdraw his mission from Kabul. It is an interesting coincidence that Burnes was recommended for a knighthood, presumably by Hobhouse, at a moment when the British Government was preparing to strengthen its ultimatum to Persia. The instructions envisaged by Palmerston on 18 July were sent to McNeill on the 27th.[3] Burnes's knighthood (and brevet promotion to Lieutenant Colonel) were gazetted at the beginning of August.[4] Robert Leech, the officer sent post-haste to Kandahar at the end of 1837 by Alexander Burnes, was rewarded at the same time with a brevet Majority. This fact seems to the author to suggest that Hobhouse was impressed by a remark in Auckland's letter of 3 May: '...I can have no doubt that the presence of Captain Burnes at Cabul has up to this time secured the neutrality of Cabul and Candahar though unhappily this may not be sufficient to save Herat...'[5]

Previously Hobhouse had uncritically accepted Auckland's view that Burnes acted hastily and without authority or judgement in promising British aid to Kandahar in December 1837. But Auckland's remark, combined with later knowledge, probably convinced him that Burnes had done right. Valuable weeks had been saved, and, besides, Burnes had put up a brave fight from beginning to end of his mission. The climate of opinion in which such a reward seemed fitting can be gauged by Hobhouse's account of an audience with the Queen on 30 July. He told her that he had spoken to the Russian ambassador about the expedition to the Persian Gulf, and that the Russian 'denied all intention, on the part of his Government, of countenancing the Persian movement towards the Indus. The Queen smiled, and said that "of course the Russians would deny participating in the aggression; but their words made very little difference, except when founded on facts".'[6]

So it was that Hobhouse wrote to Auckland through the Secret Committee on 2 August, approving of the Kharg expedition and enclosing a copy of Palmerston's declaration about the Anglo-Persian Treaty.[7] Palmerston also sent McNeill a copy of the Secret Committee dispatch.[8] Thus the Foreign Office and the Board of Control jointly endorsed everything that Auckland and McNeill had done so far. In the middle of August they heard of events in Persia and India in the middle of May—of the Russian intrigues at Herat and of Auckland's decision to negotiate with Runjeet Singh. The Meshed dispatches arrived on Palmerston's desk on

21 August, and on the 24th Palmerston replied by expressing the government's full approval of McNeill's withdrawal from the Shah's court and camp.[9] This is how Palmerston saw the situation on 25 August, when he sent copies of the Meshed dispatches to Hobhouse:

...The true Measure to take would be to make a great operation in Affghanistan; to push on Runjeet Singh, send an English Corps to act with his army; to drive the Persians out of Affghanistan and to re-organise that country under one Chief; and to pay Runjeet by giving him Peshawar and Cashmeer.

A good Affghan state in connection with British India would make a better Barrier than Persia has been, because it would be more under our Controul.

We should have the same kind of geographical Pull upon such a state that Russia has upon Persia.[10]

Almost immediately there arrived a letter from the Governor of Bombay, Sir Robert Grant, informing Hobhouse of Auckland's intentions and the scope and course of the negotiations in June. Palmerston was

very glad to find that Auckland is in so vigorous a mood...

...I quite agree with you [he told Hobhouse] that Affghanistan is the Quarter where the real work is to be done...The presence of an invading British army in Persia would create such agitation and so much Insurrection among the Persians, that the Schah would afterwards become still more dependent if possible upon Russia; and that is not what we want. The advantage of operations in Affghanistan is, that there we aim directly at the object we mean to attain; and whatever we accomplish there, we can afterwards maintain it; and we are not striking a blow in one place in order to produce an effect in another. I think Auckland should be encouraged in his Course; and when he has set up Soojah ool Moolk in Caubul and Candahar, he might leave Kamran Shah Herat, and get Ghoorian back for him—I should be glad to see that old Rogue Dost Mahommed, and those wretched Creatures of Candahar turned out as they deserve...[11]

On the same day, 27 August, Palmerston and Hobhouse compared notes about Auckland's latest private letter (the one written on 17 June), and they agreed that the Governor General, once he saw that Herat could hold out for three or four months longer, would probably 'be induced to take some vigorous measures which may be in Time to save the Place'.[12]

As usual on these occasions, Wellington's opinion was consulted. The result was a memorandum, which Melbourne received and passed on to Palmerston, who replied:

Thank you for this; it is a very sensible paper, and takes a good practical view of the matters in question. The result seems, on the whole, to be favourable to the course which Auckland is pursuing, and shows that the Persian Gulf is the place for a demonstration and a diversion, but that Affghanistan is the quarter where our strength must be employed for real defence.[13]

McNeill, however, was pressing for action in southern Persia as the quickest way of dismaying and frightening the Shah and of rescuing Herat from the Russians. By now Lord Melbourne was helping to rally sceptical members of the Cabinet in support of his Secretary of State and against the idea of mounting military operations in Persia. He wrote in that sense to Lord John Russell on 26 September. He concluded that it was impossible to give directions from London, and that the matter must be left to Auckland's judgement. '...But if he follows McNeill's advice it may bring us into collision with Russia and Persia...'[14]

On the 27th Palmerston again expressed full approval of McNeill's actions, as reported at the end of July.[15] Lord John Russell wrote in some alarm to Melbourne on that day, and again on the 29th. Palmerston thought it was time to intercede, and so on 1 October he wrote to Russell from Windsor:

...McNeill is far the ablest man we have ever had in Persia, and few men understand better than he does the bearing of Persian affairs upon our interests in India. He knows the Persians well and is as good a judge as anybody can be of the best mode of dealing with them.

The matter in question is of great importance for it is manifest that the success of the Shah of Affghanistan would be full of danger and embarrassment to us in India; and that consequently it would tend greatly to our security to get the Shah back again into his own dominions. He is in this matter acting avowedly as the Tool of Russia; and the proceedings of Russia in Affghanistan are certainly as direct an approach to British India as it is *at present* in her power to make. She has opened her first parallels, and it would not be wise in us to delay defensive measures till she has reached the glacis. Auckland and his advisers seem to be of this opinion, but we do not as yet know what course they mean to pursue. I am against McNeill's suggested march of 5,000 men from Bushire to Ispahan and Teheran. I think that if any real movement of troops should become necessary such movement would for very many reasons be better made in Affghanistan itself...

This is most important evidence for the unanimity of Palmerston, Hobhouse, and Auckland at the moment of decision in 1838. Palmerston also felt confident in the general approval of Wellington. We see that Lord John Russell had not paid very much attention so far to the dispatches from Persia, and that he must have suspected McNeill of being unjustifiably sensitive to Persian slights. Palmerston was trying to reassure him. McNeill's alarming proposal that an army should march into southern Persia was at least partly the result of poor communications between Persia and India that summer. When he made the proposal he did not yet know about the signing of the treaty and the decision to send a British contingent with Shuja into Afghanistan. But his proposal served one useful purpose. It aroused the interest of other ministers who had been reluctant to grapple with the problem hitherto. Russell's interest in the matter is a fair sign of the excitement caused by McNeill's dispatches when they reached London at the end of September. By forcing ministers to reject a march into Persia from Bushire McNeill unwittingly compelled them to consider an alternative. Palmerston's letter to Russell continued by admitting that an expedition of the kind proposed by McNeill would, if successful, involve less trouble and expense in the long run, but this was not enough:

...I wish you would send for McNeill's despatches and read them through. I think you will acquit him of impetuosity and violence, and be rather of the opinion that he has acted with discretion and judgement; certainly he has not acted with haste or without reflection...I believe Hobhouse has written to Auckland to explain why we should not like to embark in a forward movement into the interior of Persia...

A small force would risk being overpowered if the Russians intervened, and then the British would be worse off than if they had stayed behind the line of the Indus. They would raise up an insurrection among men who could not afterwards be effectively protected. In any case Britain did not seek to dethrone the Shah of Persia; she wanted to strengthen him once he had turned his back on Afghanistan. Hobhouse had therefore told Auckland, Palmerston said,

...that on the contrary any forward movement into Affghanistan would, if successful, be clear gain, and should thus make a permanent barrier for India. That our chance of success would be much greater, because there we are strong and Persia weak, and Russia would not come there to the aid of Persia. She might join Persia to repel an invasion from without; she would not join Persia to assist Persia in invading and conquering a neighbour if that neighbour is defended by England; at the same time the movement in Afghanistan might require a greater effort and a larger expense, while the mere leading troops to Bushire, if they went no further, would be comparatively easy and cheap. Hobhouse was to say to Auckland that the Government is sure he will have adopted the course which he and his counsellors will have thought on the whole best, and that he will be supported.

My own belief is that our demonstration, together with the gallant resistance of the people of Herat, will have induced the Shah to abandon the siege and retire, and if that should be the result we shall have had a good escape, and we shall then be able to enter into an alliance with the Affghans and make with them the proper arrangements for their future security and our own.[16]

Palmerston was then at Windsor, where the Cabinet met to discuss the crisis revealed by McNeill's letters. It is clear that Melbourne and his colleagues half expected Auckland to follow McNeill's advice about a Persian expedition. Hobhouse, who had earlier argued in favour of such an expedition, asked his staff at the Board of Control to gather together some facts about routes and distances. The questions and answers are preserved in the Broughton Papers, and on the back of the memorandum containing them one can discern some scribbled pencil notes in Hobhouse's handwriting. Among the most legible are the following:

...not to go if not gone—if gone not to move into the interior—if movement is begun not to stop—protect Karak...[17]

It is possible that the notes were scribbled at a Cabinet meeting. However that may be, Palmerston wrote to McNeill[18] on 12 October, advising him against the proposed march into Persia, and Hobhouse enclosed a copy of the Foreign Office dispatch with his own instructions to Auckland later in the month. We have seen that Lord John Russell had his doubts about the Government's policy in Persia. Another doubter was Lord Howick, the Secretary at War. Melbourne wrote to Lord John Russell about Howick's doubts on the 13th:

There is a good deal in Howick's letter, and I shall, of course, send it to Palmerston. He will be able to state facts with more certainty, but it is my impression that McNeill remonstrated with the Shah quite sufficiently to justify any measures which we may have taken or may take...

...The course which Howick recommends as to the troops at Karak is exactly that which we have adopted; and though it appears to me necessary and tending to peace to make a remonstrance to Russia, I quite concur with Howick that that remonstrance ought not to be couched in a haughty or even an unfriendly tone, because Russia certainly may issue a counter-manifesto, the tone of this country, of the Parliament, and of the Government having been very hostile to her both with reference to Poland and to Circassia, and some steps having been taken which, in my opinion, were uselessly irritating. With respect to interference in Afghanistan, Howick will differ, and what he says is plausible; but I am afraid his policy will not do in the least. If all Afghanistan becomes hostile how long will Runjeet Singh remain friendly, and how long will the various nations within our own frontier remain quiet?

I agree with Howick in being very unwilling to lay down that there must be war between us and Russia, and even if I came to that conclusion I would, upon the whole, delay it as long as possible. But it will not do to rely rather upon her weakness than our strength; nor can I by any means consider the Turkish and Polish campaigns a proof of that weakness...Howick's policy is well, if we have time and temper for it, but it is a policy which is not within our power, and Russia may force us to depart from it at any moment...[19]

Thus we see that Howick shared a widespread view of Indian affairs—one which we have already encountered and discussed earlier in this book. Melbourne gave a powerful answer to those who favoured the more passive policy. He showed that Russia held the initiative as the power advancing in Asia; whereas Britain was on the defensive. Not only Palmerston thought of India as a beleaguered fortress, with its glacis in Afghanistan and Persia. Perhaps more interesting than this evidence of agreement between Melbourne and Palmerston is the section of the letter to Russell which deals with past provocations against Russia. The mention of Circassia recalls Palmerston's questionable activities (with the help of David Urquhart) in 1836 and 1837. A letter from Wellington to Aberdeen, to be quoted more fully later, included the otherwise unintelligible remark: '...It appears that the Emperor of Russia imitated our example and encouraged a little private war in Asia...'[20]

A few days after Melbourne wrote his letter to Lord John

Russell a dispatch arrived in London from McNeill, relaying good news from Colonel Stoddart in Herat. Stoddart had arrived at Herat with the ultimatum on 11 August, and the Shah had yielded on the 12th, though he did not in fact turn his back on Herat before 9 September. It was not only the ultimatum that checked the Shah; his army's morale was very low, and the Russians had done little to recover their prestige since the fiasco of 24 June. McNeill's dispatch of 11 September, reporting the Shah's decision, concluded with an interesting argument that there should be no slackening of defensive measures:

...It might appear to be unjust or ungenerous in me to feel or express any doubts of the good faith of the Persian Government on this occasion, but after the repeated violation of the promises made to me in camp by the Shah himself I feel it is my duty to doubt, and I trust that the Government of India, with the knowledge it possesses of what passed in camp while I was there, and the evidence it now has of the effect produced by strong measures, will not be deterred by the promises of the Shah or his ministers, from prosecuting with vigour the only course which, as it appears to me, can retrieve our position or re-establish our influence in Central Asia. Colonel Stoddart mentions that Dost Mahomed Khan of Cabool had intimated to the Shah that hostile preparations against him were in progress both on the part of the English and the Sikhs. If this information be correct, he will have an opportunity of testing the value of the alliances he has recently formed as compared with that of a friendly connection with England.[21]

Nothing of what has just been quoted was published when papers were tabled in Parliament in 1839. The dispatch reached the Foreign Office on 17 October, when Hobhouse was putting the finishing touches to his instructions to Auckland and when Palmerston was preparing to send a note to Nesselrode. Palmerston hurriedly wrote a letter to Hobhouse about the need to secure Herat for the future, proposing even a British garrison and British resident: '...It is evident that Affghanistan must be ours or Russia's; and *this Time* we have the choice in our own Hands.'[22] The Secret Committee's dispatch to Auckland ordered the restoration of Shah Shuja to the throne of Afghanistan. There is no need to quote it at length here, for its message has been conveyed in the letters of Palmerson and Melbourne to Russell. But there are two details which have been overlooked in the past. For instance, Hobhouse left it to Auckland's discretion to make one more effort to conciliate Dost Muhammad Khan. Other writers have made much of this, for Auckland did not make a fresh approach to the Emir. But the original draft in Hobhouse's handwriting uses a word far removed from the language of conciliation. Hobhouse told Auckland that he might send an officer to Dost Muhammad with his 'final commands'. If these were rejected, the army should cross the frontier. In the dispatch as sent by the Secret Committee on 24 October the word 'commands' has given way to 'demands'. But nothing else of any importance changed. The second detail deserving notice is that the dispatch acknowledged the possibility that the retreat of the Shah from Herat, the renewal of friendly relations with Persia, and the Shah's full reparation for the indignities suffered by the British Mission might make the expedition into Afghanistan unnecessary. But even then he must recover his influence in Afghanistan. Now critics of Auckland have said that the failure of the siege of Herat made the expedition totally unnecessary. But the Shah's retreat was only one step towards a settlement of the Anglo-Persian quarrel. The Shah retreated, but friendly relations were not restored for a long time, and reparation was slow in coming. How could Auckland throw his whole policy into reverse and at the same time recover British influence in Afghanistan? As always, simultaneous alliances with the Barukzai brothers and the Maharajah Runjeet Singh were out of the question. Hobhouse's dispatch left England by the Malta packet on 27 October. On that day Hobhouse received dispatches from India in almost exactly the same sense. Thus, thanks mainly to the influence of the middleman in Persia, John McNeill, Auckland's decision to advance and the Cabinet's instructions to advance beyond the Indus crossed each other; they were identical in every important respect.[23]

In that same week Palmerston drafted the tactful remonstrance which Melbourne (agreeing with Howick) had suggested sending to St Petersburg. He had already had two interviews with the Russian ambassador, Count Pozzo di Borgo, in London earlier in October, and the ambassador had reported their conversations to Count Nesselrode. Palmerston asked as politely as he could whether the intentions and policy of Russia towards India were to be deduced from the words of the Russian Government or the actions of Count Simonich. He did not have to wait long for an answer. On 11 November Count Pozzo di Borgo came to him with a note from Nesselrode. As in 1837, so in 1838, Nesselrode denied that the Russian Government had any hostile intentions towards the British in the East. If Simonich had done what he was accused of doing, he was directly contradicting instructions from St Petersburg. Instead of plodding through the note itself, let us see what Melbourne and Palmerston made of it. Let Melbourne speak first:

I have desired Palmerston to send you [i.e. Lord John Russell] the despatch which Pozzo has received from St Petersburg. It is so important that you ought to see it...The Russian despatch is evasive as to the past, and gives bad reasons and makes false excuses for the course they have taken, but for the present and future it is satisfactory. Its propositions are that Russia should engage by all means in her power to restrain the Shah of Persia from further aggression in Afghanistan; that we should retire westwards [*sic*] from Karak; and that hereafter we should act together in concert at Teheran with a view to the preservation of peace in Central Asia. All this is very well, and there cannot be any doubt that we ought to lose no time in closing with the proposal. At the same time the measures which have been taken by Russia have been so decidedly hostile, and have so evidently only been arrested and prevented by our firm language and decided attitude, that we would hardly venture to trust—if, indeed, we ever could have done so—either to her friendship or to her moderation...[24]

Palmerston speaks second, in a letter to Hobhouse:

...It seems to me that as to the future we ought to accept this as satisfactory, and that we ought to let Nesselrode off easy as to the past. If, indeed, we were disposed to answer him controversially as one would do an opponent in the House of Commons, one might cut him up unmercifully...But that would be useful only if we wanted to lay the ground for a rupture; whereas what we want is to carry our points without a rupture; and as the Russians are disposed quietly to back out, it is not for us to criticise their gait in so doing...[25]

A little later they learned that Nesselrode had backed down completely, having recalled Simonich and having disavowed his actions and the actions of his agents. Palmerston's victory was overwhelming, thanks to McNeill and Auckland. The Queen, meanwhile, had asked for a map of Asia from the Foreign Office on 1 November, and on the 5th Hobhouse had acknowledged Auckland's warlike announcements by expressing full approval and remarking upon the similarity between their respective schemes.[26] Hobhouse now began to stress the condition that every possibility of negotiation with Kabul and Kandahar had been tried, for *he* knew how far the Russians had retreated. But there was no retreat on his part from full support for Auckland's venture.[27] When a long retired Persian hand, Sir Henry Willock, complained of the folly of setting up the 'superannuated puppet' Shuja, Hobhouse wrote on the back of his letter: 'His opinion that it would be better to spend 50,000 tomauns annually in keeping up a force in Persia officered by English than restore Shah Soojah. The details are founded on assumptions. I do not think much of the paper.'[28]

Indeed it was true that Willock had no access to official papers, and that his knowledge of Persia was long out of date. But he scored a palpable hit in damning Shuja as a puppet. As long ago as 4 July Auckland had told Macnaghten that 'without permitting unreasonable pertinacity or scruples to thwart us, he would not treat the Shah as a mere puppet but be disposed to give a considerable attention to his opinions and feelings'.[29] There was always a danger that Shuja would appear to be a puppet, and Auckland recognized it early. That was why he always showed such interest in reports of Shuja's popularity or the lack of it in Afghanistan. In fact he was given every reason in 1838 to believe that Shuja would be popular and acceptable. He kept an open mind on the subject, and cautiously backed him up with a British army.

The news of the raising of the siege of Herat in September reached the British Government on 10 December. It came from Stoddart through McNeill, who was still in camp near Tabriz. McNeill was as confident as ever that this was no time to slacken in defence of British India. He recommended immediate measures to give strength and security to Herat 'and to convince the gallant defenders of that city, and through them all the inhabitants of Central Asia that England is not unmindful of the allies who may suffer serious losses in defending their common interests; and that she is ready to acknowledge the sacrifices, and reward the valour and constancy by which she has gained so much'.[30]

John McNeill did not try to claim more than his share of the credit. He highly praised Eldred Pottinger and Charles Stoddart for their work at Herat. The main part of his own work was done in little more than two and a half years from the publication of the *Progress and Present Position of Russia in the East*. What would Wellington and Aberdeen think of Britain's position nine years after the Treaty of Adrianople? A letter from Wellington to

Aberdeen, written from Stratfield Saye on 10 December, gives several clues to the answer to that question, showing once again that Whig and Tory were fundamentally at one on the strategy for the defence of India. Aberdeen was on his estate in Scotland, and Wellington gave him the political gossip (remarkably well-informed gossip) of the capital, which he had just visited. Wellington said:

...You will have seen that we must have spoken out to Mahomed Aly; and that our fleet has been cruising in the Mediterranean and Levant in conjunction with the Turkish fleet. This is certainly not much liked by the Emperor Nicholas. The Treaty of Commerce still less. Pozo's [*sic*] observation upon the first was 'il faut empêcher les Turcs de faire et dire des sottises. Lord Ponsonby is a man who would spoil any affair. C'est un fou! qui embrouillera tout!' Then as to the Treaty of Commerce he says it is all very fine if it can be carried into execution.

The Austrians applaud it to the skies; particularly its Liberality in making it common to all nations.

From this it appears that the Govt. have at last done what they ought to have done eight years ago; as between the Sultan and Mohamed Alli, and that there is in consequence in a certain degree a renewal of friendly relations, and a revival of our influence at the Porte.

This of course delights the Austrians. But this is not all. It appears that the Emperor of Russia imitated our example; and encouraged a little Private War in Asia. The King of Persia had in his army engaged in the siege of Herat a Corps of Russian Deserters, commanded by Russian officers, said to consist of 1,000 men. It was possibly true. The Russian Ambassador was in the Camp at the siege, and very busy in the operations, and of course cognizant of this Battalion of Deserters.

You will have heard that the Govt. in the course of the summer sent some troops from India to take possession of two islands in the Persian Gulf. This expedition enlightened the King of Persia. The commercial consequences in this kingdom might have been fatal to his Authority. Revolutions were menaced in all quarters.

Besides this a very large Armament was ordered in India.

The Consequence of all has been that the Siege of Herat has been raised. The Emperor of Russia has made a communication to this court, stating that he is authorised by the King of Persia to offer his Mediation to produce a reconciliation with the Queen of England. He takes to himself the Merit of having persuaded the King of Persia to raise the siege of Herat.

I understand that Lord P. says that the Conduct of the Emperor would have justified War; but that he will not disturb the Peace of Europe.

Pozo [*sic*] hinted to me that he had denied that the island in the Persian Gulf should be evacuated; upon which if Lord P. is wise he will not allow him to say a word.

The Austrians are delighted with all this. They feel that the Emperor Nicholas has been humiliated in Asia; and they talk of our Successes in the East as decisive; and as establishing our influence permanently.

I don't know whether the raising the Siege of Herat will stop the March of the troops in India. This was intended; and I hope that it may still...[31]

What a lot of useful and enlightening information the duke packed into his letter to Aberdeen! We know now that the duke of Wellington and his circle were delighted with the shape of British policy in the East at the end of 1838. There is not a word of criticism, but there is a sting in the last sentence. There might come a time when he would argue that the raising of the siege of Herat made the expedition unnecessary. But in the author's view of Wellington's attitude it would have been easy for Palmerston to show him the wisdom of continuing. In fact Palmerston wrote to Lord John Russell five days after the duke wrote to Aberdeen. Palmerston, of course, had by then had official confirmation of the raising of the siege. He returned Howick's letter, the one which Russell had sent to Melbourne in October and which had then found its way to him. He said that McNeill and Auckland had cut the knot which Howick feared to untie:

What he says of the real weakness of the Russians for aggressive war is quite true; but the knowledge of that fact ought rather to encourage us to make a stout stand against her systematic encroachment on Peace; as we ought to be convinced that she is always pushing on as far and as fast as she can go without war; but that whenever she finds that perseverance in encroachment will lead to forcible resistance, she will pull up and wait for some more favourable opportunity of carrying on her schemes.[32]

On 20 December Hobhouse received and showed to his colleagues Auckland's Simla Manifesto of 1 October. This was in effect a declaration of war upon the states of Kabul and Kandahar, and it will be considered in some detail in the next chapter, which describes the operations of the Army of the Indus. To the relief of Hobhouse and his colleagues the Simla Manifesto made the quarrel appear entirely as one between India on the one hand and Persia, Kabul and Kandahar on the other. As Auckland said in a private letter to Hobhouse:

...It will be for others to judge of my case, and I will say nothing of it, except that I could have made it stronger if I had not had the fear of Downing Street before my eyes and thought it right to avoid direct allusion to Russia...[33]

This was as well, for on 20 December Palmerston told Pozzo di Borgo that Her Majesty's Government accepted Count Nesselrode's explanations and would refrain from holding an inquest on the 'many passages' in his dispatch which were open to challenge. On Christmas Eve Wellington again wrote to his old colleague Aberdeen. At the very end of his letter he said: 'You will have seen Lord Auckland's Declaration. How is Shujah ool Moolk to be maintained on his Throne?'[34] But Hobhouse and the other members of the Cabinet gave no hint of disapproval when they acknowledged the Simla Manifesto in a Secret Committee dispatch on 26 December. The new cordiality (on the surface) with the Russians could already be observed in relations between Palmerston and Pozzo di Borgo at the beginning of February. We find Palmerston telling Russell on 3 February:

Pozzo agreed with me yesterday that the Persians ought to evacuate that place [Ghorian] because they had it not in 1834, when England and Russia came to an agreement about Persian affairs...This Karak seems to be a good marketable commodity in this negociation...

Palmerston added that Auckland would be able to help Kamran Mirza of Herat with officers and money and perhaps some artillery:

...and this could be done with great ease when Sir John Keane has got possession of Cabul and Candahar.[35]

This brings us back to the common ground between Palmerston's Persian and Auckland's Afghan policy—the desire to preserve Herat at all costs. Hence Palmerston's interest in getting the Persians out of Ghorian, a fortress covering the approach to Herat. Palmerston had his talk with Count Pozzo di Borgo on 2 February; three days later the Queen opened the second session of the thirteenth Parliament of the United Kingdom of Great Britain and Ireland. Her speech included a reference to the retirement of her Minister from Teheran and the expression of a hope that a satisfactory adjustment of differences would soon allow friendly relations to be re-established:

The Home Government supports Auckland

...Events connected with the same differences have induced the Governor General of India to take measures for protecting British interests in that quarter of the world, and to enter into engagements, the fulfilment of which may render military operations necessary. For this purpose such preparations have been made as may be sufficient to resist aggression from any quarter, and to maintain the integrity of my Eastern dominions.[36]

Palmerston had foreseen that the Opposition would ask for papers, but he also saw from his vantage point at the Foreign Office that the publication of papers could be most embarrassing. 'The objection to giving Papers', he said in a letter to Hobhouse, 'is that our case against Russia is *too good* a one to be made out against a dear ally. It would be a terrible shewing up for Nicholas; not but that he richly deserves it.'[37] As expected, Peel moved for papers as soon as he decently could after the Queen's speech, for this was his first opportunity for months to challenge the Government's policy in the East. He had had the mortification in December of seeing both *The Times* and the *Morning Chronicle* praising Auckland to the skies. Wellington had also taken pleasure in the humiliation of the Russian Emperor, but then he was never a good *party* man. Peel wanted power for his party, so that he might reform the creaking administrative system which had escaped the Whig zeal for change since 1830. Hobhouse warned Auckland to expect 'formidable parliamentary attacks' upon his policy, and Auckland replied that he regretted this, not because he feared criticism but because he foresaw 'with what extreme embarrassment and weakness all Indian Government must be carried on if every measure, even in its progress, is to become the subject of party contention'.[38] Peel and his colleagues now sought to do exactly that, at a time when a British army was on the move and at a time when Palmerston was engaged in the delicate operation of restoring a cordial façade to Anglo-Russian relations so that he might see Unkiar Skelessi into the waste-paper basket.

Hobhouse and Palmerston now had to decide what to publish. Hobhouse wrote a short memorandum on the subject early in February:

If any of the Secret Papers regarding the pending operations in India, further than the Declaration of the Governor General already before the Public, and the Tripartite Treaty which has been placed on the Table of the Court of Directors, are produced, it is submitted that the *whole* ought to be produced. Otherwise justice will not be done to the policy which the Indian Government is pursuing, which policy is not only intimately connected with, but may be said to be founded upon the conduct of Persia and Russia.

But the production of all the Papers is liable to very serious objections:

First—It would necessarily raise most embarrassing questions regarding the state of our relations with Russia.

Secondly—It would put the Enemies of Great Britain in possession of most important information regarding the means of conquering the Indian Empire and of counteracting the measures in progress for defending it, and

Thirdly—It might embarrass and weaken those measures by raising a premature discussion, and create unnecessary alarm in the Public Mind.

Hobhouse looked back over the previous occasions on which Indian Papers had been published and saw that they had never been published in full. In particular he noted that the Board of Control had never published letters *from* the Court of Directors or Secret Committee, even when specifically requested.[39] William Cabell, assistant secretary at the Board of Control, then proposed a way of presenting the British case in conformity with Hobhouse's three reservations. First, Cabell said, lay before Parliament a copy of the Tripartite Treaty and the 1833 Treaty (between Runjeet and Shuja) on which it was founded. This was duly done on 18 February, exactly as Cabell suggested. He went on, in his memo of 14 February:

It would be difficult in the first instance to make any other selection that would not be liable to the objection of disclosing what would be inconvenient to the public interest to publish or of offence to Russia by an uncalled for exposure of the proceedings of her Agents whose acts have been disavowed...

Cabell predicted that the Opposition would thereupon call for further papers and launch a furious attack on the proceedings of the Governor General:

...The line to be taken in vindication of his Lordship would be that no other course was open to his adoption than that which he was forced at last to pursue—by the substitution of a friendly for an unfriendly power in Affghanistan—the existence of which had become inconsistent with the tranquillity of India...

One could then quote the treaty between Persia and Kandahar under Simonich's guarantee, which was designed to set up a power in Afghanistan independent of the British Government, supported by Persia and assisted by Russia (if Simonich's guarantee had been confirmed by his government):

...In making this statement credit might be given to the Emperor of Russia and Count Nesselrode for their disavowal of the acts of Count Simonitch and of the statements of Captain Vickovitch—but as they were calculated at the time to do us as much injury, as the confirmation of them could have effected, the Governor General had no course left to him but to oppose the establishment of such a power, fraught as it was with danger to our interests in India...

Next Cabell proposed that it would be easy to vindicate British policy in Persia by saying that the Afghan article of the Treaty of Teheran could not be held to apply to a state of circumstances in which Persia, by her treaty with Kandahar, had set herself in opposition to the Government of India:

...A statement to this effect, made in the face of Parliament and of the Country, could not, it is conceived, fail to carry full conviction to the mind, and to bring forth an unequivocal declaration from all parties in favour of the Governor General...If due care be taken in such a statement to separate the Emperor and Count Nesselrode from the acts of Count Simonitch and Captain Vickovitch, which they have in effect disavowed, Russia could take no just cause of offence at such a proceeding...

Once this separation had been made, Cabell went on, there would be no objection to telling Parliament what McNeill and Auckland had reported about Simonich and Vitkievitch. It would also be possible to publish a selection of Foreign Office papers between McNeill and Palmerston, together with correspondence concerning the Russian disavowal of the agents:

...At the same time might be presented from the India Board, a selection from the despatches of Sir Alexander Burnes and other British functionaries in regard to the proceedings of Captain Vickovitch both previously and subsequently to the retreat of the Shah from before Herat...

The production of these papers, Cabell argued, would show the country what danger India had been in, and how the Governor General and John McNeill had averted it.[40]

Advance to the Hindu Kush 1838–1839

The author of this work has quoted Cabell's memorandum at length, and Hobhouse's original memorandum in full, because since the time of Kaye—indeed since 1842—Melbourne's Government has been accused of garbling the Indian Papers to make a bad case look passable. Sir John Kaye waxed exceedingly indignant about the garbling and never paid any attention to other possible motives. The words of Hobhouse and Cabell offer a corrective to the view presented by the moralists of the Kaye and Durand schools. We shall hear how Hobhouse and his colleagues defended themselves against the charge of dishonesty when we come to consider the events of 1842.

Apart from a few scattered references by McNeill to Britain's commercial interest in Central Asia we have heard little in the last few chapters about the considerations which first turned British eyes in India towards Afghanistan and the territories beyond the Hindu Kush. But Auckland and his colleagues never lost sight of the commercial objectives in the political confusion. The Indus was to be a golden highway for British goods destined for Central Asia, and, if the Indus could be a highway, why not the Oxus? On 12 February Thomas Love Peacock, at that time Examiner of Correspondence at the Board of Control, wrote a memorandum on Central Asia. He addressed it to Cabell for Hobhouse's attention on the 14th. Its conclusion serves to remind us of what Melbourne and his ministers had in mind during their war of nerves with Russia:

...The policy of Bokhara has been for a considerable time pacific and commercial; that of Khiva appears to be gradually becoming more and more so. The injury which their commerce sustains by the wandering Toorkomans may be in a great measure obviated by opening to commercial navigation the Oxus and Jaxartes rivers, which appear to offer an uninterrupted navigation of nearly two thousand miles, through the Aral Sea between Kilef on the Oxus and Kokaun on the Jaxartes. The question is not whether this shall be done, but whether England or Russia shall do it. Steam vessels of 70 horse power, with sliding keels for the Aral, may be conveyed in frame from the Indus to the Oxus. In this way we may establish a commercial intercourse mutually beneficial, preoccupying this important navigation, and tending to secure the friendship of the states on its borders.[41]

On 18 February Hobhouse took Cabell's advice and released for publication the Tripartite Treaty of 1838 and its ancestor, the treaty of 1833 between Runjeet Singh and Shuja. On 28 February, at which time the papers had not yet reached the House of Lords, Ellenborough rose to ask Melbourne what treaty had been made with Sind for the march of troops through that territory. He said it was also of importance to know whether the hostility of Dost Muhammad had not been provoked and justified by British acquiescence in the expedition undertaken by Shuja in 1834. Melbourne replied that he thought it would be found there was no paper which would bear out the 'noble Lord's apprehension that the honour and character of the British Government had been at all compromised in the way suspected by the noble Lord'.[42] At the beginning of March Melbourne received privately from Ellenborough a request for papers about events leading up to the war. Melbourne passed the request to Hobhouse, and Hobhouse authorized on 8 March the publication of fifteen treaties of various dates, with Persia, Sind, Kabul, Lahore and Bahawalpur. By this time Ellenborough was ready to present the Tory case against the Whigs. He moved for more papers on 19 March, saying that there were two questions arising out of the conduct of the Governor General of India—whether it was justifiable and whether it was politic. One might assume from the evidence already produced, he said, that the conduct was a folly; it remained for the evidence to be produced to determine whether it were a crime. Aberdeen also took part in the exchange on 19 March, and a nettled Melbourne replied by accusing the Tories of being too apt to forget, for the sake of party advantage, all regard for the real interests of the country.[43] But Wellington did not join the Tory pack on this occasion. Earlier in the month he had taken the trouble to write to Palmerston to relay a story said to originate with one of the aides de camp to the Emperor Nicholas. This aide de camp was said to have seen on the Emperor's desk a document bearing the words 'approved by the Emperor' and recommending that twenty-seven sail of the line, fifteen frigates, and several transports, with thirty thousand troops, should be sent to the East Indies to seize upon the capitals of the three Indian Presidencies. The duke thought that the story was not altogether to be despised, and Palmerston took it seriously enough to check with the British ambassador in St Petersburg. Here we see a good example of the contrast between Wellington's point of view and Ellenborough's at this stage. Wellington certainly had reservations about the move to restore

Shuja to the throne of Kabul, but he fully understood the Whig Government's anxiety to prevent Afghanistan from falling under Russian influence.[44] Another anecdote shows the duke's sentiments even more clearly, though Stanhope, who has preserved the story, seems to have got the date wrong. Stanhope said under date of 9 March 1839:

I saw the Duke for a few minutes in the morning at Apsley House...In the evening we met him at dinner at Sebastiani's, and he took us afterwards in his carriage to the Opera, and from thence to a party in Cambridge House...I spoke to him for a little on the alarming news from India. He closed that subject by saying with a smile, 'if the Duke of Wellington were twenty or thirty years younger, he ought to be on horseback and on the field with Runjeet Singh, instead of being called in to arrange the affairs of the maids of honour and the Palace'.[45]

This incident is more likely to have taken place on 9 May, when Wellington was in the thick of the crisis over the Queen's Whig ladies, and when the news from India spoke of military operations in Sind on the way to Afghanistan. But the date is less important than the attitude which the incident reveals. At the end of March, after consulting Palmerston, Hobhouse released for publication a collection of sixty-one dispatches written between 1831 and 1835. Palmerston had meanwhile gone through many more recent papers: 'I have gone through these Papers and have marked in Pencil the Passages which I think ought to be omitted...'[46] The clerks at the India Board were kept very busy for the next few weeks.

The bulk of the Indian Papers reached Parliament at the end of March and the beginning of April. Hobhouse issued these in four more collections, those already mentioned having been numbered one to three. Indian Papers Number Four consisted of Auckland's key dispatches of 12 May and 13 August; Number Five was an account of Burnes's mission to Kabul, given in the form of twenty-seven dispatches and extracts from dispatches written between May 1836 and April 1838; Number Six was an attempt, by means of dispatches and extracts from dispatches, to show the activity of Russian agents in Afghanistan in 1837 and 1838; and Number Seven was a collection of dispatches relating to the occupation of Kharg. A separate publication, unnumbered, reproduced part of a dispatch from the Court of Directors to the Governor General dated 20 September 1837. No attempt was made to disguise the fact that extracts were extracts, but equally no attempt was made

226

to show by points of ellipsis (thus...) where the omissions occurred in the text. This seems to the author to have been Hobhouse's biggest mistake. A second mistake was the division of the Burnes correspondence into two collections with separate themes. This was over-sophisticated, to say the least. It so confused Kaye that in his 'ungarbled' dispatches of 1859 he showed papers as suppressed in 1839 which had in fact been published. The reader will find a table analysing the 1839 and 1859 compilations in the appendix to this book. Meanwhile the author believes that Hobhouse and Cabell withheld certain dispatches and parts of dispatches from the publication for the precise reasons stated by them in February 1839. It was not desirable to give new offence to the Emperor of Russia; for the Tsarevitch was at that moment preparing for a visit to England as a token of their new friendly relationship.[47] It was unwise to publish the whole story while military operations were in progress; it was also unwise to provoke a public discussion, which could not but be controversial, in the middle of the army's advance. Thus considerations of diplomacy, security in the modern sense of the word, and morale made Hobhouse withhold much of the information available. But the biggest single reason was the need to keep the Russians quiet and friendly. Exactly the same considerations dictated Palmerston's treatment of the 'Correspondence relating to the Affairs of Persia and Affghanistan' when the time came for publication in April 1839. A confidential print preserved at the Public Record Office can with certainty be identified as Palmerston's personal copy of the original collection, exactly as he presented it to his colleagues in the Cabinet. A comparison of the marginal instructions to the printer and the published version in the Parliamentary Papers of 1839 proves this point beyond reasonable doubt. Palmerston deliberately diluted the anti-Russian content of his and McNeill's dispatches; he disguised to some extent the close connexion between Foreign Office and India Board; and in the process he suppressed his own part in the formation of policy in India. For instance, the collection as presented to the Cabinet contained the Secret Committee dispatch of 25 June 1836, authorizing Auckland to interfere in Afghanistan at his discretion and showing that Palmerston gave the signal to send it. There is no sign of the dispatch in the published papers.

It is only fair to mention that the published papers made many old Indians shake their venerable heads in sorrow and disgust. But how could they judge without knowing the whole story, and how could Palmerston tell the whole story without damaging national interests? Metcalfe said he greatly lamented Auckland's proceedings:

It seems to me that we have needlessly and heedlessly plunged into difficulties and embarrassments, not without much aggression and injustice on our part, from which we can never extricate ourselves without a disgraceful retreat, which may be more fatal in its consequences than an obstinate perseverance in a wrong course. Our sole course is to resist the influence of Russia, and our measures are almost sure to establish it ...We may succeed, and if we do, the first impression will be imposing on all our Indian enemies, and so far advantageous, but this benefit will be ephemeral. The only certain results, even in the event of brilliant success in the first instance, are permanent embarrassments and difficulties, political and financial, which it is most unsatisfactory to contemplate.[48]

Metcalfe's view was exactly what it was in 1836, when he and Auckland argued the matter out in India, and Auckland's answer—that the most passive policy is not always the most pacific—should command just as much respect. It is more difficult to understand Ellenborough's attitude in 1839. A memorandum which he composed in April of that year is so reminiscent of Burnes in some passages that the author suspects (without being able to prove) that it incorporates what Burnes wrote to him from Kabul. We know that Burnes did write to Ellenborough from Kabul once. He may have done so at the end of 1837, when he felt that the Indian Government was paying too little attention to his defence of Dost Muhammad. However that may be, Ellenborough blamed Bentinck for enabling Shuja to attack the Barukzais in 1834. He said that Auckland should have given money to Kabul and Kandahar, restrained Shuja and Runjeet Singh, and told Runjeet Singh to be satisfied with what he had. Lord Ellenborough said that the Russians had as much right as the British to cultivate commercial and political relations with Afghanistan. The present policy would lead to a collision with Russia. He advocated 'a policy purely defensive and conservative of the status quo in all India'. Could this be the same Lord Ellenborough who predicted war with Russia along the Indus, the man who later annexed Sind after inflicting retribution upon the people of Afghanistan? Knowing how Wellington felt in

1838, and knowing how close Wellington and Ellenborough were in their views, the author can only suppose that the memorandum was a sketch for some future attack on Whig policy, designed to wound but not to reflect the author's real views. Apart from signs of insincerity one can find mistakes of fact and judgement in the memorandum. For instance, Ellenborough supposed that it would have been possible to unite Afghans and Sindians against the Persians because they were all Sunnis and the Persians were all Shias. The Sind emirs were not in fact all Sunnis. Moreover, Ellenborough advocated taking a firm line with Runjeet Singh as if that were the simplest measure in the world, or as if Runjeet Singh were just another petty chieftain instead of a king with a formidable army under European officers. We have to remember that, unlike any other Indian prince, Runjeet Singh had a superbly trained and equipped artillery, and it was artillery and good discipline that counted against the brave but undisciplined Asian armies of those days. Ellenborough's strongest point was that a British army in Afghanistan would find itself in a false military position, with difficult communications between it and its source of supply and reinforcement in India. But it was never intended that a British army should stay in Afghanistan for longer than was necessary to establish Shuja in control again. It seems very likely that Ellenborough was only making party points.[49]

During the period before and after publication of the Indian Papers Lord Palmerston continued his correspondence with the Russian government. On 25 February Pozzo di Borgo had told him that Russia considered the matter closed.[50] On 25 March he learned officially from St Petersburg that Simonich and Vitkievitch had both been recalled, and that the new Russian Minister in Teheran, Duhamel, had announced that 'the intention of the Emperor has been and will continue to be not to maintain with Affghanistan any other than purely commercial relations'. At the same time Palmerston learned Nesselrode's reaction to his prudent warning in January that discussion in Parliament might oblige his Government to publish communications exchanged on this subject. Nesselrode said that the Emperor saw no inconvenience in publication. And so, on 4 April, Palmerston replied through Pozzo di Borgo, expressing the British Government's great pleasure at the turn of events. He added that he and his colleagues still hoped for the restoration of good relations with the Shah of Persia, but this depended on the

Shah himself (for the Shah had not yet given redress for the insults endured by McNeill's mission in 1838).[51] This letter from Palmerston to Pozzo di Borgo is the last item in the collection of dispatches presented to the Cabinet in April; one can almost see Palmerston point to it and its immediate predecessors as the best possible reason for discretion in publishing Foreign Office and India Board dispatches. One can also imagine him telling his colleagues that if the Russians could be kept quiet Britain might well be able to undo the damage done by the Treaty of Unkiar Skelessi. Palmerston very nearly missed the opportunity to accomplish this diplomatic coup in the Near East, for Melbourne took his resignation to the Queen on 7 May. The Whigs were tired and tottering in all but their foreign policy. But the Queen saved them by insisting on keeping her Whig ladies-in-waiting. By the 10th she was writing to Melbourne: 'As the negotiation with the Tories is quite at an end, the Queen hopes Lord Melbourne will not object to dining with her on Sunday?'[52]

Palmerston turned thankfully back to his papers at the Foreign Office and to the task of making the Tsarevitch feel himself among friends. The Russian prince's visit was a great success, and on 25 May the British ambassador in St Petersburg reported that 'the Russian Court and people are much gratified with the reception of the Hereditary Grand Duke in England'. A new chapter was starting in Anglo-Russian relations, but Russia had not quite finished with the old. On the same day Clanricarde reported that M. Vitkievitch had arrived in St Petersburg ten days previously, and that on the night of the 20th he committed suicide: 'The cause is said to have been the disapprobation and disavowal of his conduct in Affghanistan by the Russian Govt. instead of the reward and promotion he expected. Count Nesselrode however denies that M. Vitkievitch's official position could have drawn him to this act.'[53]

Palmerston's success in conciliating the Emperor was timely. The Turkish army crossed the border into Syria, which Muhammad Ali held as tributary of the Sultan, in the month of May, intent upon punishing the unruly Egyptian Pasha but destined for a humiliating defeat at his hands. The Treaty of Unkiar Skelessi was still, in theory, in force. It was now Palmerston's mission to ensure that the treaty would never be invoked.

CHAPTER 10

THE ARMY OF THE INDUS

...I have been discussing this morning with the Commander in Chief what shall be the name of his army—and we have decided that it shall be the 'Army of the Indus'.

AUCKLAND to Prinsep, 20 October 1838

In the summer of 1838, in a hundred camps and cantonments throughout India, officers and men of the British and British Indian armies began to stir themselves and shake off the torpor induced by a dozen years of peace. One veteran of the Burmese war, Colonel William Dennie of the Queen's 13th Regiment of Foot, wrote home at the end of August that they were 'on the eve of something momentous'. But he knew nothing for certain. 'They say we are going to fight the Persians or Russians.'[1] Colonel Dennie, like many other officers that summer, began to look forward to promotion and perhaps a share of any prize money that came his regiment's way. The Company's infantry regiments were already recruiting additional men, in accordance with the Governor General's promulgations of 30 June and 28 August, to such effect that by the time the expedition got under way the number of men under arms in India had grown from 190,000 to about 203,000.[2] On 10 September the Governor General formally directed his Commander in Chief to assemble an army for the march into Afghanistan, and Fane in his turn ordered the chosen regiments to rendezvous at Karnal by the last day of October. Alexander Burnes, meanwhile, was sent ahead to win the co-operation of the rulers of states along the army's intended route.[3] Lord Auckland was rapidly approaching the point of no return, and in letters home in the third week of September he assured his colleagues that having taken his line he would 'pursue it with energy and vigour'. But he was still uncertain about the current of national feeling in Afghanistan. 'I cannot but be anxious, but all our accounts have hitherto been good.' It was in these letters home that he reacted to the first news of Muhammad Ali's claim to independence. He hoped that he would not have to detach troops to Baghdad and the Red Sea at such an inconvenient moment. 'What more may be done in that quarter, or

231

in the Persian Gulph must very much depend upon what I shall hear from Mr McNeill and from home.'⁴ But, prudent as ever, he told the Governor of Madras that in certain circumstances he might be called upon to fit out (from one of his western ports) an expedition to the Persian Gulf. Having taken that precaution, he added: '...I cannot think that the Shah will force us into a serious diversion on the side of Fars, and I sincerely hope that there will be no such difference between England and Egypt as to bring India into the quarrel towards Bagdad and Syria.'⁵ As if anxieties about Nepal and Ava were not enough to distract him, Auckland now had to think about the possibility of action against Muhammad Ali on the shores of Arabia, and, to crown his troubles, the Sind emirs were reverting to old habits. To be fair to them, they had ample reason for taking offence.⁶ Only a few months after accepting a British Resident in Hyderabad they had been presented with a bill in commutation of nearly thirty years of unpaid tribute to the ruler of Kabul. We cannot blame them for objecting to a settlement, however tidy and conducive to peace, in which they were never consulted, and which was to cost them a very large sum of money. But it was unwise of them to write to the Shah of Persia. Auckland heard about their letters of submission to the Shah at the beginning of September. Only Sobdar, apparently, had remained loyal to the alliance with Britain, and Auckland told Carnac that they were 'justifying any measures of vigour which we may decide upon taking against them. Colonel Pottinger writes upon their conduct with extreme wrath, and he would not be hastily excited against them ...'⁷ Colvin, for his part, urged Pottinger to make the most of a 'golden opportunity'. If he could fix a subsidiary force in Sinde 'upon the opening which this affair has presented to you, without seriously obstructing the primary object of success to the Candahar expedition, you will, I need not say, have conferred a most essential benefit upon your country—such as would form a noble crowning triumph to your long and honourable career of service...'.⁸ The price of forgiveness could be pitched as high as Pottinger thought fit, in other words. As we have observed before, the British in India did not allow their scruples to obstruct the establishment of their influence in Sind. The territory and the river within its borders were too important to them for that.

During the latter part of September Auckland and Macnaghten carefully drafted a declaration of the government's reasons for helping to restore Shah Shuja. This was no easy task, for Auckland wanted 'to keep Indian politics apart from those of Europe'. He had to write his declaration in such a way that the quarrel would 'stand as one between India and Persia, between the Governor General and the Chiefs of Afghanistan, and not come for umpirage to Downing Street—or be the cause there of remonstrance or embarrassment...'.[9] This was Auckland's small but valuable contribution to the maintenance of the peace of Europe, and he made it at considerable personal cost. Kaye never gave him any credit for it. The Simla Manifesto of 1 October 1838 is in effect a declaration of war, and we should not expect it to be objective and impartial and completely honest. For instance, it starts by painting the British attitude to the navigation of the Indus in the purest white of altruism and legitimacy:

...It is a matter of notoriety that the treaties entered into by the British Government in the year 1832, with the Ameers of Sindh, the Newab of Bhawalpore, and Maharajah Runjeet Singh, had for their object, by opening the navigation of the Indus, to facilitate the extension of commerce, and to gain for the British nation in Central Asia that legitimate influence which an interchange of benefits would naturally produce...

Ellenborough, who initiated the first Indus survey and all that flowed from it, saw commerce and influence as sharp weapons against Russia. But Auckland denied himself the luxury of mentioning Russia. The Simla Manifesto emphasized the commercial reasons for sending Burnes to Kabul in the first place, and then gave this very Sikh account of Jamrud:

...While Captain Burnes, however, was on his journey to Caubul, information was received by the Governor General that the troops of Dost Mahomed Khan had made a sudden and unprovoked attack on those of our ancient ally, Maharajah Runjeet Singh...

It is true that the attack was sudden; it would be true to say that it was unexpected; but it is far from true to say that it was unprovoked. Provocation cannot easily be proved. Those forts built by Hari Singh near the entrance to the Khyber, so provoking to Dost Muhammad, were innocent defensive works to Runjeet Singh, and Runjeet Singh was Britain's ally. Therefore, for the purposes of the Simla Manifesto, the attack had to be unprovoked. The Manifesto went on to praise the Maharajah for his restraint after Jamrud and to describe the influence of Persia's unfriendly policy upon the conduct of Dost Muhammad Khan. The truth suffered its worst wounds in this section of the Manifesto. Here Dost Muhammad appeared as the villain, 'urging most unreasonable pretensions', or 'avowing schemes of aggrandizement and ambition', or threatening in furtherance of his schemes 'to call in every foreign aid that he could command'. Therefore, the Manifesto said:

...the hostile policy of the latter chief showed too plainly that, so long as Caubul remained under his government, we could never hope that the tranquility of our neighbourhood would be secured, or that the interests of our Indian Empire would be preserved inviolate...

Just as the attack on Jamrud had been 'unprovoked', so the attack upon Herat by the Persian army was 'a most unjustifiable and cruel aggression', resisted heroically by a garrison with justice on its side. The Manifesto dealt in similar terms with the rest of the story of the Herat crisis, and linked Persia and Kabul and Kandahar as co-conspirators against 'the rights and interests of the British nation in India'. It said:

...In the crisis of affairs consequent upon the retirement of our Envoy from Caubul, the Governor General felt the importance of taking immediate measures for arresting the rapid progress of foreign intrigue and aggression towards our own territories. His attention was naturally drawn at this conjuncture to the position and claims of Shah Shooja ool Moolk...

The rest can be inferred from Auckland's previous dispatches. 'Pressing necessity, as well as every consideration of policy and justice, warranted us in espousing the cause of Shah Shooja ool Moolk, whose popularity throughout Afghanistan had been proved to his Lordship by the strong and unanimous testimony of the best authorities...' These were strong and confident words, disguising Auckland's private uncertainty. The Manifesto continued with an account of the Sikh part in the project and a statement of the advantages to be expected from the Tripartite Treaty:

...Various points have been adjusted, which had been the subjects of discussion between the British Government and his Highness the Maharajah, the identity of whose interests with those of the Honourable Company has now been made apparent to all the surrounding states. A guaranteed independence will, upon favourable conditions, be tendered to the Ameers of Sindh, and the integrity of Herat, in the possession of its present ruler, will be fully respected; while by the measures completed, or in progress, it may reasonably be hoped that the general freedom and security of commerce will be promoted; that the name and just influence of the British Government will gain their proper footing among the nations of Central Asia; that tranquility will be established upon the most important frontier of India; and that a lasting barrier will be raised against hostile intrigue and encroachment. His Majesty, Shah Soojah ool Moolk, will enter Afghanistan, surrounded by his own troops, and will be supported against foreign interference and factious opposition by a British army. The Governor General confidently hopes that the Shah will be speedily replaced on his throne by his own subjects and adherents; and when once he shall be secured in power, and the independence and integrity of Afghanistan established, the British army will be withdrawn. The Governor General has been led to these measures by the duty which is imposed upon him of providing for the security of the possessions of the British Crown; but he rejoices that, in the discharge of his duty, he will be enabled to assist in restoring the union and prosperity of the Afghan people. Throughout the approaching operations, British influence will be sedulously employed to further every measure of general benefit, to reconcile differences, to secure oblivion of injuries, and to put an end to the distractions, by which, for so many years, the welfare and happiness of the Afghans have been impaired. Even to the chiefs, whose hostile proceedings have given just cause of offence to the British Government, it will seek to secure liberal and honourable treatment, on their tendering early submission, and ceasing from opposition to that course of measures which may be judged the most suitable for the general advantage of their country.[10]

Auckland and Macnaghten had done their work well. Russia was never mentioned, and, if truth suffered, European peace survived. The Home Government, as we have seen in chapter 9, was duly grateful. Meanwhile there were contradictory reports from Afghanistan of the fate of Herat. On 7 October Colvin said that they were in good heart at Simla 'about these reports of the retreat of the Persians'.[11] But on the 17th he quoted a letter from a 'French man of Cabool, dated the 16th of last month', destroying that hope.[12] A few days later the hope was revived. There was to be no turning back, for McNeill had removed the last doubt when he said that Herat must be secured as well as saved *before* the Russians reached Khiva. Auckland felt that he had reasonably strong support from home, even if specific instructions were not yet forthcoming. McNeill's letter of 5th August had arrived in the fourth week of October, just before the September mail from London.

To McNeill the Governor General replied on 24 October, explaining what was afoot and, incidentally, revealing some of his personal quality as a judge and leader of men:

...Sir Henry Fane will have the command of the army—and we have no better soldier—and Mr Macnaghten will represent me with Shah Shoojah—and India has no abler man. In the event of perfect success he will remain at Cabool and apply himself to the reconciliation of differences and to the consolidation of the strength of Afghanistan. Captain Burnes will be attached to him and will undertake special missions in advance. He is now at Shikarpore...

Auckland concluded this letter to McNeill by saying:

...For yourself I can only say that I feel most grateful towards you, as I am sure that the Government at home will feel, for the ability and the determination with which you have wrestled against circumstances of no ordinary difficulty.[13]

Within a few days of writing to McNeill the Governor General had to consider whether it would be necessary after all to send a second Bengal division into Afghanistan, and whether Sir Henry Fane would need to go. He published his decision to continue the operation on 8 November, for he was now certain that the Persians had withdrawn. He said that the withdrawal was a 'just cause of congratulation', but he would 'continue to prosecute with vigour the measures which had been announced, with a view to the substitution of a friendly for a hostile power in the eastern province of Afghanistan...'. On 13 November he told the Bombay Commander in Chief, Sir John Keane, that he would succeed Fane as controller of the expedition, and on the 15th Auckland told Hobhouse:

...I have agreed with Sir Henry Fane that the campaign is not likely to be now *tali vindice dignus*, and he will remain in India until the period shall arrive for his return to England...[14]

There is nothing in the Auckland Papers to support the claim that Sir Henry Fane withdrew from a project for which he never had any enthusiasm and with which he consistently disagreed. On the contrary, there is evidence that, having already made arrangements for his retirement to England, he volunteered for one last campaign on condition that the army should be one worthy of his command. When the Army of the Indus lost one of its divisions before the campaign had even started, he decided 'to adhere to his original resolution of returning home as soon as his successor shall arrive'. The private letter to Hobhouse just quoted was the one in which Auckland acknowledged the September mail from home.[15] In it he learned of Burnes's promotion and of Hobhouse's opinion that the offer of money and assistance to Kandahar in December 1837 was perfectly proper. Auckland had disavowed the offer and had reprimanded Burnes for making it without authority. A lesser man would not have written to Burnes as Auckland did on 5 November:

...My private letters speak in high terms of your proceedings in Cabul, and I may in candour mention that upon the one point upon which there was some difference between us—the proposed advance of money to Candahar—opinions for which I have the highest respect are in your favour. I do not grudge you this and am only glad that a just tribute has been paid to your ability and indefatigable zeal...[16]

In his letter to Hobhouse the Governor General defended his disavowal of Burnes's offer, but without vehemence or rancour:

...I may be thought right again when it is known that whilst we might be offering a purse, Russia was offering a kingdom, and that we should not only have committed a political blunder, but have been dupes also in the disposal of our money—Yet do not think that I have even for a moment undervalued the extraordinary merit of Captain Burnes. I have never been served by anyone possessed of so much vigour and elasticity of action, or of more willingness for good, and I rejoice in the distinction which you have given to him...[17]

Let us consider for a moment the circumstance on which Auckland was commenting. The Government at home, surveying the whole of the correspondence from Persia and India and Afghanistan up to the end of May, judged only two men worthy of special distinction at that stage—Alexander Burnes, for his work at Kabul and Kandahar, and Robert Leech, for his conduct at Kandahar. Auckland could have reacted in several different ways, but, being what he was, a man of character and depth, he was undisturbed by the implied criticism of his own action. It so happens that Auckland and his advisers in Calcutta were looking about at the beginning of November 1838 for someone to take Macnaghten's place in the Secretariat. One of those whose names were suggested was Henry Torrens, an assistant secretary on Auckland's staff, alleged by Masson to have exerted sinister influence over the Governor General with Colvin's help that summer. Torrens did not get the job, for Auckland said of him that, notwithstanding his acknowledged ability and industry, he lacked the necessary experience, authority and standing to take first place in the government under the Governor General. Surely, if Torrens could influence Auckland to make war against his better judgement, he could influence the speed of his own promotion. Another man got the post, on his merits as an official.[18]

What of Eldred Pottinger, who had worked so hard at Herat? At home in England his exploits seemed to outshine those of Alexander Burnes, and some people professed not to understand why Burnes got a knighthood and Pottinger got nothing. The full story of the Burnes mission could not be told, and the story of Eldred Pottinger's adventure became a legend. In fact Colonel Pottinger's nephew was made Political Agent at Herat with a salary of one thousand rupees a month, backdated to the opening of the siege. Auckland wrote to Hobhouse: '...I hope that this will not be thought extravagant. His chivalrous adventure, his admirable conduct and their extraordinary results ought to be on record and upheld...'[19]

So Eldred Pottinger *was* rewarded, and generously, for the siege had lasted ten months. In 1839 he received a brevet Majority and the 'Companionship of the Most Honourable Military Order of the Bath'. Meanwhile his Uncle Henry was still struggling with the emirs of Sind and his own anger at the return of Alexander Burnes to Pottinger 'territory'. When Colvin congratulated Burnes on 21 November he had to warn him to 'drop all appearance of controversy' in his correspondence with Colonel Pottinger, 'like a good fellow'. They had not really made up the quarrel which started in 1836. Pottinger's task in Sind was now to revise the treaty arrangements with the emirs so that the British Government might establish a subsidiary force there and free the Indus traffic from all tolls. He was also to break up the old confederacy and establish each chief as an independent ruler in his own territory under British protection. This last was Pottinger's own idea, supported by Auckland.[20] The British were in a strong position to exact new terms from the emirs, for Sir John Keane and his contingent were about to land at the mouth of the Indus after sailing from Bombay, and the Bengal troops were gathering on the left bank of the Sutlej at Ferozepore. The combined forces numbered about twenty thousand men, not counting Shuja's hastily assembled contingent of six thousand camp-followers. Moreover, since the assembly at Ferozepore coincided with Auckland's state visit to the Punjab, the Sikh army was also out in force. The Talpura princes cursed the interfering English, but there was little they could do.

John Colvin was a young man with romantic ideas about Britain's role in the East, and his letters from Auckland's camp at this period may be said to reflect quite accurately the confidence and sense of destiny among British officers in 1838. The world had never seen an empire quite like that of the British in India, and there seemed to be no end to the adventure on which they had been launched in the East less than a hundred years before. 'We have gained a golden opportunity', Colvin said, 'for confirming ourselves in a position across the Indus and establishing a just impression of our power throughout Central Asia.' In another place he wrote of the 'glorious news from Herat', immediately adding: 'Let us press on as we are pressing on, and in six months hence we shall have a footing across the Indus and in Central Asia which will consolidate our power in India for another century.'[21] Enthusiasm for the campaign, which was not necessarily the same thing as enthusiasm for the policy which made the campaign necessary, was so high that Fane had to draw lots to decide which regiments should stay behind when it was publicly announced that only one Bengal division would cross the frontier. Fane's resort to the luck of the draw is more understandable if one remembers the capacity of Indian army officers for quarrelling and controversy. Fane would never have heard the last of it if he had made a deliberate choice. The announcement of the reduction in the force was made on 27 November, the day on which Auckland and his two sisters arrived at Ferozepore. On the 29th, which was a Thursday, Runjeet Singh and his escort crossed the Sutlej not far from Sobraon. He rode on an elephant surrounded by his household cavalry. The two most successful military organizations on the sub-continent vied with each other in their skill at manœuvre in the field and in the gorgeousness of their appointments and apparel. A royal salute greeted the Maharajah at the British camp, where he dismounted and entered the Governor General's tent. Emily Eden, always a wry observer of the Indian scene, thought that he looked 'exactly like an old mouse with grey whiskers and one eye'.[22] He looked anything but the fabled Lion of Lahore. Yet he had only to lift a finger to obtain instant obedience. There he sat in Auckland's tent, awaiting his present from the British nation. The bands played rousing marches, and the guns boomed, and in came Major General Sir Willoughby Cotton, newly appointed commander of the Bengal Column of the Army of the Indus, with a portrait of Queen Victoria. Emily Eden herself had painted it, relying partly on memory and partly on an old print. Her brother had had it framed at Delhi in gold and jewels. This was not the only present, nor was it the most costly, but it was clearly intended to be the centre-piece. After more formal courtesies and expressions of mutual regard the Maharajah and his escort retired to their own camp. On Friday it was Lord Auckland's turn to cross the Sutlej. He entered a camp not unlike his own, peopled by smartly uniformed warriors under a European military discipline. Auckland could look around him and privately confirm the estimate of Sikh military strength which had always made him chary of offending Runjeet Singh. The ceremonies of the previous day were reversed, but this time the Maharajah suggested a private interview on Saturday afternoon. According to Kaye, who got the story from Havelock, this formal visit to the Sikh camp degenerated into a party at which there was 'an unseemly display of dancing girls' and evening entertainment 'still less decorous'. But in fact Auckland stayed only a short time on Friday. He returned for the private interview on Saturday afternoon, during which they talked business for an hour and a half until half past five. Then the nautch and the fireworks began. Runjeet Singh, who was famous for his capacity for strong drink, passed round the cup and said to Auckland: 'There is truth in people when they drink—now shake hands with me and tell me you are my friend.' Auckland did so, and they parted.[23]

Now we must move down river to Lower Sind. On 28 November some of Keane's Bombay troops moved to the chosen camping ground at Vikkur. It soon became clear that the sulking Sind emirs (sulking with reason) had made no attempt to gather transport or provisions for their 'allies'. Keane therefore sent Captain James Outram, his aide de camp, to arrange for a supply of boats and pack animals from Cutch. By the last day of the month the whole of the Bombay Division was in camp at Vikkur, awaiting anxiously for Outram's return. Colonel Pottinger called on Sir John Keane at Vikkur to report on the progress of his negotiations with the emirs, and left him in no doubt that they were being difficult. Outram returned to camp on the 12th, and the camels arrived from Cutch on the 19th. It was just as well, for Pottinger had just heard that the emirs were quietly assembling an army while professing friendship. Pottinger therefore asked the Government of Bombay to send the strong brigade which had been held in reserve there for such an emergency. Thanks to Outram the Bombay Division already ashore was able to march from Vikkur to Tatta in the last week of December. Keane set up his headquarters there on the 28th. But his transport and supply problems had only just begun.

At Ferozepore the Bengal troops were still deep in the other military world of drill movements and ceremonial. But on 2 December Shuja's contingent started its march under the critical eye of the regular soldiers. It was generally agreed that the only respectable unit in view was the troop of Bengal Horse Artillery which Shah Shuja had borrowed from the British. On the 3rd Runjeet Singh came to inspect the army of his ally. Rather more than ten thousand men were on parade in his honour, and he admired all that he saw with his one good eye. On the next day he came to view the artillery park. He took great interest in it because he fully understood the importance of good guns and gunners in modern war. The British had flattered him by including two brand-new howitzers among his presents a few days before this visit. Having seen and praised the guns of the Army of the Indus, the Maharajah ended the evening with wine and fireworks at Auckland's tent. He left his hosts with promises of an interesting entertainment for the following day, for he had cunningly let the British show their wares first. At daybreak on Wednesday 5 December Auckland and his staff rode over to Runjeet's camp to watch his military review. A few days later Auckland wrote to Hobhouse: 'On Wednesday morning was a review of his troops, about eight or nine thousand in number, and I must say that in equipment, in steadiness, and in precision of manœuvre they seemed to be in no respect inferior to our own army...'[24]

Emily Eden later remarked on what she heard from her brother and his officers when they returned from Runjeet's camp:

All the gentlemen went at daybreak yesterday to Runjeet's review, and came back rather discomfited. He had nearly as many troops as Sir Henry Fane had; they were quite as well disciplined, rather better dressed, repeated the same military movements and several others much more complicated, and, in short, nobody knows what to say about it, so they say nothing, except that they are sure the Sikhs would run away in a real fight. It is a sad blow to our vanities! You won't mention it to the troops in London—we say nothing about it to those here.[25]

In a letter to McNeil a few days after the review Lord Auckland said he had been 'very much struck with the admirable appearance' of the Sikh troops.[26] There can be little doubt that he congratulated himself on having maintained the alliance with Runjeet Singh and avoided all causes of offence after the affair at Shikarpur in 1836. Similarly Runjeet Singh was glad to be at peace with his powerful neighbour.

Auckland wondered what would become of that large Sikh army once it lost its powerful leader. Indeed, he told Hobhouse that once matters were settled in other quarters his first care would be to strengthen his defences on the frontier with the Punjab.

On the 6th Auckland and his personal staff left the soldiers to their trade and set out for Amritsar and the next stage of his visit to the Punjab. At Ferozepore the Governor General took leave of Sir Henry Fane, 'and with regret, for though he has a temper and a bearing difficult to deal with, he has on the other hand many excellent qualities. I have throughout my career in India been with him upon terms of unreserved confidence, and I fear that upon many subjects I may not always have so able an adviser...'[27] But, although he had *seen* the last, Auckland had not heard the last of Sir Henry. The Horse Guards were slow in selecting a new Commander in Chief for India, and Sir Henry Fane remained in his post as little more than a spectator for several months more. During that time he kept up his customary correspondence with Lord Auckland. They were always frank with each other, and Auckland had to contend with the unwanted and often unhelpful criticisms of an underemployed general. He bore it all with his usual patience and good nature. But neither Auckland nor Fane expected such a long wait for the new Commander in Chief when they parted on 6 December. Fane left the operational command to Sir Willoughby Cotton, and embarked with his headquarters staff in a boat which would carry him down the Indus and keep pace with the army's march, starting on 10 December.

For every soldier who marched on that day and on the succeeding days there were at least three camp-followers. In spite of Fane's general instruction that officers and their units should travel light there was an enormous train of baggage animals. At least one regiment took its pack of foxhounds into Afghanistan,[28] and the comforts of the officers' mess were not neglected. After marching fourteen miles the army halted at Mamdot and pitched camp— or rather most of the army pitched camp. The three regiments of native infantry in William Nott's brigade refused to do so because they had not been granted extra allowances for service beyond the Indus. The mistake was quickly corrected, and there was no further hint of mutiny.[29] But the incident reflected upon Brigadier Nott, who was in temporary command of the division, under Cotton. Subsequent marches were uneventful as far as Rohri, which the army reached on 24 January.

Lord Auckland had reached Lahore on 21 December, having reported to the Secret Committee on his orders to Cotton, Keane, and Macnaghten, and on the evident earnestness and sincerity of Runjeet Singh 'in his professions of attachment to his alliance with the British Government'.[30] He had also, incidentally, placated Captain Wade, who was sore at the honours accorded to Burnes, by promoting him to Lieutenant Colonel. He mentioned this in a letter to India House on the 15th, when he also said:

...I rode yesterday with Runjeet Singh up a line of thirty thousand of his troops and one hundred pieces of cannon, everything being perfectly in order and equipped. His proceedings to me are all most cordial and friendly. He is in the strongest health and spirits and though we are accustomed to speculate on his death there is no apparent reason why he should not yet live for some years...[31]

The visit to Lahore opened cheerfully enough, but on the 24th, when all was prepared for 'a programme of amusements for six days', Auckland received a message from the Maharajah, asking him to send his doctor to examine him. Auckland's doctor found Runjeet Singh 'feverish and low'. All amusements were cancelled, and Auckland began to wonder whether the end was near. But Runjeet rallied on the 27th and was strong enough to receive him on the 28th for a little while. The long-awaited meeting between Governor General and Maharajah, which had opened so propitiously, was ending in gloom and foreboding. Auckland even fell from his horse and received a severe shaking on the day of his last interview with Runjeet Singh. The Greeks would surely have said that the gods were reminding the two potentates of their human frailty. Runjeet's reminder took a particularly unpleasant form:

...The old man's illness threw a languor over the last days of my visit, for all were in some degree uneasy about him, and the increase which weakness had given to the paralytic affection of his mouth made my last visits painful as well to myself as to him...[32]

Auckland was referring to the traces of Runjeet Singh's stroke of two years before, a stroke which had left him with damaged facial muscles. Nevertheless, Auckland ventured the opinion, based on the limited medical advice available to him then, that Runjeet Singh's life might 'with prudence be continued for some years'. In fact the old man had only six more months to live. On the 29th he sent his son and principal chiefs to say goodbye to his British visitors. On that day Auckland answered a letter from the Governor of Madras, who seems to have questioned the wisdom of going ahead with the expedition now that Herat was safe. Auckland replied:

...The retreat of the Persians from Herat is indeed a great event, but it will make comparatively but little change in my measures. Russian Agents are notoriously active in Afghanistan and I have but two days ago received letters (not of a late date) from Mr McNeill urging me to relax in no exertions to establish British influence at least as far as Herat —and this I have no doubt is right in the present aspect of European politics and I am much rather disposed at least to keep up our army to its present numbers than anywhere to reduce it...[33]

In this revealing letter to Lord Elphinstone he not only showed the continuing influence of McNeill's opinion; he also made a correct assessment of the state of European politics. But he was always just a little sceptical, even when he had weighed all the factors in the situation. He kept his sense of proportion when others, Macnaghten or Colvin, on one side, or Fane and Masson, on the other, lost theirs. In that same letter Auckland took a little further his first thoughts about the Sikh army. He could only speak of Runjeet's army as he had seen it at reviews, where it had appeared excellent in equipment and perfect in its manœuvres, 'but it has no doubt a very defective organisation and is far from well officered'. Was he indulging in wishful thinking? It seems that he was, for he had told Hobhouse only a few weeks earlier that he would have to strengthen his defences along the Sutlej before long.

Earlier we saw that Burnes travelled ahead of the Bengal column, negotiating with the chiefs along the army's route. First he obtained the co-operation of the Khan of Bahawalpur, who did what he could, but not enough, to satisfy the generals who followed on Burnes's heels. According to one staff officer who witnessed Fane's durbar at Bahawalpur on 30 December, the Khan was ill at ease, as if conscious that his state had done less for the army than was promised. He had every reason to feel ill at ease. More than thirty-five thousand hungry soldiers and camp-followers had just swept through his territory. They had behaved well, but could he really be sure that they would all leave in two days' time? Besides, when the Bengal column soaked up Bahawalpur's provisions other people had to go hungry. He was much relieved when they crossed the frontier into Khairpur in the middle of January. Burnes had by that time signed, sealed and obtained ratification of a treaty with Rustum, the Khan of Khairpur. Rustum was an old man, and he told Burnes that other invaders of India might be resisted but if one of the armies of Britain were swept away another would come in its place. Burnes wrote: '[He said] that such power induced him alike to fear and rely upon us; that he was henceforward the submissive and obedient servant of the British.'[34] The treaty brought Khairpur permanently under British protection, and the Khan accepted a British Resident at his capital and placed the conduct of his foreign relations entirely in British hands. But the most immediate benefit, from Britain's point of view, was the right to occupy the island fort of Bukkur, between Rohri and Sukkur, in time of war. Colonel Pottinger, meanwhile, was trying to persuade the emirs of Lower Sind to be as sensible as Rustum. At one stage he suggested accepting a tract of land near Tatta as a substitute for payment of support costs for the proposed subsidiary force in Sind. His Government was horrified, and on 13 December rejected the suggestion outright, for Auckland 'judged it above all things desirable to give no colour to imputations of a desire of territorial aggrandizement, in connexion with the plan of defensive policy which circumstances have forced upon the Government in India'.[35] This last phrase, from an official dispatch, was no mere form of words. It echoes a passage in one of Auckland's private letters to Hobhouse, in which he said:

...The magnitude of the measure in which I am embarked is alarming even to myself, and it will be for others to pronounce whether I am attempting at too great a hazard and at too great an expense to establish and to maintain a British influence throughout the nations of Central

Asia; or whether it would have been safer to leave Herat, Khiva, Cabul and Candahar either to the occupation of Russia or to the exercise of the political agency of that power, combined with Persia against us. I have looked upon my course to be strictly one of self-defence. I embarked in it most painfully and unwillingly, but having so embarked I will, please God, manfully go through with it...[36]

CHAPTER II

MARCHING TO KANDAHAR

...To gain over the Chiefs and people and to use and trust and please them, is the first, second and third commandment...

COLVIN to Macnaghten, 5 February 1839

...Our public affairs are prospering much, but I will not bore you with details. We really are within sight of going home, dearest Theresa, but it makes me shiver to think of it. I am so afraid something will happen to prevent it...

EMILY EDEN to Lady Theresa Lister, 17 June 1839

To be vindicated is sweet; to be ordered to do exactly what one has already started to do is triumph. Lord Auckland knew that triumph on 16 January 1839 when a dispatch marked 'Most Secret' and signed by the Secret Committee arrived at his camp. Did his hands shake as he broke the seal? Did Colvin urge him on as he fumbled with the heavy packet of dispatches from London? They would have been inhuman had they not opened the dispatches with more than usual excitement. What they found was more than Auckland had ever expected:

...I have more than once described to you the difficulties and the political intricacies with which I have had to deal, and though in every case I might have looked for favourable consideration and support I did not dare to look forward to this coincidence of opinion, and as the first announcement of my proceedings relieved you, so have your letters relieved me from a heavy load of anxiety...[1]

At the beginning of February he had the satisfaction of being able to tell Major General Cotton that Wellington had submitted one of his usual memoranda to the Home Government in November. The duke had been led into unfounded criticism by a report that the army was to descend the Indus in boats. He wondered how the army would move when it regained dry land, since it would have no pack animals with it. But in numbers he considered the army 'amply sufficient, with reserves at Shikarpore and Ferozepore. It was greater indeed than any which had been brought together during the whole of his residence in India. He suggests

247

nothing for which we have not already provided...'[2] Thus the British Government in India basked in the military approval of the duke of Wellington and the unstinted support of the Home Government at the beginning of 1839. Auckland shared the credit with McNeill and Palmerston for taking action which had 'lowered the tone' of the Russians most effectively.[3] Then at the end of February he heard that the news of Russia's humiliation and of the Indian army's move had produced a 'a most salutary effect' in the Courts of Europe.[4] Hobhouse's reservations about the wording of the Simla Declaration and the demand for money from the Sind emirs did not worry him unduly. What mattered was that the Secret Committee had stated, as recently as 26 December: '...It is sufficient for us to repeat our approval of the general course of policy which you have resolved to adopt...'[5]

Auckland no longer felt so lonely in his responsibility. He had been at his loneliest for ten days in January. William Macnaghten took leave of him and Colvin on the 6th at Ferozepore, and started on his way to the camp and court of Shah Shuja. The first of the approving dispatches from home did not arrive until the 16th. John Colvin's youthful enthusiasm was all very well, but it was no substitute for the experience and judgement of William Macnaghten. Emily Eden thought of him as '*our* Lord Palmerston, a dry sensible man, who wears an enormous pair of blue spectacles and speaks Persian, Arabic, and Hindustani rather more fluently than English'.[6] Her brother greatly admired Macnaghten but was also a shrewd judge of the man's faults. '...Macnaghten almost always does well and displays admirable talent and spirit, though he sometimes overdoes...'[7] Nevertheless, as he had said before, India had no abler man. Auckland was always inclined to encourage a good man to use his talents and abilities to the full; he did not dwell upon faults or hold inquests over past errors, unless he had to. Perhaps he was sometimes too forgiving, but no one who has ever had to lead men is likely to doubt that Auckland erred on the right side in preferring encouragement to the whip.

Macnaghten caught up with the Shah and his contingent near Shikarpur on the 31st. By that time the contingent, commanded by Major General Simpson, had crossed the Indus by boat a few miles north-east of Rohri. The Shah was not at that time very popular with the British officers, some of whom complained to Auckland's staff about his arrogance and discourtesy to them. In

order to assert his authority he kept them standing in his presence
for long periods. One of the complaints reached Colvin through
Burnes, who was told to let Macnaghten settle the matter, and
Colvin told Todd (now a political agent under Macnaghten) to
impress upon the Shah that it was necessary for him to adopt 'a
conciliatory and properly liberal demeanour' towards his own
people. 'It is not only his own success, *but the character of our
whole policy* which is involved in his finding a willing reception from
the Afghans. Our agents should ever bear in mind this essential
fact.'[8] But it was not long before Macnaghten reported that Shah
Shuja spoke of his people as a 'pack of dogs'. Confident as always,
Macnaghten assured Auckland that Shuja could be reformed, and
for a while he was right.

While Macnaghten was on his way from Ferozepore to Shikarpur
there were disturbing reports of the unfriendly disposition of the
Sind emirs. Burnes gave the news to Fane and Cotton when he
joined the Bengal column on the frontier between Bahawalpur and
Khairpur on 14 January. At first Auckland was inclined to postpone the settling of accounts with the emirs in the belief that
nothing must be allowed to delay the expedition to Afghanistan,
but he acknowledged that they might compel his army to take
action and he had to leave the tactical decision to the generals on the
spot. The distance between him and the army left him with no
alternative.[9] Colonel Pottinger sent Lieutenant Eastwick with a
copy of the new treaty proposals to Hyderabad in the middle of the
month. Eastwick embarked with Outram and another officer on the
17th for the journey by river steamer (then a great novelty) to the
capital of Lower Sind. He had to tell the three emirs that they must
pay twenty lakhs of rupees to Shuja in return for his abandonment
of all claim to supremacy and tribute in the years to come. Only
Sobdar was excused from paying, for he had not corresponded
with the Shah of Persia when the others betrayed their alliance with
Britain. The emirs were also to be told about the subsidiary force,
for which they would pay, and the abolition of all tolls on the Indus.
Colonel Pottinger authorized Eastwick to say that 'the smallest act
of hostility will plunge matters beyond the chance of recall'.[10]
Colvin, in a letter to Macnaghten, was a little more specific: '...I
trust that the Ameers are not going to delay you, but if they do all
that can be said is that they must pay for it dearly. A thoroughly good
settlement of Lower Sinde would make up for any postponement

of our great Candahar movement...' But, Colvin added, 'if Sinde be *tolerably* safe and quiet in the rear, then all efforts must be directed to *getting* on. It is to be remembered that through our alliance with Runjeet Singh and our means for moving fresh troops down the Sutlej we can always hold a most effective check over the Sindians, however inveterate their bad spirits...'[11]

Eastwick and his companions arrived off Hyderabad on the 20th, and during the next few days, while the emirs were discussing Pottinger's proposals, Outram reconnoitred the fortress. He cheerfully concluded that artillery could breach the walls without any great difficulty. On the afternoon of the 22nd the emirs sent for the British mission, greeted Eastwick and his friends very warmly, and said after long discussion that they could not answer Pottinger yet. Outram judged that the emirs were playing for time. He noted in his diary that within the last twenty-four hours orders had been issued for the immediate assembly of all fighting men at the capital. Eastwick agreed with him, and reported by messenger to Sir John Keane (then about fifty miles away at Tatta) that the emirs were likely to resist his further advance. As it happened, Keane had already decided to move a little nearer to Hyderabad. On the 23rd he led his Bombay troops into a new camp at Jerruck, just over half-way from Tatta to the capital. Eastwick, however, had not yet had a definite reply from the emirs. He asked for one, but no reply came. Fearing attack, he and his mission stood to all night. The morning of the 24th came, and there was still no reply. After a few hours Eastwick judged that the hostility of the Baluchis round about, together with the words of one who claimed to know that the terms had been rejected, justified him in re-embarking for the return journey. He encountered the Bombay division at Jerruck on the 25th, and Keane at once decided upon a combined assault on Hyderabad by Bombay and Bengal troops. Eastwick told Pottinger, who must privately have admitted some justice in the remark, what Nur Muhammad had said on reading the treaty proposals: 'Since the day that Sind has been connected with the English there has always been something new; your government is never satisfied...'[12] Independently of Keane the officers commanding the Bengal division had already decided to march on Hyderabad when Keane wrote. One has to speak of the 'officers commanding' because Fane, although officially no more than an onlooker, was still directing the Army of the Indus from his river-boat. Cotton was in overall command of Bengal troops, and Nott was temporarily commanding the division. Cotton's headquarters reached Rohri on the 24th. Fane was already there, and so were the engineers, who had been building a bridge of boats for several days. But the bridge was not complete, and Fane, with the agreement of Alexander Burnes as senior political agent present, concluded that there was time for a move against Hyderabad. At a ceremony for the handing over of the ratified Khairpur treaty on 26 January, Sir Henry Fane told Rustum that *his* army had wasted enough time in treating with the Hyderabad chief: '...I will now march down and attack him; and if you like I will show you the troops I shall send to do it.'[13] Orders for the march were issued on the 27th, but none moved until the army had taken possession of Bukkur fort. This was done at sunset on Tuesday 29 January, when the British ensign flew for the first time from a building on the territory of Sind.

Burnes and Cotton returned to the left bank and to thoughts of the march on Hyderabad. A cavalry brigade and two brigades of infantry, supported by horse artillery and field guns, were standing by, waiting for the order to advance. Each infantryman had twenty-five rounds in his pouches and one hundred and twenty-five in boxes carried by pack animals. Extraordinary rumours of the gold and silver to be found in the Hyderabad treasury excited the officers and men, who looked forward to a share of the prize money. It would be unworthy to claim that greed was the only motive of Fane and Cotton in deciding to turn south; it would also be naïve to say the opposite, that the purest professional and political motives governed all their actions. Sir Henry Fane, who always thought that he could do the Governor General's job better than the Governor General, assured Auckland in a letter written at this critical moment that the subjection of Sind was of 'infinitely paramount importance to any consideration about Shah Shooja ool Moolk and Afghanistan'. We shall see a little later how firmly Auckland put him in his place. Meanwhile Auckland was fretting about the daily evidence of his army's willingness to turn away from its main objective. He told Cotton on 28 January, by which time it was too late, that 'it would indeed be a great public misfortune if the expedition to Afghanistan were crippled or delayed...'.[14] On the day after the occupation of Bukkur the Bengal troops detailed for duty against Hyderabad began their march along the left bank of the Indus. No one, from the retiring Commander in Chief down to the newest subaltern, thought to cross the river and reconnoitre the country between Shikarpur and the entrance to the Bolan Pass. It was as though the army had corporately decided that a campaign in Sind was to take the place of the Afghan expedition. The soldiers marched for a week under the command of the efficient but irascible Major General Nott. Let him describe what happened on the evening of 6 February, as he wrote it in a letter to his son:

...I had given out my orders last evening for the column to march this morning at four o'clock. I went to bed at nine last night, and was roused out of my sleep by an express, bringing a note from Sir Henry Fane, who is ten miles ahead of me, saying that the Ameers had come to terms, and directing me to halt the 1st and 2nd Brigades where we now are, until further orders. Thus I have lost two or three lacs of rupees by the timely wisdom of these violent Ameers. However, I have also lost the grilling I should have had in this horrible climate. I suppose we shall now retrace our steps to Bukkur, pass the bridge of boats which we have thrown over the noble Indus; and then, hurrah for the Bolan Pass and Affghanistan—for poverty, a fine climate, and a gallant race of people.[15]

It was exactly as Nott predicted, except that the unreconnoitred route between Shikarpur and the Bolan Pass proved to be the stuff of nightmares. His column turned about and marched northwards from Kandiaro on 10 February. On the same day Keane's Bombay column, having received the submission of the emirs, started its march up the right bank of the Indus. The emirs had yielded on the 1st of the month, signed the draft treaty on the 3rd, and paid half of their twenty lakhs on the 7th. They dispersed their hastily assembled army, so that there was no sign of it when the Bombay column arrived at Kotri, opposite Hyderabad, on 4 February. So it was that the Sind emirs bowed to the military and political dominance of the British in India. The donkey, after much bucking and kicking, surrendered meekly to the monkey and its goad—for the time being. One more fling was to be allowed to the emirs before they lost their independence for ever.

At this time a young subaltern of Bengal Engineers, Lieutenant Henry Durand, made a note in his diary of an amusing conversation with Charles Masson, who was still clinging to the skirts of the Army of the Indus:

He gave us a very amusing account of Burnes's rencontre with Captain Vicovich at Cabul. This Russian officer reached Cabul 'with a pair of black kid gloves, a French translation of Burnes's travels, and a long Persian letter, well powdered with gold leaf, purporting to be from the Emperor of Russia'. The Afghans, of whom Mr Masson speaks highly, laughed at this soi-disant envoy, and discredited him in toto. Had Burnes had the sense to laugh too, all would have gone well; but he took the thing seriously, lost his head, and was himself the person who induced the Afghans to consider Captain Vicovich in the light of an accredited envoy.[16]

It is significant that Charles Masson was finding a receptive audience for his slanderous stories among Tory officers on the banks of the Indus in January and February 1839. The hated Whig Government had, after all, neglected *them* and honoured this conceited subaltern from Montrose, Alexander Burnes. Hobhouse had had an anonymous letter to that effect at the beginning of January, alleging that Burnes had never 'performed any great military or civil service', and insinuating that his honours were the result of a 'job'.[17] Durand later became Ellenborough's private secretary, and stood in the same relation to Auckland's successor as Colvin stood to Auckland. He is not an unbiased witness.

But Henry Durand, in January 1839, was a very small cog in a big military machine. William Macnaghten was furious when he heard that that machine was being used against Sind when it should be on its way to Afghanistan. He told Colvin that Cotton had sent his men on a wild-goose chase. 'If this goes on, as it is now doing, what is to become of our Afghan expedition? Burnes's letters are most unsatisfactory.'[18] Burnes, as we saw earlier, had given his blessing as political agent to the diversion southwards. Auckland and Colvin had by no means ruled out such a diversion; they devoutly hoped that it could be avoided. Macnaghten, however, wrote a 'decided' letter to Major General Cotton against the whole project, and presumed to give him orders, which he was not entitled to do as a 'political'.[19] Both Auckland and Colvin reproved him for this. They judged that the letter would poison Macnaghten's relations with the General unless he made amends, and they were right. Macnaghten and Cotton thrashed the matter out at a meeting on 20 February, and after much argument they parted very good friends—happily for the success of the expedition. By that time they were at Shikarpur. The Bengal column had completed its crossing by the bridge of boats two days earlier. Auckland subsequently took great pride in the achievement of the engineers responsible for the bridge, which consisted of seventy-four large boats lashed together. It was five hundred yards long, and it stood up well to the passage of more than 38,000 men, 30,000 camels, and all the artillery and wheeled transport, as well as the cavalry's horses. Sir Henry Fane said goodbye to the Army of the Indus in an order of the day on the 16th, congratulating all ranks on their exemplary discipline and good behaviour during a march of about six hundred miles. Then he boarded his river-boat and started the long journey to the sea and Bombay.

At that moment it would have been prudent to wait for General Keane and the Bombay column at Shikarpur. Keane would then have taken over command of the whole expedition and have made sure that the two columns worked as one. But Macnaghten was anxious to get on, and letters from the Governor General informed him of a serious new deterioration in Anglo-Persian relations.[20] Moreover, he heard and believed a report that Afghans were occupying the Bolan Pass. As the Bombay column was more than a hundred miles down river on the 20th, Macnaghten and Cotton agreed (during their stormy interview) that the Bengal column should press on without delay. Cotton gave his orders for the march on 21 February, but found time to manœuvre his troops in the presence of Shah Shuja, whose own contingent was improving but was still far from being a well-trained and disciplined army. The inhabitants of Larkana, about sixty miles south-west of Shikarpur, had reason to remember the contingent's lack of discipline, for on 4 February it had plundered their town in the course of a punitive foray. Auckland also reproved Macnaghten for allowing the Shah to divide his force when a slight demonstration would have sufficed. It is charitable to suppose that a proper reconnaissance of the terrain ahead would have been made if the Bengal column had waited for Keane. As it happened, there was no time left for the task when Macnaghten and Cotton decided to push on. But part of the agreement, against Macnaghten's better judgement, was that Shah Shuja and his contingent should stay behind for a while until more camels became available. On the day of Cotton's departure with the Bengal column from Shikarpur the announcement of Cotton's intention to move reached Sir John Keane near Sehwan.

Auckland heard both good and bad news in January. The Home Government approved of his actions, but in Herat, whose preservation was one of the prime aims of the expedition, there had been a stupid quarrel between the two British officers in residence and the king's minister, Yar Muhammad. The quarrel had broken out at the beginning of November. Eldred Pottinger, as political agent, and Colonel Charles Stoddart, as McNeill's representative, took very seriously their duty to discourage the slave trade which had long given Persia an excuse for attacking Herat. They forgot that this was only a secondary duty; their first was to help the government of Herat to strengthen its defences, which were also, in British eyes, the defences of India. According to Colvin the two British officers 'behaved as senselessly as our bitterest Russian enemy could desire'. With an utter want of judgement, tact and temper, though acting from good intentions, they had contrived, Colvin said, to entangle themselves in a personal quarrel and had been ordered to leave the city. Stoddart left Herat on his way to Bokhara on 3 November; Eldred Pottinger clung on in spite of insults for a few months longer. Colvin addressed Burnes as Scot to Scot:

...Why is it that Englishmen everywhere are rough, overbearing, without tact and address, and more disliked by foreigners than any other people? Pottinger endeavoured to make an Utopia of justice and forbearance among these rude and hungry Afghans, fresh as they are from a prolonged and desperate contest, and the result is that he with his schemes is sent out of the country, and the check that he might, by wiser means, have maintained, is totally lost...[21]

Auckland was equally vexed, but he saw a way out. He let it be known that he considered the quarrel a purely personal one, in which the British Government was not involved. He did not expect the quarrel to have any serious ill consequences. Wade then chimed in with some remarks which tell us a great deal about Britain's imperial history:

...There is nothing more to be dreaded or guarded against, I think, in our endeavour to re-establish the Affghan monarchy than the overweening confidence with which Europeans are too often accustomed to regard the excellence of their own institutions and the anxiety that they display to introduce them in new and untried soils...The people of these countries are far from ripe for the introduction of our highly refined system of Government or of Society, and we are liable to meet with more opposition in the attempt to disturb what we find existing than from the exercise of our physical force...[22]

Auckland also thought that Burnes had made a mistake in treating the matter as a quarrel between governments. Colvin spoke for him when he said in a letter to Macnaghten: 'It will be an immense comfort to us when we know that you are actually at Shikarpur.'[23] The author cannot help thinking that Auckland and Colvin were a little hard on Eldred Pottinger, who was young and inexperienced and really no match for the wiles of Yar Muhammad. But at the same time one must remember that the British Government, at home and in India, considered the friendship of Herat to be indispensable. That friendship might be unpalatable to many English men and women who viewed the barbaric ways of Kamran and Yar Muhammad with contempt, but it had not been unknown for such people to forget their more tender scruples when their interests were threatened, and so it was that the British Government in India declined to support Eldred Pottinger in his efforts to reform an obnoxious regime in Herat. He lingered on at Herat, submitting to insults worse than any that McNeill had borne from the Persians, until the arrival of a new British mission a few months later. He was neither the first nor the last to discover that national interests and strict morality are frequently incompatible. Meanwhile Lord Auckland was surveying a far wider field than that between the mouths of the Indus and the border of Turkestan. On 19 January Bombay troops acting on his orders took possession of Aden, just as the Home Government hoped they would. As Palmerston wrote to Hobhouse on 1 January, '...the only thing to do is to send a Force sufficient to take and keep the Place. It seems to me that it would be very soft in us to give it to the Imaum of Muscat, and that we ought to make it a British Possession. In our Hands Aden will become of great Importance in a Military and Naval and Commercial Point of View....[24] Auckland was also planning to send Rear Admiral Frederick Maitland and the 74-gun *Wellesley* into the Persian Gulf, where it could be ready either to back up the garrison at Kharg or to dissuade Egyptian forces from making an attack on Bahrain. He hoped that he would not be called upon to take any further military action in support of the Home Government's policy towards Muhammad Ali Pasha.[25] He had more than enough to do on the borders of India. As it happened, Admiral Maitland had work to do at Karachi before he could sail into the Persian

Gulf. At the beginning of February his flagship, the *Wellesley*, and a smaller vessel, the *Algerine*, accompanied the Bombay reserve force which had been requested by Pottinger and Keane. The force consisted of about three thousand men under Brigadier Valiant, who travelled in the *Wellesley* with the 40th Foot (now part of the Lancashire Regiment). As they approached Karachi at least one cannon-ball caused a splash ahead of them. It had been fired by the garrison of the fort at Manora Head. Was it a salute or a warning? Some fishermen led Maitland to believe that the garrison consisted of three thousand men, and that he would be resisted. Therefore he reduced the fort to rubble in short order with the aid of his seventy-four guns. Valiant personally commanded the landing party, but had no work to do when he reached the shore. The fort no longer existed, and in any case the garrison had been very small. The Governor of Karachi did not delay before handing over the city to the British commander.[26] There seems to be no truth in the romantic story, first told by Kennedy and passed on by Kaye, that the commander of the Manora garrison answered a first call for surrender by shouting: 'I am a Baluchi and will die first,' and answered a second by firing a shot at the British ships.[27] Colonel Pottinger argued that the shot was a customary salute, fired in exactly the same way and for the same reason as salutes from the lighthouse at Bombay. He said that the garrison consisted of sixteen men armed with swords, who were standing admiring the flotilla when the firing began.[28] But the Government chose to accept the Admiral's account that 'no attention was paid to his pacific overtures before he felt himself compelled to resort to force'.[29] It seems most likely that misunderstanding born of suspicion caused Maitland to open fire, and there is even a possibility that he positively hoped for an excuse to do so. When Lord Auckland reported the affair to the Secret Committee he said that the landing of the reserve force was likely to be opposed, that the *Wellesley* levelled the sea face of a small fort from which a shot had been fired, that the garrison of the fort was very small, and that the Governor of Karachi had capitulated and handed over military possession of the port.

...we have thus gained the occupancy of a military post, of which all reports are most favourable, and which is likely to become of much interest and importance... I forwarded instructions to Colonel Pottinger to state that under the circumstances under which the military control over Kurrachee had been acquired by us, the retention of our hold over it was a matter the determination of which rested wholly in our own discretion, and that such retention, at least during the present operations of our armies in Afghanistan, must be considered indispensable...[30]

For one reason and another Lord Auckland and his successors went on considering Karachi indispensable until 1947. But in 1839, in spite of the constant threat of cholera, Karachi was a very useful acquisition, both commercially and militarily. After doing his part at Karachi and receiving fresh orders the Admiral made a voyage up the Gulf in the *Wellesley*. Auckland was anxious about Anglo-Persian relations at that moment, and he wanted to be sure that his troops could continue to hold Kharg. Colvin, however, thought of Kharg Island as more than a bargaining counter in diplomatic negotiation. He said that it would be of value 'when the Scythian thinks of having a dockyard at Bushire'.[31] The Scythian, of course, was Russia. The source of Auckland's anxiety about Anglo-Persian relations (mentioned earlier as a factor in the premature advance of the army from Shikarpur) was McNeill's announcement that his mission was about to withdraw from Teheran again. He sent the news in the first week of December 1838 and Auckland received it exactly two months later. Auckland explained the significance of this to Hobhouse in his letter of 9 February:

...Even if it were possible now to stay proceedings the last news from Persia would make me eager to advance. The garrison and artillery left in Ghorian—The activity of Russian agency in Candahar—The conduct of Mahommed Shah—all circumstances prove that if we do not succeed in Afghanistan the base of Russian operations against India will be advanced from Teheran to Cabul and Candahar. I shall be sorry to advance the bounds of our direct influence and should have been glad to see the countries to our west remain in undisturbed neutrality, but this has not been allowed me...[32]

The mood of this letter, regretful yet determined, is utterly different from that of his private secretary. One is reminded of Melbourne's remark to Palmerston—that 'the Black Sea and the Caucasus and those great empires enflame the imagination wonderfully'. John Russell Colvin's enthusiasm for the fray is apparent in every line of his letter to Macnaghten on 5 February—and in the underlinings to which he was addicted:

[The Shah] has come back disgraced and weakened and he finds that he has been frightened by 500 Sepoys. He *will submit no more than he has done*, and the chain of Persian and English alliance is, I think, effectually severed. Persia will now go over to Russia entirely, and it will depend *solely* on the degree in which Russia may be prepared to commit herself with us in Europe whether we shall have opposition and trouble of a serious kind to encounter in Afghanistan. The pear is fast ripening, and England must prepare herself for an arduous struggle. We in India have done our part, and all that we desire is to hear of your being able to make an efficient advance. . . [33]

But, for reasons already touched upon, it was not at first a very efficient advance. The supreme commander was still with his Bombay troops, several marches behind, and the Bengal column had started from Shikarpur without proper military preparation on 23 February. Cotton's advance was slow because of the shortage of forage and water along the route. It took him more than a week to reach the frontier between Upper Sind and Baluchistan, and even then his artillery park and a brigade of Native Infantry remained at Shikarpur because of the shortage of camels. It is probable that the camels then available would have sufficed for essential stores and equipment, but no attempt was made to dispense with unnecessary loads and followers. Major General Nott looked around for a scapegoat and chose his old favourite, the General from England who had deprived a good Company man of high command. In a letter to his family he showed a serious lack of faith in the Commander in Chief. He said that Sir John Keane's appointment was from the first 'a dirty job' which had 'paralyzed and nearly given a death blow to an enterprize which ought to shed a lustre over our councils, and the moral effect of which ought to be felt by the whole world'. He implied that Keane had allowed thoughts of the riches of Hyderabad to seduce him from his duty to the state. [34] It is difficult at this distance to judge how much of the criticism was purely personal to the touchy and censorious writer of the letter. Nevertheless, Nott's strictures deserve attention for the light which they throw on the military jealousies and quarrels of those days. Keane had some glaring faults, but he was a fine soldier, and a lucky one. The news of his faults travelled ahead of him; the army of the Bengal Presidency had to wait for proof of his efficiency, good leadership, and good luck.

On 4 March the head of the Bombay column was at Larkhana, and there Keane took stock of the supply and transport problem. He had sent a complaint to Auckland about the Bengal column's misuse of camels on 1 March, and Outram had ridden ahead on that day to discuss the problem with Macnaghten at Shikarpur. Outram returned to Keane's headquarters on the 4th. Keane and Macnaghten started off on the right foot by agreeing that the Shah's contingent should get on in accordance with the Governor General's directive, '...for it is upon this contingent that we must ultimately depend for the maintenance of British influence in Afghanistan ....'.[35] Keane decided to leave at Shikarpur for the time being the Bengal Division's Second Brigade, formerly Nott's command but temporarily in the hands of William Dennie. He also resolved to leave three of his Bombay Infantry Regiments near Sukkur under Brigadier Gordon, and to lead the remainder of the Bombay column to Quetta by a short cut if he could find one. Accordingly the Shah's contingent marched from Shikarpur on the 7th, leaving William Dennie and his brigade without transport to look after the depot. Dennie was furious. He put the worst possible construction on Keane's decision and sent the following letter to Keane's military secretary:

...I cannot but lament, in common—I have no doubt—with His Excellency and the members of his whole force, that two regular and disciplined armies, brought together from so great a distance and at so much difficulty and cost, should, at the very moment of united action, be thus maimed and dismembered, merely for the purpose of keeping together a mass of raw levies, like the Shah's contingent, whose carriage and supplies would suffice for the Bengal or Bombay divisions, and who would again be much better employed if left here for formation and instruction; whereas, in their present state, they must prove worse than worthless in advance. Can this be done in the vain hope of giving plausibility to the fiction, of the 'Shah entering his dominions surrounded by his own troops' when the fact is too notorious to escape detection and exposure, that he has not a single subject or Affghan amongst them!—his army being composed of camp followers from the Company's military stations...?[36]

Dennie did himself no good with Sir John Keane by sending his letter. Keane had no time for officers who questioned his orders, especially those who presumed to criticize government policy, and who contributed anonymous dispatches to the Indian newspapers containing that criticism. The fact that Dennie had exposed a weakness in Auckland's policy was beside the point. Auckland did not need Dennie to tell him that the Shah's contingent as it stood was unsatisfactory. Meanwhile he could not allow the expedition to take on the appearance of a British invasion with conquest as its object.

On 10 March Cotton reached Dadhar, a day's march from the entrance to the Bolan Pass. His camp followers had been on half rations for two days, and he now had no more than one month's supplies. The replenishments which he had expected at Dadhar were derisory. Major Leech had tried but failed to gather together good stocks from the Baluchi chiefs in the area, and as these chiefs were subordinate to Mehrab Khan of Kalat we need not wonder that Mehrab Khan was soon blamed for all the army's trials. Murder and plunder, obstruction and the withholding of supplies were all charged to his account. When Cotton fully understood his predicament he decided that he must press on to Quetta and await Keane there. Meanwhile the political agents would have to work doubly hard to obtain supplies from the Khan of Kalat. Auckland was shocked to learn of the army's plight when he heard from Keane and Cotton in the middle of March. He took part of the blame for Cotton's premature advance from Shikarpur and consequent embarrassments, but he could not help feeling that it was right to push on as quickly as possible and that Keane had been dawdling. He was disappointed in the commissariat officers, who had behaved as though the Bengal and Bombay columns were rivals for the stocks available instead of one force. He could not understand why they had not yet taken delivery of five or six thousand fresh camels which had been sent to Shikarpur, and he was critical of Burnes and Leech for neglecting to survey the route accurately before the Bengal column started out.[37] To Macnaghten he wrote on the 17th of his surprise at 'how imperfect have been all the arrangements for an advance from Shikarpore to Dadur'. By the 22nd his surprise had become 'grievous disappointment', but he relied on the excellent spirit of co-operation between Keane and Macnaghten to put matters right.[38]

Keane, meanwhile, was anxious to bring the Bombay and Bengal columns to Quetta at the same time. Between 11 and 13 March his troops moved out of Larkhana in three groups on their way to Gandava, hoping to find an easier pass than the Bolan for the last stage of the journey to Quetta. They reached Gandava on the 21st and rested while the route was surveyed. Keane and an escort of sepoys and part of the 1st Bombay Light Cavalry left the Bombay Division at Gandava on the 23rd and raced ahead to take command at last of the combined army. He could not afford to wait any longer. The Bengal column entered the Bolan Pass on the 16th, having spent six days at Dadhar while the engineers prepared a passable road. Shah Shuja's contingent, several marches in the rear, did not reach Dadhar until the 27th, by which time Keane and his escort had caught it up on the road. While the Bengal troops were negotiating the Bolan Pass, Sir Alexander Burnes was on his way to Kalat for talks with Mehrab Khan, who favourably impressed the mission by sending an escort so that they should have an unmolested journey from Dadhar to his capital. Macnaghten wrote to Auckland from Bhag on the 19th that the army in its progress through Baluchistan had earned a great deal of hostility. He very much feared that Burnes might be led to recommend an attack on Kalat.[39] But he did not then know that Burnes was on his way to see Mehrab Khan. He changed his mind when he heard the full story of the Bengal column's adventures among the plundering Baluchi tribesmen, and there soon came a time when he suspected Burnes of being too soft towards the ruler of Kalat. At the end of the month Burnes made an agreement with Mehrab Khan. In return for one and a half lakhs a year (about £15,000 sterling) Mehrab Khan agreed to acknowledge the supremacy of Shah Shuja and to do all in his power to make communications safe between his frontier with Sind and his frontier with Afghanistan. He also promised to help to procure supplies and transport. But during the course of the negotiation Mehrab Khan made some remarks which Burnes could not resist quoting to Macnaghten: that instead of relying on the Afghan nation the British had inundated the country with foreign troops; that all the Afghans were discontented with the Shah; that Dost Muhammad was a man of ability and resource; and that

...though we could easily put him down by Shah Soojah, even in our present mode of procedure, we could never win over the Afghan nation by it...

Mehrab Khan, as reported by Burnes, also tried to make British flesh creep by telling them what lay ahead:

...Wait till sickness overtakes your troops—till they are exhausted with fatigue from long and harassing marches, and from the total want of supplies; wait till they have drunk of many waters; and wait, too, till they feel the sharpness of Afghan swords.[40]

On the 26th the Bengal column at last reached Quetta, '...a most miserable mud town, with a small castle on a mound, on which there was a small gun, on a rickety carriage. The peach and almond trees were in blossom.'[41] It had been an exhausting journey, made miserable by sharp stones underfoot, the attacks of plunderers, and bitterly cold nights. At Quetta Cotton realized that he had full rations for only ten days, and after some initial hesitation he put his fighting men on half rations and further halved the daily amount allowed to the camp-followers. The morale of the Bengal troops, both Europeans and sepoys, was low by now, and it was not improved by the knowledge that one of the political agents had suggested returning to Shikarpur. Major William Hough's enraged snort can almost be heard as we read his comment on the proposal: 'We should have been in a pretty position, with hordes of Belochees, etc., attacking our flanks!!!...'[42] Cotton paid no attention to the proposal, but sat tight and waited for Sir John Keane. He can have derived but little comfort from the encouraging letters in which Auckland and Colvin reported the approval and good wishes of the Home Government. 'The Eyes of Europe are upon you,' Colvin wrote. 'Go on and prosper.' If the eyes of Europe could have seen the state of the Army of the Indus at the end of March the Russians would have recovered completely from their humiliation at the hands of Britain. Sir Willoughby Cotton went to meet Sir John Keane and William Macnaghten on 4 April and reported to them on the sad state of his division. He made an unfortunate impression on Macnaghten:

...Sir Willoughby is a sad croaker; not content with telling me we must all inevitably be starved, he assures me that Shah Soojah is very unpopular in Afghanistan and that we shall be opposed at every step of our progress. I think I know a little better than this...[43]

Indeed Macnaghten had been predicting for at least a fortnight that the rulers of Kandahar would not resist. His optimism was boundless and infectious. In the end it led him into one risk too many. Keane and he made a good and confident pair, and their arrival at Quetta helped to lift the spirits of the Bengal troops. Keane's first action on arriving there on the 6th was to congratulate all ranks on 'the admirable manner in which their duties have been conducted, and for the good conduct and soldier-like behaviour of the troops during a march of more than 1,100 miles'. He privately told Macnaghten that the whole army must move on without delay. 'The fact is,' Macnaghten wrote to Colvin, 'the troops and followers are nearly in a state of mutiny for food, and the notion of waiting for such a person as Mehrab Khan, who has done his best to starve us, seems utterly preposterous...'[44] Keane quickly adjusted the chain of command now that he was in position as Commander in Chief. Cotton lost his army command and resumed charge of the 1st or Bengal Division. Major General Willshire, who had brought the Bombay troops in good order from the mouth of the Indus to the Bolan Pass (having eventually abandoned the search for an easier route to Quetta) was confirmed in command of the 2nd or Bombay Division. The effect on Major General William Nott was like a slap in the face. He felt that his seniority entitled him to command of one of the two divisions, and he was not afraid to tell Sir John Keane what he thought. The following dialogue took place in Keane's tent after a long and acrimonious discussion:

NOTT Well, your Excellency, I trust that I have left no ill impression upon your mind. I see the whole affair; I am to be sacrificed because I happen to be senior to the Queen's officers.

KEANE Ill impression, Sir! I will never forget your conduct as long as I live.

NOTT Oh! Your Excellency, since that is the case, I have only to wish you a very good evening.[45]

Nott was a good general, but he was a Company general who had never seen service outside India. Keane was a veteran of the Peninsular War and it was not unnatural for him to favour officers of similar military upbringing. But, however unjust the relegation might appear to Nott, the Commander in Chief had a right to expect cheerful acceptance of his orders and dispositions from every officer and man in his charge. Nott, like Dennie before him, chose to question and challenge those orders. A man of more saintly temperament than the unforgiving Keane would have had to show Nott and Dennie who was really in command. Just as Dennie stayed at Shikarpur in spite of his protests, so Nott stayed at Quetta and nursed his grievance.

At about this time Alexander Burnes returned from Kalat with his new agreement with Mehrab Khan. He found that Macnaghten had already lodged an official complaint to the Governor General about the conduct of Mehrab Khan and had made proposals for dealing with him. By this time Macnaghten had made up his mind that Mehrab Khan was the 'implacable enemy' of the British. He told Colvin, for instance, that Sir John Keane was burning for revenge:

...There never was such treatment inflicted upon human beings as we have been subjected to on our progress through the Khan's country. I will say nothing of Burnes's negotiations. His instructions were to conciliate, but I think he has adhered too closely to the letter of them. The Commander in Chief is very angry...[46]

It was useless for Burnes to plead that Mehrab Khan's subjects were themselves short of food because of a poor harvest in 1838, and that there was little or no grain to be found in the country. It was useless to argue that the Baluchi tribesmen would plunder and murder whether Mehrab Khan approved or no. The accumulated anger and frustration of the advancing army were turned upon the ruler of Kalat, even by a Macnaghten who only three weeks earlier preached conciliation. But Macnaghten may have relished the prospect of a quarrel with Mehrab for another reason. Kalat, Shal, Mastung and Kachhi commanded the lines of communication between Sind and Kandahar. It is not so surprising, therefore, to observe Macnaghten, at the beginning of April, urging the annexation of the last three and a campaign of retribution against the first. The annexed territory would be added to the dominions of Shah Shuja, and a friendly ruler would be established in Kalat— or so Macnaghten hoped.

Sir John Keane had been in camp at Quetta less than forty-eight hours when the army resumed its advance, accompanied this time by the Shah's contingent. Between 7 and 12 April they travelled from Quetta to Qila Abdullah, at the foot of the Khojak Pass, without great difficulty. The Bombay column, meanwhile, was struggling through the Bolan Pass. For many days it had had the unenviable task of marching past the decomposing corpses of men and animals lost by the Bengal Division and the Shah's contingent. The plundering and killing continued whenever opportunity offered itself to the Baluchis, and we find Outram at Quetta on the 16th recording the faithlessness and duplicity of Mehrab Khan, who had not yet paid his respects to Shah Shuja in accordance with the treaty and who had kept up close communication with Dost Muhammad himself.

The Khojak Pass was not as long as the Bolan, but it was much steeper in places. Captain Augustus Abbott of the Bengal Artillery led his experimental Camel Battery over the pass on the 13th and 14th. He had little to say about the journey, which took him into Afghanistan for the first time, except to note that on the morning of the 14th they saw the plain of Kandahar spread out below them from a height of about 2,500 feet: 'Well, the scenery was very pretty, and the vegetation very pleasing, but the pass was a dreadful one for our baggage.' In fact every wheeled vehicle had had to be manhandled over the worst slopes, and it took several days to sort out the baggage of the various units.[47] On top of this the army was still a target for marauders, some of whom carried off two elephants belonging to Macnaghten on the 19th. During this first halt on Kandahar territory Macnaghten and Keane heard a report that about 1,500 horsemen were preparing to attack the camp under one or more of the Kandahar chiefs. Keane issued new standing orders and appointed a Brigadier of the Day, who had to report personally to the Commander in Chief before going off duty. In a tented camp, even on enemy territory, there was still some time for leisure. Augustus Abbott records that he dined with the Commander in Chief on the 19th: 'We had a pleasant party and he was on his good behaviour.'[48] Earlier in this narrative there was a reference to Keane's glaring faults. One of them was a violent temper, and another was the habit of swearing like a trooper. In short he was a good officer but not a great gentleman, and he had offended many men during his career. It cost him the job of Commander in Chief for the whole of India, for when Hobhouse consulted the duke of Wellington about the succession to Fane's former post the duke said that a Commander in Chief must have great respectability and a high character. 'I do not think Keane will do', the duke said, and Hobhouse had to look elsewhere.[49] But Auckland was more charitable. He was glad that Keane was not to be the next Commander in Chief, but he praised him as a good soldier 'with a singleness of purpose and a forte volonté which I should not have found in another'. It was true that Keane had a 'sad and intractable temper', Auckland said. He put it down to ill health, and remarked: 'Do not let what you know of his temper tell against him. He has done admirably well.'[50]

On 20 April some horsemen arrived from Kandahar, but not in anger. There were about two hundred of them under one Haji

Khan Kakur. He and his men had defected from the larger band whose arrival had put the camp on the alert on the 19th, and they now tendered their submission to Shah Shuja. Macnaghten was jubilant. On the 21st the Bengal Division resumed its march towards Kandahar, and on the 23rd the Kandahar chiefs, brothers of Dost Muhammad, fled beyond the Helmand River. Their people had no love for them, for they employed extortioners to farm the revenues of the Kandahar state. Shah Shuja, accompanied by William Macnaghten, Alexander Burnes and a small escort, approached the city on Wednesday 24 April, taking a risk which Keane would never had allowed if he had known. During the last three miles Shuja received deputation after deputation and the acclaim of thousands of people. He visited the shrine where the Prophet's Shirt was venerated, and stood before the tomb of his grandfather, Ahmed Shah. Burnes and Macnaghten witnessed the moving scene and persuaded themselves that Shuja was genuinely loved and respected. They retired for the night to the Shah's camp outside the city, and on the morning of the 25th Shuja formally took possession of Kandahar. As the head of the Bengal column approached the walls the soldiers heard the crash of a royal salute and the rattle of a *feu de joie*. All around them, after months of privation, they could see fields of wheat and barley and trees laden with fruit. Villagers stood on the roofs of their houses to witness the arrival of the 'feringhees', who came pouring over the plain in their red coats and tall hats, accompanied by a sad apology for cavalry. The journey from Shikarpur had indeed taken a terrible toll of horses as well as of pack animals. That afternoon Macnaghten and Burnes sat down in their tents and described the Shah's reception at Kandahar in letters to Lord Auckland and his circle. Alexander Burnes's account particularly pleased Lord Auckland, who sent copies to many of his friends and colleagues in England and India, for it seemed to vindicate the policy of direct support to Shah Shuja after months of anxiety.[51] Macnaghten also exulted in the warmth of the welcome received by Shuja. He made the generals, Cotton being prominent among them on that account, eat their words about the unpopularity of the new king and the prospect of resistance at Kandahar. Certainly the mood of the army had changed for the better since the arrival at that city. The discomforts of the march from Shikarpur, the loss of comrades and the loss of property began to look less serious as the days of rest continued. Macnaghten told Emily Eden that they seemed to have 'dropped into a paradise' peopled by 'the finest race of Asiatics' he had ever seen.[52] Both he and Burnes reported that Dost Muhammad Khan was likely to follow the example of his brothers and run away when the army approached Kabul. The prestige of the politicals was high at Kandahar, and the army faithfully went about its own pressing business in the knowledge that it would have to stay there for at least a month. As Lord Auckland wrote to the Governor of Madras at the end of June (by which time the army had recuperated at Kandahar for two months):

...I wish that I could feel with you that Afghanistan is settled—and yet I lay my account for many a troublesome difficulty in that direction—but Sir John Keane and Macnaghten have made an excellent beginning, and I may at least admit that our prospects of success are altogether most promising...[53]

CHAPTER 12

A KING RESTORED AT KABUL

...There is much in all this to fill and raise the mind—the un-
resisted advance of British Armies from Bombay and Kurnal to the
Centre of Afghanistan; the foundation laid for reorganising a
nation; the designs of powerful and insidious enemies anticipated
and, we may trust, baffled; the good will of a great Mahommedan
population to forces composed chiefly of Englishmen and Hindoos;
the opening for extending civilisation over a great portion of the
earth. Here is abundant matter for deep, yet pleasing, reflection.
It will be something in after life to have been a near observer, and
in some sort a sharer, amid events so novel, so important, and so
striking... JOHN COLVIN to Lancelot Wilkinson, 27 May 1839

The army that marched into Kandahar at the end of April 1839
was very different from the one that left Ferozepore five months
earlier. For one thing, it was no longer so heavily loaded; the high
mortality among camels and the attentions of the Baluchi plunderers stripped the army of much of its fat. We are told that at
Ferozepore 'many young officers would as soon have thought of
leaving behind their swords and double-barrelled pistols as march
without their dressing cases, their perfumes, Windsor soap, and
eau de cologne'.[1] At Kandahar they were lucky if they could find a
change of clothes in time for the grand review marking Shah
Shuja's restoration on 8 May. Some of the men were in a worse
plight, having lost or thrown away much of their heavier (and
warmer) clothing during the march from Shikarpur. Officers and
men had endured much together, but they had so far been cheated
of real action. The Sind emirs had climbed down, and the sirdars
of Kandahar had run away. The reckoning with Mehrab Khan had
been postponed, and there would be a long wait at Kandahar while
the cavalry refitted and Shuja established his power. Nevertheless,
there were some compensations for those who escaped the fevers
that ran through the camp. From 6 May 'well conducted soldiers'
were allowed into the city,[2] and there was an extra allowance of
liquor for the men on the Queen's birthday. William Dennie wrote
enthusiastically to his mother and sisters about the good food to be
found at Kandahar. There were fruits of all kinds: '...apples,

269

grapes, cherries, apricots, mulberries, plums (or greengages rather) with pomegranates...Milk, butter and cheese are excellent... Mutton, here, surpasses everything I ever saw or tasted in any part of the world.'³

The 'Bombay Ducks', as the men from Bengal called them, marched into camp outside Kandahar on 4 May, longing to relax and to share in the enjoyment of Macnaghten's 'paradise'. But they had little enough time for relaxation, for Sir John Keane ordered a grand review in honour of the newly restored king. Soldiers of both Presidencies took part in the parade, wearing their best white trousers for the occasion. The review took place at sunrise on the 8th, while it was still reasonably cool, well outside the city walls. Outram, who organized it, and Hough, who witnessed it, show no disappointment in their accounts about the alleged indifference of the people of Kandahar. It is curious that Kaye, who had access to the accounts of Outram and Hough, preferred the one one written by Captain Henry Havelock, for the latter officer was not present at the review. His description of the parade is at best second-hand. Havelock was honest about this: '...unless I have been deceived, all the national enthusiasm of the scene was entirely confined to his Majesty's immediate retainers. The people of Candahar are said to have viewed the whole affair with the most mortifying indifference...'⁴ Yet Major Hough estimated the number of Afghan spectators at between three and four thousand. Perhaps the discrepancy is of little account after so many years. Nevertheless, it seems to the author that one ought to trust the evidence of the men who saw the event for themselves. It is very clear, moreover, that Kaye was anxious to prove that Shuja was already unpopular. The chiefs and people of Kandahar (other than the departing sirdars) welcomed Shuja on 24 and 25 April. The grand review on 8 May was the British army's formal tribute to the newly installed monarch. It is true that Shuja was disliked by some officers, but it has not been proved that Shuja was unpopular at Kandahar as early as the second week of May 1839.

Auckland had been assured by at least four officers familiar with Afghan politics that Shuja would receive a warm welcome, but he frequently expressed doubt on this score and he anxiously looked for news of Shuja's progress in the art of pleasing. For instance, his private secretary said on 16 January (in a letter to Macnaghten):

...The great security for the obtaining of onward supplies, as well as for all else in this enterprise, is to rouse the Afghan feeling heartily and generally on our side. This will, I well know, be your thought by day and your dream by night...[5]

Auckland was delighted to hear at the beginning of March that Shah Shuja had somewhat relaxed the strict etiquette which he demanded from British officers in his presence. He told Wade on 7 March:

...I have very gratifying accounts of Shah Shoojah's popularity with our officers. He seems to have become conscious that extreme formality is not consistent with good campaigning, and his excellent manners have made him much liked...[6]

But not all of those around Shah Shuja had excellent manners. Auckland told Hobhouse on 1 April that 'the Shah has a train of ragamuffins about him, from amongst whom there is a danger of excesses...'. Meanwhile, the man closest to Shah Shuja, William Macnaghten, was forming his own opinion. He put it in writing on 6 June in a letter to Auckland from Kandahar. Shuja, he said, was 'a mild, humane, intelligent, just and firm man. His faults are those of pride and parsimony...' The fault of pride appeared to the tribal chiefs 'in a more glaring light from its contrast with the behaviour of the Barukzye usurpers, who, in order to preserve their power, were compelled to place themselves on a level with their adherents...' But Macnaghten was not without hope, as he put it, that 'His Majesty will gradually assume a more condescending demeanour, or at all events that his subjects will become more reconciled to the distant formalities of their Sovereign'.[7]

Royal parsimony, of course, could be disastrous in a country where peace had to be bought from tribal chiefs with the aid of annual subsidies. Otherwise peace had to be enforced through costly expeditions. Either method was expensive, and we need not wonder that Macnaghten had to distribute large sums of money in the early days of the march through Afghanistan. Kaye's expression of moral disapproval of this system reflects a curiously naïve attitude:

...Early in the campaign, Macnaghten had encouraged the conviction that the allegiance of the Afghans was to be bought—that Afghan cupidity would not be proof against British gold. So he opened the treasure chest; scattered abroad its contents with an ungrudging hand;

and commenced a system of corruption which, though seemingly successful at the outset, wrought, in the end, the utter ruin of the policy he had reared...[8]

From time immemorial the only way of rousing Afghan feeling heartily and generally on the side of any particular ruler had been one requiring the expenditure of blood, or money, or both. Shuja, in the early days of the campaign, had not yet organized the collection of revenues. He was still heavily dependent on his British sponsors. But it is ridiculous to condemn the methods used by Macnaghten as a system of corruption introduced by British officers. This is to indulge too extravagantly an otherwise creditable sense of shame and revulsion at the cruel facts of life in the world outside the study walls.

Within a few days of reaching Kandahar the envoy and the Commander in Chief turned their minds to the pursuit of the sirdars. They determined to send about 1,500 men and two guns after the fugitives as early as 2 May, but for a week agents passed between Kandahar and the camp of the sirdars, bearing offers of peaceful submission. In the end the sirdars rejected Shuja's terms and Keane ordered Brigadier Robert Sale to lead an expedition against them. Sale assembled a composite force drawn from the Bengal Division and from the Shah's contingent. It included a company from his own regiment, the 13th Light Infantry, and its total strength was about 1,700 men and no less than nine guns. But the sirdars did not wait for them at Girishk; they made off towards the Persian frontier shortly after rejecting the peace terms offered from Kandahar. Sale had just started the dangerous crossing of the Helmand River, using rum casks for an improvised raft, when a messenger arrived with his recall orders. He and his expedition re-entered Kandahar on the 29th, exactly seventeen days after their departure. Some officers, including Havelock, have questioned the wisdom of letting the sirdars get away in the first place, but it was entirely in accordance with Auckland's instructions that Keane and Macnaghten attempted to reconcile them to Shuja's rule and the prospect of pensioned exile in India. In any case they were not by themselves a serious threat to security in Kandahar, whose people hardly pined for their return. Let us always remember that the system of government was one in which the ruler sold to the highest bidder the right to collect taxes in a particular district, or leased that right to an individual in return for services rendered. It is possible that Shuja lost whatever affection he had won from the people of Kandahar when they observed that Mirza Muhammad Tugee was still in power as chief revenue collector. Macnaghten told Auckland in June that this official, formerly employed by the sirdars, was now working for Shuja. Mirza Muhammad was 'much addicted to oppression...His chief, if not his only, recommendation is his perfect understanding of the resources of the country...'[9] Could Macnaghten have influenced Shuja to change the system, or at least the man who profited by it? There is no evidence that he even tried. What mattered to him was that Shuja should establish his power quickly; reforms could come later. The people of Kandahar and its dependencies, meanwhile, hardly noticed any change.

Another of Macnaghten's responsibilities was to cultivate friendship with Shuja's nephew at Herat. Major D'Arcy Todd therefore rode out of Kandahar with a salute of eleven guns ringing in his ears on 21 June, charged with a mission to Shah Kamran and his vizier Yar Muhammad. His subordinate political officers were Captain James Abbott and Lieutenant Richmond Shakespear of the Bengal Artillery. His escort consisted mainly of sappers, but there were also a few gunners and, to complete the mission, two assistant surgeons. He carried with him 200,000 rupees (£20,000) with which to pay for good will and the repair to Herat's defensive works.[10] By this time, incidentally, the Governor General had forgiven Eldred Pottinger for his earlier mistakes at Herat. He told Hobhouse that this young officer had deserved much credit for holding his ground in circumstances of extreme difficulty. 'It cannot be denied', he said, 'that it will be extremely difficult to fix our relations with a government so loose and suspicious as that of Herat upon a satisfactory and secure footing.'[11] Later he remarked that he 'would be satisfied for the present with putting Herat in a condition and humour for defence and with using our influence for the abolition of slavery and for the establishment of good government...'.[12]

One is reminded of the mistake that originally got Eldred Pottinger into trouble with the Governor General. Where were British officers to draw the line between influence and interference? The pursuit of important political ends would often cause them to overlook or to acquiesce in instances of very bad government. Macnaghten's acquiescence in the appointment of Mirza Muhammad

Tugee to his old post at Kandahar is a good example of this difficulty. The murder of Lieutenant Inverarity on 28 May is another. Lieutenant Inverarity and his friend Lieutenant Wilmer, both of the 16th Lancers, went fishing on the banks of the Arghandab on a Tuesday afternoon. On their way home they were attacked. Wilmer parried the sword blows of his assailant and ran for help. Inverarity was less fortunate, and he died a few minutes after Wilmer returned with an escort to rescue him. The attackers escaped, but feelings ran high, and some officers favoured exemplary punishment. Four Afghans appeared before a British military court and were found guilty of stealing twenty-three camels on 2 June. Hough sentenced them to be hanged on the spot where Inverarity had been murdered, as a warning to the many other robbers in the neighbourhood. But Shah Shuja pointed out that the four prisoners were *his* subjects, and one of his secretaries produced evidence which persuaded the Shah that the men were innocent. Hough challenged the evidence and Macnaghten sided with him, but Shuja supported the secretary and the four prisoners went free. Hough was certain that they were the robbers, but he was powerless: '...The Duke of Wellington would not under such circumstances have made over robbers to the Spanish or Portuguese governments...'[13]

The moral of Hough's tale is that an imperialist who aims at the establishment of influence instead of conquest sets himself a much more difficult task. Whether Shuja was right or wrong in freeing the prisoners is less important than the fact that in the last resort the British had to bow to his will in the matter. The hanging did not take place, and for one reason only, because the British did not enter Afghanistan as conquerors. Hough heard on 9 June that eighty more camels had been stolen, and he said that the crime was the result of letting the four prisoners go free. 'Not having the fear of Death before their eyes,' he said, the villagers had taken to their old trade of thieving.[14] As it happened, the Shah soon accepted the need for exemplary punishment. According to Outram he 'caused to be blown away from a gun a Ghiljee who, in an attempt upon our camels, had killed a camel man and wounded a trooper of cavalry'.[15] The Ghiljees, or Ghilzais in the modern spelling, were members of a large tribal confederation inhabiting the hills between Kandahar and Ghazni, on either side of the valley of the Tarnak River. The Ghilzai chiefs had spurned the Shah's attempts to conciliate them. When he sent them money and copies of the Koran they kept the money and returned the books, thus signifying rejection of his offer. Like the Baluchis before them they set out to annoy Shah Shuja and his allies without risking a head-on collision, and they too were marked down for retribution.

On 10 June Sir John Keane published orders for the march to Kabul, intending to start on the 15th, but he had no intention of repeating the mistakes made at Shikarpur and he postponed the army's departure to wait for the convoy bringing grain from beyond the passes. The convoy came in on the 23rd, and the orders for the march were re-issued. Macnaghten made Robert Leech his political agent at Kandahar, and Keane left behind the 37th Bengal Native Infantry, a company of Bengal Foot Artillery, and some ordnance stores, including his four 18-pounder siege guns. Shah Shuja's contingent left a battalion of infantry, two troops of artillery, and some cavalry. Keane had taken the decision to leave behind his siege guns at the end of May. Nothing happened in June to make him change his mind. Yet his army's next objective was a fortress famous throughout Asia, the fortress of Ghazni. Why did he suppose that he could dispense with his siege guns? It seems that he asked his chief engineer, Major George Thomson, for an opinion. Thomson consulted two officers who knew Ghazni. One of them, Major D'Arcy Todd, was a gunner of long experience. The other, Major Leech, was an engineer. They assured him that he would not need his siege guns to break down the walls of Ghazni. Besides, the siege guns were very heavy and the bullocks which usually pulled them were very weak. Thomson therefore advised Keane to leave the guns behind. In some accounts the affair of the siege guns has been confused with a report that Macnaghten at one time recommended leaving half of the army at Kandahar. He did recommend it, but not because he laughed at those who expected opposition on the road to Kabul. The fact is that he, and Auckland with him, were worried about the prospect of a renewed Persian campaign against Herat. Letters from Auckland and Colvin at the end of May speak of an army of 40,000 assembling near Teheran, and indeed it was the fear of having to rush to the defence of Herat that caused hesitation at Kandahar.[16] But by the middle of June the danger had passed. The safety of Herat was 'a sine qua non of our policy' on 9 June, and so it remained, but on the 13th Colvin felt justified in urging Macnaghten to press on to Kabul: '...On all this, however, you will act with your better knowledge in your own discretion. I give you only my personal notions and wishes from this—The fact that I have to convey to you is that danger to Herat from the Persians is *not imminent*.'[17]

The result of the correspondence mentioned here was Todd's mission to Herat, described earlier in this chapter. None of the correspondence was available to such junior officers as Henry Durand and Henry Havelock, and Macnaghten's behaviour has therefore been presented in terms more critical than he deserved. He never had an opportunity to defend himself.

We have now reached Thursday 27 June 1839, the day of the departure of the Army of the Indus from Kandahar and the day of the death of Maharajah Runjeet Singh, the Lion of Lahore. Let us now consider the state of affairs in the Punjab since the turn of the year, and let us briefly look at the view which Lord Auckland saw from his desk. Far too many accounts have reflected the personal and partisan views of men who saw only one corner of the picture. The Punjab, of course, had been selected as the route of a diversionary thrust towards Kabul, superintended by Claude Wade. Runjeet Singh's state of health was a constant source of anxiety to Auckland and his staff, and Colvin and Auckland shared their worries with Macnaghten in letters written at the beginning of February. For instance, Colvin wrote:

...Runjeet Singh's health appears to be extremely precarious. May he live for at least another twelve months. What convulsions his death at this juncture would give rise to it would be vain to conjecture. But you are in strength on the south of the Punjab, and we shall soon have 12,000 men ready at hand here...[18]

At the beginning of March they heard from Wade that the Maharajah was still unable to articulate. One of Wade's letters said that Runjeet's illness had 'greatly impaired the vigour of his government, and to obey his orders or not greatly depends upon the views and prejudices of his officers'. Auckland, who realized that Wade was far from Lahore and therefore dependent on second-hand accounts, told Hobhouse that this gloomy view of Runjeet's condition was greatly exaggerated in his opinion.[19] Wade reached Peshawar on 20 March and found Sikh officers reluctant to fulfil all their obligations under the Tripartite Treaty. He suggested that the Governor General should protest to the Lahore Durbar. But Auckland was unwilling to quarrel. He replied by offering to make an advance payment of the Sikh share of the money extracted from the Sind emirs. The remaining ten lakhs would be an ample hold over the Maharajah.[20] Nevertheless Auckland, through his private secretary, instructed George Clerk, the Resident at Ambala, to go on a mission to Lahore—officially to inquire after the Maharajah's health but unofficially to study the political scene and to investigate Wade's complaints. Clerk would also be able to let the Sikh Durbar know that Auckland disapproved of their reported intention to reinstate Sultan Muhammad Khan at Peshawar.[21] One can imagine Auckland's feelings when he heard of this report. After all that had happened in 1838 it was capricious, to say the least, to think of restoring Peshawar to the Barukzai family.

While he was still waiting for Clerk's report Lord Auckland received the news of the capture of Kandahar. To his horror he saw that Macnaghten wanted to pay a visit to Lahore as soon as Kabul was safe, and to persuade Runjeet Singh to modify the treaty in one or two respects, for Shah Shuja was then somewhat petulant about some of its terms.[22] Auckland quickly headed him off. He said that the envoy could not be spared until Shuja was well established at Kabul and Herat was secure. '... We will discuss the proposition again in another month, or sooner if possible.'[23] In the current delicate state of Sikh politics it would have been foolish to re-open questions settled in the Tripartite Treaty. Ten days after writing to Macnaghten, however, Auckland was able to report that Clerk had found Runjeet Singh animated and friendly, though speechless. The old man had even ordered his gunners to fire a salute in celebration of the fall of Kandahar.[24] But Wade was not to know this in his outpost at Peshawar. Claude Wade, the man who had campaigned on Shuja's behalf for so many years, and whose estimate of Shuja's popularity in Afghanistan had so impressed Hobhouse, now went to the opposite extreme and proposed leaving Dost Muhammad in possession of Kabul and giving British military support to one of the contenders for Runjeet's throne when Runjeet died. He was also in despair about his own career, for all he had to show for his efforts was a local promotion to Lieutenant Colonel. He offered to resign, and was rebuked for his pains:

... It is strongly felt here that your place of duty is where you can best serve the immense national interests which are involved in Lord

Auckland's scheme for the settlement of Afghanistan—and you may be assured that it is in the discharge of that duty that you will most surely promote your own credit and reputation. Every energy should be devoted with singleness of heart and purpose to that one paramount end...[25]

The news of the Maharajah's death reached Auckland at the end of June, and as soon as it was confirmed he ordered minute guns to be fired at Simla, one for each year of Runjeet Singh's life. To Hobhouse he wrote of his anxiety about the effect of the Maharajah's death upon his military preparations at Peshawar. He added:

...I need not tell you that I sincerely lament the loss of our old ally, nor need I give [sic] you that I will use my best endeavours with those who stand in his place to preserve unimpaired the relations which have so long subsisted between the British Government and the Punjab...[26]

Fortunately for Auckland and his plans the Sikh princes and generals kept the peace and restrained those officers who sought to undo Runjeet Singh's links with Britain. It was a time for political intrigue, and not for war.

Throughout 1839 Auckland felt very keenly the lack of an active Commander in Chief. Fane was old and tired, but not too tired to shower the Governor General with political as well as military advice from his place in the wings. The General felt ill used because the Horse Guards had kept him waiting in India while they endlessly debated the choice of his successor. In a private letter to Hobhouse Lord Auckland said that Fane had complained of the uncertainty and inconsistency of the home authorities

with some injustice, for there has been but little of certainty or consistency in his own movements. But I believe him to have found out on his march to Ferozepore that he has no longer the constitution which is necessary for the conduct of active operations in the field, and he was glad when the retreat of the Persians from Herat gave him a good ground for retiring. He is, as I have often told you, though an excellent soldier, a difficult man to deal with.[27]

At the moment of writing that letter to Hobhouse the Governor General was reflecting on the latest of Fane's letters from Sind. Fane, as we noted in chapter 11, considered the subjection of Sind to be more important than the march into Afghanistan, and told Auckland so in plain soldier's language. Auckland replied that the suspension of the Afghan expedition would be 'a real calamity in regard to European as well as to Asiatic policy', though military prudence might occasion some delay.[28] [It really was intolerable that Fane, by now only an 'amateur', according to Colvin, and a 'spectator and counsellor', according to Auckland, should be trying to dictate policy while Auckland had to do without the necessary services of a Commander in Chief at his headquarters.] In May Auckland again lamented the anomaly of Fane's position, for Fane was still in Bombay, having had three attacks of illness. 'In the meantime I am without a Commander in Chief, and this should not be...'[29]

Fane's successor, Sir Jasper Nicolls, arrived from England at the end of the year, and the brave old veteran sailed for home. He died at sea off the Azores early in 1840. It is a pity that Kaye thought fit to enlist Sir Henry Fane as an uncompromising opponent of the expedition into Afghanistan. He disagreed with Auckland on several occasions, it is true, but the evidence of his correspondence with the Governor General and of Auckland's correspondence with others persuades the author that Fane's ill health and the reduction in the size of the expedition were much more powerful factors affecting his decision.

We saw in chapter 11 that the emirs of Sind signed a draft treaty for Colonel Pottinger at the beginning of February 1839. Auckland congratulated Pottinger on his part in obtaining the promise of 'a permanent establishment of our power and our influence on the banks of the Indus', and gave him permission to take six months' leave in Bombay.[30] At the same time he reproved Colonel Pottinger for pursuing his personal quarrel with Burnes, even to the point of wishing to resign. Auckland was glad that Macnaghten and Burnes had become reconciled after a disagreement of their own, but he was pained to see that Pottinger bore a grudge against Alexander Burnes. To Macnaghten he wrote:

...I have before written to you of his [Burnes's] merits, of which I think most highly and of his failings which are, to say the least of them, sometimes exceedingly provoking. You may know how bitterly Col. Pottinger complains of him, in some respects with reason and in others without reason—and certainly without establishing a case for his own retirement in consequence from his position in Sinde...[31]

To Keane, on the same subject, Auckland wrote of his hope that a rest in Bombay would help Colonel Pottinger to forgive and forget.[32] To Farish he remarked that the Colonel was sensitive and that Burnes was often petulant—'and petulance from him to such a man as Col. Pottinger is to say the least of it exceedingly misplaced...'.[33]

Lord Auckland did his best to soothe Colonel Pottinger's ruffled feelings, but the task was not easy, for at the same time he had to tell Pottinger that some important changes would have to be made in the text of the treaty with the emirs, without changing its 'essential spirit and character'.[34] The Governor General had been trained as a lawyer, and Pottinger started life as a soldier. Colonel Pottinger's text had to be extensively revised by Auckland himself, and in the process the treaty became somewhat harder on the emirs. For instance, he wrote in a clause providing for the military occupation of Karachi. Finally, on 11 March 1839, Auckland ratified the treaty and sent it back for ratification (or rejection) by the emirs. His dealings with the emirs are the least creditable of all his actions as Governor General, but he was not alone in failing to see that they were being treated unjustly. The Talpura family had no friends among the British:

...The Ameers have committed many a fault and many a blunder. They have neither been wise in their treachery nor brave in their hostility, and they have yielded without dignity, and write 'we are now the ryots of the British Government.' I sincerely hope however that they will have profited by the lesson which they have received. Their river has been liberated from toll—our power will have been established on its banks and their collective power of mischief will have been broken. Yet each of them may be prosperous and happy in the condition of separate independence under British protection, as are the Sikh chiefs of the countries which I have lately transited...[35]

He was referring to the Sikhs who had long lived under British protection on the left bank of the Sutlej. He clearly felt elated by the success of his policy in Sind, and he almost immediately drafted a long dispatch to the Secret Committee, explaining what he had done.[36]

Having returned the treaty to Pottinger, the Governor General gave careful thought to the lines of communication through Baluchistan and Upper Sind. In April he appointed Ross Bell, his magistrate at Delhi, to the new post of political agent at Shikarpur. Ross Bell, like so many civil and military officers in India at the time, had some personal faults which were aggravated by the extreme heat of the plains, but Auckland could forgive much to a man who was 'experienced and remarkably energetic and able'. Remarkable energy and ability were not so commonplace that he could scrutinize personality very closely. Colvin summed up Bell's mission: '...to superintend the measures which...have been directed for organising and controlling the country from Bukkur westwards. We must make friends of the petty chiefs, and set Belochis to catch Belochis, and all will come right...'[37]

At the same time as he appointed Bell to Shikarpur the Governor General instructed Eastwick to act as Resident at Hyderabad in Pottinger's absence on leave. Once again Auckland overlooked an official's defects and valued his 'energy and arrangement and resource'—qualities which 'are greatly wanted in this direction'[38] In his detailed instructions to Ross Bell on 18 May Auckland showed what he meant by that last remark. He privately and confidentially told Bell exactly what had gone wrong with the arrangements for the march from Shikarpur to Quetta. He went over arguments which we have already heard—the commissariat's neglect and the failure to reconnoitre the route, and so on—and he added that the presence of Brigadier Gordon and his three battalions of Bombay Native Infantry and the appointment of Eastwick to act in Pottinger's stead 'have enabled me to give instructions towards the correction of the evils which had occurred, but though these officers have ably and zealously seconded me, you will find that much indeed remains to be accomplished'. Those who have uncritically accepted the charge that Auckland was inefficient might well ponder the instructions which he gave to Bell. He thought of every necessity: shelter for the troops; security of communications, to be obtained in co-operation with the chiefs; the improvement of political relations with the chiefs of Upper Sind; the proper organization of commissariat arrangements which had been contradictory and inconsistent; clarity and method in financial accounting; and, most important of all in the long run, commerce and navigation on the Indus. Bell and the officers working with him should aim to have two new steamers working on the river before the end of 1839, and should be prepared for a fortnightly convoy of merchandise in existing vessels from 1 June between Ferozepore and Bukkur. In the course of this letter Auckland made a remark which shows how sensitive he was to criticism about the twenty lakhs extracted from the Sind emirs in place of unpaid tribute. He said that Ross Bell should 'always bear in mind that this payment by Sinde is not to be considered in the light of a *mulct*. It is much below an equivalent for the claims of Afghanistan upon Sind and for the protection which will be derived from the British Government..'[39] The fact was that Hobhouse, while officially approving of the use of the Indus for military traffic and the temporary occupation of Shikarpur in this emergency, doubted the expediency of exacting the twenty lakhs from the emirs and hoped that that part of the treaty might be revised.[40] Nevertheless, he did not insist on revision when Auckland defended the clause in terms similar to those used in writing to Ross Bell, and he seems to have raised the objection only because it was so easy for political opponents to treat the payment as a mulct of dubious morality. In February Hobhouse both officially and privately urged the need for caution in considering the future of Afghanistan. He did so at a time when parliamentary attacks were imminent, and so it is not surprising to find in the dispatch of 18 February from the Secret Committee a sentence saying:

...We could never sanction any arrangement having for its object territorial acquisitions in Central Asia, but we shall consider you justified in stipulating for the permanent residence of a British Resident at the capital of Afghanistan and also for the permanent employment of a disciplined force raised for the Shah's service under British officers...[41]

Replying privately to these words of warning in May, Lord Auckland reassured Hobhouse that he would not pledge himself rashly. He said his dreams for futurity were

much more of steamers on the Indus and of the merchants of Central Asia, Cashmere and Hindostan, meeting the merchants of Europe and America at Tatta and Mithunkote, than of military posts—but we must first establish security and put aggression at a distance...[42]

It was Hobhouse's business to restrain Auckland whenever it seemed necessary, and he mistakenly thought it necessary when he read Auckland's dispatch of 13 March in the middle of the Cabinet crisis in May. But the troops were still in motion and he merely reserved for another occasion his remarks about the new arrangements with the emirs of Sind. He also had doubts about Auckland's use of the word 'garrison' when referring to future military arrangements at Herat, Kabul, and Kandahar. There was an unpleasant hint of permanence in the use of that word. For the time being, however, he congratulated Auckland on all that he had done so far, and he reiterated the British Government's view of the expediency of saving Herat from Persian aggression and of preventing the encroachments of any power from the westward.[43] Hobhouse saved until July his comments on the arrangements with Sind and his graver warnings against appearing to entertain designs of conquest or ascendancy throughout the whole of Afghanistan.[44] By then the British Government was deep in the diplomatic struggle to restrain Muhammad Ali and so deprive Russia of the opportunity to act as the sole protector of the Porte. Indeed throughout the first half of 1839 Auckland was showered with copies of letters and dispatches between London and Alexandria, Constantinople, Baghdad, and Bushire. It was somewhat galling in the middle of a difficult military operation to learn that Palmerston had warned Muhammad Ali against trying to establish his military and naval power on the shore of the Gulf, and that the warning implied the threat of counter-action from British India, for there were no direct instructions from the Secret Committee.

I am most impatient [Auckland told Hobhouse on 10 May] for instructions from you upon the subject of Bahrein and of the measures of the Egyptians upon the shores of the Persian Gulf. I passed for Sir Frederick Maitland directions such as I thought would meet with the least hazard the tendency of our foreign policy, but I have felt my responsibility in doing so and should be sorry to see new quarrels spring up in new places...[45]

What had happened was that in the course of successful operations against the Wahabites in Nejd the Egyptian army had come within striking distance of Bahrain. It was in the knowledge of that fact that Auckland had sent Rear Admiral Maitland in the *Wellesley* to cruise along the Gulf earlier in the year.

The author sees more than coincidence in the fact that Hobhouse started issuing unnecessary warnings to Auckland in July. The Russians had to be kept quiet, for, as Palmerston had earlier written to Lansdowne on 17 June:

The object now to be attained is to stop Mehemet Ali, and Mehemet Ali is weak, and England, France, Austria, and Russia are, outwardly at least, and professedly, agreed to stop him. If we let him go on, we shall have to stop Russia; and Russia is strong, and Austria might not help us against her...[46]

Advance to the Hindu Kush 1838–1839

At that time the Turkish army was on the march in Syria, and Ibrahim Pasha was advancing against it. The two armies collided at Nezib on 24 June, and the Turks were routed. The death of the Sultan and the defection of his fleet within three weeks of that defeat left the Porte tottering and in no condition to refuse the envoys of the five powers when they presented their joint note in Constantinople on 27 July. Britain, France, Russia, Austria and Prussia jointly assumed responsibility for settling the dispute. This piece of diplomacy owed everything to Palmerston's planning, and we can see why his colleague Hobhouse thought it necessary to avoid any direct offence to Russia in Central Asia at that moment. But it is only fair to note also that Auckland's treatment of the Sind emirs looked like a precedent, which Hobhouse could not pass without comment. Moreover, though Hobhouse did not hear of it immediately, Macnaghten and Auckland were already discussing the possibility of leaving part of the regular army in Afghanistan for a while after the end of the campaign:

...The only objection is that of expense, but it would be an act of extravagance to leave our work incomplete, and our strength should not be recalled *to this distance* until Afghanistan is settled and the integrity of Herat well assured. You will remember, however, that it is not only you and I who have to determine these matters and that every step must be measured as well with reference to the urgency of the case as to the opinions of others. Above all things we must look with earnestness and with perfect faith to the redemption of our promise that, the object of securing our frontier being accomplished, our military interference will be withdrawn—but the restored monarchy will not be strong until something of order and efficiency shall have been given both to its military and civil institutions, and it would perhaps be more politic to give something of European command and discipline to Afghans themselves than to leave even for a time (probably at an equal expense) garrisons in their country. The time for determining on these questions has not yet come, but you and Sir John Keane will weigh them well...[47]

Auckland told Hobhouse about this privately on 18 June, in a letter received in London at the end of August, and Hobhouse was predictably anxious about its implications. He expressed his disquiet to Auckland in a reply dated 16 September. Auckland replied in his turn on 13 November, in terms which Hobhouse must have found it difficult to answer:

A king restored at Kabul

...If the end, to be aimed at, be an independent power in Afghanistan strong enough to resist aggression, bound to us by alliance and by interest and opening to our commerce its resources and its communications, we must for a time support the Shah where we have placed him. I am as impatient as you or anyone can be to withdraw our regular force. Its distance from our provinces and from all reinforcements is a source of anxiety and uneasiness to me and I shall be rejoiced when every Bengal regiment shall have recrossed the Sutlej...

He held out the hope that all would have returned by October 1840, and he clinched his argument by saying:

...I feel that our objects cannot be effected without an expense that will be objected to, and it may be hard to calculate in money the value of such an outwork to our Empire or of the commerce which a free communication with Central Asia may open to our merchants. But if we recede our enemies will advance, and whilst I would act with prudence I would at least endeavour to retain the advantages which we have gained...[48]

We have moved rather far ahead in dealing with the question of leaving some troops in Afghanistan, and we shall return to the question later. Meanwhile, it is useful to note that Macnaghten and Auckland discussed the possibility as early as May and June 1839.

It is time now to return to Keane's army, which set out from Kandahar on 27 June along the road to Ghazni and Kabul, led by its horse artillery and cavalry, Sale's brigade of infantry, and Keane and his staff. The troops marched in the early hours of each morning, by moonlight at first, for the days were excessively hot. According to Augustus Abbott, who always contrived to march near the front with his immaculate battery of six-pounders, the temperature reached 100° Fahrenheit at times. Their journey was uneventful, in spite of the unseen Ghilzai horsemen then moving on a parallel course, and they reached their half-way house, Mukur, on 14 July. There was no shortage of supplies now, and the climate was delightful because they had climbed out of the valley to a place more than seven thousand feet above sea level. A stir of excitement went through the army on the 18th, when the leading column reached Mashaki, for Keane received information that Dost Muhammad's supporters would oppose the advance at Ghazni. Keane immediately ordered the columns strung out behind him to close up by forced marches. On the 20th, when Keane's order had

285

been carried out, Outram noted: '...the minarets of Ghazni are actually in sight.' On that very day, more by chance than by close co-ordination, Claude Wade and his eleven thousand, of whom rather more than half were Sikhs, arrived at Jamrud, close to the entrance to the Khyber Pass. Both columns were therefore poised for action against fortresses—one man-made at Ghazni, the other a formidable natural obstacle opposite Jamrud.

Outram had sighted Ghazni's pinnacles across a spacious plain, which now gave Keane room to manœuvre. He set his army in motion again early on Sunday 21 July. The infantry marched on the left, with their left leading; the guns used the road itself; and the cavalry moved on the right, with its right leading. Muhammad Hyder Khan, the Dost's son and Governor of Ghazni, observed the advance from the battlements, confident that his fortress could hold out for several months if necessary. But he had already been betrayed. Early on that Sunday morning a deserter from Ghazni joined the advancing British and sepoy columns with his few followers. His name was Abdul Rashid Khan, said by Hough to have been a nephew of Dost Muhammad, and he soon proved to be very useful to his new friends.

About a mile from Ghazni the main body of the army halted while Sale's brigade and a company from one of Abraham Roberts's regiments cleared some walled gardens commanding the approach to the fortress. Then Keane called up his artillery and fired at the walls from seven hundred yards, drew an answering fire, which he measured, and broke off the duel after about three quarters of an hour. During that time the army suffered its first casualties in action, for some of Sale's infantrymen were engaged in a duel of their own with marksmen on the walls, and the marksmen were using long muskets supported on rests. The jezail, as this weapon is called, is very accurate when fired from a rest, even at long ranges. While the firing was going on, Keane heard a report that his baggage train was about to be attacked, and he sent two of his cavalry regiments to reinforce the rearguard. Having withdrawn all troops to positions out of range of Ghazni's guns, he then instructed his chief engineer to inspect the fortifications as closely as he could with safety. The appearance of the chief engineer and his staff, escorted by infantry and cavalry, provoked more gunfire from the fortress, whose defenders were feeling over-confident after obliging Keane to withdraw out of range. George Thomson, the chief engineer, must have felt depressed when he observed the strength of the fortifications and remembered the four siege guns which were lying idle at Kandahar. But Abdul Rashid Khan had told Keane and his staff that the Kabul gate of Ghazni was only lightly fortified. All other gates but this had been bricked up. Thomson studied the Kabul gate through his telescope and ascertained that this was so. Consequently Keane decided to move the whole army to positions astride the Ghazni–Kabul road. He knew that the Kabul gate had been left unblocked because the garrison expected reinforcements from Kabul, and Thomson had assured him that the most practical method of entry was to blow up the stout timber barricade at that point and rush in. How much use was the information given by Abdul Rashid Khan? It is arguable that Thomson would have seen for himself, without prompting, that one gate was weaker than the others, and that he would have felt obliged in any case to recommend the use of explosives at that point. But Keane might not have ordered the reconnaissance until he was embroiled in an attempt to breach the south-western face of the fortress. Abdul Rashid Khan showed them where to look first for the weak point in Ghazni's defences, and saved them time, men, and ammunition. And so, on that Sunday afternoon, Keane's army began to change its ground, skirting the fortress and staying always out of range of its guns. This, as Kaye shrewdly observes, was the moment when the Barukzai chiefs and their horsemen could have done real damage, for it took the army about twenty hours to shift itself from one side of the city to the other. But Keane, whatever else he was, was a lucky general, and the Afghans did not attack.

Early on the Monday morning Sir John Keane and members of his staff rode to a commanding position on the heights east of Ghazni and laid their plans for the assault. The plans were bold and simple—an artillery bombardment, a diversion on the south side of the city by an infantry regiment, the destruction of the gate, and an assault by a storming party of European infantry (both Queen's and Company's). All was to take place by night. The boldness and simplicity of the plan still take the breath away. We have to remember that the gateway was more like a tunnel than a large door, and that Keane determined to carry out the whole attack in the dark and dead of night. So many things could have gone wrong for an unlucky general or an over-cautious one. Being bold, breezy and confident, Keane made his decision, informed his senior officers, and prepared for the coming night's work.

The early afternoon of the 22nd, however, was taken up by a skirmish with some Afghan horsemen and infantry bearing the green banner of holy war. Outram, with his usual dash and presence of mind, took command of a company of the Shah's troops and led them in a successful flanking attack on the Afghans occupying the heights above the Shah's camp. He descended again with about fifty prisoners and returned to his post as aide de camp to Sir John Keane. The prisoners belonged to the Shah. They would have been better off if they had surrendered to men of the Army of the Indus, for when they came before Shah Shuja there was a furious altercation. Shuja was insulted, and one of the prisoners stabbed one of his attendants. Hough convinced himself that the other attendants then rushed upon the prisoners and slaughtered them all, without orders from Shah Shuja. 'This', he said, 'I believe to be the real fact; and I made particular inquiries.' Outram treated the whole affair in his usual laconic style, describing the stabbing of the attendant as 'an offence for which the whole are said to have atoned with their lives'. Havelock stated that 'after repeated warnings to desist from their traitorous invectives' the most 'audacious of them were carried out, and beheaded by the royal executioners'. These three officers were at Ghazni in positions close to the high command, and the only thing that their accounts have in common is that some of the prisoners were killed after the stabbing of an attendant. Kaye, whose voice throbbed with eloquent moral indignation when he came to describe the episode, quoted an anonymous witness to the execution, said to be 'an officer of the highest character'. This officer caught a glimpse of the execution in progress and reported immediately to the tent of the envoy and Minister, William Macnaghten. But the evidence is marred by the anonymity of the witness. Macnaghten himself put the number of men executed at thirty-six, and stated that Keane knew in advance that the executions were going to take place. But another anonymous officer, quoted by Buist, said that Keane did not know, and that he was furious when he heard of such butchery within the limits of a British camp. The controversy—hardly surprising when we consider the failure of senior officers to agree on the facts—reached the Indian press and caused Auckland great embarrassment.

By the time the sun went down on the 22nd every unit commander knew where to go at the appointed time. Blustery winds sprang up and concealed the noises of preparation in the British lines. For a while there was moonlight, but the moon set at about half past ten and the last dispositions had to be made in almost complete darkness. By two o'clock everyone was in position. Most important of all, the storming party had arrived at the rendezvous, close to the two ancient pillars which stand beside the road some seven hundred yards from the Kabul gate, and the engineers were ready there with their explosives—three hundred pounds of powder in twelve sandbags. The storming party consisted of an advance, or 'forlorn hope', of 240 men under Lieutenant Colonel Dennie of the 13th Light Infantry, and a main column. The officer in command of the whole storming party was the senior colonel in Dennie's regiment, Brigadier Robert Sale, otherwise known as 'fighting Bob'. Shortly before three o'clock the engineers and Dennie's 'forlorn hope' moved down the road towards the gate. According to Dennie the main column under Sale failed to observe their departure, thus causing a nearly fatal delay. But not every witness agrees with Dennie on this, and Dennie had an axe to grind when he wrote his account of the proceedings. Durand, the subaltern responsible for laying the powder and lighting the portfire, has left the most detailed account of what happened at the gate. According to him the explosion party was challenged and came under fire from the walls when it was within one hundred and fifty yards of the gate. Nevertheless, Durand and his men reached the gateway with their loads. There they were comparatively safe as long as they stayed close to the wall. Unable to dislodge them with small-arms fire the defenders resorted to showering them with stones and bricks, which did little damage. Durand had some difficulty at first in lighting the portfire, but he could be thankful that the feint attack had already started in the south and that the artillery bombardment was under way. Within two minutes, though each second seemed like an hour to the engineers, the job was done. The charge exploded, destroying the timber of the gate and bringing down heaps of rubble. Durand's immediate superior, Alexander Peat, was a little stunned by a blow on the head and hastily concluded that the explosion had failed to make an opening for the infantry. There was a moment of confusion. Peat ran towards the main column with his false report, while Durand looked for a bugler to sound the advance. Dennie, meanwhile, had been waiting under cover for the explosion. He had with him one company from each of the European infantry regiments of the Army of the Indus—the 2nd (or Queen's Royals), the 13th Light Infantry, the 17th (later Royal Leicestershire Regiment) and the 1st Bengal European Infantry (later H.M. 101st and part of the Royal Munster Fusiliers). Dennie leapt towards the gate with his 'forlorn hope' and clambered over the rubble into the tunnel-like entrance. This is how Dennie described the moment six days later:

We succeeded. I was at the head of all; the first man in the breach, the first to enter that gateway, and the first armed Britain that entered Ghuznee! The place is famed in eastern story, and our achievement, having been enacted on ground so classical, will thus gain celebrity. I escaped unhurt again, thank God, and was, with my party, in the body of the fort before the main column followed. Our cheers told those without we were masters of the stronghold of central Asia...[49]

But where was the main column under Sale? We know of two breathless and probably concussed engineer subalterns who were looking for it with contradictory messages. According to Dennie, the chief engineer George Thomson was near the gate at the time of the explosion and sent yet another engineer subaltern, Lieutenant Pigou, to look for Sale and to hurry him up. Dennie says that Pigou had to run all the way back to the pillars (seven hundred yards away), and that he there found Sale's men still waiting for the order to fall in. Sale gave the order to fall in and advance along the road, and Pigou ran back towards Thomson. But Peat then arrived with his false report of failure and induced Sale to halt. Fortunately Thomson himself arrived with the true story, and the advance resumed. Thomson's own official report throws a discreet veil over Sale's delay: '... There was some delay in getting a bugler to sound the advance, the signal agreed on for the assaulting column to push on; and this was the only mistake in the operation...'

Hough says that Sale was only a hundred yards behind Dennie at the moment of the explosion, and this is probably closer to the truth of the matter, for William Dennie was tormented by jealousy when he wrote his account, Sale having been given all the credit for the success of the storming party. Sale's delay nearly cost him his life. It gave some of the Afghan defenders time to reoccupy the gateway, and one of them nearly overpowered 'fighting Bob', wounding him in the face with a cut from his sabre. It was a desperate fight for a time in and around the debris of the Kabul gate, but it was not without a moment of comedy. Large pieces of masonry fell among the fighters beneath the arch of the gateway, and one of them owed his life to having placed an 'unexpired portion' of chupatty under the crown of his hat. Sale and his main column, consisting of the remainder of the four regiments represented in the 'forlorn hope', fought their way eventually into the city itself, but by that time it was about four o'clock. Dennie and *his* men were approaching the citadel, and by five o'clock Ensign Frere of the 13th Light Infantry was able to hoist his regiment's colours there.

Casualties among the attackers were relatively light—only 17 dead and 165 wounded—but the defenders suffered severely, having been taken entirely by surprise. At least 500 of them fell during the storm, and about 100 were cut down by the cavalry outside the walls as they tried to escape. There were many prisoners. Augustus Abbott thought that the garrison kept a very poor look-out, allowing batteries to move unopposed along a road which could have been enfiladed from the walls. But he made no allowance for the noise of the wind and the darkness of the night. He only took account of the prisoners' bewilderment at being so surprised. They do not, he wrote, 'seem to understand such energetic proceedings'. When Afzul Khan, the Dost's eldest son, saw the colours of the 13th Light Infantry on the citadel of Ghazni at first light on 23 July, he hastily ordered his five thousand horsemen to mount and ride to Kabul. He was in such a hurry that he left behind his elephants and most of his baggage. He, too, had been taken by surprise. He had hoped for a conventional siege and the opportunity for raids on the besiegers. Alternatively, if Keane had tried to advance on Kabul without first reducing Ghazni, Afzul Khan would have joined with Muhammad Hyder Khan in attacking the invaders' rear while Dost Muhammad faced them on the Kabul road.[50] The last thing that any of the Afghan chiefs expected was a successful storm by night. Dost Muhammad heard the news of the fall of Ghazni late in the afternoon of the 23rd. He was astounded, but he was also practical. He sent for his brother, the Nawab Jubbar Khan, and instructed him to ride to Ghazni with proposals for a peaceful settlement. He would give up the throne of Kabul if he could be Shuja's vizier (or prime minister).

A few hours after the capture of the city Sir John Keane dictated his order of thanks to the victors. He said he could hardly do justice to the gallantry of the troops. He singled out the chief engineer and three of his officers, Durand, Peat and Macleod, for special praise on the 'scientific and successful manner in which the Cabul gate (of great strength) was blown up'. Then he praised Brigadier Sale and his men, as if Sale had been the first to enter after the explosion. Dennie was mentioned without special distinction, but Sale was told that Keane felt deeply indebted to him 'for the manner in which he conducted the arduous duty intrusted to him in command of the storming party'. On the following day Keane made partial amends to Dennie, but he still withheld credit from him and heaped praise on Sale in his dispatch to Lord Auckland. He described the capture of Ghazni as 'one of the most brilliant acts it has ever been my lot to witness, during my service of 45 years, in the four quarters of the globe'. Privately, according to Buist, Keane said later that Ghazni was 'but a rotten hole after all', but its capture would give the Whigs another year in office. It is difficult to judge the accuracy of Buist's report. Keane may have said it much later, but there is no reason to believe that he thought his army's achievement anything but brilliant on 23 July 1839. Dennie thought so too, and wanted due recognition of his own part in the affair. On the 24th he had a distressing interview with the Commander in Chief and, like Nott at Quetta in April, he retired hurt and angry, convinced that he was being victimized. He later wrote that by the time Sale and his men entered the Kabul gate the 'forlorn hope' under his command had reached the opposite gate and was 'in full and perfect possession, having overcome, unhelped and unaided, all opposition. This is as notorious to thousands as the sun at noon-day...'[51] Notorious or not, the fact received no official recognition at the time.

Two days after the battle for Ghazni the force under Claude Wade's superintendence entered the Khyber Pass, and it captured the fort at Ali Masjid on the 26th. With Wade were just under five thousand men in the service of Shah Shuja, commanded by Shuja's eldest son, Timur, and just over six thousand Sikhs, commanded by Colonel Shaik Bussawun. There were two ways of obtaining passage through the pass. One could pay or one could fight, and sometimes one both paid and fought. On this occasion Wade's eleven thousand had to fight, and they lost 22 men and had 158 wounded before Ali Masjid fell into their hands. Their next objective would be Jalalabad.

Nawab Jubbar Khan entered the British camp at Ghazni on the 28th. He gave his brother's message and learned that Dost Muhammad could only hope for honourable exile in British India if he surrendered. He asked nothing for himself, impressed his hosts with his dignity in such a crisis, and returned home on the 29th. It is said that he put the following question to the British envoy during his visit: 'If Shah Shuja is really a king, and come to the kingdom of his ancestors, what is the use of your army and name? You have brought him by your money and arms into Afghanistan. Leave him now with us Afghans, and let him rule us if he can.'

Macnaghten was unimpressed, being convinced that the Barukzais had damaged their reputation irreparably by consorting with the hated Persians. On the 30th Keane and his army resumed their march. A small garrison was left at Ghazni, where the citadel, being spacious and airy, served as a hospital for the sick and wounded. On 1 August Keane received the bad news of the death of Runjeet Singh, but it was balanced within forty-eight hours by the report that Dost Muhammad's followers had deserted him and that Dost Muhammad himself had fled with a faithful few towards Bamiyan. Keane decided to send Outram and a small force of cavalry in pursuit, and Haji Khan Kakur, the Afghan who had thrown in his lot with Shuja near Kandahar, was detailed to accompany Outram's men with about two thousand horsemen. Haji Khan Kakur displeased Outram first of all by bringing only three hundred horsemen, and as the days went by Outram's suspicions deepened. It became obvious that Haji Khan Kakur was deliberately slowing up the pursuit so that Dost Muhammad could get away. In fact Outram eventually had to report failure.

On the 6th Keane's army camped at Nanuchi, about three miles west of Kabul, and on the following day the king made what was meant to be a triumphal entry into the city. Accounts of his reception by the people vary as much as those of the enthusiasm displayed for him at Kandahar. Kaye quotes Havelock's vivid description of the cavalcade that left the British camp on that Wednesday afternoon, but he neglects the same writer's account of the interest shown by the people in what was happening. Havelock makes it quite clear that although there was little personal affection for Shuja there was great public satisfaction in the change of government. He saw ready acquiescence, or something more, in the faces of the many Afghan spectators of the Shah's entry into Kabul. Hough rather complacently wrote that the people began to acknowledge the beneficial effects of the change from anarchy to monarchy. Buist, summarizing the impressions of other witnesses, says that the attitude of the crowds was respectful but decorous, and even cold. Strangely enough, there seems to be no evidence to support Kaye's statement that the cavalcade was more like a funeral procession than a triumph. But Kaye was writing with the benefit of hindsight. On 7 August 1839 the people of Kabul recognized and respected a former king but showed him that he would have to work to earn their love and permanent allegiance.[52] It was not a foregone conclusion that he would fail to win their affection.

The Army of the Indus had now completed the task given to it by the Governor General in 1838. It had been generally well behaved so far, and one can be sure that critics of the policy which led it into Afghanistan would long ago have used atrocity stories as ammunition if atrocities had been committed. In fact the army's record was virtually blameless, apart from a few brawls and some rough handling of Baluchi villagers under provocation. The only atrocity on record was the execution of the Shah's prisoners, and that could not be laid at Keane's door. Some of the soldiers found the leisure and pleasures of life at Kabul too much for them, and Hough says that there were some 'irregularities' in the first week after their arrival. On 12 August Keane limited the issue of passes to soldiers noted for their sobriety and steadiness. But as soon as one task was completed another came their way. Outram returned to Kabul empty-handed but with a story that quickly put Haji Khan Kakur behind bars. Towards the end of the month the army heard of the murder of Lieutenant Colonel Herring, commanding the 37th Bengal Native Infantry, on the road from Kandahar to Kabul. The punishment of the murderers was one of several tasks confided to James Outram on 25 August. He was told to lead a mixed expedition, mainly of men of the Shah's contingent, into the Ghilzai country between Kabul and Kandahar to instal new chiefs and to arrest those who had opposed or failed to co-operate with Shuja earlier in the advance. Also at this time Keane and Macnaghten were considering the measures to be taken against Mehrab Khan of Kalat and the disposition of the regiments which would stay behind when the bulk of the Army of the Indus retired. They already had authority from Auckland to do this, and his minute of 20 August was little more than a formality confirming the decision to leave some regular troops in Afghanistan. On 1 September William Dennie wrote to his family:

> ...The war may now be considered at an end, the King being once again on his throne. The 13th with two sepoy corps have been selected to remain here on the breaking up of the army on its return to India. The king and envoy, seeking warmth and safety in the plains, retire to Jalalabad...[53]

Outram's expedition into the Ghilzai country left Kabul on the 7th, the day of a grand military review in honour of Shah Shuja. Wade's force had arrived from Jalalabad, so that the combined military strength of Shah Shuja and his allies was assembled for the first time in one place. There were rather more than 13,000 under Keane, 6,000 in Shah Shuja's contingent under British officers, almost 5,000 under the Shahzada Timur, and upwards of 6,000 Sikhs, a grand total of about 30,000 fighting men. On the 14th Sir John Keane issued a general order thanking the troops for their services. He told them that the Queen was being asked to allow them to wear the Ghazni medal awarded by Shah Shuja. The Shah caused Auckland some embarrassment by instituting an order of the Durrani Empire (unfortunate word) at this time. Senior officers, political and military, were generally placed in the 1st and 2nd classes, but five Majors, two Captains, and one Lieutenant Colonel, who happened to be Keane's military secretary, were given a special place in the 2nd class because of their 'excellent and efficient service during the whole campaign, and at the assault and capture of Ghuznee'. William Dennie was not one of them. He found *his* name in the list of Lieutenant Colonels commanding battalions or regiments, who automatically qualified for the 3rd class, and he declined an honour which fell so far short of what he thought he deserved. Junior subalterns, however brave and efficient, found no place in the honours. Captain Peat, whose false alarm nearly caused disaster at Ghazni, was one of those included in the 2nd class. Lieutenant Durand got nothing, and Sergeant Robertson, who helped him to lay the charge at the gate, was also neglected. But in those days individual non-commissioned officers and men were rarely noticed.

Advance to the Hindu Kush 1838–1839

Dost Muhammad's escape, though disappointing, did not at first give Keane and Macnaghten much anxiety. But as September advanced they heard disquieting reports of his activities beyond the Hindu Kush. They sent a small force to watch the passes, and even contemplated sending an expedition against him, but in the end they thought it more reasonable to wait for the spring. Nevertheless, as a precaution, they decided to keep nine infantry battalions in Afghanistan for the time being instead of three. Major General Thomas Willshire assembled the Bombay Division on 18 September and set out from Kabul with orders to punish Mehrab Khan on his way home. A messenger went on ahead with orders for William Nott, commanding the troops in the Quetta district. Keane told him to hold his troops in readiness for service under Willshire if required. But this unwelcome news did not reach Nott until the middle of October. It was unwelcome because he had expected to be given the task of punishing Mehrab Khan of Kalat.

After Willshire, the next to leave was Wade, accompanying the Sikhs and those of Timur's men no longer required there. The unwanted troops of the Bengal Division left Kabul under Keane on 15 October. The Bengal troops remaining in Afghanistan shared garrison duties in the principal towns with men of the Shah's contingent. Of the two European regiments one, the 13th Light Infantry, was at Kabul, and the other, the 1st Bengal European Regiment, was at Jalalabad. The other seven were regiments of Bengal Native Infantry. Cotton remained in command of the regular division, which also included some cavalry, artillery, and engineers, and William Dennie was happy again because the change of plan made him a brigadier once more, with an independent command at Kabul. Outram, meanwhile, had finished his work among the Ghilzais and was marching with Willshire's force by a previously unused route from Maruf to Quetta. William Nott moved out of Quetta on his way to Kandahar on 26 October, still smarting from the insult of being ordered to take instructions from Willshire. Indeed he had written to the Deputy Adjutant General at Kabul: 'I conceive myself to be senior to local Major General Willshire, and therefore can obey no orders originating with that officer, nor can I serve under him. . . .' This was an ill-considered and unfortunate letter. It cost him command of the whole division in Afghanistan, for Auckland was about to put him in Sir Willoughby Cotton's place when the mutinous letter came to his notice.

Cotton had to stay on. It might be argued that the whole course of events in Afghanistan in 1840 and 1841 would have been different if Nott had taken command at the end of 1839. Major General William Elphinstone might never have been sent to Kabul. But William Nott stubbornly declined to conceal his resentment of the favour shown to Willshire, and his career suffered accordingly. One can hardly claim that he suffered unjustly on this occasion.[54]

On 7 November the leading units of Keane's returning column pitched their camp at Peshawar. They had a brush with the hot-tempered 'Khyberees' before they said goodbye to Afghanistan, just to remind them that they had been lucky under a lucky general for the past few months. Ali Masjid's Sikh garrison had been evicted by the Khyberees with heavy loss just before the Bengal troops reached the area, and Keane made it his business thereafter to supply and garrison the fort until its permanent occupants arrived from Jalalabad. The Khyberees' farewell to the departing Bengal troops on 22 November was an audacious raid on the baggage party. Eventually the tribesmen resumed a life of comparative peace and quiet in return for a subsidy from Shah Shuja, in accordance with time-honoured custom. Keane and what remained to him of the Army of the Indus marched from Peshawar towards Attock on the 23rd.

In October news had reached Kabul of a Russian expedition from Orenburg towards Khiva. Macnaghten and Burnes were rattled and started pressing Auckland to mount a new expedition towards the Oxus. We shall hear soon how he reacted, but for the time being it is sufficient to note that on his own initiative Macnaghten sent part of Roberts's brigade towards Bamiyan to watch the route by which invaders from the north would attempt to cross the Hindu Kush.

The Bombay Division had reached Quetta on the last day of October. There it found a regiment of native infantry belonging to Nott's brigade. Willshire absorbed it into his Kalat expeditionary force, which marched from Quetta on 4 November and attacked and captured Kalat on the 13th. Let Emily Eden describe the battle:

Last night, when we were playing whist, I saw X. fidgeting about behind G's chair with a note in his hand...It turned out to be another little battle, and a most successful one. The Khan of Khelat was by way of being our ally and assistant, and, professing friendship, did himself the pleasure of cutting off the supplies of the army, when it was on its way to Cabul; set his followers on to rob the camp, corresponded with Dost Mahomed, etc.

...It was all done in the Ghuznee manner—the gates blown in and the fort stormed—but the fighting was very severe. The Khan and his principal chiefs died sword in hand, which was rather too fine a death for such a double traitor as he has been; and one in six of our troops was either killed or wounded, which is an unusual proportion. They found in the town a great many of our camels and much of the property that had been pillaged from the army. Also there will be a great deal of prize money. Another man has been put on the Khelat throne, so that business is finished.[55]

Alas, Emily Eden spoke too soon. But the smell of success was very sweet in government circles at the end of 1839. Nawaz Khan, a convenient claimant to the ownership of Kalat, was installed in Mehrab's place. Shal, Mastung and Kachhi were annexed on behalf of Shah Shuja, as Macnaghten had suggested in April, but Mehrab Khan's widow and stepson escaped, and the stepson, Nusseer Khan, then only 14, lived to fight another day.

Auckland now offered James Outram the political agency at Hyderabad in Lower Sind, for Colonel Pottinger had at last decided to return to England for a spell.[56] Outram had done well in Afghanistan, both in military action and in political work among the Ghilzais. He at once accepted his important new post, although it did not carry Pottinger's rank of Resident. Outram had also made himself useful to Willshire at Kalat, and Auckland was more than usually pleased with the efficiency and success of that operation. Auckland had never doubted that Mehrab Khan deserved a 'heavy account of retribution for the injuries which he has done to us'.[57]

In December 1839 Lord Auckland could look back on a successful, though at times most dangerous, series of political and military operations. He had averted war with Nepal and Ava. He had made a settlement in Sind which fell far short of conquest but promised great advantages to Great Britain, commercially and strategically. He had managed to keep clear of conflict with the Egyptians in Arabia while showing them, in anticipation of Palmerston's wishes, that they would not be allowed to take Bahrain. He had been supported at home by eminent Tories as well as his own Whig colleagues. No less a Tory than Sir Richard Jenkins, then chairman of the Court of Directors, gave him an assurance of unqualified support in May and renewed the assurance in October when some Tories renewed their attacks on Auckland's policy.[58] The question, as always, was whether he was right or wrong to send his army across the Indus. As he wrote to Hobhouse in July:

...I have always felt with you how much success or failure would affect the question of right or wrong, but much higher considerations have been involved in success or failure than those of praise or blame to me or of attack and defence to you, and I am but the more happy that all hitherto promises favourably and that your publication of papers has made men acquainted with our case and convinced the candid of its justice. I retract my praise of Ellenborough. He must well know the mischief which may ensue from a partisan agitation of great measures yet in progress in India...[59]

It is interesting to note that Jenkins backed Auckland to the hilt at a time when Ellenborough was working for party advantage. A phrase of Auckland's, used in a compassionate letter to Fane, seems to the author to apply in the quite different context of Ellenborough's attitude. He said he had always thought 'that there is more of wantonness than of malevolence in the world'.[60] The Tories were torn between a jealous admiration of what the Whigs were achieving in Central Asia and a desire to bring them down at all costs. In the autumn the attacks were so strong that Hobhouse felt compelled to ask Auckland for new ammunition. He wanted urgently to know what commercial advantage would 'be derived from the recent course of measures as regards the whole line of the Indus and the Punjab streams'.[61] But the news of Dost Muhammad's flight and the peaceful restoration of Shuja at Kabul reached London at the end of October and silenced many of the critics, as Auckland (somewhat cynically) had always expected. The Peel Papers include a letter of advice from Wellington to Sir Robert Peel, written on 18 December 1839, which admirably illustrates the Tory dilemma. The duke told Peel that it was undesirable that he 'should have at this moment the option even of taking charge of the Government'. The composition of the Queen's Household would occasion the same difficulties as in May. It would be better, he said, to think in terms of a declaration of want of confidence in the Government. He listed the many points on which the Tories disagreed with the Whigs—on military and naval expenditure, Canada, the Eastern Question, the French in Africa, Minorca, the

monetary system in Britain, Ireland, the Scottish church, and
education. But

...I have left out of consideration the state of affairs in Central Asia,
and on the Indus, which, however, must eventually come under our
consideration. But I am convinced that those who are so clamorous
to turn out the Government are not prepared for the adoption of the
measures which must be adopted in order to enable any honest man to
perform his duty, who may undertake to conduct the Government...[62]

Why did the duke of Wellington leave Central Asia out of consideration on 18 December? Was it because that was the day when
the Court of Proprietors of the East India Company met to hear
and approve (with only one dissenting voice, that of Sir Charles
Forbes) a series of resolutions by the Court of Directors, thanking
and applauding the Indian Government and Army? Peel's party
did not dare to attack the Government on that issue. There is good
reason to believe that Wellington, for one, did not want to. He
knew too much about the origins of the policy so successfully pursued in 1839 by the Whigs.

Auckland was, of course, consulted by Hobhouse about the
distribution of honours at the end of the campaign. Keane deserved
high reward, and Cotton had done well; Sale should have a higher
decoration than his present one; but 'a braver, a more skilful and
a better officer' than George Thomson, chief engineer in the Army
of the Indus, 'does not exist in any service'. Auckland told Hobhouse that he was giving

orders of merit to the native sappers and miners who through bullets
and blue lights carried the powder bags to the gate of Ghuznee. Captain
Peat of the Bombay army was next to Captain Thomson and Sir John
Keane writes in terms of rapture of the two subalterns Durand and
Macleod who were present. They are too young for you, but I like to
mention them...

In fact Durand was overlooked in the distribution of honours, just
as he had been overlooked when Shah Shuja awarded the Order of
the Durrani Empire. The author cannot help thinking that Durand
let this oversight rankle, so that by the time he became Ellenborough's private secretary he was ready to believe anything ill of
those who organized the march into Afghanistan. Lord Auckland
spoke very highly of Macnaghten's merits on this occasion, and he
warned Hobhouse that in addition to anything else that might be

done for Macnaghten he anxiously hoped that he might be given a seat on the Supreme Council in Calcutta. 'He might if his services had not been otherwise required have fairly looked for the chief place in these [the North-West] Provinces upon my return to Calcutta.' Burnes, Wade and Colonel Pottinger were also mentioned approvingly. 'I have thus named to you those who, as it seems to me, had the good fortune to be most eminent, and if you wish to go further I cannot do better than refer you to Sir John Keane's general order...'[63]

In anticipation of honours from home Auckland published his own general orders thanking the army for its services in 1838 and 1839:

...The plans of aggression by which the British empire in India was dangerously threatened, have, under Providence, been arrested. The chiefs of Cabool and Candahar, who had joined in hostile designs against us, have been deprived of power, and the territories which they ruled have been restored to the government of a friendly monarch. The Ameers of Sinde have acknowledged the supremacy of the British government, and ranged themselves under its protection. Their country will now be an outwork of defence, and the navigation of the Indus within their dominions, exempt from all duties, has been opened to commercial enterprise. With the allied government of the Sikhs the closest harmony has been maintained; and on the side of Herat the British alliance has been courted, and a good understanding, with a view to common safety, has been established with that power.

For these important results, the Governor General is proud to express the acknowledgements of the government to the army of the Indus, which alike, by its valour, its discipline, and cheerfulness under hardships and privations, and its conciliatory conduct to the inhabitants of the countries through which it passed, has earned respect for the British name, and has confirmed in Central Asia a just impression of British energy and resources...

· The subsequent references to individual officers in these general orders were a model of tact and fairness. Dennie and Durand, for instance, were among those specially commended. Every regiment in the service of the East India Company during the campaign, provided that it had proceeded beyond the Bolan Pass, was authorized to place 'Affghanistan' on its colours and 'such of them as were employed in the reduction of the fortress of that name' were authorized to add 'Ghuznee' to theirs. The Queen's regiments were told that the Governor General would recommend her Majesty to grant the same distinction to them.[64]

Advance to the Hindu Kush 1838–1839

Auckland had one final disagreeable task in December. He had to repress the active spirits of William Macnaghten. But he did it kindly, and to such effect that the envoy, who had been much and (as Auckland thought) needlessly alarmed by the Russian move towards Khiva, wrote at the New Year:

...I think it probable that your Lordship's expectation of being able to withdraw the whole of the regular army at the end of the ensuing hot season will be realised, provided there be no appearance of external aggression and I am permitted to organise troops for the internal tranquillity of the country on the footing which will be hereafter officially explained...[65]

The year 1839 therefore ended with a question mark where Auckland would have liked to see a full stop. Hobhouse provides the most fitting comment upon that period of uncertainty amid triumphs:

Of all our colleagues, the one that was most pleased with these successes was Lord Palmerston; and I always found in him a cordial sympathiser in every variety of fortune, more particularly in success—a very rare quality—at least I have found it so: for many of those who are willing to stand by a friend in adversity are but lukewarm applauders of victory. This does not arise from jealousy or indifference, but from a dislike of exaggeration, as was the case with Lord Melbourne, who, I heard, had been laughing, with the Adjutant General, at the taking of Ghuznee. I was not a little annoyed at this, and wrote to Lord Melbourne entreating him to be a little more reserved in his comments when communicating with persons not in the Cabinet. He answered me with his usual kindness; saying that the affair was brilliant, but that he was in the habit of thinking nothing settled until completely finished. Subsequent events showed how right his rule had been, and how properly applied in the case of our Afghan triumphs.[66]

RETURN TO THE INDUS 1840–1842

CHAPTER 13

VICTORY AND OVER-CONFIDENCE

...Our George has done very well in India, has he not? You know
we always thought highly of him, even in his comical dog days...
Now I think he has done enough, and might as well go home, but
none of the people at home will hear of it, and this month's des-
patches have made me desperate...

EMILY EDEN to Lady Campbell, 17 July 1840

A new Russian ambassador arrived in London in September 1839.
Baron Brunnow brought assurances from the Emperor that Russia
would co-operate actively with her European allies, even with
France if necessary, to curb the ambition of Muhammad Ali of
Egypt. After the battle of Nezib, in which the Sultan's troops fared
so badly, the five powers had stepped in at Constantinople and
Alexandria with an offer of mediation. At the moment of Brunnow's arrival in England the French were humming and hawing
over the terms to be offered to Muhammad Ali, and the Russian
Government was delighted to observe the growing isolation of the
French in their cradle of revolutions. Brunnow now repeated the
assurances given through Pozzo di Borgo in June.[1] Russia would
not invoke the Treaty of Unkiar Skelessi—she would even let it
lapse—if the Powers acted effectively together. This was music to
Palmerston's ears, for he wanted two things above all—the abandonment of the Treaty of Unkiar Skelessi and the confinement of
Muhammad Ali to his 'original shell of Egypt'.[2] Here were the
Russians, swearing to help him in both enterprises, and it was now
for the Powers, whether four or five, to agree on their proposals
to Sultan and Pasha. Muhammad Ali must be kept in check, Lord
Palmerston wrote: 'by words if possible; but if not, by deeds'.[3]
Important interests were at stake, for the Pasha was not only looking for expansion on the shores of the Mediterranean. He aspired
to power on the Arab shore of the Persian Gulf as well as in Yemen
and Nejd, and Hasa submitted to his general in 1839. Palmerston
made it very clear to the Pasha that Britain would never allow him
to establish Egyptian military and naval power along the Gulf.[4]
Moreover, the Egyptian challenge came at the very moment when

the new Commercial Treaty between Britain and the Porte was beginning to take effect. France, in offering so much as sympathy to the Pasha, was indirectly threatening most important British interests; and, as relations between Britain and France cooled, so relations between Britain and Russia became unusually warm. But Palmerston never relaxed his vigilance, and he crowed with Hobhouse over the British successes at Ghazni and Kabul and the discomfiture of the Emperor. Clanricarde wrote to him on 18 October saying, 'The Emperor was poorly and in low spirits; I will venture to say he heard of our success at Ghuzni and Caboul.'[5] At that very moment the Emperor was engaged in a project with which he hoped to make Palmerston poorly and in low spirits and to convince the world that Russia was also a formidable power in Central Asia.

All went well for the Emperor at first. The expedition under General Perowski started from Orenburg with well-defined objectives. It was to restore security to the caravan routes across the desert north of Khiva and to put a stop to the practice of seizing Russian subjects and selling them into slavery. The expedition was also to confirm in that part of Asia 'the influence which rightly belongs to Russia, and which alone can serve as a guarantee for the maintenance of peace'.[6] Clanricarde reported the start of the expedition to Palmerston on 30 November, and said that Brunnow had been instructed to explain the whole project to Her Majesty's Government. Clanricarde did not think that the project had any chance of success.[7] He certainly expressed no alarm, and in this he was at one with Lord Auckland, who had found Macnaghten and his Kabul colleagues almost frantic with anxiety based on reports of the approach of a monstrous Russian army. Macnaghten and Cotton had even contemplated sending an expedition beyond the Hindu Kush to meet the approaching Cossacks. Auckland had stamped out the panic with creditable firmness at the beginning of December.

The Governor General was mindful of the political turmoil which a successful Russian operation against Khiva would cause in Central Asia, but he ridiculed fears of an imminent Russian expedition to the northern slopes of the Hindu Kush. He doubted Russia's capacity for the task, and he was persuaded by political intelligence from home that open hostility against British India on the part of Russia was out of the question at that time. Moreover,

he suspected Macnaghten of encouraging Shuja to press ancient
territorial claims beyond the mountains in the direction of Balkh:

> ...I only want to know of Shah Shooja that he is becoming an Afghan
> king and drawing his subjects about him, that his Afghan levies are
> making progress towards efficiency, that his contingent is in a condition
> to give him support, and Police and Revenue and Commerce have
> favourable prospects. He will yet have sufficient difficulty with the pred-
> atory tribes of the mountains within his frontier, and he should strongly
> repudiate every notion of cupidity and mistrust beyond it...[8]

Time and time again Auckland had to tell Macnaghten that the
answer to all his problems lay in consolidating Shuja's power and
influence inside Afghanistan, and not in incorporating Herat and
the cis–Oxus territories of Turkestan into his kingdom. He argued
that the knowledge of Shuja's strength in his own country would
spread far and wide and earn him legitimate respect and influence
among his northern neighbours. But first he must learn to be more
of a citizen king among his own people.[9] Meanwhile the sending of
fresh armies from India was out of the question, for Auckland was
already beginning to feel the strain on his finances, and, although
he and Hobhouse agreed that a heavy outlay for a few years would
yield a handsome commercial return for decades, there were problems nearer home demanding troops and money. Nepal and Ava
presented a permanent danger of war, and the Punjab was still
reeling from the shock of Runjeet Singh's death. Auckland discussed the Kabul panic in his monthly private letter to Hobhouse
on 21 December. But Hobhouse sat in Cannon Row and betrayed
a state of mind more akin to that of Macnaghten than to Auckland's.
On the 26th Hobhouse completed a Secret Committee dispatch in
which he cordially approved Auckland's warnings to Shuja to
abjure territorial claims. But he also remarked that

> in case any other Power should endeavour by force of arms to establish
> an undue influence in that part of Central Asia you may be justified in
> pursuing a policy totally different from that which we have recom-
> mended to you. We say this in reference to intelligence which has just
> reached us...of preparations having been made to despatch a body of
> Russian troops from Orenburgh against Khiva and Bokhara...[10]

So we can now see how the news of the advance on Khiva
changed Hobhouse's attitude to the British military presence in
Afghanistan. After all that he had said about avoiding even the

appearance of conquest, he now thought it advisable to give Auckland discretion to act beyond the Hindu Kush. On Colvin's evidence the change was most noticeable. At the end of November and beginning of December, when Brunnow was being so helpful, the British Government was inclined to believe that Russia would not dare to take a step in Central Asia. On reading letters written at that time Colvin reported to Macnaghten:

> ...It will be curious to see whether in spite of all appearances and belief at home Russia will venture on establishing herself at Khiva. The very highest authority in such matters describes Russia as 'quite overpowering' in her words and acts of friendship. There is a very difficult knot to be untied about Turkey and Egypt, and if Russia stands fairly by England, as she has begun by doing, in the efforts to unravel it, she will have given a credible evidence of her present intentions. But they are slippery fellows, these Muscovites.[11]

One can imagine how 'the very highest authority in such matters', no doubt Palmerston himself, reacted when he heard of the Khiva expedition. The Russians had tricked him again, and just at the moment when he was planning to commit Auckland to superintendence of operations against China. He remained on cordial terms with Brunnow, but there were barbs in the exchanges that began to pass between London and St Petersburg in January 1840. Brunnow protested that a conquest of Khiva was out of the question. Russia had no more intention of making Khiva a dependency than Britain had of permanently occupying Afghanistan. How could Palmerston's interpretation of the affair (as a move hostile to British India) be justified at a time when Russia was trying so hard to re-establish harmony with Britain? Palmerston refused to be put off. Perowski's declaration included a reference to the 'legitimate influence' which belongs to Russia in that part of Asia, whereas Khiva was an independent state far distant from any Russian territory. He rejected the attempt to draw a parallel between Khiva and Afghanistan, and Brunnow said he would ask Nesselrode to obtain the necessary assurances from the Emperor himself.[12] As it happened, Clanricarde had already had an interview with the Emperor, who told him flatly that Perowski's was a punitive expedition—'to punish the Khan of Khiva and establish tranquility for the future in that country'.[13] Palmerston at once interpreted the latter phrase as a sign that Russia intended to make Khiva politically dependent upon her. On 3 February he wrote a strongly worded dispatch to Clanricarde for the attention of the Russian Government:

...it would not be fair or candid, on the part of Her Majesty's Government, to conceal from the Cabinet of St Petersburgh, that such a state of things, being in all respects similar in nature and tendency to that which was attempted by Russian agents in Persia and Afghanistan, would oblige the Governor General to take such defensive measures as might appear to be requisite for ensuring the future defence and tranquillity of the dominions of Her Majesty in that part of the world. Her Majesty's Government would sincerely regret that such a state of things should arise, but it would not be of their seeking, and the responsibility thereof would not rest upon them...[14]

But the dispatch was never sent in that form. Someone, possibly Melbourne, persuaded Palmerston to soften the wording, and the British and Russian Governments preserved their newly established harmony. In the middle of February, however, Palmerston hinted to Hobhouse that Auckland might now give serious attention to the affair. He agreed with Auckland that the Russians were unlikely to move beyond Khiva this time, but what if they left Khiva a Russian dependency instead of an independent state?

...This may require serious consideration on our part and on the part of Auckland; for their next move will be to do the same thing with Bokhara, and then they have the waterway of the Oxus open to them through a friendly country to the Foot of the Hindoo Coosh. Whether any alliances can be made by us with the rulers of Balkh and the adjoining states, and with Bokhara is a question which you can best determine...It seems pretty clear that sooner or later the Cossack and Sepoy, the Man from the Baltic and He from the British Islands will meet in the Centre of Asia. It should be our Business to take Care that the Meeting should be as far off from our Indian Possessions as may be convenient and advantageous to us. But the Meeting will not be avoided by our staying at Home to receive the visit. As to Herat I own that nothing in these Letters seems to me to disprove the Importance of making that Place our outpost in Affghanistan, nor the Practicability of doing so...[15]

Without waiting to see what Auckland might think about these propositions Palmerston broached them with Brunnow, who was most concerned lest Auckland order a movement beyond the Hindu Kush. Palmerston said that this was unlikely if the Russians retired from Khiva without leaving a garrison behind. But, he said,

Auckland might think it necessary to make some move 'as a set off against the Incorporation of Khiva into the Russian political system, if that should be one of the Consequences of the Expedition by means of a Reorganisation of the Govt. of Khiva...'[16] Brunnow urged Palmerston to relay the Russian explanations and assurances to Auckland without delay. The letters just quoted served as guidance to Hobhouse in the drafting of a dispatch to Auckland at the end of February. Palmerston read and fully approved of the draft, in which Hobhouse expressed a guarded disappointment at the Governor General's decision not to annexe Herat for Shah Shuja. To Palmerston it was all perfectly simple. If Britain neglected Herat, then Russia would soon establish her hold on it through the Persians—'and thus Russia will have obtained the Command of the two great Roads to the Indus; the one by Ghorian and Herat to Candahar, the other by Khiva Bokhara and Balkh to Caboul...'[17] And so Hobhouse sent his dispatch through the Secret Committee on 29 February. The government of Herat, by dishonouring its treaty with Britain, had given ample provocation, and it was to be regretted that Kamran Shah had not been held to his commitments. Still, it was fortunate that Auckland had left a large part of his army west of the Indus, for

we think it by no means improbable you may be obliged to order a portion of that force to the defence of Herat...

...In conclusion we have to say that we consider the consolidation of the restored monarchy of Shah Shooja as indispensable to the complete success of the policy which you have lately pursued, and that, should you be called upon to extend your direct influence either to Herat or to the north of the Hindoo Coosh we shall support you with an entire confidence in the judgement which has hitherto characterized all your proceedings.[18]

A few days later Palmerston heard from St Petersburg that his suspicions had been justified, for Nesselrode had at last admitted to Clanricarde that one of the objects of the Khiva expedition was to dethrone the Khan of Khva and give the throne to his brother.[19] Brunnow had been either uninformed or disingenuous when he said that Russia had no political object in view beyond that of asserting a legitimate influence in the area.

At the beginning of January 1840 Lord Auckland was at Agra. He hoped to spend several months there, superintending normal Calcutta business by means of letters and minutes and giving a

large part of his attention to affairs in the North West. From Agra
he could keep an eye on Macnaghten's work in Afghanistan during
a critical period. But on the morning of 7 January he received a
letter which sent him hurrying back to Calcutta and the council
table from which he had so long been absent.[20] The letter made him
responsible for fitting out and supervising a naval and military
expedition to the coast of China. Palmerston expected a great deal
from his friend and former Cabinet colleague. In collaboration
with Hobhouse he required Auckland to keep Muhammad Ali out
of Aden and Bahrain, the Persians and Russians out of Herat, the
Russians out of southern Turkestan and Afghanistan, and numerous petty kings and princes out of territories owned or controlled
by British India. Now he wanted him to send an expeditionary
force to China to obtain redress for insults and confiscations and to
open the China coast to international trade. In the author's view
this venture distracted Auckland during a period when affairs in
the North-West required all or nearly all of his concentration. He
inevitably left Macnaghten with more discretionary authority than
was good for him, and it is remarkable that he managed to exercise
as much control as he did. He was henceforward condemned by
Palmerston's restless world vision to work in Calcutta, when the
crisis in Central Asia demanded his presence at least eight hundred
miles further west. But let it not be forgotten that he laid the foundations for the settlement of Britain's commercial relations with
China in 1842. His mastery of official business was complete,
whether he was dealing with education or the salt monopoly or
great expeditions beyond the frontiers of India.

On the whole Auckland was 'pleased with the aspect of affairs
in the North West' at the end of January 1840. By then he had
ordered Willshire, whose troops had halted in Sind during the
Kabul panic about approaching Cossacks, to resume his march and
embark with his men for the voyage to Bombay. He still expected
to be able to withdraw all British troops from Afghan territory by
October, trusting that Shuja's power could be confirmed in his
dominions in 'but a few months'.[21] But he was not firm enough
with Macnaghten in ruling against such petty expeditions as the
one which Colonel Orchard led from Jalalabad to Pashat in
January. Macnaghten thought to please the king by sending regular
soldiers with the troops detailed to depose the chief at that place.
Orchard attempted on a smaller scale, and by day, what Keane had

achieved at Ghazni, but he lacked Keane's judgement, good luck, and sheer self-confidence. Moreover, the gate of the fort was too strong and the powder was too wet. Pashat's defenders, though they ran away when darkness came, proved that British troops in small detachments were just as fallible and vulnerable as any others. Augustus Abbott, who commanded the field guns at Pashat, thought it a 'dirty little expedition', costing 'thirty lives of fighting men, about a dozen camp followers drowned or frozen to death, and about 120 camels'.[22] Both Auckland and Hobhouse regretted the expedition, but both accepted Macnaghten's claim that it was necessary. Therefore they advised against such expeditions in general and left it to Macnaghten to judge the merits of each particular case.[23] In fact Pashat established a precedent which seriously damaged the British position in Afghanistan. Hitherto it had been possible to argue that the British and sepoy regiments were simply in transit, ready to leave as soon as the king was strong enough to defend his own frontiers, and that he was responsible for the country's internal security. Hobhouse foresaw (in July 1839) the danger which would arise if the Governor General established permanent garrisons of British troops in the principal cities of Afghanistan. 'The inevitable consequence', he said, 'would be to render us responsible not only for the political relations but the internal tranquillity of Affghanistan...'[24]

Auckland had never intended to establish permanent garrisons, and Hobhouse's misunderstanding of his intentions had long since been cleared up in February 1840, but the fact remains that already British troops had fought alongside men of Shuja's contingent in an internal police action. Hobhouse may well have been less critical on this occasion than he would have been in July 1839 because he was conscious of a new Russian threat. That threat from the north meant that British troops might have to stay longer in Afghanistan, and if Shuja's own forces were slow to achieve efficiency it might be necessary on occasion to stiffen them with British troops against internal disturbances as well as external aggression. But from every point of view it was a most unsatisfactory departure from the Government's original principles.

In March the British officers in Afghanistan caught the Cossack fever again. Auckland and the members of his council refused to be rattled by the fevered reports from Kabul, even when letters from home showed that the Russian force was much larger than Clanricarde originally supposed. To Macnaghten, whose eyes were once again on the passes through the Hindu Kush, Auckland advised calm concentration on the work of strengthening Shah Shuja in his own country. 'If Napoleon had gathered strength at Warsaw', he wrote, 'he would not have found disaster at Moscow.'[25] Nor did he give way to panic when dispatches from London revealed the feelings of Palmerston and Hobhouse on hearing Russian explanations in January. He authorized Macnaghten to send an agent to the Russian camp—then thought to be at or beyond Khiva—to request an explanation of Russian military operations in Central Asia. Colvin privately said that the object was to 'alarm the Russian Commanders as to the responsibility they will incur if they do not confine themselves within the limits avowed by their Government in Europe...'[26] Then, on 15 April, Auckland stated his case against further advances in a wise and statesmanlike dispatch to the Secret Committee. He acknowledged all the dangers and inconveniences to be expected if the Russians established themselves at Khiva and Bokhara. He said that the British Government was entitled to offer

decided opposition to any scheme which may have for its object the permanent superiority of Russia in Turkistan.

Impressed with these views we have seen with much satisfaction the firm and distinct manner in which Her Majesty's Government has noticed the indications of an intention to prosecute such a policy under cover of the more avowed objects of the present expedition; and we would fain entertain the hope that the remonstrance addressed to the Russian Cabinet may lead to the relinquishment of such intentions. But we must be prepared for disappointment, and we would state therefore that, after the most anxious deliberation, we have come to the conviction, which we feel it to be our duty at once to communicate to your Honourable Committee, that it would scarcely, under any circumstances, be consistent with any prudent application of the means and resources of India that its Government should enter on a direct contest in arms within the states of Turkistan, in order to arrest or counteract their submission to the authority of Russia...

Auckland ended by standing firm on his policy of strengthening the restored Afghan monarchy and by declaring that 'we must mainly look to the exertion of our power in Europe for the purpose of checking, beyond the limits of Afghanistan, the unjustifiable advances of Russian aggression'.[27] He was held back by many considerations of policy, and not least by thoughts of money. It did not take him long, after reading the dispatches about Khiva, to understand that the troops would have to stay in Afghanistan a while longer. Indeed, the Russian expedition to Khiva, failure though it was to all outward appearances, succeeded in sabotaging the British effort to establish peace and tranquillity in Afghanistan under a restored monarch. A study of Russian state papers might even reveal that this was what the Emperor intended, but, whether he intended it or not, he distracted the British in Afghanistan from their principal task, and at a critical moment.

At the end of April Auckland also rejected once again the proposal that he should annexe Herat on behalf of Shah Shuja. He still favoured conciliation, and he argued his case in public and private correspondence with great force. He had neither troops nor money to spare for fresh enterprises beyond Shuja's frontiers, for he had expensive military and naval commitments from Aden to Chusan. He sometimes suspected the Home Government of leaving him to do all the work while Palmerston and Hobhouse indulged in diplomatic fencing with the Russians. Strangely enough, the moment of awakening from the dream in which all British troops retired from Afghanistan by October came both for him and for Hobhouse at the beginning of May. Hobhouse had been studying a paper of Macnaghten's on the character of the principal Afghan chiefs; and did not like what he read:

...If what he says is strictly true I see no chance of your being ever able to withdraw your troops from Cabul, and Shah Shooja appears to entertain no such wish or expectation. Yet a permanent or even a prolonged occupation of that Country is not and was not contemplated by any of us...[28]

The letter just quoted was written on 4 May 1840. Exactly a week later Auckland said in his own monthly private 'budget' to Hobhouse that 'it seems probable that the promised withdrawal of all our troops will not take place in the ensuing autumn...'[29]

Yet honours had been awarded in December as if the most important work was finished. Auckland was now an earl, Macnaghten a baronet, and so on. But it took only a few months to persuade the authorities in London and Calcutta that they had a long haul ahead. For one thing, Dost Muhammad was out of their reach, and although his host, the Emir of Bokhara, treated him more like a prisoner than a guest, he was a potential menace to the new system established in Afghanistan. The tribes of Afghanistan and the petty Baluchi states astride the western passes were also more difficult to deal with than anyone had expected. The Baluchis, especially, resented the British interference which had detached three of their regions from Kalat and placed them under Shuja's sovereignty. Moreover, the military and political officers in Upper Sind and Baluchistan meddled clumsily in affairs which needed the utmost care and understanding. Auckland placed great trust in Ross Bell, his representative in Upper Sind, but he was poorly served in the long run. Meanwhile he still thought it possible to plan for a commercial fair at Sukkur (in January 1841), and he spurred on the crews of his Indus steamers in spite of discouraging reports of the uncertainty of currents, inconstant depth, and twists and turns which defied the longer vessels to negotiate them. He felt sure that they would eventually hit upon the ideal design for an Indus river steamer, and then there would be a regular traffic of passengers and merchandise. Had not Russian goods already disappeared from the shops of Kandahar ? The Indus and the markets of Central Asia were never far from his thoughts, and in this he was at one with Palmerston, Hobhouse, and many other Englishmen of his day.

We left Palmerston and Hobhouse, at the end of February, pondering on the strategy which would keep Russia away from the two great roads to the Indus. At the end of March Hobhouse sent to Auckland copies of a report by the Secretary of State on their conversations with Baron Brunnow. It is clear from this report that Palmerston and Hobhouse together gave Brunnow to understand that the Russian Government was risking a war with Britain in Asia by advancing to Khiva. It is also clear that they hinted at the possibility of a clash in Turkestan between the Russians and the *army of India*. They said that it was highly probable that Auckland would send a force to Balkh if Khiva became a Russian dependency.

...Baron Brunnow expressed his regret at this and said that if both Parties went on in this way, the Cossack, on one side, and the Sepoy, on the other, might meet in Central Asia. Sir John Hobhouse said he thought this very likely, that indeed it seemed to him certain to happen, if the Russian Government continued its present system in Asia. That he should feel great regret at such an event, but no alarm. That he was quite

easy as to the result of such a conflict as far as British interests in the
East are concerned, but that he should view it with deep concern in
consequence of its necessary bearing upon the European relations between England and Russia; and that at a moment when the two Governments seem to have come to so good an understanding upon many
great and important questions on which they had been supposed to have
previously differed, he should undoubtedly look upon any collision
between them in Asia as a great misfortune...[30]

In other words, Russia could not expect to be a friend in Europe
while pursuing an anti-British policy in Asia, and the 'great and
important questions on which they had been supposed to have
previously differed' were none other than the integrity of the
Ottoman Empire and the independence of Persia and Herat. We
can see that Palmerston and Hobhouse were on the high ground in
these discussions. Britain's military presence in Afghanistan
enabled them to argue from strength, though no one yet knew just
how costly and precarious that presence would soon become. Their
arguments carried great weight in St Petersburg later in the year.
For the time being the crisis still had to be faced. Almost as soon
as the failure of the first Khiva expedition was announced, another
was mooted, by way of the Caspian. That idea was found to be
impracticable, but still the Emperor, who considered his honour to
be at stake, pressed for an expedition which should set out in 1841.
It was all very well for Palmerston and Hobhouse to threaten
military action beyond the Hindu Kush as if they were speaking for
Auckland. His view at the beginning of May was unchanged:

...I have throughout very much entertained the views upon which you
write in regard to an advance in our name or in that of Shah Shooja
beyond the Hindoo Koosh in the direction of Khoolum or Balkh, and I
have believed that it is the wiser policy to consolidate strength within
Afghanistan and to rest upon the influence which a confirmed power
would give to the new dynasty and upon the confidence which would be
created by a policy of moderation towards neighbouring states. Yet
circumstances may occur which will make it impossible for us strictly to
pursue this line of prudence...[31]

So Auckland wrote to the Governor of Bombay at the beginning
of May. It was always his instinct to pursue a prudent policy, but
he was never afraid to move forward if circumstances made such a
move unavoidable. His misfortune, or rather one of his several
misfortunes, was to be served by men who lacked his common

sense. Even Sir James Carnac, who received the letter just quoted, had apparently recommended taking advantage of Sikh weakness in order to acquire the Punjab. Macnaghten, irritated by constant intrigues between Britain's Sikh allies and enemies of Shuja in Afghanistan, could hardly wait for the day when the Punjab would be, as he termed it, 'macadamised'. But Auckland firmly and with good humour put a stop to such talk. He had promoted Wade away from a post that had begun to be too much for him, and had put George Clerk in his place at Lahore. He told Clerk of the grievances felt at Kabul, but his orders encouraged conciliation: '...You will protect the right and you will conciliate the friendly and be firm with the unfriendly, and yet you will not easily be goaded into violent measures though possibly you may have to look forward to their being forced upon us...'[32]

Auckland sent a copy of these instructions with a private letter to Macnaghten, reminding him that 'even if things were very much more pressing than, I hope, they are, you should know for us that it is not in India convenient, or even possible, from May to November, to assist our best friends or to quarrel with our worst enemies'.[33] He never ceased to wonder at the folly of officers who overlooked such simple facts as climate and season, and at the appetite of so many officers and men for a fight with the Sikhs. Hobhouse, commenting at this time on some similar but earlier instructions to Clerk, thought Auckland's policy of forbearance and moderation towards the Sikhs 'very judicious'.[34]

At the beginning of May, as far as the British Government was concerned, the immediate crisis over Khiva was in abeyance. Baron Brunnow 'begged' Palmerston to 'entreat' Hobhouse to write to Auckland by the mail of 4 May, counselling him not to send his army beyond the Hindu Kush. Palmerston wrote:

...I said I would tell you what he had said; and that I thought it very likely you would do what he wished; and that indeed we should probably have no wish whatever to occupy Balkh unless the Russians should advance to Khiva. Perhaps you will let me or Brunnow know what you may do on this matter.[35]

Hobhouse wrote to Auckland that very day, passing on Brunnow's message, but, as we know from Auckland's previous correspondence, the message was unnecessary. One wonders whether Brunnow begged and entreated with such abandon as Palmerston described. But it is quite clear that the Russians were disconcerted by the firmness of Palmerston and his colleagues. The irony of the situation, as we discovered earlier in this chapter, was that the Russians had won a victory without knowing it. John Colvin, as usual, spelled it out more clearly than anyone else: '...The bad part of this Russian advance is that it will probably force us to keep our regular troops in Afghanistan for a second season, and we may be compelled to a loan to carry us through...'[36]

The British Government now gave more attention once again to the quarrel between Turkey and Egypt. Russia was still friendly and co-operative on that issue, even when James Abbott, a subaltern sent from Herat to Khiva at Christmas 1839, turned up at Orenburg in May 1840 and told the astonished General Perowski that he had important messages from the Khan of Khiva to the Emperor. Palmerston brazened it out and said that Britain was perfectly free at all times to communicate with the independent state of Khiva, and that Abbott's was a temporary mission with a temporary object—to obtain the release of Russian captives.[37] Perowski asked his Government for instructions, and was told to send Abbott to St Petersburg. Palmerston at that time was deep in the toils of European diplomacy in search of a settlement of the Eastern Question, and he agreed with the British Minister at St Petersburg that Abbott ought to come to London without delay, as soon as he had handed over the Khan's message to the Russian Government.[38] He could not afford to lose Russian support at that moment, for he had already offended France (and some of his own Cabinet colleagues) by insisting that Muhammad Ali should give up Syria. It is well known that he offered to resign on this issue on 5 July 1840, that Lord Melbourne shepherded all his colleagues, willing and unwilling, into line behind him, and that on 15 July Britain, Russia, Austria and Prussia formally agreed to uphold the Sultan against Muhammad Ali and to insist on an Egyptian withdrawal from Arabia, northern Syria, Adana, and Crete. This is not the place for an extended account of the crisis between Britain and France in 1840. Others have done full justice to Palmerston's triumph. But it is worth remembering that British interests interlocked in Western and Central Asia, and that Abbott's adventures in Turkestan were not unconnected with events further west. Auckland's actions and decisions were important factors in Palmerston's diplomacy. The threat of Indian military intervention beyond the Hindu Kush kept Russia amenable, and Muhammad Ali was squeezed out of Arabia as much by the exhibition of British power in India and along the Persian Gulf as by the diplomacy of the Powers in Europe.

When James Abbott arrived in St Petersburg at the end of July with letters and presents from the Khan of Khiva, the Emperor declined to receive him. Bloomfield, the British Minister, wrote to Palmerston on 1 August:

...I had hoped to have turned the favourable feeling towards England caused by the convention of the 15th July to some account, but His Imperial Majesty at present appears resolved not to entertain the question of terms offered by the Khan of Khiva, and General Perowsky is continually ready to urge the necessity of a fresh expedition and to counteract the more peaceable projects of some members of the Government...

One of the more peaceable members of the Russian Government at that time was Count Nesselrode himself. He, like Brunnow, was fully aware of the risk of war with Britain over Central Asia:

...After Captain Abbott had left Count Nesselrode, His Excellency asked me what I should write by this Messenger. I said that the communication I had to make was very simple: that I did not find any disposition here to admit of negotiations about Khiva, and that I regretted to see that the Russian Government were not desirous to give up their plans upon Khiva, and thereby get rid of a subject which will be a perpetual cause of irritating discussion with Her Majesty's Government. Count Nesselrode finished by observing that they did not intend to take possession of Khiva, but that they must endeavour to obtain respect for Russia in that country, obtain security for her subjects, and establish that just influence to which she is entitled...[39]

But Nesselrode seems to have influenced the Emperor after all, for John Bloomfield reported a marked change of tone a week later. The Emperor had agreed to enter into negotiations with the Khan if the Russian captives were returned. Bloomfield thought that Russia would still try to attack Khiva in 1841 but for the moment her tone was moderate. This was because proposals of peace had been offered through a friendly power which had become acquainted with her objects in Central Asia and which was in a position to adopt precautionary measures to prevent her from establishing herself at Khiva. He also felt that the Russian Government's tone had been moderated by Brunnow's report of what Palmerston and

Hobhouse had said earlier in the year about the risk of a collision in Central Asia. In the words of a précis of this letter in one of Palmerston's letter-books:

...The Imperial Government dreads nothing more than a collision with Great Britain in Central Asia; they are aware of their weakness and inability to meet us on equal terms, and yet they feel that their position entitles them to some share of the influence exercised by Great Britain...[40]

The wording of the remainder of this letter (a copy of which was sent to Auckland by the Secret Committee) makes it clear that 'influence' was a euphemism for markets. In fact, as Bloomfield forecast, the Emperor did offer terms to the Khan of Khiva, though Palmerston and Hobhouse continued to treat reports of the Emperor's peaceful intentions with the deepest suspicion.[41] Auckland also saw good reason to doubt the Emperor's sincerity, as he wrote to Clanricarde in September. He said the Russians had long coveted Khiva

as a point in advance towards our Indian territories...

...Yet no one can see more forcibly than I do the possible inconveniences which may grow out of the present position of this question, which, though it has not yet lost its amicable tone and character has too plainly a tendency to angry and serious collision. I need not tell you how anxious I am to avoid such an end, nor how strongly I feel the false position in which England and Russia may possibly be placed in wrangling and in fighting across the deserts of Central Asia. I know however the fault hitherto not to have been mine, and I am doing my best to check the zeal of our officers and to insist that the visits of our countrymen to Khiva shall be but temporary and that there shall be no organising at present and without further provocation of expeditions to Balkh or Bokhara or to other places beyond the Hindoo Coosh, and if on your part you can promote a good understanding upon these points you will indeed render excellent service to both countries.[42]

In September Russian moderation was even more noticeable, for Nesselrode told Bloomfield that there was now a fine prospect of settling the Khiva business. He had heard that a British officer, a subaltern called Richmond Shakespear, had agreed at Khiva to accompany a Khivan ambassador and, what was more, a group of Russians released from captivity, on their journey to Russian territory.[43] Then Brunnow told Palmerston in London that the news of Shakespear's feat of persuasion had caused the Russian Government to give up the Khiva expedition at last. Hobhouse heard of this from Palmerston at the end of the month, on being urged by his colleague to attend a Cabinet meeting to defend the proposed terms for a settlement of the Turkish-Egyptian quarrel. By that time, of course, hostilities had begun between the allies and the Egyptians in Syria, the Sultan had ordered the deposition of Muhammad Ali, and Britain had come perilously close to war with France. Palmerston told Hobhouse why he thought this Cabinet meeting so important:

...I tell my colleagues that if we give way now it will be to the menaces of France, and that if we so yield when backed by all Europe, all Europe will treat us henceforward like a nation afraid to fight. France will take Morocco and Tunis in spite of our teeth, and will settle every other matter her own way, Russia will do what she likes in Asia, and the disputed territory will be laid hold of by the United States.

Brunnow told me today officially that the Khyva Expedition is finally given up. Lt. Shakespear had reached Khyva and had persuaded the Shah to restore all the Russian prisoners, and he was going with them to Orenburgh.[44]

There we see how closely the Eastern and Central Asian questions were linked in Palmerston's mind. If Britain backs down now, he says, 'Russia will do what she likes in Asia...'. But, to Palmerston's eternal credit, Britain did not back down, and the peace party in France agreed to the withdrawal of Muhammad Ali from Syria and recognition of him as hereditary ruler of Egypt. On 10 October Bloomfield reported the arrival in Orenburg of Richmond Shakespear and four hundred prisoners, and quoted Nesselrode as saying that he 'rejoiced to see that our differences in Asia as well as in Europe were now settled'.[45] In due course the Russian Government published officially its decision to abandon the project of an advance upon Khiva. This was important, but it was overshadowed by the successful completion of Palmerston's diplomatic campaign against Muhammad Ali. The Pasha retired into his Egyptian shell after all. Palmerston was a national hero and no longer reviled by the Tories, for the time being. Would he have achieved as much if he had allowed the Persians and Russians to establish themselves in Afghanistan in 1838? If Britain had stood aside on that occasion and had weakly acquiesced in a Russian advance, she would have had to employ much of her strength and financial resources in measures for the defence and internal security of her Indian Empire. France and Egypt would have been able to carry out their plans against Turkey. No one could have stopped the Russians advancing towards Khiva. The *whole* of Britain's Asian policy would have been in ruins, and it is arguable that Palmerston would have had little opportunity to settle the commercial dispute with China. Indeed, in the author's view, the advance into Afghanistan was the foundation of Palmerston's success.

In many ways 1840 was a year of disillusionment and disappointment for Auckland and his colleagues of the Supreme Council, yet it ended as well as it began, on a note of triumph. We have already seen that both Auckland and Hobhouse wakened early to the fact that it would take a long time to establish Shuja securely on his throne, and that it would be a costly business. Auckland himself had hoped to be able to send home his resignation towards the end of the year, but he realized as early as the end of March that he would have to postpone his decision for a few months. But his friends in London would not hear of his resignation, and they made their feelings of trust in Auckland's great ability perfectly clear in the July dispatches on which Emily Eden made such an unhappy comment (in a letter quoted at the opening of this chapter).

In the spring Auckland's policy could be summed up as follows: hold on to Aden as a means of discouraging Muhammad Ali from maintaining ambitions in Arabia and of guarding against French adventures on the horn of Africa; hold on to the island of Kharg as long as possible, in the hope that it might become the 'Singapore of the Persian Gulf'; encourage the government of Herat to recover Ghorian from the Persians but leave Herat independent in alliance with Britain; consolidate Shah Shuja's power in the rest of Afghanistan and lead him to rely more and more on his own contingent and civil authorities; watch the passes over the Hindu Kush but do not stir beyond them unless the Russians make it absolutely necessary to do so; introduce order and good government in Upper Sind and Baluchistan and conciliate the tribes as much as possible, but in any case keep open the line of communications through those territories to Kandahar; similarly keep the goodwill (or its nearest equivalent in the violent habits of the Khyberees) of the tribesmen whose villages dominate the Khyber Pass; and at the same time maintain correct and cordial relations if possible with the emirs of Lower Sind, the government of the Punjab, and the rulers of Nepal and Ava. And if these were not big enough tasks there was full-time work for one man of his standing in the management of the expedition to China. Meanwhile there were a hundred and one internal matters to be thrashed out at the council table in Calcutta. No one who has read Auckland's monthly private letters to Hobhouse can accuse him of inefficiency, or indecision, or concentration on foreign at the expense of internal affairs.

One of his biggest anxieties was always caused by the quarrelling and peevish disposition of many of his officers. He took a characteristically understanding and tolerant view of their failings:

...This evil falls very heavily upon me and my time is too often occupied upon the flippancy of petty differences. It pervades every branch of the service, and is found in the church as well as in the army and the civil government. I ascribe much of it to liver and to climate, and men will not be good tempered when the thermometer is at more than 100. My liver however is as yet untainted, and I bear all as well as I can and endeavour to do more by friendly remonstrance than by angry interference...[46]

For instance, in April 1840 he received an angry complaint from William Dennie about Lord Keane's failure to give credit where credit was due in the Ghazni dispatch. He was fond of Keane in spite of his faults, and a lesser man would have thrown Dennie's letter aside rather than risk collision with the fiery and newly ennobled victor of Ghazni and Kabul. But instead he made inquiries, wrote sympathetically to Dennie, explaining that he had no direct power in the matter, and passed Dennie's memorandum to Lord Hill at the Horse Guards with a covering letter bearing witness to reports from many quarters of Dennie's gallantry at Ghazni. In earlier chapters we saw how Auckland dealt with other officers who became involved in petty quarrels—Burnes and Pottinger, Wade, Masson, even Macnaghten himself. He never thought it profitable to attempt to correct the irremediable personal defects of otherwise talented and useful public servants. He had to be especially tactful in dealing with Macnaghten, who was much inclined to sulk if Auckland criticized his measures too freely. For instance, during the summer of 1840 Macnaghten fought hard for permission to act beyond the Shah's frontiers, as if such action would magically solve all his problems in Afghanistan. Auckland refused him and relations between them became strained for a while, but as usual Auckland's forbearance and good nature—the qualities which made some fire-eaters call him, with a sneer, 'the amiable Lord Auckland'—prevailed over the momentary pique of his subordinate, and the subordinate did what he was told. But on this occasion Auckland granted one concession. He gave Macnaghten discretion to advance against Kulum, a small state formerly in subjection to Kabul, if such an advance ever became absolutely necessary. But that was as far as Auckland would let him go beyond the Hindu Kush.[47] It was as far as he ever allowed his envoy in Kabul to consider moving outside the boundaries allotted to Shuja in the Tripartite Treaty of 1838, and he only conceded the point because he was persuaded that Kulum had become a 'nest of malcontents' on the main commercial highway between Kabul and the lands beyond the Oxus.

In his letter to Hobhouse on 11 June Auckland reported: 'I have passed an uneasy and laborious month since I last wrote to you, and have had more than my usual share of anxiety. Yet I am not sure, now that the month is over, that I have much, with the exception of one disaster, to complain of. . .'[48]

The disaster had happened near Kahan, in the Marri country of Baluchistan, on 16 May. The Marris had been plundering along the road to Quetta from Shikarpur, and the British political agent had decided to instal a small garrison—and a tax-gatherer, according to Buist—in Kahan itself. This was a typical instance of the foolhardiness of Ross Bell and his associates. Not only was it madness to station fewer than three hundred men in a hill fort in the heart of hostile tribal country; it was lunacy to send men on any kind of march in the fierce heat of May. Auckland was in Calcutta, and Ross Bell was far from any superior officer. Captain Brown commanded the new Kahan garrison, which occupied the fort on 11 May. On the 16th he sent his camels back under escort, having unloaded supplies for four months of garrison duty. The young subaltern in charge of the escort, Lieutenant Clarke, encountered no opposition for the first few miles, and so he sent half of his men back along the road to Kahan. The Marris ambushed and killed most of them long before they reached the fort. Clarke and the remainder of the escort also walked into an ambush, from which only a few emerged alive. The Marris collected the camels and the baggage and began to give their attention to the business of laying siege to the intruders at Kahan. Clarke had died bravely on the mountainside from which the Marris had risen up in ambush. 'Thus', says Buist, 'in a single day, did the 5th Bombay Native

Infantry lose 148 men.'[49] When Auckland reported this to Hobhouse he made passing reference to trouble among the Ghilzais along the road between Kabul and Kandahar. He said that Macnaghten 'promises details of a glorious little victory gained by the Shah's troops against Ghilzais'. This was the victory of the Shah's troops under Captain Anderson at Tazi, near Kalat-i-Ghilzai. William Anderson's force of about 1,200 men of all arms, with not a regular British soldier or sepoy among them (except for officers), defeated about 2,000 Ghilzais at Tazi on 16 May, and temporarily restored peace to the country on either side of the Kabul–Kandahar road.[50] We can imagine how delighted Auckland was to hear the news. He thirsted every day for evidence that the Shah's own troops were capable of policing the country for him. But the dispatches from Anderson were soon followed by slightly less welcome reports that a force under Colonel Newton Wallace, including his own regiment, the 2nd Bengal Native Infantry, had linked up with Anderson to sweep the Ghilzai country in June. On 15 June an official reminder was sent to Macnaghten that it was the Governor General's

first desire that you should succeed in assisting the Shah to establish an effective national government. He has much regretted that His Majesty has not found himself yet able to select a Minister in whom he can confide and through whom he could control the various tribes and districts subject to his authority without the frequent exhibition of British intervention...[51]

But Auckland had to accept that the campaign against the Ghilzais was a special case, requiring particularly strong forces to make it effective. One of Macnaghten's many complaints against the Sikhs at this time was that they had allowed their Barukzai feudatories at Peshawar to harbour some of the principal Ghilzai chiefs during the winter of 1839–40. The chiefs had taken refuge there after Outram's campaign among them in the autumn of 1839, and now they were out in force. But the efficiency (and in some instances the ruthlessness) of the combined operation against them in May and June disheartened them, and they eventually accepted an annual stipend in return for promises of good conduct. On 30 June Cotton, as Commander in Chief of the regular troops in Afghanistan, was able to report that all was quiet again in the Ghilzai country, that the Khyber and Jalalabad tribes were at peace, and that the family of Dost Muhammad Khan (including the Nawab

Jubbar Khan) was on its way to seek asylum among the British in India.[52] The Nawab and his relatives arrived at the British camp at Bamiyan on 3 July. Only Dost Muhammad and two of his sons, Afzul and Akbar, remained at Bokhara as unwilling guests, and the Dost was even then planning his escape. There have been some picturesque accounts in the past of how he dyed his beard to make escape easier, but at the time British officials were equally prepared to believe that the escape had been engineered by 'foreign agents' to cause trouble for the British in Afghanistan.[53]

In June Macnaghten had put in a request for reinforcements. Auckland waited for firmer news of the fate of the Russian expedition to Khiva and then decided that it would be sufficient to send two regiments of Bombay Native Infantry to Kandahar and betweeen 1,500 and 2,000 recruits for the regiments in the Kabul area. If no new circumstances arose, he said, he hoped to be able to 'withdraw something in proportion' in the spring of 1841.[54] To Hobhouse he quoted glowing accounts by Cotton of the health and good behaviour of the troops at Kabul, where there was 'the utmost cordiality between our troops and the inhabitants of the city'. But Auckland was far from satisfied:

> ...I must confess that much less progress has been made in that organisation of national feeling and national strength which are essential to the perfect consummation of our plans in Afghanistan, and Macnaghten frequently writes of his difficulties, and of the divisions and of the long habits of rapine and intrigue which have for very many years prevailed in that country—and yet he seems to be making some progress and writes with good spirits upon his progress in the difficult task of reforming the army in which he is at present engaged. It must be remembered that but ten months have elapsed since our army entered Cabul, and that the renovation of such a country cannot be the work of a day, more particularly as schemes of agitation have been at work on more sides than one...[55]

It was in this letter that Auckland reported the submission of the rulers of Kulum and Kunduz to Shah Shuja. He said that neither of them was to be trusted, but their professions of friendship might be taken as good symptoms. In fact their professions of friendship did not long survive the agreement, and the Wali of Kulum gave his support to Dost Muhammad a few weeks later. Auckland had authorized Macnaghten to place troops as far north as Kulum if necessary, though he insisted that there should be no 'red coats even there. We cannot afford them to you.'[56] This was the result of Macnaghten's constant pressure in favour of an advance to Balkh, and the compromise at his expense eventually influenced the Wali's attitude to Dost Muhammad. The Wali was also alarmed by the restless northward probing of the political agent at Bamiyan, Dr Lord. It is only fair to the Wali to take note of a remark made by Hobhouse on one of Dr Lord's more scatter-brained schemes:

> ...We entirely concur in the condemnation expressed by Sir William Macnaghten in his letter to Mr Lord of the 9th of April, of the predatory warfare against the King of Bokhara [who still detained Stoddart in cruel confinement] suggested by that gentleman. Our policy is to induce by conciliation the states of Toorkestan to adopt the arts of peace, not to compel them by irritation to continue the practices of war...[57]

Unfortunately for Auckland, many of his political agents, being young and adventurous subalterns with little military experience, were all too likely to irritate where they should have conciliated.

July, August, and the first half of September were uncomfortable months for the British beyond the Indus, and Auckland was sadly disappointed in some of his best men. His letter to Hobhouse on 15 August reviewed a month 'of more than usual anxiety and uneasiness'.[58] Captain Bean, the political agent at Quetta, had been besieged by Baluchi tribesmen for several days, and there were fears for the safety of Kalat. (Auckland privately complained to Cotton that Bean should never have been left with only two hundred men at Quetta.[59]) Relations with Herat were disturbed because Major Todd had advanced British money to finance a Herati expedition against Ghorian and had seen it pocketed by Yar Muhammad. Todd had returned to Herat 'baffled and disgusted'. But Auckland was at least consistent in his Herat policy:

> ...Yar Mahomed plays false both with us and Persia, and dare not quarrel with or rely upon either, whilst he exerts himself in every artifice to obtain money from Major Todd—and I am not surprised at the uncertainty of his proceedings, for scarcely a month elapses without a discussion upon the necessity of his expulsion from Herat...[60]

Macnaghten had once again been pressing for an advance on Herat, and Auckland was just as firm as ever in refusing permission. Only twenty-four hours before writing to Hobhouse he had had to restrain Macnaghten once again:

...I have yet seen no other practicable policy in regard to Herat than that which is at the same time the honest one, of endeavouring to give Yar Mahomed confidence in his position, upon which would be based a willingness to defend it, and of having aid in readiness for his relief in the event of his being attacked...[61]

He left Macnaghten in no doubt of his opposition to ventures against Herat and quarrels with the Sikhs. Thus he rejected the proposals made by the envoy on 20 July, frankly and firmly as always. Auckland reported yet another attempt to persuade him in his September letter to Hobhouse, and as he realized that Macnaghten had support for his views in England he told Hobhouse that he would 'scarcely undertake the expedition for four millions of money'. He warned Hobhouse that it would probably cost them a million a year to hold Herat. This was dispiriting enough for a Cabinet minister basking with Palmerston in the glories of British foreign policy at the end of 1840. But Auckland had 'more than one disaster to lament' since he last wrote to Hobhouse. There had been minor losses at Bajgah and Bajaur, and one serious failure at Kalat. The Baluchi insurgents had besieged and received the surrender of the city from the British agent, and had deposed Nawaz Khan and installed the young son of Mehrab Khan as Emir. Nawaz had all too readily given up his chiefship, and was discredited beyond recall. Nusseer Khan had the backing of the tribes, and Auckland was inclined to recognize him as Emir once order had been restored and he had made his submission.

...I am inclined [Auckland wrote] to think that it will be enough if we appear in strength, and that there will be very little of military conflict. But there must be very careful arrangements, and errors which have been committed must be repaired, and I trust that an honourable and satisfactory settlement may be accomplished, so as to allow of reinforcements being sent at an early period to Candahar...[62]

These were hardly the sentiments of a warrior and a conqueror, and indeed Auckland was neither. He felt 'mortification and disappointment'[63] at the loss of Kalat, but he also felt a degree of guilt and regret, as we can see when we study the official instructions sent to Ross Bell on 11 September. Shal, Mastung and Kachhi had been most unceremoniously wrenched away from Kalat and given to Shuja in 1839, and he could hardly have expected tribes whose submission to Mehrab Khan had merely been nominal to submit with good grace to the British and their Afghan ally. The trouble was that he had been lulled by the reports of Ross Bell into thinking that all was well except for the usual lawlessness of professional plunderers.

Shortly before writing to Hobhouse in September Auckland received from Kabul a memorandum by Burnes upon the internal affairs of Afghanistan, with a commentary by Macnaghten. Both had felt strongly the need to take action against Herat and intriguing Sikhs, but they disagreed profoundly about Shuja: '...Burnes's paper is clever, though written too much in the spirit of criticism which one feels, who sits upon the coach box and sees another hold the reins—and the picture drawn by him is not a cheerful or encouraging one...'

Burnes gave many instances of misgovernment and the resulting discontent (for which the British were blamed), and suggested reforms, such as the appointment of an energetic minister to take the place of the doddering old man who used to run Shuja's household at Ludhiana and was now ostensibly head of the government. Macnaghten leapt to Shuja's defence. He drew attention to the difficulties in the way of attempting internal reforms, and he praised the Shah for his attempts to abolish objectionable taxes, to superintend the Government, and to improve the administration of justice. Macnaghten hoped to show that conditions were as good as they could be expected to be so soon after the restoration of Shah Shuja, and he tried to bias Auckland against Burnes's point of view by imputing to Burnes a most unworthy motive. Sir Alexander, Macnaghten said, wanted to prove him wrong, 'since by doing so, when he succeeds me, his failures would thus find excuse and his successes additional credit. This is all natural enough...'[64]

Auckland's own depressed comment upon all this was that it would only prove to Hobhouse that there were great difficulties to contend with, and that they were not yet surmounted. Meanwhile, Dost Muhammad was gathering support at Kulum, and Macnaghten, for once guilty of an understatement, said that his situation was far from comfortable. The troops in northern outposts had had to fall back on Bamiyan, and William Dennie was sent from Kabul with a mixed force of Shah's and Company's troops to reinforce the garrison there. He left Kabul on 7 September, and so did many citizens who daily expected a savage army of Uzbeks to appear over the northern horizon with Dost Muhammad at their head. Kaye tells us that at the height of this crisis (on 9 September) Macnaghten wrote privately to Henry Rawlinson, the officer who had taken over the political agency at Kandahar from Leech, expressing his indignation at Auckland's refusal to move troops against Herat and to speak roughly to the Sikhs. According to Kaye he said that 'such drivelling was beneath contempt'.[65] As well as admitting the impropriety of such a remark from the envoy to a junior officer at Kandahar, we who have the advantage of hindsight can judge much better than they who was drivelling and who was talking sense. Of all the officers and public servants under Auckland there was one with a fatal flaw of over-confidence in his own judgement—and he was Sir William Hay Macnaghten. If only he had had a fraction of the common sense and humility of the Governor General, we might now have a very different story to tell. But he had great ability and talent, great courage and resolution, and a reputation and attainments which, on Auckland's own recommendation, promised him a place at the council table in Calcutta once his work in Kabul was finished. Burnes once made an apt but malicious comment on Macnaghten, to the effect that he always had his eyes on the horizon and was therefore liable to miss what was under his nose.

On 11 September Dennie heard that Dost Muhammad, accompanied by his son Afzul Khan and the Wali of Kulum, had led his makeshift army into the former British post at Syghan, not more than thirty miles from Bamiyan. Dennie also heard that the Afghan levies had mutinied at Bamiyan, and that one company had already gone over to the Dost. As soon as he arrived there he disarmed the remainder of the levies, and prepared to face the Afghan chief and his 6,000 Uzbek horsemen. He did not have long to wait. Away to the west William Nott had just earned the displeasure of the Governor General by taking the law into his own hands in an incident at Kandahar. Some servants of Prince Timur, Shuja's son, had been plundering and oppressing people who had taken refuge in and near the British camp. Nott could have told Timur what was going on; he could have framed a tactful protest. He could have moved his camp away from the area of Timur's operations to dissociate himself from the actions of Timur's servants. So Auckland argued in a dispatch to the Secret Committee, explaining why Nott had been reprimanded. What Nott did on the spur of the moment was to arrest the plunderers and oppressors and have them flogged on his own responsibility. This coincided with a complaint from Shah Shuja that the actions of some British officers were lowering him in the eyes of his subjects, and showing him as a person without independent authority in his own country. Nott's motives were admirable, of course. He saw acts of oppression going unpunished, and he wished to show the people who trusted him that a British officer would not stand by and see them maltreated. But it was beyond dispute that he had no jurisdiction in the matter, however flagrant the crime. Auckland's official comment to the Secret Committee was that Nott had shown himself unfit 'for duties of any very delicate nature in the existing posture of affairs in Afghanistan'.[66]

The mention of this severe reprimand is necessary because it helps to explain the bitterness of Nott towards Auckland and Macnaghten in all that he wrote at this period. Yet Auckland had not written him off completely; in a letter from Auckland to Carnac we see Nott described as 'an officer highly esteemed in our army'.[67] In other words, Nott was a fine soldier but a poor diplomat. He did his part in Baluchistan that autumn by re-occupying Kalat, but he omitted to consult Ross Bell about the timing of his march. It is hardly surprising that Lord Auckland, who had once thought of offering him Cotton's post at Kabul, passed him over when the post became vacant again in November. It is difficult to believe that even the most partisan supporter of Nott and opponent of Auckland's policy could acquit the General of insubordination.

Long before Nott left Kandahar a relief column under Major Clibborn had been sent from Sukkur on its way to the beleaguered garrison commanded by Captain Brown at Kahan, in the heart of the Marri country. In order to reach Kahan it was necessary to negotiate the Nufoosk Pass, and on 31 August Clibborn reached the foot of the pass and observed hundreds of Marri tribesmen occupying the heights. He had been led to believe that there was plenty of water near the foot of the pass, but none was found, and his men had to attempt an assault up a narrow defile in terrible heat without it. The Marris drove Clibborn's men down the hill, but quickly ascended again under the hail of shrapnel and small-arms fire from the main body of troops in the plain. The water shortage made Clibborn abandon all hope of winning the Nufoosk Pass from the Marris, and so, on the night of 31 August / 1 September 1840 he marched his men back the way they had come, leaving behind most of his stores and equipment. Auckland called it 'a sad blow in the loss of reputation, of life and of property'. Casualties had been heavy on both sides, but Clibborn's loss was the heavier in proportion, for he had more than a quarter of his 850 men killed or wounded. There were no further disasters in that area after Clibborn's. Captain Brown eventually talked his way out of Kahan, having discovered that the Marri chief was civil and polite and ready to parley. The Marris gave him a safe conduct to the plains in return for the abandonment of Kahan. A whole chapter could be devoted to the campaign which restored a kind of peace to Upper Sind and Baluchistan in the winter of 1840, but the details of those far off-battles are not now in dispute, and it is sufficient to note in passing that Auckland had to pay heavily in men, money, and reputation for the eventual settlement. He had always counselled Ross Bell to treat the people of the area with conciliation, and had supported him, though there was fault on both sides, in an earlier dispute between Bell and the military commander who advocated stern repression. But Auckland cannot escape responsibility for the original injustice of the partition of Kalat. Even making allowances for Nott's personal grievances, and his tendency to write letters of vitriolic comment in which all men but he were villains, one must admit a large grain of truth in one of his remarks:

...the authorities are never right, even by chance, and although most of them are stupid in the extreme, they fancy themselves great men, and even possessed of abilities and talents. They drink their claret, draw large salaries, go about with a numerous rabble at their heels—all well paid by John Bull (or rather by the oppressed cultivators of the land in Hindostan)—the Calcutta treasury is drained of its rupees, and *good natured* Lord Auckland approves and confirms all. In the meantime, all goes wrong here. We are become hated by the people, and the English name and character, which two years ago stood so high and fair, has become a bye-word. Thus it is to employ men selected by intrigue and patronage! The conduct of the one thousand and one politicals has ruined our cause and bared the throats of every European in this country to the sword and knife of the revengeful Affghan and bloody Belooch, and unless several regiments be quickly sent, not a man will be left to note the fall of his comrades. Nothing but force will ever make them submit to the hated Shah Soojah, who is most certainly as great a scoundrel as ever lived...[68]

And so on. Nott's picture is a cruel caricature, motivated by personal spite as much as by genuine feeling for the people, but the element of truth in the picture shines through the distortions very clearly. Some political agents abused their local powers, and Auckland, far away in Calcutta, gave too much trust to the worst of them. Not that political agents invariably escaped censure. But Ross Bell and his assistants had too much freedom from control, and, as we have noted, Auckland was taken completely by surprise when the insurrection started in Ross Bell's area. No one told him that the estates which the Brahui chiefs held rent-free (except for feudal military obligations) under Mehrab Khan had been made subject to rent under Shuja.[69]

One thing that heartened Auckland when he reflected on the setbacks in Ross Bell's area that autumn was that the disturbances did not spread to Afghanistan itself. 'Neither Ghilzyes, nor Khyberees, nor Candaharees gave trouble, and...Huzarees and the population about Bameean behaved well towards us.' They continued to behave well when Dost Muhammad approached, and Dost Muhammad's only active supporters, be it remembered, were at that time Uzbeks from beyond the Hindu Kush. Macnaghten was hard pressed at Kabul and inclined to see conspirators behind every door. 'The Afghans', he said, 'are gunpowder, and the Dost is a lighted match.' He had to admit to Auckland that there was no such thing as an Afghan army and that it was essential to reinforce the regular troops immediately.[70] But William Dennie shamed Macnaghten into silence by scattering Dost Muhammad and his Uzbeks in a single action near Bamiyan on Friday 18 September. As usual the artillery proved its worth againstly lightly armed horsemen, and Dennie, in his order of the day, offered his 'particular thanks to Lieutenant MacKenzie, commanding the two pieces of horse artillery, to whose admirable practice the result of the day is mainly attributable...'.[71] There was nothing specially dramatic about the battle of Bamiyan. Dennie's advance guard made contact with the Dost's and drove it in, and Dennie suddenly woke up to the fact that he had a whole army against his half brigade:

...To have sent back for reinforcements would have caused delay, and given confidence to the enemy...The enemy had got possession of the chain of forts before us reaching to the mouth of the defile. They drew up and attempted to make a stand at each with the main body, while their wings crowned the heights on either side; in dislodging them from the latter, I am sorry to say, the Goorkhas suffered. After four or five rallies, seeing our steady and rapid advance, the whole force opposed to us lost heart, and fled in a confused mass to the gorge of the pass. I now ordered the whole of the cavalry in pursuit, who drove them four miles up the defile, cutting down great numbers, and scattering them in all directions, many throwing away their arms and escaping up the hills...The Dost and his son Mahomed Ufzil Khan, and the Wallee, owed their escape to the fleetness of their horses, and were last seen with not more than two hundred followers around them...[72]

That was Dennie's own account, written in a letter to Sir Willoughby Cotton a few hours after the battle. Suspecting that Dost Muhammad would try to re-assemble his army, Dennie patrolled the country north of Bamiyan for a week after the battle, but found nothing but abandoned equipment. At the end of September the Wali came to terms and promised not to help Dost Muhammad and his sons again. At the same time Macnaghten sent a brigade under Sale into Kohistan, fearing that the Dost would now find willing supporters there. Sale had orders to punish hostile chiefs and thus to deter the Kohistanis from joining Dost Muhammad. Burnes accompanied the expedition, which grimly stormed fort after fort, sometimes successfully and sometimes, as at Jugla, with great difficulty. The rebel chiefs slipped away during the night, so that the honours of the fight were even. Macnaghten, with his usual tendency to overstatement, called this petty affair a reverse.[73] The destruction of forts and villages occupied Sale's brigade throughout October.

The news of Dennie's victory reached Calcutta in the middle of the second week of October. Auckland immediately sent warm congratulations to Macnaghten and Cotton, for he was sure that this victory marked the turn of the tide. 'It has rarely happened that a public event has given me so much pleasure,' he told Macnaghten,[74] and in his official dispatch to the Secret Committee he described Dennie's feat as 'this brilliant achievement...which, with reference to the small number of our troops engaged and their being all natives cannot fail to be productive of the best moral effect'. He also reported that Dost Muhammad was to be offered a stipend of at least one lakh per annum (£10,000 sterling) if he accepted asylum in India.[75] Auckland was involved at that moment in a delicate negotiation with the Sikhs, who had been accused of intriguing against Shah Shuja. He wanted as always to maintain the Anglo-Sikh alliance—something which few Englishmen in India seemed prepared to do indefinitely. He had called upon them to hand over to Shuja the Ghilzai refugees at Peshawar and to summon the Barukzai sirdars from that place to Lahore. Now he told them that he intended to send a brigade of reinforcements through the Punjab to Kabul, and that they must give it passage in accordance with the Tripartite Treaty which was still in force. He was prepared to fight if the Sikhs resisted this proposal, but 'we may yet remain friends if the passage of our brigade be cheerfully granted'.[76] In the event the Anglo-Sikh alliance survived, perhaps at least in part because the Sikhs were suddenly weakened by the deaths of Maharajah Karak Singh and Nao Nehal Singh at the beginning of November 1840. The British brigade passed through the Punjab without disturbance.

We come now to an episode which other writers have invested with a false romantic quality. Kaye in particular has given the impression that Dost Muhammad Khan won a victory at Parwan Durrah on 2 November. Let us say rather that he left the field with his honour intact after a brief skirmish with part of Sale's brigade. The sowars of the 2nd Bengal Cavalry made his path easier by turning tail and leaving their officers to fight off about two hundred of his horsemen, a disgrace for which the regiment paid by having its number and name deleted from the Bengal army list. Dost Muhammad escaped once more, but realized that further resistance was useless. On the day after his brave encounter with Sale's brigade he rode into Kabul and dismounted in the courtyard outside Macnaghten's residence. There he met Macnaghten, who was just returning from his evening ride with his political assistant, George Lawrence. Macnaghten instinctively understood that the Dost paid him a great compliment by surrendering personally to him, and he and his officers went out of their way to treat him with honour and respect. In fact many officers who had suffered under Shuja's strict court etiquette formed a very high opinion of the Dost, though they learned to beware of his violent temper. Sir William Macnaghten had good reason to feel thankful for the unexpected change in British fortunes in Afghanistan. His optimism was shared by Auckland, who thought that the surrender would have 'infinitely beneficial' consequences, and who told his agent in Baghdad that the surrender of Dost Muhammad 'gives hopes of permanent tranquility in that quarter'.[77] Colvin told Macnaghten that 'we look to next year as one, if our wishes can be effected, of *repose* and internal improvement in Afghanistan, during which also we may bring the enormous British expenditure on account of that country within more distinct and moderate limits. . .'.[78] The news of Dost Muhammad's defeat at Bamiyan (but not yet the news of his surrender) reached London on 8 December, at the same time as that of Muhammad Ali's submission and that of the occupation of Chusan by British troops. Palmerston called it a 'flight of good news',[79] in a letter that day to Granville, and he congratulated Hobhouse with all his heart on the Bamiyan victory, calling it 'the crowning finish to your Affghan Triumph'.[80] A few days later he read some dispatches from Auckland and sent them back to Hobhouse with this comment:

. . .Auckland fights his way on capitally, and overcomes his difficulties one after another as they arise. I have no fears for our ascendancy in Affghanistan, except as to the expense of maintaining it; but if that country had become Persian and Russian you would have had to spend much more in defending our possessions east of the Indus. . .[81]

Hobhouse, as we shall see in the next chapter, was less sanguine than Palmerston about 'our ascendancy in Affghanistan', and he was about to present Auckland with an ultimatum. At Kabul the snow lay deep on the ground and enforced a peace which Burnes once likened to that of Vesuvius after an eruption. But even then a fresh rebellion was gathering strength among the Durrani tribes and the Ghilzais were waiting only for the spring. A certain Colonel Shelton, considered to be 'a great tyrant in his regiment', and a Major General William Elphinstone were about to take their posts in Kabul.

CHAPTER 14

THE MOUNTING COST OF
INTERVENTION

...The state of supineness and fancied security of those in power
in cantonments is the result of deference to the opinions of Lord
Auckland, whose sovereign will and pleasure it is that tranquility
do reign in Affghanistan; in fact it is reported at Government
House, Calcutta, that the lawless Affghans are as peaceable as
London citizens; and this being decided by the powers that be, why
should we be on the alert?

LADY SALE'S Journal, 2 November 1841

Lady Sale's bitterness is understandable, but its target, Lord
Auckland, was less deserving of censure than she thought. Let us
consider, for instance, the appointment of Major General Elphinstone and Colonel Shelton to their posts in Kabul. William George
Keith Elphinstone, grandson of the tenth Baron Elphinstone, was
born into a family noted for its public and military service. His
Uncle George was a popular hero of his time as Viscount Keith;
his first cousin was Mountstuart Elphinstone, a former Governor
of Bombay and historian of India; his second cousin was the thirteenth Baron Elphinstone, Governor of Madras from 1837 to 1842.
Most people would agree that a well-born ensign of the 41st Foot,
as William Elphinstone was in 1804, started life with certain advantages. But, even in the days of purchased commissions and
patronage, merit was not altogether disregarded. William Elphinstone commanded the 33rd Foot at Waterloo and remained with
it until 1822, having been awarded a C.B. for his services. He was
not alone among veterans of the wars against the French in returning to full-time military service after a long period on half pay, and
by 1837 he was a major general and eligible for the command of a
division. The gentlemen at the Horse Guards sent him to India in
1839 to take command of the Benares Division at Meerut. Perhaps
his highly placed friends thought that a change of climate would
alleviate his suffering from gout. However that may be, they
thought him as well qualified as any other officer of his rank for
command of the Benares Division.[1] Auckland had no part in the

selection of Elphinstone, but certainly expressed no disquiet when he first heard of the appointment in the latter part of 1839. The Horse Guards had kept him waiting for more than a year for a successor to General Fane as Commander in Chief, and had left him with a senile officer in command of the Bengal troops. Auckland trusted that he would 'do well enough in Bengal when General Elphinstone arrives'.[2] He and his sisters had known Elphinstone in their youth, well enough for Emily Eden to refer to him affectionately as Elphy Bey. In November 1840 Auckland heard that Cotton was retiring from his Kabul command because of ill health. He therefore consulted his Commander in Chief, Sir Jasper Nicolls, who agreed that they should at once offer the post to Elphinstone 'if his health should be such as to enable him to undertake such a command and his wishes should lead him to do so'.[3] Auckland wrote to Elphinstone on 14 November:

...We are both of opinion that it could not be given to anyone who would exercise its functions so efficiently as you would—and if the station were but agreeable to you it would from personal as well as from public feeling be most gratifying to me to see you in it—and I should hope that you would find the bracing hills of Cabul more congenial to your constitution than the hot plains of India...If from health or from other cause you should not favourably regard this uncertain offer I will ask you at once to intimate such a decision to me, and it will give me time, though I should do so most reluctantly, to look in other quarters for another successor to this command...[4]

Elphinstone therefore knew that he could decline the offer if he was not well enough. He also knew that Nicolls and the Governor General considered him to be the man most fitted among the major generals in India for the command at Kabul. He accepted on 26 November,[5] mildly surprising Auckland, who half expected him to plead ill health as an excuse for staying at Meerut. Auckland told Macnaghten on the 28th: '...I hardly know where I should look if he should refuse...' But what kind of General was Auckland looking for? He thought of William Elphinstone as 'an excellent soldier and of remarkably mild and conciliating manners'.[6] This was important. He wanted an efficient soldier, but he did not want one who was restless for action and irritable in the face of official restraint. Nevertheless, Auckland felt he could not do better among the senior officers available. On this occasion he did not consider Nott's qualifications, for Nott had given offence to too many people, including Shah Shuja. As we saw in chapter 13, he was a fine soldier but a poor diplomat, and Elphinstone was considered to be excellent in both callings. He was also popular with the officers and men under his command. Colvin summed up the situation when he told Macnaghten (in his letter looking forward to 1841 as a year of repose and internal improvement in Afghanistan) that 'the best General we have to send you has seen no Indian Service, and this will be an additional reason with you for peaceful councils. Colonel Shelton, another officer of some standing who has gone to Afghanistan is thought a great tyrant in his regiment and may on this account be wanting in some degree in the most useful influence possessed by a Commander.'[7]

The choice of Colonel Shelton, a one-armed veteran of the Peninsular War, as Brigadier of the Kabul garrison under Elphinstone is more questionable, since his worst fault was known in advance. But efficient officers with long service and good records were not so plentiful as one might suppose. John Shelton had the Indian experience that Elphinstone lacked. In theory the officer commanding in Afghanistan and the officer commanding the brigade at Kabul made a perfect team. In practice the combination proved disastrous. But the author seriously questions whether Auckland and his advisers should be blamed for making this choice of major general and brigadier, in the circumstances of November 1840. This is how Auckland privately briefed William Elphinstone on 18 December:

...Though I am impatient gradually to withdraw our regular troops from that country, I feel that, before we can do so, the new dynasty must be more strongly confirmed, than it yet has been, in power, and that there must be better security than is yet established against menace or aggression from the extreme North or West. I always hope however that the duty of the officer in command in Afghanistan will be rather that of maintaining a strong attitude, and of directing the distribution of the troops and the measures necessary for their health and comfort, than of conducting active operations. He will no doubt frequently be urged to send forces upon service in support of local interests, and schemes of greater measures will often be brought to his notice, but he should act upon all of them with extreme caution and reserve and should rather encourage the growth of the strength and resources of the country under his protection than allow the force under his command to be regarded as its sole support and dependence. The events indeed of last year have proved that we cannot count with certainty upon that quiet course of affairs which we should desire—and if active exertions should be called for I know that it will be ably directed by you...[8]

Indeed Auckland had no reason to believe that Elphinstone would fail him. We must do him the justice of believing that he made his choice with due consideration for the public interest, and not simply accept the ancient jibe that he was guilty of jobbery. And in view of what his letters reveal we might also question the accuracy of the statement that Sir Jasper Nicolls proposed Nott for the command and was overruled.

Sir Willoughby Cotton left Kabul because he was not in good health. Brigadier Abraham Roberts (father of Lord Roberts of Kandahar), who commanded the Shah's contingent, gave up his post because he was dissatisfied with it. He could not agree with Macnaghten on the means to be used in order to develop a national army in Afghanistan. Auckland was aware that there was fault on both sides, but he could spare Roberts more easily than he could spare Macnaghten, and so he treated a letter of complaint from that officer as an offer of resignation, and he offered the post to Brigadier Anquetil.[9] He admitted that he had not foreseen that the presence of a large regular force in Afghanistan would place the officer commanding the Shah's troops too much in the shadow of the Major General. He gently reproved Macnaghten for treating Roberts with less formal respect than his command merited, and both he and Colvin informally urged him to work more happily with Anquetil than he had worked with Roberts.[10] But, whether Roberts, or Anquetil, or some other senior officer commanded the Shah's troops, the post was of little importance while a division of regular soldiers remained in the country. The sapling could not thrive in the shadow of the mature oak.

At the end of December, when Elphinstone and Shelton were about to enter Afghanistan, Auckland felt that circumstances were 'most favourable to the promise of peace, though the great difficulty yet remains, of organising an honest and friendly government, and of reconciling this wild and divided country to anything like well regulated order...'[11].

Everything was going right for Britain in her relations with the rest of the world, but there was this constant, nagging doubt about the future policy in Afghanistan. Hobhouse conveniently forgot his strictures of July and September 1839, on the need to avoid actions which would make Britain's military presence in Afghanistan look like permanent occupation. On the last day of 1840 he sent through the Secret Committee a long and important dispatch which amounted to an ultimatum to Auckland. The man who had been so impatient in 1839 for news of the withdrawal of regular troops now regretted that so many had been withdrawn before the Shah's own forces were ready to take their place:

> ...and it is more for the sake of providing against future calamities than to censure past errors that we pronounce our decided opinion that for many years to come, the restored monarchy will have need of a British force, in order to maintain peace in its own territory, and prevent aggression from without. We must add, that to attempt to accomplish this by a small force, or by the mere influence of British residents, will, in our opinion, be most unwise and perilous, and that we should prefer the entire abandonment of the country, and a frank confession of complete failure, to any such policy...

Hobhouse was sure that Auckland had no middle course which he could pursue with safety and honour between considerable reinforcement and speedy retreat. But this was not all. Hobhouse had been studying the documents in the controversy between Burnes and Macnaghten on the internal administration of Afghanistan. He preferred Macnaghten's judgement to Burnes's, but he observed that there was just enough common ground between their two opinions to justify the belief that 'serious mistakes have been made in the administration of affairs, both civil and military, in the restored Affghan monarchy and in the immediately contiguous states'. In future the British would have to take a much closer interest in Afghanistan's internal affairs:

> ...We trust that His Majesty will have the good sense to perceive that he cannot be treated altogether as an independent sovereign, and that it is only by implicit deference to the advice of your Minister at his Court that he can maintain his position. We do not see how it is possible so to choose the public functionaries and to make such arrangements in Affghanistan as shall conceal the fact that the British are masters of the country, and that the authority of the Shah can be upheld only by their agency...The Affghans have a right to expect that they should be gainers by the change of masters; and as we alone have the power to redress their grievances the continuance of those grievances must reasonably be imputed to us...[12]

The news of Dost Muhammad's surrender reached London by way of the French telegraph from Marseilles on 6 January,[13] and

Hobhouse became more cheerful under the influence of Palmerston's heart-warming words:

> ...It is a proud Triumph of British Character that a Man driven by us from his Kingdom, pursued to be taken Prisoner, and defeated in the Field, should have fled not from us but to us, and should have sought Refuge from the Sharpness of our Sword under the Shelter of our Generosity. This single incident is of itself more glorious than many victories.[14]

But Hobhouse saw no reason for going back on his solemn warning to Auckland, and his next dispatch to India reaffirmed what had been said on 31 December. Auckland must either retreat and admit failure, or reinforce his regular troops in Afghanistan and prepare for a long stay.[15] But Auckland was well aware of the problems described by Hobhouse. It is a travesty of the truth to say with Nott's editor that Lord Auckland was head of an 'infatuated Government, lulled by the specious representations of Sir William Macnaghten'.[16] What was missing from Auckland's calculations at this time, however, was a proper assessment of national feeling in Afghanistan. He saw a number of wild and independent tribes who had to be disciplined and gradually tamed into becoming good citizens under Shuja. He did not yet understand that they might all, in spite of their differences, feel united in opposition to Shah Shuja and his British sponsors. But he understood the strength of the religious feeling which could be roused against the British, and Colvin acknowledged in a letter to Macnaghten at the end of 1840 that it was 'our real and very serious weakness...Time may possibly abate it, but no short time...'[17] Perhaps the best answer to Stocqueler and other detractors is the quality of Auckland's advice to Major General Elphinstone on 8 February:

> ...I need not dwell upon the importance of our position in Afghanistan. It is strongly felt in England as well as in India, and the extension and maintenance of our influence towards (and even beyond) the Caspian Sea, towards Meshed and Tehran, depend upon our being considered to be strong and safe at Cabul and Candahar. At the same time I am extremely desirous that our reputation of strength should rather rest upon good organisation than upon military successes and considerations of economy lead me anxiously to wish that the withdrawal of a consierable portion of our regular military force may at no very distant date be securely ordered. But this cannot be done immediately. The Shah's

army must be reformed. The contingent under British officers must be completely organised. Men's minds must become accustomed to the new order of things, and our relations with Persia and Russia must be determined, before the presence of an imposing force can be dispensed with...[18]

In fact there was in Afghanistan at the beginning of 1841 a division of regular troops, and there were at least as many again between Shikarpur and Quetta. When Hobhouse saw what forces Auckland had at his disposal he hastened to assure the Governor General that these dispositions 'for the complete maintenance of our position in the recently occupied territories, are in accordance with the views which we have already communicated to your Lordship in Council'.[19] Hobhouse thus made amends in March for his lack of confidence in Auckland at the end of December 1840. But the damage had already been done. Auckland confessed himself a 'little vexed' at Hobhouse's 'wavering tone' and unreasonable impatience for a solution in Afghanistan. He thought that Hobhouse had 'touched much too roughly a subject of great difficulty and delicacy'; but, being the reasonable man he was, Auckland then acknowledged that the Secret Committee dispatch of 31 December had been written at a time of discouragement and alarm about the British position in Afghanistan.[20] He was not easily roused to anger at any time. But all his calculations were upset, all this delicate framework of strength and conciliation was shaken and cracked, by the news that reached him in the middle of March. After all that he had written and said upon the Herat question, Major Todd had broken off relations with Yar Muhammad and had left the city. What was worse, Rawlinson in Kandahar and Macnaghten (then in Jalalabad, wintering with Shah Shuja) had taken it for granted that he would sanction an expedition against Herat, and had called on Ross Bell for some of his troops.

Yar Muhammad was at the best of times a difficult man to deal with, and he had duped Todd more than once, but Todd had no authority for the action he took in breaking off relations, or for the demands which led to his quarrel with the Herat government. It was true that Yar Muhammad had been intriguing with the Persian Government against the British. Rawlinson also suspected that there was collusion between Aktur Khan, the leader of the Durrani rebellion of December 1840, and Yar Muhammad. Major Todd could have presented a convincing case against the head of the Herat government, and should have presented it to his own Government before taking action. He could have temporized with Yar Muhammad while waiting for his Government's decision. There was no urgency. Instead, at the beginning of February he stopped the British subsidy and refused to pay a penny more until Yar Muhammad gave him some guarantee of good conduct, such as admitting a British garrison to Herat. Yar Muhammad refused, and insisted on payment of the British subsidy as usual. Todd was no match for Yar Muhammad. He had a choice between the humiliation of resuming subsidy payments and departure with the whole of his mission. He chose to leave on 10 February 1841.

Auckland heard of Todd's departure on 15 March and immediately raised the matter at a council meeting. His policy was unchanged. Herat must be encouraged and assisted to defend her independence against all comers, but British troops must not advance to Herat unless the city was in imminent danger of being attacked. The British force at Kandahar, reinforced by troops from below the passes, could move to counter such a threat at any time, if absolutely necessary. At the council meeting it was agreed that the government should disown Major Todd:

...His Lordship in Council has read the account of Major Todd's proceedings with extreme surprise, concern, and disapprobation. They are directly at variance with all the orders received by him. They are inconsistent with the most obvious dictates of sense and prudence and they may involve his government in the most unexpected and serious embarrassments...

Rawlinson was to assume responsibility for conducting relations with Herat:

...He will state to the Vizeer that the proposition for the introduction of a British garrison into Herat was made entirely without the authority of the government in India; that that government has no desire or design to interfere in Herat affairs; that its object is merely that Herat should be independent and safe from foreign assault; that it was willing for that purpose to grant a fixed pecuniary aid to the Herat authorities; that it has heard with regret and displeasure of the Vizeer's groundless apprehensions and improper intercourse with the Persian officers; that it would still be willing, on being assured of his fidelity, to renew relations with him, on the footing previously authorized; but that it will rest with himself to seek for that renewal, while the British government wishes no further to control him than by stating that it never can permit him to make over Herat to the Persian Government, the enemies of the independence of the Afghan states...[21]

It has sometimes been said that Auckland was not fortunate in having Sir Jasper Nicolls as his Commander in Chief, and a diary entry quoted by Kaye lends substance to the criticism of that officer. We find him signing the official dispatches at the council table and whispering to Auckland 'that if Herat was to be occupied by us against the will of the Vizier, the present circumstances were very propitious. We had a large body of troops at hand, and probably their plans were not matured.'[22] Yet Lord Auckland had been over the arguments for and against an advance many times in the council chamber. The project could only be justified, such was its expected cost, in the extremest emergency. Nicolls himself admitted that an expedition to Herat was beyond the Indian Government's means at that moment. But he still whispered temptation into Auckland's ear. Fortunately Auckland knew his own mind. As he wrote to Macnaghten on the 16th: '...Under present circumstances our presence at Herat would be hazardous, burdensome, and unprofitable, and it could not be maintained...'[23]

On the 22nd the whole council—including Nicolls—signed the formal reply to Hobhouse's instructions of 31 December 1840. It consisted of three minutes, one from each of the civilian members of the council. Auckland's naturally carried most weight, but he did not hesitate to draw attention to Prinsep's forecast of financial ruin when he wrote privately to Hobhouse on the 21st. His own minute calmly disposed of Hobhouse's suggestion that he had left his regular forces in Afghanistan weaker than they should have been, and recalled in passing the Secret Committee's direct orders against the permanent military occupation of posts in Afghanistan. On Hobhouse's criticism of the civil administration he argued that 'the rooted habits of a people and of a national administration are not to be changed in a day or two at our will'. He quoted many letters in which he had called Macnaghten's attention to the need to improve the civil administration. Change could only come gradually. He regretted that Shah Shuja had so far not been able to maintain his position by his own means, but had had to rely in every civil disturbance on British troops. Yet there was improvement in this department as well as in the civil government. Shuja himself had many good qualities. In the meantime the British in

Afghanistan were 'not regarded merely as friends and supporters, but the whole authority and force of the government are supposed to be in our hands, and we are charged even with the abuses which which we cannot control, but which seem to derive strength and aid from our presence'. He agreed with Hobhouse that the restored monarchy would need British military assistance for many years, and he asked whether the political advantages outweighed the expense, and whether the British forces could recede with credit. Certainly, he argued, 'if Russia has now receded from her move upon the Oxus it is mainly from the influence which our position in Afghanistan has given us the means of exercising at Khyva...'. Then he turned to the question of expense. The British commitment in Afghanistan was costing about a million pounds a year, of which the maintenance of the Shah's forces and 'political expenses' accounted for almost half. Other items within the total were the extra allowances for troops serving beyond the Indian frontier (£100,000), extra commissariat charges (£250,000), additional expenses in Sind (£80,000), and the maintenance of a steam flotilla on the Indus (£30,000): '...It is mainly this large extraordinary disbursement which causes the present yearly deficiency of revenue as compared with our expenditure, of not less than a crore and a quarter' (which was in those days £1,250,000).

Auckland then quoted the latest confirmed figures, showing that the venture beyond the Indus had caused a deficit of a crore and a quarter up to the end of April 1840. (Kaye, quoting entries in Nicolls's journal, hints that Auckland knew the deficit to be much higher but concealed the fact from the Secret Committee. But Nicolls, as a soldier scribbling in a private journal, seemed to think that Auckland could write his minute on the basis of the Accountant General's rough estimate of what the deficit would be at the end of April 1841. It was quite clear from Auckland's minute, in any case, that the deficit would have increased by at least a crore and a quarter between the end of April 1840 and the end of April 1841.) Auckland declared that the Indian Government could not for long maintain such an annual deficit. But revenues would gradually improve, and it might be possible to economize in civil expenditure. Eventually the revenues of the Punjab might be added to those of the rest of India. Since a withdrawal would cause an unfavourable public reaction, it would have to be timed to give as small an impression of weakness as possible: '...It ought for instance to be deferred till a period when we may have been able to secure some striking improvement of our position towards the Indus.'

Finally Auckland stated the policy to which he was led by all these considerations. He would continue to hold the main cities of Afghanistan in strength; he would restrain Shah Shuja from territorial expansion; he would leave the independent tribes to themselves as much as possible; he would strive to keep Herat safe from Persian agression, but without occupying the city in advance while Yar Muhammad was alive and in power; he would keep a strong force in Afghanistan while helping to bring forward a genuine Afghan army; and he would avoid all direct interference in internal affairs while giving advice tactfully in order to prevent oppression and correct abuses. Thus he hoped to show the Secret Committee that his Government was not in the pressing embarrassment envisaged in the dispatch of 31 December, 'and that the very serious question which it raises is not one which ought yet to be definitively discussed and decided'. A copy of this minute, with marginal annotations by Macnaghten, is preserved in the Auckland Papers at the British Museum. He considered Auckland's minute to be 'an admirable paper'. He reminded critics that the Tripartite Treaty had expressly forbidden British interference in Shuja's internal affairs, and saw no cause for disappointment in the fact that Afghanistan had not become stable under Shuja in little more than a year and a half. As for Shuja himself, 'there never was a man who has been so cruelly calumniated...'. We might allow Macnaghten all this and more, but what are we to make of the blithe confidence of a man who could write, as he did in the margin of Auckland's minute, that the peace and prosperity of Afghanistan were so much improved that even the Khyberees were giving up plundering and becoming merchants?[24] Macnaghten's over-confidence, in the spring and summer of 1841, appears in everything he wrote, but it is nowhere as obvious as it is in his remark about the tribesmen of the Khyber Pass.

Auckland knew all about Macnaghten's optimism, and usually made allowance for it. For his own part, he saw many difficulties ahead, but none so difficult as that of finance, which (as he told Hobhouse) 'weighs with seriousness and anxiety upon my mind'.[25] Colvin put it more bluntly to his friend Macnaghten: 'Money, money, money is our first, our second and our last want. How long we can continue to feed you at your present rate of expenditure I

347

cannot tell. To add to the weight would break us down utterly.'[26]
It was in his March letter to Hobhouse that Auckland summarized
the views of Henry Thoby Prinsep, a member of his council.
Prinsep, he said, had originally opposed the expedition beyond the
Indus, but he saw that the plans of 1838 would have successful
results in the distant future:

...He looks upon the abandonment of our position as impossible without danger and dishonour, would take a more direct share than has been
taken in the government of the country, and would be inclined, if it were
possible, to sanction the proposed advance upon Herat. He thinks that
our present force is at least as much as the country can feed and rates our
expense at a crore and a quarter, ending in the unhappy admission that
the maintenance of our position in Afghanistan must end in financial
ruin unless there should be some prospect of providing an additional
crore to the net revenues of India...

Auckland then showed that Prinsep had also envisaged a future
in which 'the revenues of Lahore or a portion of them should fall
into our hands'. But Prinsep underestimated the difficulty of annexing the territories not yet subject to British rule in India. His own
inclination was 'to provide for immediate exigencies and stand firm.
If we can do so and be strong and there should be a calm instead
of the storm which is threatened we may reconsider our position...'
The storm, of course, was the one building up over Herat. We can
well understand why Auckland was so bitter about Todd's brain-
storm and the fecklessness of those officers who started moving
troops in February as though a march on Herat was the simplest
thing in the world. But there was one crumb of consolation for
Auckland at the end of March. He received a copy of a letter from
Palmerston to Hobhouse indicating there was no immediate necessity for action at Herat, since Russia was friendly and disposed to
keep Persia in check. Palmerston characteristically (and justifiably)
remarked that he did not know how long this would last, and that it
would not be wise to relax too much in the precautions taken in
Asia.[27] Nevertheless, Auckland was cheered by the prospect of an
agreement between Britain and Russia to abstain from 'further
encroachment in Central Asia'. He told Macnaghten about it in
one letter, and sternly reproved him in another for 'unthinking
eagerness' to march on Herat. '...I must again beg you upon the
considerations which I have before stated to view your position
soberly...'[28]

The mounting cost of intervention

At the beginning of April the Indian Government announced the opening of a 5 per cent loan whose purpose was to enable it to maintain the current rate of expenditure until the end of 1842. Subscriptions came in slowly at first, but they totalled well over £1,000,000 by the end of July, and stood at about £2,200,00 in the middle of November.[29] The initial sluggishness of the subscribers has often been mentioned, as if it was a sign of a lack of confidence in the Government, but not the steady and satisfying growth of the funds subscribed between July and November—a growth which would seem to indicate solid confidence rather than the lack of it. However that may be, Auckland felt that the subscribers had given him a little breathing-space, and in his letter to the chairman of the Court of Directors on 19 November he was able to report that 'our treasuries are easy at present'. The tragedy was that the breathing-space came too late.

Blow after blow fell on Auckland's head in 1841. He was still repairing the damage done by Todd's recklessness at Herat when he heard of the unsatisfactory settlement accepted by the British plenipotentiary with the expeditionary force off the coast of China. He knew that it would never please Palmerston, who had given specific instructions, and he remarked to George Clerk, his agent at Ambala, that 'things have been sadly mismanaged for me at my extreme flanks of China and Herat'.[30] In the event, Elliot, the plenipotentiary, suffered the same fate as Major Todd. He was recalled in disgrace. But Palmerston sent out in his place Sir Henry Pottinger, formerly Resident in Sind, one of the hardest negotiators in the business of diplomacy, and his choice was confirmed by the Tories when they came to power in September. Auckland took the Chinese blow bravely and went on with his uphill struggle in Afghanistan. He issued official instructions to Macnaghten to start a very tactful course of advice to Shuja and his ministers (such as they were) on internal administration.[31]

As always, Auckland had also to keep his eye on the Punjab and other neighbours. The Punjab at that moment was in turmoil. Since the death of the Maharajah and his heir at the beginning of November, the Sikh army had sadly declined from its former magnificent state. Sher Singh, the new ruler, was weak, and his soldiers were rapidly becoming a mob. George Clerk at one stage offered British help to restore order if that should be required, but the offer was not taken up, and Auckland was thankful not to

349

be embroiled in new quarrels. But he wrote to Maharajah Sher Singh at the end of April, remonstrating with him over the Durbar's apparent inability to control its mutinous soldiers, and warning him with infinite courtesy that the safety and interests of other powers might become vitally concerned if the excesses continued.[32] Sher Singh could only put one construction on these words, and, as it happens, Emily Eden has interpreted them for us in one of her letters. Writing to her brother Robert in England about the unrest in the Punjab, she said:

> ...It is not actually any business of ours, but it interrupts our communications with Afghanistan; and, in short, it is obvious that it might at last furnish one of those pretences for interference England delights in, and when once we begin I know (don't you?) what becomes of the country we assist—swallowed up whole...[33]

The Commander in Chief also had in mind the possibility of a British intervention in the Punjab, and he was equally frank about it in his diary. 'Unless a large accession of Punjab territory comes in to connect us safely with Caubul, and to aid our very heavy expenses, we must withdraw...'[34] This was no more than Auckland and Prinsep had envisaged in their minutes, but Auckland was much less enthusiastic for the fray than most of his associates and officers. Yet even he had been seduced by the thought of the revenues which would come his way if the Punjab fell into anarchy and if Britain were forced to intervene, and in the spring and summer of 1841 he worried constantly about the state of his financial affairs.

In his May letter to Hobhouse the Governor General had before him Macnaghten's marginal notes on the minute of 19 March. He quoted these to Hobhouse[35] as evidence of the gradual improvement in affairs in Afghanistan, and he wrote gratefully to Macnaghten about them.[36] To the chairman of the Court of Directors he wrote that his financial position *alone* gave him uneasiness at the beginning of May.[37] What pleased him more than anything else was the news that Persia was about to withdraw its garrison from Ghorian. The garrison marched out of Ghorian after occupying the place for three and a half years, and the way apparently lay open for the return of Sir John McNeill to Teheran, the evacuation of Kharg by the British, and the signing of a commercial treaty. Then the government of Herat, being at odds with the British in

India and Afghanistan, offered submission to the Shah of Persia. It is interesting to see how the Home Government and Auckland's council separately reacted to the news from Persia and Herat. Palmerston and Hobhouse heard the news at the end of May, and on 1 June the Secretary of State addressed the following personal note to the president of the Board of Control:

...I have read Col. Sheil's Despatches about Persian affairs, and am decidedly of opinion with you, that Auckland ought to be instructed to take possession of Herat, and of Ghorian also if it should not have been evacuated by the Persians; and that Shah Kamran ought to be put aside, and the territory of Herat should be restored to the Kingdom of Caubul.

Kamran Shah has broken his Engagements with us doubly. He has offered not only to ally himself with but to submit himself to the King of Persia; and he has marched an army Eastward to threaten us in Candahar. It seems to me that if we were to submit to such Proceedings we should be at once abandoning Herat to the Persians and Russians, and that we should seriously derogate from our Position in Central Asia.

...In fact I look upon it that as between Russia and England whichever gets to Herat first *will keep it*; and I think it is of vital importance to our Indian Empire that Russia should not have Herat. The only way of preventing it is that we should go thither ourselves. Now the present moment is peculiarly favourable for such a measure. You have troops already on the Helmund, half way from Candahar to Herat; and Kamran Shah has given us just cause of war, which if we pass over he may consider himself for the future at liberty to do towards us anything he likes. The Iron is hot; let us strike it; if we let it grow cold it will be too hard for our blows.[38]

Hobhouse readily agreed with Palmerston's proposal, and hurriedly drafted a dispatch to Auckland to that effect. On the 3rd Palmerston asked him to send copies of his draft to other members of the Cabinet 'as a thing that Melbourne and John Russell have agreed to'. Palmerston had discussed the proposal with two of his Cabinet colleagues (Morpeth and Baring) in the House of Commons the previous evening; they had acquiesced but 'did not remember the subject having been mooted in Cabinet'.[39] In other words, if Morpeth and Baring had not spoken up, the dispatch might have gone off to India before the matter had come to the attention of most Cabinet ministers. Hobhouse did as Palmerston suggested, and the completed dispatch was ready for transmission on 4 June, the day on which Sir Robert Peel gained a majority of one in the House of Commons on a motion of no confidence in the

Whig Government. The dispatch gave Auckland instructions ('unless circumstances now unknown to us should induce you to adopt a different course') to advance an army for the occupation of Herat and the annexation of that city and its dependent territories to the kingdom of Kabul. In it Hobhouse acknowledged that Auckland had been prudent in his military dispositions in Afghanistan, in accordance with the Secret Committee's instructions of 31 December, and, what is more important, that Auckland had no safe alternative to the continued expenditure of a crore and a quarter annually on the maintenance of Britain's position in Afghanistan.[40] Whether because of the vote of no confidence or because another letter from Auckland arrived that day, Hobhouse had to write a less warlike dispatch on the 5th, only twenty-four hours after completing the first one. Auckland had told him that an expedition to Herat would take months to prepare, cost millions of pounds, and demand an army of 12,000 men of all arms. The occupation of Herat would add a million a year to the cost of British commitments beyond the Indus. It is hardly surprising that the Secret Committee's dispatch of 5 June authorized Auckland to take all precautions and even to abstain from mounting an expedition to Herat if he judged it necessary. Nevertheless, Hobhouse said that 'the good policy of annexing the Herat territory to Eastern Afghanistan is all but unquestionable'.[41] So it was that the tottering Whig Government retreated within twenty-four hours from the brink of a new war in Central Asia. Palmerston shortly afterwards concluded that the Persian evacuation of Ghorian, even in the strange circumstances of Herat's offer of submission, justified him in sending Sir John McNeill back to Teheran to resume normal diplomatic relations with the Persian Court, and McNeill did so with great success.[42] Looking back at this episode in the last months of the Whig administration the author of this work finds it remarkable that Palmerston and Hobhouse were still so jittery about Herat (or 'tetchy', to use Nesselrode's word) in June 1841. Palmerston seems to have given little serious thought to the cost and difficulty of the course proposed, and at the moment of crisis he and Hobhouse disregarded all recent signs of Russian goodwill and leapt to the alert like a pair of frightened sentries.

Auckland's reaction was much more circumspect. The news reached him at the beginning of the second week in July. On the 11th he authorized Rawlinson to tell Yar Muhammad that he regarded his submission to Persia as null and void, and that the British Government would 'take its own measures for the security of its interests, as circumstances may appear to require, without any regard to the views or purposes of that Court' (meaning Herat).[43] But he privately advised Macnaghten that he did not expect the march of armies, disagreeable though the news from Herat might be,[44] and he was delighted to read a few days later in the Secret Committee's dispatches of 4 and 5 June that the Home Government had had second thoughts on hearing of the difficulties. In any case he strongly suspected that Yar Muhammad would try to play off British against Persians and Persians against British for as long as it would be profitable to him, and that true submission to Persia was unlikely. Events proved him right.

Throughout the summer Macnaghten sent him glowing reports of peaceful improvements in Afghanistan, making light of the renewed trouble among the Ghilzais and the Durranis. In the middle of June, for example, Macnaghten gently reproved Rawlinson for taking such a gloomy view of the Durrani rebellion and of the British position generally.[45] He did so almost at the moment when Auckland was writing to him that 'we have in these countries a much stronger national spirit to deal with than many of us had calculated upon...'.[46] Yet he was prepared to give Macnaghten the benefit of the doubt, and his letters home frequently included references to the envoy's confidence and reports of peace and prosperity. He told Macnaghten on 11 July:

You can hardly do better than proceed as you are proceeding. You must fix a strong and permanent check upon the Ghilzais. You must secure every communication and collect and establish force at Candahar, and until this is done, unless you can depend upon Afghan instruments, you must bear with a little vapouring and disturbance and withholding of revenue beyond the Helmund. Your account of the country near to Cabul is very satisfactory...[47]

The trouble was that Auckland had become accustomed to these frequent outbreaks among the tribes. He saw them, and Macnaghten encouraged him to see them, as nothing more than tribal unruliness, to be shrugged off, perhaps, as 'vapouring and disturbance and withholding of revenue'. Macnaghten even referred to the Durrani rebels as 'perfect children' in a letter once again rejecting Rawlinson's warnings about national feeling, and after the victory of the troops from Kandahar against Aktur Khan and his Durranis in August Macnaghten made his notorious claim that 'the country is perfectly quiet from Dan to Beersheba'.[48]

In June, as we saw earlier, the Whigs were defeated on a motion of no confidence in their administration. Melbourne advised the Queen to dissolve Parliament, and in the subsequent election the Conservatives, as they were now frequently called, won a handsome majority in the House of Commons. Auckland heard the result on 16 August and immediately decided to send his resignation home. Many a matter, he said, was unsettled in India, but he felt he had been in India long enough, and he hoped to embark in March at the latest. He warned Hobhouse that Major General Elphinstone's health was failing and that Sir William Macnaghten, who frequently complained of illness, could not be expected to stay much longer in Afghanistan.[49] He did not, as Lady Sale alleged, consider the Afghans to be as peaceable as London citizens, but he was convinced that the British position in Afghanistan was 'much more insecure from financial than from military difficulties',[50] and he assured Sir John McNeill on 22 August that

the tenure of our position in that country is occasionally not without its difficulties, but I trust that it is improving. The Eastern districts have been particularly tranquil. We have found enemies in the Ghilzye and Dooranee tribes, but they have at least learnt that 5,000 of their insurgents can be beaten by 500 of our troops. At the date of my last accounts there was no considerable body anywhere in arms.[51]

One of the last acts of the Secret Committee under the Whigs that summer was to inform Auckland of the appointment of Sir William Macnaghten as Governor of Bombay in succession to Sir James Carnac. The Committee sent Hobhouse's dispatch by the mail that left London at the beginning of August, thus demonstrating the Government's confidence in the security of the British position in Afghanistan. The newly elected House of Commons, with its large Conservative majority, met for the first time on 24 August. On Friday the 27th it met to debate Sir Robert Peel's censure motion against the men still occupying the Government benches. Hobhouse tells us in his memoirs that Lord John Russell wound up for the Whigs, and that the House divided at half past two on the Saturday morning, when the ayes outnumbered the noes by 360 to 269. The president of the Board of Control walked home through the deserted Westminster streets to Berkeley Square, where he arrived at about half past three 'most happy that this long agony had ended at last'.[52] That most loyal of loyal Whigs, Lady Palmerston, would have been shocked by such talk. She told her friend Mrs Huskisson in a letter written that day that people were tired of a Government

that was always struggling, and then, as John Russell says, so grossly misrepresented. It is perhaps better the Tory party should be so large, with so many internal dissentions they must split and fall to pieces; and will do so the more readily from having less to fear from the Whig Party. Our tactics must be to be quiet and give them rope...The Queen is very much annoy'd as you may suppose, but she has wonderful courage and firmness and will bear it all with composure. It is impossible that Melbourne should not be also very much vexed...Altogether it is provoking to everybody, feeling too how well the country has been governed and how everything has prospered at home and abroad...[53]

But was everything as prosperous as Lady Palmerston liked to think? Certainly not at home. Abroad, Afghanistan was exacting a heavy tribute from the Indian treasuries, and the China dispute was still unsettled. In their anxiety to take over and set all to rights at home, the Conservatives had inherited two particularly heavy foreign responsibilities. The Whig argosies were somewhere at sea, with many a storm before them, and their new owners had to ask themselves whether they would ever come to port. Lord Ellenborough was soon at his desk at the Board of Control, and his first duty as president was to instruct Auckland through the Secret Committee to suspend orders for the advance of troops upon Herat—'unless you should be already engaged in the execution of those orders'.[54] On the 6th he wrote a very civil letter to Auckland, privately hinting that a change of policy was likely. He wondered whether Auckland would want to be responsible for applying a policy of which he might not entirely approve, but he was convinced that 'your execution of whatever policy you carry into effect will be distinguished by the same ability which has been generally acknowledged in the execution of your former measures'.[55] Ellenborough moved very cautiously. Apart from suspending the previous Government's orders for a march on Herat, he changed nothing for the time being. In a memorandum for the Queen's eyes he pointed out that an annexation of Herat was capable of damaging relations with Russia. '...Your Majesty cannot but be sensible of the difficulty of maintaining in Europe that good understanding with Russia which has such an important bearing upon the general peace, if serious differences should exist between Your Majesty and that Power with respect to the States of Central Asia.' He also made the point that a further advance of 360 miles into Central Asia 'could not but render more difficult of accomplishment the original intention of Your Majesty, publicly announced to the world, of withdrawing Your Majesty's troops from Afghanistan as soon as Shah Shoojah should be firmly established upon the throne he owes to Your Majesty's aid'. These considerations alone would have prompted the Government to think again about the Herat orders, he said, but financial considerations were also important. One wonders how the Queen, Whiggish as she still was in 1841, reacted when she read Ellenborough's next remark: '...Your Majesty must be too well informed of the many evils consequent upon financial embarrassment...' But she could hardly disagree with Lord Ellenborough's closing remark: '...Her Majesty's Government should have especial regard to the effect which the protracted continuance of military operations in that country, still more any extension of them to a new and distant field, would have upon the finances of India, and thereby upon the welfare of eighty millions of people who there acknowledge Your Majesty's rule.'

The Queen's reply is significant, and it accords with the other evidence available, that Peel's Government did not plan any sudden withdrawal from Afghanistan. She thought that the 'course intended to be pursued—namely to take time to consider the affairs of India without making any precipitate change in the policy hitherto pursued, and without involving the country hastily in expenses, is far the best and safest'.[56] In a second letter to Auckland, written on 19 September, Ellenborough gave more evidence of the Government's caution. He had not yet been able to bring Afghan policy before the Cabinet, but the latest accounts from Persia gave hope that a commercial treaty would soon be completed. His own, Palmerstonian words were: '...Our last accounts from Persia lead to the hope that our last demand, as to the commercial treaty, will be complied with, and thus we shall be enabled to evacuate Karak.' But he then went on in a completely different vein from Palmerston's. 'This would afford the best opportunity for commencing a retrograde movement to the Indus provided the affairs of Afganistan begin to assume a settled appearance. My idea is that the Shah's troops commanded by our officers should be

356

raised to 12,000 men as a preliminary measure.' Palmerston might never have spoken of a 'retrograde movement', but on this evidence Ellenborough was not departing so far from Whig policy. He was proposing to withdraw regular troops, but only if Afghanistan became stable, and, moreover, he was proposing to make the Shah's British-officered contingent much larger. This was very much what Auckland had wanted to be able to do for months, except that Auckland and his Whig colleagues were not so optimistic about the timing of the withdrawal of regular forces from Afghanistan. Ellenborough ended his letter to Auckland by wishing that he could persuade him to stay on as Governor General, 'for I feel satisfied that we should go on well together', and by noting that he was determined to resign and come home.[57] In fact Ellenborough did not yet have Auckland's resignation in front of him, but Hobhouse had shown him parts of Auckland's private letter of July, and had told him that the Governor General did not want to stay in India after the end of 1841. It was Palmerston who advised Hobhouse to do so, in a note written only a few days after the Peel administration was formed. Having given the advice, he said:

...I am afraid the Tories will throw away the high Position which we have established for British interests in the East; Aberdeen, whom I saw, as it was right and proper I should, in order to explain to him any Points on which he might want information, said he thought we had been *too hard* upon the Shah of Persia; and Ellenborough I believe has always condemned our Conquest of Afghanistan. This Govt. will infallibly discredit themselves before twelve months have passed over their heads, but I fear that they will also in that time have done serious mischief to our National Interests at home and abroad—Our friends are steady and zealous.[58]

At the beginning of October Auckland's letter of resignation arrived in London. There was much consultation between Peel and Wellington, and between Queen Victoria and Lord Melbourne (whom she still privately consulted from time to time). Peel immediately thought of Ellenborough as the best qualified man to succeed Auckland, and could think of only one drawback—'a tendency to precipitation and over-activity'. He supposed that Ellenborough would have very good and steady advisers in India.[59] Wellington agreed with Peel about his merits, but did not think that Peel could rely safely upon the members of the council in Calcutta to check Ellenborough's 'active habits and disposition...I think,

357

however, you may rely upon Lord Ellenborough's sound sense and discretion...'.[60]

Melbourne told the Queen that he was very glad to hear of the appointment of a man of such great abilities, knowledge of India, industry, and accurate habits of business. '...He has hitherto been an unpopular man and his manners have been considered contemptuous and overbearing, but he is evidently much softened and amended in this respect, as most men are by time, experience, and observation.' As for the appointment of Lord Fitzgerald to succeed Ellenborough at the Board of Control, Melbourne said, 'It is upon the whole an adequate appointment.'[61] Ellenborough had his appointment approved by the Court of Directors, and began to prepare for the long voyage to India. Fitzgerald installed himself at the Board of Control and formed a very favourable opinion of Auckland's abilities and statesmanship, as revealed in the official dispatches and minutes. He must have spoken too admiringly of Auckland in Peel's presence, for Peel went out of his way to try to turn Fitzgerald against Auckland. He sent him a copy of a memorandum submitted by Henry Willock (who had canvassed his opinions once before, in 1838, in a memorandum to Palmerston), and said:

Enclosed is a paper which will be interesting to you.

It contains a demonstration of the folly of our advance beyond the Indus—and its ruinous consequences to the finances of India.

Lord Auckland may have conducted himself with ability and activity in small matters—but his policy in respect to the Affghan country, and the restoration of Shah Soojah, will far outweigh in fruit of evil any good which he may have effected in India.[62]

In fact Fitzgerald did not change his high opinion of Lord Auckland, much to Peel's disgust. Peel was not very well informed on Eastern affairs, and his acceptance of Willock's arguments does him little credit, for Willock had no recent knowledge of the East, being an armchair critic of no great distinction. Fitzgerald was so little moved by Peel's letter—the result of intense indignation about the financial burden in Afghanistan—that his first dispatch to India through the Secret Committee, on 25 October, could well have been written by Hobhouse himself.[63] All was approbation and agreement, and Ellenborough sailed on 6 November with views unchanged from those which he expressed to Auckland in September.

We left Auckland at the moment of his firm decision to resign

358

and go home. He knew that he had to look for a successor to Major General Elphinstone, and he told Macnaghten that Nott was in the running. '...I think highly of him as a soldier, and apparently he has not been wanting in hearty cooperation with Major Rawlinson, but he seems to judge with a sourness and occasionally to express himself with an indiscretion much to be regretted...'[64] He also heard in September that Macnaghten had been promoted, and that he would have to appoint a successor. Should it be Burnes? There was a time when he would have had no doubt about Burnes's qualifications for the succession, but now he wondered whether the appointment would be wise. Burnes had admirable qualities, but there were defects as well as merits, as Colvin said in a letter to Macnaghten:

...For that post a calm and balanced judgement—a temper marked alike by fortitude and moderation—nerve and firmness in critical emergencies—the experience of public affairs which leads men to be tolerant of unavoidable losses and defects—a reputation so established as to leave no room for the suspicion that the success of others may be regarded with coldness—a large and liberal mind which rises above favouritism—these are all of them qualifications eminently requisite—on the other hand Burnes possesses a peculiar experience and perhaps a peculiar influence which may be most valuable...Is Burnes really a fit and safe person to be appointed Envoy at Cabool? We could arrange to give him, I should add, a Residency in India...

On the same day Colvin told Macnaghten, in a separate letter, that the general feeling in England was in favour of withdrawal from Afghanistan, 'though of course by some prudent and measured course of retrocession...'.[65] But Macnaghten had already heard the rumour, as Kaye shows us in quoting his letter of 25 September to Thomas Robertson at Agra: '...If they deprive the Shah altogether of our support I have no hesitation in saying (and that is saying a great deal) they will commit an unparalleled political atrocity...'[66]

And so, at the end of September 1841, it was common knowledge in India and Afghanistan, at least among officials (and spies), that Auckland had sent home his resignation, that Macnaghten was moving soon to Bombay as Governor, that the officer commanding British troops in Afghanistan was a sick man who would soon give up his post and return to India, and that the new Government in London intended to withdraw all regular forces from Afghanistan as soon as it could find an honourable and face-saving excuse for doing so. In addition, the envoy and Minister was convinced that the entire country could be kept in order by the Shah's troops, with the help of one European regiment at Kabul and another at Kandahar, and that he would soon be able to reduce the British outlay in Afghanistan to thirty lakhs (£300,000) per annum, for progress made in pacification and subjugation was 'perfectly wonderful'. In the circumstances just explained it is hardly surprising that certain Afghans now began to think of speeding the departing British on their way.

CHAPTER 15

RISING AT KABUL

...Our great experiment of consolidating Afghanistan is, in short,
a failure, except at a cost which, even if we could, for any period
continue to bear it, would be wholly disproportionate to its object.
It will probably, therefore, not be persevered in beyond the point
which the honour of our arms or obvious present expediency may
demand. We must console ourselves with having successfully
warded off a pressing danger, with having gained most valuable
knowledge, with having, as I think, greatly exalted the reputation
of our excellent troops—and with having extended our authority
very largely towards what all will regard as a proper barrier, the
Indus...

JOHN RUSSELL COLVIN to his father, 22 December 1841

The confidence of the British in their military position in Afghanistan had its roots in the defeat and surrender of Dost Muhammad
Khan at the end of 1840. Kabul and the surrounding country
remained quiet during the military operations of that autumn, and
only the Kohistan chiefs showed themselves willing to join forces
with the former emir. Sale's expedition put a stop to their plans.
Thereafter, there was occasional trouble with the Durranis north
and west of Kandahar, and with the Ghilzai tribes between Kandahar and Kabul. Both tribes had been accustomed to a considerable degree of independence under former rulers, but the new
order threatened to strengthen the central government at the
expense of their chiefs. The Durranis also had a genuine grievance
about the system of revenue collection, which was oppressive. This
and similar injustices were in the process of being corrected during
1841, under British influence, but the British were trying to do in
a year or two the work of decades or even centuries. Tribal ties were
still so strong in Afghanistan in 1965, at the time of the first general
election under a new democratic constitution, that only about 20
per cent of the electorate went to the polls. Those who voted lived
chiefly in the big towns. The tribes went their own way.

Troops from Kandahar defeated Durrani forces under Aktur
Khan in January and July, and again in August; the latter victory
was so striking that Macnaghten concluded that the Durrani insurrection was at an end. 'The victory of the Helmund was very

361

complete. . . .'[1] In May and August the Ghilzais also suffered heavily in combat with troops from Kandahar. The British and their sepoys, and the Shah's British-officered regiments, all had two priceless advantages—discipline and artillery. The Afghan tribes usually had very little of either. But they eventually found other ways of winning their battles.

Once the main Durrani and Ghilzai forces had been dispersed Macnaghten congratulated himself on the peace and quietness of the country, although he still found work for the troops. In spite of all Auckland's warnings it was still customary to send out punitive expeditions from Kabul and Kandahar on the king's behalf, and those expeditions invariably included British Indian regiments. Brigadier Shelton's first duty on entering the country had been to lead such an expedition from Jalalabad in February. In September, when Macnaghten was writing so cheerfully, it was considered necessary to send one expedition north from Kandahar into the Teree country, and another from Kabul to Zurmat. At the same time Sir William Macnaghten started to economize at last. The eastern Ghilzais, who lived among the rocky defiles between Kabul and Jalalabad, had been quiet while their western cousins had been at war in the summer. They had been very quiet for a long time, largely because their chiefs were receiving a subsidy of 80,000 rupees. Macnaghten judged that he could safely halve their subsidy, and he summoned them to Kabul to hear his decision. The subsidy was not a British innovation; the chiefs had exacted similar tribute from previous rulers of Kabul as a reward for good behaviour. To tamper with it was to invite trouble. Macnaghten took the risk, and the chiefs took deep offence at his action. He wrote to Auckland on 8 October, saying that the local rebellion raised by these chiefs could easily be suppressed, and that he was preparing to leave Kabul for India on the 20th. He expected to be in Bombay by the middle of December.[2] Major General Elphinstone was due to accompany him and the column of regiments returning to India.

On Saturday 9 October Elphinstone sent the 35th Native Infantry forward to clear the Khurd Kabul Pass, the first big obstacle on the route to Jalalabad. There the 35th and its supporting cavalry and artillery found the Ghilzais in full, hostile possession of the entrance to the pass. The troops halted on Sunday and their commanding officer, Thomas Monteith, asked for more men from Kabul. That night the Ghilzais raided Monteith's camp near

Butkhak with help from some of the armed retainers of certain of the Kabul chiefs, though the extent of this collusion was not understood at the time. Twenty-four sepoys were killed or wounded. Macnaghten thought it particularly provoking that the trouble had broken out while the best part of a brigade was absent from Kabul on the Zurmat expedition. He was still confident that the Ghilzais' rebellion could be put down, and that the country would then be quieter than it had ever been before. On Monday Sale led the 13th Light Infantry and some supporting troops to relieve Monteith and the 35th Bengal Native Infantry at Butkhak. Together the two regiments forced the pass on Tuesday. Then Sale took his own regiment and most of the supporting troops back to Butkhak, leaving Monteith and his men at Khurd Kabul. Sale, who had been wounded in the ankle during the engagement, wanted to wait at Butkhak for the return of the Zurmat expedition, so that the regiments marching to India could form a united force. It had long been decided that the regiments with longest service in Afghanistan would go home in 1841, and that fresh units would move up to take their place with the November convoy. In the middle of October the troops of the Kabul garrison were in a hazardous position, with Monteith warding off Ghilzais at Khurd Kabul, Sale waiting at Butkhak, and little more than one Bengal infantry regiment in the cantonment just outside the walls of Kabul. Fortunately the remainder of the garrison arrived from Zurmat on the 17th. Macnaghten had hoped to clear up the trouble by negotiating with the Ghilzais, but he reluctantly admitted that they would have to be 'thrashed' after all, and he sent an infantry regiment (the 37th Bengal) and supporting arms to Sale at Butkhak, ready for the fight. He still had a strong brigade in cantonments. At this point it may be useful to recall that Macnaghten had suggested in September that the two fresh regiments would not be needed and could be turned back from Peshawar. Auckland refused this offer, 'and would not commit the error of too rapidly reducing our military strength in Afghanistan'.[3] In one of his October letters to London he said that he did not adopt 'all of Sir William's sanguine views and would have the government yet to lay its account for the occasional recurrence of hazard and of difficulty'.[4] Once again events proved him right.

On 22 October Sale, who now had a brigade under his command, moved from Khurd Kabul towards Tezin. He was preparing to attack the first of the Ghilzai forts when the political agent announced on the 23rd that the chiefs had come to terms. It was all very well for Durand to write years later that this was a time for action—'for striking and not for talking',[5] but some allowance must be made for the circumstances of the time, and Durand had the benefit of hindsight. Durand knew, and we know, that the Ghilzai rising was the prelude to a national insurrection. But there was no reason to believe that such an outbreak was imminent in October. The Ghilzais saw Sale coming with his redcoats and his field guns, and they hurriedly concluded their agreement with Captain Macgregor, the political agent. They did not recover the whole of their subsidy, but they extracted 10,000 rupees as the price of a safe passage and the restoration of peace.[6] Sale felt confident enough to send the 37th Native Infantry back to join the escort which was to accompany the departing envoy and general. He marched on the 26th, and soon discovered that the Ghilzai chiefs had been faithless or unable to control their own men. His rearguard was engaged in a continuous running fight, which occupied him until he reached Gandamak on 30 October. There he halted to count casualties and gather strength. More than a hundred of his troops and camp followers had been killed or wounded since the conclusion of Macgregor's agreement with the Ghilzai chiefs.

The first day of November found Macnaghten and Burnes confident and indeed complacent. Burnes called on the envoy to wish him a safe journey to Bombay, and, according to Macnaghten himself, congratulated him on his 'approaching departure at a season of such profound tranquility'. Macnaghten hoped that 'the business last reported' (the attack on Sale's rearguard) 'was the expiring effort of the rebels'. He congratulated Rawlinson on the peaceful state of affairs in the Kandahar area.[7] At that very moment a group of conspirators was forming with the earnest intention of speeding the British on their way. We have it on the authority of the two principal diarists of these events that Burnes was warned in good time, and that he scoffed at the warning.[8] He would not even ask for a strong guard for his house in the city, where he lived and roamed as freely as if he was in Bombay. We have to remember that the British garrison at Kabul had been lulled by long periods of peace and quiet into relaxing ordinary military precautions. The king and his troops occupied the vast and crumbling Bala Hissar at the south-east corner of the city. Many officers and their families lived, like Burnes, in houses within the city walls. The British and

British Indian regiments occupied hurriedly constructed temporary cantonments about a mile from the Kohistan gate of Kabul. They were neither a fort nor an open camp. This is how Brigadier Shelton described them:

...Never having been much in cantonments, I went round and found them of frightful extent—the two sides of the oblong, including the two mission compounds, about 1,400 yards each, the two ends each 500, with a rampart and ditch an Afghan could run over with the facility of a cat, with many other serious defects. The misfortune of this was that so many troops were necessary for the actual defence of the works, that only a few could be spared for external operations...[9]

The cantonments stood beside the main Kabul–Kohistan road, about half-way from the city to the village of Beymaroo, and slightly to the north of the Kabul River. The country round about was dotted with forts or fortified houses belonging to Afghan chiefs. Two of the nearest ones were used by the British garrison. In one they kept their powder and ammunition (the magazine fort), and in the other they kept much of their food (the commissariat fort). The cantonments faithfully reflected the compromise on which the British presence in the country was based. They were not conquerors, and therefore the British did not occupy the Bala Hissar, which was the ruler's palace as well as being the strongest fortress at Kabul. They were the king's allies, and therefore could assume that the king's supporters were their friends. They felt that they were among friends at Kabul. In the circumstances they felt justified in taking just enough care to keep out thieves and plunderers. They dared not build anything more permanent. Indeed they planned for every emergency but the one that came upon them.

The second day of November 1841 was the third Tuesday of the month of Ramadan, a month in which Muslim tempers are proverbially short. We know this because Dr James Burnes preserved a translation of a message from the chief conspirators to the leaders of the Afridi tribes astride the Khyber Pass:

...The fact is this, that on the third Tuesday of the blessed month Ramzan in the morning time it occurred, that with other heroic champions stirring like lions, we carried by storm the house of Sickender Burnes. By the grace of the most holy and omnipotent God the brave warriors, having rushed right and left from their ambush, slew Sikander Burnes with various other Feringees of consideration, and nearly 500 battalion men, putting them utterly to the sword, and consigning them to perdition...[10]

From about 6 a.m. onwards the people in cantonments could hear firing and tumult in the city. Lady Sale's Afghan servant reported that she had been threatened and reviled on her way to work, and she and other Afghans brought strange rumours of mob violence in the city. At about 8 a.m. a messenger handed Macnaghten a note from Burnes reporting the outbreak, but this was followed almost immediately by a story that Burnes and two other officers at his house had been murdered. It was said that Burnes had made an unsuccessful attempt to quieten the crowd by addressing it from the gallery of his house. The treasury administered by the Shah's military paymaster, Captain Johnson, had been plundered and its guard slaughtered. Macnaghten sent Lady Sale's son-in-law, Lieutenant Sturt, with orders from Major General Elphinstone, who was not only a sick man but also suffering from the effects of a heavy fall from his horse on Monday evening. Sturt was to tell Shelton to march at once to the Bala Hissar. He was to act on his own judgement after consulting the king. At the same time Macnaghten sent one of his political assistants to warn the king that Shelton and his men, who had been camped for some time outside cantonments, were on their way to help. Shelton received his orders shortly after 9 a.m., and he prepared to act upon them. But less than an hour later he received a message from the Bala Hissar, saying that the king did not want him to come. It seems that at this critical moment Shah Shuja was too proud to admit that he needed British troops to keep order in his own capital city. Shelton sent Sturt to the Bala Hissar to find out what was going on, and eventually, at about midday, received orders to come to the Bala Hissar after all. 'I then marched in,' Shelton recorded 'when the king asked me, as well as I could understand, who sent me, and what I came there for.' The king had, in fact, acted promptly on becoming aware of the extent of the riot. He had sent some of his own troops into the narrow streets of the city to disperse the mob, and Macnaghten and Elphinstone at first thought that this would be enough. But the Shah's men were driven back, and Shelton gave them covering fire as they took refuge in the Bala Hissar. Shelton and his men also went into the palace fortress. It was already afternoon, and the mob still controlled the city.

Rising at Kabul

It is easy to complain that the British garrison achieved nothing that day. Vincent Eyre was particularly bitter about it, though he generously made allowances for Major General Elphinstone's sickness. But the author of this study has lived through the events of 2 November 1841 many times in his imagination and still finds it impossible to believe that the garrison could have done more that day. The outbreak started in the heart of a city of narrow streets, and it was mid morning before anyone understood the full extent of the trouble. There was no delay in sending orders to Shelton, who had a strong body of troops close at hand. Shelton was not lacking in energy or resolution at the moment of crisis. But Kabul was Shah Shuja's capital. The riot, which was all it was at the beginning, was his affair, and his own troops failed because they were helpless and unable to manoeuvre in the narrow streets. Their two field guns were useless to them. Shah Shuja wasted the morning and early afternoon with this venture, and instead of displaying his independence he finished the day more dependent than ever on the military power of his British allies. They, for their part, were in no fit state to suppress a *national* uprising with the resources available to them at Kabul. Major General Elphinstone saw this clearly, and perhaps too clearly, from the start:

My dear Sir William,

Since you left me, I have been considering what can be done tomorrow. Our dilemma is a difficult one. Shelton, if reinforced tomorrow, might, no doubt, force in two columns on his way towards the Lahore Gate, and we might from hence force in that gate and meet them. But if this were accomplished what should we gain? It can be done, but not without very great loss, as our people will be exposed to the fire from the houses the whole way. Where is the point you said they were to fortify near Burnes's house? If they could assemble there, that would be the point of attack; but to march into the town, it seems, we should only have to come back again; and as to setting the city on fire, I fear, from its construction, that it is almost impossible. We must see what the morning brings, and then think what can be done. The occupation of all the houses near the gates might give us a command of the town, but we have not means of extended operations. If we could depend on the Kuzzilbashes, we might easily reduce the city.

Yours truly,

W. K. Elphinstone[11]

367

As Kaye himself admitted, it was not as easy as it looked: precipitate repressive action might have done more harm than good in the long run. In that sense, Elphinstone cannot really be blamed for the events of 2 November. Yet his letter to Macnaghten reveals a hesitant and negative attitude which almost invariably destroys confidence in the military commander possessing it. By nightfall on 2 November the officer commanding British troops in Afghanistan ought to have been giving firm orders for the next day's operations. Whatever private doubt he entertained, he should not have been seen to have any doubt at all about the successful outcome of the struggle.

The garrison took heart early on Wednesday morning, when Major Griffiths led the 37th Native Infantry into cantonments after a harassing march from his camp several miles from the city. He had been waiting there for the convoy which was to take the envoy and others back to India, but Elphinstone summoned him back to Kabul as soon as the trouble started. The regiment arrived in very creditable order, and its presence enabled Elphinstone to send a reinforcement to Shelton in the Bala Hissar. Orders had already gone to Nott, calling for a brigade of reinforcements from Kandahar, and to Sale, urging him to return to Kabul with all his men. But muddle and indecision plagued the garrison on the day after the outbreak. Lady Sale noted that 'many projects were entered into, for the purpose of putting down the rebellion, but none were put into practice'. It seems certain that Macnaghten and some others were still unwilling to believe that they had more than a local outbreak on their hands. The result of the muddle and indecision, and of the paralysis to which Lady Sale drew attention, was that the young subaltern in charge of the detachment guarding the commissariat fort evacuated the place without waiting for relief. By this time, in any case, the Afghans were taking full advantage of the tactical disabilities of the men in cantonments. They occupied as many forts as they could round about, and kept up a constant sniping. Some officers were already in favour of abandoning the ill-sited cantonments and transferring the whole garrison to the Bala Hissar. In Eyre's view the loss of the commissariat was fatal:

It is beyond a doubt that our feeble and ineffectual defence of this fort, and the valuable booty it yielded, was the first *fatal* blow to our supremacy at Cabul, and at once determined those chiefs—and more particularly the Kuzzilbashes—who had hitherto remained neutral, to join in the general combination to drive us from the country...

The first attempt to recover the commissariat fort was a failure, and men on duty on the walls could see their food, medical supplies, and rum being plundered with impunity. The other forts in Afghan hands were so sited that it was suicide to try to approach the commissariat fort from cantonments. The garrison tried to capture one particularly troublesome fort commanding the approach to the commissariat fort, but by the time they succeeded there was nothing left of the commissariat stores. The commissariat officers had to buy provisions as best they could (and at high prices) from neighbouring villages.

By the end of the first week of the Kabul garrison's ordeal, the chiefs leading the insurrection had set up one of the Dost's cousins, Nawab Zaman Khan, as king, and Macnaghten was busily trying to buy support among the Kuzzilbashis. Major General Elphinstone was already looking ahead, with painful clarity, to the time when, with all men against them, the British in Kabul would have neither food nor ammunition. There were times when the General seemed to be the only one prepared to face disagreeable facts. Unfortunately for the men under his command, he saw clearly but was incapable of choosing a consistent course of action for them to follow with hope as well as courage. Their gallant actions, as described by Eyre on 6 November, when they captured Muhammad Sharif's fort and scattered the Afghans who ventured to challenge them in the open country, seemed to lead them nowhere. Elphinstone recalled Shelton and part of his detachment from the Bala Hissar to cantonments on the 9th. He felt that he could no longer bear the burden of command alone.

John Shelton had been cooped up in the Bala Hissar for a week, during which time his men could only fire half-heartedly into the city in the hope of setting fire to the houses of the insurgent leaders. He was brave, and he was efficient in his profession, but he was a friendless, gloomy man—what other soldiers called a croaker. He judged that the whole garrison would be doomed to destruction if it tried to withstand a siege, and that its best hope was to make a dash for it to Jalalabad. In cantonments, where he arrived at about 7 a.m. on 9 November, he found low morale and 'anxiety on every countenance'. At that moment they had provisions for only a few days. Elphinstone placed him in command of the cantonments, but the two men soon clashed. According to Shelton, the Major General prevented him from giving 'such orders and instructions as appeared to me necessary'. According to Elphinstone, his Brigadier was unco-operative and 'contumacious', always finding fault and obstructing the execution of his orders. Shelton, he said, 'appeared to be actuated by an ill feeling towards me'.[12] Indeed, it would have been much better for the garrison if, as Elphinstone said, Robert Sale had stayed behind. Yet Shelton covered himself with glory for a few hours on 10 November. He led his own regiment, the 44th Foot, together with the 37th Native Infantry and one of the Shah's regiments, in a desperate assault on the Rikabashee fort, from which the Afghans were firing at will into the cantonments. At one moment the assault seemed to have failed, and all agreed that Shelton's coolness and bravery rallied the men and ensured victory. On the envoy's recommendation, moreover, Private Stewart of the 44th was promoted to Sergeant on the spot for setting such a good example of steadiness to his wavering comrades at the height of the battle. The fruits of this victory were considerable, for the Afghans, who lost at least 150 men, killed and wounded, evacuated other neighbouring forts containing more than fifty tons of grain. The men of the garrison triumphantly carried about half of this quantity into cantonments before nightfall, but, according to Eyre, they lost the other half because Shelton would not allow his men to stay and guard all the forts during the night. In spite of its own heavy casualties in the action of 10 November, the garrison as a whole was in good heart. Lady Sale remarked: 'The events of today must have astonished the enemy after our supineness, and shown them that when we have a mind to do so, we can punish them.' In after years eminent critics blamed the Kabul garrison for staying on the defensive, but Macnaghten put his finger on the essential weakness of its position when he told Macgregor (the political agent with Sale) that the Kabul garrison was not strong enough for both offensive and defensive operations.[13] With one more brigade at its disposal it could have at least tried to take the city from the insurgents. But there was only one brigade at Kabul. Who would guard the cantonments while that brigade took the field in force? Could half a brigade mount effective operations against an enemy whose strength increased every day? How could the British be sure that the Afghans would oblige them by bringing an army into the field? The Afghan confederacy truly held all the advantages, having shrewdly ensured that Sale's brigade was well out of range when the insurrection started. The chiefs could afford to bide their time.

Sale and his fellow officers faced a cruel decision when the orders for the recall of their brigade arrived from Kabul. They could see that their presence at Kabul might well turn the scales against the insurgents, but they were more than seventy miles from the city, and the Ghilzais were waiting for them in the passes. If they obeyed they would have to abandon three hundred sick and wounded men. They were not strong enough to force the passes *alone*. Sale had every personal reason for going back, for his wife, daughter, and son-in-law were still at Kabul, but at the moment of decision he thought of the men under his command. The decision itself was a joint one, since Sale had called a council of war to discuss the recall orders. From Gandamak the brigade started its march to Jalalabad on 11 November, and it occupied that place two days later. The people at Kabul could not be expected to view the decision dispassionately. Macnaghten, for instance, told Macgregor that Sale's brigade must return 'if you have regard for our lives or for the honour of our country'.[14] By then the Kabul garrison had provisions for only ten days.

Macnaghten wrote that letter on the day after a successful sortie against an Afghan force which had started bombarding cantonments with two guns sited on the Beymaroo heights. When night fell one of the guns was safely spiked, and the other was on its way to cantonments, having been captured by the defenders. Vincent Eyre's comment is full of foreboding:

This was the last success our arms were destined to experience. Henceforward it becomes my weary task to relate a catalogue of errors, disasters, and difficulties, which, following close upon each other, disgusted our officers, disheartened our soldiers, and finally sunk us all into irretrievable ruin, as though Heaven itself, by a combination of evil circumstances for its own inscrutable purposes, had planned our downfall.

On that Sunday, 14 November, Major General Nott received *his* orders to send a brigade from Kandahar to Kabul. Maclaren's homeward-bound brigade had been halted on the 10th when Nott heard that one of his detachments had been massacred on escort duty between Ghazni and Kabul. Now Maclaren was sent along the road to Kabul. Meanwhile Sale's brigade was settling down at Jalalabad, and on the 14th Monteith led a force of more than a thousand men in a sweep of the surrounding country. During this sortie some of the men saw a lone Afghan among the rocks over-

24-2

looking the southern face of Jalalabad. He was playing what looked uncommonly like a set of bagpipes, and showed no fear of the bullets whipping past his head. Thereafter the British soldiers called the place Piper's Hill.

On the 15th, early in the morning, two dirty and bloodstained officers rode into cantonments with a horrifying tale of the fate of the Charikar detachment. They had been attacked and besieged, first at Lughmani and then at Charikar, from 3 November to the 13th, when what remained of the Gurkha regiment, starving and waterless, tried to march to Kabul. By that time all discipline had vanished, and many of the men were killed or captured in the hills. The two officers who were received 'by their brethren in arms as men risen from the dead' were Major Eldred Pottinger, who had been political agent in Kohistan, and Lieutenant J. C. Haughton, adjutant of the Gurkha regiment in the Shah's service. Haughton owed his life to Pottinger, who had stayed with him at a time when he was ready to lie down and die rather than move another step with his terrible wounds. The position of British arms in Afghanistan was now becoming brutally clear. Nott was strong at Kandahar, but had a brigade out in the open, making its perilous way to Kabul. There was a regiment of native infantry in Ghazni, and one of the Shah's regiments held Kalat-i-Ghilzai fort. Small detachments dared not move about in the open, and they were doomed if they stayed in remote outposts like Charikar. There was a brigade at Kabul, and another at Jalalabad. The Afghans had chosen the moment of greatest weakness, and now winter was fast approaching.

On 18 November Macnaghten's inclination was that they should try to hold out in cantonments rather than retreat to Jalalabad or take refuge in the Bala Hissar. Shelton was the leading advocate of a march to Jalalabad, and others were uncertain whether to stay where they were, in the hope of getting reinforcements from Kandahar, or to move in with Shah Shuja. The great disadvantage of the latter course was that it could not be done without the sacrifice of a great deal of property which would be needed during the winter siege.[15] Few people knew it in cantonments, but Macnaghten was still in touch with various chiefs in the hope of dividing the confederacy. But he was not making much progress. His one hope lay in reinforcement from Kandahar. Meanwhile it was decided that the garrison ought to take possession of Beymaroo village, which was a source of forage and provisions as well as a nest for snipers. There were two attempts to take the village, on the 22nd and the 23rd, and both failed miserably, mainly because the British neglected to take advantage of the chaos produced among the Afghan defenders of the place by the first shots. Thousands of Afghans streamed out of Kabul towards the Beymaroo hills to help their friends; and, instead of quietly occupying a village in the early hours of 23 November, the British troops found themselves involved in a battle out in the open. They gave a good account of themselves in the end, but their victory was not decisive. They fumbled and made mistakes in conditions which had always favoured them in the past. Vincent Eyre gloomily recorded that 'this day decided the fate of the Kabul force'. Lady Sale watched the battle from the roof of her house, using the chimney as a shield against stray bullets, and she concluded, with all the authority of the General's lady, that the misfortunes of the day were mainly attributable to Shelton's bad generalship. She said he had taken up an unfavourable position in the field after his first fault in neglecting to surprise the village and occupy it, 'which was the ostensible object of the force going out'.

In the circumstances it need not surprise us that on Wednesday 24 November Macnaghten and Elphinstone agreed to avail themselves of the offer of negotiation made to them on behalf of the confederate chiefs. Two days earlier the chiefs had been strengthened by the arrival in Kabul from Bamiyan of Muhammad Akbar Khan, the Dost's second son. The first interview between Macnaghten and a deputation from the chiefs took place on the 25th. The chiefs demanded unconditional surrender, and Macnaghten sent them packing. But there was sleet on the morning of the 26th, and snow, which soon froze, in the afternoon. Where was the dividing line between heroism and folly in such conditions? The chiefs had asked for too much. They judged that a few days would make their offer look more acceptable. By the end of the month it was common knowledge that offers and counter-offers were passing between Macnaghten and various chiefs, and no one thought it advisable to resist when the Afghans burned the one and only bridge across the Kabul river about a quarter of a mile from cantonments. The bridge was destroyed on 5 December; on the 6th the garrison lost one of their tactically important forts in discreditable circumstances. The garrison had lost the will to fight because its commanders made no secret of their lack of faith in eventual victory. Macnaghten twisted and turned in an effort to ward off the evil day of capitulation. In his desperation he accused the troops of cowardice, but he had to admit that with only a few days' provisions in store there was little to be done. Elphinstone argued that the defence of an extensive and ill-selected cantonment would not admit of distant expeditions in search of supplies among hostile people.

So it was that on Saturday 11 December Macnaghten and three of his officers went out to meet the chiefs on the plain south-east of cantonments. Macnaghten took with him a draft treaty, whose preamble accepted that the continuance of the British army in Afghanistan in support of Shah Shuja was displeasing to the great majority of the Afghan nation '. . . and whereas the British government had no other object in sending troops to this country than the integrity, happiness and welfare of the Afghans, and, therefore, it can have no wish to remain when the object is defeated by its presence, the following conditions have been agreed upon . . .'. In short, the British would return to India unmolested; they would send back Dost Muhammad and his family, and Shuja could either stay or return to India with the British. The two sides would exchange hostages to guarantee observance of the treaty, which envisaged perpetual friendship between the two countries in spite of all that had happened. The ever-optimistic Macnaghten even included an article providing for a British Resident at Kabul and an Afghan promise that no alliance would be concluded with any other power without British consent. All the assembled chiefs, Barukzais, Ghilzais, Populzais, Kuzzilbashis and others, accepted these terms and asked that they should be put in writing without delay. The objections raised by Akbar Khan were overruled, and Macnaghten returned with Captains Lawrence and Mackenzie to cantonments, having handed over Captain Trevor as a hostage to prove his sincerity. Then the chiefs proposed that Shuja should remain king, marrying his daughters to leading Afghan noblemen like themselves, and abandoning his distasteful custom of keeping them waiting for hours at his gate and of standing on royal ceremony. This, more than any other fault, made them hate Shah Shuja. But the king refused. The British troops in the Bala Hissar were withdrawn under the not very efficient escort of Muhammad Akbar Khan, and the confederate chiefs—still united, to the astonishment of Macnaghten, after more than a month of insurrection—insisted that the garrison should give up its outlying forts in return for provisions. This was done, much to the disgust of Vincent Eyre, who thought that the move placed the garrison completely at the mercy of the Afghans. The march to Jalalabad should have started, in accordance with the treaty, on or about 15 December, but the departure was delayed from day to day while fresh points were raised. Five inches of snow fell on the 18th. On the following day Macnaghten wrote orders for the evacuation of Kandahar, Ghazni (which was under siege at that moment), and Jalalabad, but at the same time he was secretly in communication with some of the chiefs. He still hoped to divide them and save himself and his Government from the humiliation of surrender. Conscious of the British garrison's weakness, the chiefs kept adding new demands. They wanted more hostages; they wanted guns and ammunition; they demanded that Shelton be handed over to them. Macnaghten temporized, and the chiefs made do with four comparatively junior hostages. All was apparently ready for the departure of the British on 22 December, for they now knew that Maclaren's brigade had returned to Kandahar on encountering the first fall of snow between that place and Ghazni.

On the 21st Macnaghten had written to Mohan Lal, who was his secret agent among the chiefs, that he was ready to stand by his agreement with the confederacy, 'but that if any portion of the Afghans wish our troops to remain in the country, I shall think myself at liberty to break the engagement which I have made to go away, which engagement was made believing it to be in accordance with the wishes of the Afghan nation'.

Akbar Khan now set a trap for Macnaghten. He had always opposed the treaty, and now he wanted to discredit the envoy and increase his own power. He sent proposals through a kinsman, Muhammad Sidiq Khan, who called on the envoy on Wednesday evening, 22 December. Shuja would remain king, with Akbar as his minister, on payment of £300,000, and an income of £40,000 a year for life. Akbar would seize the foremost Ghilzai leader, Aminullah Khan, and hand him over to the British, who would take possession of the Bala Hissar and the fort which commanded the route between that place and cantonments. The British troops would remain at Kabul until the spring, when they would leave Afghanistan as if of their own accord. This, at any rate, is Eyre's

375

version of the story, and he at least was there and heard what happened from Colin Mackenzie, one of Macnaghten's political agents. Macnaghten had already given presents to Akbar Khan, including a carriage and pair and a brace of pistols, and Lady Sale knew enough of what was going on to write in her journal that 'the envoy, in taking the part of M. Akbar Khan, has given him the means of doing much harm...'. On Wednesday evening, after dinner, Macnaghten accepted Akbar's proposals, signed a paper listing the terms, and arranged to attend a meeting with Akbar on the following morning. He asked Elphinstone for two regiments of infantry and two guns, to be ready for secret service, and at 11 a.m. on Thursday he summoned two of his assistants, Captains Lawrence and Mackenzie, to his side. He also called Captain Trevor, who had long since been returned by his captors in Kabul in exchange for other hostages. Mackenzie had already been instructed to buy a handsome Arab horse from one of the officers, and when he had done so, without at first knowing that it was a present for Akbar Khan, he arrived at Macnaghten's office and found the envoy alone. Macnaghten told him about the arrangement with Akbar Khan. 'I immediately warned him that it was a plot against him,' Mackenzie later told Eyre. But Macnaghten replied: 'A plot! let me alone for that, trust me for that.' Mackenzie said he consequently offered no further remonstrance. At about midday the envoy and his assistants mounted their horses and prepared to leave cantonments. Macnaghten noted that the regiments which he had requested were not ready, and uttered a complaint about this new piece of inefficiency. But according to Mackenzie, a note was already on its way to the envoy from Elphinstone, though it arrived too late, refusing to comply because the action proposed was too risky. Macnaghten now told Lawrence and Trevor what he had told Mackenzie, and when one of them remarked that it seemed a dangerous scheme, he brushed the remark aside by saying that if the scheme succeeded it would be worth all risks. In Mackenzie's version the envoy said that a thousand deaths were preferable to the life he had lately led. Mackenzie then remembered the gift horse and went back for it. As he caught up with the other three again he observed that the small cavalry escort had halted on Macnaghten's instructions. He had a strong presentiment of danger, but he went forward and joined the others, who were seated on horse-cloths. Macnaghten then handed

over the horse, for which Akbar thanked him, and when Macnaghten remarked that there were more people present than seemed
advisable at a secret conference, Akbar assured him they were all
in the secret. Suddenly Lawrence found himself disarmed and
gripped firmly by one of the chiefs, who told him to come along
if he valued his life. Mackenzie was surrounded by armed men.
He saw Akbar Khan and Sultan Jan dragging the envoy down the
hillock on which they had been seated, and Lawrence saw the
envoy lying on the ground, 'his head where his heels had been,
and his hands locked in Muhammad Akbar's, consternation and
horror depicted in his countenance'. Both lost sight of Trevor, and
both narrowly escaped death as their captors hurried them away to
the big fort which had been mentioned in the 'agreement'.
Mackenzie remembered Akbar being congratulated by the mob
and shouting at him in derision: 'You'll seize my country, will
you?' Neither Mackenzie nor Lawrence saw Macnaghten and
Trevor die, but it appeared afterwards that Trevor was hacked to
pieces after falling from his rescuer's (or captor's) horse, and that
Akbar Khan struck the first blow at least at Macnaghten. One of
the Afghans in the mob beside the hillock flourished a severed
human hand under the noses of Lawrence and Mackenzie. But
they were well guarded, and that evening they were moved to
Muhammad Akbar's house in the city, minus their watches, rings,
and silk handkerchiefs. Akbar never formally admitted killing
Macnaghten, but he did once claim that the envoy drew a sword
which had been concealed in a sword stick, and that he had been
unable to protect him from the fury of the crowd. But according to
another British officer, Captain James Skinner, Akbar shot Macnaghten with the pistols which had been given to him on the
previous day, and the mob then hacked at the body with their
long knives. The remains were displayed prominently at the entrance to the Kabul bazaar. But what became of the escort? The
troopers had halted at some distance from the place of rendezvous,
and the whole coup was over before they could do anything about
it. Nor were they eager to intervene. The subaltern in command of
the escort went back to the cantonments for help, but none was
forthcoming. Lady Macnaghten did not know whether her husband
was dead or alive. One nameless Hindu jemadar of the escort
alone made any effort, and he was cut to pieces for his pains. On the
following day Akbar asked one of the prisoners how to repair his

new pistols, and when they observed that both barrels had recently been discharged he volunteered the information that he had fired them at a cavalryman who charged at him during the mêlée. Mackenzie described this as a defence made 'without any accusation on our part, betraying the anxiety of a liar to be believed'.

There was a conference of the leading chiefs in the confederacy on the 24th, and new terms were sent across to cantonments. Pottinger was now the senior political agent, and he was in a weak position because he had no answer to the charge that Macnaghten had violated the treaty by plotting. The new clauses in the treaty stipulated that the British should leave behind all but six of their guns, the whole of their treasure, and all the married men and their wives and children. On Christmas Day Pottinger (who had refused to give up married families) wrote to Jalalabad informing Sale's political agent that the Kabul garrison was about to march to join the brigade there. Another letter went to Rawlinson at Kandahar, advising the withdrawal of the Kandahar garrison. But on the 26th the chiefs made new demands, this time for money, and Pottinger argued at the council of war that it was no longer possible to treat with such treacherous people. He said they should either stay where they were or fight their way to Jalalabad, but the other senior officers overruled him. Guns and treasure were handed over, sick and wounded were placed in the care of some of the Kabul chiefs. On New Year's Day, after Pottinger had been compelled to send instructions for the withdrawal of the Jalalabad garrison, the eighteen chiefs in the confederacy sent in the ratified treaty, which clearly promised safe and unmolested passage between Kabul and the frontier. In most respects the treaty was very similar to the one proposed by Macnaghten on 11 December. The names of the signatories, in the spelling adopted by the translators at the time, were as follows: MAHOMED ZEMAUN KHAN, Meer Hajee Khan, Sekundur Khan, Darweesh Khan, Allee Khan, M. Akbar Khan, M. Oosman Khan, Gholam Ahmed Khan, Gholam M. Khan, Khan M. Khan, Abdool Khalik Khan, Ameen Oolah Khan, Meer Aslan Khan, Sumud Khan, M. Nasir Khan, Abdoolah Khan, Ghuffoor Khan, and Meer Alteb Khan. 'This is the treaty...' they said, 'from which articles we will not depart.'[16]

On the morning of Thursday 6 January 1842 some 4,500 troops (and some of their families) and more than 12,000 camp-followers marched out of the cantonments. There were five infantry regiments (H.M. 44th, the 5th, 37th and 54th Regiments of Bengal Native Infantry, and the Shah's former 6th Regiment); a regiment of Bengal Light Cavalry (the 5th); several squadrons of irregular horse (Anderson's and Skinner's); six guns of the Bengal Horse Artillery; three guns of the mountain train; and a group of sappers and miners. The women and children travelled with the main body in the centre of the column. Nawab Jubbar Khan had been detailed to provide the escort promised by the treaty, and at 10 a.m., when the march had already started, he asked Elphinstone to wait for twenty-four hours because his men were not ready. It was too late. As the garrison moved out the plunderers moved in behind them. At 2 a.m. on Friday morning all the men and women of the garrison were in camp at Bygram, about five miles from Kabul. On the horizon they could see the glow of the fire which now consumed their cantonment.

On Friday they marched again, this time towards the Khurd Kabul Pass. By this time most of the men of the Shah's 6th Infantry had absconded, preferring beggary or slavery in Kabul to death on the road to Jalalabad. It was bitterly cold. Throughout the morning they were constantly harassed by Afghan plunderers, more or less organized, but there was still plenty of fight in the remaining infantry regiments. Later in the day Akbar Khan arrived with an escort and said that he had been sent to help them on their way to Jalalabad. He claimed that their sufferings were their own fault, since they had chosen to march before the chiefs were ready. Yet they had marched on the agreed day. Akbar Khan now began to haggle over the treaty. He stipulated that they must not go beyond Tezin until Sale had evacuated Jalalabad. Meanwhile he would find them food and firewood. They spent Friday night close to the entrance to the Khurd Kabul Pass, where the column began to disintegrate and the intense cold took many victims. On Saturday morning the Ghilzais waited for the column at the entrance to the pass, and the men of the 44th Foot dispersed them with a spirited bayonet charge. Akbar Khan now proposed sending emissaries to clear the Ghilzais from the pass, but in return he demanded Pottinger, Lawrence, and Mackenzie as hostages. Elphinstone had no choice but to comply, and the journey through the terrible defile was as bloody as if Akbar had never intervened. Eyre estimates that three thousand men and women, some of them with children, died that day. Lady Sale was wounded in the arm as she

379

galloped through. Her son-in-law, Lieutenant Sturt, died of the wounds he received there. The cold took more victims that night. Akbar was still playing the part of protector, and on Sunday morning he took a number of families, men, women and children, under his wing. He again promised food and fuel, and again provided none. There were many deserters from the regiments of irregular horse. Sunday night's frost killed most of the remaining sepoys, and on Monday morning only the European soldiers were in any condition to fight. The camp-followers had long since broken away from the main body, and were trying to make their own way to safety. They died in hundreds or lingered on for days, immobilized by frostbite. What remained of the main column reached Tezin that afternoon, having refused to throw away weapons and rely on Akbar's protection. By 8 a.m. on the 11th, Tuesday morning, they were still ten miles short of Jagdalak, and less than half way to Jalalabad. Akbar had thrown up his hands and claimed that the Ghilzais were no longer controllable by their own chiefs. He still hovered close to what remained of the Kabul garrison. The 44th Foot, reduced to fewer than 200 men by now, forced a path to Jagdalak on Tuesday under constant fire from Ghilzai marksmen. There they rested while Elphinstone, Shelton and Paymaster Johnson went into Akbar's camp for a conference. Akbar detained them there for the night, and the conference with the Ghilzai chiefs on Wednesday morning was inconclusive; it soon became apparent that Elphinstone and his companions were prisoners or hostages. According to Abbott, however, Elphinstone smuggled out a message to the few officers and men still alive, urging them to make a run for it. This they did after nightfall. Captain Souter of the 44th wound the regimental colours round his waist before leaving Jagdalak, and on Thursday morning, when the survivors could only be numbered in tens, he probably owed his life to that fact. Some say that a bullet struck the colours and failed to penetrate his body; others claim that an Afghan thought the rich fabric of the colours a symbol of his rank, making him worthy of ransom. However that may be, Captain Souter was one of a small group of officers and men who were taken prisoner instead of being slaughtered on 13th January.

Only one man reached Jalalabad on that disastrous day. He was Dr William Brydon, an assistant surgeon in the Company's service, who survived to take a heroic part in the defence of Lucknow in

1857 and to enjoy retirement in Scotland. He arrived at Jalalabad at about noon on the 13th, 'on a wretched pony, wounded, and with his sword broken'.[17] The melancholy scene inspired at least one Victorian painter, and for a long time there was a legend that Dr Brydon was the sole survivor of the Kabul garrison. In fact he was one of a lucky few—the hostages, the families, the sick and wounded who had been left behind by treaty, and the stragglers who either found their way back to Kabul or reached Jalalabad in ones and twos during the last fortnight of January. Dr Brydon was the only European to reach Jalalabad. Those who had been 'rescued' by Akbar Khan migrated from fort to fort in January and finally came to rest in relatively comfortable quarters at a place called Buddeabad, where other captured survivors joined them one by one. On 18 January, the day of their arrival, Lady Sale recorded: 'We number 9 ladies, 20 gentlemen, and 14 children. In the tykhana (cellar) are 17 European soldiers, 2 European women, and 1 child (Mrs Wade, Mrs Burness, and little Stoker).' From time to time in her journal and Eyre's we find that they also shared their quarters with fleas. But they were lucky to be alive, and thanked God for their survival.

The Jalalabad garrison at that time was busy with the repair of its fortifications and the daily round of collecting forage and provisions. They even took to cattle-stealing, bringing in 175 bullocks on the 30th and 734 sheep on 31 January. Though constantly annoyed by snipers and bodies of horsemen they were masters of the country round about, for the time being. But Akbar Khan was planning a campaign against them, and they had hard work ahead. The earthquake of 19 February shook down the new works that had cost them so much effort, and all was to do again, but they were not disheartened. By then they had passed their crisis, having decided at a council of war in the middle of February that they should hold out until relieved by troops from Peshawar. Nott, meanwhile, had not been idle at Kandahar. On 12 January, when the remnant of the Kabul garrison was suffering terribly, he had taken the offensive against Durrani tribesmen on the Arghandab, a river about five miles west of Kandahar. The Durranis now had Shuja's son, Prince Sufter Jang, at their head, for he had defected in December. Nott's victory against the Durranis reminded the Afghans that British troops with a strong and secure base and plenty of comrades in reserve were not lightly to be challenged in the field, and that the successful insurrection at Kabul had depended on shrewd timing, British errors, and treachery at the last.

We have now followed the tragic decline and fall of British power at Kabul from the moment of proud complacency in September to the humiliation of January 1842. It is now necessary to consider the effect of these events, as they unfolded, on the Government in Calcutta, and on those officers and political agents who were in a position to act swiftly on the North-West Frontier.

Captain Henry Lawrence (one of the three Lawrence brothers who had such distinguished careers in India) sent the first news of the Kabul outbreak to George Clerk, the agent at Ambala, on 14 November. Their instinctive reaction was to order regiments forward from Ferozepore to Peshawar, and to call for more troops from Ludhiana.[18] The 64th Bengal Native Infantry crossed the Sutlej on its way to Peshawar on 18 November, followed two days later by the 60th Native Infantry. Fresh regiments had in any case been warned for service in Afghanistan, but there was previously no sense of urgency. Auckland was at first somewhat irritated by Clerk's action, which he heard of on 25 November. He could not see how the march of a brigade could possibly influence events at Kabul, since the regiments could hardly hope to reach that city before April. At that moment he knew only that there had been an outbreak of violence in Kabul, and he was confident that the Kabul garrison could deal with it.[19] Two more regiments crossed the Sutlej on the 26th. At the end of November Auckland received further letters showing the extent of the trouble in eastern Afghanistan. He called for a meeting of his council, but first he wrote to Sir Jasper Nicolls:

...I need not tell you that these communications very greatly distress me and leave room for very formidable and serious speculation...The question with us is, what is to be done?—and I propose to have a special council tomorrow. It seems to me that we are not to think of marching fresh armies for the re-conquest of that which we are likely to lose...

Auckland considered briefly the possibility that the insurrection might not be as serious as it seemed:

It is however I fear more likely that the national spirit has generally roused, and in this case the difficulty will not be one of fighting and gaining victories, but of supplies, of movement, and of carriage. For either supposition the troops in Afghanistan are sufficiently numerous. They would but be encumbered by greater numbers, and even if large reinforcements could be sent from our provinces they could not arrive before the crisis will have passed. If the end is to be disastrous, they would but increase the extent of the disaster. I approve however of the advance of the two regiments which have been sent to Peshawar, and I should like some addition to be made to their strength. At Peshawar they may afford a strong point of support either for retreat or for advance—and whether Brigadier Sale's two regiments fall back upon them, or they advance to Jalalabad, there will be a respectable force for any object...

The clarity of Auckland's thought at such an early stage of the crisis is more striking when one reads his letter-books than it is when one sees Kaye's rather haphazard selection from his letters to the Commander in Chief. This letter of 1 December ended with the thought that the result of the crisis in progress would have to be decided by the forces on the spot. Meanwhile there would be a good reserve at Peshawar and another in Upper Sind. In India itself there would be a good force with a strong disposable body for any new emergency.[20] As he told Anderson in a letter the next day, the season and the difficulty of terrain and transport would make any attempt to reinforce Kabul out of the question. He made the same point for the benefit of Robertson at Agra, and he added that, while he approved of the march of up to six regiments to Peshawar, it would not be prudent to weaken any further the military strength of 'our own provinces'. He wanted at least 12,000 men to be on call in the area bounded by Agra, Delhi, Meerut and Karnal.[21] His council agreed with him that an enterprise of reconquest was beyond the Government's means; that a rescue operation could not be mounted during the winter months; and that 'at present safety to the force at Cabul can only come from the force itself'.[22] Auckland felt depressed beyond measure when on 4 December he received Lady Sale's account of events up to 9 November. He wrote to Macnaghten a letter which was almost certainly delivered too late, if at all. He already foresaw what would be the fate of the Kabul garrison, but he ventured to hope that it might yet save itself:

...And yet, under the most favourable events I would have you share in the feeling which is growing strongly upon me—that the maintenance of the position which we attempted to establish in Afghanistan is no longer to be looked to, and that after our experience of the last few weeks it must appear to be, if not vain, yet upon every consideration of prudence far too hazardous and costly in money and in life for us to continue to wrestle against the universal opinion, national and religious, which has been so suddenly and so strongly brought in array against us. And it will be for you and for this government to consider in what manner all that belongs to India may be most immediately and most honourably withdrawn from that country.[23]

On military matters he wrote with firmness and efficiency to Nicolls, and it was certainly not his fault if Brigadier Wild eventually had to rely on the Sikhs at Peshawar to supply him with field guns. Auckland supposed, however, and Nicolls does not seem to have contradicted him, that one brigade with artillery would be sufficient to force the Khyber Pass. He discouraged, but did not forbid the sending of the second brigade, for he was always conscious of his responsibility to defend India itself against those who might hope to exploit momentary British weakness. He told Nicolls that there were three possible results of the crisis in Afghanistan: all might be lost at Kabul, and then it would be necessary to withdraw 'troops from other quarters'; secondly, the former positions might be almost entirely regained, and then the government would have to consider future policy very carefully; and, thirdly, the position might be held with great difficulty, requiring a strong effort from Kandahar and Ferozepore for relief.[24] 'Even in the worst case the language held should be one of confidence, though perhaps of uncertainty of determination.' In short, he fully expected his successor (whom he soon knew to be Ellenborough) to plan a withdrawal, and he did not want to commit him too firmly to any particular course of action. Colvin had to write to George Clerk on Sikh affairs, and gently reminded him that it was not the Government's intention, 'at every sacrifice of blood and treasure, to reassume its position across the Indus—in fact to reconquer Afghanistan and permanently to hold it, though against the deep-rooted feeling of its people, by sheer force...'.[25] We must remember that all was still uncertain. There could as yet be no talk of retribution, for the Kabul garrison was still in one piece as far as people knew in Calcutta. It was Auckland's job to look ahead, and he did not like what he saw. He shrewdly hit upon the Kabul garrison's real weakness on 15 December, when he told a correspondent in Bombay that the 'difficulty in Afghanistan is not in beating the enemy, but in moving and feeding the troops'.[26]

On the 18th, he heard, though he was little comforted by the news, that the Persians had at last signed the Commercial Treaty, and that McNeill now expected him to evacuate Kharg. He fully expected the Persians to make trouble again over Herat as soon as they saw an opportunity.[27] On the 22nd he sent the first connected narrative of Afghan events to the Secret Committee, envisaging an early withdrawal from the whole of Afghanistan. In a private letter to Ellenborough on the same day he wrote of the humiliation that such a withdrawal would bring:

> ...It had throughout been my hope that security to Herat and Afghanistan against aggression might have been established at Teheran, and that a transfer of our interference in Afghanistan to national institutions and authority might presently have taken place. But this hope can scarcely now be sustained, and it may be thought better to bear the taunt of abandonment than to persevere in what promises to be a fearful and, financially at least, a ruinous struggle. I would however in any case strongly maintain our positions at Shikarpore and at Curachee, and I shall be glad to see our new alliance with Belochistan cordially and permanently established. If our position at Cabool should be held good, other questions of military movement and of policy may arise and the time is not yet come for any absolute resolution—nor can we yet attempt to foresee the difficulties or advantages which would attend any course that may be now laid down, but I am compelled at present to the belief that the end which should be aimed at ought not to be other than that which I have, under other and more adverse contingencies, contemplated...I have been much and deeply affected by what has passed, more so than I can well describe, but I hope that I have looked at all coming difficulties with firmness, and I have omitted no exertion to meet them...[28]

Auckland re-addressed that letter to Lord Fitzgerald before it left India, having just heard that Ellenborough was on his way. For a more personal, more direct statement of the trend of official opinion in Calcutta at that moment we should turn to John Colvin's letter to his father, an extract from which prefaces this chapter. In short, 'our great experiment of consolidating Afghanistan is a failure...'.[29] In view of what happened in 1842, it is also worth noting that Auckland wrote to his colleagues that Ellenborough was the best choice that the new government in London could have made, and that he and Ellenborough had been 'old and intimate friends'.[30]

At the end of December Brigadier Wild arrived at Peshawar

with his four regiments and with gunners who had been expecting to take over the guns of Abbott's battery in the normal course of events. Nicolls cheerfully advised Wild to borrow some guns from the Sikhs at Peshawar, which he did. Unfortunately they were not in as good condition as they should have been. Wild wanted to wait for the second brigade (which crossed the Sutlej under Brigadier McGaskill on 4 January), but the messages from Sale in Jalalabad were most pressing. He determined to take a risk, which might have been justified if he had advanced with his whole force to break into the Khyber Pass. But instead, acting without careful planning and impeded by unhelpful Sikhs, he split his brigade in two and sent half of it to the rescue of the fort at Ali Masjid, just inside the pass, which was beleaguered by the Afridis. His subsequent operations failed miserably because of the initial error. The Sikh auxiliaries mutinied, the sepoys wavered under the fire of the Khyber tribes-men, and the Sikh guns broke down one by one. By the end of January the entire brigade was licking its wounds at Jamrud, where it would have done better to await McGaskill in the first place.[31]

As January advanced Auckland became more and more uneasy about the conduct of his military commanders at Kabul. All the accounts from that place up to 23 November made him feel that they were lacking in 'spirit, prudence and address'.[32] It was all very disheartening. He heard on 5 January of the failure of the garrison to secure provisions and supplies. He told Nicolls that he was

prepared for everything but for such misdirection, and misconduct of our troops. I can make no further suggestions to you until I know more; but you may shortly have to consider what instructions should be issued to General Sale, and as to whether it may not be better that he should fight down, than that Brigadier Wild or General Pollock should fight up, the pass, but this must greatly depend upon the manner in which matters may end at Cabool...[33]

The Governor General learned on 20 January of the murder of Sir William Macnaghten and the preparations for the retreat to Jalalabad. His immediate reaction was to authorize Nicolls to send forward another brigade and 'to be prepared to march onwards if necessary'.[34] George Clerk had by this time met Sir Jasper Nicolls near Karnal, and had made it clear that he favoured a big effort to regain Kabul as a matter of honour and dignity. Nicolls reminded him of Auckland's views, as expressed before the full extent of the disaster was known, and left Clerk in no doubt that he agreed with the Governor General.[35] It so happened that while Clerk and Nicolls were discussing future action Auckland was writing to the chairman of the Court of Directors:

...The general impulse here is to active exertion, to retribution, and to measures which may retrieve our honour and military character. I feel myself obliged to look at things more calmly, and I would yet act upon the instructions which we gave on Dec. 3rd and decide immediately upon no other policy than that of advancing only for objects of rescue...[36]

On the same day he assured the president of the Board of Control that he would not rashly encourage his officers to run into new dangers. '...my present purpose is that only of gathering strength, and I will rather attempt to stem than immediately to turn the course of events...'[37] This was surely wise policy for a Governor General in the last few weeks of his term of office. It must be for Ellenborough to decide whether to commit large bodies of troops and large sums of money to an operation for revenge and the recovery of military reputation. Auckland could do no more than prepare the military means for any operation that Ellenborough might choose to undertake. This he did with his usual calm and efficiency, so that Ellenborough had only, as it were, to turn the tap when he arrived. On the 28th he started writing a letter-journal to Ellenborough on the main issues of Indian foreign policy, and especially on recent events in Afghanistan. He had just heard with anger as well as sorrow that the Kabul garrison had been preparing to retreat at the turn of the year, and that those in Kabul had ordered the Jalalabad brigade to leave Afghanistan. He strongly approved of Sale's determination to question the order. Then, on 30 January, all his worst fears were confirmed. He heard of the arrival of Brydon at Jalalabad and the carnage in the passes between that place and Kabul. He immediately published a proclamation to the effect that 'the most active measures have been adopted, and will be steadfastly prosecuted, for expediting powerful reinforcements to the Afghan frontier, and for assisting such operations as may be required in that quarter for the maintenance of the honour and interests of the British Government...'. In it he also spoke with loathing of 'a faithless enemy, stained by the foul crime of assassination', and guilty of 'consummate treachery'.[38] The active measures mentioned in the text included the forming of four depots of 2,000 recruits each, to supply deficiencies, and the raising of an additional regiment of irregular cavalry. He had, of course, already authorized the advance of a third brigade towards the frontier. But, as Colvin indicated to Clerk that day, '*For the present*, then, it is not intended to re-enter Afghanistan with a view to re-conquest, retaliation, punishment, or any other name by which a second invasion might be described.'[39] The decision must be Ellenborough's, or so his underlining seemed to say. If Auckland were to have remained, however, it seems unlikely that he would have willingly undertaken a campaign of retribution. He wrote on 3 February that he would rather withdraw the garrison from Jalalabad.[40] Yet we must make allowance for the mood of a man who had just heard of Wild's utter failure at the Khyber Pass, and of the trouble among the Sikhs in the Peshawar area. He began to suspect that Peshawar without willing Sikh co-operation would be a dangerous base of operations.

On 5 February the tide began to turn. Major General George Pollock arrived at Peshawar on that day and began to take matters in hand. He was a patient man, and he proposed to move not a moment before he was ready. Morale was low among the sepoys and many were in hospital. On 8 February H.M. 9th Foot marched in from Karnal, and the news travelled rapidly to Jalalabad, where it persuaded Sale and others who had hesitated that they were right to vote for staying until relieved. In fact, Auckland's fears and anxieties about the Sikhs would have been allayed by later news of the co-operative attitude of Gulab Singh. But his time in India was running out, and his last act was to give careful instructions to Pollock to do nothing more than effect the safe withdrawal of the garrison at Jalalabad and maintain a strong position on the frontier. He informed the Secret Committee of his decision on 19 February, two days before Ellenborough's ship hove in sight of Madras.[41] As Durand describes the moment, the scene leaps to life. We see the passengers leaning on the ship's rails, idly gazing at the town and fort, and we sense the mounting excitement as the crew spells out the tragic message conveyed by the signals on the Madras flagstaff:

...Whatever dreams of a peaceable rule, rendered illustrious by the advancement of the internal prosperity and civilisation of India, Lord

Ellenborough might have entertained and eloquently depicted on leaving England, or indulged during a four months' voyage, were thus at once sternly dissipated by the ominous welcome which awaited him...[42]

The outgoing and incoming Governors General were in very different moods at that moment. Auckland was cast down, and it would hardly be an exaggeration to say that his heart was broken. All his plans had broken down in circumstances of 'horror and disaster of which history has few parallels', he told Hobhouse in one of his last letters from Calcutta:

...I cannot blame myself for not having foreseen these dangers, for I omitted no reasonable precaution, although up to the very date of the insurrection the tone of all those whose observation should have been best, of Macnaghten, Burnes, Genl. Elphinstone, Pottinger, was that of unlimited confidence in the growing improvement of our position at Cabul. They wished me not to take measures for replacing the regiments named for withdrawal, which I refused, and all were found to be ill prepared on the day of trial...

He recalled how the British officers had laboured to improve the administration, and how they had found that such an administration raised every chief against them:

...I still think that if there had been foresight of preparation, or vigour of action in the beginning, much of the evil which has occurred, would have been averted. But there was no limit to the confidence of security ...The leaders were spiritless and the troops became dispirited and bad. The season was severe, provisions were failing, and in the end there seems to have been no thought but that of raising [*sic*] life—and the attempt to do so made in the manner least likely to be honourably successful. The accounts received give the praise to Sir William Macnaghten, and he perished. The details of the suffering and of the loss of life which have since reached me have been appalling, and I not only feel this most acutely, but I also feel the many circumstances of embarrassment and danger with which this empire will be threatened as I leave it. I have been greatly depressed but I have not the less laboured. I am doing our best to repair our military strength. I look upon our affairs in Afghanistan as irretrievable, but I would maintain the best and boldest attitude that is yet allowed to us, and we must yet encounter risks in the endeavour to save what may be saved, from the wreck. For there is yet many a point of deep and painful anxiety in regard to the insulated posts in which detachments of the army are placed, and I fear that we are doomed to hear of more horrors and disaster...[43]

Return to the Indus 1840–1842

Auckland wrote thus to his old colleague, expecting sympathy and understanding. Hobhouse merely found the letter 'dispiriting' and a sign of 'lamentable panic'.[44] But Hobhouse, as we shall see, continued to believe for a time after the Kabul disaster that it was possible to re-establish the British position in Afghanistan as though nothing had happened. Auckland and Ellenborough knew better, but Ellenborough, fresh from his long sea voyage, and insulated from the many difficult problems which then weighed Auckland down, reacted immediately like the men of Calcutta when they heard the news of the murder of Sir William Macnaghten. He wrote to Peel from Madras Roads on 21 February:

...the honour of our arms must be re-established in Afghanistan *before it can be safe* to contemplate as a practical course our withdrawal from that country. Every difficulty should be encountered and overcome for the preservation of India...[45]

Ellenborough's ship anchored at Calcutta on 28 February 1842. Almost immediately, as Auckland had foretold, a new disaster occurred. Ghazni, the city whose name had been made part of British military history and embroidered on the colours of many fine regiments, fell to the merciless Ghilzais.[46]

CHAPTER 16

THE ARMY OF RETRIBUTION

...Whatever course we may hereafter take must rest solely upon
military considerations, and hence, in the first instance, regard to
the safety of the detached bodies of our troops at Jellalabad, at
Ghuznee, at Khelat-i-Ghilzye, and Candahar; to the security of our
troops, now in the field, from all unnecessary risk; and finally to the
re-establishment of our military reputation by the infliction of some
signal and decisive blow upon the Afghans, which may make it
appear to them, to our own subjects and to our allies, that we have
the power of inflicting punishment upon those who commit
atrocities and violate their faith, and that we withdraw ultimately
from Afghanistan, not from any deficiency of means to maintain
our position but because we are satisfied that the king we have set
up has not, as we were erroneously led to imagine, the support of
the nation over which he has been placed...

LORD ELLENBOROUGH to Sir Jasper Nicolls, 15 March 1842

The new Governor General swept into Government House at
Calcutta like a *nouveau riche* owner surveying a crumbling family
mansion before the family had moved out. His brisk and pro-
prietorial orders and his haughty manner with officers and servants
alike assaulted the ears of the Edens like the blows of the wood-
man's axe in the Cherry Orchard. He horrified Emily Eden by
having his cavalry escort exercised in her flower garden. He was
not the man to meet Auckland's mood and lift him out of his
despondency. Though they had been friends they were of very
different temperaments. It is very revealing of Ellenborough's
character that he asked Peel unsuccessfully before leaving London
for the old title of Captain General as well as that of Governor
General. He had always regretted that he could not be a soldier,
and now he had an opportunity to direct the armies of India from
the seat of power. His ship anchored at Calcutta on the last day of
February; on 1 March he wrote an encouraging letter to Major
General George Pollock at Peshawar. 'I rejoice', he wrote, 'that the
first act of my government has been to express approval of the
conduct of a good soldier...'[1] The letter must have been invigorat-
ing, even inspiring, for the troops assembled at Peshawar. The
army had long resented the abuses of the system which gave more
power of decision to junior officers acting as political agents than

391

to field officers and, occasionally, to generals. Auckland had been blamed for the abuses, though the system, if properly applied, was a sensible one. Now the soldiers saw a Governor General who admired, respected, and was prepared to trust them:

> ...Do all you can for the efficiency and comfort of your troops. Keep them as much as possible in mass. Do not without absolute necessity incur the risk of a failure which might dishearten them. When you strike a blow let it be a heavy and decisive one. These are my views and they seem to be yours. Depend upon my constant and zealous support...

Now Auckland had often written letters to his generals with similar advice. In his quiet way he had managed and led the fieriest senior officers in the army in India. One has only to recall his correspondence with Fane and Keane. But Ellenborough adopted a completely different style. He wrote as though he were a Field Marshal addressing his assembled generals from a prancing charger. At its best the style was inspiring; at its worst it was rodomontade. In March 1842 it was just what the army needed.

For nearly a fortnight, while Auckland waited for his ship, the two proconsuls shared Government House and discussed future policy. They agreed that Shuja's failure to win the allegiance of the people of Afghanistan, and the consequent awakening of national and religious feeling against Shuja's British supporters, had destroyed the basis of the policy which led the British into Afghanistan. Three days after Auckland's departure Ellenborough issued instructions to his Commander in Chief, for transmission to other generals, confirming that he intended to withdraw from Afghanistan as soon as he honourably could: '. . .we withdraw ultimately from Afghanistan, not from any deficiency of means to maintain our position but because we are satisfied that the king we have set up has not, as we were erroneously led to imagine, the support of the nation over which he has been placed...'[2]

Ellenborough's first letter to Peel from Calcutta gave a progress report and praised Pollock, Nott and England (then preparing to lead a relief column to Kandahar) as 'prudent and sensible men'. In it Ellenborough stated that he had strengthened the expedition to China.[3] Peel's Government, of course, had inherited two Eastern wars from the Whigs, and Ellenborough hoped to extricate himself from both wars 'with honour' by the end of 1842. He realized that this would not be easy, especially when he heard at the beginning of April that Ghazni had fallen. He told Peel on 5 April that he was leaving Calcutta to be nearer the North-West Frontier and thus speed up communications with the army.[4] He started his journey on the 6th.

The Ghazni detachment, having lost access to its water supply, had surrendered in accordance with a solemn agreement. On 6 March Lieutenant Colonel Palmer and his men evacuated the citadel at Ghazni in the belief that they would be allowed to march unmolested to Peshawar. But they had been tricked. Fighting started again on the 7th and ended in a second surrender on the 10th. Many sepoys were killed. Others were enslaved. The ten surviving officers were held as hostages.[5]

At Jalalabad the siege opened in earnest at the beginning of March. Akbar Khan's army was growing every day, and Shuja, in theory still king, wanted to know when Sale and his men would retire in accordance with the December agreement. Sale advised Shah Shuja to write to General Pollock, 'under whose orders we are now serving'. On the 11th the garrison showed its teeth. Sale sent William Dennie out with about 800 men to inspect the fortifications in front of Akbar's position. They drove the Afghans from the breastwork, raised among the ruined walls of an older city, and returned to the town, pursued by Akbar's horsemen. The guns mounted on the walls of Jalalabad caused many casualties among the pursuers. Dennie was able to report to Sale that, contrary to rumours then current, no attempt had yet been made to undermine his defences. But from noon to sunset on the following day the garrison was under continuous fire. As Augustus Abbott wrote: '...We are now in a state of siege; our works are strong enough to resist any Afghan force, but there is cover within eighty yards of the walls, and the enemy hems us in daily...'

Nevertheless, foraging parties went out under escort on most days, and the escort usually had to fix bayonets before the attackers would leave them in relative peace to cut grass.[6]

Sale, meanwhile, was in frequent communication with Pollock, who was still waiting for additional cavalry in camp at Khoulsir, near Peshawar. The messengers risked death or disfigurement as they passed between the two camps, and so they carried their messages on tiny scraps of paper which were sometimes inserted into quills, or baked in cakes, or, as one young subaltern noted, carried 'in an unusual receptacle behind'.[7] Pollock received

Ellenborough's first letter on 15 March, and word soon spread that the new Governor General was prompt to approve the efforts of his army. At last, on 30 March, the long-awaited cavalry and horse artillery came in, and Pollock gave orders for the first move since 9 February. So it was that the division advanced on the last day of March to a new camp only two miles from the entrance to the Khyber Pass. Every man in the division knew that the object of the march was to relieve Jalalabad, but no one knew for certain what would happen then. James Cumming of the 9th Foot wrote: 'It is thought that, the relief of Sale being accomplished, we shall return immediately to Peshawar—I fervently hope not, but I believe no one knows excepting Pollock himself. . .'[8] There was already a general feeling that honour would not be satisfied unless British power was felt again at Kabul itself.

Major General William Nott continued in command at Kandahar, assisted by Major Henry Rawlinson. There was no formal siege, but the Durrani tribesmen round about had flocked to the standard of Prince Sufter Jang, a disappointed and disaffected son of Shah Shuja. Rawlinson saw this ferment as no mere 'transient disturbance'. He concluded that the British army was engaged in a regular national war, and that the Kandahar garrison would have to struggle throughout the summer against a large tribal army. On 3 March he began to evict about five thousand men, women and children from the city. The eviction took three days, and undoubtedly caused much human suffering. But there were villages close by, and if we should think Rawlinson's decision heartless we might remember that the people of Ghazni let in the besiegers who eventually massacred or enslaved Palmer's sepoys, and that Ghilzais guarding Akbar's European and Indian prisoners at Buddeabad on 3 March led the frostbitten sepoys out into the fields to die. On the 7th William Nott advanced with the bulk of his garrison against the hovering Durranis. There was a brief skirmish on the 9th, but Nott never made contact with the main force, for the Durranis had doubled back to Kandahar and were hoping to crush the depleted garrison before he returned. All day long and far into the night on the 10th the Durranis threw themselves against the Herat gate of Kandahar, but their attempt miscarried. The defences were too strong and the guns were too accurate for them. Nott and his two brigades re-entered the city on the 12th in the knowledge that they had been outmanœuvred by the Durranis and saved from disaster by the coolness and heroism of the few hundred officers and men left behind on the 7th. But they felt strong and confident—confident enough to take the initiative again on Good Friday, 25 March. They chased the Durrani horsemen to the bank of the Arghandab, and were fully prepared for a battle on the following morning, but by that time their enemies had gone.

While Pollock was assembling his force at Khoulsir in February and March a brigade was on its way to Kandahar under Brigadier Richard England. It marched from Dadhar on 7 March towards the Bolan Pass and Quetta, where part of it arrived on the 16th. Brigadier England then made a tragic mistake. He pushed on without waiting for the remainder of his brigade, half expecting that Nott would have sent troops to meet him half-way. He left Quetta with two incomplete infantry regiments and small detachments of cavalry and horse artillery on the 26th. On the 28th he met opposition at Haikalzai, whose heights provided perfect cover for the tribesmen barring his route. After a costly attempt to storm the heights Brigadier England decided to return to Quetta and to try again when he had a complete brigade. His impatience to get on had cost him about a hundred killed and wounded. On 1 April Brigadier England was once more at Quetta. This time he took the precaution of writing to General Nott, who replied with instructions to march his brigade to the southern end of the Khojak Pass, arriving not later than 1 May. By that date a brigade from Kandahar would be waiting for him at the northern end of the pass.[9]

The first news of the Kabul insurrection had reached London early in January. By the end of February the Home Government realized that the Kabul garrison had been in terrible danger at the turn of the year, and public interest and concern were kept alive by the publication of letters and journals from Lady Sale. On Thursday 10 March the president of the Board of Control wrote a hurried note to the Queen about dispatches received 'within this hour' from Bombay. Thus she learned of the murder of Sir William Macnaghten and the surrender of the Kabul Garrison and its subsequent catastrophe.[10] The full extent of the loss sustained was not known at first, and Greville wrote:

...The Duke of Wellington told me at court on Friday that there must have been either the grossest treachery or the most inconceivable imbecility, and very likely a mixture of both, as they often go together.

Auckland, who writes (as is natural) in great despondency, says that the whole thing is unintelligible to him, for, as far as they know, the 5,000 British troops at Cabul were never assailed by above 10,000 or 12,000 Afghans, irregulars armed with matchlocks and spears, while our force was provided with artillery and all the appurtenances of war. According to all our notions and all former experience, a British force could always put to flight or destroy native tribes ten times more numerous. The Duke said that the captivity of the women would produce an effect from one end of Asia to the other, such as Europeans could form no idea of...[11]

Wellington went on saying it, in common with many of his colleagues, for weeks. He was at Stratfield Saye on the last day of March, putting the finishing touches to a dispatch addressed to Lord Ellenborough. It was a rainy day, and instead of riding with his guest, Lord Stanhope, he read out what he had written to Ellenborough.[12] Peel was so impressed by this dispatch that he took a copy to the Queen and asked her to read it, 'that she might see what a resource she had in any difficulty'. He said that for 'comprehensiveness of views, simplicity and clearness of expression, and profound sagacity' it was equal 'to any production of the meridian of his glorious career'.[13]

Wellington started by saying that Britain's moral force and political power and influence appeared to have received a blow

from the effects of which we shall not recover for some time. There is not a Moslem heart from Pekin to Constantinople which will not vibrate when reflecting upon the fact that the European ladies and other females attached to the troops at Cabul were made over to the tender mercies of the Moslem Chief who had with his own hand murdered Sir William Macnaghten, the representative of the British Government at the Court of the Sovereign of Affghanistan. It is impossible that that fact should not produce a moral effect injurious to British Influence and Power throughout the whole extent of Asia, and particularly among the Moslem population of the British Dominions in the Peninsula of India and the Dependencies thereof...

The duke cautiously gave it as his opinion that vigour and energy were lacking in the command of the troops at Kabul, and that it was this defect that caused the deterioration of military qualities in men who had always been more than a match for native armies. Turning to political aspects of the crisis, he said:

...It is impossible for me to form a judgement of what ought to be the political object to be attained in the North West of India after the termination of this campaign. . . It will remain for the British Government in India to determine what course it will take in relation to its engagements in Central Asia. Whether we are to act offensively, and enter the country again, or to carry on our operations with more caution, I earnestly recommend that we should consider maturely our main position in Hindostan, that that should be effectually secured without loss of time. . .

Wellington then foreshadowed the completion of the British defensive system in India and the Anglo-Sikh wars:

. . . It is true that the Seik Govt. is in an unsettled state, and not what it was when governed by Runjeet Singh, at the commencement of the war in Affghanistan. But the weakness of the Government or the absence of all Government in the Punjab, and the possibility of Hostility in that part of the Seik State, would be an additional inducement to the British Government to attend to the Defences of our own excellent Frontier, even if the consequences of the state of confusion in the Government of the Punjab should eventually require the active interference of the British Government in order to settle the Govt. of the country, whose tranquility is so essential to its own protection and safety. . .

His strategy required an army upon the Sutlej, 'supported by the fortresses of Delhi, Agra, and Allahabad, and having the protected Seik states behind it'. Such an army would be safe from frontal attack. Its right would be on the Himalayas, and could not be turned. Its left, protected by a desert, would also be secure. But the Indus river-crossing at Bukkur would need to be secured, and gunboats would have to patrol along the Indus to protect the army's left. (In other words, Ellenborough cannot afford to relinquish that control of Sind which Auckland made an essential part of *his* policy.) Next Wellington warned Ellenborough against the evil of placing too much power in the hands of political residents and agents. He said that the practice was 'a Novelty and an abuse of modern times, arising out of jealousy of the powers of military officers'. He concluded his dispatch with this inspiring challenge:

. . . If you should succeed in these measures, you will save the British nation from the Ruin and Disgrace of the loss of this great Empire; and you will acquire throughout the world the reputation and respect which you deserve. It is impossible to impress upon you too strongly the Notion of the importance of the Restoration of Reputation in the East. Our enemies in France, the United States, and wherever found are now rejoicing in Triumph upon our Disasters and Degradation. You will teach them that their triumph is premature. If anything else should occur to me you shall hear from me.[14]

There was little that the Prime Minister could add to Wellington's dispatch. Nevertheless, Peel wrote to Ellenborough on 6 April, mixing encouragement with an appeal for caution. It would probably be necessary to take decisive measures to retrieve Britain's military credit and to prove to the world that treachery should not go unpunished. 'But we shall lose nothing alternately by acting cautiously and deliberately—by securing ourselves against the risk of even greater disasters in Hindoostan, or of reiterated failure in our attempt to inflict just retribution on the immediate objects of our vengeance...'[15]

II

Caution and deliberation were two of Major General Pollock's many military qualities. He waited while the Sikhs organized their diversion on his left. He waited while the political agent tried to buy an easy passage for his division through the Khyber Pass. But while he waited he planned. He saw the Khyberees, or Afridis as we now more accurately call them, building an enormous sangar across the mouth of the pass. He saw their fires burning on the hills immediately to the right and left of the opening, and he saw their white flag, signifying 'Victory or Death'. He proposed to meet the defenders on their own ground, by crowning the heights on either side of the entrance to the pass. What was the point of battering his division's head against that sangar while Afridis fired their bone-shattering iron balls from jezails sited on the high ground? He would take the high ground and destroy their advantage. Then he would press on to Ali Masjid and Jalalabad. But where would he go then? Let James Cumming, writing his last letter home, answer that question. The date is 4 April, 1842: '...The Candahar army advances on Cabul, succouring Kelat-i-Gilzie and Guznee on its way, and meets the army of the Indus at the former place...'[16]

It is most interesting to note that Pollock's intention was common knowledge in the British camp at the beginning of April, for Pollock did not yet have authority to march further than Jalalabad, and Nott had other worries. But whatever he might do later, Pollock first had to break into the Khyber Pass. At half past three on Tuesday morning, 5 April, without benefit of fifes, bugles or drums, Pollock's division moved towards the pass in three columns. Brigadier Wild, who had bitter experience of war in the Khyber Pass, commanded the centre column's advance guard, but his men had no fighting to do that day. That was the business of the left and right crowning columns, each of which was led by elements of the 9th Foot. Before the Afridis were properly awake the crowning columns were half-way up the heights commanding the entrance to the pass. The startled tribesmen manning the sangar looked up and saw red coats where they had expected to see their comrades. The rest was comparatively easy for Pollock's division. 'Fancy English troops crowning heights, with the thermometer at 100 or 115 degrees, or even more—yet they can and will do it,' said James Cumming on the eve of the assault. He found that he could do it, and make his men follow him, but a ball from a jezail killed him instantaneously as he proved that he could.[17] When the job was done the whole division moved up to Ali Masjid, where it halted on the 6th.

Up at Jalalabad, late on 5 April, spies arrived with a report that Pollock had failed to win an entrance. The report seemed to be confirmed when Akbar's guns fired a salute on the morning of the 6th. In reality he was celebrating the death of Shuja, who had been assassinated just outside Kabul the day before, but the Jalalabad garrison assumed that the salute was in honour of those who had repelled Pollock's division. Some of the officers took the view that their only chance lay in attacking Akbar's army in the open country. After hearing the salute Augustus Abbott, Captain Oldfield, and 'other fiery spirits' went to Major General Sale and urged him to order an attack. Sale refused. Abbott proposed mounting an attack in spite of Sale, but only a few officers agreed, and his mutinous project was abandoned. But after two hours of reflexion Sale sent for Oldfield and withdrew his opposition. He and his staff then heard the 'cheering intelligence' that Pollock had forced the Khyber Pass after all, and all differences were forgotten in the pre-parations for the attack which started a few minutes before five on the morning of 7 April. Three columns of infantry marched out of the Kabul gate of Jalalabad, accompanied by about two hundred cavalrymen and a battery of nine-pounders. Two infantry regiments shared the honours. William Dennie commanded 500 men of his own regiment, the 13th Light Infantry, and Thomas Monteith led his 35th Bengal Native Infantry in a column of the same strength as Dennie's. Henry Havelock commanded the third column, of 350 men, drawn from those two regiments and from the garrison's sappers. Akbar's camp was two and a half miles from the walls, but he had detachments in some old forts along the route. In one of these the Afghans were wide awake. Instead of leaving them behind, for they could do no real harm, Sale ordered Dennie's column and the guns to silence them while the other two columns pressed on. But Akbar's cavalry took advantage of the sudden weakening of the advance, and Monteith and Havelock sent an urgent request to Sale for artillery support. Sale then saw his error and ordered the guns and Dennie's column to resume their advance. But the diversion had ended William Dennie's long military career. He was killed while leading the 13th against the fort in an unnecessary attack ordered by his old comrade, 'fighting Bob' Sale. They buried him at Jalalabad, and marvelled that Sale and Dennie, officers of the same regiment, successful in battle in the open field, should have had such different careers. Sale had the good luck to be noticed and liked; Dennie had bad luck and a bad habit of 'croaking'. But a week before he died he received the recognition which had eluded him in the past. He heard that Queen Victoria had made him one of her aides de camp. On 7 April he died before he could see his regiment's triumph against Muhammad Akbar Khan. Abbott's guns drove away the Afghan cavalry, and the infantry columns forced Akbar's men to abandon their camp. Abbott wrote:

... We took four guns, great numbers of tents and much valuable property, and I cannonaded the retreating column until it was a mile distant. Sale burned the tents, which was a great pity. I purchased for 600 rupees a beautiful MacCabe's gold repeater, found in Akbar's tent, and shall keep it as a memento of 7th of April, 1842...[18]

The four guns were, in fact, part of the lost equipment of the massacred Kabul garrison. The Afghans tried to use them against Sale's men on the 7th. Akbar himself directed their fire at one point. But the effective use of artillery was still a foreign mystery to Afghan warriors, like disciplined ranks and the fixed bayonet, and so the guns were abandoned.

Akbar and his followers, who were now fewer every day, made their way into the hills, taking the British prisoners with them. Akbar impressed the officers among them by making light of his defeat at Jalalabad and praising Sale's troops, so that Eyre credited Akbar with 'the liberality which always marks the really brave...'[19] But Eyre's opinion was not widely accepted in the fresh division which joined Sale at Jalalabad on 16 April. The further Pollock's men advanced and the more they heard and saw of what had happened in January the more intent they became on revenge.

Ellenborough congratulated Pollock on his success at the entrance to the Khyber Pass in a letter written on 19 April.[20] He had only just heard the news, but it did not affect the decisions which he transmitted to the Commander in Chief and to Nott and Pollock on that day. He had to weigh Pollock's success and Sale's cheerful defence of Jalalabad against the disturbing news from Ghazni, Kandahar, and Haikalzai: Palmer and his garrison defeated; Nott outmanœuvred; England checked on his way to relieve Nott. He was fearful of the effect of these reverses on the morale of his sepoys. 'All these things', he wrote in a letter to Henry Hardinge, 'have and must be expected to have a very injurious effect on the minds of the troops.'[21] He therefore ordered Nott to withdraw to Quetta, and thence to Sukkur once circumstances permitted. At the same time he issued orders for the withdrawal of all the troops under Pollock and Sale into positions in which they might have certain and easy communications with India, but authorized a delay if negotiations for the release of the prisoners were at a delicate stage or if military operations (whether for the rescue of the prisoners or the repulse of an Afghan attack) were in progress. He was not at that moment confident that any of his troops could safely inflict a 'signal and decisive blow' upon the Afghans.[22] But on the morning of the 21st he heard of the Jalalabad garrison's success against Muhammad Akbar Khan. It was exactly what he wanted. He immediately wrote to the Prime Minister:

At last we have got a victory, and our military character is re-established. Sir Robert Sale has completely defeated the Afghans under the walls of Jalalabad...

But, delighted as he was, Ellenborough saw no reason for changing his plans:

...I am satisfied that the momentary success of Sale and of Pollock must not lead us to change our view of what ought to be our permanent policy. We must draw back our forces into positions in which they may have certain and easy communications with India... The victory of Jalalabad does not change my opinion...[23]

Ellenborough told the president of the Board of Control (in another private letter written on the 21st) that he had 'gasped for this victory as all around us gasp for the rains'. On the outside of this letter one can still read four lines of Italian verse:

Io la bevo	I drink it,
Io l'anelo	I pant for it,
Come beve la cicala	As the cicada drinks
La ruggiada del cielo	The dew from heaven.

He determined to make the most of the successes in the eastern sector. He had a salute and a *feu de joie* fired at Benares, where he heard the news, and he ordered the commanders of all the principal military stations throughout India to fire a salute in honour of the Jalalabad garrison.[24] And in a proclamation of that date he first used the phrase by which the defenders of Jalalabad have ever since been known—'the illustrious garrison'. But he was always impulsive, and, although he could not be accused of panicking, he was certainly guilty of self-deception. The victory at Jalalabad was not, by itself, sufficient to re-establish his country's military reputation in Asia. He had not yet received Wellington's dispatch of 16 March, which made so much of the need to re-establish that reputation, and he underestimated the strength of public feeling at home about the disgrace and humiliation suffered by the British at Kabul.

Nevertheless, in a letter to Pollock on 28 April, he took cautious account of the possibility that Pollock might advance on Kabul. He recognized that this might happen because of the absence of serious opposition, the divisions among the Afghan chiefs, and Pollock's desire to show the flag again at Kabul. What he said could be interpreted as a grudging authorization for an advance on Kabul. Pollock so interpreted it. But Ellenborough added:

... You will understand that it will in no respect vary the view which the Governor General previously took of the policy now to be pursued... The only safe course is that of withdrawing the army under your command at the earliest practicable period into positions within the Khyber Pass where it may possess easy and certain communications with India ...[25]

It so happened that Pollock received this letter at about the same time as he received the orders to withdraw from Afghanistan.

Ellenborough had instructed Nicolls to issue them on the 19th, when he was in Benares and Nicolls was in Simla. Nicolls did not send the orders immediately, probably because he expected Ellenborough to amend them on hearing of the success at Jalalabad, and they eventually left his headquarters on the 29th. Since these also contained qualifications, Pollock felt safe in remaining at Jalalabad and collecting carriage cattle for a future move, whether forward or backward. In his reply to Ellenborough, dated 13 May, he argued compellingly against an immediate withdrawal. '...I fear that it would have the very worst effect—it would be construed into a defeat, and our character as a powerful nation would be entirely lost in this part of the world.' He reminded Ellenborough that negotiations for the release of the prisoners were still in progress. If he were to retire at that moment 'it would be supposed that a panic had seized us. I therefore think that our remaining in this vicinity (or perhaps a few marches in advance) is essential to uphold the character of the British nation...' Finally he recommended that Major General Nott should remain for a while at Kandahar and eventually advance to Kabul in concert with Pollock's troops.

...Under any circumstances I should not advocate the delay of the troops either at Candahar or on this side beyond the month of November; and in this arrangement advertence must be had to the safety of the Khyber, which I consider the Sikhs would gladly hold if they were allowed to take possession of Jellalabad.[26]

William Nott, for his part, had already signified to the Governor General that he would not be able to 'retire below the passes' before October. A letter accepting this proposition followed hard upon the peremptory orders to retire of the previous month. But he still had no discretionary authority to march his army to Kabul. Brigadier England, this time leading his whole brigade, kept his appointment with the brigade from Kandahar at the Khojak Pass at the end of April. He had imitated Pollock in dealing with the tribesmen opposing him at Haikalzai on 28 April. His men crowned the heights on either side of the objective and scattered the men who had done so much damage in March. The brigade from Kandahar and the brigade from Quetta, having joined forces at the Khojak, entered Kandahar on 10 May.

In letters to former Cabinet colleagues on 17 May the Governor

General again argued his case for treating the victory at Jalalabad as his 'signal and decisive blow' and withdrawing all his troops to India. To Hardinge he said:

I hope the government have come to the same conclusion to which I have, that the garrison of Jallalabad having been relieved with credit to our arms there is no sufficient reason for maintaining 30,000 men beyond the Indus, and 24,000 of those men in perpetual danger where they can have no secure communications with India. I say nothing of the expense, but this year it will be enormous...[27]

The same message went to Peel, Wellington, and Fitzgerald, that there was no object in keeping troops beyond the Khyber and Khojak passes. He told them also that the troops would be needed in India, where some of the native states were in ferment. To Wellington he played a variation on the theme that all political agents were villains. '...I must tell you that in not ordering the army to Ghuznee and Cabul without the means of movement or supply, and in giving up the irrational schemes of extending our dominions to the westward I stand alone and have to withstand against the whole monstrous body of political agents. I have acted altogether in all that I have done upon my own judgement...'[28] But in reality it was the army and not the 'monstrous body of political agents' that wanted to advance to Ghazni and Kabul before returning to India. It was certainly true, on the other hand, that Ellenborough acted, in everything he did, upon his own judgement. He resented all criticism, and treated advice as criticism. His arrogance offended Whig and Tory alike in Calcutta, and many an angry letter spread the story of his rudeness in London society. Yet he is not altogether to be blamed. He found the heat intolerable, and said as much to Peel. He was working a sixteen-hour day and was personally responsible to the Home Government for the conduct of two Eastern wars. And Auckland's tolerance of human failings (as long as they co-existed with notable energy and talent) had permitted certain petty abuses which angered Ellenborough. For instance, he suspended a civil servant who dared to publish his opinion that the Kabul garrison was guilty of cowardice in the face of the enemy.[29] Auckland had allowed the Indian press a degree of freedom which verged on licence in time of war, and too many officers and officials under his regime had used that freedom without being punished for their indiscretion.

At the end of May, though short of transport, both Pollock and

Nott were waiting for some hint from Ellenborough that a march to Kabul was in order. Pollock was still negotiating with Akbar for the release of prisoners, and Akbar was involved in a complicated political struggle at Kabul between the rival contenders for the vacant throne. The beleaguered garrison of Kalat-i-Ghilzai, on the road from Kandahar to Ghazni, beat off a concerted Ghilzai attack on 21 May, though outnumbered two to one. Nott, meanwhile, had sent an expedition to bring off the garrison. The expedition, consisting of a brigade under Colonel Wymer, had nothing to do but help the defenders to raze the fortress and return to Kandahar with them. In Wymer's absence Nott had one final battle with the Durranis on 29 May near Kandahar. He reckoned that his 1,500 men faced an army of 8,000 with 2,000 in reserve, and he was understandably jubilant when the Durranis broke and ran:

...How I should like to go to Caubul! It is wonderful that the people in Hindostan should be so panic-struck; and they seem to believe that our Sepoys cannot stand the Afghans. Now, I am quite sure, and should like to try it tomorrow, that 5,000 Bengal Sepoys would lick 25,000 Afghans.[30]

But Ellenborough was still set on bringing the troops back to India, even if their actual departure had to be postponed. He told Peel:

We shall be unable now to bring back the two armies until the cool season, and they want carriage to a vast extent, to enable them to move at all. The cost will be enormous, but I do trust that by means of this cost and of these measures we shall be in a state of security by January...I really believe that the late events in upper Afghanistan and the manner in which the conduct of the troops has been spoken of and rewarded have altogether re-established the spirit of the army. The feeling of humiliation is gone, and they know that good conduct will be appreciated. There is however really no officer who can execute orders and no civilian who will. I speak of the political people. They are deeply poisoned by vain ambition and they do not act fairly with the governor general. Two I have put out—more must probably go. They will soon learn that there is a government. Major Generals Nott and Pollock have not a grain of military talent. The latter has fallen into the hands of two or three young political assistants and has not acted lately upon his own view of what is right. He would otherwise have been before now on the left bank of the Indus, and safe...[31]

We now see how Ellenborough hoped to conceal the fact that Pollock and Nott had evaded compliance with his orders to retire to the Indus. The generals were inefficient and one was ruled by political agents. Only the Governor General was blameless. But Ellenborough was wrong in supposing that the Home Government sided with him against the generals who wanted to march to Kabul, as we shall see later in this chapter. The letter just quoted was in reply to Peel's of 6 April, and it is reasonable to suppose that Ellenborough had studied Wellington's dispatch of 31 March by then. The dispatch must have been in the back of his mind throughout the month of June as he studied reports from Kandahar and Jalalabad. At the end of the month he heard that Nott had not only been reinforced but had routed the Durranis near Kandahar and relieved the garrison of Kalat-i-Ghilzai. Nott had also announced the arrival of a convoy of 3,000 camels. Pollock, meanwhile, was in strength at Jalalabad, and as eager as ever to march to Kabul. Ellenborough judged that conditions were now favourable for the 'signal and decisive blow' which he had recommended on his arrival in India. If his army could have retired immediately after the victory at Jalalabad, he would have been able to say that the blow had been struck and honour satisfied. But, as he told Pollock at the beginning of June, 'the retirement after six months of inaction before a following army of Afghans will have an appearance of a different and less advantageous nature'. It would be for Pollock's consideration whether his large army 'which would beat in open field everything brought against it in Afghanistan, should remain entirely inactive during the period which must now apparently elapse before it can finally retire'.[32] So it came about that on 4 July Lord Ellenborough issued new orders to Pollock and Nott. They were to undertake a combined advance on Kabul if Nott judged his forces and transport sufficient for the task. But the orders to Nott were cautiously worded. The general was given the option of retiring by way of Kabul or by way of Quetta.[33] Kaye called the letter to Nott a masterpiece of Jesuitical cunning, but Ellenborough explained his motives in a long letter to the duke of Wellington, and the duke fully agreed with him, that '...the case is one in which, at this distance, I could not direct an advance, but, at the same time, I should hardly be justified in continuing to prohibit it. It is entirely a question of commissariat.'[34] He used a similar form of words in letters written on the same day to Peel and

Fitzgerald. If ever there was a case for allowing a general the exercise of his own judgement and discretion this was surely it. Ellenborough knew that Pollock and Nott *wanted* to march to Kabul. He was confident that Pollock *could* do so. But he could not be certain that Nott's army was in a fit state to go by that route. He therefore reminded Nott of all the hazards ahead and let him judge for himself whether the march was possible. The author fails to see anything Jesuitical in the instructions. Ellenborough has also been accused of disguising Nott's advance on Kabul as a retirement. But Ellenborough wanted both parts of his army on the Sutlej—that is, at Ferozepore. A glance at the map will show that there is little to choose between the two routes in point of distance if Ferozepore was the goal. We must also remember that Nott's division consisted largely of Bengal sepoys, returning to the Bengal Presidency, not to Bombay.

Nott accepted his responsibility gladly, and after weighing all the advantages and hazards he decided upon marching with most of his men to Kabul and thence to the plains. Long before he received this information Ellenborough took it for granted that Nott would go to Kabul. He told Pollock on 23 July:

...The object of the combined march of your army and Major General Nott's upon Cabul will be to exhibit our strength where we suffered defeat, to inflict just, but not vindictive retribution upon the Affghans, and to recover the guns and colours as well as the prisoners lost by our army...You will as long as the season permits you to remain with perfect security rely upon your own force and upon that alone for the effecting of your objects and exert that force vigorously—giving every proof of British power which is not inconsistent with the usages of war and the dictates of British humanity. But you will never forget that after so exhibiting that power you are, without allowing yourself to be diverted therefrom by any object, to obey the positive orders of your government to withdraw your army from Affghanistan...[35]

He followed up these instructions a week later with a letter warning Pollock not to become involved in king-making:

...We desire only that the Afghans shall have a government capable of maintaining and willing to maintain the relations of peace and friendship with its neighbours, and such a government, when satisfied that it has the character of permanence, we shall be forward to recognise. We desire to see firmly established in Affghanistan a friendly and an independent government. It was because the government of India thought it had reason to believe that the government of Cabool was forming connections which were inconsistent with its independence and evinced hostility to the British power that an army was directed to march upon the Indus and a sovereign, having hereditary claims and supposed to be not only friendly towards us but popular with his former subjects, was supported in his endeavour to repossess the throne. That sovereign is no more. Any engagements, whatever they may have been, have died with him, and we are now at liberty to concur in the establishment of the independence of Affghanistan under whatever government or person the Afghans may prefer...[36]

That was as near as Ellenborough ever came to admitting that the previous Government was justified in its measures in Afghanistan. It is a pity that he never brought himself to say it publicly. But party feeling was too strong in him.

III

We last heard of the prisoners at the beginning of April, when Muhammad Akbar Khan had them moved to a new fort in the hills between Jalalabad and Kabul. They had often had to rough it, but their condition was very different from the luridly imagined nightmare of popular belief in England. On several occasions Akbar Khan protected them from less merciful Afghans, and his interest in their welfare seemed to transcend what was expedient to him as the 'owner' of a valuable bargaining counter. But he sometimes overestimated their capacity to endure a harsh climate, hard riding, and unhygienic quarters. Major General Elphinstone was already sick when they moved from Buddeabad, and the journey to Tezin through soaking rain brought him close to death. The prisoners arrived at Tezin on the 19th, and on the following day Mrs Waller, wife of a subaltern of horse artillery, gave birth to a daughter (the fourth child to be born since the prisoners were taken). The proud parents, truly English in adversity, named the girl Tezeena. After only two days most of the prisoners were moved again at short notice, and the upheaval proved too much for Elphinstone. He died in the evening of 23 April, much lamented by many of his fellow prisoners and especially by the private soldiers, one of whom dressed up as an Afghan to escort the General's coffin to Jalalabad. Akbar offered to send the body there for burial, and after a false start, during which Ghilzais desecrated the coffin and wounded Private Miller, he made sure that the remains reached Jalalabad as promised. There the General was buried with military honours. It would perhaps be uncharitable to link Akbar's humanity on this occasion with the fact that he was just opening negotiations with Pollock, but the two events were very close together, and Akbar was in a weak position politically. Aminullah Khan, lord of the Logar Valley just to the south of Kabul, had transferred his unstable affections from Akbar's family to Shuja's once again. Kabul politics were such that no one was much surprised by this defection. Aminullah, after all, had once been Shuja's loyal supporter, until he turned against Shuja and instigated the Kabul insurrection.[37] Now, in April 1842, he suddenly gave his support to Prince Fath Jang, one of Shuja's sons. Fath Jang took possession of the Bala Hissar and demanded that all the European prisoners should be handed over to him. Civil war was imminent, and many of the more peaceable citizens left Kabul for the country. Meanwhile Captain Mackenzie, one of the political agents among the prisoners, arrived in Jalalabad on 25 April with Akbar's offer of terms. He returned at the end of the month with a letter from Major General Pollock, who was prepared to pay a ransom of two lakhs of rupees (about £20,000) for the prisoners. It so happened that Ellenborough had written to Pollock only a day or two earlier saying that he would exchange but not ransom prisoners.[38] Therefore Pollock's offer was repudiated before it was sent, in effect. Pollock sent word to Ellenborough of the negotiations the moment Mackenzie left. Mackenzie reported to Akbar Khan, rested, and set off once again with new proposals from his trusting jailer. Akbar wanted an amnesty for himself and some of his associates, assuming that the British intended to re-establish themselves in Afghanistan. If they only intended to take revenge and then leave the country he wanted the government of Kabul and their recognition. He also asked for two lakhs a year and a lump sum of eight lakhs to start with. The authority for this version of Akbar's terms is Sir John Kaye, and his account of the matter is circumstantial, documented, and convincing,[39] but it is only fair to add that Lady Sale reported that Akbar Khan wanted friendship and not money. One can only suppose that Akbar was too proud to tell his prisoners that he was trying to sell his support to the British. By now Kabul was the scene of daily fighting between the factions, and Aminullah Khan, having tried and failed to get hold of the group of prisoners who had always been in Kabul, had taken refuge in the Bala Hissar.

409

Akbar Khan and his supporters now undertook a regular siege of the great fortress, while Fath Jang wrote anxious letters to Jalalabad to urge the British on. Soon Akbar's faction had the upper hand, and Fath Jang was just about to recognize Akbar as vizier and Aminullah as deputy vizier when Nawab Zaman Khan intervened. He said that *he* was the chief of the Barukzai party, and that Akbar had no right to treat with Fath Jang without his authority. The negotiations broke down.

On 15 May Ellenborough rebuked Major General Pollock, first for giving the slightest encouragement to Fath Jang in his hopes of British recognition, and secondly for even considering the possibility of treating with Akbar Khan—'the acknowledged murderer of the late Sir William Macnaghten' and the man who 'deceived and betrayed a British army into a position in which it was destroyed'.[40]

But Pollock was still refusing Akbar's terms, and Mackenzie reported to Akbar in the middle of May. At that moment Ellenborough received an account of the opening of the negotiations and confirmed that he would only consent to an exchange of prisoners.[41] They, meanwhile, were living very comfortably (by comparison with previous experience) in a house about three miles from Kabul. The politics of that city were daily becoming more complicated. Akbar Khan defeated Fath Jang in June after springing a mine under one of the Bala Hissar's towers and bombarding the fortress with heavy ordnance. But Fath Jang was not Akbar's only rival, and there followed an uneasy truce. Each of the faction leaders occupied a tower in the Bala Hissar—Fath Jang for the Durranis, Akbar and Zaman for the opposing factions of the Barukzais, Muhammad Shah Khan (Akbar's ally) for the Ghilzais, and Khan Shereen Khan for the Kuzzilbashis, or Persian colony in Kabul. The quarrel between the rival Barukzai leaders was acute, and on 21 June the prisoners learned that Akbar had outwitted Zaman with a *coup de main* whose success rested on bribery and betrayal. The Kuzzilbashis reluctantly submitted to Akbar's supremacy, and Akbar reverted to an older tradition and proclaimed himself vizier under Fath Jang as king. He gained control of the original Kabul prisoners—those who remained as hostages and invalids in January—and removed them to the Bala Hissar. His own group of prisoners remained in their house outside the city. Mackenzie was now seriously ill, and Akbar sent Captain Troup as his envoy to

Pollock at Jalalabad. Troup started his journey on 10 July, but he was back again on the 27th with no definite reply from Pollock. According to Eyre the negotiation was just about to yield a result—an exchange of prisoners and British withdrawal from Afghanistan—when Pollock received Ellenborough's order to march on Kabul in concert with Nott's army. Akbar was bitterly disappointed, but prepared to send Troup and another officer, George Lawrence, back to Jalalabad to conclude the negotiations without delay. Before they left he heard of Pollock's plan, which Troup had tried to keep secret, to advance on Kabul. He became very angry and threatened to send all the prisoners into slavery in Turkestan, but he still sent Troup and Lawrence to Jalalabad. Pollock, who was busy with his preparations for the advance on Kabul, sent them back with an inconclusive reply, and in any case, though he did not yet know it, instructions were on the way from Ellenborough to try Akbar Khan, if caught, for the murder of Sir William Macnaghten.[42] Akbar heard Pollock's non-committal reply on 9 August. On the 7th Nott had marched out of Kandahar, and on the 9th he was on his way to Kabul with upwards of 6,000 of his best men—the 40th and 41st Regiments of Foot (later parts of the Lancashire and Welch Regiments), five regiments of Bengal Native Infantry, and strong detachments of artillery and cavalry. Pollock started his march from Jalalabad with about 8,000 men on the 20th. As soon as he heard the news from Jalalabad Akbar Khan sent his prisoners under escort towards Bamiyan, and, observing the gradual decline of support for his cause at Kabul, did what he could to gather an army to oppose Pollock. At least the Ghilzais were still with him.

The British forces now in motion saw themselves as an Army of Retribution, and behaved like one. Theirs was a very large and very ugly punitive expedition, and Lady Sale's journal entry for 21 August may serve as a reasonably accurate impression of their mood:

...Once again in power, here, I would place Akbar, Mahommed Shah, and Sultan Jan hors de combat; befriend those who befriended us, and let the Afghans have the Ameer Dost Mahommed back, if they like. He and his family are only an expense to us in India; we can restore them, and make friends with him. Let us first show the Afghans that we can both conquer them and revenge the foul murder of our troops; but do not let us dishonour the British name by sneaking out of the country, like whipped pariah dogs...As to the justice of dethroning the Ameer

Dost Mahommed, and setting up Shah Soojah, I have nothing to say regarding it: nor regarding our policy in attempting to keep possession of a country of uncivilised people, so far from our own; whence all supplies of ammunition, money, etc. must be obtained. Let our Governors General and Commanders in Chief look to that; whilst I knit socks for my grandchildren: but I have been a soldier's wife too long to sit down tamely whilst our honour is tarnished in the sight and opinion of savages...[43]

We must remember that Lady Sale claimed to have heard Akbar Khan describing how he plotted the massacre of the Kabul garrison, and that she was writing not simply for her own amusement but for a circle of readers in England, to whom she had become a popular heroine. It is not too difficult to see that her audience would be largest among Tories. Her strong language was probably mild compared to that of the soldiers, whether British or Indian, for there were too many reminders along the route of what happened to comrades since November 1841.

While waiting at Jalalabad for orders to advance, Pollock had administered a first dose of retribution by sending a brigade into the Shinwari country south of the city. The troops burned forts and villages and felled trees, arguing that the tribesmen could only be made to feel their punishment if they were deprived of irreplaceable amenities. Pollock's men followed the Shinwari precedent on the march to Kabul. Nott, meanwhile, had reached Mukur without firing a shot. Soon after resuming his march from that place on the 28th he saw his cavalry worsted in an encounter with Afghan horsemen. In the afternoon some shots were fired at his column from a fortified village. More shots were fired as a company of the 40th Foot went to investigate, and according to Rawlinson (whose journal Kaye quotes), about a hundred of the village's men were 'butchered'.[44] Augustus Abbott, serving under Pollock, took part in a punitive raid on villages near Gandamak towards the end of August:

...We destroyed all the vineyards, and cut deep rings round trees of two centuries' growth. It is lamentable to see the mischief done, but the example was quite necessary. We treated them well in November, and they attacked our rear the moment we moved from Gundamuck...[45]

The men of Sale's brigade, who had suffered much on their march to Jalalabad in the previous November, had long memories. Back now to the western sector. On 30 August William Nott was in camp at Ghoaine when Shamshuddin, Governor of Ghazni, appeared on the field with about 12,000 men. Nott went out to meet them with half of his force and after 'a short and spirited contest', in which the Afghans fought boldly and gallantly, cheering as they advanced, Nott's men put them to flight. The Afghans left behind their guns, tents and ammunition, and Nott boasted to Ellenborough that given one more hour of daylight he would have destroyed the whole of Shamshuddin's infantry. His casualties were mainly among the cavalry. Nott halted for one day at Ghoaine and then resumed his march. The original dispatch reporting this engagement, written in tiny script on a single sheet of paper not much larger than a bus ticket, can be seen among the Ellenborough Papers at the Public Record Office.[46] By the morning of 5 September Nott was close to Ghazni, from which Shamshuddin had sent his officer prisoners to Kabul in August. Before pitching camp Nott sent troops to clear the Afghans from the heights overlooking the city, and once that was done he had positions prepared for the four 18-pounder siege guns—the four guns which Keane had left behind in Kandahar in 1839. But Shamshuddin and his followers evacuated the city during the night. Nott remembered the fate of the Ghazni garrison earlier in the year and thought of the sepoys sold into slavery or cut down in the snow. He wrote to Ellenborough: '...I directed the city of Ghuznee with its citadel and the whole of its works to be destroyed...'[47]

By 9 September his engineer officer, Major Sanders, had done what was required of him, but according to his report he did not destroy the whole city. He blew up the citadel and breached the walls, setting fire to some houses. They were still in flames when the army resumed its march to Kabul, carrying with it the 'gates of the Temple of Somnath'[48] as required by Lord Ellenborough.

Fath Jang escaped from Kabul at the end of August and arrived unheralded in Pollock's camp at Gandamak on 1 September. In spite of Ellenborough's rebuke Major General Pollock treated the prince as a prince, and had a salute fired in his honour. The prince accompanied the army on its grim march to Kabul—grim because of what the soldiers saw just after leaving Gandamak on the 7th. Abbott's description of the scene can hardly be bettered:

...We left Gundamuck at daylight on the 7th, and at three miles reached a conical hill, where our unfortunate Cabul force made its last hopeless and desperate stand. The hill is literally covered with skeletons, most of them blanched by exposure to the rain and the sun, but many having hair of a colour which enabled us to recognise the remains of our own countrymen. From thence to the Soorkhaub, we saw but few bones, but at the ford of the river there was a considerable heap, and some caves contained the bodies of Hindoostani people recently murdered. The whole road from Soorkhaub to Jugdulluck was similarly marked, and it is useless to attempt any account of the horrible sight. Suffice it to say, we passed skeletons thrown into heaps of eighty and a hundred.[49]

At Jagdalak the Army of Retribution came face to face with four thousand Ghilzais in a strong position on the heights above the pass. When the guns had dislodged the Ghilzais from their sangars the infantry in three columns chased them from ridge to ridge until they fled in confusion. This was no cold-blooded act of vengeance against villagers. Infantrymen accustomed to the life and battles of the plains dashed up steep slopes to fight men who had lived among mountains all their lives. The mountain-dwellers did not stay to fight. But so far Pollock's army had not had to contend with Muhammad Akbar Khan since leaving Jalalabad. Pollock halted at Tezin on 12 September, and Akbar Khan, who by this time had about 16,000 men under his command, decided to oppose him there. On Tuesday 13 September he saw his supporters flee in all directions after being chased, like the Afridis before them and like the Ghilzais at Jagdalak a few days earlier, from ridge to ridge and rock to rock. For a while the Afghans had fought with great courage, but their enemy had mastered their own 'peculiar style of warfare' (as Kaye called it), and nothing could withstand the advance of those vengeful Englishmen and sepoys. Akbar acknowledged defeat and fled into Kohistan. Pollock's army camped within sight of the walls of Kabul two days later, and the British flag flew again from the Bala Hissar on Friday 16 September. A detachment of Kuzzilbashi horsemen rode with Pollock's military secretary, Sir Richmond Shakespear, to rescue the prisoners who had been taken to Bamiyan. They, in fact, had already regained their freedom with the help of money and Kuzzilbashi influence over their jailer. Nevertheless, they were delighted to see their rescuer. Only Brigadier Shelton marred the occasion by rebuking Captain Shakespear for failing to pay his respects to him as senior officer present the moment he arrived. As if it mattered whether Shakespear saluted Shelton or kissed Lady Sale on both cheeks. But Brigadier Shelton never changed.

The Army of Retribution

One can imagine William Nott's disappointment when he camped near Kabul, two days after Pollock had arrived, and saw the British flag already flying from the citadel. He sulked in his tent for a while, but Pollock made all right by calling on him at his camp. Later they disagreed about policy towards the factions at Kabul, but Pollock was clearly in command and Nott had to submit to his decision. One of Pollock's decisions was to send a brigade under McGaskill to punish Aminullah Khan at Istalif, north of Kabul. McGaskill's men attacked Charikar as well as Istalif before returning to Kabul in October. Akbar Khan was still in Kohistan in September, and was still hoping that the British might come to an understanding with him. On the 27th the very last prisoner to be released came into the British camp, escorted by an Afghan who brought a letter from Akbar. This prisoner, Captain Bulstrode Bygrave, paymaster at Kabul in 1841, had lost the toes of one foot as the result of frostbite earlier in the year, and Akbar had taken a fancy to him and treated him kindly. Indeed he took Bygrave with him when he fled into Kohistan after the battle of Tezin Pass. Now Pollock had achieved what he had been sent to achieve. He had recovered all the prisoners and had exhibited British strength where British troops had previously suffered defeat. But had he inflicted just retribution without being vindictive? What is the difference between just retribution and vindictive retribution? Ellenborough's fine-sounding distinction between the two was rather vague, and left Pollock in reality with considerable latitude. On the whole, Pollock was worthy of the trust that Ellenborough placed in him, but his choice of the Kabul bazaar as the scene of the final act of retribution was unfortunate. On 9 October he instructed his chief engineer to destroy the bazaar, laying his charges in such a way that other parts of the city would not suffer. He justified his choice by recalling that the insurgents had displayed Macnaghten's mutilated remains at the entrance to the bazaar in December 1841. Though he sent a strong detachment of troops to guard against excesses the rumour spread that Kabul was to be given up to plunder. On the day of the explosion, 10 October, some men evaded the guards at the main gates and entered the city to loot and pillage at will.

On the 12th, by which time strict military discipline had been restored, Pollock led the combined armies away from Kabul. Fath Jang had abdicated, and another of Shuja's sons, Prince Shapur, was temporarily Emir of Kabul with Pollock's tacit approval. He lasted only as long as it took Akbar Khan to return to Kabul and gather together a few influential supporters. The British army reached Jalalabad without incident, and took care to destroy the fortifications which Sale's garrison had restored to such good effect during the siege. Then the army split into three columns for the journey to Peshawar by way of the Khyber Pass. Pollock's column, in the van, had no trouble, but the Afridis took a heavy toll of stragglers and baggage as the other two columns threaded the pass. The Afridis thus had the last word after all, and instead of a stately procession there was an undignified scramble to be free for ever of the 'good old trap'. But Ellenborough made sure that the Army of Retribution received its full measure of pomp and ceremony, promotion and reward. He was there to welcome it when the army crossed the Sutlej by a bridge of boats during the last fortnight of December and assembled, like an earlier Army of the Indus, at Ferozepore. He even held a review for the benefit of the Sikhs, but whereas the celebrations of December 1838 showed the world the strength of the Anglo-Sikh alliance, those of December 1842 prefigured the Anglo-Sikh wars and the annexation of the Punjab. The Maharajah Sher Singh did not attend the parade.

CHAPTER 17

AFTERMATH AND EPILOGUE

Rejoice, great Mistress of the Sea,
The Affghans and Chinese are whack'd;
All hail, tremendous fall in tea:
Welcome, ye dollars nicely sack'd.
Boil, Britannia—thy kettle boil away;
Sing Roo, Too, tooit-tooit-tooit-tooit-tol di day...

'Boil, Britannia'; or 'Punch's Paean', 3 December 1842

In a dispatch to the Secret Committee at the end of April 1842 Lord Ellenborough confirmed his intention to liquidate the previous Government's arrangements in Afghanistan.[1] Henceforward, he said, the Government of India would be content with the limits which nature appeared to have assigned to its empire. Peel and his colleagues were neither surprised nor disappointed, but they thought it expedient to keep the news to themselves for the time being. Public opinion was not yet prepared for such an admission of failure, and the Whigs would not hesitate to exploit the slightest hint of retreat from the positions won under their regime. Palmerston was unrepentant, and put the whole disaster down to military incompetence. Indeed his wife blamed Lord Fitzroy Somerset and the duke of Wellington for sending Major General Elphinstone to India against the wishes of John Hobhouse. 'It is shocking', she told her brother Frederick, 'to think of such loss of life, all owing to a job, for there is no doubt that they might still be safe in Cabul, had the troops behaved as they ought...'[2] It was a time for recriminations, and the Tories were as eager as the Whigs for the fray. Some, of course, were more eager than others. Benjamin Disraeli was one of the more eager young Tories. On the last day of May he challenged Hobhouse to explain 'why he had adopted such a course with respect to the despatches of a British Minister at a foreign court as to induce that person to say that the proceeding was a piece of trickery and fraud'. He was referring to the publication of a letter from Burnes, condemning in those terms the suppression of dispatches and parts of dispatches written by him when papers were presented to Parliament in February and March 1839. Burnes's letter, published after his death, accompanied a selection of dispatches as originally written. Hobhouse defended himself with the greatest confidence and spirit against Disraeli, and at the end of it all he wrote an account of the exchange in the Commons in his private diary. The diary entry corresponds almost exactly with what was said in the House of Commons, and there is not the slightest trace of embarrassment or bad conscience in what he wrote for his most personal records. Since Kaye has made so much of the charge against Hobhouse it should be salutary to see how Hobhouse defended himself:

...Mr D'Israeli asked me his question as to the alteration and suppression of Burnes's papers, which he said Burnes himself in a private letter now published had stigmatised as a trickery and a fraud. I made a brief reply—that of the 36 letters of Burnes presented by me to Parliament 30 were given as extracts only, and that such omission was usual and could not be called suppression—that there was no desire to conceal Burnes's preference of Dost Muhammad and his Candahar brothers. Indeed letters were given which distinctly showed it—that no alteration had been made except such as was inevitable in order to avoid giving personal offence in questions where such offence might be productive of serious and mischievous results—that as to Burnes's private letter—the man who had published it was no friend to the memory of that lamented officer—as it was a gross violation of public duty and private confidence to make use of official knowledge against the authorities under whom a functionary acts—and I added that although we had exercised a sound discretion as to the selection of the papers, yet it was a matter of perfect indifference to me personally if all that was written and received during the time I was at the Board of Control was published—our successors had all the documents and if they thought the production of them advisable might produce them. The conversation dropt—Palmerston and Russell approved my answer. Peel, Graham and Stanley seemed to me to acquiesce in what I had said about omissions and to hesitate as to alterations. The fact was I would not tell what these alterations are without running the risk of doing what I wanted to avoid—viz—criminating the Emperor of Russia. As I was walking home I saw Mr Baillie, who had given the notice about Burnes's letters. He told me my answer was quite satisfactory...[3]

On 3 June Hobhouse was at Lansdowne House, listening to a concert of English music, when he encountered Lord Fitzgerald, his successor at the Board of Control. Fitzgerald, of course, had had nine months in which to master the business of the India Board and to study the principal dispatches to and from India for the previous five years. He told Hobhouse, who made a note of the fact in his diary that evening, that he thought it his duty as a minister and a gentleman to acquit Hobhouse and his colleagues of having improperly altered—or interpolated—those papers. Fitzgerald reserved his opinions as to Auckland's policy but deprecated all discussion for the time being:

...I told him that he would have to insert a paragraph in the Queen's speech at the opening of the next session—congratulating the parliament on the tranquillisation of Affghanistan—He shook his head and sighed. Ld Minto told me that Ld Fitzgerald had guarded himself more than necessary in respect to Auckland's policy and that his caution amounted to condemnation. Baron Brunnow told me that he was much gratified at the way in which I had answered D'Israeli and had noticed it in his last despatch to his Government. He understood that I had refrained from detailing the nature of the alterations made in Burnes's papers and he spoke in strong language of the complete failure of the present Cabinet to conciliate the French...[4]

Baron Brunnow was the Russian envoy in London. It is strange that Hobhouse had not yet discovered that Peel's Cabinet was planning to pull out of Afghanistan. He might have guessed as much when Fitzgerald shook his head and sighed instead of continuing the conversation. A few days later news arrived from India of the successes at Jalalabad and the Khyber Pass and the failures at Ghazni and Haikalzai. It seems that Peel and his colleagues did not immediately understand that Ellenborough intended to treat the victory over Akbar Khan as the 'signal and decisive blow' of his first orders to Sir Jasper Nicolls. If they did understand what he was doing they gave no inkling of it in public. As far as anyone knew in London the British army was still advancing. Meanwhile recriminations and arguments based on hindsight were common coin. Hobhouse discovered that David Urquhart 'is the man who is putting up D'Israeli against our Persian and Indian policy', and David Urquhart, as we saw in a previous chapter, had a grievance against Palmerston. In anticipation of a further debate on the Afghan expedition Hobhouse began preparing his speech on 18 June. On the day before the debate he had 'some very agreeable talk' with one of the daughters of Lord Cowley after dinner.

She seemed to be sure that he [the duke of Wellington] did not approve of the Affghan expedition, i.e. of the policy of it, and asked me whether, between friends, I did not think it a mistake. I told her my opinion...

This is one proof among many that there is a general impression conformable to that meaning, since our disaster at Caubul—but *only since*...[5]

On Thursday evening, 23 June, H. J. Baillie, seconded by Benjamin Disraeli, moved for papers on the Afghan war. Hobhouse found that the first two speeches were an 'elaborate attack on the Affghan expedition—to which D'Israeli added some personalities against me and concluded with arraigning all Lord Palmerston's foreign policy. They knew little of the real subject in debate...' His reply was a speech lasting from half-past seven to ten o'clock. He nobly defended Auckland against the partisan charges advanced by the first two speakers and he mercilessly reminded the Tories opposite of their praise for the military measures at the time and their failure to raise any objection to the Government's Central Asia policy while they were in opposition. Only Peel had expressed reservations (as to policy but not as to military measures) in February 1840. But he had not condemned the policy.

Sir, we did not claim a share of the praise then, but we will not shrink from partaking the blame now, with the late Governor General. For I repeat, the policy was ours no less than his...Lord Auckland and the Cabinet came, without previous concert, to the same conclusion, that a movement across the Indus was indispensable for the very safety of our Eastern Empire—and what we thought then we think now...

Hobhouse recalled a more recent opportunity for the expression of Tory dissent—the opening of the 1841 session of Parliament. But there was none. The critics waited until after the disaster:

...I confess that a great disaster has occurred, and I need not say how deeply I deplore it—but it is a military defeat—nothing more. It has nothing to do with the policy of the proceeding, unless it can be proved to be the inevitable consequence of our position in Affghanistan, which I am sure it cannot be proved...

He repeated his earlier assertion that the Parliamentary Papers of 1839 afforded a full and fair view of, and a complete justification for, the expedition to the westward of the Indus. He said he brought Russia into the argument reluctantly, but he did so, and he asked:

...What, then, was the natural conclusion of Lord Auckland [in the face of Russian intrigues]? The natural conclusion was, that the time so often foretold was at last approaching, and that the mighty power of the North was now at last menacing our eastern dominions. Sir, we were called upon to act in regard to Russia as we found her at the time...

Then Hobhouse defended himself more fully against the charge of garbling:

Was the Governor General to act uniformly upon all that was told him by one British agent? Was he not to consider others too?...It has been said that all the documents were not laid upon the Table, and that parts had been omitted. That is true: but there has been no garbling of the papers. Various parts were withheld, and very reasonably so; and if I were still the Minister, and those papers were called for, I should do the like again. To have published all that Sir A. Burnes said, would have answered no good purpose. The only object required to be shown was, what was the cause of the war. I do not mean to say that Sir A. Burnes did not maintain opinions different from Lord Auckland; and as I stated the other day, the late Government published three of Sir A. Burnes's letters, in which he gave a decided opinion in preference of Dost Mohamed against the pretensions of any other person. We had no objection, nor did we make any attempt to conceal Sir A. Burnes's opinion. I am, however, happy to say, that the charge of unfairly garbling the documents in our office, merely to make out our own case, has been completely disposed of by the new President of the Board of Control, who, having access to all the papers in question, has, with manliness and candour, which might well be counted upon from him, declared the other day, in the House of Lords, that we are not in any way liable to that imputation...

He went on to recall the arguments of Masson and Wade in favour of Shuja in 1838, and Burnes's own judgement that Shuja had a good chance of success. But he did not need to say much more, for he had already convinced many of those who had stayed to listen to him on the Tory benches. He ended by saying:

...Sir, I sit down impressed with the deep conviction with which I arose to address the House, that Lord Auckland was not only justified in the course he pursued, but that had he pursued any other he would have rendered himself amenable to the censure, and more than to the censure, of the British Parliament and British public.

Hobhouse's diary tells us that he was much applauded by his own party and treated very civilly by his opponents. Peel was subdued in reply, and Hobhouse's diary contains a fair summary of his speech:

...Peel then spoke very quietly. He said I had an excuse for speaking in detail, but that he as responsible minister ought to maintain silence—that the production of the papers might revive discussion as to circumstances no longer in existence—that whatever Russian policy might have been formerly, we were now on the most friendly terms with Russia—that he agreed with me in saying that our disasters were to be repaired, and would be, but would give no opinion as to Lord Auckland's policy. He thought I had understated the financial difficulties. He ended by trying to show that in 1839 he had shown more disapproval of the Affghan war than I had given him credit for...

Palmerston made a rollicking speech in defence of the Melbourne Cabinet's Indian and foreign policies, and taunted the Tories with their silences in 1839 and their wisdom after the event. Peel was visibly irritated by Palmerston's devil-may-care attitude, so different from Hobhouse's sensible and convincing defence, and there were some ironical cheers as Palmerston sailed on with all his gun ports open. But he made one extremely sensible observation, which Sir John Kaye would have done well to notice before maligning the Melbourne Cabinet: that no government ever publishes its agents' dispatches *in extenso*, 'and if they did so, the agents would cease to write despatches worth receiving'. It was left to Lord John Russell to wind up for the Whigs. He likened the Tories to vultures assaulting a fallen and wounded soldier, for they had 'waited to make an attack till a cloud of misfortune had darkened our triumphs in India'. But he was glad to see that the case they had made was 'so utterly weak, and he thought its failure must convince the House of the policy of the proceedings that had been adopted'. Baillie attempted to withdraw his motion, but the Radical Joseph Hume insisted on a division, being by no means convinced that Peel ought to aid and abet the Whigs in concealing evidence from the House of Commons. Eighty-four members voted in the early hours of the Friday morning, and of those only nine supported the motion. The rest followed their leaders and let the matter drop.[6] It is a pity that Kaye did not follow their example. But he was a man with a mission to preach against the unfettered actions of Governors General in India, and he was so stubborn in his belief that Auckland's policy was entirely his own that he ignored convincing evidence then available and persisted in saying that the Home Government was only an accessory after the fact. He persisted in his belief even when he had access to the records of the

Secret Committee. The result is that later writers have reproduced his opinion without question and have ignored the readily available evidence of Hansard for 23 June 1842. If Peel's Cabinet was prepared to absolve Hobhouse of the charge of garbling (and indeed to have its president of the Board of Control say so in the House of Lords) why should Kaye be believed? He was convinced that the Auckland policy was a misguided policy, and that the decision to withhold and shorten dispatches was motivated by a feeling of guilt. The author of the present work submits that Kaye was seriously mistaken, and that Hobhouse's defence was honest and politically sound.

Hobhouse's speech also satisfied the Russian envoy, with whom he had a long conversation on 1 July. They discussed the news just received by way of the telegraph from Marseilles—that Pollock had arrived at Jalalabad and England at Kandahar. Brunnow's manner, Hobhouse wrote in his diary that day, was just as friendly as ever. 'He had no doubt of our speedily recovering Affghanistan.'[7] That must have been the instinctive reaction of many people in London on the 1st of the month. But on the 4th the dispatches themselves reached London. Fitzgerald reported to Queen Victoria:

From the seat of war the intelligence is most satisfactory...Recent events have not, however, changed the views of Lord Ellenborough as to the general policy which he recommends to be pursued. He regards as the best result of that success which has attended the Arms of Your Majesty that it admits of withdrawing, without dishonour, the British force to positions of safety, having certain and uninterrupted communications with the British territory.[8]

Peel wrote encouragingly to Ellenborough on the 6th, but intimated that he would like to see the remaining summer months used to good effect in Afghanistan. He wanted the prisoners released, but above all he wanted the evacuation, when it came, to have 'the *appearance* of a deliberate act, the necessity for which was not imposed by purely military considerations, but which was the consequence of civil and diplomatic arrangements dispensing with any probable necessity for our intervention and permitting our withdrawal from the country'. In truth he was very angry with Ellenborough for ordering the immediate withdrawal of the troops, though he realized that he had no alternative but to approve of a policy already resolved on and in course of execution. 'Advance to

Cabul may be unwise', he wrote to Fitzgerald, 'but I should have been inclined to keep our troops in their present positions, or on the frontier, until some sort of settlement had been made in Afghanistan, and should appear to be the result of our recent successes...'[9] The Cabinet, however, was not united on this. Stanley told Ellenborough that he could not regret the course he had taken,

unless it should have, as I fear it may, an unfavourable effect on the minds of the natives, that the murder of our ambassador and the massacre of the garrison will remain unavenged. Except for retribution we have no object in remaining an hour in Candahar or advancing on Caubul; and from what you say I fear our armies are not in a state to advance, or to encounter another action in Caubul. We shall, I have no doubt, be violently attacked for our retreat; but the real authors of the evil, be it what it may, are those who even counselled the advance. I do trust however that you will have taken effectual steps to secure the restitution of the prisoners, who seem to be in more, rather than less danger, from the unsettled and disorganised state of the Affghan chiefs...[10]

Wellington also wrote to Ellenborough, and his opinion was that the only reason for lingering in Afghanistan was that the presence of British troops might facilitate the release or exchange of the prisoners. He said:

...You will quit Affghanistan with honour if you can bring away the prisoners. But on the other hand there must be limits to the expense and risk of such an operation. The right of your army under General Pollock must not be exposed to the consequences of passing another winter beyond the Khyber, nor the left beyond the Bolan Pass...[11]

Peel was embarrassed, not least because he found himself in disagreement with Wellington, and Wellington was unsparing in his admiration of Ellenborough's measures. We do not have to look far for the reason. Wellington and Ellenborough had agreed that the Government's measures in Afghanistan should be guided entirely by military considerations. The safety of the army and the security of India were not to be risked for doubtful political advantages, and it followed that the great soldier and his pupil were indifferent to the clamour of politicians and the press. But how long would the Government be able to keep it secret that Ellenborough had ordered the British army to withdraw without delay? The Cabinet knew at the beginning of July. By the beginning of August the newspapers were making much of a rumour of withdrawal. Hobhouse noted in his diary that Ellenborough was condemned for this order 'even by the Times and other Conservative papers in the strongest terms. It can hardly be true...' Palmerston faced Peel with the rumour in the House of Commons. '...Peel gave an evasive answer...' and Palmerston taunted him with uncomfortably accurate scraps of Indian gossip about the reaction of the generals to Ellenborough's orders.[12] The debate itself, one of the last of the session, was interesting because it showed Palmerston as an unrepentant believer in the policy of maintaining a permanent British presence in Afghanistan. Peel made some telling points in reply. Palmerston's boasts of the great foreign and commercial successes of the previous administration looked somewhat less convincing by the time Peel had reminded the House of their cost in money and international goodwill.

The session ended on 12 August, and ten days later the Edens arrived and took up residence in their house at Kensington Gore. Peel was about to leave London for the country when he received a note from Auckland, offering to call. Peel postponed his departure and later described the interview that took place on the 24th in a letter to Fitzgerald:

...He was very friendly and cordial. I asked him if I might speak to him on Indian affairs with perfect unreserve. He said I might.

...The most important declaration that Lord Auckland made was in favour of the abandonment of Afghanistan as soon as it could be decently effected.[13]

We must give Peel the credit of knowing what Auckland said at their private interview. But Charles Greville heard a more detailed account of the interview from Sir James Graham, the Home Secretary:

...Auckland said that Peel received him with great civility and cordiality; and Graham told me that Peel had found Auckland by no means disposed to adopt and countenance all Palmerston's views and opinions; that he had been very guarded, and said nothing indicative of any difference of opinion between himself and his political friends, but that he had spoken like an honest man, looking to the true interests of the country under actual circumstances, and not to any mere party purpose. It was the impression of Peel, clearly, that Auckland does not contemplate the reoccupation of that country, unless it be merely for the purpose of recovering our honour and restoring our supremacy...[14]

425

Return to the Indus 1840–1842

There is a striking discrepancy between what Peel told Fitzgerald and what Greville heard from Graham. How frank was Auckland during that interview with the Prime Minister towards the end of August? Whether he *declared* himself in favour of permanent withdrawal or simply left Peel with a strong *impression* that that was his view, it is clear that he arrived home believing that the restoration of Shuja had been a failure. He had had plenty of time to reflect on the long voyage home, and reflexion simply confirmed the view that he had formed in the closing months of his term at Calcutta. But he was enough of a party man to wait and see what line his political friends were taking. In a sad interview with Hobhouse on 26 August he expressed no opinion as to future policy towards Afghanistan. It seems that he was more candid with the Prime Minister than he was with Hobhouse, who wrote a long diary entry on their conversation when he got home that evening.[15] It is unthinkable that Hobhouse would have omitted to mention a declaration of the kind attributed to Auckland by Peel. The solution to this puzzle must be that Auckland wished to remain a member of the Whig inner circle. By the middle of September, indeed, he was saying in Greville's hearing that British authority should be established permanently 'in those countries' once Kabul had been reoccupied.[16] Thus he lent his support to the current Whig campaign against the policy of retreat. He had to choose between publishing his private views and remaining loyal to his political friends, and he chose loyalty. The only other explanation is that Palmerston and Hobhouse convinced him in a fortnight that the views he had held for nine months were misguided, that they cheered him up, in other words. This would be a convenient theory for those who have argued that Auckland was weak and easily influenced by stronger characters. But it does not match the character revealed by our study of the Auckland and Broughton Papers.

At the end of August the press campaign against the policy of retreat was at its height. 'Ellenborough', so Hobhouse confided to his diary, 'seems positively to have ordered the retreat from Afghanistan, and he is most unsparingly and I think justly abused for that dastardly policy.'[17] The indispensable and ubiquitous Greville met Sir Charles Metcalfe at that time and described him in his diary as 'the greatest of Indian authorities'. Metcalfe, it appears, told him that he was always opposed to the Afghan expedition and could never understand how Auckland could have been induced to undertake it. But Metcalfe thought that the British Government had no alternative but to re-establish its authority at Kabul and then make a treaty with a ruler chosen by the Afghans themselves. Greville continued:

...The opposition continually taunt the present Government with having approved of Auckland's policy, when it appeared likely to be successful, and now finding fault with it when unexpected failure and disaster have occurred. Graham, however, told me that his party had all along disapproved of it, that the four greatest authorities on Indian affairs had been opposed to it; viz. the D. of Wellington, Lord Wellesley, Sir Chas. Metcalfe, and Mountstuart Elphinstone; and that he had got up the whole question with the intention of bringing it before the House of Commons, and had only been prevented by the Duke of Wellington, who would not suffer it to be done. The Duke, who, from the moment when any question has assumed a national character, sets aside every party object, said that we had now gone so far, and the country was so completely committed in this measure, that nothing must be done to mar its execution, and that it would produce a very serious and prejudicial effect if a large minority of the House of Commons should pronounce a condemnation of it. Accordingly Graham was obliged to be silent, and the consequence of that silence is to afford the Opposition a fair pretext for saying that their policy met with no opposition and no objections, while success appeared likely to crown it...[18]

Greville somewhat overstated the purity of Tory motives in remaining silent from 1839 to 1841, but we have already seen in a previous chapter that the duke of Wellington advised Peel (at the end of 1839) to postpone consideration of policy in Central Asia, and the picture of the duke in this section of Greville's diary is immediately recognizable. It is as well to remember, however, that Aberdeen influenced *The Times* to support Palmerston's foreign policy during that period.[19] It is always difficult to disentangle party sentiment from national feeling on these occasions, and the explanation of Tory silence put forward by Graham (according to Greville) argues a self-discipline verging on the superhuman and the incredible. Pious followers of this Tory hagiography have uncritically accepted Greville's, or rather Graham's, estimate of Wellington, Wellesley, Metcalfe and Elphinstone as the four greatest authorities on Indian affairs. Were they? Metcalfe was the only one of the four with recent knowledge of Indian affairs based on actual Indian experience, and the Tory Government of 1834–5 showed no disposition to make *him* Governor General. Wellesley and Elphinstone had long since retired from public life. Only Wellington had had recent access to the most secret records of the Board of Control, and he, it appears, had been instrumental in preventing a Tory attack on the Whig Government's Central Asian policy.

While the press was clamouring for the recovery of the prisoners and against the still unconfirmed orders to withdraw from Afghanistan the members of Peel's Cabinet were sadly divided. They heard at the turn of the month that Ellenborough had given Nott discretion to advance on Kabul if he could. The duke of Wellington was full of admiration for his protégé's decision, but others could not afford to be so contemptuous of public opinion. Stanley wrote to Ellenborough on the 5th:

The accounts of your Indian proceedings will leave us, till the next mail, in a state of anxious suspense. I have not yet seen the official papers; but Fitzgerald tells me that you have authorised Nott to advance, *if he can*. The early disclosure of your orders for the retreat was most unfortunate; and I am afraid it will have given a character of vacillation and uncertainty to your counsels, which they do not deserve. Of the ultimate necessity for the abandonment of Affghanistan I have not the least doubt—nor, to do him justice, has your predecessor, whom I have not seen, but who, I hear, has not hesitated frankly to express his opinion to Peel. I confess my great anxiety is about our prisoners, and especially the women. I think anything and everything else may be defended, whatever course be taken; but the abandonment of the prisoners would be a serious stain, and excite a loud, and I am afraid, a well-founded cry against us in the country. We shall look with intense anxiety for the next reports. You have an awful task in hand; God send you well through it...[20]

Stanley made it sound as though not only the safety of the Indian Empire but also the fate of the Peel administration depended upon Ellenborough. Sir Robert Peel, meanwhile, was engaged in an angry correspondence with Fitzgerald over the terms of the official dispatch to be sent to India. Peel said he had promised acquiescence and full support of the Government of Lord Ellenborough, but 'approbation I could not express, seeing that I think his first orders were precipitately given...'. He wanted Fitzgerald to write strongly about the prisoners, whereas the duke of Wellington thought strong words unnecessary. In fact the argument was academic, for the prisoners were released before the September dispatches were half-way to India. But the correspondence shows how Peel and many of his colleagues responded to the force of public opinion. Peel was also angry with Lord Ellenborough because he had taken it upon himself to write directly to the Queen, and because so many reports were reaching London of the Governor General's insolence towards senior officials in India.[21] It was said that he treated the members of his council like so many clerks,[22] and it is certain that he withheld from his own Commander in Chief, Sir Jasper Nicolls, a member of that council, the information that Nott was authorized to march on Kabul.[23] Ellenborough boasted that only two or three people would be privy to the secret, and Nicolls was not one of them.[24] So it is not surprising that Peel disapproved of the form in which Ellenborough's orders went to Nott. 'It places him, in my opinion, in an embarrassing situation, by devolving specially upon him an extent of responsibility which he ought not to bear...'.[25] Henry Hardinge, the Secretary at War, influenced Peel's view of the matter by telling him that Nott was unlikely to accept the challenge. In the author's opinion Peel was wrong to take such a jaundiced view of Ellenborough's instructions to Nott, and Hardinge made an unnecessarily pessimistic judgement of Nott's willingness to accept responsibility. But they were all under strong pressure from public opinion. As Greville wrote:

...The Whig papers are attacking Ellenborough with the greatest asperity and doing all they can to divert public attention from the original expedition and its subsequent disasters, and to fix the general indignation upon him for the policy he is disposed to adopt. It is still, however, very little known to the world what has occurred, and what is meditated, but I cannot doubt from the tenor of the few observations I have heard from both Graham and Fitzgerald, that Government have made up their minds to renounce all idea of permanent conquests and establishment in Afghanistan. The English Public will be satisfied if they get back the prisoners, which is what they think most about, and though they will be dissatisfied and disappointed if some sort of vengeance is not executed upon Akbar Khan, they will on the whole be happy to be extricated from such an embarrassing and expensive scrape...[26]

One of the more effective Whig arguments against Tory policy on this issue was that Ellenborough, during his brief period at the Board of Control in September and October 1841, had expressed

approval of Auckland's forward policy. Ellenborough found it easy
to refute the allegation as made by Palmerston, but it is quite clear
from his correspondence with Auckland at that time that he would
have liked Auckland to remain Governor General, and that he
considered a 'retrograde movement to the Indus' to be dependent
upon the affairs of Afghanistan beginning to assume a settled
appearance.[27] This was what Auckland had always wanted. No
wonder the Whigs were so successful in their propaganda campaign against the Government in August and September 1842. But
the success was to be short-lived, partly because it became known
that Auckland had intended to fall back on Peshawar rather than
recapture Kabul after the massacre. If Ellenborough was wrong to
order a withdrawal, how could Lord Auckland be right? 'Auckland apparently does not admit this,' Greville noted, 'and both
parties are anxious to enlist his opinions and intentions on their
side.'[28] It was becoming much more difficult for Auckland to keep
to himself the secrets of a period when he was serving a Tory
Government. The same scruples that made him place himself at
Peel's disposal on returning to London would cause him to observe
a gentlemanly discretion among former colleagues. His was a
difficult position. He was privy to the secrets of a Government
which he and his friends opposed in Parliament, and men of both
parties were trying to claim him as a supporter on Afghan policy.
In fact his intention at the beginning of the year had not (as we
have seen) been to withdraw in panic, but to rescue the Jalalabad
garrison from danger, and to maintain a force as close to the frontier as possible with safety among the then unsettled Sikhs.
Certainly he believed that the time had come to abandon Britain's
position in Afghanistan, but he did not seek to commit his successor either to precipitate advance or to panicky withdrawal. His
measures were provisional, pending Ellenborough's arrival, and
they were also sensible, for little or nothing could be done while
the passes were under snow. But these considerations were not
clearly understood in London, where many people simply envisaged a stark choice between immediate energetic action and
ignominious retreat in December and January. Eventually Auckland felt compelled to make his position clear to Palmerston, who,
to his credit, accepted that Auckland's measures had been provisional and not simply spineless. He sent the letter to Hobhouse,
who referred to it in his diary on 8 October:

...Indian Mail—good news—advance ordered on Caubul—a letter from Palmerston including one from Auckland which he has written to show what his views and intentions were in regard to Affghanistan after he heard of the disasters at Caubul. It seems clear to me that he was prepared for, if not proposing, a retreat to Peshawar in the first instance, if not a retreat behind the Sutledge—also that he wrote to others e.g. Ld Fitzgerald pretty much in the same dispiriting tones as he used in writing to me, and that Peel will one day quote him to excuse Ellenborough's order to retire from Affghanistan...[29]

The good Indian news that day was that Nott had accepted the task of advancing on Kabul. There was relief in Downing Street, but Peel and Fitzgerald, to name only two, were still critical of Ellenborough for first ordering an immediate withdrawal and then leaving the march on Kabul to Nott's discretion. Only Wellington was prepared to give the Governor General full approval:

...You have stated clearly your objects. You have afforded them [i.e. the generals] ample means, and you have suggested the mode of execution with all the reasons in favour of and against your suggestions, the latter formed upon the knowledge acquired by experience. You could not do more. You might have done less. I concur in all your objects. I think your generals ought to be successful in carrying into execution your views...[30]

The existence of a disagreement on this issue between Peel and Wellington is interesting, but it is insignificant beside the general feeling that Kabul must be re-occupied, however briefly. As Peel wrote to Ellenborough, it would be a 'consolation to millions whose feelings have been wounded by our late disasters and would aid us materially in bringing to a conclusion those relations with Afghanistan in which we have been involved by the presumptuous and reckless folly of others...'.[31] Peel may not have known it, but he and Palmerston were in agreement on one point. Though inclined to be more censorious than others of his party on this issue, Peel had (as we saw earlier) argued in favour of retiring only after making 'civil and diplomatic arrangements dispensing entirely with any probable necessity for our intervention'. He had also mentioned the possibility of a settlement with a new Afghan government. By the beginning of October Palmerston seemed to admit the possibility of withdrawing from the country on similar conditions. At any rate he said in the letter to Hobhouse already quoted, on 5 October, that once at Kabul the British army could not go back 'without having made some secure and permanent arrangement for the political connexion of Affghanistan with British India'. This is not the language of a man who wished to recover the position established under Macnaghten and Shuja, but it does show that Palmerston was as much convinced as ever of the folly of leaving Afghanistan to the Persians and Russians.[32]

In October no one save the duke of Wellington had a good word to say for Ellenborough. His reputation sank even lower when Peel and his colleagues heard that the other members of the Supreme Council in Calcutta had lodged an official complaint with the Secret Committee. They complained that he had kept them in ignorance of his measures, in violation of the Act of Parliament regulating the system of government in India. They did not dispute his authority to act without their approval, but they strongly resented being kept in complete ignorance of what was afoot. Fitzgerald anxiously consulted Peel and Wellington, fearful that the news of this complaint would leak out and cause the Government embarrassment in the House of Commons. '...Will Hobhouse, will the friends of Auckland, or will Palmerston allow such topics to sleep?' The duke of Wellington came to the rescue with sage advice, which Fitzgerald passed on to Ellenborough in a private letter.[33] The storm blew over, but the 'Chairs' registered yet another black mark against Ellenborough's name for future reference.

Palmerston continued to grumble about the Tory Government's conduct of affairs, especially foreign affairs. He felt that Aberdeen was too submissive, and that if the policy of meekness continued Britain would have to look for

some less timid power who may kindly be disposed to take us under its protection.

No doubt for valuable consideration we could prevail upon our dear Friend the Czar to take us under his wing, and his Conditions would probably be acceptable to many, as he would most likely be satisfied with being allowed to relieve us from the sin of selling opium to the Chinese, and from the crime of attempting to defend our Indian Empire by civilizing Affghanistan.[34]

In fact Aberdeen was not doing too badly, though Palmerston the Whig could scarcely be expected to admit it. Aberdeen had sensibly left Palmerston's China policy more or less undisturbed. True, he had instructed Pottinger not to press for *permanent* tenure of an offshore island, but Pottinger deliberately exceeded his instructions on this point and obtained an island colony (Hong Kong), as Palmerston had always wanted.[35] Aberdeen did not complain. The news of the Anglo-Chinese Treaty negotiated by Sir Henry Pottinger arrived in London on 22 November, along with the first news of the successes in Afghanistan. Stanley gravely inquired of Peel whether a *feu de joie* would be in order, and Peel replied that there was never better reason for one.[36] Accordingly Stanley ordered the officers commanding batteries in Hyde Park and at the Tower to fire a salute in honour of 'these glorious successes'. Stanley crowed to Queen Victoria in fair imitation of Viscount Palmerston:

> ...It is difficult to estimate the moral effect which these victories may produce, not on Asia merely, but throughout Europe also. At the same moment your Majesty has brought to a triumphant issue two gigantic operations, one in the centre of Asia, the other in the heart of the hitherto unapproachable Chinese Empire...The Governor General of India is free, without discredit, to enter upon measures of internal improvement, and, having established the supremacy of British power, to carry on henceforth a more pacific policy...[37]

To his colleagues in London, as well as to the earl of Clare, Ellenborough sent copies of the proclamation which he signed on 1 October, in the very room in which Auckland signed his Simla Manifesto on 1 October 1838. The text of Ellenborough's proclamation, in which he publicly repudiated the policy of his predecessor, can be found in an appendix to this book. He knew that the proclamation would make the Whigs angry, but he told Peel that 'the people of England will approve of it, and all military men will say I am right'.[38]

Peel answered Ellenborough's private letter on 3 December. 'Everyone feels', he said, 'that since the battle of Waterloo no tidings have reached this country so important as those which simultaneously announced the termination of hostilities in Central Asia and in China...' He told Ellenborough that his proclamation had indeed provoked much angry comment, and not only in Whig circles. Could a Governor General censure a previous Government, he gently asked, without appearing to censure the Queen in whose name the Government had acted? Nevertheless, Peel added, the policy outlined in the proclamation was wise and based on just reasons.[39] Another who thought the policy in the proclamation wise was the Russian ambassador, Baron Brunnow. On 30 November he sent a copy to Count Nesselrode:

...Cette proclamation manifeste la détermination du Gouverneur Général d'effectuer l'évacuation de l'Afghanistan, de retirer les forces Anglaises sur la rive gauche de l'Indus, en les repliant jusque sur le Sutledge, et de restreindre désormais la domination de la Cie. des Indes dans les limites que la nature paraît avoir assignées à son empire...

This confirmed, Brunnow said, what Peel, Aberdeen, and Ellenborough himself told him at the end of 1841. The proclamation proved the foresight and calm wisdom of the Emperor in restraining the Shah of Persia through the Russian Minister in Teheran at the beginning of 1842, when the Shah gave signs of wishing to exploit a momentary British weakness. Indeed, Brunnow wrote, if the Emperor had not caused Count Medem to join the British envoy in restraining the Shah of Persia, then Lord Ellenborough would not have been able to carry out his policy of withdrawal. Peace was now assured:

Je la crois plus assurée que jamais, du moment où l'Angleterre, replaçant sagement entre elle et nous les déserts qui nous séparent comme une large zone de neutralité, rentre spontanément dans les limites que la nature a assignées a son empire aux Indes.

One has to give the Russian Government of that time full marks for astuteness. Had the Shah of Persia moved on Herat at the beginning of 1842 the British would have stopped him and Tories might well have become converts to the Whig belief that the only way of keeping Herat secure was to maintain Britain's influence and military power in Afghanistan, at whatever cost. But the Russian Minister joined in restraining the Shah, and his Government was able to persuade Aberdeen and Peel that Russia sincerely wanted peace in Central Asia and had no appetite for territorial expansion there. By the end of 1842 the Russian and British ministers in Teheran were working together in complete harmony, a harmony reminiscent of the honeymoon period of 1834. The only difference was that Palmerston was no longer at the Foreign Office to advise the Queen's representatives to 'have their horses always saddled'. At the beginning of January 1843 Baron Brunnow wrote to thank Ellenborough for sending him a copy of the proclamation. He told the Governor General that the British and Russian envoys in Teheran were now engaged in a mediation between Turkey and Persia:

...This Anglo-Russian mediation, giving to all oriental people an evident proof of the good understanding between the two great powers, will produce, I trust, a very useful impression upon the mind of the Asiatic nations at large, who constantly were speculating upon the supposed jealousy of England and Russia. It is particularly with the intention of counteracting and correcting these mistaken views that both our governments have joined in this mediation, which I had the honour of proposing to Lord Aberdeen's acceptance, and which he most kindly agreed upon...[40]

So it was that Britain severed her ties with Afghanistan while Russia, untroubled by the vigilant Palmerston, obtained a subordinate treaty from the Khan of Khiva under the threat of an expedition from Orenburg. And in 1844, the very year in which Emperor Nicholas and Count Nesselrode made private visits to Britain, the Russians established themselves on the banks of the Aral Sea, which receives the waters of the Amu Daria and Syr Daria (Oxus and Jaxartes).

But we have moved far ahead of those who studied the proclamation in London at the beginning of December. The Whig leaders were appalled by the proclamation and resentful at the Tory assumption of all the credit for the successes in China. As usual Palmerston could depend on the *Morning Chronicle* to back him up. That newspaper proclaimed that the Tories had merely inherited the right policy from Viscount Palmerston, and that the success owed nothing to them.[41] Princess Lieven received a very cool answer from Lady Palmerston when she incautiously (or was it deliberately) praised Peel as a 'firm and powerful minister'. Lady Palmerston reminded her that Palmerston laid the foundation for Peel's success in China, and the Princess confessed to making a 'very great blunder...It is obvious from what you say that the credit for your glorious success in China is due entirely to Lord Palmerston...'[42] It is difficult to find a higher and more faithful Tory witness than Charles Greville, and yet he, as well as the Whigs, found Ellenborough's proclamation 'very objectionable in many respects'. He noted that people in general approved of the policy now proclaimed but disapproved of the proclamation's tone and its indirect slur on Auckland and men not alive to defend themselves:

...On the whole Ellenborough has not given satisfaction to any party or set of men. Conservatives complain of him as well as Whigs. He has

435

given personal offence in India and political offence here, and the appointment, from which great things were expected, has turned out ill. The Duke of Wellington, however, is perfectly satisfied with what he has done, and as the Government meant to support him before all his successes, much more will they do so now.[43]

Greville also found a mood of bitterness in the Auckland household, 'and no wonder'. The Edens and Ellenborough had always been friends in spite of party differences, but now they found him publicly condemning Auckland's own measures for the defence of India. They would have been even more disgusted if they had known what Ellenborough was writing to Peel and his colleagues. In order to excuse his unpopularity with the Court of Directors he told Peel that they disliked him because 'I am here to extirpate jobbing, and I succeed the most corrupt of administrations, under which almost every office was given from views of private patronage, and very commonly to promote the connections of Directors'. He said he was unpopular with the press because he refused to divulge secrets, and that the civil service disliked him merely because he showed favour to the army. (In other words, he was the only honest man in Calcutta official circles. He was the only one in step.) 'I have travelled in all seasons with no more comfort than a Cadet...What I want more than anything else is support in Parliament. As to honours for myself I do not value them one rush. I value nothing but Power.'[44] He was enraged when he read the London newspaper attacks in October, and he more than once threatened to resign unless ministers expressed their full confidence in him in Parliament. He so offended Fitzgerald, who was in authority over him, that Fitzgerald offered to resign. Peel told Fitzgerald to stand his ground:

...Inform Lord Ellenborough that he has had every support which it was possible for him to receive, but that you will insist upon your right, and your duty, freely to express your opinion upon every act and every matter of public concern connected with the administration of affairs in India...[45]

Peel had reason to feel angry with Ellenborough in January, for Parliament was about to reassemble, and certain of Ellenborough's measures, or military measures for which he was ultimately responsible, were likely to be attacked in the House of Commons. Ugly stories were circulating in London about the devastation committed by Pollock's army, and many people were laughing at the Governor General for writing such a foolish proclamation about the Gates of Somnath. This was the proclamation in which he had addressed the princes of India: '...The gates of the temple of Somnauth, so long the memorial of your humiliation, are become the proudest record of your national glory, the proof of your superiority in arms over the nations beyond the Indus.' He forgot, or chose to ignore, that many of the princes, as good Muslims, were more likely to resent than to take pride in the recovery of the gates, for Mahmoud of Ghazni was a Muslim conqueror of superstitious Hindus in their eyes. Of course he was right to attempt to awaken Indian national (as opposed to sectarian) feeling, but the attempt was premature.[46]

Peel's main reason for disquiet, however, was still secret. He was uneasy about Ellenborough's intentions in Sind, where Charles James Napier had been given supreme military and political command in August. Henry Hardinge warned his brother-in-law, Lord Ellenborough, that Peel was 'alarmed lest you should have given too much rope to Napier in this Scinde affair...'.[47] This was precisely what Ellenborough had done. Napier had arrived at Karachi on 9 September 1842 with instructions to find out whether the emirs had contravened the existing treaty, and to negotiate in any case for its revision. As Ellenborough wrote to Peel on 18 October: he wanted Karachi and Sukkur and Bukkur ceded to Britain in redemption of the annual sums paid by the emirs for the maintenance of the British subsidiary force. 'I wish to have nothing else on the Indus.' He mentioned the advantages of Sukkur as an emporium, and the usefulness of the Indus as a route not only for the movement of British manufactures into India but also for the speedy transport of troops and equipment. 'This is no more than what I looked forward to twelve years ago.'[48] We can see at a glance that he had been reading Auckland's minutes, and that Auckland's minutes had been framed, on Ellenborough's admission, in accordance with the policy laid down by Ellenborough himself in 1830. One comment needs to be made, however. Ellenborough told Peel that this was no more than he had looked forward to twelve years earlier. But he had looked forward to very much more, and notably the substitution of British for Russian manufactures in the markets of Central Asia. It was not tactful to mention such hopes in 1842.

At the beginning of November Ellenborough received a long memorandum from Napier, accompanying a list of complaints (prepared by Outram) against the emirs.[49] Almost as soon as he completed the list Outram found himself deprived of his post. Ellenborough had dissolved the Sind–Baluchistan Political Department and decreed that the officers serving as agents should return to regimental duties. Napier was now in sole command, both political and military. He told Ellenborough that he could either evacuate Sind, in which case future events would bring the British back to the banks of the Indus, or he could take advantage of the breaches of treaty committed by the emirs to make his occupation of Karachi, Bukkur, Sukkur and Shikarpur permanent. He was emphatic that Shikarpur must remain in British hands as a commercial centre of importance and a central point of communication 'where the British government would learn what was going on in Asia'. This was the substance of Napier's recommendations but it was clear that he would not hesitate to finish once and for all with the Sind emirs when the opportunity presented itself. It is not the purpose of this book to explain in detail how the British in India gained possession of Sind, but, as we have seen from the beginning of our study of the Afghan War, control of the navigation of the Indus for commercial and military purposes was a constant theme of correspondence between the Secret Committee and the Governor General. It should not therefore be surprising that Ellenborough instructed Napier to negotiate for terms very similar to those proposed in the memorandum. He was to take advantage of the emirs' misbehaviour to gain permanent possession of Karachi, Rohri, Sukkur and Bukkur. Shikarpur was not mentioned. The emirs should be asked to grant the right to cut wood along the banks of the Indus (for burning in the boilers of steam vessels), and there should be a uniform currency—with the Queen's head on one side.

...My ultimate object [said Ellenborough] is the entire freedom of internal trade throughout the whole territory between the Hindoo Coosh, the Indus and the sea, and I only await the favourable occasion for effecting this purpose and for introducing uniformity of currency within the same limits...

It would be diverting to find out how Ellenborough proposed to exert his influence for this purpose as far north as the Hindu Kush, having just relinquished a hard-won influence in Afghanistan. But

438

to do so would be to wander too far from the main narrative, which now brings us to the moment when Ellenborough sent the draft treaties to Napier. He did this on 14 November, and in an accompaying letter he looked forward to the construction of one big entrepot embracing Sukkur, Bukkur and Rohri in 'the city of Victoria on the Indus'.[50] As soon as Napier had possession of Sukkur he should build a large serai for merchants, combining the beauty of the East and the fortifications of the West. On the same day he wrote to Stanley, remarking by the way that he was 'quite charmed with Sir C. Napier'. He also wrote to Peel on the 15th:

...The violations of treaty by the Ameers rendered some punishment unavoidable. I considered well what we ought to demand and I do not think I have gone beyond what was expedient and just...They are all the descendants of invaders and the worst of all possible rulers...No one will regret their expulsion from India...[51]

These were the sentiments which caused Peel to feel alarmed at the beginning of February, and which caused Lord Fitzgerald to send a warning against precipitate military action and Hardinge to give his brother-in-law a little friendly advice. But the warnings were too late. On 14 February 1843 fighting started at Hyderabad, where the emirs at last abandoned the pretence of negotiation and decided to try their luck in battle. This was only a skirmish, however. On the 17th Napier defeated the combined forces of Hyderabad, Khairpur and Mirpur at Miani. There was a second battle, and another victory for Napier, at Dubba on 26 March. Napier assumed the title of Governor of Sind in March, but there was one more battle before annexation. Sher Mahomed of Mirpur, defeated at Dubba, tried once more to win his independence at Shahdadpur in June. Napier's commander on this occasion was General Jacob, who defeated Sher Mahomed on 13 June. In August Sind became part of British India.

While the battle of Miani was deciding the fate of the Talpura dynasty, members of Parliament in London were studying a bluebook just laid on the table of the House of Commons. The correspondence published therein on 14 February had a sobering effect upon Ellenborough's critics, so that his brother, Henry Law, was able to report that publication 'immediately produced a very favourable change of opinion. All idea of dividing upon the Vote of Thanks to you was at once abandoned...'[52]

The votes of thanks in the two chambers were accordingly carried without dissent, save for the Radical Joseph Hume's lone protest in the House of Commons. The vote in the House of Commons was so worded, however, that only Hume could readily quarrel with it: 'that the thanks of this House be given to the Right Honourable Lord Ellenborough, governor general of the British possessions in the East Indies, for the ability and judgement with which the resources of the British Empire in India have been applied in the support of the military operations in Affghanistan'. The voting took place on 20 February, and members of Parliament then had only to wait for a week or so for a debate on policy. First of all Roebuck introduced his motion for a committee to inquire into the circumstances which led to the hostilities in Afghanistan. Palmerston had written to Hobhouse, warning him to come home for the debate, but it was not necessary. Roebuck did not make any personal attack on Hobhouse, though he questioned once again the papers tabled in Parliament in 1839. Palmerston and Russell answered Roebuck's criticisms to their own and to their party's satisfaction, but the man who mattered was Peel. He opposed the motion on the grounds that it was impolitic to disturb the currently friendly relations with Russia. Hobhouse, who knew the truth of the matter, thankfully noted in his diary that Peel had behaved well in positively denying that there had been any garbling of the papers presented to Parliament in 1839, and in that thankful mood he questioned the propriety of Vernon Smith's motion against the proclamation on the gates of Somnath. '...It was a party affair, I think, a false move, but the majority was less than usual—84.'[53] Peel also thought it a party affair. At least he told the Queen on the following day that the debate had 'a strong infusion of party zeal'.[54] And Palmerston, who relished the opportunity to counterattack, told Hobhouse that, once the debate on Smith's motion was over, 'that will about finish our Indian discussions unless the next Mail should bring us some fresh Freaks of our most absurd Governor General'.[55] He did not in fact have long to wait, and then he chose to remain silent. On 10 April he told Hobhouse:

...It is rather entertaining to see Ellenborough turned Conqueror so soon after his reflections upon us for having gone beyond the natural limits of the Sutlej; but I should be sorry to check him in his Career of victory by any questions or Criticism in the H. of Cms. When he has got back to Candahar and Cabool, then will be the Time to crow over him.[56]

Well, Ellenborough never did get back to Kandahar and Kabul. He annexed Sind, but the Government at home was too well acquainted with the territory's strategic value to repudiate him. Its members complained and questioned the morality of the trans-action, but in the end they acquiesced, and the Court of Directors of the East India Company impotently objected too late. When Ellenborough completed the annexation of the Gwalior state, they remembered one of their remaining privileges. They were still empowered by law to recall a Governor General who failed to please them, and so they did. Wellington and Peel tried to stop them, but the law was on the side of the Directors, who had borne too many of Ellenborough's insults to relent, and the Governor General who thought himself a Viceroy fifteen years too soon returned to England and an earldom in the autumn of 1844. His brother-in-law, Sir Henry Hardinge, succeeded him in Calcutta, just in time to meet the shock of the first war against the Sikhs. It soon became clear to the world that the natural frontier assigned to the British Empire in India was one that included Sind *and* the Punjab, as James Mill had so quietly forecast in 1832:

I consider that we have nothing between us and the most desirable frontier everywhere, but the territory of Runjeet Singh. If we were threatened on the north west frontier, for example, by an invasion of the Russians, we should, in self defence, be obliged to take possession of the country to the foot of the hills, as we could not leave an intermediate space, in which the enemy might establish themselves...[57]

The thought had also crossed the minds of Bentinck and Auck-land, Wellington and Ellenborough, among others, in the years between Mill's evidence and the annexation of Sind and the Punjab.

The recall of Ellenborough coincided with the visit to England of the Emperor of Russia and Count Nesselrode. Relations between Great Britain and Russia were very close, and there was a merciful lull in their long Central Asian rivalry, but, just as surely as the British approached their natural frontier on the sub-continent, so the Russians moved forward in the territories beyond the Hindu Kush. Dost Muhammad, meanwhile, free since the end of 1842, preserved his independence at Kabul and looked to the eventual unification of his country under one king, as Burnes and McNeill had done in the days of Runjeet Singh. In the end he was even allowed to take Herat.[58] The debate on the morality of Britain's policy before and during the First Afghan War outlived all who had a part in making it. Kaye published serious charges against some of the leading figures in the controversy, yet a majority in the House of Commons could never be found for any motion supporting Kaye's charges. Let Palmerston, the man who, after all, contributed most to the framing of the policy, have the last word. He wrote to Hobhouse (by then Baron Broughton) from his house in Piccadilly on 19 March 1861, when he was 76 and still very active:

My dear Broughton,

We have had a most bitter attack this evening in the House of Commons upon our Afghan War and Papers, but it ended in a triumphant majority against Dunlop, a bitter old Scotch lawyer. It was really too bad to put us on our defence about a Transaction which happened upwards of twenty years ago.

Yours sincerely,

Palmerston[59]

APPENDIXES

THE INDIAN PAPERS

In the table set out below column three shows whether the document summarized in column two was published in the collection of papers presented to Parliament in 1839. Column four shows whether that document was published in the collection made for Parliament by Sir John Kaye in 1859, when he attempted to restore the 'garbled papers' to their original state.

Date	Contents	1839	1859	Remarks
1836				
31 May	Dost Muhammad welcomes Auckland to India and asks for guidance in his quarrel with Runjeet	Yes	No	—
22 Aug.	Auckland's reply: abjures intervention in Sikh-Afghan affairs; preaches Commerce; proposes to send an agent one day	Yes	No	—
5 Sept.	Official instructions to Burnes on his Indus mission; little or no political content	Yes	No	—
1837				
20 Apr.	Dost to Burnes: desires British aid against Sikhs	No	Yes	Shows Dost's rooted hostility to Sikhs
27 Apr.	Tsar to Dost: friendly; non-committal reply to an earlier letter from Dost Muhammad	No	Yes	Implicates the Emperor
15 May	Auckland to Dost: tells him Burnes is coming on commercial business	Yes	No	—
15 May	Official modification of September orders to Burnes: possibility of using good offices between Sikhs and Afghans; keep an eye on Russian and Persian activities in Central Asia	No	Yes	Shows Dost in a *bad* light. Implicates Russia. Otherwise a questionable omission

445

Date	Contents	1839	1859	Remarks
31 July	Burnes receives letters from Dost and Mirza Sami Khan. Persian envoy at Kandahar and coming to Kabul	No	Yes	Could be offensive to Runjeet Singh
1 Aug.	Burnes sends above to Macnaghten	No.	Yes	—
9 Sept.	Burnes reports on Persian and Russian relations with Kandahar	Yes	Yes	Parts deleted in 1839 stressed Russian intrigue and mentioned 15th May orders
10 Sept.	Burnes acknowledges an official dispatch of 31 July about possibility of a Sikh-Afghan settlement	No	Yes	—
11 Sept.	New instructions for Burnes: a more political mission than was first envisaged	No	Yes	A questionable suppression; see 15 May
24 Sept.	Burnes reports his arrival at Kabul	Yes	No	Innocuous
4 Oct.	Burnes reports on Persian influences at Kabul	Yes	No	Shows Dost's preference for British
5 Oct.	Burnes reports on first talks with Dost	Yes	Yes	Slight cuts in 1839 in references to Peshawar
9 Oct.	Burnes acknowledges Masson's great help	No	Yes	Of no political consequence
20 Oct.	Burnes reports on Russian commerce in Central Asia	No	Yes	Dispensable
24 Oct.	Burnes writes to Kandahar chiefs	Yes	Yes	
25 Oct.	Dost writes publicly to his brothers at Kandahar	Yes	Yes	Edited, but not suppressed (as Kaye indicates)
25 Oct.	Dost writes privately to them	Yes	Yes	
28 Oct.	Wade stresses importance of Herat's independence	Yes	No	Extract only in 1839
31 Oct.	Burnes reports on letters to Kandahar	Yes	Yes	Editing in 1839 does not conceal Dost's good disposition towards Britain
15 Nov.	Burnes reports arrival of letter from Simonich	Yes	Yes	Kaye indicates suppression where there is none
19 Nov.	Burnes transmits terms of proposed treaty between Persia and Kandahar	Yes		—
20 Nov.	Wade's comments on Burnes's letter of 4 Oct.	Yes		
29 Nov.	Wade writes on overtures from Kabul and Kandahar separately to Persia earlier in 1837	Yes	Yes	Wade balances Burnes's liking for Dost
2 Dec.	Burnes reports at length on Kabul politics, including an appreciation of Dost's merits	No	Yes	The least justifiable omission of all
2 Dec.	Macnaghten repeats that British policy would still favour the Sikhs in any Sikh-Afghan war	No	Yes	See 15 May and 11 September 1837

Date		Col 1	Col 2	Notes
20 Dec	Burnes reports the arrival of Vitkievitch	Yes	Yes	Much edited to reduce anti-Russian flavour
22 Dec.	Burnes offers Kandahar brothers British aid	No	Yes	Suppresses reference to Kandahar offer which Auckland disavowed
22 Dec.	Burnes confirms that Vitkievitch is a Russian agent, and encloses a copy of the Emperor's letter	Yes	Yes	All references to Emperor deleted
23 Dec.	Burnes reports his offer to Kandahar brothers	No	No	See 22 Dec.
23 Dec.	Burnes to Auckland, privately, on Vitkievitch and future British policy at Kabul	Yes	Yes	Drastically cut in 1839; Ellenborough may have seen a copy of this
25 Dec.	Burnes gives instructions to Leech for his mission to Kandahar	No	Yes	Suppressed; see 22 Dec. (Kandahar)
26 Dec.	Burnes reports on Leech's mission to Kandahar	No	No	Suppressed; see 22 Dec. (Kandahar)
27 Dec.	Macnaghten to Burnes, reminding him of his terms of reference	No	No	See 15 May, 11 Sept, 2 Dec.
1838				
1 Jan.	Wade to Macnaghten, casting doubt on Burnes's view of Kabul politics	Yes	No	Wade's comments on a suppressed dispatch!
18 Jan.	Burnes on site and prospects of the proposed Indus trade fair	No	Yes	Dispensable
20 Jan.	Macnaghten to Burnes, including a reprimand about the offer to Kandahar	Yes	Yes	Mainly a reprimand which Burnes would not have wanted published; therefore much edited
20 Jan.	Auckland to Dost on the progress of Burnes's mission so far	Yes	No	Evidence of Dost's friendly disposition; fair statement of terms
22 Jan.	Burnes reports that Dost is paying no attention to Vitkievitch	No	Yes	Proof that Dost prefers British
26 Jan.	Burnes to Macnaghten, on Dost's views on Peshawar	Yes	Yes	Much edited; omissions sometimes questionable
26 Jan.	Dost to Auckland, saying that delay may cause difficulty	Yes	No	—
29 Jan.	Burnes reports on Russian promises to Kandahar (naming the Emperor)	Yes	No	—
1 Feb.	Burnes reports on Russian ambitions in the direction of Khokand	No	Yes	Could be offensive to the Emperor
7 Feb.	Burnes comments on Herat affairs	No	Yes	Too strong a plea for Barukzais
10 Feb.	Burnes reports on a Sikh intrigue against Dost	No	Yes	Could be offensive to Runjeet Singh

447

Date	Contents	1839	1859	Remarks
18 Feb.	Burnes describes Vitkievitch's activities at Kabul	Yes	Yes	Much edited, and not always reasonably
23 Feb.	Burnes answers Macnaghten's of 20 Jan.	Yes	Yes	Virtually complete if collated
4 Mar.	Burnes reports on alleged messages from Vitkievitch to Runjeet Singh	Yes	Yes	—
5 Mar.	Burnes reports the latest hitch in negotiations	Yes	Yes	Much detail omitted
7 Mar.	Burnes reports that Dost has yielded at last	No	Yes	Dispensable because Dost changed his mind almost immediately
7 Mar.	Macnaghten tells Burnes about Sikh views on Peshawar	No	Yes	—
13 Mar.	Burnes reports renewal of negotiations	Yes	Yes	Much detail omitted
17 Mar.	Burnes reports on proposed Persia-Kandahar treaty under Russian guarantee	Yes	Yes	Illustrates Vitkievitch's activities
21 Mar.	Wade argues against dealing further with Dost	No	Yes	Suppresses arguments *against* Dost
21 Mar.	Dost asks Auckland for a little encouragement and power: he wants British intervention on his behalf at Peshawar	Yes	No	Shows Dost in a good light
21 Mar.	Burnes report sthat thes irdars are waiting for a British reply	Yes	No	—
24 Mar.	Burnes brings his account of the negotiations up to date	Yes	Yes	Shortened, but not drastically
28 Mar.	Macnaghten to Burnes	No	Yes	Suppresses well reasoned statement of *British* case.
11 Apr.	Dr Lord says there is a suspected Russian agent at Balkh	Yes	No	—
23 Apr.	Dost tells Burnes he has given up hope of help from British	Yes	Yes	—
25 Apr.	Burnes reports end of mission and encloses Dost's letter	Yes	Yes	—
27 Apr.	Auckland replies to Dost's of 21 Mar. and withdraws good offices	Yes	No	—
27 Apr.	Macnaghten instructs Burnes to leave Kabul	Yes	Yes	Much detail omitted
27 Apr.	Auckland to Secret Committee on need to remonstrate with Russians about Vitkievitch	Yes	Yes	—
28 Apr.	Dost to Auckland, summing up negotiations	Yes	No	—
30 Apr.	Burnes sends Dost's letter and writes from Jalalabad about Vitkievitch	Yes	Yes	Virtually complete if collated

APPENDIX 2

GENERAL NAPIER'S COMMENTS ON
THE KABUL INSURRECTION

Charles James Napier, the conqueror of Sind, read Vincent Eyre's *Military Operations at Cabul* (5th ed.), in 1843, with a pencil in his hand. He made more than sixty marginal notes, most of them violent and sarcastic, and signed his name to the last of them. His copy of the book is in the India Office Library. What follows is a selection from the notes:

Eyre	Napier
P.75. Shelton refused to post a guard at a small fort containing grain.	It seems to me that to Shelton may be traced the whole misfortune of this army.
P.106. If the garrison had occupied the Bala Hissar '...a large party would probably ere long have been formed in our favour'.	God's blood had you not 5,000 men? What other *party* did you want? Your very *camp followers* were enough to have defeated the enemy.
P.106. Shelton's objections to moving to the Bala Hissar.	He ought to be shot. He was if this book be true the *real* author of all ill.
P.112. Major Swayne's failure at Beymaroo.	Just like you all! A set of idiots in command of brave men.
P.115. November 23rd was the day that decided the fate of the Cabul garrison.	It was decided when Macnaughten [*sic*]—Elphinstone and Shelton were made your leaders! The blame of Macnaughten belongs to Lord Aukland [*sic*] Elphinstone and Shelton. Was this not pure imbecility and want of moral courage want of everything military.
P.116. Shelton objected to storming Beymaroo.	This man was the evil spirit of the force!
P.133. Attempt to be fair to Shelton.	He merits nothing but contempt for never losing sight of what was disgraceful to do. The retreat was infamous. he ought to have been *shot* for *speaking of it*.
P.137. Possibility of negotiating is mentioned for the first time.	Bah! How can you treat with men who cannot control their troops. Judge! Macnaghten seems to have had no clear vision of the native character nor any moral principle. He was a degree better than Shelton and that is all.
P.138. Two delegates from the chiefs enter cantonments to parley.	Two rascals came to me from these Mahoms and I heard them *in public before the soldiers* and then kicked them out of the camp frightened to death lest I should hang them! They wanted me to lay down my arms and quit Sinde under the Amers protection.

Appendix 2

Eyre	Napier

P.143. Eyre regrets having to mention facts affecting honour of a British regiment.

No—not in the least. this affects those two fellows McNaghten and Shelton and *no one else.* if I was despotic the last should be with the first.

P.147. Elphinstone's thoughts on retreat.

Poor driveler.

P.152. Terms of the evacuation agreement.

I would have proposed to them to *seize the Punjaub* and *divide it between us*! and when I joined Genl Sale I would make my *Salaam* the moment I passed the Khyber Pass! McNaghten does not seem to have had the head even to negotiate.

P.154. A tribute to Macnaghten's courage.

Bah! if a man whose egregious folly caused the destruction of a whole army is thus to be lauded praise is not worth having! I would rather have the white of an egg to clean my boots.

P.155. Macnaghten was in many essential points a great man.

Jesus of Nazareth What disgusting stuff is this! a man whose exceeding folly has stained the annals of his country with dishonoured arms and caused the destruction of 15,000 people 'a great man!' his name is a bye word and a disgrace.

P.191. A crowd of Afghans was observed.

Why did you not cut their throats?

P.192. The envoy gave Akbar a horse costing 3,000 rupees.

Ass! Public thief!

P.193. Akbar thanked the envoy for the pistols which he had given him.

Had he fired them into his guts he wd have shown some sense.

P.193. The murder of Macnaghten and Trevor.

Idiots you deserved it all.

P.227. Lady Sale suffered a slight wound in the arm.

It entered her *elbow* and was cut out at *her wrist*, a 'slight wound' God forgive me but with the exception of the women you were all a set of sons of bitches and you who pretend to record facts call this a slight wound! The devil you do! Had you half as bad a one (for I saw it) you would have walked out of action in no time I'll warrant or you are a better man than I believe you to be, tho' I never put much faith in your half and half fellows who pretend to be *moderate* and tell 'only what they saw.'— if you speak truth your history is not worth a damn.

[signed] C. J. Napier

Note. Shelton was exonerated at a court martial early in 1843. Vincent Eyre ended a distinguished career as a Major General after nearly thirty years in India.

A PROCLAMATION MADE AT SIMLA,
1 OCTOBER 1842

The government of India directed its army past the Indus in order to expel from Afghanistan a chief believed to be hostile to British interests and to replace upon his throne a sovereign represented to be friendly to those interests, and popular with his former subjects.

The chief believed to be hostile became a prisoner, and the sovereign represented to be popular was replaced upon his throne: but, after events which brought into question his fidelity to the government by which he was restored, he lost, by the hands of an assassin, the throne he had only held midst insurrections, and his death was preceded and followed by a still-existing anarchy.

Disasters unparalleled in their extent, unless by the errors in which they originated, and by the treachery in which they were completed, have in one short campaign been avenged upon every scene of past misfortunes; and repeated victories in the field, and the capture of the cities and citadels of Ghazni and Cabul, have again attached the opinion of invincibility to the British arms.

The British army in possession of Afghanistan will now be withdrawn to the Sutlej.

The Governor General will leave it to the Afghans themselves to create a government amidst the anarchy which is the consequence of their crimes.

To force a sovereign upon a reluctant people would be as inconsistent with the policy as it is with the principles of the British government, tending to place the arms and resources of that people at the disposal of the first invader, and to impose the burden of supporting a sovereign without prospect of benefit from his alliance.

The Governor General will willingly recognise any government approved by the Afghans themselves, which shall appear desirous and capable of maintaining friendly relations with the neighbouring states.

Content with the limits nature appears to have assigned to its empire, the government of India will devote all its efforts to the establishment and maintenance of general peace, to the protection of the sovereigns and chiefs of its allies, and to the prosperity and happiness of its own faithful subjects.

The rivers of the Punjab and the Indus, and the mountainous passes,

29-2

and the barbarous tribes of Afghanistan will be placed between the British army and an enemy approaching from the west—if, indeed, such an enemy there can be—and no longer between the army and its supplies.

The enormous expenditure required for the support of a large force in a false military position, at a distance from its own frontier and its resources, will no longer arrest every measure for the improvement of the country and of the people.

The combined army of India and of England, superior in equipment, in discipline, in valour, and in the officers by whom it is commanded, to any force which can be opposed to it in Asia, will stand in unassailable strength upon its own soil; and for ever, under the blessing of providence, preserve the glorious empire it has won in security and honour.

The Governor General cannot fear the misconstruction of his motives in thus frankly announcing to surrounding states the pacific and conservative policy of his government.

Afghanistan and China have seen at once the forces at his disposal and the effect with which they can be applied.

Sincerely attached to peace for the sake of the benefits it confers upon the people, the Governor General is resolved that peace shall be observed, and will put forth the whole power of the British government to coerce the state by which it shall be infringed.

By order of the Right Honourable the Governor General of India,

T. H. Maddock

Secretary to the Government of India,
with the Governor General.

BIBLIOGRAPHY

MANUSCRIPT SOURCES

BRITISH MUSEUM (ADD. MSS.)
Aberdeen 43043–44, 43060, 43063–64, 43089, 43144.
Auckland 37689 to 37713.
Bligh 41272–73, 41285.
Broughton 36467 to 36474, 43744–45, 46915.
Heytesbury 41558–59.
Palmerston 48535–36.
Peel 40409–10, 40420, 40467, 40471, 40514.
Wellesley 37313, 37415.

PUBLIC RECORD OFFICE
Ellenborough Papers, PRO 30.12 *passim.*

INDIA OFFICE LIBRARY
Sir Charles Napier's marginal comments in a copy of Vincent Eyre's
Military Operations at Cabul..., I.O.L. MSS. Eur. B. 199.

OFFICIAL RECORDS

Correspondence relating to the Affairs of Persia and Affghanistan,
printed solely for the use of the Cabinet. Palmerston's annotated copy.
PRO F.O. 539.1 and 2.
Correspondence relating to the Affairs of Persia and Affghanistan—
an edited version of the above. Printed as part of Parliamentary Papers
1839, XL.
Indian Papers, Collections 1 to 7 and one unnumbered dispatch, Parliamentary Papers 1839, XL.
The Indian Papers restored by Sir J. W. Kaye, Parliamentary Papers
1859 (Session 2), XXV.
Report from the Select Committee appointed to inquire into the present
state of the Affairs of the East India Company, etc. Political or Foreign
Affairs, House of Commons Reports 1831–32 (735–vi), XIV.1.

Hansard.

London Gazette.

India Office Records:
(a) Board's Drafts of Secret Letters and Dispatches (I.O.R./B.D.);
(b) Bengal Secret Letters, etc. (I.O.R./S.L.).

PUBLISHED PAPERS

Abbott, Major General Augustus. *The Afghan War...*, ed. C. R. Low.
R. Bentley and Sons, 1879. From Abbot's *Journal.*
Cumming, James Slator. *A Six Years Diary.* Martin and Hood, 1847.

Bibliography

Dennie, William. *Personal Narrative of the Campaigns*... William Curry, Dublin, 1843.

Eden, Hon. Emily. *Up the Country*, Letters written to her sister, etc. 2 vols. London, 1866.

Eden, Hon. Emily. *Miss Eden's Letters*, ed. V. Dickinson. Macmillan, 1919.

Greville, Charles. *Greville Memoirs*, ed. Lytton Strachey and Roger Fulford. 8 vols. Macmillan, 1938.

Hobhouse, John Cam, Baron Broughton. *Recollections of a Long Life*. 6 vols. John Murray, 1909.

Lamb, William, Lord Melbourne. *Lord Melbourne's Papers*, ed. L. C. Sanders. Longmans, 1889.

Law, Edward, Lord Ellenborough. *Political Diary*. 2 vols. Bentley and Sons, 1881.

Law, Edward, Lord Ellenborough. *India under Ellenborough*, ed. Sir Algernon Law. John Murray, 1926.

Metcalfe, Charles, Lord Metcalfe. *Life and Correspondence*, ed. Sir J. W. Kaye. 2 vols. London, 1854.

Nott, Sir William. *Memoirs and Correspondence*, ed. J. Stocqueler. 2 vols. London, 1854.

Peel, Sir Robert. *Papers and Letters*..., ed. C. S. Parker. 3 vols. John Murray, 1899.

Russell, Lord John. *Early Correspondence*, ed. Rollo Russell. 2 vols. T. Fisher Unwin, 1913.

Stanhope, Philip, Earl Stanhope. *Conversations with the Duke of Wellington*. John Murray, 1888.

Temple, Emily, Lady Palmerston. *Letters*, ed. T. Lever. John Murray, 1957.

Temple, Henry, Lord Palmerston. *Life and Correspondence*, ed. A. E. Ashley. 2 vols. Bentley and Sons, 1879.

Temple, Henry, Lord Palmerston. *Regina v. Palmerston*, ed. B. Connell. Evans, 1962.

Victoria, Queen. *Letters*, ed. A. C. Benson and Viscount Esher. John Murray, 1908.

Wellesley, Arthur, duke of Wellington. *Despatches, Correspondence and Memoranda*. 8 vols., John Murray, 1867–80.

CONTEMPORARY NARRATIVES

Buist, George. *Outline of the Operations*... *Times*, Bombay, 1843.

Burnes, Sir Alexander. *Travels into Bokhara*... 3 vols., John Murray, 1834.

Burnes, Sir Alexander. *Cabool: being a Personal Narrative*. John Murray, 1842.

Burnes, Dr James. *Narrative of a Visit to the Court of...the Ameers of Sinde*... Government of Bombay, 1829.

Durand, Sir Henry. *The First Afghan War and its Causes*. London, 1879.

Evans, George de Lacy. *On the Designs of Russia*. London, 1828.

Bibliography

Evans, George de Lacy. *On the Practicability of an Invasion of India.* London, 1829.

Eyre, Vincent. *Military Operations at Cabul...* John Murray, 1843.

Haughton, John. *Char-ee-kar...* Provost and Company, 1879.

Havelock, Henry. *Narrative of the War...* 2 vols. London, 1840.

Hough, William. *Narrative of the March...* London, 1841.

Masson, Charles. *Narrative of Various Journeys...* 4 vols. London, 1842-3.

Mohan Lal. *Journal of a Tour...* Calcutta, 1834.

Mohan Lal. *Life of the Amir Dost Mohammed Khan.* 2 vols. London, 1846.

McNeill, John. *Progress and Present Position of Russia in the East.* London, 1836.

'Non-Alarmist'. *A Few Words on our Relations with Russia.* London, 1828.

Outram, James. *Rough Notes of the Campaign...* Bombay, 1840.

Pottinger, Henry. *Travels in Beloochistan and Sind.* Longmans, 1816.

Sale, Florentia (Lady Sale). *Journal of the Disasters...* London, 1843.

OTHER VICTORIAN WORKS

Boulger, D. C. *England and Russia in Central Asia.* 2 vols. W. H. Allen, 1879.

Boulger, D. C. *Lord William Bentinck.* Oxford, 1892.

Colvin, Sir Auckland. *John Russell Colvin.* Oxford, 1895.

Forbes, Archibald. *The Afghan Wars...* Seeley and Co., 1892.

Fortescue, Sir John. *History of the British Army.* 13 vols. Macmillan, 1899.

Griffin, Sir Lepel. *Ranjit Singh.* Oxford, 1890.

Kaye, Sir J. W. *History of the War in Afghanistan.* 3 vols. London, 1857-8.

Kaye, Sir J. W. *Lives of Indian Officers.* 2 vols., London, 1904.

Krausse, Alexis. *Russia in Asia.* Grant Richards, 1899.

Lushington, Henry. *A Great Country's Little Wars.* London, 1844.

Rawlinson, Sir Henry. *England and Russia in the East.* London, 1875.

Trotter, Lionel. *Earl of Auckland.* Oxford, 1890.

GENERAL

Archbold, W. A. J. Chapter xxviii, *Cambridge History of the British Empire*, vol. iv, *British India.* Cambridge, 1929.

Bearce, George. *British Attitudes towards India.* Oxford, 1961.

Bullard, Sir Reader. *Britain and the Middle East.* Hutchinson, 1951.

Caroe, Sir Olaf. *The Pathans.* Macmillan, 1958.

Caspani, E. and Cagnacci, E. *Afghanistan, Crocevia dell'Asia.* Milan, 1951.

Cecil, Algernon. *Queen Victoria and her Prime Ministers.* Eyre and Spottiswoode, 1953.

Cecil, Lord David. *The Young Melbourne.* Constable, 1939.

Cecil, Lord David. *Lord M.* Constable, 1954.

Costin, W. C. *Great Britain and China 1833-1860.* Oxford, 1937.

Court, W. H. B. *Concise Economic History of Britain.* Cambridge, 1954.

Dorling, Captain H. Taprell. *Ribbons and Medals.* George Philip, 1946.

Edwardes, Michael. *Asia in the European Age.* Thames and Hudson, 1961.

Bibliography

Fraser-Tytler, Sir W. K. *Afghanistan, a Study...* Oxford, 1950.
Freeman-Greville, G. S. P. *Muslim and Christian Calendars.* Oxford, 1963.
Gail, Marzieh. *Persia and the Victorians.* Allen and Unwin, 1951.
Graves, Philip. *Briton and Turk.* Hutchinson, 1941.
Groseclose, Elgin. *Introduction to Iran.* Oxford, 1947.
Guedalla, Philip. *Palmerston.* Ernest Benn, 1926.
Haas, William. *Iran.* Columbia University, 1946.
Hobsbawm, E. J. *The Age of Revolution...* Weidenfeld and Nicholson, 1962.
Huttenback, Robert. *British Relations with Sind...* University of California, 1962.
Ilchester, Earl of. *Chronicles of Holland House.* John Murray, 1937.
Imlah, J. A. H. *Lord Ellenborough, a Biography.* Cambridge, Mass., 1939.
Jackson, Donovan. *India's Army.* Low, 1940.
James, David. *Lord Roberts.* Hollis, 1954.
Keith, A. B. *Constitutional History of India.* Methuen, 1936.
Laver, James. *British Military Uniforms.* Penguin, 1948.
Lewis, Bernard. *The Emergence of Modern Turkey.* Oxford, 1961.
Little, Tom. *Egypt.* Ernest Benn, 1958.
Low, S. J. M. and Sanders, L. C. *History of England during the Reign of Queen Victoria.* Longmans, 1907.
Marlowe, John. *Anglo-Egyptian Relations, 1800–1953.* Cresset, 1954.
Mersey, Viscount. *Viceroys and Governors General of India.* John Murray, 1949.
Mitchell, B. R. and Deane, P. *Abstract of British Historical Statistics.* Cambridge, 1962.
Panikkar, K. M. *The Founding of the Kashmir State.* Allen and Unwin, 1953.
Sheppard, Eric. *Short History of the British Army.* Constable, 1926.
Spear, Percival (ed.). *Oxford History of India.* 3rd ed. Oxford, 1958.
Sykes, Sir Percy. *History of Persia.* 2 vols., Macmillan, 1930.
Sykes, Sir Percy. *History of Afghanistan.* 2 vols. Macmillan, 1940.
Thompson, Edward and Garratt, G. T. *Rise and Fulfilment of British Rule in India.* Macmillan, 1934.
Thomson, David. *England in the Nineteenth Century.* Penguin, 1950.
Trevelyan, G. M. *British History in the Nineteenth Century.* Longmans, 1922.
Trevelyan, G. M. *History of England.* Longmans, 1926.
Ward, Sir A. W. and Gooch, G. P. *Cambridge History of British Foreign Policy.* 2 vols. Cambridge, 1939.
Waterfield, Gordon. *Layard of Nineveh.* John Murray, 1963.
Webster, Sir Charles. *Foreign Policy of Viscount Palmerston.* 2 vols. Bell, 1951.
Wilson, Sir Arnold. *The Persian Gulf.* Oxford, 1928.
Woodruff, Philip. *The Men who ruled India.* Cape, 1953.
Woodward, Sir Llewellyn. *The Age of Reform.* Oxford, 1962.
Young, George. *Egypt.* Ernest Benn, 1927.
Young, G. M. (ed.). *Early Victorian England.* 2 vols. Oxford, 1934.
Zinkin, Maurice and Zinkin, Taya. *Britain and India...* Chatto, 1964.

NOTES

INTRODUCTION

1 Spear, *Oxford History of India* (3rd ed.), p. 601.
2 Woodward, pp. 217–40, 417–18.
3 Ward and Gooch, *Cambridge History of British Foreign Policy*, II, 199–211.
4 Webster, II, 752.
5 Thompson and Garratt, p. 375.
6 Kaye, *Afghanistan*, I, 403.
7 Sheppard, p. 190.
8 Fortescue, in Young's *Early Victorian England*, I, 355–6.
9 Archbold, *Cambridge History of the British Empire*, IV, 520.
10 Trotter, *Auckland*, p. 75.
11 Thompson and Garratt, p. 342.
12 Woodward, p. 417.
13 Edwardes, *Asia in the European Age*, p. 61.
14 *D.N.B.* on Ellenborough, under Law, Edward Earl of.
15 Sale, 24 Dec. 1841.
16 Masson, *Narrative of Various Journeys*, III, 451–479.
17 Buist, *Outline of the Operations*, p. 46.

CHAPTER I, pp. 3–17

1 Surrendered 3 Nov. 1840, released November 1842.
2 Reached Lahore 20 Jan. 1843.
3 Emily Eden to her sister 1 June 1841, Eden, *Letters*.
4 Buist's phrase. *Outline of the Operations*, preface, p. iv.
5 Dalhousie's minute 14 March 1854, I.O.R./S.L. enclosures.
6 Shakespeare, *Macbeth*, I, iii.
7 Broughton, *Recollections*, v, 6, 5 October 1836.
8 Cobbett, *Political Register*, 16 Apr. 1808.
9 *Hansard*, 3rd series, vol. XIX, 10 July 1833.
10 Landing at Alexandria, 1 July 1798.
11 1 August 1798.
12 The earl of Mornington became Marquess Wellesley in 1799.
13 Wilson, *Persian Gulf*, p. 254.
14 Keith, *Constitutional History of India*, pp. 113–14.
15 Treaty of Finkenstein, 4 May 1807.
16 A letter dated 11 Oct. 1807, Huttenback, p. 5.
17 Proclaimed Pasha, May 1805; recognized by the Porte, November 1806.
18 Little, *Egypt*, p. 58, and Young, *Egypt*, p. 39.
19 Archbold, *Cambridge History of the British Empire*, IV, 487.
20 Dispatch dated 29 June 1810, I.O.R./B.D. III, first series.
21 Battle of Aslanduz, on the River Aras.
22 Sykes, *Persia*, II, 314.

23 Emily Eden to Charles Greville 10 July 1838, Eden, *Letters*. '...We have a Shah Shujah all ready to lâcher at Dost Mahomed if he does not behave himself!'

CHAPTER 2, pp. 18–31

1 Ward and Gooch, *Cambridge History of British Foreign Policy*, II, 6–7.
2 Trevelyan, *History of England*, p. 630.
3 Nikolai Nikolaievich Muraviev, *Journey in Turkmenia...1822*.
4 Webster, I, 276.
5 Little, *Egypt*, pp. 60–1.
6 Woodward, p. 216.
7 Ward and Gooch, *Cambridge History of British Foreign Policy*, II, 90–2.
8 Lewis, *Emergence of Modern Turkey*, p. 78, describes the massacre of the Janissaries, 15 June 1826.
9 Canning succeeded Liverpool 10 Apr. 1827. Canning died 8 Aug. 1827, a month after the Treaty of London, in which Britain, France and Russia agreed to intervene to prevent a collision between Turk and Greek. The allied fleet sank most of Ibrahim's at Navarino, 20 October 1827.
10 *Hansard*, 3rd series, Jan. 1828.
11 Secret Committee to Governor of Bengal, 2 Dec. 1828, I.O.R./B.D. VII, 1st series.
12 Ward and Goach *Cambridge History of British Foreign Policy*, II, 100.
13 Sykes, *Persia*, II, 317–20.
14 Treaty of Turkmanchai, 23 Feb. 1828.
15 Fighting started in March; war was declared on 26 Apr. 1828.
16 See note 11.
17 Wellington to Ellenborough 9 Oct. 1828, Wellington, *Despatches*, v, 117–19.
18 Negotiated March, ratified by the Shah Aug. 1828.
19 Secret Committee to Governor of Bengal 13 Dec. 1828, I.O.R./B.D. VII, 1st series.
20 Kaye, *Metcalfe*, II, 197.
21 Melville was his immediate predecessor at the Board of Control (Ellenborough, *P.D.* I, 219–20).
22 *Ibid.* I, 224, 25 Sept. 1828.
23 *Ibid.* I, 232–3, 1 Oct. 1828.
24 *Ibid.* I, 227, 26 Sept. 1828.
25 Huskisson, Palmerston, Dudley, Grant and Lamb (later Melbourne) resigned at the end of May 1828.
26 Ward and Gooch, *Cambridge History of British Foreign Policy*, II, 99.
27 Ellenborough, *P.D.* I, 94, 29 Apr. 1828.
28 *Ibid.* I, 149, 17 June 1828.
29 *Ibid.* I, 209, 6 Sept. 1828.
30 George de Lacy Evans spoke for the anti-Russians in his book *On the Designs of Russia* (1828). An anonymous pamphleteer, 'Non-Alarmist', answered him on behalf of the pro-Russians.
31 Wellington to Aberdeen 7 Nov. 1828, Wellington, *Despatches*, v, 225–6.

32 Ellenborough, *P.D.* II, 25, 29 Apr. 1829.
33 Wellington to Aberdeen 22 Apr. 1829, Wellington, *Despatches*, V, 591.
34 Ellenborough, *P.D.* II, 78, 30 July 1829.
35 Wellington to Aberdeen 25 Aug. 1829, Wellington, *Despatches*, VI, 106–7.
36 Ellenborough, *P.D.* II, 88, 22 Aug. 1829.
37 Treaty of Adrianople, 14 Sept. 1829.
38 Heytesbury to Aberdeen 30 Sept. 1829, Heytesbury 41558, fos. 241–3.
39 Wellington to Aberdeen 11 Oct. 1829, Wellington, *Despatches*, VI, 212–19.
40 Ellenborough to Wellington 18 Oct. 1829, *ibid.* pp. 238–9.
41 Aberdeen to Heytesbury 31 Oct. 1829, Aberdeen 43809, fos. 106–17.
42 Aberdeen to Heytesbury 7 Nov. 1829, *ibid.* fos. 118–19.
43 Heytesbury to Aberdeen 25 Nov. 1829, Heytesbury 41559, fos. 65–6.
44 Heytesbury to Aberdeen 27 Nov. 1829, *ibid.* fo. 67.
45 Aberdeen to Heytesbury 13 Dec. 1829, *ibid.* fos. 81–2.
46 Ellenborough, *P.D.* II, 149–50, 16 Dec. 1829.
47 *Ibid.* II, 122–3, 29 Oct. 1829.
48 *Ibid.* II, 123–5, 30 Oct. 1829.
49 *Ibid.* II, 144, 9 Dec. 1829.
50 *Ibid.* II, 149–50, 16 Dec. 1829.

CHAPTER 3, pp. 35–49

1   High Tories offended by Catholic emancipation, 15 Nov. 1830.
2   Aberdeen to Heytesbury 7 Nov. 1829, Aberdeen 43809, fos. 118–19.
3   Ellenborough, *P.D.* II, 151, 18 Dec. 1829.
4   Ellenborough to Wellington 19 Dec. 1829, Wellington, *Despatches*, VI, 327–8.
5   Secret Committee to Governor of Bengal 19 Dec. 1829, I.O.R./B.D. VII, 1st series.
6   Ellenborough, *P.D.* II, 153, 20 Dec. 1829.
7   Heytesbury to Aberdeen 18 Jan. 1830, sent to Bengal with a dispatch from the Secret Committee to the Governor of Bengal, I.O.R./B.D. VII, 1st series.
8   Secret Committee to Governor of Bengal 12 Jan. 1830, I.O.R./B.D. VII, 1st series.
9   Creevey's Diary, 26 June 1830; also Greville, same date.
10 Palmerston to Lady Cowper, Guedalla p. 122.
11 *Hansard*, 3rd series, Nov. 1830, debate on the King's speech.
12 15 Sept. 1830.
13 James Burnes, *Narrative of a Visit*, pp. 120–1.
14 Malcolm to Bax 23 July 1830, Wellington, *Despatches*, VIII, 227–9.
15 Burnes, *Bokhara*, I, 2.
16 James Burnes, pp. 3–4, 23 Oct. 1827.
17 Ellenborough, *P.D.* II, 37, 16 May 1829.
18 Minute of 9 Nov. 1828, Kaye, *Metcalfe*, II, 197–8.
19 Comments on a letter dated 30 Oct. 1830, I.O.R./S.L. enclosure.

20 Secret Committee to Governor of Bengal July 1831, I.O.R./B.D. VII, 1st series.

21 Pottinger to Bombay Government 20 March 1831, Huttenback.

22 Burnes sailed from Hyderabad 23 Apr. 1831, Burnes, *Bokhara*, I, 44–5.

23 *Ibid.* I, 131, 20 July 1831.

24 On or about 9 Sept. 1831.

25 Boulger, *Lord William Bentinck*, p. 169 25 Oct. 1831,

26 Spear, *Oxford History of India*, p. 598.

27 Prinsep to Pottinger 22 Oct. 1831, I.O.R./S.L. enclosures.

28 Burnes, *Bokhara*, I, 158.

CHAPTER 4, pp. 50–80

1 Burnes, *Bokhara*, I, 137–8, 4 May 1832.

2 Trevelyan, *History of England*, p. 672.

3 House of Commons Reports 1831–2 (735–vi), XIV, 16 Aug. 1832.

4 An alliance for eight years in the first instance, 8 July 1833.

5 Burnes, *Bokhara*, III, 199–201.

6 Huttenback, 2 July 1834, p. 28.

7 Burnes, *Bokhara*, I, p. 15, 17 Jan. 1832.

8 *Ibid.* I, 17, 18 Jan. 1832.

9 *Ibid.*, from the Preface

10 Kaye, *Lives*, II, p. 41.

11 Burnes, *Bokhara*, I, 98–9.

12 *Ibid.* p. 100.

13 Mohan Lal, *Journal of a Tour*, p. 64.

14 Burnes, *Bokhara*, I, 150.

15 Kaye, *Afghanistan*, II, 143.

16 Kaye, *Lives*, II, p. 29.

17 Burnes, *Bokhara*, II, 334.

18 *Ibid.* II, 342–5.

19 *Ibid.* I, 165.

20 30 May 1832.

21 Burnes, *Bokhara*, I, 291.

22 *Ibid.* II, 443–4.

23 Mitchell and Deane, *Abstract of British Historical Statistics*, pp. 182, 282, 313–14, 217–18.

24 Burnes, *Bokhara*, II, 189.

25 *Ibid.* p. 199.

26 *Ibid.* pp. 136–7.

27 *Ibid.* I, 175.

28 P.P. 1839 Indian Papers 3.

29 *Ibid.*

30 Boulger, *Lord William Bentinck*, p. 170.

31 Bentinck to Runjeet Singh 30 Apr. 1833, *ibid.*

32 Hough, *Narrative of the March*, p. 416.

33 Caspani and Cagnacci, *Afghanistan, Crocevia dell'Asia*.

34 Ellenborough PRO 30.12.28.5, unpublished journal, p. 112.

35 *Ibid.* p. 125, 8 Jan. 1835.

36 Ellenborough to Heytesbury 11 Feb. 1835, Ellenborough PRO 30.12.29, part 1(2).

37 Ellenborough to Fitzgerald 10 Jan. 1843, Ellenborough PRO 30.12.77.

38 Sykes, *Persia*, II, 324–5.

39 Palmerston to Bligh 16 June 1834, sent to Bengal with a Secret Committee dispatch, I.O.R./B.D. VIII, 1st series.

40 Bligh to Palmerston 2 July 1834, *ibid.*

41 Secret Committee to Governor General July 1834, *ibid.*

42 Palmerston to Bligh 5 Sept. 1834, Palmerston PRO F.O. 539.2, fo. 4.

43 Palmerston to Bligh 5 Sept. 1834, Bligh 41285, fo. 165.

44 15 Nov. 1834. Melbourne had been Prime Minister since June.

45 Ellenborough journal entry, 18 Dec. 1834, PRO 30.12.28.5, p. 80.

46 Ellenborough to Peel 10 Jan. and Peel to Ellenborough 12 Jan. 1835, Peel 40410, fos. 5 and 19.

47 Ellenborough to Peel 12 Jan. 1835, Peel 40410, fos. 30–1.

48 Heytesbury to Peel 16 Jan. 1835, *ibid.* fo. 160.

49 Bligh to Wellington 26 Jan. 1835, Bligh 41273, fos. 13–14.

50 Bligh to Wellington 5 March 1835, *ibid.* fos. 27–8.

51 Secret Committee to Governor General 9 Feb. 1835, I.O.R./B.D. IX, 1st series.

52 Masson, III, 316–21.

53 Secret Committee to Governor General 7 March 1835, I.O.R./B.D. IX, 1st series.

54 Palmerston to Temple 10 March 1835, Palmerston, Ashley ed.

55 An unidentified secretary at the Foreign Office to Henry Fox, quoted in Ilchester, *Chronicles of Holland House*, p. 194.

56 Hobhouse to Heytesbury 4 May 1835, Peel 40420, fo. 130.

57 Minute by Bentinck 13 March 1835, full text in Boulger, *Lord William Bentinck*, pp. 177–201.

58 Secret Committee to Campbell 1 July 1835, I.O.R./B.D. IX, 1st series.

59 The complete text is at PRO F.O. 539.2, fo. 7. The extract is in P.P. 1839, correspondence relating to the affairs of Persia and Afghanistan.

60 Auckland to Hobhouse 30 July 1835, Broughton 36473, fos. 36–7.

61 Broughton, *Recollections*, V, 45.

62 Cecil, *Lord M*, p. 254; also Eden, *Letters*, Sept. 1835.

63 Cecil, *Lord M*, pp. 345–52.

64 *D.N.B.* David Urquhart, 1805–77.

65 Lady Cowper to Mrs Huskisson 5 Jan. 1836, Palmerston, Lever ed.

66 Ellis to Palmerston 13 Nov., 24 Dec. and 30 Dec. 1835, Palmerston PRO F.O. 539.2, fo. 7.

67 Ellenborough journal entry, 18 Dec. 1834, see note 45.

CHAPTER 5, pp. 81–101

1 Friday 4 March 1836.
2 Melbourne to Palmerston 7 Jan. 1836, Guedalla, p. 168
3 Ellis to Palmerston 8 Jan. 1836, Palmerston PRO F.O. 539.2, fos. 7–8.
4 Ellis to Palmerston 15 Jan. 1836, *ibid.* fo. 8, p. 168.
5 Ellis to Palmerston 15 Feb. 1836, *ibid.* fo. 10.
6 Auckland to Clarke 2 Apr. 1836, Auckland 37689, fos. 8–9.
7 Melbourne to Palmerston 17 Feb. 1836, Guedalla, p. 168.
8 Melbourne to Palmerston 29 Feb. 1836, *ibid.*
9 McNeill, *Progress and Present Position of Russia in the East*, pp. 130, 140, 146, 150–1.
10 Ellis to Palmerston 25 Feb. 1836, Palmerston PRO F.O. 539.2, fos. 10–11.
11 Minute of 4 May 1836, Auckland 37709, fos. 14–15.
12 Auckland to Hobhouse 2 June 1836, Broughton 36473, fos. 57–9.
13 Auckland to Carnac 28 May 1836, Broughton 36473, fos. 51–6.
14 Ellis to Palmerston 1 Apr. 1836, Palmerston PRO F.O. 539.2, fo. 11.
15 Appointment gazetted on 25 May 1836.
16 Melbourne to Palmerston 15 May 1836, Guedalla, p. 168.
17 Ellis to Palmerston 10 Apr. 1836, Palmerston PRO F.O. 539.2, fos. 11–12. Palmerston and Auckland both received it in July.
18 Secret Committee to Governor General 18 May 1836, I.O.R./B.D. IX, 1st series.
19 Secret Committee to Governor General 7 June 1836, *ibid.*
20 Macnaghten to Ellis (but received by McNeill) 20 June 1836, Auckland 37690, fos. 8–11.
21 Auckland to Hobhouse 20 June 1836, Broughton 36473, fos. 70–8.
22 Cecil, *Lord M*, pp. 261–3.
23 Palmerston to McNeill 23 June 1836, Palmerston, PRO F.O. 539.2, fo. 18. The enclosure is at fos. 14–15.
24 Secret Committee to Governor General 25 June 1836, I.O.R./B.D. IX, 1 series.
25 Minute of 19 Aug. 1836, Auckland 37709, fos. 98–114.
26 Macnaghten to Wade 22 Aug. 1836, Auckland 37690, fos. 1–3.
27 Auckland to Hobhouse 26 Aug. 1836, Broughton 36473, fos. 79–82.
28 Auckland to Hobhouse 31 Aug. 1836, Broughton 36473, fos. 83–90.
29 Dost Muhammad to Auckland 31 May 1836, P.P. 1839 Indian Papers 5.
30 Auckland to Dost Muhammad 22 Aug. 1836, *ibid.*
31 Bentinck to Shah Shuja 20 Oct. 1832, P.P. 1839 Indian Papers 3.
32 Macnaghten to Wade 27 Sept. 1836, Huttenback, quoting Punjab Government Records.
33 Macnaghten to Burnes 5 Sept. 1836, P.P. 1839 Indian Papers 5.
34 Colvin to Pottinger 1 Sept. 1836, Auckland 37690, fos. 5–6.
35 Macnaghten to Pottinger 26 Sept. 1836, I.O.R./S.L. enclosure.
36 Colvin to Pottinger 29 Sept. 1836, Auckland 37690, fos. 12–13.

37 McNeill, *Progress and Present Position*, pp. 128–9.
38 Macnaghten to Pottinger 26 Sept. 1836, see note 35.
39 Auckland to Metcalfe 24 Sept. 1836, Auckland 37689, fos. 29–31; see also Auckland to Hobhouse 7 Oct. 1836, Broughton 36473, fo. 91.
40 Governor General to Secret Committee 26 Sept. 1836, I.O.R./S.L. XXIII, 1st series.
41 Metcalfe to Auckland 15 Oct. 1836, Auckland 37689, fos. 39–41.
42 Auckland to Metcalfe 28 Oct. 1836, Auckland 37690, fo. 15.
43 Auckland to Melville 17 Nov. 1836, Auckland 37708, fo. 20.
44 Auckland to Hobhouse 17 Nov. 1836, Broughton 36473, fo. 99.
45 Colvin to Pottinger and Burnes 3 Nov. 1836, and Burnes to Colvin 16 Nov. 1836, Auckland 37710, fos. 43–5.
46 Auckland to Fane 23 Nov. 1836, Auckland 37708, fos. 23–4.
47 Auckland to Hobhouse 24 Nov. 1836, *ibid.* fo. 24.
48 Auckland to Carnac same date, *ibid.* fo. 25.
49 Colvin to Wade 25 Oct. 1836, Auckland 37690, fo. 17.
50 McNeill to Palmerston 8 Oct. 1836, Palmerston PRO F.O. 539.2, fo. 20.
51 McNeill to Palmerston 3 Nov. 1836, *ibid.* fo. 21.
52 Macnaghten to McNeill 21 Nov. 1836, Palmerston PRO F.O. 539.1, fos. 3–4.
53 Burnes, *Cabool, A Personal Narrative*, p. 1.
54 Minute of 25 Dec. 1836, Auckland 37690, fos. 19–22.

CHAPTER 6, pp. 102–134

1 Auckland to Carnac 5 Jan. 1837, Auckland 37689, fos. 21–5.
2 Auckland to Sullivan 7 January 1837, *ibid.* fos. 26–7.
3 Palmerston to Durham 16 Jan. 1837, Palmerston PRO F.O. 539.2, fo. 5.
4 Durham to Palmerston 24 Feb. 1837, *ibid.*
5 Simonich to Nesselrode 28 May 1837, *ibid*, fo. 6; contained in Durham to Palmerston 15 July 1837, *ibid.*
6 Palmerston to McNeill 4 Aug. 1837, *ibid.* fo. 32.
7 Burnes, *Cabool*, p. 11.
8 Governor General to Secret Committee 2 Jan. 1837, I.O.R./S.L. XXIII, 1st series.
9 Auckland to Grant 14 Jan. 1837, Auckland 37690, fos. 26–8.
10 Colvin to Pottinger 6 Feb. 1837, Auckland 37690, fo. 30.
11 McNeill to Macnaghten 22 Jan. 1837, Palmerston PRO F.O. 539.2, fos. 23–6.
12 Auckland to Carnac 15 Feb. 1837, Auckland 37690, fos. 31–6.
13 Auckland to McNeill 24 Feb. 1837, *ibid.* fos. 47–50.
14 McNeill to Palmerston 20 Feb. 1837, Palmerston PRO F.O. 539.2, fos. 26–7. There had been doubts about the genuineness of Ellis's Kabul envoy, but the one seen by McNeill was accepted.
15 McNeill to Palmerston 24 Feb. 1837, *ibid.* 1, fo. 3.
16 McNeill to Burnes 13 March 1837, Kaye, *Afghanistan*, 1, 304.

17 Auckland to McNeill 30 March 1837, Auckland 37690, fos. 77–8.
18 Macnaghten to McNeill 10 Apr. 1837, Palmerston PRO F.O.539.2, fo. 33.
19 Auckland to McNeill 10 June 1837, Auckland 37691, fos. 12–14. Kuzzilbashis, a colony of Persian settlers of the Shiite persuasion in Kabul, were powerful supporters of Dost Muhammad.
20 Undated, probably late April, Kaye, *Metcalfe*, II, 306.
21 Auckland to Fane 15 March 1837, Auckland 37690, fos. 63–5.
22 Auckland to Hobhouse 9 Apr. 1837, Broughton 36473, fos. 128–46.
23 Dost Muhammad to Burnes 20 Apr. 1837, P.P. 1859.
24 Auckland to Dost Muhammad 15 May 1837: complete text in Palmerston PRO F.O. 539.2, fo. 39; extracts in P.P. 1839.
25 Macnaghten to Burnes 15 May 1837, enclosed in I.O.R./S.L. XXIII, 1st series, dispatch of 5 Aug. 1837.
26 Burnes, *Cabool*, p. 71.
27 Burnes to McNeill 6 June 1837, Buist, *Outline of the Operations*.
28 Colvin to Burnes 26 July 1837, Auckland 37691, fos. 57–60.
29 Minute of 14 June 1837, Auckland 37691, fos. 16–18.
30 Minute of 19 June 1837, *ibid.* fos. 30–4; also Auckland to Lock 15 June 1837, *ibid.* fos. 18–20.
31 McNeill to Palmerston 30 June 1837, Palmerston, PRO F.O. 539.1, fos. 5–7.
32 McNeill to Auckland 4 July 1837, *ibid.* 2, fo. 45.
33 Simonich to Rodofinikin 23 July 1837, Palmerston, PRO F.O. 539.2, fo. 6.
34 Dost Muhammad and Mirza Sami to Burnes, undated, probably mid-July, P.P. 1859.
35 Auckland to Hobhouse 8 Sept. 1837, Broughton 36473, fo. 187.
36 Minute of 9 Sept. 1837, Auckland 37691, fos. 126–31.
37 Macnaghten to Burnes 11 Sept. 1837, P.P. 1859.
38 Colvin to Burnes 13 Sept. 1837, Auckland 37691, fo. 133.
39 Colvin to Wade 13 Sept. 1837, Auckland 37692, fos. 1–2.
40 Burnes, *Cabool*, p. 142.
41 Buist places this at pp. 171–2 of Wood's *Journey to the Oxus*.
42 Burnes to Macnaghten 24 Sept. 1837, P.P. 1839 Indian Papers 5.
43 Burnes to Macnaghten 5 Oct. 1837, P.P. 1839 Indian Papers 5, and P.P. 1859.
44 Burnes to Macnaghten 4 Oct. 1837: a complete text is in Palmerston, PRO F.O. 539.2, fos. 59–61; and extracts in P.P. 1839 Indian Papers 5.
45 Burnes to Macnaghten 9 Oct. 1837, P.P. 1859.
46 Palmerston to Queen Victoria 8 Oct. 1837, Connell.
47 Auckland to Hobhouse 9 Oct. 1837, Broughton 36473; also in Auckland 37692, fos. 13–19.
48 Burnes to Macnaghten 31 Oct. 1837, P.P. 1839 and 1859; complete text in Palmerston, PRO F.O. 539.2, fos. 64–6.
49 Burnes to an unidentified correspondent 30 Oct. 1837, quoted in Buist, *Outline of the Operations*.
50 Macnaghten to Burnes 2 Dec. 1837, P.P. 1859.

51 Burnes to Macnaghten 15 Nov. 1837, P.P. 1839 and 1859; complete in Palmerston PRO F.O. 539.2, fos. 68–9.
52 McNeill to Palmerston 30 Oct. 1837, Palmerston PRO F.O. 539.1, fo. 9.
53 Burnes to Macnaghten 19 Nov. 1837, P.P. 1839 Indian Papers 6; complete in Palmerston, PRO, F.O. 539.2, fos. 69–70.
54 Burnes, *Cabool*, p. 248.
55 Auckland to Carnac 10 Dec. 1837, Auckland 37692, fos. 33–47.
56 McNeill to Palmerston 30 Oct. 1837, Palmerston PRO F.O. 539.1, fo. 9.
57 McNeill to Palmerston 25 Nov. 1837, *ibid.* fos. 10–11.
58 McNeill to Palmerston 27 Nov. 1837, *ibid.* 2, fos. 41–2.
59 Burnes to Macnaghten 20 Dec. 1837, P.P. 1839 Indian Papers 6, and P.P. 1859; author's italicization, not Burnes's.
60 Kohendil Khan to Burnes December, and Burnes to Kohendil Khan 22 Dec. 1837, P.P. 1859.
61 Emperor Nicholas to Dost Muhammad 27 Apr. 1837, enclosed with Burnes to Macnaghten 22 Dec. 1837, *ibid.*
62 Burnes to Macnaghten 23 Dec. 1837, *ibid.*
63 Burnes to Leech 25 Dec. 1837, *ibid.*
64 Burnes to Auckland 23 Dec. 1837, P.P. 1839 Indian Papers 6, and P.P. 1859.
65 Burnes, *Cabool*, p. 262.

CHAPTER 7, pp. 137–173

1 Auckland to McNeill 15 Sept. 1837, Auckland 37692, fos. 3–6.
2 Broughton, *Recollections*, v, 116–17, 19 Jan. 1838.
3 Auckland to Hobhouse 6 Jan. 1838, Auckland 37692, fo. 71.
4 Wade to Macnaghten 28 Oct. 1837, P.P. 1839 Indian Papers 5.
5 Macnaghten to Wade 13 Nov. 1837, Palmerston PRO F.O. 539.1, fo. 24.
6 Wade to Macnaghten 1 Jan. 1838, P.P. 1839 Indian Papers 5.
7 Auckland to Dost Muhammad 20 Jan. 1838, *ibid.*
8 Macnaghten to Burnes 20 Jan. 1838, P.P. 1839 Indian Papers 6 complete in P.P. 1859 and in Palmerston, PRO F.O. 539.2, fo. 50.
9 Colvin to Burnes 21 Jan. 1838, Auckland 37692, fo. 91.
10 Auckland to McNeill 27 Jan. 1838, *ibid.* fo. 106.
11 Governor General to Secret Committee 8 Feb. 1838, I.O.R./S.L. XXIII, 1st series.
12 Auckland to Hobhouse 13 Feb. 1838, Broughton 36473, fos. 222–7.
13 Burnes to Macnaghten 26 Jan. 1838, P.P. 1839 Indian Papers 5, and P.P. 1859, the latter a full text.
14 Dost Muhammad to Auckland 26 Jan. 1838, P.P. 1839 Indian Papers 5.
15 Burnes to Macnaghten 26 Jan. 1838, *ibid.*; also P.P. 1859.
16 Burnes to Macnaghten 5 March 1838, *ibid.*
17 Burnes to Macnaghten 7 March 1838, P.P. 1859 only.

18 Burnes to Macnaghten 13 March 1838, P.P. 1839 Indian Papers 5, and a full text in P.P. 1859.

19 Macnaghten to Burnes 7 March 1838, P.P. 1859 only.

20 Macnaghten to Burnes 28 March 1838, *ibid.*

21 Auckland to Hobhouse 9 Apr. 1838, Broughton 36473, fos. 234–42.

22 Burnes to Macnaghten 26 Jan. 1838, see note 13.

23 See note 18.

24 Burnes to Macnaghten 24 March 1838, P.P. 1839 Indian Papers 5, and a full text in P.P. 1859.

25 Dost Muhammad to Auckland 21 March 1838, P.P. 1839 Indian Papers 5 only.

26 See note 24.

27 Wade to Macnaghten 21 March 1838, P.P. 1859 only.

28 Governor General to Secret Committee 23 Apr. 1838, I.O.R./S.L. XXIII, 1st series.

29 See chapter 6, note 29.

30 McNeill to Palmerston 23 Feb. 1838, Palmerston PRO F.O. 539.1, fos. 16–17.

31 McNeill to Auckland 7 March 1838, mentioned in Auckland to Hobhouse 3 May 1838, Broughton 36473, fos. 243–8; McNeill to Palmerston 8 March 1838, Palmerston PRO F.O. 539.1, fo. 23.

32 Auckland to Dost Muhammad 27 Apr. 1838, P.P. 1839 Indian Papers 5 only.

33 Macnaghten to Burnes 27 Apr. 1838, P.P. 1839 Indian Papers 6, and full text in P.P. 1859.

34 Governor General to Secret Committee 27 Apr. 1838, I.O.R./S.L. XXIII, 1st series.

35 Governor General to Secret Committee 1 May 1838, *ibid.*

36 Macnaghten to McNeill 1 May 1838, Palmerston PRO F.O. 539.2, fo. 76.

37 Auckland to Hobhouse 3 May 1838, Broughton 36473, fos. 243–8.

38 Palmerston to McNeill 12 Feb. 1838, Palmerston PRO F.O. 539.2, fo. 44.

39 Palmerston to McNeill 16 March 1838, *ibid.* 1, fos. 14–15.

40 Secret Committee to Governor General 20 March 1838, I.O.R./B.D. IX, 1st series.

41 Palmerston to McNeill 7 Apr. 1838, Palmerston PRO F.O. 539.2, fos. 48.

42 These letters between Sheil, Palmerston and Hobhouse are all in Broughton 36469, fos. 5–14.

43 Secret Committee to Auckland 10 May 1838, I.O.R./B.D. IX, 1st series.

44 Burnes to Macnaghten 30 Apr. 1838, P.P. 1839 Indian Papers 5 and 6, complete in P.P. 1859.

45 Burnes to Wade 5 May 1838, P.P. 1859.

46 See note 44.

47 Bonham to Palmerston 7 Apr. 1838, Palmerston PRO, F.O. 539.2, fo. 71–2.

48 McNeill to Palmerston 11 Apr. 1838, *ibid*, 1, fo. 26.

49 McNeill to Auckland 11 Apr. 1838, *ibid*. fos. 24–5.

50 Palmerston to McNeill 18 May 1838, *ibid*. 2, fos. 52–3.

51 Secret Committee to Governor General 19 May 1838, I.O.R./B.D. IX, 1st series.

52 Palmerston to McNeill 21 May 1838, Palmerston, PRO, F.O. 539.1, fo. 24.

53 Minute of 12 May 1838, I.O.R./S.L. enclosures; part in P.P. 1839 Indian Papers 4.

54 Governor General to Secret Committee 22 May 1838, I.O.R./S.L. XXIII, 1st series.

55 Masson, *Narrative of Various Journeys*, III, 486.

56 Colvin to Macnaghten 22 May 1838, Auckland 37693, fos. 1–2.

57 Palmerston to Hobhouse 18 June 1838, Broughton 46915, fos. 89–90.

58 Muhammad Ali's announcement 15 May 1838 (Tom Little, *Egypt*, pp. 61–2). The Secret Committee informed Auckland of this on 7 June 1838 (I.O.R./B.D. X, 1st series).

59 Palmerston to Campbell 7 July 1838.

60 Palmerston to Ponsonby 13 Sept. 1838.

61 The Treaty of Balta Liman, 16 Aug. 1838.

CHAPTER 8, pp. 174–206

1 Todd to Burnes 23 June 1838, Broughton 36473, fos. 306–7.

2 3 June 1838, P.P. 1839, correspondence relating to Persia.

3 McNeill to Palmerston 25 June 1838, Palmerston PRO F.O. 539.1, fos. 40–1.

4 McNeill to Palmerston 25 June 1838, *ibid*. fos. 36–9.

5 Colvin to Macnaghten 22 May 1838, Auckland 37693, fo. 4.

6 Colvin to Macnaghten 1 June 1838, *ibid*. fos. 16–17.

7 Auckland to Macnaghten 1 June 1838, *ibid*. fos. 15–16.

8 Governor General to Secret Committee 13 Aug. 1838, I.O.R./S.L. XXIII, 1st series.

9 Auckland to Macnaghten 10 June 1838, Auckland 37693, fos. 31–2.

10 Burnes to Macnaghten 2 June 1838, P.P. 1859.

11 Masson to Macnaghten 8 June 1838, Broughton 36473, fos. 370–6.

12 Colvin to Pottinger 13 June 1838, Auckland 37693, fos. 38–9.

13 Auckland to Grant 15 June 1838, Auckland 37693, fos. 44–5.

14 Auckland to Hobhouse 17 June 1838, Broughton 36473, fos. 262–7.

15 Auckland to Macnaghten 14 June 1838, Auckland 37693, fo. 41.

16 Burnes to Macnaghten 19 and 20 June 1838, P.P. 1859.

17 See note 14.

18 Auckland to Fane 21 June 1838, Auckland 37693, fos. 51–4.

19 Masson, *Narrative of Various Journeys*, III, 489–90.

20 Auckland to Macnaghten 9 July 1838, Auckland 37693, fo. 89.

21 Auckland to Ross 3 July 1838, *ibid*. fo. 73.

22 The Tripartite Treaty, P.P. 1839 Indian Papers 1.

23 Colvin to Macnaghten 25 June 1838, Auckland 37693, fos. 55–6.

24 Minute of 2 July 1838, *ibid*. fos. 69–71.

25 Auckland to Macnaghten 1 July 1838, Auckland 37693, fo. 66.
26 Colvin to Macnaghten 12 July 1838, *ibid.* fos. 98–9.
27 Auckland to Prinsep 8 July 1838, *ibid.* fos. 80-2.
28 Todd to Burnes 23 June 1838, see note 1.
29 Auckland to Hobhouse 10 July 1838, Broughton 36473, fos. 281–8.
30 Colvin to Macnaghten 12 July 1838, Auckland 37693, fos. 96–8.
31 Auckland to Hobhouse 12 July 1838, Broughton 36473, fos. 304–5.
32 Governor General to Secret Committee 13 Aug. 1838, see note 8.
33 Burnes to Burnes 22 July 1838, Kaye, *Afghanistan*, I, 366.
34 Burnes to Burnes 23 Aug. 1838, *ibid.* p. 367.
35 Colvin to Burnes 4 Aug. 1838, Auckland 37694, fo. 2.
36 Masson, *Narrative of Various Journeys*, III, 492.
37 *Ibid.* p. 495.
38 Auckland to Hobhouse 12 July 1838, see note 31.
39 Emily Eden to Charles Greville 10 July 1838, Eden, *Letters*.
40 Auckland to Hobhouse 23 Aug. 1838, Broughton 36473, fos. 308–18.
41 Auckland to Fane 24 Dec. 1838, Auckland 37694, fos. 170–1.
42 Colvin to Burnes 24 Dec. 1838, *ibid.* fo. 171.
43 Governor General to Secret Committee 13 Aug. 1838, see note 8.
44 Macnaghten to Pottinger 13 Aug. 1838, I.O.R./S.L. enclosures.
45 Auckland to Keane 15 Aug. 1838, Auckland 37694, fos. 12–14.
46 Colvin to Pottinger 15 Aug. 1838, *ibid.* fos. 14–15.
47 Auckland to Ross 21 Aug. 1838, *ibid.* fo. 20.
48 Auckland to Skinner 21 Aug. 1838, *ibid.* fo. 19.
49 Colvin to Sutherland 20 Aug. 1838, *ibid.* fos. 18–19.
50 Auckland to Hobhouse 23 Aug. 1838, see note 40.
51 Colvin to Wade 24 and 27 Aug. 1838, Auckland 37694, fos. 28 and 31.
52 Colvin to Lynch 28 Aug. 1838, *ibid.* fo. 34.
53 Colvin to Hodgson 28 Aug. 1838, *ibid.* fos. 31–3.
54 McNeill to Hennel 10 July 1838, Palmerston PRO F.O. 539.2, fos. 77–8.
55 McNeill to Stoddart 10 July 1838, *ibid.* fos. 78–80.
56 McNeill to Palmerston 30 July 1838, *ibid.* I, fo. 42.
57 McNeill to Stoddart 10 July 1838, see note 55.
58 McNeill to Palmerston 1 Aug. 1838, Palmerston, PRO F.O. 539.1, fo. 43.
59 McNeill to Palmerston 2 and 3 August 1838, *ibid.* 2, fos. 81–3; McNeill to Auckland 5 Aug 1838. Auckland's answer is in Auckland 37694, fos. 94–5.

CHAPTER 9, pp. 207–230
1 Palmerston to McNeill 22 June 1838, P.P. 1839.
2 Palmerston to Hobhouse 18 July 1838, Broughton 46915, fo. 93.
3 Palmerston to McNeill 27 July 1838, Palmerston PRO F.O. 539.1, fo. 27.
4 *London Gazette*, knighthood, 6 Aug.; brevet, 7 Aug. 1838.
5 Auckland to Hobhouse 3 May 1838, Broughton 36473, fos. 243–8.
6 Broughton, *Recollections*, v, 159, 30 July 1838.

7   Secret Committee to Governor General 2 Aug. 1838, I.O.R./B.D. x.
8   Palmerston to McNeill 6 Aug. 1838, Palmerston PRO F.O. 539.2, fo. 72.
9   Palmerston to McNeill 24 Aug. 1838, *ibid.* fos. 75–6.
10 Palmerston to Hobhouse 25 Aug. 1838, Broughton 46915, fos. 105–6.
11 Palmerston to Hobhouse 27 Aug. 1838, *ibid.* fos. 107–10.
12 Palmerston to Hobhouse 27 Aug. 1838, *ibid.* fos. 111–12.
13 Palmerston to Melbourne 9 Sept. 1838, Sanders, *Melbourne*, p. 453.
14 Melbourne to Russell 26 Sept. 1838, *ibid.* p. 452.
15 Palmerston to McNeill 27 Sept. 1838, Palmerston, PRO, F.O. 539.2, fos. 78 and 80.
16 Palmerston to Russell 1 Oct. 1838, Russell, II, 222–6.
17 Broughton 36469, fo. 145, pencil notes.
18 Palmerston to McNeill 12 Oct. 1838, Palmerston, PRO F.O. 539.2, fos. 85–6.
19 Melbourne to Russell 13 Oct. 1838, Sanders, *Melbourne*, pp. 454–5.
20 Wellington to Aberdeen 10 Dec. 1838, Aberdeen 43060, fos. 182–90.
21 McNeill to Palmerston 11 Sept. 1838, Palmerston PRO F.O. 539.1, fos. 44–5.
22 Palmerston to Hobhouse 18 Oct. 1838, Broughton 46915, fos. 131–2.
23 Secret Committee to Governor General 24 Oct. 1838, I.O.R./B.D. x, 1st series.
24 Melbourne to Russell 14 Nov. 1838, Sanders, *Melbourne*, pp. 455–6.
25 Palmerston to Hobhouse 14 Nov. 1838, Broughton 46915, fos. 137–8.
26 Secret Committee to Governor General 5 Nov. 1838, I.O.R./B.D. x, 1st series.
27 Secret Committee to Governor General 4 Dec. 1838, *ibid.*
28 Willock to Palmerston 1 Dec. 1838, Broughton 36469, fo. 202.
29 Colvin to Macnaghten 4 July 1838, Auckland 37693, fos. 74–5.
30 McNeill to Palmerston 6 Oct. 1838, Palmerston PRO F.O. 539.1, fos. 45–6.
31 Wellington to Aberdeen 10 Dec. 1838, see note 20.
32 Palmerston to Russell 15 Dec. 1838, Russell, II, pp. 238–9.
33 Auckland to Hobhouse 13 Oct. 1838, Broughton 36473, fos. 331–8.
34 Wellington to Aberdeen 24 Dec. 1838, Aberdeen 43060, fos. 196–9.
35 Palmerston to Russell 3 Feb. 1839, Russell, II, 246.
36 *Hansard*, 3rd series, vol. XLV, 5 Feb. 1839.
37 Palmerston to Hobhouse 28 Jan. 1839 Broughton 46915, fos. 151–2.
38 Auckland to Hobhouse 10 May 1839, Broughton 36474, fos. 1–6; and Auckland to Jenkins 21 May 1839, Auckland 37696, fos. 24–5.
39 Undated memorandum among papers for Jan. 1839, Broughton 36470, fos. 19–21; also undated note, *ibid.* fos. 556–7.
40 Cabell's memorandum 14 February 1839, *ibid.* fos. 103–10.
41 Peacock's memorandum, same date, *ibid.* fos 85–92.
42 *Hansard*, 3rd series, vol. XLV, 28 Feb. 1839.
43 *Ibid.* vol. XLVI, 19 March 1839.
44 Broughton, *Recollections*, V, 177–8.
45 Stanhope, *Conversations*, pp. 136–7.

46 Palmerston to Hobhouse 20 March 1839, Broughton 46915, fo. 161.
47 Clanricarde to Palmerston 25 May 1839, Palmerston 48535, fo. 328.
48 Kaye, *Metcalfe*, 11, 200–201.
49 Ellenborough's memorandum 23 Apr. 1839, Law, *India under Ellenborough*.
50 Russian note delivered 25 Feb. 1839, Palmerston PRO F.O. 539.2 fo. 99.
51 Russian note 25 March 1839, and Palmerston to Pozzo di Borgo 4 Apr. 1839, both P.P. 1839.
52 Queen Victoria to Melbourne 10 May 1839, Cecil, *Melbourne*, p. 326.
53 Clanricarde to Palmerston 25 May 1839, see note 47.

CHAPTER 10, pp. 231–246

1 Dennie, *A Personal Narrative*, 22 Aug. 1838.
2 Buist, *Outline of the Operations*, p. 79.
3 Macnaghten to Burnes 6 Sept. 1838, P.P. 1859.
4 Auckland to Lushington 17 Sept. and to Hobhouse, 19 Sept. 1838, Auckland 37694, fos. 47–53.
5 Auckland to Elphinstone 21 Sept. 1838, *ibid.* fos. 53–4.
6 Auckland to Prinsep 10 Sept. 1838, *ibid.* fo. 42.
7 Auckland to Carnac 12 Oct. 1838, *ibid.* fo. 67.
8 Colvin to Pottinger 11 Sept. 1838, *ibid.* fo. 44.
9 Auckland to Hobhouse 15 Nov. 1838, Broughton 36473, fos. 339–52.
10 Simla, 1 Oct. 1838, I.O.R./S.L. enclosure.
11 Colvin to Wade 7 Oct. 1838, Auckland 37694, fos. 64–5.
12 Colvin to Wilkinson 17 Oct. 1838, *ibid.* fos. 77–8.
13 Auckland to McNeill 24 Oct. 1838, *ibid.* fos. 94–5.
14 Auckland to Hobhouse 15 Nov. 1838, see note 9.
15 Auckland to Elphinstone 6 Nov. 1838, Auckland 37694, fos. 101–2.
16 Auckland to Burnes 5 Nov. 1838, *ibid.* fo. 101.
17 Auckland to Hobhouse 15 Nov. 1838, see note 9.
18 Auckland to Morrison 12 Nov. 1838, Auckland 37694, fo. 107.
19 Auckland to Hobhouse, see note 9.
20 Auckland to Pottinger 21 Nov. 1838, P.P. 1859 Colvin to Pottinger; same date, Auckland 37694, fos. 125–6.
21 Colvin to Hodgson 11 Nov. and Colvin to Burnes 21 Nov. 1838, Auckland 37694, fos. 106 and 126–7.
22 Eden, *Up the Country*, 30 Nov. 1838.
23 Auckland to Hobhouse 9 Dec. 1838, Broughton 36473, fos. 359–68.
24 *Ibid.*
25 Eden, *Up the Country*, 6 Dec. 1838.
26 Auckland to McNeill 8 Dec. 1838, Auckland 37694, fo. 137.
27 See note 23.
28 Eden, *Up the Country*, 7 Nov. 1839, when the foxhounds were returning.
29 Abbott, Hough and Nott confirm this incident, 12 Dec. 1838.
30 Governor General to Secret Committee 14 Dec. 1838, I.O.R./S.L. XXIII, 1st series.

31 Auckland to Lushington 15 Dec. 1838, Auckland 37694, fo. 148.
32 Auckland to Hobhouse 2 Jan. 1839, Broughton 36473, fos. 409–16.
33 Auckland to Elphinstone 29 Dec. 1838, Auckland 37695, fos. 4–6.
34 Burnes, *Cabool*, p. 52.
35 Governor General to Secret Committee 13 March 1839, I.O.R./S.L. XXIV, 1st series.
36 Auckland to Hobhouse 15 Nov. 1838, see note 9.

CHAPTER 11, pp. 247–268

1 Auckland to Hobhouse 9 Feb. 1839, Broughton 36473, fos. 419–30.
2 Auckland to Cotton 3 Feb. 1839, Auckland 37695, fos. 54–5.
3 Colvin to Cotton 2 Feb. 1839, *ibid.* fo. 54.
4 Colvin to Cotton 25 Feb. 1839, *ibid.* fo. 88.
5 Secret Committee to Governor General 26 Dec. 1838, I.O.R./B.D. X, 1st series.
6 Emily Eden to Charles Greville 10 July 1838, Eden, *Letters*.
7 Auckland to Hobhouse 18 June 1839, Broughton 36474, fos. 63–8.
8 Colvin to Todd 11 Jan. 1839, Auckland 37695, fo. 19.
9 Auckland to Farish 13 Jan. 1839, *ibid.* fo. 15.
10 Pottinger to Eastwick 13 Jan. 1839, I.O.R./S.L. enclosures.
11 Colvin to Macnaghten 16 Jan. 1839, Auckland 37695, fos. 31–2.
12 Eastwick to Pottinger, see note 10.
13 Hough, *Narrative of the March*, 26 Jan. 1839.
14 Auckland to Cotton 28 Jan. 1839, Auckland 37695, fo. 45.
15 William Nott to Charles Nott 7 Feb. 1839, Nott, *Memoirs*, I, 102.
16 Durand, *The First Afghan War*, p. 42, 31 Jan. 1839.
17 'Zeta' to Hobhouse 1 Jan. 1839, Broughton 36470, fos. 22–3.
18 Macnaghten to Colvin 5 Feb. 1839, Kaye, *Afghanistan*, I, 415.
19 Macnaghten to Cotton 7 Feb. 1839; Auckland's reproof: Auckland to Macnaghten 19 Feb. 1839, Auckland 37695, fos. 78–9.
20 Auckland to Macnaghten 5 Feb. 1839, *ibid.* fo. 59.
21 Colvin to Burnes 17 Jan. 1839, *ibid.* fo. 34.
22 Wade to Auckland 31 Jan. 1839, Broughton 36473, fo. 431–3.
23 Colvin to Macnaghten 16 Jan. 1839, Auckland 37695, fos. 31–2.
24 Palmerston to Hobhouse 1 Jan. 1839, Broughton 46915, fos. 145–6.
25 Auckland to Taylor 1 Feb. 1839, Auckland 37695, fos. 56–7.
26 Buist, Durand and Hough agree on the story so far.
27 Kaye, *Afghanistan*, I, 418.
28 Pottinger to Maddock 6 July 1839, I.O.R./S.L. enclosures.
29 Maddock to Pottinger 2 Sept. 1839, *ibid.*
30 Governor General to Secret Committee 13 March 1839, I.O.R./S.L. XXIV, 1st series.
31 Colvin to Macnaghten 5 Feb. 1839, Auckland 37695, fo. 58.
32 Auckland to Hobhouse 9 Feb. 1839, see note 1.
33 Colvin to Macnaghten 5 Feb. 1839, see note 31.
34 Nott, *Memoirs*, I, 105–6, letter of 14 Feb. 1839.
35 Auckland to Keane 24 Feb. 1839, Auckland 37695, fos. 85–6.
36 Dennie, *A Personal Narrative*, letter of 9 March, 1839.

37 Auckland to Keane 13 March, and to Cotton 14 March 1839, Auckland 37695, fos. 119–120.
38 Auckland to Macnaghten 17 and 22 March 1839, Auckland 37695, fos. 121 and 125.
39 Macnaghten to Auckland 19 March 1839, Kaye, *Afghanistan*, I, 429–30.
40 Burnes to Macnaghten 30 March 1839, *ibid.* 424–5.
41 Hough, *Narrative of the March*, 26 March 1839.
42 Hough, *ibid.*, and Buist, *Outline of the Operations*, 27 March 1839.
43 Macnaghten to Auckland 4 Apr. 1839, Kaye, *Afghanistan*, I, 431–2.
44 Macnaghten to Colvin 6 Apr. 1839, *ibid.* 432–3.
45 Nott, *Memoirs*, I, 117–21.
46 Macnaghten to Colvin 9 Apr. 1839, Kaye, *Afghanistan*, I, 433–4; also to Auckland 6 Apr., a letter quoted in Secret Committee to Governor General 13 Sept. 1839, I.O.R./B.D. XI, 1st series.
47 Abbott, *Journal*, entry dated 14 Apr. 1839.
48 *Ibid.* entry dated 19 Apr. 1839.
49 Broughton, *Recollections*, V, 209–10, 3 July 1839.
50 Auckland to Hobhouse 25 Sept. 1839, Broughton 36474, fos. 132–41.
51 Burnes to Auckland 25 Apr. 1839, Broughton 36474, fos. 43–5.
52 Macnaghten to Emily Eden 25 Apr. 1839, Eden, *Up the Country*, entry of 23 May 1839.
53 Auckland to Elphinstone 26 June 1839, Auckland 37696, fos. 119–20.

CHAPTER 12, pp. 269–302

1 Nott, *Memoirs*, I, 91.
2 Hough, *A Narrative of the March*, 6 May 1839.
3 Dennie, *A Personal Narrative*, 15 Jun. 1839.
4 Havelock, *Narrative of the War*, II, 22–3.
5 Colvin to Macnaghten 16 Jan. 1839, Auckland 37695, fos. 31–2.
6 Auckland to Wade 7 March 1839, *ibid.* fo. 108.
7 Macnaghten to Auckland 6 June 1839, Broughton 36474, fos. 122–7.
8 Kaye, *Afghanistan*, I, 435–6.
9 Macnaghten to Auckland 6 June 1839, see note 7.
10 Hough, Outram and Buist, *see* Bibliography.
11 Auckland to Hobhouse 25 May 1839, Broughton 36474, fos. 7–12.
12 Auckland to Hobhouse 18 June 1839, *ibid.* fos. 63–8.
13 Hough, *Narrative of the March*, 7 June 1839.
14 *Ibid.*, 9 June 1839.
15 Outram, *Rough Notes*, 17 June 1839.
16 Auckland to Burnes 27 May 1839, Auckland 37696, fo. 42.
17 Colvin to Macnaghten 9 and 13 June 1839, Auckland 37696, fos. 74–7 and 87–8.
18 Colvin to Macnaghten 5 Feb. 1839, Auckland 37695, fo. 58.
19 Auckland to Hobhouse 1 Apr. and 10 May 1839, Broughton 36473, fos. 446–53, and 36474, fos. 1–6.
20 Colvin to Wade 1 Apr. 1839, Auckland 37695, fos. 138–9.
21 Colvin to Clerk 6 Apr. 1839, *ibid.* fo. 141.

22 Macnaghten to Auckland 25 Apr. 1839, Kaye, *Afghanistan*, I, 438–9
23 Auckland to Macnaghten 27 May 1839, Auckland 37695, fos. 43–4.
24 Auckland to Hobhouse 6 June 1839, Broughton 36474, fos. 54–8.
25 Colvin to Wade 7 June 1839, Auckland 37696, fos. 66–8.
26 Auckland to Hobhouse 14 July 1839, Broughton 36474, fos. 104–9.
27 Auckland to Hobhouse 9 Feb. 1839, Broughton 36473, fos. 419–30.
28 Auckland to Fane 10 Feb. 1839, Auckland 37695, fo. 63.
29 Auckland to Hobhouse 10 May 1839, see note 19.
30 Auckland to Pottinger 22 Feb. 1839, Auckland 37695, fos. 81–2.
31 Auckland to Macnaghten 28 Feb. 1839, *ibid*. fos. 97–8.
32 Auckland to Keane 1 March 1839, *ibid*. fos. 99–100.
33 Auckland to Farish 3 March 1839, *ibid*. fo. 104.
34 Colvin to Pottinger 9 March 1839, *ibid*. fos. 109–10.
35 Auckland to Hobhouse 12 March 1839, Broughton 36473, fos. 436–44.
36 Governor General to Secret Committee 13 March 1839, I.O.R./S.L. XXIV, 1st series.
37 Colvin to Willoughby 19 Apr. 1839, Auckland 37695, fo. 157.
38 Auckland to Prinsep 19 Apr. 1839, *ibid*. fos. 160–1.
39 Auckland to Bell 18 May 1839, Auckland 37696, fos. 11–14.
40 Secret Committee to Governor General 4 Dec. 1838, I.O.R./B.D. x, 1st series.
41 Secret Committee to Governor General 18 Feb. 1839, *ibid*.
42 Auckland to Hobhouse 10 May 1839, see note 19.
43 Secret Committee to Governor General 13 May 1839, I.O.R./B.D. x, 1st series.
44 Secret Committee to Governor General 8 July 1839, *ibid*.
45 Auckland to Hobhouse 10 May 1839, see note 19.
46 Palmerston to Lansdowne 17 June 1838, Guedalla. p. 424
47 Auckland to Macnaghten 15 June 1839, Auckland 37696, fos. 91–3.
48 Auckland to Hobhouse 18 June and 13 November 1839, Broughton 36474, fos. 63–8 and 172–80.
49 Dennie, *A Personal Narrative*, 29 July 1839.
50 Kaye, *Afghanistan*, I, 456.
51 Dennie, *A Personal Narrative*, written down in 1840.
52 Havelock, Hough, Buist, Kaye, 7 Aug. 1839.
53 Dennie, *A Personal Narrative*, letter of 1 Sept. 1839.
54 Nott to Deputy Adjutant General 14 Oct. and Auckland to Keane 5 Dec. 1839, Nott *Memoirs*, I, 147–50; also Auckland to Hobhouse 21 Dec. 1839, Broughton 36474, fos. 188–99.
55 Eden, *Up the Country*, entry dated 4 Dec. 1839.
56 Auckland to Outram 1 Dec. 1839, Auckland 37697, fo. 6.
57 Auckland to Hobhouse 25 May 1839, see note 11.
58 Auckland to Jenkins 14 July and 23 Dec. 1839, Auckland 37696, fos. 177–8, and 37697, fos. 57–9.
59 Auckland to Hobhouse 14 July 1839, see note 26.
60 Auckland to Fane 17 July 1839, Auckland 37696, fo. 191.
61 Colvin to Wade 13 Dec. 1839, Auckland 37697, fo. 29.

62 Wellington to Peel 18 Dec. 1839, Peel, II, 416–20.
63 Auckland to Hobhouse 15 Oct. 1839, Broughton 36474, fos. 158–65.
64 Havelock, *Narrative of the War*, Appendix.
65 From Auckland to Hobhouse 23 Jan. 1840, Broughton 36474, fos. 203–10, quoting Macnaghten's of 1 Jan.
66 Broughton, *Recollections*, v, 231–2, 31 Oct. 1839.

CHAPTER 13, pp. 305–336

1 Nesselrode to Pozzo 17 June 1839, Ward and Gooch, *Cambridge History of British Foreign Policy*.
2 Palmerston to Bulwer 1 Sept. 1839.
3 Palmerston to Hobhouse 12 June 1839, Broughton 46915, fo. 167.
4 Palmerston to Ponsonby and Campbell 10 May 1839, sent to India with Secret Committee dispatch of 11 May, I.O.R./B.D. x, 1st series.
5 Palmerston to Hobhouse 31 Oct. 1839, quoting Clanricarde, Broughton 46915, fos. 181–2.
6 Perowski's manifesto. Berowski, a different man, died at Herat.
7 Clanricarde to Palmerston 30 Nov. 1839, I.O.R./B.D. xi, 1st series.
8 Auckland to Macnaghten 7 Dec. 1839, Auckland 37697, fos. 12–13; also Colvin to Macnaghten 5 Dec., *ibid.* fo. 10.
9 Auckland to Macnaghten 10 Dec. 1839, *ibid.* fo. 21.
10 Secret Committee to Governor General 26 Dec. 1839, I.O.R./B.D. xi, 1st series.
11 Colvin to Macnaghten 19 Jan. 1840, Auckland 37697, fos. 130–1.
12 Palmerston to Clanricarde 24 Jan. 1840, I.O.R./B.D. xii, 1st series.
13 Clanricarde to Palmerston 14 Jan. 1840, *ibid.*
14 Palmerston to Clanricarde 3 Feb. 1840, *ibid.*
15 Palmerston to Hobhouse 14 Feb. 1840, Broughton 46915, fos. 196–9.
16 Palmerston to Hobhouse 17 Feb. 1840, *ibid.* fos. 202–3.
17 Palmerston to Hobhouse 28 Feb. 1840, *ibid.* fos. 204–5.
18 Secret Committee to Governor General 29 Feb. 1840, I.O.R./B.D. xii, 1st series.
19 Clanricarde to Palmerston 24 Feb. 1840, Palmerston 48536, fo. 16.
20 Auckland to Robertson 7 Jan. 1840, Auckland 37697, fo. 100.
21 Auckland to Hobhouse 23 Jan. 1840, Broughton 36474, fos. 203–10.
22 Abbott to a friend 1 Feb. 1840, Abbott, *Journal.*
23 Auckland to Hobhouse 16 Feb. 1840, Broughton 36474, fos. 229–34; also Governor General to Secret Committee, 15 Feb. and 16 March, I.O.R./S.L. xxv, 1st series.
24 Secret Committee to Governor General, 8 July 1839, I.O.R./B.D. x, 1st series.
25 Auckland to Macnaghten 22 March 1840, Auckland 37698, fos. 89–90.
26 Colvin to Macnaghten 12 Apr. and Maddock to Macnaghten 13 Apr. 1840, *ibid.* fos. 125–7 and 134–6.
27 Governor General to Secret Committee 15 Apr. 1840, I.O.R./S.L. xxv, 1st series.

28 Hobhouse to Auckland 4 May 1840, quoted to Macnaghten by Auckland 29 June 1840, Auckland 37700, fos. 74–5.

29 Auckland to Hobhouse 11 May 1840, Broughton 36474, fos. 280–9.

30 Palmerston to Clanricarde 24 March 1840, I.O.R./B.D. XII, 1st series, a copy sent to India.

31 Auckland to Carnac 1 May 1840, Auckland 37699, fos. 37–8.

32 Auckland to Clerk 6 May 1840, *ibid*. fos. 58–9.

33 Auckland to Macnaghten 6 May 1840, *ibid*. fos. 60–2.

34 Marginal comment by Hobhouse on the Governor General's dispatch to the Secret Committee 8 May 1840, I.O.R./S.L. XXV, 1st series.

35 Palmerston to Hobhouse 4 May 1840, Broughton 46915, fos. 210–11, and see note 28.

36 Colvin to Bayley 12 May 1840, Auckland 37699, fos. 83–5.

37 Palmerston to Hobhouse 25 May 1840, Broughton 46915, fo. 212–15.

38 Palmerston to Bloomfield 7 July 1840, I.O.R./B.D. XIII, 1st series, a copy sent to India.

39 Bloomfield to Palmerston 1 Aug. 1840, *ibid*.

40 Bloomfield to Palmerston 7 Aug. 1840, *ibid*.

41 Secret Committee to Governor General 4 Sept. 1840, *ibid*.

42 Auckland to Clanricarde 14 Sept. 1840, Auckland 37701, fos. 102–3.

43 Bloomfield to Palmerston 26 Sept. 1840, I.O.R./B.D. XIII, 1st series, a copy sent to India.

44 Palmerston to Hobhouse 29 Sept. 1840, Broughton 46915, fos. 221–2.

45 Bloomfield to Palmerston 10 Oct. 1840, I.O.R./B.D. XIII, 1st series, a copy sent to India.

46 Auckland to Hobhouse 25 Sept. 1839, Broughton, 36474, fos. 132–41.

47 Governor General to Secret Committee 4 June 1840, I.O.R./S.L. XXV, 1st series.

48 Auckland to Hobhouse 11 June 1840, Broughton 36474, fos. 294–301.

49 Buist, *Outline of the Operations*, 16 May. 1840

50 *Ibid*. Durand and others agree.

51 Torrens to Macnaghten 15 June 1840, Auckland 37700, fos. 54–5.

52 Cotton to Auckland 30 June 1840, quoted in Auckland to Carnac 23 July 1840, Auckland 37700, fos. 132–3.

53 Governor General to Secret Committee 13 Sept. 1840, I.O.R./S.L. XXV, 1st series.

54 Auckland to Cotton 9 July 1840, Auckland 37700, fos. 93–4; also Governor General to Secret Committee 11 July 1840, I.O.R./SL. XXV, 1st series.

55 Auckland to Hobhouse 10 July 1840, Broughton 36474, fos. 328–37.

56 Auckland to Macnaghten 16 July 1840, Auckland 37700, fos. 115–17.

57 Secret Committee to Governor General 17 Aug. 1840. I.O.R./B.D. XIII, 1st series.

58 Auckland to Hobhouse 15 Aug. 1840, Broughton 36474, fos. 338–47.

59 Auckland to Cotton 16 Aug. 1840, Auckland 37701, fo. 30.

60 See note 58.

61 Auckland to Macnaghten 14 Aug. 1840, Auckland 37701, fos. 12–14.

62 Auckland to Hobhouse 18 Sept. 1840, Broughton 36474, fos. 348–55.
63 Governor General to Secret Committee 13 Sept. 1840, I.O.R./S.L. XXV, 1st series.
64 Auckland to Hobhouse 18 Sept. 1840, see note 62; also Kaye, *Afghanistan*, II, 67–8.
65 Macnaghten to Rawlinson 9 Sept. 1840, Kaye, *Afghanistan*, II, 81.
66 See note 63.
67 Auckland to Carnac 15 Sept. 1840, Auckland 37701, fo. 109.
68 Nott to his family 29 Sept. 1840, Nott, *Memoirs*, I, 256.
69 Auckland to Bean 5 Apr. 1841, Auckland 37704, fos. 121–2.
70 Macnaghten to Auckland 12 Sept. 1840, Kaye, *Afghanistan*, II, 82–3.
71 Dennie, *A Personal Narrative*, Order of the Day, 19 Sept. 1840.
72 Dennie to Cotton 18 Sept. 1840, *ibid.*
73 Macnaghten, probably to Rawlinson, 4 Oct. 1840, Kaye, *Afghanistan*, II, 89–90.
74 Auckland to Macnaghten 10 Oct. 1840, and Auckland to Cotton, same date, Auckland 37701, fos. 174–5.
75 Governor General to Secret Committee 16 Oct. 1840, I.O.R./S.L. XXV, 1st series.
76 Auckland to Hobhouse 18/19 Oct. 1840, Broughton 36474, fos. 361–70.
77 Auckland to Macnaghten 28 Nov. and to Taylor 4 Dec. 1840, Auckland 37702, fos. 128–30, and 37703, fo. 5.
78 Colvin to Macnaghten 13 Dec. 1840, *ibid.* fos. 22–4.
79 Palmerston to Granville 8 Dec. 1840, Ashley, pp. 400–1.
80 Palmerston to Hobhouse 8 Dec. 1840, Broughton 46915, fo. 240.
81 Palmerston to Hobhouse 12 Dec. 1840, *ibid.* fos. 241–2.

CHAPTER 14, pp. 337–360

1 *D.N.B.* Elphinstone, William.
2 Auckland to Hobhouse 25 Sept. 1839, Broughton 36474, fos. 132–41.
3 Auckland to Cotton 13 Nov. 1840, Auckland 37702, fos. 79–80.
4 Auckland to General Elphinstone 14 Nov. 1840, *ibid.* fos. 85–6.
5 Auckland to Elphinstone 18 Dec. 1840, Auckland 37703, fo. 33.
6 Auckland to Macnaghten 28 Nov. 1840, Auckland 37702, fos. 128–30.
7 Colvin to Macnaghten 13 Dec. 1840, Auckland 37703, fos. 22–4.
8 Auckland to Elphinstone 18 Dec. 1840, *ibid.* fo. 33.
9 Auckland to Roberts 12 Nov. and to Anquetil 22 Nov. 1840, Auckland 37702, fos. 72 and 111–12.
10 Auckland to Macnaghten 12 Nov. and 28 Nov., and Colvin to Macnaghten 13 Dec. 1840, Auckland 37702, fos. 77–8 and 128–30, and 37703, fos. 22–4.
11 Auckland to Hobhouse 22 Dec. 1840, Broughton 36474, fos. 429–35.
12 Secret Committee to Governor General 31 Dec. 1840, I.R.O./B.D. XIII, 1st series.
13 Greville, *Memoirs*, 7 Jan. 1841.
14 Palmerston to Hobhouse 7 Jan. 1841, Broughton 46915, fos. 245–6.

15 Secret Committee to Governor General 29 Jan. 1841, I.O.R./B.D xiv, 1st series.

16 Stocqueler, ed. Nott, *Memoirs*, I, 285–6.

17 Colvin to Macnaghten 13 Dec. 1840, see note 7.

18 Auckland to Elphinstone 8 Feb. 1841, Auckland 37703, fos. 151–3.

19 Secret Committee to Governor General 23 March 1841, I.O.R./B.D. xiv, 1st series.

20 Auckland to Carnac, Robertson and Macnaghten 26 Feb. 1841, Auckland 37704, fos. 35–9.

21 Maddock to Macnaghten 15 March 1841, *ibid*. fos. 63–5.

22 Kaye, *Afghanistan*, II, 397, Nicolls' journal 15 March 1841.

23 Auckland to Macnaghten 16 March 1841, Auckland 37704, fos. 65–6.

24 Minute of 19 March 1841, Auckland 37704, fos. 84–94.

25 Auckland to Hobhouse 21 March 1841, Broughton 36474, fos. 466–74.

26 Colvin to Macnaghten 21 March 1841, Auckland 37704, fos. 70–1.

27 Palmerston to Hobhouse 2 Feb. 1841, I.O.R./B.D. xiv, 1st series, a copy sent to India.

28 Auckland to Macnaghten 23 and 25 March 1841, Auckland 37704, fos. 96 and 103–4.

29 Auckland to Lyall 8 July and 19 November 1841, Auckland 37705, fos. 156–7, and 37706, fos. 173–5.

30 Auckland to Clerk 6 Apr. 1841, Auckland 37704, fos. 125–6.

31 Maddock to Macnaghten 5 Apr. 1841, *ibid*. fos. 124–5.

32 Governor General to Maharajah Sher Singh 26 Apr. 1841, Auckland 37705, fo. 27.

33 Emily Eden to Robert Eden 12 Apr. 1841, Eden, *Letters*.

34 Kaye, *Afghanistan*, II, 149, Nicolls' journal 20 May 1841.

35 Auckland to Hobhouse 12 May 1841, Broughton 37474, fos. 542–7.

36 Auckland to Macnaghten 9 May 1841, Auckland 37705, fo. 51.

37 Auckland to Lyall 8 May 1841, *ibid*. fos. 46–7.

38 Palmerston to Hobhouse 1 June 1841, Broughton 46915, fos. 257–60.

39 Palmerston to Hobhouse 3 June 1841, *ibid*. fos. 263–4.

40 Secret Committee to Governor General 4 June 1841, I.O.R./B.D. xiv, 1st series.

41 Secret Committee to Governor General 5 June 1841, *ibid*.

42 Secret Committee to Governor General 28 June 1841, I.O.R./B.D. xv, 1st series.

43 Maddock to Macnaghten 11 July 1841, Auckland 37705, fo. 163.

44 Auckland to Macnaghten 11 July 1841, Auckland 37706, fo. 1.

45 Macnaghten to Rawlinson 13 June 1841, Kaye, *Afghanistan*, II, 123.

46 Auckland to Macnaghten 12 June 1841, Auckland 37705, fos. 110–12.

47 Auckland to Macnaghten 11 July 1841, see note 44.

48 Macnaghten to Rawlinson 2 Aug. and to Robertson 20 Aug. 1841, Kaye, *Afghanistan*, II, 130.

49 Auckland to Hobhouse 20 Aug. 1841, Auckland 37706, fos. 46–8.

50 Auckland to Macnaghten 21 Aug. 1841, *ibid*. fos. 55–6.

51 Auckland to McNeill 22 Aug. 1841, *ibid*. fo. 59.

52 Broughton, *Recollections*, VI, 42–3, 28 Aug. 1841.
53 Lady Palmerston to Mrs Huskisson 28 Aug. 1841, Lever.
54 Secret Committee to Governor General 4 Sept. 1841, I.O.R./B.D. XV, 1st series.
55 Ellenborough to Auckland 6 Sept. 1841, Ellenborough PRO 30.12, and Peel 40471, fos. 216–25.
56 Undated memorandum Sept. and Queen Victoria to Ellenborough 19 Sept. 1841, Victoria, *Letters*, I, 326–9.
57 Ellenborough to Auckland 19 Sept. 1841, see note 55.
58 Palmerston to Hobhouse 7 Sept. 1841, Broughton 46915, fos. 265–6.
59 Peel to Wellington 6 Oct. 1841, Peel, II, 576.
60 Wellington to Peel 7 Oct. 1841, *ibid.* pp. 576–7.
61 Melbourne to Queen Victoria 12 Oct. 1841, Victoria, *Letters*, I, 346–7.
62 Peel to Fitzgerald 17 Oct. 1841, Peel, II, 580.
63 Secret Committee to Governor General 25 Oct. 1841, I.O.R./B.D. XV, 1st series.
64 Auckland to Macnaghten 3 Sept. 1841, Auckland 37706, fo. 70.
65 Colvin to Macnaghten 26 Sept. 1841, *ibid.* fos. 94–6.
66 Macnaghten to Robertson 25 Sept. 1841, Kaye, *Afghanistan*, II, 150–2.

CHAPTER 15, pp. 361–390

1 Macnaghten to Robertson 20 Aug. 1841, Kaye, *Afghanistan*, II, 130.
2 Macnaghten to Auckland 8 Oct. 1841, quoted by Auckland to Nicolls 29 Oct., Auckland 37706, fo. 147.
3 Auckland to Nicolls 20 Oct. 1841, *ibid.* fos. 126–7.
4 Auckland to Lyall 21 Oct. 1841, *ibid.* fos. 131–2.
5 Durand, *The First Afghan War*, 23 Oct. 1841.
6 Sale, *Journal*, p. 23.
7 Macnaghten to Macgregor and Rawlinson 1 Nov. 1841, Kaye, *Afghanistan*, II, 162–6.
8 Lady Sale and Vincent Eyre, sources for much of this chapter.
9 Shelton quoted by Kaye, *Afghanistan*, II, 208.
10 James Burnes to James Carnac 1 Feb. 1842, Wellesley 37313, fo. 135.
11 Elphinstone to Macnaghten 2 Nov. 1841, Kaye, *Afghanistan*, II, 410.
12 Shelton's statement, see note 9; Elphinstone's memorandum, quoted by Eyre.
13 Macnaghten to Macgregor 9 Nov. 1841, Kaye *Afghanistan*, II, 210.
14 Macnaghten to Macgregor 14 Nov. 1841, *ibid.* pp. 224–5.
15 Macnaghten to Elphinstone 18 Nov. 1841, *ibid.* pp. 237–8.
16 The full text of the treaty of 1 Jan. 1842, the date of ratification, is in Kaye, *Afghanistan*, II.
17 Abbott to a friend 18 Jan. 1842, Abbott, *Journal*.
18 Kaye, *Afghanistan*, III, 15–16.
19 Auckland to Nicolls 25 Nov. 1841, Auckland 37706, fo. 193.
20 Auckland to Nicolls 1 Dec. 1841, *ibid.* fos. 197–8.

21 Auckland to Anderson and Robertson 2 Dec. 1841, *ibid.* fos. 198–9 and 200–1.
22 Auckland to Nicolls 2 Dec. 1841, *ibid.* fos. 201–2.
23 Auckland to Macnaghten 4 Dec. 1841, *ibid.* fos. 202–3.
24 Auckland to Nicolls 5 Dec. 1841, *ibid.* fos. 205–6.
25 Colvin to Clerk 8 Dec. 1841, Auckland 37707, fos. 14–15.
26 Auckland to Anderson 15 Dec. 1841, *ibid.* fos. 23–5.
27 Auckland to Nicolls 18 Dec. 1841, *ibid.* fos. 38–9.
28 Auckland to Ellenborough 22 Dec. 1841, *ibid.* fos. 48–55.
29 John Colvin to James Colvin 22 Dec. 1841, *ibid.* fos. 64–7.
30 Auckland to Nicolls and Lyall 23 Dec. 1841, *ibid.* fos. 59–60 and 61–3.
31 Based partly on Auckland's letter-journal for Ellenborough, starting 28 Jan., and partly on Abbott's letter of 25 Jan.
32 Auckland to Nicolls 1 Jan. 1842, Auckland 37707, fos. 82–3.
33 Auckland to Nicolls 6 Jan. 1842, *ibid.* fo. 93.
34 Auckland to Nicolls 21 Jan. 1842, *ibid.* fos. 110–111.
35 Kaye, *Afghanistan*, III, 24, Nicolls' journal 23 Jan. 1842.
36 Auckland to Lyall 23 Jan. 1842, Auckland 37707, fos. 117–21.
37 Auckland to Fitzgerald 23 Jan. 1842, *ibid.* fos. 123–4.
38 Proclamation by the Governor General 31 Jan. 1842.
39 Colvin to Clerk 31 Jan. 1842, Auckland 37707, fos. 134–5.
40 Auckland to Nicolls 3 Feb. 1842, *ibid.* fo. 145.
41 Governor General to Secret Committee 19 Feb. 1842, I.O.R./S.L. XXVII, 1st series.
42 Durand, *The First Afghan War*, 21 Feb. 1842.
43 Auckland to Hobhouse 18 Feb. 1842, Auckland 37707, fos. 187–8.
44 Diary entry 3 July 1843, Broughton 43745, fo. 164.
45 Ellenborough to Peel 21 Feb. 1842, Ellenborough PRO 30.12.89.
46 Ellenborough to Peel 5 Apr. 1842, *ibid.*

CHAPTER 16, pp. 391–416

1 Ellenborough to Pollock 1 March 1842, Ellenborough PRO 30.12.98.
2 Ellenborough to Nicolls 15 March 1842, *ibid.* 83.
3 Ellenborough to Peel 22 March 1842, *ibid.* 89.
4 Ellenborough to Peel 5 Apr. 1842, *ibid.*
5 Eyre, *Military Operations at Cabul*, Appendix.
6 Abbott, *Journal*, letter of 12 March 1842.
7 Cumming, *Six Years Diary*, entry for 7 March 1842.
8 *Ibid.* entry for 31 March 1842.
9 Nott to England 18 Apr. 1842, Kaye, *Afghanistan*, III, 439–40.
10 Fitzgerald to Queen Victoria 10 March 1842, Victoria, *Letters*, I, p. 385.
11 Greville, *Memoirs*, 14 March 1842.
12 Stanhope, *Conversations*, p. 274, entry for 31 March 1842.
13 Peel to Arbuthnot 5 Apr. 1842, Peel, II, 535.
14 Wellington to Ellenborough 31 March 1842. The original is in Ellenborough PRO, 30.12; also a copy in Wellesley 37415, fos. 142–53.
15 Peel to Ellenborough 6 Apr. 1842, Ellenborough PRO 30.12.37.

16 Cumming, *Six Years Diary*, entry for 4 Apr. 1842.

17 *Ibid.*

18 Abbott, *Journal*, entry for 7 Apr. 1842, and letter of 26 April.

19 Eyre, *Military Operations*, 11 Apr. 1842.

20 Ellenborough to Pollock 19 Apr. 1842, Ellenborough PRO 30.12.98.

21 Ellenborough to Hardinge 18 Apr. 1842, *ibid.* 30.12.89.

22 Ellenborough to Fitzgerald 20 Apr. 1842, *ibid.* 30.12.77.

23 Ellenborough to Peel 21 Apr. 1842, *ibid.* 30.12.89.

24 Ellenborough to Fitzgerald 21 Apr. 1842, *ibid.* 30.12.77.

25 Ellenborough to Pollock 28 Apr. 1842, *ibid.* 30.12.98.

26 Pollock to Ellenborough 13 May 1842, *ibid.* 30.12.65.

27 Ellenborough to Hardinge 17 May 1842, *ibid.* 30.12.89.

28 Ellenborough to Wellington 17 May 1842, *ibid.* 30.12.89.

29 Ellenborough to Fitzgerald 9 May 1842, *ibid.* 30.12.77.

30 Nott to Hammersley 2 June 1842, Kaye, *Afghanistan*, III, 317.

31 Ellenborough to Peel 7 June 1842, Ellenborough PRO 30.12.89.

32 Ellenborough to Pollock 1 June 1842, *ibid.* 30.12.98.

33 Ellenborough to Pollock 4 July 1842, *ibid.*; also to Nott, same date, PRO 30.12.95.

34 Ellenborough to Wellington 6 July 1842, *ibid.* 30.12.89.

35 Ellenborough to Pollock 23 July 1842, *ibid.* 30.12.98.

36 Ellenborough to Pollock 29 July 1842, *ibid.*

37 Lady Sale and Vincent Eyre are the sources for the story of the prisoners and of Kabul politics.

38 Ellenborough to Pollock 25 Apr. 1842, Ellenborough PRO 30.12.98.

39 Kaye, *Afghanistan*, III, 218–12.

40 Ellenborough to Pollock 15 May 1842, Ellenborough PRO 30.12.98.

41 Ellenborough to Pollock 21 May 1842, *ibid.*

42 Ellenborough to Pollock 3 Aug. 1842, *ibid.*

43 Sale, *Journal*, entry for 21 Aug. 1842.

44 Kaye, *Afghanistan*, III, 329.

45 Abbott, *Journal*, 24 Aug. 1842.

46 Nott to Ellenborough 31 Aug. 1842, Ellenborough PRO 30.12.6/4.

47 Nott to Ellenborough 8 Sept. 1842, *ibid.*

48 Ellenborough to Nott 4 July 1842, see note 33.

49 Abbott, *Journal*, letter to a friend 12 Sept. 1842.

CHAPTER 17, pp. 417–442

1 Governor General to Secret Committee 30 Apr. 1842, I.O.R./S.L. XXVII, 1st series.

2 Lady Palmerston to Lord Beauvale 6 May 1842, Lever.

3 *Hansard*, 3rd series, vol. LXIII, 31 May 1842, the date of an entry in Hobhouse's diary, Broughton 43744, fo. 49.

4 *Ibid.* fo. 53, diary entry for 3 June 1842.

5 *Ibid.* fos. 61–3, entries for 18 and 22 June 1842.

6 *Hansard*, 3rd series, vol. LXIV, 23 June 1842, the date of an entry in Hobhouse's diary, Broughton 43744, fos. 63–6.

7 *Ibid.*, entry dated 1 July 1842, fos. 70–1.

8 Fitzgerald to Queen Victoria 4 July 1842, Victoria, *Letters*, I, 406–7.

9 Peel to Fitzgerald 6 July 1842, Peel II, 586.

10 Stanley to Ellenborough 6 July 1842, Ellenborough PRO 30.12.37.

11 Wellington to Ellenborough 6 July 1842, Wellesley 37415, fos. 154 ff.

12 Hobhouse's diary entry for 7 Aug. 1842, Broughton 43744, fo. 95; also for 12 Aug. 1842, *ibid.* fo. 97.

13 Auckland to Peel 23 Aug. 1842, Peel 40514, fos. 181 and 183; also Peel to Fitzgerald 5 Sept. 1842, Peel II, 589 ff.

14 Greville, *Memoirs*, entry for 3 Sept. 1842.

15 Hobhouse's diary entry 26 Aug. 1842, Broughton 43744, fos. 101–4.

16 Greville, *Memoirs*, entry for 11 Sept. 1842.

17 Hobhouse's diary entry 31 Aug. 1842, Broughton 43744, fo. 106.

18 Greville, *Memoirs*, entry for 3 Sept. 1842.

19 *History of the Times*, I, 296–7.

20 Stanley to Ellenborough 5 Sept. 1842, Ellenborough PRO 30.12.37.

21 Peel to Fitzgerald 8 Sept. 1842, Peel II, 590; also Peel to Fitzgerald 9 Sept., *ibid.* p. 591.

22 Hobhouse's diary entry 8 June 1842, Broughton 43744, fo. 56.

23 Kaye, *Afghanistan*, III, 456, Nicolls' journal.

24 Ellenborough to Peel 6 July 1842, Ellenborough PRO 30.12.89.

25 Peel to Fitzgerald 11 Sept. 1842, Peel, II, 591–2; also Peel to Fitzgerald 8 Sept., *ibid.* p. 590.

26 Greville, *Memoirs*, entry for 11 Sept.

27 Ellenborough to Peel 19 Sept. 1842, Ellenborough PRO 30.12.89.

28 Greville, *Memoirs*, entry for 24 Sept.

29 Palmerston to Hobhouse 5 Oct. 1842, Broughton 46915, fos. 271–2; also Hobhouse's diary entry for 8 Oct., Broughton 43744, fos. 109–10.

30 Wellington to Ellenborough 9 Oct. 1842, Ellenborough PRO 30.12.6/4.

31 Peel to Ellenborough 24 Sept. 1842, *ibid.* 30.12.37.

32 See note 29.

33 Fitzgerald to Peel 19 Oct. 1842, Peel, II, 595; also Peel to Fitzgerald 2 Nov. 1842, *ibid.* pp. 596–7. They discussed the Duke's letter.

34 Palmerston to Lansdowne 4 Nov. 1842, Guedalla p. 210.

35 Pottinger to Aberdeen 29 Aug. 1842, PRO F.O. 17.57.

36 Peel to Stanley 23 Nov. 1842, Peel 40467, fo. 303.

37 Stanley to Queen Victoria 23 Nov. 1842, Victoria, *Letters*, I, 440–2.

38 Ellenborough to Peel 5 Oct. 1842, Ellenborough PRO 30.12.89.

39 Peel to Ellenborough 3 Dec. 1842, *ibid.* 30.12.37.

40 Brunnow to Nesselrode 30 Nov. 1842 and Brunnow to Ellenborough 2 Jan. 1843, *ibid.* 30.12.37.

41 Greville, *Memoirs*, entry for 27 Nov. 1842.

42 Princess Lieven to Lady Palmerston 27 Nov., Lady Palmerston to Princess Lieven 1 Dec., and Princess Lieven to Lady Palmerston 5 Dec. 1842, Lever, p. 238.

43 Greville, *Memoirs*, entries for 30 Nov., 6 and 8 Dec. 1842.

44 Ellenborough to Peel 27 Oct. 1842, Ellenborough PRO 30.12.89.

45 Fitzgerald to Peel and Peel to Fitzgerald 12 Jan. 1843, Peel, III, 3.

46 Proclamation of 16 Nov. 1842.

47 Hardinge to Ellenborough 6 Feb. 1843, Ellenborough PRO 30.12.37.

48 Ellenborough to Peel 18 Oct. 1842, *ibid.* 30.12.89.

49 Napier's memorandum 17 Oct. 1842, Law, *India under Ellenborough.*

50 Ellenborough to Napier 4 and 14 Nov. 1842, Ellenborough PRO 30.12.96.

51 Ellenborough to Stanley 14 Nov. and to Peel 15 Nov. 1842, *ibid.* 30.12.89.

52 Henry Law to Ellenborough 13 March 1843, Law, *India under Ellenborough.*

53 Hobhouse's diary entry 19 March 1843, Broughton 43745, fo. 115.

54 Peel to Queen Victoria 10 March 1843, Victoria, *Letters,* I, 468–9.

55 Palmerston to Hobhouse 9 March 1843, Broughton 46915, fos. 277–8.

56 Palmerston to Hobhouse 10 Apr. 1843, *ibid.* fos. 279–80.

57 James Mill to the Select Committee 16 Aug. 1832, House of Commons Reports, 1831–2 (735–vi) XIV.1.

58 In 1863, just before he died.

59 Palmerston to Hobhouse 19 March 1861, Broughton 46915, fo. 343.

INDEX

Abbas Mirza, 60, 66

Abbott, Captain Augustus: approaching Kandahar, 266; and Ghazni, 285; at Ghazni, 291; at Pashat, 312; at Zurmat, 362–3; at Jalalabad, 380, 386, 393; advocates offensive, 399–400; on punitive measures, 412

Abbott, Captain James: at Herat, 273; at Khiva and St Petersburg, 318–19

Abdul Majid, Ottoman Sultan (reigned 1839–61), 305, 318

Abdul Rashid Khan, 286–7

Aberdeen, see Hamilton-Gordon

Aboukir Bay, Battle in (The Nile,) 8

A'Court, Sir William, Baron Heytesbury: in St Petersburg, 26–9, 38; on Russian aims, 39–40; Governor General designate, 65, 69; appointment rescinded, 73; views recalled, 111

Adana, 52, 318

Aden, occupied, 256; importance of, 311, 314, 322

Adinanagar, 169, 170, 180, 186

Adrianople, Treaty of, 1829: British reaction to, 27–9; effect of, 52, 54; recalled, 84, 217

Affghanistan, campaign honour, 301

Afghanistan: first British contact with, 14; byword for anarchy, 17; other mentions, *passim*

Afghans: vengeful, 16; claim to Sind, 42; disunity of, 108–9; weapons of, 91–2, 262; Shuja's contempt for, 165; attitudes of towards Shuja, 184–5, 262, 266, 270, 293–4, 374; Nott's opinion of, 252, 405; 'as peaceable as London citizens', 337, 354; conspiracy among, 360, 364–5

Afridis, or Khyberees, 297, 322, 333, 347, 365, 386, 398–9, 414, 416

Agra: Auckland in, 310–11; Robertson, in 359, 383; as fortress, 397

Ahmed Shah, founder of Durrani empire (reigned 1747–73), 9, 14, 48, 267

Aktur Khan, Durrani chief, 343, 353, 361

Alexander I, Tsar of Russia (reigned 1801–1825): at Tilsit, 10; against Napoleon, 15; and Europe, 18; death of, 29

Alexander II, Tsar of Russia (reigned 1855–81): in England as Tsarevitch, 227, 230

Algerine, warship, 257

Ali Masjid, fort, 292–3, 297, 386, 398–9

Allahabad, fortesss, 397

Allard, General Jean François, 102

Ambala, 277, 349, 382

Amherst, William Pitt, Earl Amherst, 40

Aminullah Khan, 375, 409, 410, 415

Amritsar, Treaty of, 1809; 14, 48, 93; Auckland's visit to, 242

Amu Darya, river, see Oxus

Anderson, Captain William, 325

Anquetil, Brigadier, 340

Apsley House, 43, 226

Aral Sea, 37, 38, 59, 76, 224, 435

Aras, river (Araxes), 22

Arghandab, river, 274, 381, 395

Army, Indian: reinforcements for, 186, 187, 191–2, 203, 231, 388; peevish officers of, 239, 323; size of in Afghanistan and Sind in 1840, 343

Army of Retribution: vengefulness of, 401, 411, 412; enters Khyber, 398–9; relieves Jalalabad, 401; recaptures Kabul, 414; withdraws, 416

Army of the Indus: first named, 231; command of, 236; loses division, 239; too much baggage, 242–3; enters Afghanistan, 266; at Kandahar, 269–76; takes Ghazni, 286–92; occupies Kabul, 294–5; at Peshawar, 297; other mentions, 219, 250, 252, 267, 270

artillery: Sikh use of, 229; gift of to Runjeet, 241; British excel with, 362; a mystery to Afghans, 400

Asiatic Journal, 16

Index

Asterabad, 100
Athenaeum, 64
Attock, river crossing,75, 118, 297
Auckland, see Eden
Austria, 52, 218-9, 283-4
Ava, 158, 191, 200, 232, 298, 307, 322
Avitabile, General Paolo, 64
Aylmer, see Whitworth-Aylmer
Azores, 279

Baghdad, 18, 205, 231-2, 283, 335
Bahadur Khan, 58
Bahawalpur, 54, 114, 225, 245, 249
Bahrain, 256, 283, 298, 311
Baillie, H. J., Tory M.P., 418, 420-2
Bajaur, 328
Bajgah, 328
Bala Hissar, fortress at Kabul, 5, 364-75 passim, 409, 410, 414
Balkh, 58, 307-20 passim
Balta Liman, Convention of, 1838; 173, 218, 306
Baluchis: fierceness of, 53; 'vapouring Belochees', 123; British and, 15, 250-81 passim, 294, 315, 322, 327, 331-2, 385
Bamiyan, 283, 297, 326-33 passim, 373, 411, 414
Baring, Sir Francis Thornhill, Baron Northbrook, 351
Barukzais, family of Dost Muhammad: feud with Sadozais, 16, 17, 72; Burnes's high opinion of, 57; other mentions, 62, 105, 120, 184, 201, 215, 271, 277, 287, 293, 325, 335, 374, 410
Basra, 205
Bassein, Treaty of, 1802, 9
Bax, John, 44
Bean, J. D., 327
Bell, Andrew Ross, 280-2, 315-43 passim
Benares, 337, 402, 403
Bengal, conquest of, 5; other mentions, 7, 13, 41, 70, 186, 191, 203, 407
Bengal Division of the Army of the Indus: at Ferozepore, 238-42; on the march, 245; Hyderabad diversion, 250-1; crosses Indus, 253-4; advance to Quetta, 254-63; in Afghanistan, 266-97 passim
Bentinck, Lord William Cavendish: Ellenborough's instructions to,

23, 35, 38, 39-42, 43-5; reports Metcalfe's views, 45; Grant's orders to, 46; meets Burnes, 47; and Runjeet, 48; his record, 50-1; on Indian defences, 51, 74-6; on Shuja's expedition, 61-2, 92-3; other mentions, 68, 81, 96, 97, 441
Berowski, a Polish 'General', 79, 129, 179-80
Beymaroo, 365-73 passim
Bhag, 262
Black Sea, 28, 52, 258
Bligh, Hon. John Duncan, 67, 69
Bloomfield, John Arthur Douglas, 318-21 passim
Board of Control: established, 6; under Ellenborough, 21, 24, 37, 44, 70, 355; under Grant, 43; under Hobhouse, 73, 77, 87, 208, 351, 354; under Fitzgerald, 358, 395, 402, 418, 419; officials of, 212, 222, 224, 226, 230; other mentions, 428, 429
Bokhara: fears for, 30, 37-41, 160, 171, 176, 206, 320; Burnes in, 47, 58-60; Russian trade with, 48, 58-9, 111; Stoddart's mission to, 166, 205-6, 255, 327; Dost's exile in, 314
Bolan Pass, 63, 252-66 passim, 395, 424
Bombay: Governors of, 8, 185, 209, 354, 362, 364; Pottinger in, 15, 279; Burnes and, 40-7, 60, 64; other mentions, 98, 101, 115, 129, 157, 178, 179, 180, 191, 203, 205, 238, 253, 257, 311, 316, 384, 395
Bombay Division: In Sind and Afghanistan, 238, 240, 250-65 passim; detachment in Aden, 256; known as 'Bombay ducks', 270; returns home, 296-7
Brahuis, 333
Broughton, see Hobhouse
Broun-Ramsay, James Andrew, Marquis of Dalhousie, 5
Brown, Captain Lewis, 324, 331-2
Brunnow, Philip Ivanovitch, Baron von, Russian ambassador: arrives in London, 305-6; conversations, 308-21 passim; Ellenborough and, 434-5; Hobhouse and, 419, 423
Brydges, Sir Harford Jones, 12-13

484

Index

Eden, (Cont.)

early life and career, 73, 77–8, 94

character and reputation, 94, 96–105 passim, 143, 196, 198–9, 204, 236, 239, 244, 323, 404, and vilification of, xv

disagreement with Metcalfe, 81, 95–8, 228

restrains Runjeet Singh, 91–9 passim

insists on Anglo-Sikh alliance, 92, 102–15 passim, 121, 134, 156, 167, 169, 180–1, 215, 278, 334–5, 350

early relations with Kabul and Kandahar, 86–96, 88, 92–92

doctrine of just interference, 86, 93, 100, 110–11

interest in Indus and Sind, 90–1, 101, 104, 194–5, 202, 280–2

opinion of Burnes, 128, 183, 187, 195, 237, 359

terms offered to Dost Muhammad, 120–2, 127, 141, 147, 156

attitude towards Dost, 93, 111–12, 167–8, 201, 334–5

military precautions, 103, 115–16, 154, 186–7, 191–2, 203

contacts with McNeill, 100–1, 107, 108, 138, 142–3, 156, 160, 236

agonizing reappraisal, 156–9

prepares for action, 165–204 passim

chooses Macnaghten, 191–2, 194, 196, 204

restraining influence on Macnaghten, 181–2, 183, 277, 302, 306–7, 323, 327–8, 348, 356, 363

his Simla manifesto, 4, 118, 219, 232–5

deplores partisan attacks, 221, 299

reaches point of no return, 231, 236, 244

reviews Army of the Indus, 239

first meeting with Runjeet, 239–44

home government approves, 247–8, 255

concern about Shuja, 217, 270–1, 325–6, 329, 345, 349, 353

seizure of Aden, 256, and Karachi, 257–8

view of Hyderabad diversion, 249, 251, 253, and army's plight, 261

opinion of Keane, 266

on Eldred Pottinger in Herat, 180, 255–6, 273

fears new Herat siege, 275

lacks active commander in chief, 278–9

on Egyptians in Arabia, 205, 283

on Nott's qualifications for command, 296, 330–31, 359

permits temporary occupation of Afghanistan, 284–5, 314, 322

views on Kalat, 297–8, 328, 332

recommends honours and thanks army, 254, 300–1

ordered to organise China expedition, 311, 349

his efficiency, 311, 323

views on Khiva and Bokhara, 312–20 passim

chooses Elphinstone, 338–40, 342–3

on Todd's conduct at Herat, 343–5, 348–9, 350–3

floats loan, 349

sends resignation, 354, 357, 359

reaction to Kabul disaster, 382–96 passim

advises against re-conquest, 384–5, 388

return to London, 425–6, 430–1

Eden, Robert John, 350

Egypt, 7–10, 51–2, 172–3, 283–4, 298, 321

Elfi Bey, 10

Ellenborough, see Law

Elliott, Captain (later Rear Admiral Sir) Charles, 349

Elliot, Sir Gilbert, Earl of Minto, 10–14

Elliot, Gilbert, 2nd Earl of Minto, 419

Ellis, (Sir) Henry, 65–91 passim, 129

Elphinstone, John, Lord Elphinstone, 232, 244, 337

Elphinstone, Mountstuart, 11, 13–14, 45, 68, 337, 427–8

Elphinstone, Major General William George Keith: career and conections, 337–8, 417; his task in Kabul, 339–40; ill-health of, 354, 359, 362; inadequacy of during insurrection, 366–76 passim; a prisoner, 380; death and burial, 408–9; other mentions, 297, 336, 379

England, Brigadier (later General Sir) Richard, 392, 395, 401, 403, 423

487

31-2

Index

Ludhiana, 17, 48, 55, 61–2, 70, 119, 139, 144, 329, 382
Lughmani, 372
Lynch, Lt., 205

Macaulay, Thomas Babington, Lord Macaulay, 7, 50
MacDonald, see Kinneir
McGaskill, Brigadier, 386, 415
Macgregor, Captain G. H., 364, 371, 378
Mackenzie, Captain (later Lt. General) Colin, 374–9 passim, 409, 410
Mackenzie, Lt. Murray, 333
Mackeson, Captain (later Lt. Col.) Frederick, 184–5, 192
Maclaren, Major James, 371, 375
Macleod, Lt., 292, 300
Macnaghten, Sir William Hay: character and reputation, xv, 330; his boundless optimism, 249, 263, 267, 323, 330, 347, 374, 389; at Simla with Bentinck, 47; correspondence with McNeill, 88, 108, 158; 'our Lord Palmerston', 94, 248; correspondence with Burnes, 113–71 passim; negotiates tripartite treaty, 169–99 passim; volunteers for Kabul, 191–2; Auckland's opinion of, 236, 248; takes up appointment, 248; criticises Sind diversion, and clashes with Cotton, 253–4; relations with Keane, 260, 261, 268; views on Kalat, 262–5 passim; in Kandahar, 267–8; use of subsidies, 271–2, 362; defends Shuja against critics, 271; favours retaining regulars, 284, 285, 295–6; exaggerated fear of Russian advance, 297, 301, 306, 313; candidate for supreme council, 300–1; his complaint against Sikhs, 317, 325; on Afghan government and internal security 311–12, 329, 341; 347, 350; urge to advance to Herat, 275–6, 327–8, 330, 343, 345, and beyond Hindu Kush, 326–7; nervous about Dost's return, 333–4; accepts Dost's surrender, 335; glowing reports from Kabul, 353–4, 360, 361, 363; governor designate of Bombay, 354, 359; indignation at withdrawal rumours, 359; plans

journey to Bombay, 362, 364; first impression of rising, 366, 368; in touch with chiefs, 369, 372; negotiations and first agreement, 373–4; readiness to escape from agreement, 375, 378; Akbar's trap, 375–7; murdered and mutilated, 4–5, 377, 386, 394, 395, 396, 410–11, 415
McNeill, Sir John: secretary of legation under Ellis, 68–9, 73; published views on Russian expansion, 83–5, 95, 110, 179, 217; envoy to Teheran, 87, 101, 170; denounces Simonich, 100–1, 103; memorandum on Afghan politics, 105; advocates friendship with Kabul and Kandahar, 106–8, rejects Auckland's instructions, 107; correspondence with Burnes, 107–8, 114; changes view on Herat, 117, 124; his mission insulted, 129, 155, 159, 168, 174, advises remonstrance, 117–18, 137, 138, 155; goes to Herat, 156, 159, 164; recommends deterrent action, 155–6, 161, 164–5, 172, 175–9; tries to dissuade Shah, 165, 174; severs relations with Persian Court, 174, 194, 197; his Meshed dispatches, 175–9, 203, 204, 208; sends Stoddart to Herat with ultimatum, 205–6; recommends expedition into southern Persia, 206, 210–11; Palmerston's praise of, 210–11, 248; reports raising of siege, 214, and urges continued action, 217; importance as middleman, 215; praises Pottinger and Stoddart, 217; returns to Teheran, 258, and quarrels again, 258; returns to Teheran and negotiates commercial treaty, 350, 352, 354, 385
Madras, 232, 388, 390
Mahmud of Ghazni, 60–1
Mahmud II, Ottoman Sultan (reigned 1808–39), 29, 51–2, 172–3, 218, 230, 284
Mahmud Shah, 9–10, 14, 16
Maitland, Rear Admiral Sir Frederick Lewis, 256–8, 283
Malcolm, Sir John, 11–13, 24, 29, 44, 45, 47

493

Index

Index

Sanders, Captain E., 413

Secret Committee: its role, 6; its powers, 37; key dispatch of 7 March 1835, 91, and of 13 June 1836, 89–90, 96, 202, 227, and of 24 October 1838, 214–15; other mentions, 10–11, 21, 104, 160, 194, 197, 202, 220, 222, 247–8, 257, 280, 307, 330, 334, 343, 345–6, 352–5, 358, 385, 388, 417, 423, 438

Sehwan, 254

Seistan, 80

Selim III, Ottoman Sultan (reigned 1789–1807), 10

Sepoys, 12, 258, 309, 312, 315, 362, 388, 394, 401, 405, 407

Seringapatam, Battle of, 8

Seton, Captain David, 11–12

Shahdadpur, Battle of, 439

Shah Shuja, or Shuja-ul-Mulk, King of Afghanistan (reigned 1803–9 and 1839–42): seizes throne, 9–10, makes treaty with Britain, 13–14, 225; loses throne, 14; loses Koh-i-Noor diamond, 17, and becomes pensioner of British 17; receives Burnes at Ludhiana, 48–9, 57; requests British aid, 51, 61; his alliance with Runjeet, 61, 169, 222–5; his bid for throne, 62–4, 74, 92, 132; his value to Auckland, 108, 169, 188, 201–2; expert opinion of his chances, 163, 183–5, 186–7, 192, 421; his insistence on his rights, 194, 277, 347; in Simla manifesto, 234–5; will he be a puppet?, 217, 220, 271, 274, 293; his contingent, 239, 241, 248, 254, 260, 262, 265, 275, 294, and British-officered forces, 340, 345, 355–6, 360–7 *passim*; haughty ways offend, 63, 248–9, 271; a reluctant 'citizen king', 249, 273, 307, 313, 316, 322; Macnaghten's opinion of, 271, 347; his 'train of ragamuffins', 271, and the Ghazni atrocity, 288; enters Kandahar, 267, 269, and Kabul, 293–4; institutes order of Durrani Empire, 295; his territorial ambitions, 306–7; his ramshackle government, 329, 342, 349, 374; ineffec-

tive in crisis, 366, 372, 375, 393; assassination of, 399, 408, 409; restoration judged failure, 426; other mentions, 105, 181–2

Shakespear, Sir Richmond Campbell, 273, 320, 414

Shal, 265, 298, 328

Shamsuddin Khan, 413

Shapur, 415–16

Sheil, Col. (later Major General Sir) Justin, 160–1, 190, 351

Shelton, Brigadier John: 'a tyrant in his regiment', 336; brave but a croaker, 369; prisoner of Akbar, 380, 414; other mentions, 337, 339, 363–75 *passim*

Sher Muhammad, 439

Sher Singh, Maharajah of Lahore (ruled 1840–3), 350, 416

Shi'a, sect of Islam, 159, 229

Shikarpur, 62, 91–9, 104, 106, 114, 169, 180–1, 183, 185, 189, 193, 196, 200 236, 249–75 *passim*, 280–1, 324, 343, 385, 438

Shinwari, 412

Shuja-ul-Mulk, *see* Shah Shuja

Sikhs, 5, 42, 48, 56, 63–4, 85, 91–2, 109, 112, 120, 165, 181–3, 229, 240–2, 280, 317, 384, 386, 388, 397, 398, 416

Simla, 47–8, 116, 125, 137, 139, 143, 148, 150, 159, 160, 170, 193, 195, 197, 199, 235, 403

Simla Manifesto of 1838, 4, 118, 219, 221, 232–5, 248, 433

Simla Proclamation of 1842, 433, 451–2

Simonich, Count Ivan: minister in Teheran, 72, 118, 134; letters to Kabul, 131; encourages Shah, 87, 100, 103–4, 129, 132; offers to Kandahar and Kabul, 127, 150, 164, 206, 223; follows McNeill to Herat, 164, 171; active in Herat, 165, 174–80 *passim*, 206, 218; fails in directing siege, 180; disavowed, 215–16, 229

Simpson, Major General F., 248

Sind: isolation of, 3, 8, 12, 15, 17, 42, 53; early British contacts with, 8, 11–13, 15, 18–19, 37, 40–2, 44–8; Pottinger's early negotiations in, 50–1, 53–5; new demands from, 93–5, 98–9, 101, 104, 112, 116;

497

Index